A MODERN ENGLISH GRAMMAR

by the same author

A MODERN ENGLISH GRAMMAR ON HISTORICAL PRINCIPLES
IN SEVEN PARTS

    I. SOUNDS AND SPELLINGS
    II. SYNTAX (FIRST VOLUME)
    III. SYNTAX (SECOND VOLUME)
    IV. SYNTAX (THIRD VOLUME)
    V. SYNTAX (FOURTH VOLUME)
    VI. MORPHOLOGY
    VII. SYNTAX

LANGUAGE: ITS NATURE, DEVELOPMENT AND ORIGIN

HOW TO TEACH A FOREIGN LANGUAGE

CHAPTERS ON ENGLISH

AN INTERNATIONAL LANGUAGE

NOVIAL LEXIKE

THE PHILOSOPHY OF GRAMMAR

MANKIND, NATION AND INDIVIDUAL

LINGUISTICA

THE SYSTEM OF GRAMMAR

ANALYTIC SYNTAX

GROWTH AND STRUCTURE OF THE ENGLISH LANGUAGE

ESSENTIALS OF ENGLISH GRAMMAR

A MODERN ENGLISH GRAMMAR

ON HISTORICAL PRINCIPLES

OTTO JESPERSEN

Part VII
SYNTAX

Completed and edited by
NIELS HAISLUND

GEORGE ALLEN & UNWIN LTD EJNAR MUNKSGAARD
LONDON   COPENHAGEN

REPRINTED IN GREAT BRITAIN
1961, 1965 AND 1974

This book is copyright under the Berne Convention. All rights are reserved. Apart from any fair dealing for the purpose of private study, research, criticism or review, as permitted under the Copyright Act, 1956, no part of this publication may be reproduced, stored in a retrieval system, or transmitted, in any form or by any means, electronic, electrical, chemical, mechanical, optical, photocopying, recording or otherwise, without the prior permission of the copyright owner. Enquiries should be addressed to the publishers.

ISBN 0 04 425012 6

PRINTED IN GREAT BRITAIN
BY ALDEN & MOWBRAY LTD
AT THE ALDEN PRESS, OXFORD

Preface

This book is the seventh and last volume of that great work by Otto Jespersen the first volume of which was published in 1909.

Before his death in 1943[1] Otto Jespersen had written Chs. I—XI and planned the rest of the book. During his last illness, when he foresaw the possibility of death before he should have finished his work himself, he expressed a wish that, in that event, I should publish the present volume.

Chs. I—V were written by Otto Jespersen (denoted hereafter as OJ) after the publication of vol. VI in 1942, and are here published with minor changes and additions by me (NH).

Chs. VI—VII were written by me immediately before the War at OJ's directions on the basis of his *Progress in Language* (London 1894) and were afterwards revised by OJ.

---

[1] Obituary notices by Danes: C. A. Bodelsen in Festskrift udgivet af Københavns Universitet i Anledning af Universitetets Aarsfest, November 1943, pp. 137—142 (in Danish); another article on O. J. by Professor Bodelsen (in English) will appear in the Bulletin du Cercle Linguistique de Copenhague. — L. L. Hammerich in Det Kgl. Danske Videnskabernes Selskabs Oversigt over Selskabets Virksomhed 1943—44 (København 1944) pp. 41—57 (in Danish), to which is appended a bibliography of O. J.'s works 1930—1943 by Niels Haislund pp. 57—63 (in continuation of C. A. Bodelsen's bibliography in A Grammatical Miscellany Offered to Otto Jespersen (Copenhagen 1930), pp. 433—457). — Louis Hjelmslev in Acta Linguistica III fasc. 2—3 (Copenhague 1942—43), pp. 119—130 (in French). — Niels Haislund in English Studies (ESts) vol. XXV no. 5 (Oct. 1943), pp. 138—143 (in English).

Ch. VIII was written by me, in part on the basis of an old MS. written by OJ (before 1920?), and was afterwards revised by OJ.

Ch. IX was written by OJ. Here, too, I have made minor changes and additions, e.g. Section 9.2_6.

The chapters on Comparison, X—XI, were originally written for vol. VI (immediately before the War), but OJ finally decided to reserve them for vol. VII. Ch. X was written by me and revised by OJ. Professor Paul Christophersen, Ph. D. (denoted by his initials in the survey below), who wrote parts of vol. VI, has written some sections on irregular comparison (11.1—11.3_4), and I have written sections 11.3_5—11.3_8, both parts being revised by OJ, who wrote the rest of Ch. XI himself.

Before his last illness OJ had written a few sections on the Articles, viz. on the morphology of the articles (12.1—12.2_8) and Border Cases (12.3—12.3_3). As he foresaw that he might not live to finish these chapters himself, he dictated a plan for the treatment of the syntactical part of the chapters on the articles, a "theory of the stages of familiarity" (cf. below, 12.4_1—12.4_4), and on the basis of this plan I have written the rest of Ch. XII (from 12.5_1 on) and Chs. XIII—XVI.

Finally 1 have written Chs. XVII—XVIII, Quantifiers and Mood.

The above account may be summarized as follows in a schematic survey (cf. the corresponding list in vol. VI p. iv):

Chapter	
I-V	OJ
VI-VII	OJ(1894)/NH/OJ
VIII	(OJ)NH/OJ
IX	OJ
9.2_6	NH/OJ

Chapter	
X	NH/OJ
XI	PC/NH/OJ
11.1-11.3$_4$	PC/OJ
11.3$_5$-11.3$_8$	NH/OJ
XII-XVIII	NH
12.1-12.3$_3$	OJ

My material for the parts written by me after OJ's death was chiefly illustrative examples from OJ's collections, in most places amply supplemented by examples collected by myself; thus the majority of illustrative examples used in the chapters on the articles are due to my own observations, but many of them originate from books formerly belonging to OJ, in many cases collected by me during his lifetime. For the chapter on quantifiers I have also occasionally benefited by some very old notes written by OJ (for lectures?).

The list of Technical Terms (pp. 648—663) was planned and begun by OJ and finished by me.

I have done my best to complete this volume in Otto Jespersen's spirit and on the lines followed by him in the other parts of the grammar. It will be for others to decide to what degree I have succeeded.

The MS. was completed before the end of the war. After the War Professor W. E. Collinson, Professor Jespersen's old friend, was kind enough to go very carefully through the chapters written by me. His critical remarks and additions, which I had an opportunity to discuss with him in London in 1946, have greatly increased the value of this part of the work, and I owe him a great debt of gratitude for his assistance.

A printers' strike in Copenhagen in 1947 held up the printing of the book, and later the reading of the proofs occasionally collided with other work I had to do.

I am highly indebted to Mr. Walt Arneson, B. A., who has gone through the whole of the MS., some of it during Professor Jespersen's lifetime, and criticized the linguistic form in which the work is presented to the reader. He has not only suggested formal improvements on many points, but also kept an open eye on the contents and offered suggestions of various kinds, particularly as regards U. S. usage.

Further I offer my cordial thanks to Professor Bruce Dickins, who, during my stay in Cambridge in 1946, read some chapters of the MS., and to Professor Paul Christophersen, who has kindly read the proofs of some of the first chapters and looked at various other sections. Both have offered valuable critical remarks.

My friend Professor O. Vočadlo of Prague during our stay in Cambridge in 1946 read some chapters of my MS. and later he has read a proof. He has not only pointed out a number of misprints which might otherwise have been overlooked, but also offered many valuable suggestions as regards the contents for which I am very grateful to him.

Finally I am glad to have an opportunity on behalf of Mr. Frans Jespersen, M. Sc., and myself to express our profound gratitude to the directors of the Carlsberg Foundation, who have not only granted personal support to me for the preparation of the MS. and given me a grant for my stay in England in 1946, but have also offered a generous subvention towards the printing of the book.

Copenhagen, May 1949. *Niels Haislund.*

Contents

	PAGE
PREFACE	v
ABBREVIATIONS AND LIST OF BOOKS QUOTED IN VOLS. II-VII	1

I. Word-Classes — 41
Introduction 1.1. Substantives 1.2. Adjectives 1.3. Verbs 1.4. Adverbs 1.5.

II. Sentence-Structure and Word-Order — 53
Principles 2.1. Central Part of the Sentence 2.2_1—2.2_6. Front-Position of Object 2.2_7—2.2_9. Front-Position of Predicative 2.3_1—2.3_3. Preposition at the End 2.3_4—2.3_6. Anaphoric Repetition 2.3_7—2.3_8. Front-Position of Tertiary 2.4—2.5. Place of Tertiaries (apart from the cases dealt with above) 2.6_1. Tertiary between S and V 2.6_2—2.6_6. Time 2.6_7. Quantifier Tertiaries 2.6_8—2.7_2. Special Cases 2.7_3. Overlapping 2.7_4—2.7_6. Imperative 2.7_7. Infinitive 2.7_8. Participles 2.7_9. Place of the Object 2.8_1. Tertiaries with Verbs 2.8_2—2.8_8.

III. Sentence-Structure. Concluded — 107
Sentences with the Empty *there* 3.1—3.2. Abbreviated Sentences 3.3_1. Front-Part Left Out 3.3_2—3.3_7. Middle Part Left Out 3.4. End Left Out 3.5. Inarticulate or Semi-Articulate Sentences 3.6.

IV. Person — 125
Introduction 4.1. First Person 4.2. Second Person 4.3. Third Person 4.4_1—4.4_5. Indirect Speech 4.4_6. Person in Verbs 4.5_1—4.5_8.

They + Numeral. *Them* as an Adjunct 4.5_3. *It* 4.6. A. Anaphoric *it* 4.6_2. B. Preparatory *it* 4.6_3—4.6_7. Cleft Sentences 4.6_8. D. Unspecified *it* 4.6_9—4.6_{11}. The Generic Person 4.7. Reflexive 48_1 ff. Simple Pronouns in a Reflexive Sense 4.8_2—4.8_3. Reflexive Pronouns as Regimens of Prepositions 4.8_4—4.8_6. Reflexive Possessives 4.9_1—4.9_2. Non-Reflexive Use of *Self*-Pronouns 4.9_3—4.9_6.

V. Sex and Gender — 174
General Remarks 5.1. Substantives 5.2—5.4. Animals 5.4_1—5.4_3. Plants 5.4_4. Pronouns 5.5—5.8. Animate and Inanimate 5.9.

VI. Case — 219
Introduction 6.1_1. Case in Pronouns 6.1_2 ff. Extraposition 6.2_1—6.2_3. Apposition 6.2_4. Relative Attraction 6.2_5—6.2_6. Preposition and Conjunction 6.3. Notional Subject 6.4_1—6.4_3. Loosely Connected Nexus 6.4_4. Position 6.4_5 ff. Before the Verb 6.5—6.6. After the Verb. Predicative 6.7. After the Verb. Subject 6.8—6.9.

VII. Case in Pronouns (Continued) — 262
Phonetic Influences 7.1—7.4. Final remarks 7.5.

VIII. Case in Nouns — 281
Introduction 8.1. Use of the Common Case 8.2. Common Case as Tertiary 8.3 ff. Tertiaries of Measure 8.3_2—8.4_7. Tertiaries of Time 8.5. Tertiaries of Space 8.6. Tertiaries of Manner 8.7—8.8. Pairs of Words 8.9_1—8.9_6. *First thing* 8.9_7. "Sixpence an ounce" 8.9_8.

IX. Case (Continued) — 306
Possessive, Genitive, and Use of *Of*. Possessive of Third Person Plural 9.1_1. Possessive of *it* 9.1_2. *My, thy : mine, thine*, etc. 9.1_3. Use of the Genitive and of Possessive Pronouns 9.2—9.5_7. Genitives as Primaries 9.5_8—9.5_9. Other Employments of *Of* 9.6. Partitive 9.7. Specializing *of* 9.8. Appositional *of* 9.9.

X. Comparison — 342
Form 10.1 ff. Orthographical Changes 10.1_7. Introduction to Classification 10.2_1. Monosyllables 10.2_2. More than One Syllable 10.2_3 ff. Sibilants, etc. 10.3_5—10.3_9. Adverbs 10.4_1—10.4_3. Group Comparatives, etc. 10.4_4—10.4_9. Regular instead of Irregular Comparison 10.5_1—10.5_2. Comparatives from Prepositions, and Superlatives in *most* 10.5_3—10.5_9.

XI. Comparison (Continued) — 367
Double Comparison 11.1_1. Parallel Increase 11.1_2. Change of Vowel, etc. 11.1_3—11.3_8. Meaning 11.4 ff. Gradual Increase 11.5_4. Latent Comparatives 11.5_5—11.5_6. The Three Degrees 11.6. A Very High Degree 11.7_1—11.7_6. Latin Comparatives and Superlatives 11.7_7. Strengthening 11.8.

XII. Determination and Indetermination (The Articles) — 403
Introduction 12.1. Forms of the Articles 12.2. Border Cases 12.3_1—12.3_3. Prosiopesis 12.3_4—12.3_5. Headlinese 12.3_6. Syntax 12.4 ff. Stages of Familiarity 12.4_2—12.4_4. Stage I. Complete Unfamiliarity (or Ignorance). The Indefinite Article 12.5. Meaning of Substantives with the Indefinite Article. *A* in Book-Titles 12.5_4. Other Uses of *A* 12.5_5—12.5_6. Distributive *A* 12.5_7. The Indefinitive Article before Words Generally Used as Proper Names 12.5_8—12.5_{10}. Indefinite Article with Quantifiers 12.5_{11}. Cardinals 12.5_{12}. Unification 12.6. Mass-Words 12.6_3. Shades of Meaning of Mass-Words with the Zero Article 12.6_4—12.6_7. Plurals 12.6_8—12.6_{11}. Names of Languages 12.6_{12}. Zero with Substantives in Certain Grammatical Functions 12.7. Object with Zero 12.7_1. Zero with Predicatives 12.7_2—12.7_{10}. Zero in Prepositional Phrases 12.8_1—12.8_3. Zero in Enumerations and Pairs of Words 12.8_4—12.8_8. Conflict between Articles 12.9.

XIII. Articles before Junctions — 471
Various Junctions 13.1—13.2. Superlatives and Ordinals as Secondaries 13.3.

PAGE

XIV. Stage Two. The Definite Article   479
Contextual and Situational Basis 14.1. Typical *the* 14.2. Generic Use of *the* 14.3—14.4. Distributive Use 14.5$_1$. Familiar *the* 14.5$_2$. *The* in Exclamations 14.5$_3$—14.5$_7$. *The* before Comparatives 14.6. Articles before Superlatives and Ordinals 14.7. Adjectives as Primaries 14.8$_1$—14.8$_5$. *All* 14.8$_6$. *Both* 14.8$_7$. The *Which*, etc. 14.8$_8$—14.8$_{10}$.

XV. Stage Three. Zero   529
Address 15.1$_1$—15.1$_4$. Familiar Persons 15.1$_5$. Legal Terms, etc. 15.1$_6$. Meals 15.2$_1$—15.2$_2$. Institutions 15.2$_3$—15.2$_4$. *Town, bed* 15.2$_5$—15.2$_6$. Names of Periods and Dates 15.3.

XVI. Proper Names   544
Introduction 16.1$_1$. Personal Names 16.1$_2$. Place-Names 16.1$_3$ ff. River-Names 16.1$_4$—16.1$_5$. Oceans, Seas, Channels, Straits, and Lakes 16.1$_6$. Countries, etc. 16.1$_7$—16.1$_8$. Islands 16.1$_9$. Mountains and Mountain Ranges 16.2$_1$. Towns 16.2$_2$. Parks 16.2$_3$. Streets and Roads 16.2$_4$—16.2$_7$. Buildings 16.3$_1$—16.3$_6$. Books, Newspapers, and Periodicals 16.3$_7$. Typical and Honorific *The* before Personal Names 16.3$_8$. Titles and Other Common Names Connected with Personal Names 16.4. Personification 16.5. Adjectives before Proper Names 16.6. Quasi-Proper Names 16.7.

XVII. Quantifiers   580
Introduction 17.1$_1$. Numerals 17.1$_2$ ff. Foreign Numerals 17.2$_1$. Uncertainty of Number 17.2$_2$—17.2$_4$. Ordinals, Fractions 17.2$_5$. Distributive Use of Numerals 17.2$_6$. 'Nothing' 17.2$_7$. *Once, Twice, Thrice* 17.3. Pronouns of Totality 17.4—17.8. Adjectives 17.9$_1$. Survey of Pronominal Quantifiers 17.9$_2$—17.9$_3$.

XVIII. Mood   623
Introduction 18.1$_1$—18.1$_2$. Indicative and Subjunctive 18.2$_1$—18.2$_2$. Form 18.2$_3$—18.2$_7$. Conditional Clauses 18.3. Temporal Clauses 18.4. Wishes 18.5. Intention or Purpose 18.6$_1$—18.6$_2$. Content-Clauses 18.6$_3$. Concessive Clauses 18.6$_4$. Indirect Speech 18.7$_1$

	PAGE
—18.7$_2$. Indirect Questions 18.7$_3$. Indefinite Relative Clauses 18.7$_4$—18.7$_5$. Imaginative *were* 18.7$_6$.	
TECHNICAL TERMS	648
GENERAL INDEX	664

ABBREVIATIONS AND LIST OF BOOKS QUOTED IN VOLS. II-VII

(In this list L = London, MM = Macmillan, N.Y. = New York,
P = Penguin, and T = Tauchnitz edition.)
Some recent novels from which very few quotations are taken,
are not included in the list.
The original year of publication is often added in parenthesis.

Abr. & Isaak = Abraham & Isaak. Ein mittelengl. misterium. Ed. R. Brotanek. 1897.
Ade A = George Ade, Artie. Chicago 1897.
adj = adjective.
adv = adverb.
AF = Anglo-French.
AHuxley, see H—.
Ainsworth JS = Harrison Ainsworth, Jack Sheppard. L n. d. (1839).
Alden U = Percy Alden, The Unemployed. L n.d.
Aldrich S = Thomas B. Aldrich, The Stillwater Tragedy. T 1880.
Alford Q = Dean Alford, The Queen's English. 8th ed. L 1889.
Allen A = Hervey Allen, Anthony Adverse. L 1934 (1933).
    S = Grant Allen, Strange Stories. L 1899.
    W =   — The Woman Who Did. T 1895.
Amr = American.
AmSp = American Speech (Periodical). Baltimore 1925 ff.
AnalS(ynt) = Otto Jespersen, Analytic Syntax. Copenhagen 1937.
Angell I = Norman Angell, The Great Illusion. L 1914.
Anstey V = F. Anstey [T. A. Guthrie], Vice Versa. L 1882.
AR = The Ancrene Riwle, ed. Morton. L 1853 [the usual name Ancren Riwle is incorrect].
Archer A = William Archer, America To-Day. L 1904 (1899).

Arden of Feversham ed. Ronald Bayne. Temple Dramatists. L 1897 (1592).
Arnold P = Matthew Arnold, Poetical Works. L 1890 (MM).
Ascham S = Roger Ascham, The Scholemaster. Arber (1570).
    T =   —   Toxophilus. Ib. (1545).
Aumonier OB = Stacy Aumonier, Olga Bardel. L 1916.
    Q =   —   The Querrils. L 1919.
Austen E = Jane Austen, Emma. T. (1816).
    M =   —   Mansfield Park. L 1897 (1814).
    P =   —   Pride and Prejudice. L 1894 (1813).
    S =   —   Sense and Sensibility. L n. d. (1811).
AV = The Authorized Version of the Bible 1611 (Facsimile ed., Oxford 1833. — 20th C. V. [or Tr.] = The Twentieth Century New Testament, L 1898 — 1901).

Bacon A = Francis Bacon, The New Atlantis, ed. Moore Smith. Cambridge 1900 [written in 1624].
    E =   —   Essays, ed. Wright. L 1881.
Bale T = John Bale, A Comedy concernynge Thre Lawes 1538, ed. Schröer (Anglia V 1882) (Quoted by verse).
Barnes Y = Margaret Ayer Barnes, Years of Grace. L 1930.
Barrie A = James M. Barrie, Auld Licht Idylls. L 1898.
    AC =   —   The Admirable Crichton. L 1923.
    M =   —   The Little Minister. L 1893.
    MO =   —   Margaret Ogilvy. T 1897.
    T =   —   Tommy and Grizel. L 1900.
    W =   —   A Window in Thrums. 6d ed.
BDS = My Best Detective Story (Anthology). L 1931.
Beaconsfield L = Benjamin Disraeli, Lothair. L n. d. (1870).
Beaumont = Francis Beaumont and John Fletcher, ed. Glover and Waller. Cambridge 1905.
(Sometimes quoted from Mermaid Series ed.)
Behn = Aphra Behn, The Novels, ed. E. A. Baker. L 1904.
Bell PrecPorc = Neil Bell, Precious Porcelain. L 1931.
Bellamy L = Edward Bellamy, Looking Backward, 2000—1887. L. n. d. (1888).
Bennett A = Arnold Bennett, Anna of the Five Towns. L 1912 (1902).

Bennett Acc	=	Arnold Bennett,	Accident. T 1929.
B	=	—	The Grand Hotel Babylon. L 1912 (1902).
BA	=	—	Buried Alive. Reader's Libr. L n.d. (1908).
C	=	—	Clayhanger. T 1912 (1910).
Cd	=	—	The Card. L 1913 (1911).
ECh	=	—	Elsie and the Child. T 1924.
GS	=	—	The Grim Smile of the Five Towns. T 1907.
H	=	—	How to Live on 24 Hours. L 1912 (1908).
HL	=	—	Hilda Lessways. T 1912 (1911).
HM	=	—	The Human Machine. L 1910.
ImpPal	=	—	Imperial Palace. L 1930.
L	=	—	Lilian. L 1922.
LM	=	—	The Love Match. T (1922).
LR	=	—	Lord Raingo. L 1926.
P	=	—	Mr. Prohack. L 1922.
PL	=	—	The Pretty Lady. L 1918.
R	=	—	The Regent. 1/- ed. L 1916 (1913).
RS	=	—	Riceyman Steps. T 1924 (1923).
T	=	—	These Twain. L 1916.
W	=	—	Old Wives' Tale. T 1909 (1908).

RBennett P = Rolf Bennett, Mr. Pyecroft. L 1933.
Benson A = Edward F. Benson, Arundel. L 1915.

B	=	—	The Babe B. A. L 1911 (1897).
D	=	—	Dodo. T 1894 (1893).
D2	=	—	Dodo the Second. T (1914).
DA	=	Robert Hugh Benson,	The Dawn of All. L n.d.
Da	=	Edward F. Benson,	Daisy's Aunt. L n.d.
DB	=	—	David Blaize. L n.d. (1916).
J	=	—	The Judgment Books. L 1895.

Benson N = Robert Hugh Benson, None Other Gods. L n.d.
     W = Arthur C. Benson, From a College Window. L 1906.

Bentley O = E. C. Bentley, Trent's Own Case. L 1936.
     T = — Trent's Last Case. L 1912.

Beow = Beowulf.

Beresford G = J. D. Beresford, God's Counterpoint. L 1918.
  PrisHartl = — The Prisoners of Hartling. (1922).

Beswick OD = Eardley Beswick, Original Design. L 1933.

Birmingham IS = G. A. Birmingham [James O. Hannay], The Inviolable Sanctuary. L n.d.
     W = — The Adventures of Dr. Whitty. L 1915.

Birrell O = Augustine Birrell, Obiter Dicta. L (6d ed.) (1884-87).

BJo = Ben Jonson, generally quoted from the Mermaid Series.
  A = — The Alchemist, ed. L. M. Hathaway. N.Y. 1903. Quoted by act and line.
  P = — The Poetaster, ed. J. H. Penniman. Boston 1913.

Black F = William Black, The New Prince Fortunatus. T 1890.
     P = — The Princes of Thule. T (1873).
     Ph = — The Strange Adventures of a Phaeton. L n.d. (1872).

Bøgholm = N. Bøgholm, Bacon og Shakespeare. København 1906.

Bosw(ell) = James Boswell, Life of S. Johnson, ed. Fitzgerald. L 1900 (1791).

Bradley M = Henry Bradley, The Making of English. L 1904.
     S = Andrew C. Bradley, Shakespearean Tragedy. L 1904.

Brett Young PC = Brett Young, Portrait of Clare. L 1929. (1927).

Bridges E = Robert Bridges, Eros and Psyche. L 1894 (1885).

Bromfield GW = Louis Bromfield, A Good Woman. N.Y. 1927.

Brontë J = Charlotte Brontë, Jane Eyre. L (Nelson) (1847).
     P = — The Professor. L 1867.
     V = — Villette. L 1867 (1852).
     W = Emily Brontë, Wuthering Heights. L 1867 (1847).

Abbreviations and List of Books. 5

Browning = Robert Browning, Poetical Works. L 1896.
Two vols.
T = — — T 1872-84.
Four vols.
Mrs Browning A = Elizabeth Barrett Browning, Aurora Leigh. T (1856).
Buchanan F = Robert Buchanan, Father Anthony. L n.d.
J = — The Wandering Jew. L 1893 (1890).
Bunyan G = John Bunyan, Grace Abounding, etc, ed. Brown. Cambridge 1907.
P = — The Pilgrim's Progress. 1st ed. 1678.
Burke Am = Edmund Burke, Speech on Conciliation with America, ed. Hammond Lamont. Boston 1898.
Burnett F = Frances Burnett, Little Lord Fauntleroy. T.
Burns = Robert Burns, Centenary edition. Edinburgh 1896.
Butler E = Samuel Butler, Essays on Life, Art, and Science. L 1908.
Er = — Erewhon. L 1913 (1872).
ER = — Erewhon Revisited. L 1910 (1901).
N = — Note-Books. L 1912.
W = — The Way of All Flesh. L 1908 (1903).
H = — Hudibras, ed. Waller. Cambridge 1906 (1663-68).
By(ron) = George Gordon Byron, Poetical Works, ed. E.H. Coleridge. L 1905.
Ch = — Childe Harold (Canto and stanza).
DJ = — Don Juan (Canto and stanza).
L = Lord Byron in his Letters, ed. V. H. Collins. L 1927.
c. = century.
Caine C = Hall Caine, The Christian. L 1897.
E = — The Eternal City. L 1901.
M = — The Manxman. L 1894.
P = — The Prodigal Son. L 1904.

Caine S = Hall Caine, The Shadow of a Crime. 1892 (1885).
Cambr St = A Cambridge Staircase (anonymous). L 1883.
  Tr = Cambridge Trifles (anonymous). L 1881.
Campbell Shl = Olwen Ward Campbell, Shelley and the Unromantics. L 1924.
Campion O = Thomas Campion, Observations . . . 1925 (1602).
Canfield SW = Dorothy Canfield, Her Son's Wife. N.Y. 1926.
Carlyle E = Thomas Carlyle, Essays. (Blackie and Son).
  F = — in Froude, Life (1,2 = First 40 Years of his Life, L 1882; 3,4 = His Life in London. L 1884).
  FR = — The French Revolution. L (Nelson) (1837).
  G = — Correspondence with Goethe, ed. Norton. L 1887.
  H = — On Heroes, Hero-Worship and the Heroic in History. L 1890 (1841).
  P = — Past and Present. L 1893 (1843).
  R = — Reminiscences, ed. Froude. L 1881.
  S = — Sartor Resartus. L n.d. (1839).
Carpenter Ad = Edward Carpenter, From Adam's Peak to Elephanta. L 1910 (1892).
  C = — Civilisation, its Cause and Cure. L 1897 (1889).
  D = — My Days and Dreams. L 1916.
  E = — England's Ideal. L 1887.
  L = — Love's Coming of Age. Manchester 1897 (1896).
  P = — Prisons, Police, and Punishment. L 1905.
Carroll A = Lewis Carroll [Charles L. Dodgson], Alice's Adventures in Wonderland. L (6d. ed.) (1866).
  L = — Through the Looking-Glass. L (6d. ed.) (1871).

Cather P = Willa Cather, The Professor's House. T 1926 (1925).
Caxton B = William Caxton, Blanchardyn, ed. Kellner. L
  1890 (1489).
  R =   —   Reynard the Fox, ed. Arber. (1481).

cf = confer.

Ch = Geoffrey Chaucer, Skeat's Six-Volume Edition. (A, B, C, etc, the Groups in Canterbury Tales. MP = Minor Poems. HF = Hous of Fame. L(GW) = Legend of Good Women. PF = Parlement of Foules. R = Romaunt of the Rose. T = Troilus.)

ChE = Otto Jespersen, Chapters on English. L 1918.

Chesterton B = Gilbert K. Chesterton, Robert Browning. L
  1906 (1903).
  Ch =   —   Chaucer. L 1932.
  D =   —   Charles Dickens. L (1913).
  F =   —   The Innocence of Father Brown. T 1911.
  T =   —   The Man who was Thursday. (1908).

Childers R = E. Childers, The Riddle of the Sands. L (Nelson).
Christie Cards = Agatha Christie, Cards on the Table. L 1936.
  LE =   —   Lord Edgware Dies. L 1933.
  3A =   —   Three-Act Tragedy. Albatross 1935.

Churchill C = Winston Churchill, Coniston. L 1906.
Clough = Arthur H. Clough, Poems and Prose Remains. L 1869. 2 vols.

Coleridge = Samuel Coleridge, Poetical Works. L 1893 (MM)
  B =   —   Biographia Literaria. (Everyman) (1817).
  Sh =   —   Lectures on Shakespeare. (Bohn).

coll. = colloquial.
Collier E = Price Collier, England and the English. N.Y. 1909.
Collingwood R = W. G. Collingwood, Life of John Ruskin. L 1905.

Collins M = Wilkie Collins, The Moonstone (The World's Classics) (1868).
      W   —   The Woman in White (ib.) (1860).
Congreve = William Congreve in the Mermaid Series. L.
      DD =   —   The Double-Dealer. (1693).
      OB =   —   The Old Batchelor. (1693).
    (Both in Works I. 6th ed. 1753).
Connington TT = J. J. Connington [A. W. Stewart], The Two Tickets Puzzle. T 1930.
Conway C = Hugh Conway [F. J. Fargus], Called Back. T 1884 (1883).
QCouch, see Quiller-Couch.
Cowper = William Cowper, Poetical Works. Globe ed. L 1889.
      L =   —   Letters, ed. J. G. Frazer. L 1912.

cp. = compare.

Crofts Ch = Freeman Wills Crofts, The Cheyne Mystery.
      G =   —   Inspector French's Greatest Case.
      St =   —   The Starvel Tragedy.
    All in Inspector French's Case Book. L n.d.
Cronin C = A. J. Cronin, The Citadel. L 1938 (1937).
      H =   —   The Hatter's Castle. L 1931.
Curme CG = G. O. Curme, College English Grammar. Richmond 1925.
      S =   —   Syntax (A Grammar of the English Language III). Boston 1931.

Dan. = Danish.

Dane FD = Clemence Dane [Winifred Ashton], First the Blade (Nelson). (1918).
      L =   —   Legend (Omnibus) (1919).
Daniel DR = Samuel Daniel, A Defence of Ryme. 1925 (1602).
Darwin B = Charles Darwin, His Life, etc, by F. Darwin. L 1892.
      D =   —   Descent of Man (1871).
      E =   —   Expression of the Emotions (1872).
      L =   —   Life and Letters, 3 vols. L 1888.
Deeping RR = Warwick Deeping, Roper's Row. L 1929.

Abbreviations and List of Books. 9

Deeping 3R = Warwick Deeping, Three Rooms. L 1930.
Defoe G = Daniel Defoe, The Complete Gentleman, ed. Bülbring. L 1890.
 M = — Moll Flanders (The Abbey Classics) (1722).
 P = — Journal of the Plague Year, ed. Brayley. L n.d. (1722).
 R = — Robinson Crusoe 1719 (Facsimile ed. L 1883).
 R2 = — Farther Adventures of Robinson Crusoe. L 1719.
 Rox = — Roxana (The Abbey Classics) (1724).
Dekker F = Thomas Dekker, The Pleasant Comedie of Old Fortunatus, ed. Scherer (1600).
 G = — The Gull's Hornbook, ed. McKerrow (King's Library 1904) (1609).
 S = — The Seven Deadly Sins, ed. Arber. L 1879 (1606).
 Sh = — The Shoemaker's Holiday, ed. Warnke & Proescholdt (1600).
Deloney = The Works of Thomas Deloney, ed. F. O. Mann. Oxford 1912.
Deutschbein ME = Deutschbein, Mutschmann, Eicker, Handbuch der englischen grammatik. Lpz. 1926.
 SNS = Max Deutschbein, System der neuenglischen Syntax. Cöthen 1917.
Devil E = The Merry Devil of Edmonton (in Gayley II).
Di Am. Notes = Charles Dickens, American Notes. (Everyman) (1842).
 D (or DC) = — David Copperfield. L 1897 (MM) (1849-50).
 Do = — Dombey and Son. L 1887 (Ch. D. ed.) (1848).
 F = — Our Mutual Friend. L 1912 (Nelson) (1865).

Di H	=	Charles Dickens,	Hard Times. L 1903 (Nelson) (1854).
L	=	—	Letters. L 1893 (MM).
M	=	—	Martin Chuzzlewit. L n.d. (Ch. D. ed.) (1843).
N	=	—	Nicholas Nickleby. L 1900 (MM) (1839).
P	=	—	Pickwick Papers. L 1890 (Chapman & Hall) (1837f.).
P [Ch&H]	=	—	Pickwick Papers. L 1911 (ib. pop. ed.).
Pw	=	—	Pickwick Papers. T.
S(k)	=	—	Sketches. T 1886 (1836).
T	=	—	Tale of Two Cities. T (1859).
X	=	—	Christmas Books. L 1892 (MM).

dial. = dialect(s), dialectal.

Dickinson C	=	G. Lowes Dickinson,	Letters from John Chinaman. L 1904 (1901).
F	=	—	in Forster, Goldsworthy Lowes Dickinson. L 1934.
Im	=	—	Is Immortality Desirable? Boston 1909.
R	=	—	Religion. L 1906 (1905).
S	=	—	A Modern Symposium. L 1906 or 1915 (1905).

Dobson F = Henry A. Dobson, Fielding. L 1889 (1883).
     P =   —   Collected Poems. L 1897.
Doren Sw = Carl van Doren, Swift. L 1931.

Doyle B	=	Arthur Conan Doyle,	The Hound of the Baskervilles. T 1902.
F	=	—	The Sign of Four. T 1891 (1889).
G	=	—	The Great Shadow. T 1893.
M	=	—	The Stark Munro Letters. T 1895.

Abbreviations and List of Books. 11

Doyle S = Arthur Conan Doyle, 1, 2 = Adventures; 3, 4 = Memoirs; 5, 6 = Return; of Sherlock Holmes. T 1893-1905.
    Sh = — Complete Short Stories. L 1929.
    St = — A Study in Scarlet. T 1892 (1887).
Dreiser AT = Theodore Dreiser, An American Tragedy. N.Y. (1925).
    F = — Free, and Other Stories. N.Y. 1918.
Drinkwater P = John Drinkwater, Poems 1908-14. L 1917.
Dryden = John Dryden, Poetical Works. Globe ed. L 1890. (Sometimes quoted from vol. 5 of Scott's ed.).
Dyboski T = Roman Dyboski, Tennysons Sprache und Stil. Wien 1907.
E = English.
E3, see below Sh.
ead = eadem (same authoress).
Earle M = John Earle, Micro-cosmographie (Arber) (1628).
Eastw = Chapman, Jonson, Marston, Eastward Hoe (in Gayley).
ed. = edition (by), edited (by).
EDD = Joseph Wright, English Dialect Dictionary. Oxf. 1898 ff. — EDG see Wright below.
EEP = Alexander Ellis, On Early English Pronunciation. L 1869 ff.
Egerton Castle K = Egerton Castle, Keynotes. L 1893.
EK = Otto Jespersen, Studier over engelske kasus. København 1891.
ElE = Elizabethan English.
Eliot, see GE.
Elizabeth Exp = Expiation, by the Author of Elizabeth and her German Garden [Countess Russell]. (1929).
    R = The Adventures of Elizabeth in Rügen. L 1911 (1904).
Ellis M = Havelock Ellis, Man and Woman. L 1904.
    N = — The New Spirit. L 1892.

12   Abbreviations and List of Books.

ElSmith Tz = Eleanor Smith, Tzigane. L n.d. (1935).
Ertz G = Susan Ertz, The Galaxy. L n.d. (1929).
Escott E = T. H. S. Escott, England. L 1887.
ESt(n) = Englische Studien (Periodical). Lpz.
ESts = English Studies (Periodical). Amsterdam.
Eton = A Day of My Life .. By an Eton Boy. L 1889.
F = French; folio.
Farnol A = Farnol, The Amateur Gentleman. L n.d. (1913).
Farquhar B = George Farquhar, The Beaux' Strategem (in Restoration Plays, Everyman 1912).
Fielding   = Henry Fielding, Works, Second ed. L 1762. (8 vols).
    JA =   —   Joseph Andrews (Everyman) (1742).
    T =   —   Tom Jones. L 1782 (1749). 4 vols.
First = My First Book, by W. Besant and 20 Other Writers. L 1897.
Flaherty I = Liam O'Flaherty, The Informer (Traveller's Libr.) (1925).
Fludyer = [R. C. Lehmann,] Harry Fludyer at Cambridge. L 1890.
Ford = John Ford, ed. Havelock Ellis in Mermaid Series. L.
Forster = John Forster, Life of Charles Dickens (Chapman and Hall) (1871—74).
    I = E. M. Forster, A Passage to India. P 1936 (1924).
Fowler KE = H. W. and F. G. Fowler, The King's English. Oxford 1906.
    MEU = H. W. Fowler, A Dictionary of Modern English Usage. Oxford 1926.
Frankau D(ance) = Gilbert Frankau, Dance, Little Gentleman! L n.d.
Franklin = Benjamin Franklin, Autobiography, ed. Macdonald. L 1906.
Franz = W. Franz, Shakespeare-Grammatik. 2 Aufl. Heidelberg 1909.
    N = Nachtrag (in 3. Aufl. 1924).
Freeman CT = R. Austin Freeman, A Certain Dr. Thorndyke. L n.d.

Abbreviations and List of Books. 13

Freeman Th = R. Austin Freeman, The Famous Cases of Dr. Thorndyke. L n.d.
    TI = — Dr. Thorndyke Intervenes. L 1935.

Froude C = James Anthony Froude, Carlyle [see above].
    O = — Oceana. T 1886.
    RC = — Relations with Carlyle.

Fulg = Fulgens & Lucres, by H. Medwall, ed. Boas & Reed. Oxford 1926 (between 1513 and 1519) (quoted by page).

fut = future.

G = German.

Galsw B = John Galsworthy, Beyond. L 1933.
    C = — The Country House. L 1911 (1907).
    Car = — Caravan. L 1925.
    D = — The Dark Flower. T 1913.
    EC(h) = — End of the Chapter. L 1935.
    F = — The Freelands. L 1916 (Nelson).
    FCh = — On Forsyte 'Change. L 1930 (or Grove ed. L 1930).
    FM = — A Family Man and Other Plays. T.
    Frat = — Fraternity. T 1909.
    FS = — The Forsyte Saga. L 1925.
    IC = — In Chancery. L 1920.
    IPh = — The Island Pharisees. L 1925 (1/- ed.) (1904).
    Loy = — Loyalties. (1922).
    M = — A Motley. T 1910.
    MP = — The Man of Property. L 1906. Pop. ed. 1915.
    MW = — Maid in Waiting. L 1931.
    P = — Plays (1 = Silver Box. 2 = Joy. 3 = Strife. 4 = The Eldest Son. 5 = The Little Dream. 6 = Justice. 7 = The Fugitive. 8 = The Pigeon. 9 = The Mob). L 1910-14.

Galsw SP = John Galsworthy, Saint's Progress. L 1919.
 SS =   — The Silver Spoon. L 1926.
 Sw =   — Swan Song. L 1928.
 T   =   — Five Tales. L 1918.
 Tat =   — Tatterdemalion. L 1920.
 TL =   — To Let. L 1921.
 WM =   — The White Monkey. L 1924.

Galton H = Francis Galton, Hereditary Genius. L 1892 (1869).
Gamelyn = The Tale of Gamelyn. Ed. Skeat. Oxford 1884.
Gammer (Gurton's Needle), page in Manly's Specimens.
Gardiner H = Samuel R. Gardiner, Student's History of England. L 1898.
Garnett Go = David Garnett, Go She Must. L 1927.
 L   =   — Lady into Fox. T 1929.
 MZ =   — Man in the Zoo. T 1929.
 T   = Richard Garnett, The Twilight of the Gods. L 1888.

Gascoigne = George Gascoigne, The Steele Glas. Arber (1576).
Gay BP = John Gay, Singspiele [Beggar's Opera and Polly], ed. Sarrazin.
Gaye, Vivandière. L.
GE A = George Eliot, Adam Bede. L 1900 (1859).
 L   =   — Life and Letters. T.
 M   =   — The Mill on the Floss. T (1860).
 Mm =   — Middlemarch. N. Y. n.d. (Burt) (1871-72).
 S   =   — Silas Marner. T or Everyman (1861).
 V   =   — The Lifted Veil. T (1859).

Gibbon M = Memoirs of the Life of Edward Gibbon, ed. Birkbeck Hill. L 1900.
Gibbs BR = Philip Gibbs, Blood Relations. L (1935).
Gilbert = W. S. Gilbert, Original Plays. First Series. L 1884.
Gissing B = George Gissing, Born in Exile. L (Nelson) (1892).
 G   =   — The New Grub Street. L 1908 (1891).
 H   =   — The House of Cobwebs. L 1914 (Constable).
 O   =   — The Odd Women. L (Nelson) (1893).

Abbreviations and List of Books. 15

Gissing R = George Gissing, Henry Ryecroft. L 1912.
Gk = Greek.
Goldsm V = Oliver Goldsmith, The Vicar of Wakefield. 2 vols. 1766 [Facsimile ed. L 1885], or ed. Stein. Oxford 1922.
Goldsmith = Oliver Goldsmith, Globe ed. L 1889.
Gosse D = Edmund Gosse, Two Visits to Denmark. L 1912.
    F = — Father and Son. L 1907.
    L = — English Literature. Illustrated. L 1903.
    P = — Portraits and Sketches. L 1912.
GP = Georgian Poetry 1911-1912. L 1912.
Gr = Greek.
Grand T = Sarah Grand [Mrs. McFall Clarke], The Heavenly Twins. L 1893.
Grattan & Gurrey OLL = Our Living Language. L 1925.
Graves Goodbye = Robert Graves, Goodbye to All That. L 1929.
    IC = — I, Claudius. L 1936.
Gray = The Poetical Works of Thomas Gray. Cooke's ed. L (quoted by page, poem, line).
Green H = John Richard Green, A Short History of the English People. Illustr. ed. L 1894.
Greene F = Robert Greene, Friar Bacon and Friar Bungay, ed. Ward. Oxford 1887 (ab. 1590).
    J4 = — James the Fourth in Manly's Specimens.
Gretton H = R. H. Gretton, A Modern History of the English People. Illustr. ed. L 1894.
GS = Otto Jespersen, Growth and Structure of the English Language. Lpz. (1st ed. 1905).
Hadow Ch = Grace E. Hadow, Chaucer and his Times. L 1914.
Haggard S = Rider Haggard, She. L 1896 (1887).
Hamerton F = Philip G. Hamerton, French and English. T.
Hammett Th = Dashiell Hammett, The Thin Man. L 1934.
Hankin = St. J. Hankin [1869-1909], Three Plays. L 1927.
Hardy E = Thomas Hardy, The Hand of Ethelbertha. T 1876.
    F = — Far from the Madding Crowd. L 1906 (1874).

16   Abbreviations and List of Books.

Hardy L = Thomas Hardy, Life's Little Ironies. L 1903 (1894).
     R = — The Return of the Native. Wessex ed. L 1912 (1878).
     T = — Tess of the D'Urbervilles. L 1892 (1891).
     U = — Under the Greenwood Tree.
     W = — Wessex Tales. L 1889 (1888).
Harpsfield M = Harpsfield's Life of More. E. E. T. S. 186. L 1932.

Harraden D = Beatrice Harraden, The Scholar's Daughter. T 1906 (1903).
     F = — The Fowler. L 1899.
     S = — Ships that Pass in the Night. L (6d. ed.) (1893).
Harris Shaw = Frank Harris, Bernard Shaw. L 1931.
Harrison IS = G. B. Harrison, Introducing Shakespeare. Pelican 1939.
     R = Frederic Harrison, John Ruskin. L 1902.
Hart BT = Frances Noyes Hart, The Bellamy Trial (Amr). 1929 (Heinemann's Omnibus Books).
Hawth(orne) = Nathaniel Hawthorne, Works. N.Y. 1900.
     S = = The Scarlet Letter L 1903 (1850).
     Sn = — The Snow Image and Other Twice-Told Tales. N.Y. n. d. (Caldwell).
     T = — Tanglewood Tales. L n.d. (Warne).
Hay B = [John Hay,] The Breadwinners. T 1883.
Hazlitt A = William Hazlitt, Liber Amoris (Routledge). (1823).
Hemingway FA = Ernest Hemingway, A Farewell to Arms. P (1929).
     OT = — In Our Time. L 1926.
Henderson Shaw = Archibald Henderson, George Bernard Shaw. N.Y. 1918.
Henley B = William E. Henley and Stevenson, Beau Austin. L. (1884).
     Burns = — Centenary ed. of Burns.

Hergesheimer MB = Joseph Hergesheimer, Mountain Blood. L 1922.
Herrick M = Robert Herrick, Memoirs of an American Citizen. N.Y. 1905.
Hewlett F = Maurice H. Hewlett, The Forest Lovers. L 1910 (1898).
    Q = — The Queen's Quair. L 1904.
Heywood P = John Heywood, The Four PP (Manly I 483ff.). Quoted by line.
    Pr = — A Dialogue of the Effectual Proverbs ... concerning Marriage (1562), ed. J. S. Farmer. L 1906.
Holmes A = Oliver W. Holmes, The Autocrat of the Breakfast Table. L 1904 (1857).
Hope C = Anthony Hope [Hawkins], Comedies of Courtship. T 1896.
    Ch = — A Change of Air. T 1893.
    D = — Dolly Dialogues. L 1894.
    F = — Father Stafford. L 1900 (6d. ed.).
    In = — Intrusions of Peggy. L 1907 (Nelson).
    M = — A Man of Mark. L (6d. ed.)
    Q = — Quisanté. L (Nelson).
    R = — Rupert of Hentzau. T 1898.
    Z = — The Prisoner of Zenda. L 1894.
Housman J = Laurence Housman, John of Jingalo. L 1912.
Howells S = W. D. Howells, The Rise of Silas Lapham. T (1884-85).
Hughes T1 = Thomas Hughes, Tom Brown's School-Days. L 1886 (1856).
    T2 = — Tom Brown at Oxford. L 1886 (1861).
Hunt A = Leigh Hunt, Autobiography. Oxford 1928 (World's Classics) (1850).
Huxley L = T. Huxley, Life and Letters 1-2. L 1900.
    LS = — Lectures and Lay Sermons (Everyman).
AHuxley AH = Aldous Huxley, Antic Hay. Phoenix Libr. 1928 (1923).

AHuxley BL = Aldous Huxley, Those Barren Leaves. T (1925).
         BNW = — Brave New World. Albatros 1933 (1932).
         CY = — Crome Yellow. L 1923 (1921).
         EG = Eyeless in Gaza. L 1936.
         Jest. Pil. = — Jesting Pilate. Phoenix Libr. (1926).
         LM = — Little Mexican & Other Stories. L 1924.
         MC = — Mortal Coils. L 1922.
         PCP = — Point Counter Point. L 1931 (1928).

ib = ibidem (same work).
id = idem (same author, cf ead).
IF = Indogermanische Forschungen.
inf = infinitive.
ing = verbal substantive in *-ing*.
Ingoldsby = The Ingoldsby Legends by Thomas Ingoldsby [Richard Harris Barham]. L 1899 (1840).
Jackson S = Holbrook Jackson, Bernard Shaw. L 1907.
Jacob G = Naomi Jacob, Groping. L 1933.
    Lie = — That Wild Lie. L n.d.
Jacobs L = W. W. Jacobs, The Lady of the Barge. L (Nelson) (1902).
James A = Henry James, The American. T (1877).
    G = Montague Rhodes James, Ghost Stories of an Antiquary. P 1937 (1910).
    RH = Henry James, Roderick Hudson. L (Nelson) (1875).
    S = — The Soft Side. L 1900.
    TM = — Two Magies. L (1898).
Jameson F = Margaret Storm Jameson, Farewell to Youth. L 1928.
Jeans MU = James Jeans, The Mysterious Universe. Pelican 1937 (1930).
Jenkins B = Herbert Jenkins, Bindle. L 1916.
Jerome NN = Jerome K. Jerome, Novel Notes. T 1894.

Abbreviations and List of Books.

Jerome T = Jerome K. Jerome, Three Men in a Boat. L 1889.
    TB = — Three Men on the Bummel. T 1900.
    TC = — Tommy & Co. L (1904).
Jerrold C = Douglas Jerrold, Mrs. Caudle's Curtain Lectures. L n.d. (1846).
Jevons L = W. Stanley Jevons, Elementary Lessons in Logic. L 1885 (1870).
Johnson L = Samuel Johnson, Lives of the Most Eminent English Poets. 4 vols. L 1781.
    R = — Rasselas, ed. Birkbeck Hill. Oxford 1887 (1759).
Johnston O = Mary Johnston, By Order of the Company. L 1914.
Jonson, see BJo.
Joyce Ir = P. W. Joyce, English as We Speak it in Ireland. L 1910.
Juliana = Juliana, ed. William Strunk. Boston 1904.
Karpf SCh = Fritz Karpf, Syntax in den Werken Chaucers. Wien 1930.
Kaye-Smith GA = Sheila Kaye-Smith, Green Apple Harvest L 1923 (1920).
    HA = — The End of the House of Alard. L 1923.
    T = — Tamarisk Town. L 1923 (1919).
Keats = John Keats, The Complete Works, ed. Buxton Forman. Glasgow 1900.
Kemp N(ine)DW = Kemps Nine Daies Wonder, ed. Dyce 1840 (1600).
Kennedy CN = Margaret Kennedy, The Constant Nymph. T (1924).
    R = — Red Sky at Morning. L 1927.
Ker E = W. P. Ker, English Literature, Medieval. L 1912.
Kidd S = Benjamin Kidd, Social Evolution. L 1894.
King O = C. Daly King, Obelists at Sea. L 1932.
Kinglake E = A. W. Kinglake, Eothen, ed. Hogarth & Collins. Oxford 1914 (1844).

King's E = H. W. and F. G. Fowler, The King's English. Oxford 1906.

Kingsley H = Charles Kingsley, Hypatia. L n.d. (1853).

Kipling B = Rudyard Kipling, Barrack-Room Ballads. 1892 (Engl. Libr.).
DW = — The Day's Work. T (1898).
J1 = — The Jungle Book. 1897 (Engl. Libr.) (1894).
J2 = — The Second Jungle Book. T 1897 (1895).
K = — Kim. L 1908 (Pocket ed.) (1901).
L = — The Light that Failed (Engl. Libr.) (1890).
MOP = — Mine Own People (Engl. Libr.) (1891).
P = — Puck of Pook's Hill. T (1906).
S = — Stalky & Co. T (1899).
ST = — Soldiers Three. T (1888).
V = — Collected Verse. N.Y. 1917.

Knecht K = Jacob Knecht, Die Kongruenz zwischen Subjekt und Prädikat. Heidelberg 1911.

Krapp CG = G. P. Krapp, Comprehensive Guide to Good English. N.Y. 1927.

Krüger = Gustav Krüger, Schwierigkeiten des Englischen. Dresden und Leipzig 1897 ff.

Kyd = The Works of Thomas Kyd, ed. Boas. L 1901 (page).

Lamb E = Charles Lamb, The Essays of Elia. L 1899 (Dent).
R = — Rosamund Gray. L 1905 (1798).

Landor C = Walter S. Landor, Imaginary Conversations, ed. Havelock Ellis. L 1886 (1824-29).
P = — Pericles and Aspasia, ed. id. L n.d. (1836).

Lang Ban & AB = Andrew Lang, Ban and Arrière Ban. L 1894.
C = — Custom and Myth. L 1893 (1884).
E = — Essays in Little. L 1891.
T = — Tennyson. L 1904.

Lat = Latin.
Lawrence L = D. H. Lawrence, The Ladybird. L 1923.
         LG = — The Lost Girl. L 1920.
         SL = — Sons and Lovers. L 1927 (1913).
Lay = Layamon, ed. E. Madden.
Lecky D = William E. H. Lecky, Democracy and Liberty. L 1896.
Le Gallienne Y = Richard Le Gallienne, Young Lives. L (1899).
Lehmann DA = Rosamond Lehmann, Dusty Answer. Phoenix Libr. 1930 (1927).
Lewes H = George H. Lewes, History of Philosophy. L 1893 (1845-46).
Lewis B = Sinclair Lewis, Babbitt. L 1922.
       EG = — Elmer Gantry. L 1927.
       MA = — Martin Arrowsmith. L 1926 (1925).
       MS = — Main Street. L 1923 (1920).
Lindsay CA = Norman Lindsay, The Cautious Amorist. L 1934.
Linklater J = Eric Linklater, Juan in America. L 1931.
        MM = — Magnus Merriman. Albatross (1933).
Locke A = William J. Locke, The Joyous Adventures of Aristide Pujol. Cheap ed. L n.d. (1912).
     BV = — The Beloved Vagabond. L (1906).
     CA = — The Coming of Amos. L 1924.
     D = — Derelicts. Cheap ed. (1897).
     FS = — Far-away Stories. Cheap ed. L n.d.
     GP = — The Great Pandolfo. L 1925.
     HB = — House of Baltazar. L 1920.
     Ordeyne = — The Morals of Marcus Ordeyne. L 1906 (1905).

Locke	S	= William J. Locke,	Septimus. L 1916 (1909).
	SJ	= —	Simon the Jester. L 1910.
	St	= —	A Study in Shadows. L n.d. (1896).
	W	= —	The Wonderful Year. L 1916.

LondE = A Book of London English 1384-1425, ed. R. W. Chambers and M. Daunt. Oxford 1931.

London	A	= Jack London,	Adventure. L 1911.
	C	= —	The War of the Classes. N.Y. 1905.
	F	= —	The Faith of Men. L 1904.
	M	= —	Martin Eden. L 1915 (Popular ed.) (1909).
	V	= —	The Valley of the Moon. L 1914 (1913).
	W	= —	White Fang. L 1908 (1906).

Longfellow = Henry W. Longfellow, Poetical Works. L 1881.

Lounsbury SU = Thomas R. Lounsbury, The Standard of Usage in English. N.Y. 1908.

Lowell		= James R. Lowell,	Poetical Works in one vol. L 1892 (MM).
	St	= —	My Study Windows. L n.d. (Scott) (1871).

Lowndes	BD	= Mrs. Belloc Lowndes,	Bread of Deceit. T (1925).
	Ivy	= —	The Story of Ivy. T 1928.

Lubbock P = John Lubbock, The Pleasures of Life. L (6d. ed.).

Lucas RR = E. V. Lucas, Rose and Rose. L 1921.

Lyly	C	= John Lyly,	Campaspe, in Manly, Specimens of the Pre-Shakespearean Drama. Boston 1900 (page).
	E	= —	Euphues, ed. Arber (1579-80).

Rose Mac(aulay)	DA	= Rose Macaulay,	Dangerous Ages (Collins 1/- Libr.) (1921).
	K	= —	Keeping up Appearances. T (1928).
	O	= —	Orphan Island. L 1924.

Rose Mac(aulay) P = Rose Macaulay, Potterism. L 1922 (1920).
              T = — Told by an Idiot. L 1923.
Mac(aulay) B = Thomas B. Macaulay, Biographical Essays. T.
          E = — Essays, Critical and Historical. T.
          H = — History of England. T.
          L = — Life end Letters, by Trevelyan (Nelson).
         WH = — Warren Hastings. L n.d. (1841).

MacCarthy = Justin MacCarthy, A History of Our Own Times. N.Y. 1880.

Macdonald F, see Franklin.

Macdonell E = A. G. Macdonell, England, Their England. Albatross 1934 (1933).

MacGill Ch = Patrick MacGill, Children of the Dead End. L 1914.

Mackenzie C = Compton Mackenzie, Carnival. L 1922 (1912).
         PR = — Poor Relations. L 1919.
         RR = — Rich Relatives. L 1921.
         S = — Sinister Street. 2 vols. L 1913-14.

Maclaren A = Ian Maclaren [John Watson], The Days of Auld Lang Syne. L 1896.

Mal, see Malory.

Malet C = Lucas Malet [Mary Harrison], Sir Richard Calmady. L 1901.

Mal(ory) = Thomas Malory, Morte D'Arthur, ed. O. Sommer. L 1889.

Mandv = Voiage and Travayle of Sir John Maundeville, ed. Halliwell. L 1883.

Mannin ChE = Ethel Mannin, Children of the Earth. P (1930).
         Conf = — Confessions and Impressions. L 1932 (1930).

Mannin M = Ethel Mannin, The Magician. L 1931.
   RS = — Rose and Sylvie. L 1938.
   W = — Women also Dream. L 1937.
Marl(owe) or Ml E = Cristopher Marlowe, Edward the Second, ed. Tucker Brooke. Oxford 1910.
   F = — Doctor Faustus.
   J = — The Jew of Malta.
   T = — Tamburlaine. All in Breymann & Wagner's ed. Heilbronn 1885 ff.
   H = — Hero and Leander, ed. Tucker Brooke. Oxford 1910.
Masefield C = John Masefield, Captain Margaret. L n.d. (Nelson) (1908).
   E = — The Everlasting Mercy. L 1912 (1911).
   M = — Multitude and Solitude. L n.d. (Nelson) (1909).
   S = — Sard Harker. L 1924.
   W = — The Widow in the Bye-Street. L 1912.
Mason Ch = A. E. W. Mason, They Wouldn't Be Chessmen. L 1935.
   R = — Running Water. L (1907).
   3G = — The Three Gentlemen. L 1932.
Massinger N = Philip Massinger, New Way to Pay Old Debts (in Gayley, Repres. Eng. Com. III).
Masterman OT = J. C. Masterman, An Oxford Tragedy. P 1939 (1933).
   WL = W. S. Masterman, The Wrong Letter. L 1926.
Matthews A = Brander Matthews, The American of the Future. N.Y. 1909.
   F = — His Father's Son. N.Y. 1896.
Maugham AK = W. Somerset Maugham, Ah King. L 1933.

Abbreviations and List of Books.

Maugham Alt	= W. Somerset Maugham,	Altogether (Collected Stories). L 1934.
C	= —	Cakes and Ale. L 1930.
F(PS)	= —	Six Stories Written in the First Person Singular. L 1931 or T 1932.
HB	= —	Of Human Bondage. L 1929 (1915).
MS	= —	The Moon and Sixpence. T (1919).
Pl	= —	Plays. 4 vols. T.
P(V)	= —	The Painted Veil. L 1925.
TL	= —	The Trembling of a Leaf. T 1923 (1921).

Maurier T = George du Maurier, Trilby. L 1894.

Maxwell BY	= W. B. Maxwell,	The Case of Bevan Yorke. L 1927.
ChN	= —	Children of the Night. L 1925.
EG	= —	Elaine at the Gates. L 1924.
F	= —	Fernande. T 1926.
G	= —	Gabrielle. L 1926.
HR	= —	Himself and Mr. Raikes. T 1929.
ML	= —	A Man and his Lesson. L 1919.
S	= —	Spinster of this Parish. L 1922.
WF	= —	We Forget Because We Must. T (1928).

Maynard Smith F = H. Maynard Smith, The Inspector Frost Omnibus. L 1933 (Benn).

McKenna M	= Stephen McKenna,	Midas & Son. L 1919.
Ninety	= —	Ninety-six Hours' Leave. L 1917.

McKenna S = Stephen McKenna, Sonia. L (Methuen) (1917).
    Sh =   —   Sheila Intervenes. L 1918 (1913).
    SM =   —   Sonia Married. L 1918.
    SS =   —   The Sixth Sense. L 1918 (1915).
McKnight EW = George H. McKnight, English Words and their Background. N.Y. 1923.
    MnE =   —   Modern English in the Making. N.Y. & L 1928.

ME = Middle English.

Medwin S = T. Medwin, Life of Shelley, ed. Buxton Forman. Oxford 1913.

Mencken BB = H. L. Mencken, A Book of Burlesques. N.Y. 1924 (1916).
    AL =   —   The American Language, 3rd ed. N.Y. 1923.
    AL^4 =   —   4th ed. 1936.

Mered(ith) E = George Meredith, The Egoist. L 1892 (1879).
    H =   —   Evan Harrington. L 1889 (1861).
    R =   —   The Ordeal of Richard Feverel. L 1895 (1859).
    SP =   —   Selected Poems. L 1919 (1897).
    T =   —   The Tragic Comedians L. 1893 (1881).

Merm. = The Mermaid Series of the Old Dramatists.

Merrick C = L. Merrick, Conrad in Quest of his Youth. L n.d. (1903).

Merriman S = H. Seton Merriman [H. S. Scott], The Sowers. L 1905 (1896).
    V =   —   The Vultures. L 1902.
    VG =   —   The Velvet Glove. L 1901.

Mi, see Milton.

Mill L = John Stuart Mill, On Liberty. L 1859 (1858).

Abbreviations and List of Books. 27

Milne P = A. A. Milne, Mr. Pym Passes By.(1st perform. 1920).
Mi(lton) A = John Milton, Areopagitica, ed. Hales. Oxford.
Poetical Works from H. C. Beeching's ed. Oxford 1900; C = Comus; PL = Paradise Lost; PR = Paradise Regained; S = Sonnets; SA = Samson Agonistes. Other titles occasionally abbreviated. Pr = English Prose Writings, ed. H. Morley. L 1889.
Mitford OV = Mary Russell Mitford, Our Village, ed. Ritchie. L 1906 (1819-32).
Ml, see Marlowe.
MM = Macmillan.
ModE (or MnE) = Modern English.
Moore EW = George Moore, Esther Waters. P 1936 (1894).
    L = — — The Lake. L 1921 (1905).
More A = Thomas More, Utopia. Arber's reprint of 2nd ed. of Robinson's transl.
    U = — — The transl. ed. J.H.Lupton. Oxford 1895.
Morley HB = Christopher Morley, Human Being. L 1933.
    TL = — Thunder on the Left. P 1937 (1926).
    M = John Morley, Miscellanies. L 1886.
Morris C = William Morris, Signs of Change. L 1888.
    E = — The Earthly Paradise. L 1880.
    N = — News from Nowhere. L 1908.
Mulock H = Dinah Mulock [Mrs. Craik], John Halifax Gentleman. T (1858).
Murray D = James A. H. Murray, The Dialect of the Southern Counties of Scotland. L 1873.
NED = A New English Dictionary, by Murray, Bradley, Craigie, and Onions. Oxford 1884-1933.
Neg. = Otto Jespersen, Negation in English. Copenhagen 1917.
Nicolson SP = Harold Nicolson, Some People. L 1930.
Norris O = Frank Norris, The Octopus. L 1908 (Nelson) (1901).
    P = — The Pit. L 1908 (ib) (1903).
    S = — Shanghaied. L (ib).
North = North's Plutarch, facsimile ed. (1579)-
NP = Newspaper (or periodical; among those most frequently quoted are The Times, Daily News, Daily Chronicle, Westminster Gazette, The Tribune; New York Times; Evening

News; Everyman; Public Opinion; The Outlook; The Bookman; Review of Reviews; The World's Work).

OE = Old English.

OF = Old French.

OHenry (B) = The Best of O. Henry. N.Y. n.d.

Onions AS = C. T. Onions, An Advanced English Syntax. Oxford 1904.

Oppenheim Laxw = E. Phillips Oppenheim, Mr. Laxworthy's Adventures. L 1913.

Oros. = Orosius, ed. Sweet.

Orr L = Mrs. Orr, Life of Robert Browning. L 1891.

Orrm = The Orrmulum, ed. R. Holt 1878.

Osborne = The Letters of Dorothy Osborne to W. Temple, ed. Moore Smith. Oxford 1928.

Otway = Thomas Otway, The Orphan and Venice Preserved, ed. McClumpha. Boston 1904(?).

Page J = Thomas Nelson Page, John Marvel Assistant. N.Y. 1909.

Palm P = Birger Palm, The Place of the Adjective Attribute. Lund 1911.

Palmer Gr = H. E. Palmer, A Grammar of Spoken English. 1924.

Parker R = Gilbert Parker, The Right of Way. L 1906 (1901).

Pascoe PS = C. E. Pascoe, Everyday Life in our Public Schools. L n.d.

Pater P = Walter Pater, Imaginary Portraits. L 1887.

— R = — The Renaissance. L 1912 (1873).

Payn S = James Payn, Sunny Stories. L.

Payne Al = L. W. Payne, Word-List from East Alabama (Univ. of Texas). 1909.

PE = Present English.

Peacock M or S = Peacock's Memoirs of Shelley, ed. Brett-Smith. L 1909.

Pegge Anecd = S. Pegge, Anecdotes of the English Language. 2nd ed. 1814.

Peele D = George Peele, David and Bethsabe, in Manly's Specimens of Pre-Shakespearean Drama II (page).

Pennell L = Elizabeth Robins Pennell, The Lovers. L 1917.

pf = perfect.

PG or PhilGr = Otto Jespersen, The Philosophy of Grammar. L 1924.

Philips L = F. C. Philips, As in a Looking-Glass. T 1886.
Phillips P = Stephen Phillips, Paolo and Francesca. L 1900 (1899).
Phillpotts GR = Eden Phillpotts, The Gray Room. T 1922 (1921).
    K = — The Three Knaves. L 1912.
    M = — The Mother. L 1908.
PhSt = Phonetische Studien. Marburg.
Pinero B = Arthur W. Pinero, The Benefit of the Doubt. L 1895.
    M = — The Magistrate. L 1897 (1885).
    Q = — The Gay Lord Quex. L 1900 (1899).
    T = — The Second Mrs. Tanqueray. L 1895 (1893).
pl = plural.
plpf = pluperfect.
Plunket Greene E = R. and E. Plunket Greene, Eleven-Thirty till Twelve. L 1934.
PMLA = Publ. of the Mod. Lang. Ass. of America.
Poe = Edgar Allan Poe, Works. L 1872.
    S = — Selections. L (1887?) (Cassell's Red Libr.).
Pope = Alexander Pope, Poetical Works. L 1892 (Globe ed.).
Poutsma = H. Poutsma, A Grammar of Late Modern English. 2nd ed. 1928; the later vols. in 1st ed.
pple = participle.
prep. = preposition.
Priestley A = J. B. Priestley, Adam in Moonshine. L 1927.
    AP = — Angel Pavement (1931).
    B = — Benighted. L 1929.
    F = — Faraway. L 1932.
    G = — The Good Companions. L 1930 (1929).
prs = present.
prt = preterit.
Progr = Otto Jespersen, Progress in Language. L 1894.
ptc = participle.
Puttenham = George Puttenham, The Arte of English Poesie. Arber. (1589).

Q = quarto.
(q) = quoted second-hand.
Quentin P = Patrick Quentin, A Puzzle for Fools. L 1936.
Quiller-Couch M = Arthur T. Quiller-Couch, Major Vigoureux. L 1907.
    T =   —   Troy Town. L n.d. (1888).
Quincey = Thomas De Quincey, Confessions of an Opium-Eater, etc. L 1901 (MM).
Raleigh M = Walter A. Raleigh, Milton. L (1900).
  S = — Style. L 1904 (1897).
  Sh = — Shakespeare. L 1907.
Rea Six = Lorna Rea, Six Mrs. Greenes. L 1929.
Read K = Opie Read, A Kentucky Colonel.
Redford W = John Redford, Wyt and Science in Manly's Specimens I 421ff. Quoted by verse (ab. 1530 acc. to NED).
Rehearsal = George Villiers, The Rehearsal. Arber. (1671).
Richardson G = Samuel Richardson, Sir Charles Grandison. L 1754.
Ridge B = William Pett Ridge, 69 Birnam Road. L 1907.
  G = — Name of Garland. T (1907).
  L = — Lost Property. L 1902.
  ME = — Mord Em'ly. L 1918 (1898).
  N = — Nearly Five Million. L 1907.
  S = — A Son of the State. L (6d. ed.) (1899).
Ritchie M = Anne Thackeray Ritchie, Chapters from Some Memoirs. T 1896.
Roberts M = Morley Roberts, The Private Life of Henry Maitland. L 1912.
[Leigh] Rogers, Wine of Fury. L 1924 (Grant Richards).
Roister = [Udall,] Ralph Roister Doister. Arber. (1553?).
Roosevelt A = Theodore Roosevelt, American Ideals. N.Y. 1901.
Rose Mac(aulay), see M—.
Royce R = Josiah Royce, Rare Questions. N.Y. 1908.
Ru(skin) C = John Ruskin, The Crown of Wild Olive. L 1904 (1866).
  F = — Readings in Fors Clavigera. 1902.

Abbreviations and List of Books. 31

Ru(skin) On P = John Ruskin, Ruskin on Painting. N.Y. 1879.
    P = — Praeterita. L 1907.
    S = — Sesame and Lilies. L 1904 (1864).
    Sel = — Selections. 2 vols. L 1893.
    T = — Time and Tide. L 1904 (1867).
    U = — Unto This Last. L 1895 (1861).
Russell Ed = Bertrand Russell, On Education. L 1926.
    FO = — Freedom and Organisation (1934).
    SE = — Sceptical Essays. L 1928.
    SR = — Principles of Social Reconstruction. L 1917.
    W = — What I Believe (1925).

Sackville-West E = V. Sackville-West, The Edwardians. T 1931 (1930).

Saintsbury = George Saintsbury, A Short History of English Literature. L 1919 (MM).

Salt Joy = Sarah Salt, Joy is my Name. L 1929.

Savage OW = R. H. Savage, My Official Wife. T 1891.

Sayers GN = Dorothy M. Sayers, Gaudy Night. L 1935.
    HC = — Have His Carcase. L 1934.
    HH = — Hangman's Holiday. L 1934.
    NT = — The Nine Tailors. Albatross 1934.
    UnnD = — Unnatural Death. L 1935.

sb = substantive.
Sc = Scottish.

Schreiner T = Olive Schreiner, Trooper P. Halket. L 1897.

Scott A = Walter Scott, The Antiquary. Edinb. 1821 (1816) (canto and stanza).
    I(v) = — Ivanhoe. Everyman (1819).
    LL = — The Lady of the Lake. Edinb. 1874 (1810).
    O or OM = — Old Mortality. Oxford 1906 (1816).

32   Abbreviations and List of Books.

Seeley E = John R. Seeley, The Expansion of England. L 1883.
    L = — Lectures and Essays. L 1895.
Selden = John Selden, Table Talk. Arber's Reprints (1689).
sg = singular.
Sh = William Shakespeare. Abbreviations of plays, etc, as in Schmidt's Shakespeare-Lexicon (As = As You Like It. R2 = Richard the Second. H4A = First Part of Henry the Fourth. Tp = Tempest, etc. Wint (not WT) = Winter's Tale. Lines numbered as in the Globe ed. Spelling as in the Folio of 1623. — Sh? E3 = Edward the Third, ed. Warnke and Proescholdt. Halle 1886.
Sh-lex. = Alexander Schmidt, Shakespeare-Lexicon. 3rd ed. Berlin 1902.

Shaw 1	= G. Bernard Shaw,	Plays. Unpleasant. L 1898.
2	= —	Plays. Pleasant. L 1898.
A	= —	Androcles and the Lion, etc. L 1916.
B	= —	John Bull's Other Island. L 1907.
C	= —	Cashel Byron's Profession. L 1901.
D	= —	The Doctor's Dilemma. L 1911.
F	= —	Fabianism. L.
Ibsen	= —	The Quintessence of Ibsenism. L.
IW	= —	An Intelligent Woman's Guide to Socialism. L 1928.
J	= —	John Bull's Other Island. L 1907.
StJ	= —	Saint Joan. L 1924.
M	= —	Man and Superman. L 1903.
Ms	= —	Misalliance, The Dark Lady, Fanny's First Play. L 1914.
P	= —	Three Plays for Puritans. L 1901.
TT	= —	Too True to be Good. T 1935.

Abbreviations and List of Books. 33

Shelley = Percy Bysshe Shelley, Poetical Works, ed. Hutchinson. Oxford 1904.
    L = — Letters, ed. Ingpen. L 1909.
    P = — [Prose,] Essays and Letters. L (Camelot).
    PW = — Prose Works, ed. R. H. Shepherd. 2 vols. L 1912.

Mary Shelley F = Frankenstein (Everyman) (1818).
Sher(idan) = Richard B. Sheridan, Dramatic Works. T.
Sherriff F = R. C. Sherriff, The Fortnight in September. T (1931).
Sidney A = Philip Sidney, Apologie for Poetrie. Arber's Reprints (wr. ab. 1580).
Sinclair R = Upton Sinclair, The Industrial Republic. L 1907.
Sitwell M = Osbert Sitwell, Miracle on Sinai. Albatross 1934 (1933).
Smedley F = Frank Smedley, Frank Fairleigh. T (1850).
Smollett R = Tobias Smollett, Roderick Random. Everyman (1748).
Sonnenschein = E. A. Sonnenschein, A New English Grammar. Oxford 1921.
Southey L = Robert Southey, Letters, ed. M. H. Fitzgerald. Oxford 1912 (World's Classics).
Spect(ator) = Addison, etc, The Spectator, ed. Morley. L 1888.
Spencer A = Herbert Spencer, Autobiography. L 1904.
    E = — Essays. L 1883.
    Ed = — On Education. L 1882 (1861).
    F = — Facts and Comments. L 1902.
    M = — Man versus the State. L 1884.

Spenser FQ = Edmund Spenser, The Faery Queen in the Globe ed.
Spies KS = H. Spies, Kultur und Sprache im neuen England. Lpz. 1925.
Stacpoole C = H. de Vere Stacpoole, Cottage.
StE = Standard English.
Stedman O = A. M. M. Stedman, Oxford. L 1887.
Steel F = Flora A. Steel, On the Face of the Waters. L (1896).
Stephen L = Life and Letters of Leslie Stephen. L 1906.

Sterne = Laurence Sterne, Works. L 1885 (Nimmo).
    M = — Tristram Shandy and A Sentimental Journey. L 1911 (MM).
Stev(enson) A = Robert Louis Stevenson, The Art of Writing. L 1905.
    B = — The Black Arrow. L 1904 (1888).
    C = — Catriona. L (1893).
    D = — The Dynamiter. 1895 (1885).
    JH = — Dr. Jekyll and Mr. Hyde. T 1886.
    JHF = — Dr. Jekyll, etc, and Other Fables. L 1896.
    K = — Kidnapped. L 1886.
    M = — The Merry Men. L 1896 (1887).
    MB = — Men and Books. L 1901 (1882).
    MP = — Memoirs and Portraits. L 1900 (1887).
    N = — New Arabian Nights. L n.d. (1882).
    T = — Treasure Island. L (Cassell) (1882).
    U = — Underwoods. L 1894 (1887).
    V = — Virginibus Puerisque. L 1894 (1881).

sth = something.
Stockton R = Francis R. Stockton, Rudder Grange (1879).

Abbreviations and List of Books.

Stoffel Int = Cornelis Stoffel, Intensives and Downtoners. Heidelberg 1901.
    S = — Studies in English. Zutphen 1894.
Storm EPh = Johan Storm, Englische Philologie. Lpz. 1892, 1896.
Strachey EV = Lytton Strachey, Eminent Victorians. L 1926 (Phoenix Libr.) (1918).
    QV = — Queen Victoria. L 1928 (ib) (1921).
Straw = Jack Straw, ed. H. Schütt. Heidelberg 1901 (1593).
Street A = G. S. Street, Autobiography of a Boy. L 1894.
    E = — Episodes. L 1895.
Strong B = L. A. G. Strong, The Brothers. L 1933 (1932).
Sutro F = Alfred Sutro, Five Little Plays. L 1912.
Sweet E = Henry Sweet, Elementarbuch des gesprochenen Englisch. Lpz. 1886.
    NEG = — A New English Grammar. Oxford 1892, 1898.
    P = — A Primer of Spoken English. Oxford 1890.
    S = — The Practical Study of Languages. L 1899.
Swift = Jonathan Swift, Works. Dublin 1785.
    J = — Journal to Stella, ed. Aitken. L 1901.
    P = — Polite Conversation, ed. Saintsbury. L 1892 (1738).
    T = — The Tale of a Tub. L 1760 (1704).
    UL = — Unpublished Letters of Dean Swift, ed. Birkbeck Hill. L 1899.
Swinburne A = Algernon Charles Swinburne, Atalanta in Calydon, etc. T.
    E = — Erechtheus. L 1876.
    L = — Love's Cross Currents. T 1905.

Swinburne SbS = Algernon Charles Swinburne, Songs before Sunrise. L 1903 (1871).
        Sh = — A Study of Shakespeare. L (1879).
        T = — Tristram of Lyonesse. L 1884 (1882).

Swinnerton S = Frank Swinnerton, Summer Storm. T 1927 (1926).

Tarkington F = Booth Tarkington, The Flirt. L n.d. (1913).
        MA = — The Magnificent Ambersons. N.Y. 1918.
        Pl = — The Plutocrat. N.Y. 1927.
        Tu = — The Turmoil. N.Y. 1934 (1915).

Tenn(yson) = Alfred Tennyson, Poetical Works in one vol. L 1894.
        L = — Life and Letters. T 1899.

Thack B = William M. Thackeray, Burlesques. L 1869.
      E = — Henry Esmond. T (1852).
      H = — History of Sam. Titmarsh and The Great Hoggarty Diamond. L 1878 (1841).
      N = — The Newcomes. L 1901 (1853).
      P = — The History of Pendennis. 1 vol. ed.; sometimes quoted from T, 3 vols. (1848-50).
      S = — The Book of Snobs. L 1900 (1848).
      Sk = — Sketches and Travels in London. L 1901.
      V = — Vanity Fair. L 1890 (1847-48).

Thenks = Thenks Awf'lly. Sketches in Cockney. L 1890.
Thomson S = James Thomson, The Seasons, etc, ed. J. L. Robertson. Oxford 1881.
Towneley = The Towneley Plays, ed. England. E.E.T.S. 1897.
Tracy P = L. Tracy, The Park Lane Mystery. L (1924?).
Trampe Bødtker C = Critical Contributions to Early English Syntax. Christiania 1908.
Trelawny R = E. J. Trelawny, Recollections of Shelley, etc. L 1906 (1858).

Trollope A = Anthony Trollope, Autobiography. Oxford 1923 (World's Classics) (1883).
    B = — Barchester Towers (Bohn's Libr.) (1857).
    D = — The Duke's Children. T (1880).
    O = — An Old Man's Love. T.
    W = — The Warden. L 1913 (Bohn's Libr.) (1855).

Twain H = Mark Twain [Samuel Clemens], Huckleberry Finn. T (1884).
    M = — Life on the Missisippi. L 1887 (1883).
    S = — The Stolen White Elephant.

Tylor A = Edward B. Tylor, Anthropology. L 1881.
US or U. S. = the United States of America.
Vachell H = Horace A. Vachell, The Hill. L 1905.
VaV (also Vices & V.) = Vices and Virtues, ed. Holthausen.
vb = verb.
vg = vulgar.

Walker L = Hugh Walker, Literature of the Victorian Era. Cambridge 1910.
    O = — Outlines of Victorian Literature. Cambridge 1913.

Walpole A = Hugh Walpole, All Soul's Night. L 1933 (MM).
    C = — The Cathedral. L 1922.
    Cp = — Captives. L 1920.
    DF = — The Dark Forest. L (Nelson) (1916).
    DW = — The Duchess of Wrexe. (1914).
    F = — Fortitude. (1913).

38   Abbreviations and List of Books.

Walpole GM = Hugh Walpole, The Green Mirror. (1918).
        OL =   —   The Old Ladies. T (1924).
        RH =   —   Portrait of a Man with Red Hair. L 1925.
        RH =   —   Rogue Herries. L 1930.
        SC =   —   The Secret City. (1919).
        ST =   —   The Silver Thorn. T 1928.
        W   =   —   Wintersmoon. L 1928.
        CN =   —   Captain Nicholas. T (1934).
Walton A = Izaak Walton, The Compleat Angler. L 1653.
Ward D = Mrs. Humphrey Ward, David Grieve. T 1892.
     E =   —   Eleanor. L 1900.
     F =   —   Fenwick's Career. L 1906.
     M =   —   The Marriage of William Ashe. L (Nelson) (1905).
     R =   —   Robert Elsmere. T (1888).
Washington U = Booker Washington, Up from Slavery. N.Y. 1905.

Waugh BM = Evelyn Waugh, Black Mischief. Albatross 1933.
      W = Alec Waugh, Wheels within Wheels. L 1933.
Wells A   = H. G. Wells, Anticipations. L 1902 (1901).
      B   =   —   Bealby. Conard. 1915.
      Bish =   —   The Soul of a Bishop. L (1917).
      Blw =   —   Mr. Bletchworthy on Rampole Island. T 1929 (1928).
      Br =   —   Mr. Britling Sees it Through. L 1916.
      Cl =   —   The World of William Clissold. L 1926.
      EA =   —   An Experiment in Autobiography. L 1934.
      EL =   —   An Englishman Looks at the World. T (1914).
      F   =   —   The Future in America. L 1907 (1906).
      Fm =   —   The First Men in the Moon. L (Nelson) (1901.
      H   =   —   The Wife of Sir Isaac Harman. L 1914.
      Inv =   —   The Invisible Man. L 1924 (1897).

Wells	JP	=	H. G. Wells, Joan and Peter. L 1918.
	K	=	— Kipps. L (Nelson) (1905).
	L	=	— Love and Mr. Lewisham. L 1900.
	M	=	— Mankind in the Making. L 1903.
	Ma	=	— Marriage. T (1912).
	N	=	— The New Machiavelli. L 1911 (1910).
	OH	=	— Outline of History. L 1920.
	Par	=	— Mr. Parman. L 1930.
	PF	=	— The Passionate Friends. L (1913).
	T	=	— Twelve Stories and a Dream. L (6d. ed.) (1903).
	TB	=	— Tono-Bungay. T (1909).
	TM	=	— The Time Machine. L 1895.
	TM*	=	— — Cheap ed. 1911.
	U	=	— A Modern Utopia. L 1905.
	V	=	— Ann Veronica. L 1909.
	WW	=	— The War of the Worlds. L 1912 (Nelson) (1898).

Westermarck M = Edward Westermarck, The History of Human Marriage. L 1894.

Wharton HM = Edith Wharton, The House of Mirth. N.Y. 1905.

White N — Percy White, The New Christians. T.

Whitman L = Walt Whitman, Leaves of Grass. Boston 1898 (1855).

Whittier = John Greenleaf Whittier, Poetical Works. Oxford ed. 1904.

Wilde	D	=	Oscar Wilde, The Picture of Dorian Gray. N.Y. n.d. (1891).
	H	=	— The Happy Prince. L 1889 (1888).
	Im	=	— The Importance of Being Earnest. L n.d. (1895).
	In	=	— Intentions. L 1891 (Engl. Libr.).
	L	=	— Lord Arthur Savile's Crime. T (1887).
	P	=	— De Profundis. L 1905.
	R	=	— The Ballad of Reading Gaol. L 1898.
	S	=	— Sebastian Melmoth. L 1904.

Wilder H = Thornton Wilder, Heaven's My Destination. N.Y. 1934.

Wilkins P = Wilkins, Pericles, ed. Mommsen. Oldenburg 1857.
Williamson L = C. N. & A. M. Williamson, The Lightning Conductor. L (Nelson).
        P =   — The Princess Passes. L (ib).
        T = D. Williamson, Twenty-Five Years Reign. L 1935.

Wister G = Owen Wister, General Grant. 1900.
WLL = Ward, Lock & Co.'s London. L 1927.
Woolf D = Virginia Woolf, Mrs. Dalloway. T 1929 (1925).
Wordsw(orth) = William Wordsworth, Poetical Works, ed. Hutchinson (Oxf. ed.). Sometimes quoted from Macmillan's 1 vol. ed.
        Lit =   — Literary Criticism. L 1905 (Frowde).
        P =   — The Prelude (book and line).

Worth S = Nicholas Worth, The Southerner. N.Y. 1909.
Wright EDG(r) = Joseph Wright, English Dialect Grammar.
        R = Elizabeth Mary Wright, Rustic Speech and Folk-lore. Oxford 1913; cf. EDD.
Wülfing = J. Ernst Wülfing, Die Syntax in den Werken Alfreds des Grossen. Bonn 1894-1901.
Yeats CC = W. B. Yeats, The Countess Cathleen. L 1920 (1892).
Yonge G = Charlotte M. Yonge, A Book of Golden Deeds. L n.d.
Young PC, see Brett Young.
Zangwill G = Israel Zangwill, The Grey Wig. L 1903.

Chapter I

Word-Classes

1.1$_1$. I have in this work *in the main* followed the traditional system of word-classes ('parts of speech'). See on the theory in general chs IV-VI of PhilGr.

Here I shall chiefly deal with the manner in which words belonging to one class are derived from words of another class, with or without change. I shall continually refer to the Morphology presented in vol VI, much of which will here be repeated in a different arrangement. The numbers in parentheses refer to vol VI if nothing is said to the contrary. Unimportant classes have been left out.

1.1$_2$. A great many English words may, if considered isolatedly (as parts of 'language'), belong to more classes than one; but in each particular application (in 'speech') they can only belong to one, and it is generally easy to determine which one. *Fight* is a vb in *they fight*, but a sb in *their fight* and *this fight*. *Walk*, in the same way, is a sb in *he takes a walk | they took a walk | two walks*, but a vb in *they walk, he walks, he (they) walked*.

Compare also:

His former love for her (sb).

He loved her once (vb).

The two words *love* are related to each other as *admiration* and *admire*.

See especially vol VI 6.1$_2$.

Substantives

1.2₁. Substantives may be formed from any word-class or from word-groups, even from sentences, as 'quotation-words', vol II 8.21, e. g. Your *late* was misheard as *light* | There should be two l's in his name | All the "Thou shalt not's" of the Bible.

Sbs (and vbs) from various word-classes with repetition: *clop-clop*, etc, vol VI 10.2. With change of vowel: *chit-chat, tittle-tattle, pitter-pat, bim-bam-bum* vol VI 10.3. With change of consonant: *hanky-panky, argle-bargle, airy-fairy, hurdy-gurdy*, etc, vol VI 10.4.

1.2₂. Sbs may be formed from other sbs with the endings

-ate, -at: cardinalate, proletariat (24.8)
-cy: chaplaincy (13.2₂), aristocracy (13.2₃)
-dom: dukedom (25.3₅)
-hood: brotherhood (25.3)
-ism: Americanism (19.9₅)
-ship: authorship (25.3₃).

These are mainly predicative nexus-sbs.

-eer, -ier, -yer: engineer, hosier, lawyer (14.5₁, 15.5)
-er: Londoner, widower (14.3₁ ff.). Cf below *-er* from vbs.
-ist: pianist, copyist (19.9)
-ite: Pittite, pittite (24.7)
-ster: gunster, barrister (15.1).

These are chiefly agent-nouns of various kinds.

-ade: lemonade (24.2)
-age: anchorage, cottage (24.3)
-ess: princess, actress, duchess (19.1)
-et, -ette: turret, cigarette, suffragette (24.6)
-ie, -y: archie, Billy, baby (13.4)
-let: brooklet (23.4)
-ling: sapling (23.5).

1.2₃. Sbs may be formed from adjs

(1) without any ending, chiefly to denote concretes (persons or things); the chief criterion is the possibility of having a pl in *-s:* the whites, natives, Liberals, elders; sweets, vegetables, evils, dailies, etc (vol II ch IX and ib 8.14). This should be kept strictly apart from the use of adjs as primaries, *the poor*, etc (vol II ch XI),

(2) with endings to denote predicative nexus-words:

-ance, -ence, -ancy, -ency: abundance, excellence, -cy, constancy (21.6₃)

-hood: falsehood (25.3)

-ice: justice (19.9₂) where *cowardice* should be added).

-th: depth (24.4₅)

-tude: exactitude (24.9₈)

-ty: nobility (24.9).

1.2₄. Sbs may be formed from vbs

(1) without any ending: approach, build (7.1 ff.).

On voice-alteration: *belief* from *believe* see vol VI ch XII; on sbs in *-tch* from vbs in *-k* see ib 12.5; on difference in stress 11.9,

(2) with one of the following endings to denote nexus-sbs:

-ade: blockade (24.2)

-age: marriage (24.3)

-al: acquittal (22.2)

-ance, -ence: frequence, importance (21.6₃, on forms in *-cy* see 21.6₅)

-ation: organization (21.7)

-ery: fishery (15.7₂)

-fication: purification (25.1₃)

-ing: breaking (21.9, cf vol V ch VIII)

-ion (*-sion*, *-tion*)*:* acquisition, addition, extension, suggestion (21.7)

-ment: banishment (21.8)

-o(u)r: error (15.6_2)
-ure: closure (15.6_1)
-y: enquiry (13.2_1),

(3) with one of the following endings to denote agents:
-er, -or: baker, protector (14.1_1 ff., -erer 14.4)
-io(u)r: warrior, saviour (14.5_2)
-ster: brewster, spinster (15.1)
-trix: testatrix (15.9_4),

(4) in -ee implying dependent nexus: nominee (13.6).

Adjectives

1.3₁. Adjectives may be formed from sbs

(1) without any ending: chief (vol II ch XIII on the relation between adjunctal use of sbs and transition into adjs),

(2) with one of the endings
-al: suicidal, commercial, sexual (22.1)
-an: Lutheran (21.1)
-ar: oracular (15.4)
-ary, -ory: fragmentary, contributory (15.8)
-ean: Jacobean (21.1_7)
-ed: talented, blue-eyed (24.1)
-en: golden, brazen, maiden (20.4)
-ern: southern (21.5_2)
-ese: journalese (19.8)
-esque: Kiplingesque (19.6_6)
-ful: doubtful (23.2)
-ic(al): heroic, hestoric(al) (22.3)
-ine: labyrinthine (21.4)
-ish: childish (19.6)
-less: endless (23.3)
-like: godlike (23.1)
-ly: scholarly (22.7)
-proof: bulletproof (25.2_8)

-ous: venomous (19.7)
-y: bloody (13.3).

Adjs may be formed from adjs with the endings
-fold: manifold (25.2$_7$)
-ish: blueish (19.6$_3$)
-ly: sickly (22.7$_4$)
-y: bluey (13.3$_6$); with repetition: goody goody, highty-flighty (13.4$_8$).

1.3$_2$. Numeral adjs from other numerals:
-th: seventh (24.4$_1$)
-teen: sixteen (irregular: thirteen, fifteen)
-ty: sixty (irregular: thirty, fifty; in spelling: forty).

1.3$_3$. Adjs may be formed from vbs with the endings
-ant, -ent: triumphant, persistent (21.6)
-ative: talkative, contemplative (25.2$_4$)
-ble: eatable, persuasible, soluble (22.6)
-ful: forgetful (23.2$_2$)
-ive: active (25.2$_1$)
-less: dauntless (23.3$_2$)
-y: quaky (13.3$_7$).

Participles, (1) in *-ing,* (2) formed in various other ways, may in some respects be considered adjs.

Verbs

1.4$_1$. Verbs may be formed from sbs

(1) without any ending: arm (6.2 ff.); with change of vowel: bleed (11.5), with change of stress: object (11.9, cf vol I 5.7), with change of consonant: prove (12.2 ff.),

(2) with the endings
-en: lengthen (20.5)
-fy: personify (25.1$_1$)
-ize (-ise): symbolize (19.4).

On transitive and intransitive uses of vbs from sbs see vol III 16.6.

1.4₂. Vbs may formed from adjs

(1) without any change: calm, black (6.9₁, 20.5₁)

(2) with the endings

-en: blacken (20.5)

-fy: clarify (25.1).

On transitive and intransitive uses of vbs from adjs see vol III 16.5.

Vbs may be formed from advs without any change: out (6.9₃).

Adverbs

1.5₁. Adverbs from substantives may be formed with the endings

-ling(s): sideling(s) (23.6)

-ly: hourly (22.9₂)

-s: needs (18.1).

1.5₂. Adverbs may be formed from adjs

(1) without any change. This depends on the OE adverbial ending *-e*, which was to some extent retained in ME: *clene, dere, faste, harde, loude, slowe*, and then disappeared.

The obsolete adj *fain* (OE *fægen* 'glad') is in ModE hardly ever used except predicatively (*he is fain to* 'he is glad to, rejoices to' passing into 'he is obliged to'); in the combination *would fain (do...)* it was originally in apposition to the subject, but was then apprehended as an adv 'gladly, willingly': Mi SA 1535 Yet Hope would fain subscribe.

1.5₃. (2) with the ending *-ly* (22.8). On words in *-ly* derived from sbs which can be used both as adjs and advs see vol VI 22.9₂; on *-lily* ib 22.9₃.

As advs = adjs which never take *-ly*, we may mention *little, less, least, much, more, enough; long; better, best, worse, worst*.

1.5₄. No fixed boundary can be drawn between adjs and advs.

(a) This is first seen in cases in which a predicative approaches the status of an adv; many instances are given in vol III 17.2 ff.: go fast, run deep, arrive punctual (Hope, 17.2₅), lie heavy, speak fair, play false, the fire burns clear, smell sweet, ring true, look foolish, etc; on the use of advs in *-ly* in such cases see ib 17.5₇.

(b) Next we have what in vol II 15.2 I termed adjective-subjunct: an adj placed before another adj in adjunctal use, functions virtually as an adv: burning hot, wide open, wide awake; uncommon good, extraordinary meek, precious poor, mighty quick, jolly beastly, terrible strong, devilish clever; bitter cold, dead tired, etc, some of these combinations, however, having a colloquial or vulgar ring. This has led to the two words *very* and *pretty* becoming in fact advs. On *new(ly)-born* and *moderate(ly) sized* see vol II 15.3.

(c) Thirdly, we have combinations like *sweep the room clean, beat one hollow*, etc, in which I think we have the adj, not the adv, as predicative in a simple nexus as object of result; see vol V 3.7, cf 3.7₂ and especially 3.8: *cut each other dead, taking things easy, catch it bad*, etc. NED looks upon *easy* in *take it easy, let one off easy* as an adv.

(d) In the familiar "This is easier said than done" most grammarians will probably take *easier* as an adv (= more easily said than done), but a different analysis is perhaps also possible: *easier* as an adj (predicative) and *said* and *done* as appositional (easier when said than when done).

In the following lists the letters (a), (b), (c), (d) refer to the above classes.

1.5₅. In several cases we have two adverbial forms, one = the adj and the other with *-ly*. These are often differentiated, the former being used of time, etc, and the latter usually of manner and often in a figurative sense.

The examples are here given in alphabetical order.

cheap: sell, buy cheap | he got off cheaply.

clean: clean shaven; Sh Cæs I. 3.35 cleane from the purpose; Carlyle SR 57 he was clean gone; I had clean forgotten it | cleanly dressed. — On *cleanly* [klenli] adj (with adv *cleanlily*) see vol VI 22.7₅.

clear: clear-cut face; the thieves got clear away; jump clear of the hedge | he expressed himself clearly; it will be clearly understood.

close: close by the house; close shaven; Ruskin S 1.196 [Nature] keeps it close sealed (c) | ib 1.481 this curse seems to follow too closely on the excess; Doyle S 1.209 you cannot guard yourself too closely.

dead: Di D 15 dead sleepy; dead certain; dead against | deadly wounded.

dear: buy dear | (figuratively) he sold his life dearly; love dearly; dearly beloved brethren (in church phraseology).

deep: deep-set eyes; Carlyle SR 89 sunk us so deep in thy troublous dim Time-Element; be deep in debts; Di Do 143 deep-laid scheming; he drinks deep | deeply offended; Ruskin S 1.205 he is thinking deeply; he deeply regrets.

direct: he went direct to Paris (without detours) | he left directly after the sermon; directly opposed tendencies.

due: due north | it was duly confirmed.

easy: take it easy (c); formerly frequent (Sh, etc) in cases where now *easily*. Cf above on *easier*.

even: even then, even if | spread evenly.

evil: formerly frequent as an adv (NED quotations up to 1693 and 1749) Sh Lr I. 1. 169 thou dost euill (sb?) | evilly disposed.

fair: promise, bid fair; copy fair (c) | deal fairly with him.

false: Dryden [q NED *s. v. spell v.*² 3] it is false spelled throughout this book; Darwin L 3.10 Lyell's memory plays him false when he says ... (a) | falsely accused.

fast: run fast; play fast and loose (a); fast asleep | fastly (rare): fastly bound.

fit: Thack P 2.32 She cried fit to break your heart; Caine M 52 I was trembling fit to drop; Parker R 15 he can sing a comic song fit to make you die; I laughed fit to die (a?) | fitly arranged.

flat: fall flat (a) | I tell you flatly.

free: I got it free of charge | he drinks freely; criticize freely.

full: full well (nearly obsolete); full many (poet.); Di Do 272 full dressed; he looked me full in the face | fully satisfied.

hard: he works hard, strives hard, it freezes hard; he is hard up; hard by the church | *hardly;* see VI 22.9$_1$ and add: Di Do 54 Joe has been hardly used; he took it hardly; hardly earned money.

high: high up in the air; play high; Di Do 285 I have looked for you high and low | highly cultivated, excited; think highly of some one.

just: just now, just at that spot (moment); I just managed it | justly accused.

late: better late than never; soon or late; he works early and late; late in the day | he was lately seen in this neighbourhood.

like: he behaved just like you | *likely* see vol VI 22.9$_4$.

loud: speak loud (a) | (more figuratively) proclaim loudly; praise loudly, cf Scott Poet. W 88 And loudly Marmion's bugle blew ... Some clamour'd loud for armour lost.

low: speak low; bow low (a); GE A 1.108 curtseying low | lowly born (N.B. *lowly* also as an adj).

near: he stood near the door; near akin (related) | it touches me nearly; not nearly enough; cf vol VI 22.9$_1$.

new: newly see vol II 15.31.

plain: speak plain (a); Sterne 26 I told you as plain as words could tell you such a thing | plainly (common).

pretty: vol II 15.22 | prettily dressed.

quick: come, go quick (a); Galsw Car 897 Under the new sun, where blood ran quicker than in this foggy land | it must be made quickly, or not at all; quickly afterwards (NED).

right: serves you right; Right Reverend; right away, through, up, down | you rightly suppose; I don't rightly know; Ruskin S 1.117 to the rightly perceiving mind.

round: round about, look round; the car will be round in a minute | tell him roundly (= 'flatly'); written roundly, but without a flourish.

scarce: as an adv archaic | scarcely (now the usual form).

short: stop short (a), break (snap) short (off) (NED) (b), cut short (c); the effect came short of their desire (='did not amount to', NED) | shortly 'briefly, abruptly, in a short time'; shortly after.

sound: sound asleep | he slept soundly; she reasons soundly; he ought to be soundly thrashed.

still: he is still alive; still better | stilly (rare; VI 22.8$_3$).

straight: walk straight before you (a); straight across; ask him straight(-)away; straight forward | straightly (same meaning; rare).

strong: he comes it strong (a); Di Ch 20 it blew so

strong; still going strong (a); Trollope D 190 go in hard and strong for committees | strongly built; he strongly opposed the measure.

swift, swiftly without difference, cf Pope 34 Nor half so swift the trembling doves can fly ... Not half so swiftly the fierce eagle moves.

wide: wide open, wide awake (b); Fox 2.115 he answers wide of the mark | widely separated; we differ widely from each other.

wrong: go wrong (a), read wrong; Spectator no. 405 several of the Words were wrong spelt, cf Storm EPh 729; Austen P 186 she has been acting wrong | wrongly (the usual adv).

On *-ly* added to superlatives (*mostly, lastly*) and ordinals (*firstly,* etc) see vol VI 22.9$_6$.

On *usual* and *more than usually* see ib 22.9$_8$ and add the quotations: Austen M 302 they sat much longer than usual in the dining-parlour | GE A 1.178 She would have wanted to put on her hat earlier than usual, only she had told Captain D. that she usually set out about eight o'clock | Hardy F 39 he called as usual to the dogs || Garnett 44 more than usually despondent | Stevenson VP 123 more than usually black thoughts.

1.5₆. *Sure* at the beginning of a sentence is seemingly an adv (Sure, you have not forgotten ...), but is really a predicative adj (without a vb), like *true,* etc. See vol III 17.9$_7$. It is placed parallel to the adv *surely* in Keats 2.155 Sure I have heard ... Surely I have traced ...

Some forms in *-less* (23.3) are frequently used as advs, e. g. in Sh *causeless, doubtless, questionless.* If these are placed in front of the sentence, they may be apprehended in the same way as *sure* above. Other words in *-less*, e.g. *blameless*, *needless*, are only used as adjs, and advs in *-ly* are formed from them. As an adj, *doubtless* is generally supplanted by *indubitable*.

Previous to (more common than *previously to*) is now a kind of composite preposition, but *previous* must be analyzed as an adjective in apposition to the whole sentence. In the same way we have *preparatory to* and *prior to:*

Examples: Lamb R 30 he was come to pass one night at Widford, *previous to* his departure for Edinburgh | Brontë P 3 my father became bankrupt a short time *previous to* his death | ib 98 what had I known of female character *previously to* my arrival? | ib 188 | Hardy F 39 he called to the dogs, *previously to* shutting them up || Di D 216 I gave Mr W. my hand *preparatory to* going away myself | Wilde In 70 he was taken back to Newgate, *preparatory* to his removal to the colonies | NED 1875 [It] seems, prior to experience, very improbable.

If *to* does not follow, *previously* has to be used: he had seen her a short time previously.

Analogously we have the group preposition *according to* and the group conjunction *according as* on the one hand, and the adv *accordingly* on the other. On the exceptional use of *accordingly* before *as* see vol VI 22.9$_4$.

Thus also *subsequent to* — *subsequently*, (rare as in Poe 340 subsequently to the period when ....) | *contrary to my wishes* | *subject to the King's consent* | *irrespective of cost*.

Chapter II
Sentence-Structure and Word-Order

2.1₁. Our chief concern here is with the fully articulate sentences, those containing a subject and a finite vb. In such sentences the vb (V) may be considered the centre, round which the other parts are grouped, the subject (S), predicative (P), and object (O) being the parts most closely connected with the verb, while tertiaries (advs, prepositional groups, clauses, etc) are more peripheral.

The relation between subject, object, and predicative in general has been dealt with in vol III chs xi-xviii; ib 17.8-9 some kinds of not fully articulate sentences have been mentioned (Who so smooth as Mr. M? | all right | She a beauty! | And we alive! | no matter | and a good thing too | Not bad, those old times | the more fool you | no matter what the consequences, etc).

Other kinds of inarticulate or semi-articulate sentences contain an infinitive, see vol V 20.2 ff. (What to do? | How account for it? | Why not do it at once? | My nephew marry a tragedy queen! | You coward, to lay your hand on your wife!, etc). — Incomplete questions (What of that?, etc) and exclamations (What for!, etc) were dealt with in vol V 25.4.

Some other types of such sentences will be dealt with below in ch III.

What determines the order in which words are arranged in speech? Here we find various principles or tendencies, which are of a more or less universal character, though by no means strictly logical; these may in certain cases be in conflict with one another, but in others they concur. They are here, for later reference, classed as A, B, etc.

2.1₂. (A) First we shall mention the principle of *Actuality:* what is at the moment uppermost in the speaker's mind tends to be first expressed. This is the reason, or rather one of the reasons, why the subject — what one is going to speak about — is generally given in front position. But it may also be the object, or the predicative, or any other element that is drawn forward in this way. Very often it is something which has just been mentioned in a preceding sentence, thus what some scholars (French, Danish, Dutch) call an 'anaphoric' pronoun (e. g. *that*, or a relative pronoun at the beginning of a clause). Such back-reference explains the front position of such words as *so* (so I am, so am I; so long a time) and *neither* (neither am I).

Examples will be given below (2.2₃).

The greater interest felt for persons than for things is in vol III 14.7₁ given as the reason for an indirect object being generally placed before a direct object. (Exceptions ib 14.7₃ff.).

But it is evident that this principle of actuality or interest if carried through might easily lead to chaos, such as is found in the jumble often heard in the speech of small children and sometimes in the careless speech of undeveloped minds.

2.1₃. (B). *Precedence of modifier.* A modifying word is generally placed before that which is modified (determined, defined, specialized) by it.

This is clearly seen in a junction, where the primary comes last:

$$\overset{5}{A} \overset{4}{\text{ not}} \overset{3}{\text{ particularly}} \overset{2}{\text{ well expressed}} \overset{1}{\text{ thought}},$$

and where a genitive precedes the other sb: *John's children*. In compounds the modifying element is as a rule placed first: *gas-light*, etc (vol VI 8.2). The same principle applies to quantifiers, whether simple or consisting of a prepositional group: *many women, a lot of money, a glass of wine*; quantifiers even are placed before other adjuncts: *many old women, much cold water, all young people*, and often before an article: *half the way, half an hour, all the servants, both the servants, many a man*.

This principle accounts for the invariable precedence of *not*, when it is a word-modifying element: not infrequently | not the slightest reason | he was found not guilty | not quite right, etc.

Further, it accounts for the difference between "Nearly all died" = 'they died with few exceptions' and "all nearly died" = 'everybody was on the verge of dying'.

In a nexus it is more difficult to apply the same principle because the relation between primary (S or O) and secondary (V) is not the same as in a junction. But in AnalSynt 33.6 I maintain that "the notion expressed by a vb is made more definite by the subject: *goes* is specified in different ways when we say that *the minister, the watch, time, a rumour goes*, etc." If this is accepted it affords a further explanation of the prevalence of the order SV, but, it must be admitted, not of the order VO, for the object specifies the vb, not inversely.

In a dependent nexus the subject also generally precedes the predicate part: *they judged me* (S) *a happy man* (P) | *this will make her* (S) *happy* (P), vol V 1.7 and ch II. Similarly the subject precedes an infinitive: *this will make the watch* (S) *go* (I); cf also nexus-sbs: *the King's* (S) *arrival* (X), and *ing*-combinations, whether the subject is in the genitive or in the common case: *on Miss Sharp('s) appearing*, etc. Cf on the whole question vol V, where exceptions are also mentioned.

A preposition is generally placed before its regimen which is 'modified' by it; similarly a conjunction is placed at the beginning of a clause.

2.1₄. (C) The principle of *Cohesion:* ideas that are closely connected tend to be placed together. Hence what is closely related to the verbal idea as the centre of a sentence is placed as near as possible to the vb: subject, object, predicative; similarly such advs as form a complement to the verbal idea, while other tertiaries may be relegated to a more peripheral place. Hence also an adjunct is placed either immediately before or immediately after its primary, and the same is done with a tertiary in relation to the secondary to which it belongs. The order of two adjuncts to the same sb is often decided by one of them forming a composite idea with the sb: poor afflicted *human nature* | in perfect *good temper* | a clever *young man* (vol II 15.15).

An apposed word is not so closely connected with the head-word as an adjunct and therefore has afterposition: Edward *the First* | William *the Conqueror* | Mr. Dimley, *the president of the club* | the City *of Rome*; a house *not his own* (see vol II 15.6 for 'semi-predicative post-adjuncts'; cf AnalSynt chs IV and XII, also ib on Extraposition). We have a closer connexion in *He himself* says so than in the synonymous *He* says so *himself*.

The power of cohesion is in some cases stronger in colloquial speech than in literary language: *isn't he ready?, won't he come?* as against *is he not ready?, will he not come?* A preposition is generally closely connected with, and therefore placed just before, its regimen, but exceptions occur, not only if the regimen is a relative or interrogative pronoun which has to be placed in front-position (cf vol III 10.2 ff.) and in the case of the 'split infinitive' (vol V 20.4), but in other cases as well (below 2.3$_4$ ff.); cf also the passives *he was talked of and sympathized with*. The role of cohesion is also seen when *each to other* and *one to another* are now supplanted by *to each other* and *to one another*, and when *nothing important* is contrasted with *no important thing* (vol II 17.32). Note also the group-genitive *the King of England's daughter* as against ME *the kinges daughter of England*.

2.1$_5$. (D) The principle of relative *Weight* also to some extent determines word-order (cf Behaghel's "Gesetz der wachsenden glieder"). Lighter elements can be placed near the centre, while heavier ones are relegated to more peripheral places: *take it off* | *take off your hat* (below, 2.8$_7$). Whole clauses are generally placed either at the very beginning or at the end of the sentence of which they form parts — thus really in 'extraposition'. Emphasis may be expressed by either of these two positions, or, in fact, as Sweet says, by putting the word in any abnormal — that is, unexpected position. The light little word *it* is frequently placed with the verb to avoid clumsy collocations, thus as subject in *It is fortunate that he has come* | *it is a pleasure to see so many people here;* as object in *I take it for granted that he will come*, etc. Similarly, in *He was a great poet, that son of the Stratford butcher, William Shakespeare — he* represents the real subject, which would be too heavy to be placed first. In this way many awkward and clumsy collocations are avoided.

A participial adj is felt to be more weighty than an ordinary adjunct and therefore is often placed after its primary: *for the time being* | *in the year following*. This is especially obvious if the participle has an object or another supplement: *in the year following his dismissal* | *an old gentleman turned eighty* (cf vol II 15.481 ff.).

By considering the relative weight of various parts, and by grouping them accordingly, the sentence is rounded off and prevented from being top-heavy.

2.1₆. (E) *Stress and Rhythm* also to some extent influence word-order. Some instances were given in vol III 14.7 to explain various arrangements of pronouns as direct and indirect objects. P. Fijn van Draat, *Rhythm in English Prose* (Heidelberg 1910, p. 123 ff.) has collected about 800 quotations to prove that the seemingly capricious position of the adv *only* is largely decided by rhythm, chiefly to avoid the clash of strong syllables. But his argument is not so conclusive as he thinks, chiefly because he operates with only two degrees of stress and overlooks the possibility of intermediate stresses (degrees 2 and 3 between 1 and 4.) — The same scholar's theory of the influence of rhythm on word-order with regard to another point has been ably criticized by E. Buyssens in ESts 1933 p. 129 ff., see especially p. 148: "Sentence-rhythm is too proteiform to be considered as determining this construction." Cf also my own criticism in vol III p. 148 of Fijn van Draat's pet theory of rhythm in quite another field. — A. Western's valuable paper *On Sentence-Rhythm and Word-Order in Mod. Engl.* (Norsk vidsk. skrifter 1908) is far less dogmatic than Fijn van Draat; it deals, in fact, chiefly with the influence of logic and stress on word-order and sentence-rhythm.

Stress is in some cases intimately connected with Actuality (A): what is uppermost in one's mind is often, though not always, emphasized.

2.1₇. (F) These were considerations determining the place of words from the point of view of the speaker. But the hearer's point of view should also be taken into consideration. It is of importance for him to know, as soon as possible, if what is said should be taken as a simple positive statement, as a negative statement, as a question, or as a wish. Hence the desirability of placing negative advs early in the sentence, and the use of the order VS in questions and in wishes. Various compromises between such arrangements and the usual order SV have been dealt with in vol V chs xxiii and xxv, see especially the General Survey vol V 25.9; others will be dealt with in the rest of this chapter.

2.1s. (G) *Tradition*, too, is an important factor in determining word-order: on a great many points a fixed word-order has become traditional, and speakers will unconsciously arrange their thoughts and words according to a certain pattern. This will change from time to time. In former times the same system was more or less carried out in English that still prevails in other connected languages, according to which the finite vb took the second place whenever there was an introductory element (*up went the flag | well might he say*), but this has to a great extent been given up (cf below $2,4_2$). On the whole the development has been towards a fixed word-order as a simple consequence of the giving up of many flexional endings which in a more highly inflected language renders a free word-order possible.

Many years ago one of my classes at the University of Copenhagen calculated statistically various points in regard to word-order in different languages. I give here only the percentages of sentences containing a subject, a vb, and an object in the order S V O:

	Prose	Poetry
Gothic	41	
Beowulf		16

	Prose	Poetry
Alfred	40	
Layamon		48
Ancrene Riwle	66	
Chaucer	84	51
Shakespeare	93	86
Milton	88	71
Pope		68
Byron	93	81
Shelley	89	85
Macaulay	82	
Carlyle	87	
Tennyson		88
Dickens	91	
Swinburne		83
Pinero	97	

Supplemental numbers were given by F. J. Curtis in Anglia Beiblatt 1908, p. 143:

Bible	94	
Kipling	95	90
Thackeray	95	
Wells	95	
Ruskin	98.5	
Darwin	99.1	
Shaw	99.8	
Meredith	94	
Stephen Phillips		80

For the sake of comparison I mention some numbers from other languages: A Danish prose-writer (J. P. Jacobsen) had 82, a Danish poet (Drachmann) 61, Goethe (poetry) 30, a modern German prose writer (Tovote) 31, Anatole France 66, Gabriele d'Annunzio 49 per cent of the same word-order. Even if I concede that our statistics did not embrace a sufficient number of extracts to give fully reliable results, still it is indisputable that English shows more regularity and less caprice in this respect than most or probably all cognate languages, without, however, attaining the rigidity found in Chinese, where the percentage in question would be 100 (or very near it). English has not deprived itself of the expedient of inverting the ordinary order of the members of a sentence when required, e. g. for the sake of emphasis or poetic expression, but it makes a more sparing use of it than German and the Scandinavian languages.

We shall now deal with Modern English word-order in more detail.

Word-Order in the Central Part of the Sentence

2.2₁. The vb (V) is the centre of a finite sentence, but it should be remembered that the formally finite vb is often accompanied by a participle or an infinitive which forms part of the verbal idea and is really the most important part notionally. Thus we have frequent collocations like *has come, is taken, is coming, will come, does come*, even with two or three 'lesser vbs': *has been taken, will be coming, will have been taken*.

If we denote the lesser vb by v, we thus have combinations like v V, v I — or v V(I) —, $v_1 v_2$ V. But in relation to the other main parts of the sentence, S and O, these combinations function like simple vbs as far as word-order is concerned. As we shall see, tertiaries may in some cases be inserted between the separate parts of such a composite verbal expression. In the following formulas V also comprises v V and v v V, unless the opposite is expressly stated. In some cases, however, it is necessary to keep v and V apart, e. g.

when a subject comes between them: v S V or v S I.

Parallel to v V we have the combinations of a vb of little notional importance with a verbal sb, which in form is identical with the (inf. of the) vb: *have a cry, a bathe, take care, give a sigh,* etc (vol VI 7.2).

It is not necessary here to give examples of the ordinary place of the subject before the vb — examples will abound in the following sections.

V S

2.2₂. This order is in some cases glottic, i. e. serves to distinguish one kind of sentence from another. Thus in questions, see the full treatment in vol V 25.5$_4$ ff.: *is he ill?* as against *he is ill*. With a full vb we have the archaic *What say you?* (vol V 25.5$_5$), where now the periphrasis with *do* is used: *What do you say?* (O v S I).

But the formula S V also occurs in questions, chiefly in short sentences when an affirmative answer seems to be taken for granted; in this case intonation is the only sign of the question (vol V 25.5$_1$): *You think so?* | *He lives here?*

Next in wishes (subjunctive): Long live the King! | Sh Tro II. 3.243 Know the whole world he is as valiant | Ro III. 2.136 Wash they his wounds with tears | R2 II. 1.139 Loue they to liue that loue and honour haue | By DJ 11.38 Praised be all liars and all lies! — Cf 18.6$_2$.

But nowadays wishes are generally expressed by a preposed *may*, which effects the compromise between the order V S and S V through v S V(I): Marlowe E 1646 long may you liue | Sh Lr I. 1.186 And your large speeches (O) may your deeds (S) approue | Austen P 284 Much good may it do them! (O v S I O¹) | Happy may your birthday be!

The contrast between the order in wishes and in

ordinary statements is well brought out in Dickinson, Europ. Anarchy 74 "The war may come," says one party. "Yes," says the other; and secretly mutters, "May the war come!"

The order S V is also found in wishes, chiefly in fixed sentences like: God bless you | God save the King! | Sh H6A III. 2.117 Yet Heauens haue glory for this victorie. — More examples below, 18.5_1 ff.

Here we may mention V S in stage-directions: Enter the King, the Queen ... (originally subjunctive, hence without -s in the 3rd pers. sg): Hankin 1.56 Is just about to go out, when enter Stella.

More rarely the same order is found in the preterit: Lawrence L 176 Entered the little lady in her finery.

The word-order V S is also found extensively in exclamations. See examples of it and of the now usual order S V in vol V 25.4_7.

Note the negative expression in Galsw M 34 How often have I not watched him (with other quotations Negation p. 98). Also without an interrogatory word: Wouldn't that be fun! = 'What fun it would be!'

Further, the inversion V S is significant in conditional clauses without any conjunction, see vol V 21.6, where a discussion is found of the connexion of such clauses with the word-order in questions.

Sometimes the order V S is occasioned by the subject being as it were an afterthought, the sentence being at first intended as elliptical, cf below, 2.2_5: Walpole W 252 Must have cost a pretty penny that thing to-night | Maugham Alt 370 Pulls you down dreadfully, this confounded malaria.

2.2₃. Finally, the difference between the two orders S V and V S is glottic when it is used to distinguish between a simple Corroboration of a remark just made (*so I am*, etc) and, on the other hand, a statement that the remark applies equally to some one or something else (*so am I*, etc). The latter type is sometimes emphasized by the addition of *also* or *too*, or after a negation, of *either*. Both types are introduced, when positive, by *so*, and, when negative, by *nor*, *neither*, or *no more*. The difference in word-order is combined with, and explained by, a difference in stress: so I ˈam: so am ˈI.

Thus we have the following types:

(a) (He is rich) So he ˈis | So is ˈshe.

(b) (I don't believe he is rich) Neither (Nor, No more) he ˈis | Neither (Nor, No more) is ˈshe.

But with the negative, the rule is not always observed.

Examples in positive statements of the order S V:

Sh Merch II. 6.44 And I should be obseru'd. — So you are, sweet | Goldsm 648 It would be well for all the publicans. — Ecod, and so it would | Di N 314 You promised me you'd find her out. — So I did | ib 320 you had better get back before dark. — Thank you, so I had | id X 26 She had a large heart! — So she had | Thack N 283 284 London is delightful, and so is the seaside | Pinero S 78 that shocks you! So it does me | Mackenzie S 1.163 I like you more than I do any other chap. — So I do you | Bennett GS 283 I've got a bad cold. — So you have! she agreed | Hope D 54 We may see somebody. So we may.

Examples of the order V S: Sh Merch II. 4.26 ile be gone about it straight. — And so will I | Swift P 69 Can you keep a secret? — Yes, I can. — Well, miss, and so can I | ib 105 she's as old as Poles. — So will you be, if you ben't hang'd when you're young | Di Do 295 his eyebrows were still black, and so was much of his hair | id D 143 your lodging will be paid by me.

So will your washing | Ruskin S xv Perhaps you are a little envious; but then — so is everybody else | Browning 1.410 The Mayor looked blue; So did the Corporation, too | Hardy F 349 Gabriel had prayed; so would she | Stevenson JHF 171 So the physician said in his prospectus; and so said all the citizens in the city | Kipling L 197 I wish I were going with you. — So do we all | Mackenzie S 1.170 I kissed Dora this morning. — So did I Winnie | Wells OH 256 the Byzantine Empire ... its monarch had a Roman title no doubt, but so for that matter had the late Tsar of Bulgaria | Meredith H 329 Now I'm cool, Tom, and so must you be | Sackville-West E 242 You are a secret sort of person, Viola ... So are you a secret sort of person, Sebastian | Mackenzie C 177 I shall always love you ... So shall I you | ib 183 I adore you. — So do I you | Bennett Acc 256 You must go to bed ... So must you go to bed, Alan answered.

Examples of both orders closely after each other: Sh As II. 3.9 'tis the rarest argument ... And so 'tis ... To be relinquisht of the artists. So I say, both of Galen and Paracelsus. — Of all the learned and authenticke fellowes. — Right, so I say. — That gaue him out incureable. — Why there 'tis, so say I too. ... Iust, you say well: so would I haue said | Shaw 2.214 *Philip:* You were wrong. *Dolly:* So were you. *Ph.:* We're forgetting our manners, Dolly. *D.:* Yes, so we are | You must go to bed now. — So I must, and so must you.

Some examples of both orders with an object may be found vol III 12.7₂ ff.

2.2₄. Examples in negative statements of the order S V: Mackenzie S 1.476 It's about time I met him. — Why, haven't you? Nor you have | ib 488 you would insist that you didn't like her playing. — Nor I did |

Sackville-West E 125 you were saying the other day that you hadn't seen Clemmie for five years. — Nor I have | Walpole Cp 183 don't you know where Bryanston Square is? ... If I did I wouldn't ... Quite right — neither you would | Di Do 301 She says you couldn't read. — No more I can! | Thack N 814 saying that I do not understand anything about business. No more I do; that is the truth | McKenna Sh 257 I didn't know you did anything. — No more I did, till this summer | Stevenson T 74 I had no thought that Mr. Trelawney would hear a word. — No more I would, cried the squire | Chesterton F 172 I thought you didn't believe in magic. — No more I did | Benson DB 157 I said nobody ever had got out of Tovey's without cribbing. — No more they have | Jacobs L 117 I'm not aware that I've said anything to be laughed at. — No more you have.

The word-order V S: AV. John 8.11 No man [hath condemned me]. — Neither doe I condemne thee | Thack (q Poutsma) Warrington did not speak. Neither did Miss Bell speak | Allingham P 36 Uncle Andrew isn't a lovable character. But then nor are any of them really | Di P 439 "Well, I never heard the like of that!" exclaimed Mary. "No more did I," said Sam | Thack (q Poutsma) The girl had no fortune; no more had Mrs. Sedley | id (q id) You do not play to win. No more do I | Shaw P 137 do you like to be reminded that you are very young? — No. — Neither do I like to be reminded that I am — middle aged. Cf with a different vb in the second sentence: Macaulay E 2.105 As the Reformation did not find the English bigoted Papists, so neither was it conducted in such a manner as to make them zealous Protestants.

2.2₅. Inversion (VS) is very frequent in a kind of short sentences appended to main sentences to make it clear who or what is meant by a pronoun used loosely in the first sentence: Di X 5 They had clear, loud, lusty, sounding voices, had these Bells | id M 8 She was the most arch and at the same time the most artless creature, was the youngest Miss Pecksniff, that you can possibly imagine | Stevenson T 11 He has a cut on one cheek, and a mighty pleasant way with him, particularly in drink, has my mate Bill | ib 89 He's no fool, is Dick | Ward E 263 it is a strange case — is Manisty's | Doyle S 1.183 It is a fine, law-abiding country is England | Wells H 329 She's not bad isn't Alice | Walpole OL 12 She was a proud and severe lady was Mrs. Payne | Zangwill G 117 They are a queer lot of muddle-heads are the police | Bennett P 68 she knew what she was about, did that young woman | id W 2.238 He will have his joke, will the doctor! | Williamson L 138 He can do a good many things, can Lord Lane | Crofts Ch 31 They know what they're about, does this gang.

The opposite order is rarer in such repetitive sentences: GE M 1.6 it is puzzling work, talking is | id S 142 Ah, she has a quick wit, my friend Priscilla has | Bennett ECh 73 They're like that, Jewesses are | Walpole Cp 274 but he was a weight on my chest that fellow was, with his long white beard | Freeman Th 325 It has given us all a dreadful turn, this affair has.

2.2₆. The same word-order V S occurs, but is not glottic, in cases where a sentence begins with some word other than the subject; the front-position may be due to various reasons, often to back-reference to something in a preceding sentence. As remarked above (2.1₈), this order agrees with a custom found extensively in all the cognate languages, but has largely been given up in PE. Very frequently we have a lesser vb, so that the order is v S V, or, in some v V S: Thack N 202 Here will be your place.

On the two orders S V and V S with an imperative see vol III 11.8$_3$ ff.

Front-Position of Object

2.2$_7$. We find front-position of the object with the word-order O V S for instance in Sh Mcb I. 5.18 What thou would'st highly, That would'st thou holily | Austen P 186 and not a note, not a line, did I receive in the meantime | Di D 611 Not another word did Mr. Dick utter on the subject | Doyle S 3.217 But no trace of the body could we find | ib 5.73 Only one little gleam of hope did I get | Locke HB 137 A sorry figure. And just such a sorry figure had cut John Baltazar [not natural].

In most cases, particularly in colloquial English, we find the order O S V, e. g. Sh Mids II. 1.233 Things base and vilde, holding no quantity, Loue can transpose to forme and dignity | Ado III. 1.106 Some Cupid kills with arrowes, some with traps | Mi PL 5.611 him who disobeyes Mee disobeyes [Latin more than English] | Keats 5.102 no one rings For coals, and therefore no coals Betty brings | Shelley Phil. View Ref. 62 Property thus acquired men leave to their children | Di D 244 talent, Mr. Micawber has; capital Mr. Micawber has not | Kingsley H 90 The priests are jealous of the deacons, and good cause they have | Carlyle SR 100 him what Graceful would ever love? | Swinburne L 219 the air that has nothing of her left it chafes me to breathe | Smedley F 2.10 The champagne breakfast on the following morning who shall describe? | Maugham Alt 140 pockets they had not | Walpole DW 141 his life had been entangled with women; some he had loved, others he had been in love with, others again had loved him | Wells OH 294 This fact the genius of Constantine grasped | id L 111 But the pneumatic glove there was no explaining.

Generally the meaning is clear; but it requires some reflexion to understand the following quotation: Shelley Adonais 4.4 when his country's pride (O), The priest, the slave, and the liberticide (S), Trampled and mocked with many a loathed rite.

The context makes the meaning clear in By DJ 16.89 They wondered how a young man so absurd (O) Lord Henry (S) at his table should endure | Longfellow 260 A blind man is a poor man, and blind the the poor man is, For the former seeth no man, and the latter no man sees.

Intentional ambiguity is found in the oracular Sh H6B I. 4. 33 The Duke yet liues, that Henry shall depose.

The rare order 3 V O S is only justified because *take place* is a set phrase = 'happen': Macaulay H 1.172 Early in 1661 took place a general election | Crofts Ch 169 there took place what seemed to be a trifling thing. Similarly with *take root* = 'thrive': Dickinson S 29 Under this shelter take root and thrive all monstrous and parasitic growths.

2.2₈. A quotation, or the beginning of one, may be considered the preposed object of a subsequent *said* or an equivalent expression. Both orders (VS and SV) may be found; VS was always used with the archaic *quoth he*, etc, and is still frequent in short insertions merely to indicate who spoke; the other order, SV, is perhaps chiefly found if the manner of utterance is indicated. This, however, does not appear clearly in the following quotations, chosen a little at haphazard: Richardson

G 54 He is, whispered she to me, as he ..., a young Baronet | Brontë V 180 Flirtation amongst the rest, subjoined I, in thought. — When do you suppose she will return to town? he soon inquired | Chesterton F 232 that's all I can tell you, went on Flambeau carelessly | Hardy F 348 which, thought she, ... || Doyle S 1.15 It came by the last post, said he ... There will call upon you to-night, at a quarter to eight o'clock, it said,... | Philips L 74 "That is plain enough," I think to myself, "and very much to the point" | ib 89 "But I assure you —" he began, nothing disconcerted | Walpole SC 71 Why not? he asked me suspiciously || Goldsm 653 For the first course a pig and prune sauce. — *Hast.* Damn your pig, I say. — *Mar.* And damn your prune sauce, say I [in the latter *I* is stressed].

2.2₉. The order V S is rare and, except in questions, archaic when the initial word is the regimen of a preposition placed at the end of the sentence: Sh Tw V. 1.57 A bawbling vessell was he captaine of | More U 47 this kinde of men muste we make most of | Gammer 96 many a good mans house haue I bin at | Spectator 179 This state of mind was I in | Quincey 11 Nothing of that sort do I pretend to | ib 181 Many a family party, consisting of a man, his wife, and sometimes one or two of their children, have I listened to | Macaulay H 2.209 What a generation of vipers do we live among!

Examples of the usual order S V in sentences with a preposition at the end will be found below, 2.3₅—2.3₆.

An indirect object cannot, like a direct one, have front-position in a sentence: *to* is required (vol III 14.8₂).

Front-Position of Predicative

2.3₁. If a predicative precedes we have the order P V S: [proverb] handsome is that (more rarely *as*) handsome does | such is life | Bennett B 232 a prince is never seriously ill until he is dead. Such is statecraft | if such is the case | Di N 609 they forget these things sometimes, and more's the pity [common, also with *the more*] | Bennett LR 390 Strange creatures were women! | Di D 484 Great was the labour; priceless the road | Ruskin F 68 'Blessed are the merciful for they shall obtain mercy' [biblical] | Kipling J 1.58 chattering, fooling, vain—vain, foolish, and chattering, are the monkeys | id V 149 Lean are the camels but fat the frails, Light are the purses but heavy the bales | Stevenson MB 188 Many and long were the conversations they held through the prison wall.

This order is not natural except with the single vb *be*; it is felt as odd even in such a combination as Medwin S 109 bitter were destined to be its fruits [better: .... were its fruits destined to be].

In the following quotation the subject would now be preposed: Swift P 125 this is it to send a fool of an errand.

Note the order with a split nexus-object: Sh Hml II 2.94 Your noble sonne is mad: Mad call I it.

The order P S V is found in the common *Certain it is that* ... and similar sentences; see, e. g., Di D 190 and nice people they were | ib 306 None of your close shavers the prince ain't | Carlyle P 176 a small Poet every Worker is | Brontë J 187 it was a lady who sang, and very sweet her notes were | Rose Macaulay P 233 Horrible, these women were; ugly, dirty | Strachey QV 48 And the governess was no fool: narrow, jealous, provincial, she might be; but she was an acute and vigorous woman.

2.3₂. This order P S V is particularly noteworthy in a stylistic trick consisting in a repetition of an immediately preceding expression (cf below, 2.3₇ f.): Brontë

V 215 I am glad to see you free, and trust that free you will long remain | ib 418 I wished him success; and successful I knew he would be | id P 187 I have one object before me now — to get that girl for my wife; and my wife she shall be [very frequent in Charlotte Brontë] | Stevenson V 124 if a person cannot be happy without remaining idle, idle he should remain | Lang T 170 his dramas were written to be acted, and acted some of them were | Bennett C 1.187 he regretted that he was like that; but like that he was | Myers M 155 If I could serve Jerningham's purposes better blind, blind I would be as long as he liked | Christie LE 89 That looks like accident, and in my opinion accident it is | Bennett P 102 Of course I'm bored. I feel all right, but bored I am | Strachey QV 57 She found him perfect; and perfect in her sight he remained | ib 77 She felt that only one thing now was needed: she must be firm. And firm she was.

2.3₃. A preposed infinitive only rarely causes the order V S: Sh Hml III. 3.38 Pray can I not.

Generally we have S V: Fielding T 3.7 Knock, indeed, he did at the door, but not with one of those gentle raps | Gissing G 66 Do something I must, or I shall fret | Mackenzie RR 40 "he will only go and spend it." And spend it Sholto did | Hope R 160 while he could run, run he would | Campbell Shl 84 Read Shelley did | Masefield W 89 Look queer, the street will, with the lock away | Norris O 366 Have her he would.

Preposition at the End

2.3₄. A preposition sometimes has end-position while what is, or should be, its regimen has front-position. For the sake of emphasis or contrast (actuality, above, 2.1₂ A) the speaker begins his sentence with an important noun or nominal phrase without exactly knowing how to continue. The preposition is generally closely connected with a vb or other words (above, 2.1₄ C). As to this order in questions and in relative clauses see vol V 25.1₄₋₇ and vol III 10.2, cf 13.9. Except in questions, we now always find S V, not V S, in such sentences; cf above, 2.2₉.

The close relation between vb and prep. is seen in such parallel phrases as Austen M 265 her temper he had good reason to depend on and to praise | Thack V 9 Many a dun had she talked to, and turned away from her father's door | Shaw P xix the pleasures of the senses I can sympathize with and share.

2.3₅. I have found some examples in Ch, many in Elizabethan English, and a great many in later books, but shall give here only comparatively few of those I have collected — arranged according to prepositions:

of: Sh Tw I.2.33 what great ones do, the lesse will prattle of | John II. 1.553 and this rich fair town we make him lord of | Bunyan G 10 This also I have taken notice of | Austen M 408 His present state Fanny could hardly bear to think of | Keats 5.89 £ 30, an ample sum I assure you — more I had no thought of | Di D 55 the length of those five days I can convey no idea of to any one | ib 404 that I'm sure of | ib 661 that I am convinced of | Carlyle FR 342 New Mirabeaus one hears not of | Stevenson K 71 even their pickles, which were the great dainty, I was allowed my share of | Meredith T 125 Politics he thought of as the dust of battle | Ruskin CWO 29 what ought to be done with them, we'll talk of at another time | Doyle S 6.107 The Indian I also thought nothing of.

on, upon: More U 145 one thinge you muste looke more narrowly vpon | Sh Cymb IV. 2.130 No single soule Can we set eye on | As III. 5.104 and that Ile liue vpon | Mi PL 9.539 Thee all things living gaze on | Di Do 225 Florence, the Captain waited on, with his strange news | Ruskin 1.303 these pencil sketches he put a few blots of colour upon | Ward D 2.97 Two things he was set on | Meredith E 418 Breakfast, you may count on, from Mr. Dale | Galsw EC 5 What he says you can rely on.

to: Ch PF 695 I wook, and bokes tok me to | Swift 3.304 All this my master very graciously consented to | Goldsm V 1.82 This I positively objected to | ib 2.82 as to your marriage with any but my daughter, that I never will consent to | Bennett ECh 176 What I say I stick to.

in: Goldsm 666 this house I no more show my face in | Burns 439 That dreary hour he mounts his beast in; And sic a night he taks the road in | Quincey 70 him I could believe in | Shaw D 283 I went off to your lodgings, and a nice mess I found everything in.

into: Carlyle SR 196 this also, by way of counterpart and contrast, the world shall look into.

for: Sh Mcb IV. 2.36 Poore birds they [gins] are not set for | BJo 3.233 Blood he thirsts for, and blood he will have | Defoe R 139 but that there was no help for | Fielding 3.559 Your youngest daughter I will provide for | Sheridan 333 This mischief you may thank yourself for | Austen P 74 my temper I dare not vouch for | Ruskin P 2.179 mere rags or dirt I did not care an atom for | GE A 207 the parson's ready to back it, that I'll answer for.

at: Sh Cor II. 2.128 our spoils he kick'd at | Wells A 97 Certain interesting side questions I may glance at here | Meredith R 329 and an undistinguished man what woman looks at.

with: Sh H4A I. 2.211 how thirty at least he fought with | Brontë P 241 and that pleasure I could have dispensed with | Di N 568 Such kindness as he knows, he regards her with | Ritchie M 15 Poor André Chenier we were all in love with | Pinero S 47 most of it you're acquainted with | Masefield S 36 Women he hardly spoke with from year's end to year's end | Bennett P 209 That I agree with | Shaw 1.34 Every few hundred pounds he could scrape together he bought old houses with | Norris P 54 There, that's over with.

In former days *withal* was often used instead of *with* in this place.

Without: Swinburne L 172 What liberty to act and think is left us, let us keep fast hold of; what we cannot have, let us agree to live without.

Various other prepositions: Sh Alls IV. 2.23 What is not holie, that we sweare not by | Ward R 1.297 his bowling they set small store by ‖ Shelley L 709 One thing, I own, I am curious about ‖ Austen M 90 the mother I could not avoid, but the son I *can* get away from | Galsw MW 124 That we must save her from somehow ‖ Morley M 172 Justice and injustice in the law, let us abstain from inquiring after ‖ Zangwill G 344 Room after room they passed through.

2.3₆. The same regimen may be dependent on two or more prepositions in the same sentence: Brontë P 269 Byron excited her; Scott she loved; Wordsworth only she puzzled at, wondered over and hesitated to pronounce an opinion upon | Carlyle H 4 Such hideous inextricable jungle of misworships, misbeliefs, men, made as we are, did actually hold by, and live at home in | Di X [p. ?] All this the fairies revelled in, and loved her for | Ruskin CWO 127 A goodly struggle in the Olympic dust, though it be the dust of the grave, the gods will look upon, and be with you in.

The following sentences are certainly unnatural: Southey L 57 Your Essays on Contemporaries I am not much afraid of the imprudence of | Shelley P 182 one thing will you take care of for me?

Cf from a comic paper: Governess: "Here is a nice book from which I shall read to you." Little Girl: "What did you bring me that book to be read out of from for?" — See also Weekley, *Saxo Grammaticus* p. 86 ff.

Anaphoric Repetition

2.3₇. By a stylistic trick, which for more than a century has been gaining ground in literature, a word is repeated and for emphasis given front-position: Mill Poetry [399] where every one feels a difference, a difference there must be | Kingsley H 78 There was to be no outrage, and no outrage there was | Hope D 104 she sighed delicately and delicately she panted | Strachey QV 228 She had settled to go to Balmoral on the 18th, and on the 18th she would go | McKenna SS 244 as long as mother thinks I must have a change, change I must have. Cf the slightly different type with a repeated adjective, as in Maxwell ML 72 Next day all went merry as merry could be.

The repeated word is a vb: Southey L 68 When he is gone, as go he will, nobody wil believe what a mind goes with him | Brontë V 199 I hardly noticed by what magic these doors were made to roll back — Dr. John managed these points; roll back they did, however | Lang T 182 The days darkened around him, as darken they must | Walpole RH 216 when the crisis came — as come he knew it would | id C 322 realise that he must dissemble. Dissembling was the hardest thing

..., but dissemble he must | Merriman S 52 when the famine comes — and come it assuredly will.

2.3₈. Such an anaphoric repetition is particularly interesting in a clause with *if* (more rarely *where*); sometimes it merely indicates a doubt on the part of the writer as to the choice of the most appropriate word: Cowper L 1.208 Forgive the bard, if bard he be, who once too wantonly made free | Austen M 380 What are my present plans, if plans I can be said to have | Brontë J 85 she was going to be taken to the region of spirits, if such region there were | Poe 177 Tell me the method — if method there is — by which ... | Di P 378 his better feelings conquered, if better feelings he had | Trollope W 88 The contentment of these almsmen, if content they be | Galsw WM 99 What, then, was the reason of the change — if change there were? | Bennett H 27 Now that I have succeeded (if succeeded I have) in persuading ... | Brett Young PC 78 This torture, if torture it was meant to be, recoiled upon her | Doyle S 4.193 he wants to find out some clue as to the burglary last night, if a burglar it was | Phillpotts K 92 as for your soul, — if soul you have || Kinglake E 173 the camels were turned loose to browse upon the shrubs of the Desert, where shrubs there were.

Several similar quotations were printed in my paper in S. P. E. Tract No. 48 (1937), p. 272.

Front-Position of Tertiary.

2.4₁. A preposed echo-word often causes the order V S with a notionally insignificant verb: Sterne M 1.28 at length, in some evil hour, — pop comes the creditor upon each | Carlyle FR 403 Crack go the whips | GE M 1.83 Snip! went the scissors | Hawthorne Sn 52 ting-a-ting-ting! goes the bell | Cronin H 154 Click-click went the needles! | Childers R 258 "Plump" went the lead.

2.4₂. In a great many cases, but without any consistency, the front-position of a tertiary (adv, prepositional group, etc) occasions the order V S.

This is very frequent with negative advs, which are placed in front in accordance with principle A (above, 2.1₂): Mackenzie S 1.87 Never was spoken so sweet a name as Maud | Locke HB 85 He was staring at the print, absorbed as never had he been in his life before | Walpole RH 186 As surely as never before in his love had he known what love truly was, so did he know it now | Mackenzie S 1.43 his own real house, where no longer did even a belated luggage train assure him of life's continuity | Ellis M 27 at no age are females taller or heavier than men | Wells Ma 1.42 Not for him was it to pretend | Hope Z 219 but not a bit did Rupert care | Macaulay H 4.273 Least of all could he harbour any thought of molesting an august assembly | Not till then did he perceive his mistake | Scarcely had he spoken these words when ...

Only has a kind of negative force: Seeley E 58 only by means of colonies was it possible to bring the wealth of the new world within the reach of our population. Cf below, 2.7₃.

With regard to other tertiaries I shall first give some examples of the old order V S (where now S V would be used, cf above, 2.1₉) and of vacillation: Marlowe J 922 And after that was I an Engineere | ib 926 And after that was I an Vsurer | ib 941 One time I was an Hostler in an Inne | Sh Hml II. 2.245 Then is doomesday neere | ib 250 Then is the world one | ib 255 Why then 'tis none to you ... to me it is a prison. Why then your ambition makes it one | ib 301 Nay then I haue an eye of you | ib III. 2.387 yet cannot you make it | ib 408 Now could I drink hot blood | ib 3.73 Now might I do it pat, now [conjunction] he is praying. — And now Ile doo't, and so he goes to Heauen, And so am I reueng'd | ib V. 1.208 Here hung those lips that I haue kissed I know not how oft | H4B IV. 3.126 Hereof comes it, that Prince Harry is valiant | AV John 11.3 Therefore his sister sent. 5 Now Iesus loued Martha. 6. When he ..., he abode. 7 Then after that, saith hee. 10 if a man walke ..., hee stumbleth. 11 These things said hee, and after that, he saith ... 12 Then said his disciples ... if ..., he shall doe well. 14 Then saide Iesus ... 16 Then said Thomas ... 17 Then when ..., hee found. 18 Now Bethania was ... 19 Then Martha ... went. 21 Then saide Martha... 36 Then said the Iewes. 41 Then they tooke away. 47 Then gathered the chiefe Priests and the Pharises a councell. 51 And this spake he. 56 Then sought they for Iesus | Bunyan G 44 Now was the battle won, and down fell I ... Now was I ... Now I began ... At the same time also I had ... 45 Sometimes, indeed, I should have ... Now was I ... Then began I ... | Swift J 15 Here must I begin another letter | Richardson G 70 Now, Lucy, will I resume the thread.

2.4₃. In recent usage V S is always used with the weak non-local *there* (cf below, ch III). With the local *there* and *here* V S is frequent if the vb is of little significance (generally short): Here comes (goes) the old man | there goes the train | there flies the aeroplane (but: there the aeroplane dives). Note Galsw Sw 150 There speaks your modern! | id SS 313 Here she was, and here was her heart's desire (different weight!).

2.44. When such advs as *out*, *up*, *down*, *away*, *over*, and also other tertiaries are placed in front, the order is generally determined by relative weight (above, 2.1$_5$ D). A short unstressed pronoun comes between the adv and the verb: Off he went, up he rushed, down I came | Goldsm 51 out she shall pack with a sussarara.

Exceptions are frequent: Austen M 420 Bitterly did he deplore ... wretchedly did he feel that ... | Brontë V 20 With curious readiness did she adapt herself to such themes as interested him | London M 100 if she could feel hunger and thirst, then could she feel love. — But a sb follows the vb.

Examples: off went the car, up rose the other fellow | Di P 94 There was a sudden bump — a loud crash — away rolled a wheel, and over went the chaise | Doyle S 3.119 I was sitting doing a smoke that very evening ... when up came my landlady | Di D 139 With morning came Peggotty; who called to me, as usual ... | Butler Er 74 Once only did Yram treat me in a way that was unkind | Kipling L 109 they laughed together, and with that laugh ended all serious discourse | Hope In 170 With her marriage would come a change | Mackenzie S 1.77 On the afternoon walks would be told stories of Miss Carthew's youth.

A similar distinction will be found below with regard to the position V 3 O or V O 3 (see 2.8$_7$).

2.45. Examples of V S after introductory word in clauses: Sh Shrew I 1.39 No profit growes, where is no pleasure tane | Austen M 279 towards the fireplace where sat the others | Galsw IC 54 Her mother had been like that, whence had come all those tears | Locke GP 161 she asked Myrtilla whom, least of all mortals, did she desire to take into her confidence | Dickinson S 60 Where is Man, the new Man, there is our Country | Maugham Alt 81 an office in which sat a stout, spectacled, bald-headed man | ib 546 she must pass two mortal hours before broke the reassuring day.

2.4₆. The order V S seems to become more and more common after *than* (in some cases to avoid having to choose between the pronominal forms *we* and *us*, etc) and after *as:* Lang T 36 Carlyle had very little more appreciation of Keats than had Byron or Lockhart | NP 1915 No more than can a woman forget her suckling child can he forget the tribulations of the people | Walpole GM 231 her old conviction that she knew him better than did the others | Merriman S 79 a Frenchman of note plays his part better than do we dull, self-conscious islanders || Macaulay E 4.120 As was the head, such were the members | Merriman S 69 She did not sway from side to side as do some people who lose themselves in the intoxication of music.

2.4₇. Inversion may be found in the second member of a composite sentence with *the* + comparative (cf vol V 21.7₄ and below, 14.6): Austen S 18 the more I know of the world, the more am I convinced | ib 34 the noisier they were the better was he pleased | Hughes T 2.33 the more he puzzled about it the less could he understand it.

2.4₈. A frequent beginning of a sentence is *Well might* with S after V. But the opposite order is also found and seems regular after *as:* Wordsw P 5.566 Well might we be glad | Brontë V 374 Well might this old square be named quarter of the Magii | Bennett W 2.325 Well might the Old Guard imagine ... | Churchill C 35 Well might Mr. Worthington tremble for his other ambitions || Di D 448 he gnashed his teeth with jealousy. Well he might. If he had the least idea how I adored his mistress, well he might | Priestley B 38 Waverton .. was looking at him curiously ... And well he might |

McKenna SM 47 they looked slightly bewildered — as well they might (also Priestley G 512 and 563).

2.4₉. If *much* or a synonym (as object or tertiary) is placed at the head of a sentence to achieve an ironical (negative) meaning, the order is generally S V except with *may* (which may, or may not, be taken as a wish): Scott A 2.7 And much good that will do when he has frightened the lad out of the country? | Galsw P 12.99 Much gratitude I get for saving you | id WM 235 Much that'd save her from some æsthetes! | Bennett RS 159 Love? A lot you know about it! | ib 237 It'll kill me; but a fat lot you care about that | Wells Ma 2.103 Much you'd care | Shaw 2.140 Much good your dying would do me! | Maugham P 215 Much she cared for what any one thought of her now || Carlyle F 3.215 Much good may Liverpool do you | Thack N 404 and much good may it do him | Shaw 2.185 and much good may they do you.

2.5₁. Both orders S V and V S are found close upon one another in Sh Hml III. 3.60 'tis not so aboue, There is no shuffling, there the action lyes in his true nature (N.B. Modern editions with comma to avoid misunderstanding: There, is no ...) | Brontë V 427 The last day broke. Now would he visit us. Now he would come and speak his farewell | Wells PF 38 With her alone I had talked of my possible work and purpose; to her alone had I confessed to ambitions ...

We should say: In the year 1603 Queen Elizabeth died — but In the year 1603 died good old Queen Bess.

2.5₂. In all cases except those now dealt with, frontposition of a tertiary does not cause inversion; thus we have the order S V after such adverbs as connect a sentence with what precedes, *accordingly, consequently, therefore, thus, again*. Thus also those marking a contrast: *on the contrary, on the other hand.* Further, after an introductory clause: *If (when, as) this happens,* etc. Other examples, which might be multiplied ad infinitum: Now that's all right | On Sunday a curious thing happened | Formerly John never complained | Happily the story ends here (= it is fortunate that ..) | Unfortunately he played at Monte Carlo. (With the last two examples compare the different meaning where we have a different word-order below, 2.6_5.).

Place of Tertiaries
(apart from the cases dealt with above).

2.6₁. The position of tertiaries forms a very difficult chapter of English grammar. How complicated this subject is, appears very clearly when we see that the exhaustive treatment of just two advs, *never* and *ever* (with the exclusion of *ever* = 'always') by E. Buissen (ESts 1939, p. 129 ff.), takes up no less ten pages.

On the place of advs and tertiaries generally, see Sweet NEG § 1833 ff., Krüger III p. 221 ff., 698, Kruisinga Hdb⁵ III p. 341 ff., Poutsma I² p. 427 ff., Western, *Sentence-Rhythm* p. 18 ff.

A tertiary (adv or adverbial group) may in PE have the following positions:

(1) in front, before both subject and vb; this has already been dealt with (2.4_1 ff.);

(2) between S and V;

(3) after S and v, but before V;

(4) between V and O or P;

(5) at the end of the sentence.

In positions (1) and (5) the tertiary may often be said to be in extraposition, in the latter case as a kind of afterthought. In either position it is often separated from the rest of the sentence by a pause; in writing by a comma.

Many advs can, according to circumstances, be placed now here, now there. Though there are certain strict rules, much depends on the speaker's or writer's individual fancy; he may desire to emphasize one element or to avoid crowding together several tertiaries.

Tertiary between S and V
Style-Tertiaries

2.6₂. First I shall deal with a peculiar use of a tertiary mentioned in my paper "Linguistic Self-Criticism" in S. P. E. Tract No. 48 (1937) as 'speakers' asides': the tertiary serves to qualify not the real content signified by the vb, but the stylistic choice of the following word, which then is strongly stressed.

As a typical example may be given 'she fairly screamed', which is = 'you may fairly say that she screamed.'

Literary examples: Swift J 473 I fairly ventured my life | Di P 39 [he] then fairly turned his back and — we will not say fled; firstly because it is an ignoble term, and, secondly, because Mr. Pickwick's figure was by no means adapted for that mode of retreat — he trotted away | id D 473 With that he fairly ran away | Hunt A 360 One of these grampuses fairly sprang out of the water, bolt upright | Stevenson T 176 Gray took his pipe out of his mouth and fairly forgot to put it back again, so thunder-struck he was at this occurrence || Galsw Ca 451 it fair sickened me to see the way they treat them | Wells T 80 he fair scared me | Bennett LR 348 I fair can't do it | Walpole Cp 168 Makes you fair sick to see me ... You fair loathe the sight of me.

Other advs similarly used:

You *properly* took my breath away | Hope D 87 When I was introduced I *absolutely* blushed | Walpole ST 220 I moved to the wall to take it down and I couldn't, I *literally* couldn't | Galsw SS 290 I *simply* can't bear the idea of England being in a fix | Bennett P 80 The car simply had to be bought | Maugham P 217 I had to see the Governor and I simply couldn't get away | id TL 205 when I saw the Chinese I *positively* started | RBennett P 62 You positively behaved like a madman | Mackenzie S 200 He *practically* never shoots now.

Thus also with quantifying advs:

Byron DJ 5.4 it [the name of Mary] *half* calls up the realms of fairy | Bennett B 152 they still *half*-expected some strange visit from Jules | Benson D 2.216 the quiver of her lips *half at least* consisted of self-pity | Walpole Cp 81 At the door he *almost* ran into Mr. Thurston | Allen A 176 Father Xavier ... seized his hat and almost fled through the door | Bennett A 211 she almost trembled | Locke W 165 I *more or less* see | Crofts St 9 Turning a corner she *all but* ran into Mrs. Oxley | Cole Corpse 95 He *as good as* told me so just now | Maynard Smith F 632 He as good as owned to us that his credit was shaken.

Cf with a clause: The Dean *as it were* brushed aside all objections.

Here we may class *quite* in GE Mm 203 I quite hoped that we should be friends | Freeman Th 162 I quite appreciate the value of dust as evidence in certain circumstances.

And *just:* Shaw P 281 I didnt give orders: I just asked him | Bennett RS 248 He just lay on his back and stared up at the ceiling | Galsw Ca 239 They just live to scrape enough together to keep their souls in their bodies | Maugham Alt 696 He only just escaped a squint. — Cf below, 2.7_3.

A colloquial adv of the same order is *jolly well* before a strongly stressed vb; in vg speech some drastic synonyms are found: Kipling S 158 because we jolly well chose | Walpole ST 96 I'm right, and you jolly well know it | Galsw WM 93 lie in bed if he jolly well pleased || ib 289 It did matter ... it *dashed well* did | ib 297 Think what you *damned well* like of my character! | Frankau Dance 125 if he says I asked him here, I suppose I *ruddy well* did ask him here | NJacob G 169 I pay cash, and what I can't pay cash for I *blasted well* do without | ib 249 It won't do! It won't *bloody well* do at all!

2.6₃. In this way a comparative with *than* may be used: *more than* = 'one might use a stronger expression': Sheridan 287 indeed he more than merited those repeated bursts of applause | Cowper L 2.14 I more than admire my author [Homer] | Byron L 212 But I more than love you, and cannot cease to love you | Brontë V 183 Now, when the pain is gone, I more than forgive | Di F 823 You and I suspect some one. — More than suspect | Poe 26 Till I scarcely more than muttered 'Other friends have flown before ... ' | James RH 27 I don't think he more than half suspects his ability | Bennett LR 322 They [newspapers] more than satisfied him | Philips L 129 there are some things which I more than dislike | NP 1919 she marries a man she no more than likes | Tarkington Pl 177 She little more than breathed it.

With a slight difference: Dryden, Ess. on Dram. Poesie: When he [Sh] describes anything, you more than see it — you feel it too | Bennett ECh 284 He no more dared ring the bell than he dared pour out the tea.

Rather ... than: Defoe R 2.30 the poor creatures rather devour'd than eat it | Brontë W 209 'If you don't let me in, I'll kill you!' he rather shrieked than said | Di D 434 I felt, rather than saw, that the resemblance was not lost on my companion || Anstey V 153 [?] the sudden question rather threw him off his guard.

Similar combinations with sbs and adjs are found in my S.P.E. paper.

In the same way *as* (or *so*) *much as* may be placed before a vb: More U 186 they neuer asmuch as dreamed therof | Heywood P 99 she not so much as dreamed that all was spent | Osborne 181 I never soe much as took the least notice on't | Defoe M 121 He never so much as asked me about my fortune | Di P 552 If she so much as rustled the folds of her hood, he could hear the ill-looking man clap his hand upon his sword | Ruskin P 1.43 if I so much as approached the parlour door | Butler N 255 if you so much as ask us to pass the melted butter we will shoot you | Stevenson T 8 The doctor never so much as moved | Walpole F 199 they had forgotten that they so much as had bodies at all | Hope Ch 235 I am not one of those women that lay hold of a man if he as much as looks at a girl | London A 192 by his silence he as much as says, 'I do things like this every day.'

2.6₄. *Sort of* and *kind of* before a strongly stressed vb may be considered stylistic tertiaries: Galsw 241 It sort of haunted you | Bennett B 95 I only sort of felt that he was a suspicious character | Wells Bish 274 then I sort of had to telegraph | Walpole RH 249 It never kind of struck me that the fog was going to worry you | Locke FS 249 I sort of interest myself in the old weapons | Dickinson in Forster's Life 218

I sort of see all the time the illusion and unimportance of these things.

The weakened character of the phrase *kind of* in American English is clearly seen from the pronunciation [kaində], spelt *kinder* or *kinda* (Sam Hellman in Am. Humour (1925) 386 I'm kinda glad to see 'em).

2.6₅. Very often this order implies a judgment on the part of the speaker: he *naturally* replied at once = 'it was natural that he ... ' Similarly *clearly:* Macaulay E 4.15 he clearly saw that ... And *evidently:* He evidently failed to grasp the situation. Cf also Ward M 283 She very *wisely* keeps her views to herself | NP 1933 He quite *correctly* asserted that ...

If, on the other hand, the adv is meant as descriptive of manner, it follows the vb: He replied naturally | He saw it clearly. Thus also: He does nothing simply (as contrasted with the use of *simply* before the vb, above, 2.6₂).

An approximation to such style-advs is found in cases like: if he *really* loves her | she *actually* forgot everything about it.

This position is frequent with those introductory advs whose front-position was mentioned above (2.5₂): The Captain *accordingly* remarked | He *therefore* (*accordingly*) set out to discover the whereabouts of N. | John, *on the other hand*, emphasized the arguments for her innocence.

An adv in this position often serves to characterize not only the action expressed by the vb, but partly also the subject; I take some quotations from Western (he terms them, perhaps not too felicitously, adj-advs; better perhaps epithet-adverbs (Palmer)): I then told Mrs. M. my disasters; and she *good-naturedly* blamed herself for not having better instructed me | my wife *artfully* introduced it | As Clive had not the remotest intention of satisfying those claims, he *composedly* prepared two treaties | G *boldly* walked forward alone. Also: Kipling S 286 his Excellency *graciously* spared him. — In all such cases the adv really adds little to the logical import of the sentence, but rather serves to give it an emotional colouring.

When other qualifying elements are added to the same vb, tertiaries of the type just described may be placed after the vb: Little Nell stood *timidly* by | His rival, who sat *despondingly* in a corner | Both she and the old man looked despondingly at it | He nodded *silently* to the other.

2.6₆. I subjoin a variety of quotations for the order S 3 V without attempting to analyze or classify them:

Sh Merch IV. 1.402 I *humbly* doe desire your Grace of pardon | Cowper L 1.258 but he *good-naturedly, though I think weakly,* interposed in her favour | Macaulay E 4.105 the history of Catholicism *strikingly* illustrates these observations | Di X 54 the Phantom *slowly, gravely, silently* approached | id P 103 it'll do her good, and she *richly* deserves it | Galsw Tat 35 What a room! Its green and beetroot colouring and the prevalence of cheap plush *disagreeably* affected him | NP 1918 To this the statesman *gently but firmly* demurred | Ward M 222 his interest in her *visibly* increased | Maxwell G 364 She *flatly* refused to see Monsieur Léon | Ruskin F 60 you *probably* will be having a dinner-party to-day | Ward M 218 she probably doesn't quite understand | ib 304 Edith *warmly* acquiesced | Royce Race Questions 43 Dead men *not only* tell no tales; they also, strange to say, attend no schools | Priestley F 284 Ramsbottom *slowly* opened his eyes, and blinked at them; he *care-*

fully adjusted his spectacles, and stared at them; a large fat smile *gradually* spread over his face; then it gradually disappeared | he *narrowly* escaped death | she *involuntarily* shrank from this ghastly object | Trollope B 159 it might be good policy, but it *also* might not.

This order seems to some extent to be literary rather than colloquial; it is sometimes promoted by the desire not to heap too many tertiaries closely together.

Time

2.6₇. Advs of time are often placed between S and V. This is the rule with *never:* He never makes a mistake, — and with *ever* when it forms a contrast to *never:* I don't think he ever makes a mistake | if he ever makes a mistake || Stevenson JHF 65 the Doctor now more than ever confined himself to the cabinet.

With other advs of indefinite time the same order is frequent, but not in the same way obligatory: He always (sometimes, occasionally, often, generally, now and then, seldom, still, etc) makes a mistake. But this applies to full vbs only, thus also *have* when not an auxiliary: Stevenson T 77 We never had a night at the "Admiral Benbow" when I had half the work. Cf below, 2.8₂ ff., on small verbs.

With some advs of time this order, as Sweet remarks, suggests sequence in time: I *now* proceed to explain ... Compare "he then went to Brighton" with "he lived then at Brighton". When *then* = 'accordingly', it often has front-position: Then it is true that he did it?

Cf also He *further* remarked that ...

Here has the same effect, while as a real local adv it is put after V: Tom's bell here rang, and Tom was summoned to the parlour.

Examples of other time-tertiaries. It will be seen that they sometimes draw other tertiaries with them: Brontë J 20 Mr. Lloyd *a second time* produced his snuff-box | Di D 162 I *rarely* heard from Miss Murdstone | ib 425 when I *at last* inquired ... | Doyle M 64 when I at last laid my hand on his collar | Bennett B 169 You *months ago* expressed the warmest satisfaction | Brontë V 23 He *rarely, it is true*, remarked on what he read | Pinero S 39 when we *next* meet I shall remember nothing [or *meet next*] | Poe S 77 when I *at last* completely came to my senses, I found ... | Doyle S 1.155 It was nearly four o'clock when we *at last*, after passing through the beautiful Stroud Valley, and over the broad gleaming Severn, found ourselves at Ross | she *at once* impressed me as a flirt.

Quantifier Tertiaries
(Cf above, 2.4$_7$ ff., 2.6$_2$ ff.)

2.6s. Some tertiaries of degree may come between S and V (note the negatives): Sh Meas II. 4.119 I *something* do excuse the thing I hate [now *somewhat;* NED: she somewhat smiled] | Defoe Rox 93 However, it *not a little* pleased me to see him so concerned | Walpole RH 227 You *a little* overestimate the situation | Black Ph 246 I don't think it *much* matters really [also: matters much] | Maugham Alt 1244 I don't think he *much* cares about seeing people | Aldington D 3 of course, nobody *much* bothered to read the lists | Bennett T 61 The piano *faintly* sounded | Benson D 2.44 Something within her *ever so faintly* resented the idea of Jack's marrying Nadine | Harraden D 30 I *so* want to get better | James RH 375 it's a riddle, and I *only half* guess | Bennett RS 246 Nothing else in her own existence *greatly* mattered to her | He *badly* wants a trashing | he *seriously* injured his foot.

The quantifier *little* (without the indefinite article) nearly means the same thing as a negative: I little thought he was such a brute. It is also placed before such verbs as *know* and *care* and a few others.

2.6₉. I give here a collection of quotations in which the same adv is in closely connected sentences put in two different places, leaving the reader to find out the reasons for this diversity; in the last quotation the difference between *can't* and the more emphatic *cannot* should be noted: BJo 3.169 I am *but* a messenger; I *but* tell you, what you must hear | Peacock Works 1.336 Might it not be a mermaid? It was *possibly* a mermaid. It was *probably* a mermaid. It was *very probably* a mermaid. Nay, what could it be but a mermaid? It *certainly* was a mermaid | Austen M 358 all this became *gradually* evident, and *gradually* placed Susan before her sister as an object of compassion | Bennett ECh 246 I suppose you are Adela, said the visitor *awkwardly*, and *awkwardly* advancing | NP 1925 Milton's mind ranged *everywhere* and *everywhere* found grist for the mill | Stephen L 483 if I *unduly* depreciate myself, I depreciate others *unduly* too | Bennett A 54 an eminent actor strolled in to us *grandiosely*, ... chatted *grandiosely*, and *grandiosely* departed | id C 1.57 Mrs. Nixon greeted Mrs. Hamps *effusively*, and *effusively* gave humble thanks for kind enquiries after her health | Beresford G 154 'I can't *really* see,' she said with a sort of moody petulance. 'I *really* cannot see why we shouldn't be married.'

2.7₁. *Than* and the element compared are sometimes placed before the comparative: Black F 2.196 who than she more capable of advising in aught concerning Lionel's welfare? | Galsw EC 258 and than that was anything more calculated to give pleasure? | Stedman O 103 Than these there are no more despicable creatures in existence | Bennett C 1.279 Than they, she had no more skill to be sociable. Cf the relative *than whom*.

2.7₂. A tertiary is sometimes placed at the beginning of a clause after *as*, though it logically belongs in the main part of the sentence: Doyle S 5.196 I propose to occupy my mind as best I may | Shaw J 195 let me take it as best I can | Gissing G 444 he went away to bear the misery as best he might | Moore Conf 5 I put my trust in the future, as well I might, for a fair prospect of idleness lay before me.

Special Cases

2.7₃. The position of some advs requires special mention. — Cf Poutsma I² 451 ff.

Again has various places; as an introductory particle it has front-position, like the synonymous *on the other hand*; in the sense 'once more' it is generally put after the vb, thus also when = 'in return, in reaction': shine again (really = 'against'). Note the idiomatic use in Di P 210 when that chap as we issued the writ against at Camberwell, you know, came in — what's his name again? (also Maxwell F 73).

Enough: 'normally follows an adj or adv which it qualifies' (NED): I am not tall enough; — but it is sometimes placed before; end-position in: a pleasant room enough (q); = 'a sufficient number or quantity of': he had money enough, enough money | Shaw P 211 not having enough great men in our influential families to go round || he proved convincingly enough...

First: he came first | when he first came, when we were first married (does not imply the possibility of a second marriage, but = 'soon after our marriage,' cf vol IV 5.9) | with front-position = 'firstly, in the first place.'

Generally: he generally made himself useful (= 'at most times') | he made himself generally useful (= 'useful in a general way').

Hardly (cf vol VI 22.9_1 and above, 1.5_5): he worked hardly || he hardly worked at all | he has hardly been seen here.

Indeed: Indeed, it is too much | it is indeed too much | he might indeed have refused | very good indeed | Will you come? I will, indeed.

Just: cf above, 2.6_2, and see Hope D 6 I just taught him ... I just slipped in a remark here and there-... I used to speak just at the right time ... A condition that he should do just what I wanted ... I didn't [care for him]. "Not a bit?" "Just as a friend."

Now introductory, front-position, cf above, 2.6_7: Now, Brown was a very young man | now he is coming, he is coming now | the population of England was then hardly a third of what it now is.

Often not, not often, see vol V 23.3_1. Cf also Rose Macaulay P 220 people often don't get on with their mothers-in-law | Bennett Imp. Pal. 151 Candour isn't necessarily the best policy. It often isn't | Maxwell EG 172 She cried a little ... Often she could not cry | Maugham Alt xvii That is a writer's supreme virtue and one upon which sufficient stress is often not laid.

Mostly: Rose Macaulay P 226 The trouble is that they mostly can't do anything of the sort. They don't mostly even know how to try. — Cf vol VI 22.9_6.

Once: he once told me [on some occasion in the past], weak stress | he told it once [not twice; stressed] | I cannot begin my work again when I have once been interrupted (Sweet) = 'once I have been interrupted.'

Only. Purists insist on placing *only* close to the word it qualifies, but as a matter of fact it is by most people placed between S and V, and stress and tone decide where it belongs, cf Ballard, *Thought and Language* 212 ff., with many quotations, Palmer Gr § 386. He did not listen; he only ˈtalked | The others listened, ˈhe only talked.

Some quotations: Sh Merch II. 8.50 I thinke he onely loues the world for him, i.e. 'he loves the world only for him' | Stevenson M 104 The illusion only endured an instant | Benson DB 308 You got down this afternoon only? — Yes, sir. I only heard this morning | Kipling S 280 He slept twenty-four hours. I only slept seventeen | Locke W 282 He only saw her when she came down late for dinner | Graves IC 423 A man only has one mother | Galsw EC 364 You don't only have to watch him, but everybody connected with him | Locke GP 294 A taxi took him to the house which now was only his on sufferance | Shaw TT 157 [journalist:] I have only been married once. I mean I have been married only once.

Note *if only:* Wells TM 87 If only I had had a companion it would have been different | Royce R 43 an animal that you can debase to whatever level you please, if you only have power.

As a limitation of what has just been said, *only* has front-position: I quite agree with you, only I think that Henry is right on some points | He is a very nice man, only he talks too much | Mackenzie C 125 He said he would have done, only you treated him so off-hand | Swinnerton S 147 [charwoman] I shouldn't a noticed it only I was scrubbin' | Salt Joy 233 I wouldn't have come home only Aunt Bessie said she was ill.

Cf the conjunction *only that* = 'except that, but for the fact that': Thack P 171 only that she remembered that the lad's father had always destined him for the College, ... very likely the fond mother would have put a veto upon his going to the University | Butler Er 128 it might easily have happened to themselves, only that they had the luck to be better born or reared | Ridge N 222 he would have passed by the crowd only that his name was called | Dickinson S 77 a plea with which I most heartily sympathize, only that he gave no indication of the basis.

Quite: he is quite a famous man | Maugham Alt 461 Dick Temple who came from quite a good county family | Mason No Oth. Tiger 31 Do you know that I hardly believed you? — You quite did not believe me, returned Strickland; = 'you quite disbelieved me', different from 'didn't quite believe me,' = 'partly'.

So am I, so I am, see above, 2.2_3 | so good | so = 'so much': My head aches so | = 'in this way. like this': So it was that he became a soldier | It is not so.

Though as an adv has end-position.

Too (really a stressed form of the prep. *to*) = 'more than desirable' is a word-modifier and precedes: too old, too badly done; = 'also' it is generally placed after the word it belongs to: She, too, was angry | here, too, he was wrong. But exceptions are not at all rare, e.g. Beswick OD 183 That afternoon was a bad one too for Tom Nellon.

Yet introductory: he is young, yet he is not without experience | he has not come yet | he has not yet been seen | in questions implying a negation ('nearly = already, but not expressing surprise, as that word' NED); cf Sheridan 275 have you sent your play to the managers yet? | Kennedy R 210 Are you married yet? = 'I thought you weren't married yet'.

Overlapping

2.7₄. Sometimes one part that would seem naturally to belong to a dependent clause is placed in the main sentence (or rather the main part of a sentence). This is especially frequent in clauses without a conjunction, so that the boundary between main sentence and clause is not outwardly marked. In sentences without a conjunction the tertiary may be considered as an introductory part of the clause: Swift J 46 I hope in a month or two all the forms of settling this matter will be over | Sweet E 29 I expect in a few years there'll be none left at all | Maugham P 109 I should have thought under the circumstances a wife's place was by her husband's side | id Pl 3.62 Well, I thought in the hot weather I'd sleep there sometimes.

Examples with *perhaps* are frequent: Galsw Frat 23 I fancied perhaps you might feel that ... | ib 90 I was hoping perhaps I might be allowed to take them | Shaw A 119 I should have sent her away, only I thought perhaps you wanted her to talk into your machines | Maugham Pl 2.244 I thought perhaps she might have done it herself | Walpole Cp 153 I think perhaps I shall sleep a little.

Similarly in Galsw EC 545 I thought possibly I might take you down to see him to-morrow | Cather P 227 I expect maybe he's had his feelings hurt here || NP 1926 we hope next month that we may be able to announce that the offers have been forthcoming.

Examples with conjunction or interrogative pronoun or adv: BJo 3.22 I hardly can perceive him, that he breathes | Phillpotts GR 85 I remember long ago, after the wedding, that he was interested in haunted rooms || Sh Ant V. 1.51 Wee'l heare him what he sayes | Tennyson In Mem. 74 I see thee what thou art | id 322 I know thee who thou art || Ch B 4391 Herkneth thise blisful briddes how they singe, And see the fresshe floures how they springe || Sh R2 III. 3.61 marke King Richard how he lookes | ib V. 4.1 Didst thou not marke the King what words hee spoke? | Swift J 159 it pitied us to see the Archdeacon, how concerned he was | Earle Phil 525 one little girl I well remember how she puzzled me.

On *I don't know exactly* (or *exactly know*) *what happened*, see vol V 25.2$_4$.

2.7$_5$. Descriptive advs (of manner) are generally placed after the vb (and as close to it as possible): It snowed heavily for an hour | she passed the night quietly | he writes badly | he dealt fairly and squarely with her | he walked away leisurely | he works very carefully, but slowly | he pronounces each syllable clearly and distinctly | he spoke simply and to the point | he averted his head respectfully | she laughed heartily | he looked at her thoughtfully | Ward M 234 she had treated her badly | ib 235 these things stood out plainly, whatever else remained in obscurity | ib 236 she walked up to him deliberately | Kipling L 82 Surely you aren't taking all the stuff in the papers seriously.

This is distinct from other uses of some of the same advs mentioned above (2.6$_2$, 2.6$_5$f.).

2.7$_6$. Sometimes the vb and adv are joined by a hyphen; thus with *to:* Jerome Idle Thoughts [T] 157 She hears the front door opened and closed-to | Pinero B 277 When Theo came-to | Hewlett F 20 Prosper clapped-to his spurs.

The adv is clearly an afterthought in Hardy L 42 the inexplicable fact absorbed Cope's attention quite | Merriman Last Hope 402 On these subjects the Marquis good-humouredly followed her advice, sometimes | Bennett A 212 ... he asked of Anna, menacingly | Graves IC 175 He said that he could not get enough reliable information locally | (q Western) What is it, whispered Edith, fearfully.

Tertiaries of time are generally placed after other advs: I saw him there lately | we expect him back again to-morrow | she met him clandestinely in the garden every evening.

Some examples of tertiaries placed between V and O: Hawthorne T 125 he had on a singular pair of shoes | Ridge G 50 the trouble of putting on again laced-up boots | NP 1911 to hold in check the insurgent democracy, — but these might be infinitely augmented.

Imperative

2.7₇. Tertiaries with the Imperative: Just fancy! | Never say die! | Never fear (Wells N 455) | Walk as fast as you can! | Do your work slowly and steadily! | Treat her kindly — but: Kindly shut the door (cf above, 2.6₅).

Infinitive

2.7₈. The order of words connected with an infinitive requires few remarks. The infinitive in a combination with small verbs has been dealt with above. Otherwise tertiaries are placed before the infinitive, either before *to* or between *to* and the infinitive (see vol V 20.4). A few special cases are illustrated in these quotations: McCarthy 2.283 It was the happy fortune of his country to have never been placed in any position of organic danger | Stevenson A 12 He will be found to have greatly enriched the meaning | Garnett L 13

Her odour abated so much by this means that he came not to notice it at all.

The object of an infinitive is generally placed after it. An isolated exception is *truth to tell*, which, however, is not invariably carried through, see e.g. Thack N 604 Truth to tell, she hardly took any notice of him | Merriman S 131 Etta, who, truth to tell, had pulled up the windows | McCarthy 2.342 About the rest of the Adullamites, truth to say, very few persons thought at all | Thack N 825 the beauty of which, to say truth, time had considerably impaired. — With the definite article probably always: to tell the truth.

Participles

2.7₉. There is, as remarked in vol VI 9.7₃, a tendency to place a particle first, which with the vb would stand after: *outstretched*, but *stretch out;* thus also *downlying*, but *lie down*, *forthcoming*, but *come forth*, etc. See also Hardy F 388 she had done so in bygone days, which, though not long gone by, seemed infinitely removed | Brontë V 169 I had to recur to gone-by troubles.

In a few cases a prepositional group is placed before a participle: as in duty bound | James RH 411 Roderick came out from the house, not, as appeared, on pleasure bent. Cf Hughes T 2.92 if we are that way inclined.

Place of the Object

2.8₁. The natural place of the object is after the vb, see below.

Exceptionally (archaically or poetically), the object is placed before the full vb: Sh Hml III. 4.9 Hamlet, thou hast thy father much offended. Mother you haue my father much offended | ib III. 3.78 I, his foule sonne, do this same villaine send To heauen | Tennyson 575 God the traitor's hope confound!

Tertiaries with Verbs

2.8₂. When the verbal expression is compounded of a small vb and a full vb (infinitive or participle) the regular order is for the tertiary to follow the small vb. This is found with all those tertiaries which are generally placed between S and V, with the exception of style-tertiaries:

He has never met her | he'll never meet her.
He is always meeting her.
He can never forget it.
He will often forget things.
He has purposely refrained from answering.
He was naturally surprised.
He had evidently forgotten his manners.

A few literary quotations will suffice: Di D 163 you have never been a lodger. You have been a friend | ib. I shall never, Master Copperfield, revert to the period without thinking of you | Rose Macaulay P 215 How did one work that? You could never tell | Squire Parodies Pref. All the parodies I have ever published, or, I imagine, ever shall publish.

2.8₃. The same order is the rule when a form of the vb *be* is followed by a predicative: S V 3 P; in fact, the second participle in the passive sentence just quoted is a predicative:

He is never (always, sometimes, often) ill.

If, however, a predicative is qualified by some complement, both positions of the tertiary are possible:

He never (always) was unkind to children, or He was never (always) unkind to children | Di D 76 Mr.

Mell never said much to me, but he was never harsh to me | Lawrence L 197 A man never is quite such an abject specimen as his wife makes him look.

If *is* or *was*, etc, stands alone, the tertiary is placed before it, and the vb receives strong stress:

(Unkind to children?) He never (always, etc) ˈis.

Similarly when other small vbs stand without a following full vb: He hasn't seen her and never ˈwill (nor ever ˈwill) | Seen her? Well, he never ˈhad.

2.8₄. Exceptional front-position of the tertiary may be occasioned in an emotionally coloured saying like "You never can tell" (Title of play by Shaw; also common elsewhere), and in a contrast like "It never ˈhas been, and never ˈwill be, necessary" | Macaulay E 4.254 But it was then, and still is, the opinion of everybody that Hastings was the real mover | Murry, Probl. of Style 9 But the perfect critic does not exist, and never has existed.

The small vb is also stressed in Di D 160 I never will desert Mr Micawber ... I never will do it | ib 180 his sister, Betsey Trotwood, never would have run away | Lawrence L 188 He's really wonderful. And he always has been the same | Butler E 255 it always has been thus, and always will be.

2.8₅. The following quotations illustrate both orders in close succession: Sheridan 269 you will never read anything that's worth listening to ... But you never will read anything to entertain one | Di P 397 to the best of my knowledge, I was never here before ... I am perfectly serious. I really never was here before | id Do 314 I am not a favourite child. I never have been. I have never known how to be | Trollope B 377 You must positively introduce me, Thorne; you positively must | Matthews F 193 she no longer wore the magic spectacles of youthful love; she was no longer a mere girl | Bennett I 514 He would never, and never could, know anything worth knowing | Childers R 156 the sea has never been my element, and never will be | Caine C 46 It has always been so, and always will be | Phillpotts M 36 your opinion was always outrageous and always will be | Merriman Last Hope 289 He had once thought that she was always conscious of the social gulf existing between them; that she always remembered that she was by birth a lady | Walpole W 422 You never have loved me?... You have never loved me?

The difference between weakly stressed *is to* and strongly stressed ¹*has to* (cf vol V 13.5) results in the word-order: she's always to assist him | she always ¹has to assist him.

2.8₆. Difficulties in placing the tertiary increase when the same sentence contains two small vbs.

Various English friends whom I asked about such sentences (some years before World War II) preferred: this will probably be said (to: this probably will be said) | examples may easily be found (to: may be easily found) | it will often be said (to: it will be often said) | the whole matter has been publicly discussed (to: has publicly been discussed) | it must also be constantly borne in mind (to: be also constantly borne in mind) | This letter does not seem ever to have reached the King's hand (to: seem to have ever..., as in MacCarthy 2.438 | He had often been there (to: be had been often there, as in Trollope W 203).

One of the editors of the NED preferred: The family of Dirkwood had been long settled in Sussex (as in Austin S 1), while the other preferred: ... had long been settled in Sussex. Scott (I 95) writes: he would have probably withdrawn himself altogether; but Dr Onions preferred: ... would probably have withdrawn himself.

In some cases my English friends thought two orders equally good: I could have easily vindicated human kind (thus Swift 3.342) or: I could easily have v. ... | Had he been always as easily repelled, Carlyle would assuredly not have deserved the praise of catholicity (Walker L 56) or: Had he always been ... | I must have indeed been shy (Butler Er 91) or: I must indeed have been shy | the whole matter has been frequently discussed, or: .. has frequently been ..

A few literary quotations without remark: Shelley L 730 You will have probably been informed of the manner | Macaulay H 1.61 the opposition which had, during forty years, been silently gathering and husbanding strength | Trollope W 67 could he have thus comprised the matter | Gissing H 183 May would have long ago bought a bicycle had she been able to afford it | Doyle S 5.257 as if they had been that instant done | Butler Er 88 the vintage had been already gathered | id ER 289 its place would be soon filled by men who would be as false | id Er 43 a thought occurred to me, which would have doubtless struck me at once | McCarthy 2.521 no popularity could have wholly prevented that result | Huxley L 1.69 I should have bitterly despised myself | Milne P 67 I should have pretty soon seen what that fellow Marcus was up to | Sweet NEG § 542 The effect ... has been already treated of.

2.8$_7$**.** Complemental advs, i.e. advs that form a sense-unit with the vb, have their place after the vb, but may be separated from it by the object, if this is a light unstressed pronoun. The rule thus is:

I give him up: I give up all hope.
put it on: put on your hat.
put it off | put off the whole thing.
he found it out : he found out their plans.
he tore it up | he tore up the letter.
he gave it back : he gave back the book.

We see here the same principle of weight (D) as above with 3 V S and 3 S V (2.4_4).

This, to some extent, may be compared with the difference between *for it* (*him*) with half-stressed prep. and *for the king* with weakly stressed *for*.

When a pronoun is stressed it may be placed after the tertiary: Sh Mcb IV. 2.51 there are lyars and swearers enow to beat the honest men and hang vp |them | Ado III. 3.91 call vp |me | Di P 215 If you want to ease your mind by blowing up somebody, come into the court and blow up |me.

The following quotations illustrate both positions: Sh H4A I. 2.106 I must giue ouer this life, and I will giue it ouer | Di F 771 I'll give up every word of it. I'll give it up, and I'll give up you | Thack P 3.206 you may give up society without any great pang ... but severe are the mortifications and pains you have if society gives up you | Brontë W 98 Will you give up Heathcliff hereafter, or will you give up me? | Fox 1.145 So I have given them up, and in fact they have given up me | Galsw WM 172 he must have picked up something in the Square — dogs were always picking things up | Bennett P 19 he had decided to give up his other club. He must give it up | Hankin 2.115 Break off this engagement. Break it off, I beg of you | Shaw C xv showmen, who set him on to fight as they might set on a dog | id P 123 Wont you cut their heads off? — What! Cut off your brother's head? — Why not? He would cut off mine, if he got the chance | Galsw FS 399 Would you like to put on your hat ...? But while she was gone to put her hat on, he frowned | Mannin ChE 74 "You did something to me when you tore up her picture," he said at last. "It was as though you tore my heart up" | Lawrence L 237 to make up his mind. Now he had made it up.

But exceptions to the rule given do occur: see your friend off — more frequent than the order in Kaye-Smith T 355 Ted's gone to the station to see off Louise and James | Walpole ST 100 I had not been able to make my mind up about the cottage | Caine P 174 when I gave Thora up to you.

2.8₈. The order V O 3 is, perhaps, especially frequent if the object is a word of such little notional importance as *matters* or *things*, as these approach the value of a pronoun. Bentley T 264 wished to clear the matter up.

A gradual approach to the now usual end-position is seen in Luke 15.6 Wycliff: he cometh hoom, and clepith togidir hise freendis and neiȝboris ... 9 sche clepith togidir freendis and neiȝboris | AV 6 he calleth together his friends and neighbours ... 9 she calleth her friends and her neighbours together | 20th C. 6 he calls his friends and neighbours together ... 9 she calls her friends and neighbours together.

Note the order with both indirect and direct object: Caine P 39 Then you will give her back her word | Meredith H 70 I'll send you up some tea presently | always: pour her out some wine.

In some cases there seems to be little if any difference between the two positions, e.g. take away one's breath, or: take one's breath away | take up one's time, or: take one's time up | turn out one's pockets, or: turn one's pockets out | we have found out all this, or: found all this out | wrap up the books, or: wrap the books up, etc.

As to cases in which it may be doubtful whether we have an adv or a prep. (think over a matter: think a matter over) see vol III 13.9_1 (1) ff.

Chapter III
Sentence-Structure. Concluded
Sentences with the Empty *there*

3.1₁. The empty, or, as I have called it elsewhere, the existential *there* differs from the local adv *there*

(1) by having weak stress and consequently having the vowel [ɛ·ə] reduced to [ə],

(2) by losing its local meaning; hence the possibility of combining it with local advs and other tertiaries, see below, 3.1_2.

(3) by being a quasi-subject, thus e.g. in an infinitival nexus and with an ing, see below, 3.1_4, 3.1_7.

(4) by the tendency to have the vb in sg form with a pl subject, see below, 3.1_4.

(5) by the word-order: *there is nothing wrong*, but *there nothing is wrong;* cf above, 2.4_3.

Thus it is not quite correct to say with NED (*there* 4) that "Grammatically there is no difference between *There comes the train* and *There comes a time when*, etc.; but while in the former *there* is demonstrative and stressed, in the latter it has been reduced to a mere anticipative element occupying the place of the subject which comes later."

3.1₂. The empty *there* can be connected in the same sentence with indications of place: Ch B 3981 For *ther-in* is ther no desport or game | Franklin 191 paquet-boats ... there were two then remaining *there* | Di X 31 The noise in this room was perfectly tumultuous, for there were more children there, than he could count | Di T 2.31 But there is no one there | Stevenson M 33 and there, sure enough, crusted with the red rust, there lay an iron shoe-buckle | id K 204 There, there are living many friends of mine || Ch G 943 somwhat of our metal Yet is ther *heer* | Bunyan P 62 and there was here enough of this | Wells TM 149 There's some magazines here | Doyle S 6.39 Here on the left hand there stands a shop window filled with photographs || Ch B 4178 a toun, *Wheras* ther was swich congregacioun | Where there is a will, there is a way || Di T 2.213 What strength there is *in these common bodies*!

3.1₃. *There* has often been described as preparatory subject, as anticipatory subject (Curme; cf *anticipative* in NED), or as introductory (Kruisinga), but these epithets are misleading, for *there* need not precede the real subject; Curme just after using his term gives the example: Men there were yet living who had seen him, etc. Other examples of the place after the subject proper, many of them in questions: Sh Merch IV. 1.47 Some men there are loue not a gaping Pigge | Mi PL 4.178 One Gate there onely was | ib 4.514 One fatal Tree there stands of Knowledge call'd | Defoe R 2.4 What there was really in this, shall be seen in its place | Di X 3 I don't mean to say that I know what there is particularly dead about a door-nail | Maugham Alt 928 what other explanation was there? | What is there to laugh at? | Shoes there were none | The reason, if reason there was. — Note that in some of these, at any rate, *is* and *was* are stressed more strongly than in sentences with the other word-order.

3.1₄. The tendency in colloquial English to use *there is* before a pl word was mentioned in vol II 6.81 and 6.82 with the explanation that *there is* in the beginning of the sentence becomes a fixed formula and is often pronounced before the speaker has considered whether it is a sg or pl word that is to follow; parallels from Danish, Italian and Russian were mentioned, and examples from Malory and later writers were given, among others of *there was you*. An earlier example is Ch T 3.865 there is but we two. And recent ones are Wells TB 2.112 They're to call on me on Wednesday, and there's got to be you for tea | Mason Witness 9 Before I came there was no one. Since I came here there has been — you | Huxley PCP 280 In the intervals, Walter darling, there's you.

This peculiarity is one of the indications of the fact that in the *there*-sentences we have not to do with a subject in the ordinary sense.

In all these sentences *there* occupies the place usually given to the subject, and might be termed a vicarious subject or quasi-subject — Wiwel uses the term *nødsubjekt* ('makeshift subject'), and Western *skinsubjekt* ('sham subject') —, while the other word is relegated to a second plane. This is especially obvious in the use of *there* as subject in infinitival and gerundial groups: *let* there be light | I don't want there to be | it was impossible for there to be (vol V 19.4) | account for there being something rather odd (ib 9.7$_9$).

There are other indications that *there* is felt as as a kind of subject. Thus the use of tag-questions: there is nothing funny about him, is there? | there will be trouble, won't there? || Tarkington F 90 No other little girl ever fell in love with you, did there? — Further answers like these, where we should otherwise have no subject: Is there any bridge going? Yes, there is | Are there any cherries? Yes, there are. — And finally the frequent occurrence of *there* at the beginning of relative contact clauses (i. e. without any relative pronoun). These otherwise always begin with the subject, as the rel. pron. as subject cannot be spared, but cf Money is just about the most useful thing there is | Bentley T 330 the disappearance of any chance there might be of the commutation of the capital sentence. Many quotations in vol III p. 148.

3.1₅. But if *there* is the subject, what about the other part: how are we to analyze it? It is as a rule more indefinite than ordinary subjects, which are the most special part of the sentence; and it does not take the usual place of a subject. Still, it must be considered the subject proper of these sentences. In AnalSynt 10.5 I analyze *There are many churches there* as 3/s V S 3, denoting by 3/s something which may either be called a tertiary or a lesser subject. This is correct enough, but there might be occasion to show that there is something unusual about both subjects, and I now propose to do this by a raised ^{m} ("modified"), exactly as I marked (ib 3.8) some unclassifiable adjuncts as 2^m; thus $3/s^m$ V S^m 3.

3.1₆. The chief use of *there*-sentences is to denote the more or less vague existence or coming into existence of something indefinite; thus very frequently with the vb *be:* There's some one at the door | If he comes, there will be trouble | What is there for dinner? | There is no time like the present | There is many a slip between cup and lip | There is no rule without some exception | There are as good fish in the sea as ever came out of it (and many other proverbs).

3.1₇. *There being* is frequent in nexus-tertiaries to indicate cause: Spectator 3 As for the rest of my infancy, there being nothing in it remarkable ... | Di Do 26 there not being room for both of them in the only boat that was not swamped, neither of them would consent to go | Stevenson MB 179 And I, there being none to settle the difference, must reproduce both versions | Di T 1.58 There appearing to be no other door ... and the keeper of the wine-shop going straight to this one, Mr. Lorry asked him.

3.1₈. The combination of *there is* with a following *-ing* was dealt with in connexion with Expanded Tenses in vol IV 14.8(4) (Shall there be gallows standing | if there were any drinks going, etc). On *there is no use -ing* instead of the more usual *it is* — see vol V 8.2₁. Cf also Kaye-Smith HA 291 there's no good making conjectures | ib 294 There's no good whispering.

3.1₉. The vb *be* is also found in passive constructions, which are very frequent in sentences with *there:* AV Matth 19.13 Then were there brought vnto him little children | Sh H4B V. 4.7 There hath beene a man or two lately killed about her | Hml V. 1.258 Must there no more be done? | Carlyle SR 73 would there not, among the idler classes, perhaps a certain levity be excited | Bentley TI 206 There had been a jeweller's window smashed.

3.2₁. Other vbs than *be* are found in *there*-sentences, but generally only those of a somewhat vague meaning, such as *come, appear, happen,* etc: AV John 1.46 Can there any good thing come out of Nazareth? [but without *there* in 20th C. V. Can anything good come out of Nazareth?] | AV Esth 4.14 then shall there enlargement and deliuerance arise to the Iewes | Defoe R 2.93 Early one morning, there came on shore five or six canoes of Indians | Spectator 189 There cannot a greater judgment befal country than .. | Keats 4.184

there has scarce a day passed but he has visited him | Carlyle FR 106 Since the year 1614, there have no States-General met in France | GE A 396 there may good come out of this | Stevenson JHF 209 In the ancient days there went three men upon pilgrimages | Dreiser F 226 Then there won't anything happen to her.

A few examples of vbs outside these categories: Mitford OV 21 There only wants a pool under the thorn to give a still lovelier reflection | Lawrence L 97 There wants a man about the place | Carlyle SR 158 That there should one man die ignorant who had capacity for knowledge.

3.2₂. Transitive vbs with objects formerly were not at all rare with *there* (NED *there* 4 b, obs.; frequent in Ch). We do not say *There took a man a walk*, but *There was a man who took a walk*. But *take place* = 'happen,' may still be found; thus also *cross her path* = 'come': Thack P 715 there took place between him and his son a violent and painful scene | Cronin C 91 On the sixth of September there took place a full meeting of the Committee | Locke HB 177 If there crossed her path a man with a strong protective arm, he was whisked away. — Cf also More U 23 There met us at Bruges they whom ...

3.2₃. A *there*-sentence may contain a predicative, e.g. Stevenson T 147 There is one thing good about all this [different from: There is one good thing] | Christie Big Four 220 At times there seemed really nothing the matter with him.

The generally indefinite character of sentences with *there* is (as already hinted above) shown by the 'subject', which in the majority of cases is indefinite. If it is a sb, it is most often accompanied by an indefinite adjunct (*a, no, some, any, many,* etc). Note that *that* and *those* as subjects here have an indefinite meaning: there was *that* in his character which ... = 'something'; there are *those* who think ... = 'some'.

3.2₄. Not infrequently, when the subject is seemingly definite, the underlying notion is really indefinite as shown by the indefinite article after *of:* Stevenson T 130 I was thinking this over, when there came ringing over the island the very cry of a man at the point of death | id M 204 it was not long before there shone in at the door the ruddy glimmer of a lantern | Jenkins B 246 ... when there reached him the sound of a motor-car | Swinnerton S 50 Beyond, there could be seen the rim of a hill | Maxwell F 31 and there passed through his mind the memory of a real boy, a boy called Cartwright || Note also *for example* in Russell FO [p. ?] The few survived had curious adventures. There were, for example, Mrs. Simmons and her daughter.

In other instances the writer might nearly as well have written *a* as *the:* Bennett C 1.194 there had begun to form in his mind the conviction that all was not quite well with the work | Galsw MW 214 When, at last, she stopped, there followed the strangest silence [= 'a very strange silence'] | id D 69 Through the leaves there came the faint far tinkle of the tea-bell | Russell FO 485 Then there awoke in me the wish to build shops of my own | Benson D 2.45 there was also in Dodo's heart the indefinable yearning for days that were dead.

3.2₅. But in some passages these explanations do not hold good; sometimes the reason for the *there*-construction seems simply to be the length of the subject which has made it difficult to place it at the beginning of the sentence; cp. the constructions with *it,* below, 4.6₈. Examples: Di T 1.212 there is, in her heart towards you, all the love and reliance of infancy itself | Collins W 419 There were also placed in her possession the clothes Lady Glyde had worn | Stevenson T 108 Then it was that there came into my head the first of the mad notions that contributed so much to save our lives | Kipling MOP 193 after the little silence that followed on the ceremony there entered the native officer who had played for the Lushkar Team | Waugh W 64 Later in the day there was announced Roy Bauer, the man on whom he relied for the remainder | Walpole Cp 21 Then there arrived Mr. Brassy, her father's solicitor, from Cater Hill | Butler W 304 then there came into his mind that noble air of Handel's: 'Great God'' | Oppenheim Laxw 94 To-night there will meet here the man whose deeds a short time ago set all London in a panic, and the bloodhounds who ... | Benson D 26 as he thought of this, there occurred to him the remark that Dodo had made that morning.

3.2₆. In sentences of the vague character generally found in English with *there*, in Scandinavian with *der*, in Dutch with *er*, in Fr. with *il y a*, in Ital. with *v'è*, there seems everywhere to be a tendency to have the V before the S; in comparing the Authorized Version with the Greek original I was struck with the frequency of *there*, where the Greek had the word-order VS.

Abbreviated Sentences

3.3₁. Alongside the fully articulate sentences considered so far (containing a subject and a finite vb) we have very frequent instances of inarticulate or semi-articulate sentences — cf the remarks in PhilGr 308 ff. on expression, suppression, and impression. We here have especially to dwell on sentences in which something is left out either through what is learnedly called prosiopesis — the beginning left out — or aposiopesis — the end left out. In both kinds we find types of sentences in which the suppression has occurred so often that at last no one thinks any more of what is left out, the remainder becoming a regular idiomatic expression which the grammarian must recognize as a complete sentence. Cf also *Language* 273.

Front-Part Left Out

3.3₂. The beginning is dropped: the speaker begins to articulate, or thinks he begins, but produces no articulate sound (either for want of expiration, or because he does not make his vocal chords vibrate till one or two syllables after the beginning of what he intended to say).

It may be a particle or even the beginning of one: Galsw P 2.22 [Of] Course you've no personal feeling in the matter (also Kipling S 59, Rose Macaulay T 208, etc) | Kipling S 154 [Be-]'Sides.

3.3₃. What is left out is very often the subject: (I) thank you, (I) beg your pardon, beseech you (Sh, etc), etc, for which I may refer to vol III 11.8$_{61}$ ff. Ib 11.8$_7$ we saw instances of something else left out besides the subject: (I am) Sorry, etc; 11.8$_{72}$ (Do you) See? | (Have you) Seen the Walworth's lately?; 11.8$_{73}$ (When you) Come to think of it, etc.

A few additional quotations: Merriman S 41 [I shall] See you later | Hammett Th 147 [I shall] Be seeing you | Di P 134 [I'm] Blessed if she didn't send 'em all to sleep | Kipling S 154 [I'm a-]'Fraid not | ib 189 [I'll be] 'Shot if I would! | Galsw F 342 [It would] Never do to really let them have such decisions in their hands | Kipling L 155 [Do you] Think so? | id S 119 [Do you re-]'Member that chap?

With the omission out of *God* in *Damn*! (ib 11.8$_{62}$), *Saue thee* (Sh Lr II. 1.1), and *Bless us*! (said the Mayor, Browning 1.408) should be compared the similar dropping at the end of a sentence (below, 3.5$_3$): in both cases the aversion to mentioning the holy name comes into consideration.

3.3$_4$. What is left out may be simply a vb: Doyle S 5.35 [Is] That you, Lestrade? | Meredith R 355 [Is] That all? | Ridge G 286 I'm going home! [Are] You coming, or are you going to stay here? | Hankin 1.54 [Does] Sir John often dine here? | Bennett C 1.342 [Will] That do? | Wells Cl 148 [Are] You coming, Billy? | Galsw P 9.18 [Did] Stephen get my note?

3.3$_5$. Very often *as* is left out before *soon as:* Swift J 491 Soon as he saw me, he left the Duke | Shelley 56 soon as the Woman came into that hall, she shrieked | Di D 679 [vg] Soon as she see him, all her fear returned upon her ... soon as she got to England | Hope C 147 soon as I got a rise | Ridge S 77 he'll have to take me to the theatre, soon as ever he gives up playing this game || Cf also Mannin W 55 likely as not he was only making out he was annoyed, to save his face | Merriman V 26 Likely as not, said Captain Cable | Hergesheimer MB 155 often as not there's shooting.

Note also the omission of *the* before a comparative: [The] More's the pity | Galsw T 166 Sooner the better.

3.3$_6$. The article is dropped (or has coalesced with the following word): Keats 5.178 Fact is, I have had so many kindnesses done me | Lewis MA 213 trouble is I can't be sensational enough | Kipling S 265 'Thing I don't understand | ib 267 'Rest of our chaps ...

3.3$_7$. An initial negative is left out in the order to a helmsman when he is too near the wind: (No) Near! (NED *near* adv. 1 c; *near* the old comparative = PE *nearer;* cf below, 11.2$_7$).

The omission of *no* before *more* seems to be confined to the South-Western counties: Phillpotts M 29 Not much of a scholar. More am I. (Other examples ib 12, 144) | ib 322 you meant that I couldn't expect that man to like me. More I do. Similarly with *either* = 'nor .. either': Quiller-Couch M 111 it so happens that I have no small change about me. Me either!, said Mrs. T. idiomatically.

Middle Part Left Out

3.4. The following small number of examples are chiefly due to rapid and slovenly pronunciation: Bennett C 1.300 Where [have] you been, old gentleman? | Norris P 351 what [are] you doing? | Ridge G 284 How [are] you going to treat me this time? | Cronin C 71 I'm glad to see you. I['ve] been back and forward here this last hour.

Cf the chiefly American: couple [of] minutes | you['d] better do it. This omission of the auxiliary leads to the (Amr) use of *done* = *did, been* = *was, were,* cf vol IV 3.8(4).

End Left Out

3.5$_1$. The final kind of abbreviated sentences, in which the end is left out, is termed aposiopesis, or, more familiarly, stop-short or pull-up sentences. — Cf PhilGr 310(2).

In the following quotations the writer has aptly characterized the state of mind that most often leads to such ellipses:

Thack V 6 "Well, I never" — said she — "what an audacious" — emotion prevented her from completing either sentence | Di Ch 24 "Well, I never!" cried Meg. She had, though — over and over again. For it was Toby's constant topic | Di Do 49 "Good heaven," said Uncle Sol. "It can't be! Well, I —" "No, nor anybody else," said Walter, anticipating the rest. "Nobody would, nobody could, you know" | Swinnerton S 229 "Well, all I can say is — " But Rachel did not say anything | Hankin 2.96 Mrs. E.: I must say! (but words fail her) | Harraden S 14 "Well, I'm blessed!" said the taller of the two, lighting a cigar. "So am I," said the other, lighting his cigar too. "Those are precisely my own feelings," remarked Mrs. R.

After saying "If only something would happen" the speaker stops without making it clear to himself how he would go on — whether "I should be happy," or "it would be better," or "things would be tolerable," or whatever he might think of. But even without any continuation the *if*-clause is taken at more than its face value and becomes, to speaker and hearer alike, a complete expression of a wish:

Harraden S 78 O, if I had only not come to Peterhof | Caine C 153 If she could only get a hearing! | Galsw FM 166 If only Ronny weren't known to be so broke.

3.5₂. But an *if*-clause without a continuation may also be simply a round-about way of stating something: Shaw StJ 103 Why, if it isnt Peter Cauchon! [= it is!] | Norris O 101 Well, if here isn't that man Annixter | Mackenzie PR 256 Well, if that isn't the best thing I've heard since I was home | Lawrence L 211 Well, if that isn't the devil | Galsw Sw 114 If that was pleasure! | id P 2.47 If you can't see that this is a special opportunity.

Or it may contain a request: Galsw FM 131 If you'll

all be handy, in case he wants to put the questions for himself.

Other similar clauses without the finishing apodosis: Di Do 181 "... they're poor, indeed; but if you come to blood, sir!" the Major gave a flourish with his stick and walked out, in despair of being able to say what you came to, if you come to that | Galsw FM 64 If you knew what a Prussian expression you've got! | Rose Macaulay K 50 Mrs. Folyot said that she was terribly sorry, but, of course, if it must be | id T 216 "So long as it makes him happier," said Rome. "Poor darling."

3.5₃. Elliptical *ever* to strengthen a superlative will be mentioned in one of the chapters on Comparison (11.8₇); a parallel is Keats 5.45 I enjoy claret to a degree | Bennett B 51 The symptoms are unusual to a degree.

And after "it's just as well" one often does not add the second member of the comparison: Brontë V 5 Mrs. Bretton did not hear it: which was quite as well | Stevenson JHF 25 it is as well we have met.

Cf also Ward M 118 [lady:] Poor Kitty! she has been in such a state of mind | ib 124 Do you know that you look such a duck this afternoon ... This hat suits you so — you are such a grande dame in it.

Further — as it is difficult in a hurry to hit upon some adequate comparison — *so glad that I cannot express it* frequently results in the inexpressible remaining inexpressed and *so* becomes = 'very much indeed', e. g. in Doyle R 54 I shall so look forward to seeing it.

Cp also Wells Fm 46 I wouldn't go up in one [a balloon] — not for ever so | Galsw WM 180 she had liked the country ever so.

3.5₄. A servant in bringing a message will say: There is no answer [waiting, or wanted] (Di N 39) | It's for

Mrs. Tanqueray, sir; there's no answer (Pinero S 168), — or Bennett A 93 A letter, and there's an answer, and he's waiting.

The stopping short before the mention of God is similar to the omission at the beginning of a sentence mentioned above (3.3₃): Galsworthy M 121 We've walked from Brighton, so 'elp me! | Shaw A 135 So help me, Governor, I never did.

A favourite beginning that is not finished is "Of all the ....," meaning 'this is the worst,' e.g. Galsw Escape 63 Well, of all the impudent villains! | Shaw M 7 I must say that of all the confounded pieces of impertinence — | Hart BT 230 Of all the little idiots! | Swinnerton S 110 Of all the cheek! he ejaculated | Priestley A 229 "Of all the confounded cheek!" Adam began.

3.5₅. The beginning of a familiar phrase suffices to suggest the continuation: I haven't the faintest (or, in coll. speech, *the foggiest*, in slang, *the groggiest*) [notion] | it's no earthly [use, Galsw SS 8 the general opinion that the League of Nations was "no earthly"] | they were head over ears [in love, id MW 116, WM 165] | Stevenson K 4 honour to whom honour [is due] | Do things regardless [of expenses] | That depends [on circumstances] | Well, I'm hanged [if I understand; Hope C 183] | My [gracious!, or God!].

3.5₆. A subject, either a noun or a clause, is often in an exclamation left without any predicate: Mackenzie PR 45 "The trouble you must have taken," Hilda exclaimed | Maugham Pl 3.67 Oh, the humiliation I endured | Galsw Ca 700 The way he sits and smiles! | Congreve 155 That my poor father should be so very silly | Di X 222 Poor girl! That I could ever hope she would be fond of me! That I could ever believe she was! | Maugham Pl 2.234 I wouldn't be a lady's companion, not for anything. What they have to put up with!

3.5₇. The end of an indefinite relative clause is often left out. This is somewhat different from the phenomenon dealt with in vol III 17.9₅₂ (2) with examples like "whatever the consequences to himself" and "however interesting to her the conversation" — clauses parallel to sentences consisting of a preposed predicative and a subject like "Queer cattle — women". In such cases there is no ellipsis.

3.5₈. But an ellipsis must be acknowledged in the following clauses with relative pronouns or adverbs in *-ever* (archaic *-soever* or *-so*):

(1) *who* (not very frequent): Di F 329 the incompetent servant, by whomsoever employed, is always against his employer | Walpole OL 230 Then there was Canon Ryle, smiling and polite to whomsoever | Merriman S 216 I am not likely to discuss it with anyone whosoever.

Thus also *what* as a primary in Stevenson JHF 78 this drug is wanted bitter bad, sir, whatever for.

(2) *what* (rarer *which*) as an adjunct, which thus comes to lose its relative power and mean 'any': Lamb E 1.119 theses to be defended against whatever impugners | Quincey 117 won in whatsoever way, success is success | Ruskin 1.415 in whatever field, it [genius] will always be distinguished by its labour | Poe 663 Beauty of whatever kind, in its supreme development, invariably excites the sensitive soul to tears | Rose Macaulay T 131 Anyhow, from whatever cause, there began at this time a slump in decadence | Bennett A 211 At whatever cost, she was bound to win | Dickinson S 73 to realize, at whatever cost of suffering, great works and great lives | Sh Wiv IV.

2.24 he curses all Eues daughters, of what complexion soeuer | Carlyle H 127 all Protestants, of what rank and function soever | Defoe R 191 no man of what kind soever || Di F 795 For whichsoever reason, or for all, he drooped his devoted head.

(3) adverbs: Mi A 33 in any twenty capacities how good soever | Fielding 3.498 a conqueror ... how ambitious, wanton, or cruel soever | Gissing G 444 It would never have been possible for him to support a wife of however humble origin | Poe 670 in subjects so handled, however skilfully, or with however vivid an array of incident | Carpenter P 59 imprisonments — how-so-oft repeated — are powerless to change the Drink habit | Black Ph 300 Young people must not play pranks with Scripture names, in however innocent a fashion.

In this way *whensoever* comes to mean 'at any time' in Sh Hml V. 2.210 now or whensoeuer — and *however* comes to be used without any feeling of ellipsis in the sense 'nevertheless.'

This ellipsis lies at the bottom of the very frequent use of *whatever* placed after a sb to strengthen an indefinite adjunct, chiefly negative (quotations in NED *whatever* 4 *b* from 1623 on): Defoe R 158 not upon any account whatever | James S 139 you took no notice of it, you know, whatever | under no pretence whàtever | (q NED) All bodies whatever are liable to the state of sonorous vibration || Ruskin Sel 1.408 a man is not educated, in any sense whatsoever, because he can read Latin | Wilde SM 159 Public opinion is of no value whatsoever.

Inarticulate or Semi-Articulate Sentences

3.6₁. In the cases so far considered the intention of the speaker, though not carried out fully, was to form a full sentence according to the usual pattern with a subject and a finite vb. But we now come to utterances of a different type, which, however, should be considered complete sentences. First we should mention such terms of politeness as: Thanks | Thanks very much | Thanks awfully | Ladies first! | After you (please) | Good morning (abbreviated: Morning) | in earlier times Good morrow (abbreviated: Morrow, Farquhar B 323) | Good day | Good afternoon | Good night.

Next, we have answers, which are complete in themselves, but cannot be understood except from the context or whole situation, e.g. Yes | Certainly | By all means | No | Not on any account, etc.

Requests are frequently expressed in inarticulate sentences: Two third Brighton return | Another bottle of the same kind | None of your cheek!

Note especially verbless sentences with the preposition *with:* Away with you! | Sh Alls IV. 3.242 off with his head | H4A II. 2.55 on with your vizards | Meas V. 1.313 to th' racke with him | Shrew Ind I 72 to bed with him. (Cf also Meas V. 121; Wint III. 3.128; Gent IV 4.22) Still in use.

With is here used in nearly the same way as in full sentences like "How is it with your health ? | "Shelley 259 What is it with thee, sister ? Thou art pale.

3.6₂. In a rapid narrative we may have a whole string of inarticulate sentences indicating swift motion: Then rapidly to the door, down the steps, out into the street, and without looking to right or left into the automobile, and in three minutes to Wall Street with utter disregard of police regulations and speed limits | Longfellow, Paul Revere's Ride: A hurry of hoofs in a village street, A shape in the moonlight, a bulk in the dark, And beneath, from the pebbles, in passing, a spark Struck out by a steed flying fearless and fleet.

3.6₃. As it is in these cases, a feeling of terseness and of vigour is also produced by the omission of verbs in a great many proverbial locutions, apophthegms, party devices, or similar sayings: Like master, like man | Shaw C 175 Every man to his taste | No cure, no pay (in Kingsley H 318 No play, no pay) | Di N 331 Wine in, truth out | One man, one vote | Once taken, never shaken | Once bitten twice shy | Quincey 30 Once a clergyman, and always a clergyman | Norris P 255 Once a speculator, always a speculator | Least said, soonest mended (Di D 476, Ridge S 20, etc) | Dickinson S 95 As with the land, so with its products | So far, so good (common) | First come, first served.

3.6₄. We have verbless word-groups serving as a kind of temporal or conditional clause followed by a main sentence introduced by *and:* Brontë P 181 one minute more and we should not have had one dry thread on us | Lawrence, Publ. Mod. L. Ass. 1909 258 A touch, and the whole may fall like a house of cards | Kingsley H xi A few more tumultuous years, and the Franks would find themselves lords of the Lower Rhineland | Stevenson MB 194 A little while ago and Villon was almost totally forgotten | Holmes A 233 he drew a long breath with such a tremor in it that a little more and it would have been a sob | Stevenson MB 326 Once found out, however, and he seems to himself to have lost all claim to decent usage.

3.6₅. In these and similar instances I have no hesitation in employing the word 'sentence'. But it is much more difficult to apply that grammatical term to some instances of what H. Straumann, *Newspaper Headlines* (London 1935), terms 'block-language':

(1) Signboards: "J. C. Mason, Bookseller;"

(2) Titles of books, articles, etc: Men and Women |

Life and Letters of Charles Lamb | Chapter II. Arrival in London | Recent Medical Discoveries;

(3) Newspaper headlines: Death of the King | Terrible Explosion, Fifty Dead;

(4) Entries in diary: Tuesday. Rain and fog. Chess with uncle Tom, walk with the girls.

Straumann's book contains many clever remarks on block-language and language in general, but his careful analysis of headlines from purely formal points of view without regard to ordinary grammatical categories is not really of the slightest assistance in understanding either ordinary sentences or his special subject. We understand a headline more or less through our transposing it into ordinary language with its usual grammar. Straumann himself seems to admit this when on p. 79 he applies the terms nexus and junction to headlines like "Steamer sunk" (nexus) and "Sunk Steamer" (junction) or "Captain Russell" (junction) and "Russell Captain" (nexus). Headlinese combinations are not in themselves sentences and often cannot be directly supplemented so as to form articulate sentences: they move, as it were, on the fringe of ordinary grammar.

Chapter IV

Person

4.1. When in grammar we speak of the three persons, we mean the distinction between:

(1) the speaker: the first person,

(2) the person (or persons) spoken to: the second person, and

(3) what is neither speaker nor spoken to: the third person.

It is easy to see that this grammatical terminology has nothing to do with the ordinary use of the word *person:* "the horse runs" and "the sun shines" are in the third person, and if in a fable we make the horse say "I run" or the sun say "I shine," both sentences are in the first person.

The distinction applies primarily to the "personal pronouns": first person *I*, second person *you* ((and the old *thou*); to the third person belong not only the personal pronouns *he, she, it*, but everything else: *the man (goes), who (goes), everybody (goes)*, etc.

First Person

4.2₁. The form *I* goes back to OE *ic*, ME often *ich*. The consonant has generally disappeared, but survives in the dialect of one part of Somersetshire in the form [itʃ, ʌtʃ], also [tʃ] before *am*. In literature this is represented in Gammer Gurton's Needle: *cham, chyll* 'I will', *chwold* 'I would', similarly in Redford. Edgar (disguised) in Sh Lr IV. 6.239 speaks the Somerset dialect: Chill not let go, zir.

The pl is *we, us*.

On *I* for *me* and inversely, see Ch VI on Case in Pronouns.

Us loses its vowel in *let's* (cf vol I 9.94, and vol V 24.1₄ on the difference between *let us* and *let's*), formerly also in other cases: Sh Mcb I. 3.125 betray's.

4.2₂. Various substitutes may be used for the pronoun of the first person sg, thus *number one* (e.g. Lytton K 354, Galsw Ca 232); further some expressions taken from the usual way of signing letters: *your humble servant* (obs.) and *yours truly::* Fielding T 3.83 this did him some disservice with your humble servant | Thack S 20 all the inhabitants of the hotel, amongst others your humble servant, (ib 150, Kaye-Smith F 217) | Thack P 1.46 Give the young one a glass, and score it up for yours truly | id N 147 why haven't you picked out some nice girl for yours truly? — While these are familiar, the following are decidedly vg: *this child* as in Ridge G 103 it may answer with some; but not with this child (also Maugham Alt 254); frequent in U.S., especially among negroes, and sometimes "improved" into *this baby* (O'Neill Emp. Jones 16 I ain't 'lowin' nary body to touch dis baby | ib 21), *this chicken* (ib 23 Takes more'n dat to scare dis chicken), or *this horse*. Other Amr. substitutes are *the old boy* (or *man*), or *your uncle* | Ade A 89 what she sees in me to get stuck on [= in love with] is what keeps *your Willie boy* guessing. Cf Mackenzie C 164 and 273 *this little girl* | Jerome NN 98 [a baby!] not *this baby*.

Occasionally a speaker uses his own name instead of the pronoun "I"; thus in Sh Cæsar and Othello often, by commentators taken as a sign of their pride (?); e.g. Cæs 1.2.17 Speake, Cæsar is turn'd to hear.

Many writers in their articles and books avoid the use of the pronoun *I* and replace it by *the author* or *the (present) writer*, whenever it is not possible to use some passive or impersonal construction.

4.2₃. As already remarked in vol II 4.52, *we* is not a normal pl (= several *I*'s, like *horses*, etc), but a pl of approximation = 'the speaker + some one else or some others'. It is therefore often necessary to specify who else is included: we gentlemen, we Yorkshiremen, we Europeans, etc.

Colloquially, *us* may be used for *me:* Mackenzie C 103 Give us a cigarette, Val. — Further in Scottish and Irish; see vol II 4.13.

Present company may be used as a substitute for *we*,

us: Caine C 186 you fancied yourself above present company.

A kind of fluctuation between two persons is sometimes found. *Some of us* and *most of us* are, strictly speaking, in the third person; therefore we should say: Most of us lost their heads.

But it is, at any rate, excusable, if the speaker includes himself, to say: Most of us lost our heads.

Similarly with *most of you*.

Compare Thack N 297 Clive and I went each to our habitation | Masterman WL 32 We will each carry on with our own line of research | ib 140 we will each keep his own counsel | Dickinson in Forster 50 then [we] went out into the night, each on our different paths.

4.2₄. A curious confusion of the two first persons is sometimes found when the speaker means "If I were you": Maugham Alt 750 I wouldn't tell him more about yourself than you find absolutely necessary | Sayers Unn. D 24 In any case, I said, I shouldn't distress yourself too much | Phillpotts GR 75 If you can even lunch with your party I should | Sayers DC 57 I should not let the matter prey on your mind in the least.

Cf vol IV 19.5(6) I would [if I were you] and 20.3(7) I should.

4.2₅. The possessive pronoun corresponding to *I* is *my, mine;* on the distinction see vol II 16.2.

Mine is always pronounced [main], but *my* alongside of the pronunciation [mai] has an unstressed form [mi], shortened from the ME form [mi·]. [mi] may still be heard, not only in vulgar speech, but on the stage, and in courts of law when addressing My Lord. Cf vol I 4.431.

Second Person

4.3₁. Now only one form *you* without distinction of number or case. Formerly four forms:

Sg. nom.	thou
Sg. oblique	thee
Pl. nom.	ye
Pl. oblique	you.

The way in which the simplification has been brought about is described in detail in Chapters 6—7 on Case in Pronouns.

On various ways of distinguishing a pl from the sg of the 2nd person see vol II 2.84, 2.87 (you people, etc.), 2.88 (you together, you all).

4.3₂. For the second person, too, we have some substitutes. First we may mention the paternal *we*, frequent from doctors and teachers and probably meant originally to denote kindness through identifying the interests of speaker and hearer; this seems to be found in many countries: Thack P 3.306 What a pretty gal we've grown | ib 354 Are we going to change our condition and give up our chambers? | Mrs. Browning A 177 we are sad to-night | Di T 2.18 (husband to wife) | Stevenson M 225 Aha! said the doctor. So we rise early in the morning, do we? | Wilde Imp 22 [clergyman to young girl] And how are we this morning? (thus Hankin 1.42 doctor to patient) | Meredith H 179 Are we enamoured of a beautiful maiden?

There are a few respectful substitutes for the simple *you*, consisting of *your* and a substantive (the verb to be put in the third person): *Your Majesty, Your Royal Highness, Your Lordship, Your Excellency, Your Grace* (to Dukes, Duchesses, and Archbishops), *your worship* (to judges).

My darling and *my own girl* may occasionally be used as fondling substitutes for the pronoun; thus Candida speaks to her husband, in Shaw 2.121 *My boy* is not looking well. Has *he* been overworking?

There is a fondling way of using *it* instead of *you* in speaking to children, which is also sometimes used from husband to wife, etc. This usage originated in the habit of half mentioning, half addressing an infant that is too small to understand what is being said to it. Sh John II. 1.160 goe to yt ['its'] grandame, childe ... and it grandame will Guie yt a plum | Mcb III. 4.66 [Lady M. to her husband] shame it selfe. Why do you make such faces? | Goldsm 668 it won't leave us, cousin Tony, will it? | Thack P 3.401 Foolish boy! she said, it shall be loved as it deserves | id N 348 | Di N 195 and 244 (Mr. Mantalini to his wife) | Caine C 151 And what's its nyme, my dear? | Shaw 2.126 [Candida petting Marchbanks ironically] Poor boy! have I been cruel? Did I make it slice nasty little red onions? | Pennell L 101 Dear old Sweetheart, keep itself well.

4.3₃. A pronoun of the second person is very often placed both before and after a term of abuse: Redford W 357 thow calat, thow | Sh Ado V. 1. 53 thou doest wrong me, thou dissembler, thou || Redford W 342 you quene, you | Sh Mids III. 2.288 Fie, fie; you counterfeit, you puppet, you | Defoe R 9 you fool you | Thack V 303 you were ready to murder your brother, you wicked Cain you | Shaw 1.214 Do you think I'll put up with this from you, you young devil, you? (also ib 2.99) | Ridge G 34 Oh, you Christy Minstrel, you!

4.3₄. Any name may be made into the second person, as in: Come here, John! | Beg your pardon, Miss Langton | What do you think, Dr Cassell? | Anything else, sir?

Here we say that *John, Miss Langton, Dr Cassell,* and *sir* are vocatives, but in English the vocative is not, as in some languages, a separate case.

Any imperative is virtually in the second person, even if seemingly addressed to a "third person". Quotations for this (Somebody call my wife | Don't congratulate me, anybody! | Search him, some of you, etc) see vol V 24.1$_6$.

4.3$_5$. The possesive pronouns of the second person are the obs. or archaic *thy, thine* and the living *your, yours*. On the difference between primary and secondary see vol II 16.231 f., 16.27 ff.

On the pronounciation of *your, yours* [juə, juəz; jɔə, jɔ·əz] see vol I 4.434.

With weak stress *your* may become [jə].

Instead of *yours* the negro and the "poor white" in the South of the U.S. alike are much more apt to say *your-all's* or *yourn*, see V. Starnes in Century Mag. May 1895 p. 155 and Mencken AL⁴ 449 with references.

Third Person

4.4$_1$. In the third person we have the forms

Sg. nom.	he	she	it
Sg. oblique	him	her	
Pl. nom.		they	
Pl. oblique		them.	

For the explanation of *she* instead of OE *heo* see Lindkvist in Anglia 45 p. 1 ff.

On the difference between *he, him — she, her — it* see ch V on Sex.

On the case-distinction see ch VI on Case in Pronouns. See below, 6.1$_3$, on dialectal *un* from OE acc. *hine*.

Him and *her* often lose [h] in weak position: *for him* [fɔr im], *to her* [tu ə], etc. *It* is now always without the *h* it had in OE *hit*. In a weak position *it* may lose its vowel: *'tis, 'twas, 'twill;* but instead of *'tis* it is now usual to say *it's*.

Instead of *them* there is a coll. form, generally considered sub-standard, *hem, 'em*, which is not historically to be considered = *them* with [ð] dropped, but is a continuation of OE and ME *hem*, of the same stem as *he*, etc. This is written in literature *'hem* (BJo), or *'em*, sometimes *'um* (e.g. Goldsm 658). Swift ridicules the use of *'um* for *them* in the *Tatler* no. 230.

4.4₂. The possessive pronouns of the third person are *his, her, hers, its; their, theirs*.

On the difference between primary *hers, theirs*, and secondary *her, their* see vol II 16.27 ff.

The most important function of the pronouns of the third person is to denote the person or thing indicated by the situation or context, thus very often as an 'anaphoric' pronoun, referring back to what has just been mentioned: When Ann saw Brown, she [= Ann] shook him [= Brown] by the hand.

The pronoun is often superfluously added after the noun, e. g. in ballad style and especially in illiterate speech: Brown, he knows (Sh Lr II 1.124 Our father he hath writ | R3 III 2.115 Your friends at Pomfret, they doe need the priest | Err V. 229 God he knows; the latest example in NED 1839 the skipper he stood beside the helm). Also before the noun: He is very clever, that boy of yours | Kaye-Smith T 222 She was a good girl, Fanny | Kingsley H 188 They were blissful months those to poor Hypatia.

4.4₃. *He* or *she* may be made definite by a following indication, thus a relative clause: Ann told it to him who sat next to her, or a prepositional phrase: Which of the ladies is your sister? She in the red dress | Spielmann, Studies in the First Folio 26 a portrait of Shakespeare when a much younger man than him of the bust. (Is NED correct when calling this archaic?).

He, she, they as antecedents of a relative clause may either be non-generic as in the sentence just above, or generic = 'any one'. Both cases were dealt with rather fully in vol III 5.1_1 ff. and III 5.1_6. Examples were also given there in which the pronoun was separated from the relative clause. As there said, many of such combinations are now literary rather than coll.; *they that* and *they who* are now supplanted by *those that* and *those who*.

A few additional examples may find their place here: Sh As II. 7.98 He dies that touches any of this fruite | AV Rom. 13.8 hee that loueth another hath fulfilled the Law | He who can't keep a penny Will never have many | Sh Ro II. 3.94 they stumble that run fast.

4.4₄. Sometimes it may be doubtful to which of several persons mentioned a *he, she,* or *they* refers. Stress is a convenient means to dispel doubt in that respect (in print often denoted by italics): Di OT 47 Oliver was not altogether as comfortable as the hungry pig was, when he was shut up ... in the grain department | Huxley L 1.225 Huxley's wife was at Folkestone for three months. ... Huxley ran down every week; his brother George and his wife also were frequent visitors | Mackenzie SA 229 Mary's hands ... were now the hands of her grandmother when *she* was fifty, fifty years ago | Maugham Alt 476 By some chance he had never met Hutchinson, though of course he knew all about him just as Hutchinson knew all about *him* | Walpole C 66 The Archdeacon was determined to fight them ... even as the Black Bishop had fought *his* enemies | Lawrence L 195 Hannele waited with her hands in her lap, and Mrs Hepburn mused, with her hands in *her* lap | Lamb E 1.181 Children love to listen to stories about their elders, when *they* were children | Walpole SC 99 and shadows moved behind the shadows, and yet more shadows behind *them*.

In Somerset a distinction is made between *Bill cut's vinger* and *Bill cut ees vinger*, the former meaning, 'Bill's own finger', the latter, 'the other man's' (Elworthy Wordbook XVII).

In formal and legal style ambiguity is often avoided by the use of *the former* and *the latter* instead of pronouns.

In Mi PL 4.600 a stressed *they* is opposed to *these*, meaning 'the former' and 'the latter' respectively: beast and bird, They to thir grassie couch, these to their nests.

4.4₅. Personal pronouns as primaries may take an adjective as a secondary: Poor little I (or me) | Rehearsal 83 that you will here with poor us still remain | Ridge G 103 Makes me shriek to see little you standing there.

Indirect Speech

4.4₆. In indirect (reported) speech a shifting of the persons is in many cases natural, a direct first person being turned according to circumstances into an indirect second person or an indirect third person, etc. The various possibilities may be thus tabulated: the direct statement (A speaking to B): "I am glad of your agreement with him" (i.e. C) may become:

(1, A speaking with C): I said I was glad of his agreement with you.

(2, A speaking with D): I said I was glad of his agreement with him.

(3, B speaking with A): You said you were glad of my agreement with him.

(4, B speaking with C): He said he was glad of my agreement with you.

(5, B speaking with D): He said he was glad of my agreement with him.

(6, C speaking with A): You said you were glad of his agreement with me.

(7, C speaking with B): He said he was glad of your agreement with me.

(8, C speaking with D): He said he was glad of his agreement with me.

(9, D speaking with E): He said he was glad of his agreement with him.

It should be remarked, however, that in the sentences 2, 5, 8, and 9, clearness would certainly be gained by the use of the name instead of one or more of the ambiguous *he*'s.

It is a simple consequence of the nature of the pl *we*, that it frequently remains unshifted, as in: "He said that he still believed in *our* glorious future as a nation."

Ambiguity may sometimes be caused by the use of the third person both for real third person (Lat. *eum, ejus*, etc) and for a shifted first person (Lat. *se, suus,* etc.). Thus in North's Plutarch 1004 "Antonius sent againe to chalenge Cæsar, to fight with him hand to hand. Cæsar aunswered him, that *he* had many other wayes to dye then so." He means Antonius, but Shakespeare took it as a shifted first person and renders it (Ant. IV. 1.4) "let the old Russian [read: ruffian] know, *I* haue many other wayes to dye."

As Brinton remarks (*Essays of an Americanist.* Philadelphia 1890, p. 324) "John told Robert's son that he must help him" may have any of six different meanings, which in some Amerindian languages are expressed by distinct pronouns.

Sometimes extra stress may show that a shifted first person is meant, as in GE M 1.244 Tom thought this sister of Tulliver's seemed a nice little thing, quite unlike her brother; he wished *he* had a little sister.

In some cases ambiguity is obviated by adding *the latter:* Thack N 401 When Miss O. quitted Madame d'Ivry's family, she spoke with great freedom regarding the behaviour of that duchess, and recounted horrors which *she, the latter*, had committed.

Some curious instances of shifting are found in these quotations: Sh Merch II. 8.22 (Shylock cries "My daughter! O my ducats ...) Why all the boyes in Venice follow him, Crying his stones, his daughter, and his ducats | Defoe G 124 will you give me leav to make an objeccion or two? The gentleman told him, with all his heart | Di D 334 As to a fish-kettle, Mrs C says, Well! would I only come and look at the range?

The shifting may even be found in imperatives and wishes expressed in the subjunctive: Carlyle FR 136 they [the Clergy] pass silently, and none cries, God bless them | Ridge G 147 what she wanted to say was, that for cleanliness and appearance and comfort, give her a horsehair sofa with a black cushion | Burns 120 An' she cry'd L—d preserve her! | Di Do 160 the dream she had, was over now, God help her! | Ward Chaucer 129 a question was how to take this money to the house. It must be done by night; so let them draw lots, and let him on whom the lot fell run to the town | Shaw P 273 Heaven forgive me for judging him ... You said just now, Heaven forgive you for judging him.

Person in Verbs

4.5₁. The distinction of the three persons applies not only to pronouns but to verbs as well. But in English this has in course of time been greatly restricted: it is found only in the present tense, and there only in regular verbs (I, you, we, they *go;* he *goes*) and *be* (I *am*, he *is;* we, you, they *are*). On *-s* in *dares* and *needs* see vol V 12.2—3. On *-th* and *-s* see vol VI ch III. In the past tense, and in the originally perfecto-present verbs, the distinction has been given up (*saw, can, may*, etc, in all persons). The old forms corresponding to *thou* have been discarded from natural speech together with that pronoun (thou *art, wert, wast, canst, mayst, goest,* etc; see vol VI ch II). The present subjunctive is always equal to the base and shows no distinction according to person; see below, 18.2$_3$ f.

On the other hand, standard English has developed a distinction in the use of the auxiliaries *will* and *shall* according to the persons, see vol IV chs XV-XXI.

The obliteration of the old personal distinction in so many verbal forms is a signal case of progress in language, as evidenced by the difficulties such distinctions produce in those cases in which they are still found. There is no difficulty in

Neither my brother nor I *saw* her, or

Neither my brother nor I *can* have done it.

But in the present tense things are not so easy. Instead of "either you or I *are* wrong," which is felt to be incorrect, or "either you or I *am* wrong," which is equally objectionable, some people will prefer the stiff and awkward "either you are wrong, or I," where one feels tempted to add "am [wrong]," which makes it still more clumsy; Dean Alford *(The Queen's English*, 8th ed. 155) proposed to say "either you or I is wrong," though he admits that" the sound is harsh, and usages would be violated." The following passages show how English writers have cut the Gordian knot in different ways:

4.5₂. (1) the verb is put in the pl (because *neither A nor B is = A and B are not):* Hunt A 295 Neither he nor I were very strong | Brontë P 181 Neither she nor I were wet | Tennyson 369 For whatsoever knight against us came Or I or he have easily overthrown | Stevenson T 168 neither you nor I are much account at the shooting | id MB xiv I question whether either I or the writer in the Review have ever encountered a good one | Harraden S 37 to imagine that you or I are going to do any good | Garnett Go 28 neither he nor I are superior | Bennett P 299 doubt as to whether you or I are the strongest | NJacob G 82 Only to-day have I understood that neither you nor I are left alone | Wells PF 106 neither she nor I were behaving as though we thought so | Father Ronald Knox in BDS 90 they were no more mystics than you or I are || Mason House Arrow 128 Have either of you two ladies received an anonymous letter? | Rhode Murder Praed 165 Have either of you any knowledge ... Have either of you any suspicions.

4.5₃. (2) the verb is attracted to the nearest subject: Greene J4 415 this king and I am one | Swift P 107 I wonder why such a handsome, strait, young gentleman as you, do not get some rich widow | Galsw D 30 Am I and all women really what they think us? | Tennyson 446 Great brother, thou nor I have made the world | Gissing G 337 Neither you nor Amy is the kind of person

to take a pleasure in disagreement | id B 413 Neither
you nor anyone else has authority over me | London A
180 all I or any other man knows | Maxwell HR 127
Neither of you are weighing your words.

4.5₄. (3) the verb is in the third person sg: Sh LL
V. 2.346 Nor God, nor I, delights in periur'd men | Scott
Iv 178 either the Prior or thou has made some alterations | Walpole Golden Scarecr. 25 I'm afraid neither you
nor I is the ideal man | Lewis EG 291 of course neither
you nor I is necessary to the progress of that great
Methodist Church | id MA 37 Either he or me has got
to get out | Shaw 1.55 [vg] You and me is too much
of a pair. — Cf Swinburne Itylus (116) could I forget
or thou remember, Couldst thou remember or I forget.

4.5₅. Similar difficulties often appear in relative clauses; the Prayer Book reads "Thou art the God that
doeth wonders," where the AV has "Thou art the God
that doest wonders" (Ps. 77.14). Cf also: Sh Shrew IV.
2.18 I am not Licio, But one that scorne to liue in this
disguise | Wiv II. 2.166 I am a gentleman that haue
spent much | John IV. 2.47 Then I, as one that am the
tongue of these | cf also Mids II. 1.34, R3 IV. 4.268,
Ado V. 2. 89 | BJo 3.117 Are you not he, that filthy
wretch, that here, in hope of prey, have ... snuffed
about .... Are you not he that have to-day .... professed | AV Judges 13.11 Art thou the man that spakest
unto the woman? | Spectator 449 I am one who live in
a continual apprehension | Cowper L 2.13 Thou only
critic of my verse that is to be found in all the earth,
whom I love | Shelley P 75 the presumption that I,
the person who now write and think, am that one mind.

4.5₆. There is a decided tendency to use the form of
the third person after *it is* (*was*) instead of the orthodox
"it is I (me) who (that) am the guilty" and "it is you

who (that) are the guilty" and even "it is not I who am guilty": Sh As III. 5.55 'Tis not her glasse, but you that flatters her | Beaconsfield L 438 It is you, my dear Lothair, that is surprising, not the world | Ward G 1.290 It's you that's being teaching Lucy these beautiful sentiments | Zangwill G 355 I'm very sorry it's me that affords you amusement | Stevenson A 86 it is yourself that is hunted down | id K 194 you that's a man of so much penetration | Barrie Adm. Crichton 77 it wasn't you who was firm | Cather P 238 I'm glad it's you that's doing this to me, Tom; not me that's doing it to you | Cronin H 633 It's not you that is to blame.

Cp "It isn't you that is wrong, but John," in which the third person in the verb may be justified by the fact that the meaning is "the person that is wrong, is John, not you."

4.5₇. Here I may mention the very frequent occurrence of a vb in the sg after *one of* (pl) + relative: Sh Alls IV. 3.323 | Boswell 2.94 Dr. Johnson exclaimed, "One of the most dreadful things that has happened in my time | Fielding 4.124 one of those who was vain enough of my own charms | Maugham Pl 4.62 I am one of the few men I know who is able to profit by experience | Priestley AP 286 one of the two or three things written during these last ten years or so that is going to live. — Frequent in newspapers.

4.5₈. Attraction is also found in Marlowe F 1380 And none but thou shalt be my paramour | Sh H4B IV. 2.121 Heauen, and not wee, haue safely fought to day (Q: God, and not wee, hath ...) | Meredith H 168 you none of you know how to meet a woman's smile. Curle L 94 Who but I am able to manage the house?

Who is = 'who is meant by' in the following sentences: Bennett P 311 We had a breakdown ... Who's we? | Maugham Pl 3.154 We were under the impression that you had a case this morning. — Who is we? | id P 64 We should go up the Western River and then by chair. — Who is we? — You and I.

The vb after such honorific substitutes for the second person as *Your Majesty* is normally in the third person sg; an exception is Sh R2 II. 2.20 so your sweet maiestie Looking away vpon your Lords departure, Finde shapes of greefe.

Cf below, 4.8$_1$, on *myself*, etc.

They + Numeral

4.5₉. In connexion with a numeral, *they* was formerly very frequent and is still not at all rare: Malory 50 they two ... they sixe | Sh Err I. 1.111 And in our sight they three were taken vp | AV Mark 10.8 and they twaine shal be one flesh.

They two, e.g. Franklin 46, Wordsw 135, Lamb R 13, Tennyson 114, Di Do 143, id N 759, Shaw D 206, Hope R 59, Allen W 87, Norris, Hawthorne S 69, Hewlett Q 24, ib 446.

Even before a sb: Malory 56 they two knyghtes.

In the oblique case, *them* + numeral is found, e.g. in Caxton R 83 the fayrest of them thre | Malory 50 eche of them V | More U 181 of them III | Sh H5 III. 2.30 I am boy to them all three, but all they three ... could not be man to me | BJo 3.247 out of them two.

But this is now generally avoided, because *them* is felt to be like the vg use of *them* as an adjunct (them boys); *them two* in Peggotty's mouth Di DC 123 is meant as vg; still we find Shaw J 225 I want to see them two meet.

Nowadays *these two* and *those two* are preferred. But the simple definite article before the numeral is perhaps just as frequent, thus in a subject: Di T 2.289 The two stand in the fast-thinning throng; also id N 206, Thack N 25, ib 624, ib 810, Tennyson 311, Ward M 355, Shaw 1.186, ib 152, Ridge L 184, Kipling L 38, id J 42, Hardy L 185, Maugham PV 208 the two of them.

And outside the subject: Austen M 150 in each of the three | Hawthorne S 18 the graver man of the two | Kingsley H 9 he left the two together | Shaw P 126 This movement brings the three in a little group to the place.

Them as an Adjunct

See NED *them* 5 (from 1596 and later), examples in vol II 16.13 from Bunyan, Di, Thack, Hardy, Shaw. It is used in vg speech as subject as well as in other positions.

It

4.6₁. OE *hit* lost its *h* in ME on account of the habitual stresslessness, cf vol I 2.942. The vowel, too, was often lost: *'tis, 'twas, 'twill*, etc, though in ordinary PE *it's* has supplanted *'tis*, probably on account of the frequency of *that's, what's* with loss of *i* in *is;* cf also *I'm, you're*, etc. After prepositions in vg speech *on't, o't* (= of it).

We have to distinguish between three functions of *it:*

(A) Anaphoric *it* — referring to something previously named:

(B) Preparatory *it* — referring to something that follows;

(C) In cleft sentences: *it is* ... ;

(D) Unspecified *it* — without any reference.

A. Anaphoric *it*

4.6₂. *It* refers back to anything previously mentioned that is not spoken of as *he* or *she* (see ch V on Sex: an infant, an animal, or a thing): Have you seen my knife? Yes, it is on that table. *It* may even refer to *nothing:* Hope R 235 well, nothing seems to be happening, does it? (also elsewhere).

This *it* has a pl identical in form with the pl of *he* and *she: they, them.*

It is used as subject, as object, as indirect object (examples vol III 14.5₂) and after a preposition.

Though *it* is a primary, it cannot take an adjunct; parallel to *all that*, we say *it* (..) *all* with *all* in apposition: Chesterton F 289 After it all, I am still glad that you are brave | The loveliness of it all | It is all very well.

We may find *it that* or *it which* with a relative clause: BJo has 1.30 it will never out o' the flesh that's bred i' the bone — now: What is bred ...

An ambiguity (not very serious) may sometimes arise when there are two antecedents to which *it* may refer: If the baby does not thrive on raw milk, boil it.

In rare cases *it* refers to a verbal action, chiefly after *do* (where *so* is generally used); in the Swift quotation we should now say *to* as representing an infinitive (cf vol V 20.5₇, on obs. *to it* ib 20.5₉). Examples: Bennett B 151 Supposing that anything could happen to me — which it can't | Swift J 4 I have not yet seen her, nor intend it | Austen S 315 she has forgiven me before she ought to have done it.

Cf also: you may go to London if you find it necessary.

In popular speech that word which *it* refers to is very often postponed till the end of the sentence: It runs very well, that horse of yours (Wright EDGr).

On the omission of *it* = what you said, etc, in *I know*, etc, see vol III 16.1₅. A few similar examples: Sh Hml III. 4.201 Alacke, I had forgot | Di P 243 I should never guess, if I were to try all night | Collins W 214 Time will show | Doyle S 1.45 And how did you find out?

B. Preparatory *it*

(Also termed anticipatory or representative *it*).

4.6₃. *It* stands as a preliminary representative of a longish group of words which follows later because its placement here would make the sentence-structure cumbersome or 'top-heavy'. It is often what I have called a "dummy subject". It heralds, as Fowler says MEU 301, a deferred subject — but may also herald a deferred object.

Preparatory *it* has already been dealt with in previous volumes in connexion with the treatment of its various functions. I give here a reference to these passages with one example each, often abbreviated, just to show the character of the phenomenon. In some cases I add a few supplementary quotations and remarks.

4.6₄. References to vol. III.

2.1₃. *It* stands for a content-clause: It seems certain that he is dead.

As subject of a nexus-object: We thought it probable that the accusation would be refuted.

As object: She would have it that all men hailed him.

As there are comparatively few vbs that require *it* before a content clause as object, some supplementary quotations will not be amiss here: Swift 3.63 the Lilliputians will needs have it, that men and women are joined together like other animals | Kennedy CN 41 report had it that she was of very good family | Sh Ado IV. 1.206 And publish it, that she is dead indeed |

4.6s.] B. Preparatory *it*. 145

Mannin W 85 he liked it that she had a good firm grip | Benson DB 243 I always rub it in that cricket doesn't matter.

2.3_6. The same without *that:* I take it he should be equal to the task | It occurred to me there was no time to lose.

2.2_7. *It* after a preposition: rely on it that I shall give you a full account.

2.4_3. Indirect question: It mattered little who filled the town.

3.7_6. Relative clauses: Was it true what Mabel had said?

4.6₅. References to vol. V.

4.3_1. In a nexus-object: I make it a rule never to look into a newspaper (4.3_4 without *it:* he thought fit to escape. Here might be added: AV Esth 3.6 hee thought scorne to lay hands on Mordecai | Swift 3.176 the King thought proper to pass a few days at a palace | Goldsm V 1.35 I always thought fit to keep up some mechanical forms of good breeding | Trollope B 356 she now thought well to show her husband that ... | Wells Fm 4 one creditor saw fit to be malignant).

9.8_5f. *It* precedes a gerund with its subject: It is no use her listening at keyholes | it seems so funny any one being frightened of me | it's no use him pretending he doesn't.

Cf 11.1_6. It's been very pleasant seeing you again.

11.1_3. *It* represents an infinitive: It is a great pleasure to see you (cf 11.2_6 Would it be asking too much of you to register the parcel?).

19.1_1. Infinitive with its subject: It is rather funny, you to be talking of power.

19.1_4f. Infinitive with its subject after *for:* It is good for a man not to touch a woman.

19.2₇. How painful it was to Marion for these people to witness it.

Note the idiomatic expression in Defoe G 42 it was as much as both the clergymen could do to keep them from quarrelling | Hope R 38 it was as much as I could do to hold the pen | Stevenson M 33 It was all that I could do to catch a trail of the sea-tangle.

4.6₆. *It* represents an inf as object: Stevenson A 54 we have it in our power to do great harm or great good | Williamson Wedding Day 166 they owed it to themselves and to him to make good marriages | Bennett LR 146 you wouldn't think she had it in her to fight.

In *find it in one's heart*, *it* was formerly absent, but it is found in recent usage: More U 79 if you ... can find in youre harte to followe some prynces courte | Sh As II. 4.4 I could finde in my heart to disgrace my mans apparell | Defoe R 283 I could not find in my heart to take him off | Bosw 2.125 He cannot find in his heart to pour out a bottle of wine | Lamb R 10 I can't find in my heart to forbid him | Di P 532 said he could never find it in his heart to stand in the way of young people's happiness | Wells Cl 450 I did not find it in my heart to do so || Collins (q Ellinger) The general has taken it into his heart to explain ...

In vol V ch XIV it is stated that in English an inf can only in certain definite cases be governed by a preposition. It should be added that a preparatory *it* often serves as a remedy: Bunyan G 123 I looked upon it as my duty to do both | I look upon it as an advantage to be able to go third class.

Only rarely do we find the representative *it* placed immediately after the inf it represents, as in Sh Ven 168 Thou wast begot, to get it is thy duty; cp. such popular expressions as "John Farnham he says," etc.

4.6₇. What we have thus seen denoted by a preparatory *it* was a clause, an inf, or an ing. Outside of these cases any group of words may be represented, chiefly, however, in such a way that the group is the equivalent of a clause, which, in fact, may have been present in the mind of the speaker: Wells Br 219 It was perfectly horrible the way that people were being kept in the dark [= how people were ...] | Collingwood R 272 It was not strictly academic, the way he used to come in | Galsw SS 49 it was uncanny the way she had left her image on his senses | Bennett P 29 It's fantastic the number of cars there are in use in America [= how many ...] | Trollope W 198 It is incredible the number of evil practices he has put down | Hawthorne S 104 It was wonderful, the vast variety of forms into which she threw her intellect | Bennett RS 47 Yes, but you see it never strikes them the inconvenience they're causing [= what inconvenience ...] | Di F 192 it's no good this sort of game | Doyle S 5.105 It's getting on my nerves, this business | Hawthorne S 157 It is inconceivable, the agony with which this public veneration tortured him! | Locke W 343 For it matters not so much the life one leads as the knowledge of the perfect way to live it.

In this way *it* may even stand for a pl noun: Wells T 56 It's extraordinary the different ways different people have of showing respect | Phillpotts M 13 Samuel tells me 'tis a pity the friends he makes | Galsw EC 444 It's extraordinary the things one can do without | Fielding 4.370 It is incredible the pains I have taken [pains sg.?].

C. Cleft Sentences

4.6₈. A cleaving of a sentence by means of *it is* (often followed by a relative pronoun or connective) serves to single out one particular element of the sentence and very often, by directing attention to it and bringing it, as it were, into focus, to mark a contrast. In AnalSynt Ch 25.4 I give a detailed criticism, which I shall not repeat here, of the view previously expressed by myself (vol III 4.6) and others — the transposition theory. The result I arrive at is that *it is* and the following connective are considered as a special kind of extraposition, symbolized by brackets [ ].

Thus I analyze

It is the wife that decides [sv] S [3^c] V

It is the wife who decides [sv] S [S^c] V

It was John we saw [sv] O S V

Who is it that cries S? [vs 3^c] V

What is it you're talking of O? [vs] S W.

Two sentences, identical in writing, but differing in meaning and intonation:

It is the country that suits her best, are

(a) S V P(12(S^c V O 3) if it means that the country previously mentioned (*it* anaphoric) suits her better than any other, — and

(b) [sv] S [3^c] V O 3 = country life suits her better than town life.

It is here he must come [sv] 3 S V

It was yesterday that he died [sv] 3 [3^c] S V

When was it that he died 3? [vs 3^c] S V.

Other examples in AnalSynt and in vol III 4.6.

The questions: *Who was it that found the key?* and *Where was it (that) they met?* ask for more precise information than the simple *Who found the key?* and *Where did they meet?* — *What is it you are doing?* presupposes a knowledge in the speaker of the second person doing something, while *What are you doing?* does not imply such a knowledge.

The Irish make an excessive use of cleft sentences: Is it reading your are? | it is angry that he was | it's right weel you look (Joyce Ir 51) | McKenna SS 164 It's yourself should have been there | ib 165 It's the fine tale ye're spoiling | Birmingham Inviol. Sanctuary 28 it's proud and pleased I am to see you home again | Cronin H 40 It's an angel you are to forgive me | Lindsay CA 26 Is it bitten you are? | frequent in Synge.

When there is no cleft sentence (i.e. when no continuation with a relative clause could be thought of), *he, she, they* are used, not *it:* (Who are those girls?) They are my sister's friends | (Who is that boy?) He is our neighbour's Jack | Barrie AdmCr 146 But they were happy days | Mackenzie S 1.313 He did not know whose tunes they were that Stella played | ib 316 "... these ferns." "They're not ferns — they're bracken."

Other examples of *they* in vol II 6.241.

D. Unspecified *it*
(Also called conceptional *it*, PhilGr 241).

4.6₉. This is often considered 'impersonal' or 'indefinite', though it really refers to something definite. Cf Sh Tw V. 1.401 The raine it raineth euery day (with the definite article; cf also the weather is fine, etc).

It is in the first place used as subject, as "the great neuter of nature," in expressions for the weather: it rains, drizzles, hails, freezes, snows, is pouring down, etc. Thus already OE Blickl. Hom. ðonne hit swiðe frēoseþ. On the origin see PhilGr 241.

ModE examples: AV Gen 2.5 the Lord God had not caused it to raine vpon the earth | Stevenson M 102 It had thundered during the day, and it promised more thunder | It is cold, warm, fine, cloudy ... | It looks like rain | It is rather close in here | Bennett HL 165 it only began to rain in earnest just as we got to the gate. — Very thoughtful of it, I'm sure! | id W 1.263 Do you think it will last long? — Not it!

Further some examples on time:

It is five minutes to six | It wants only a few minutes to six | It is long till Christmas | It was a long a time before I got hold of him.

It is Friday today (but also with the day of the week as subject, without *it:* Today is Friday | Doyle M 18 yesterday was my birthday). Note in a nexus-tertiary: Being Sunday, all shops were shut — quotations vol V 6.9 (also with *it*).

On distance:

It's a long way to Tipperary | London V 327 It is forty miles from Oakland to San José | It is not far from here to Brighton.

Unspecified *it* as subject is found in: It says in the Bible: Thou shalt not steal | Bennett A 90 It says in the "Signal" that trade is improving (= it is said in ...).

4.6$_{10}$. Unspecified *it* is very often used as the object of an otherwise intransitive *vb*. Idiomatic phrases thus evolved possess a certain affective colouring by containing *it* = 'the thing you know, which I need not specify'. A great many examples were given in vol VI 6.8$_7$ of vbs = sbs + *it*, arranged after the character of the sb (names of persons: *lord it;* names of inanimate things: *cab it;* other sbs: *Aldershot it;* adjs: *brave it*).

A few additional examples: Marlowe E 671 Now let vs in, and feast it roiallie (also Dekker F 588) | Sh Err IV. 4.65, cf other vbs Sh-lex p. 600b | Kemp NDW 2 to foote it | Maxwell F 18 We pig it with the artists and other riff-raff | Kennedy CN 24 one of you must leg it up to the hotel | Doyle S 5.277 he legged it as hard as he could run.

With or without *it:* Marlowe E 1519 thou wilt fight it to the last | Goldsm V 1.38 we can walk it perfectly well ... if we walk to church in this trim | Byron 643 I battle it against him, as I battled in highest Heaven | Shaw TT 57 you can jump out to dress yourself and hop it from here.

Walk it and *hop it* (where the vb may be formed from the sb) form the transition to other vbs of movement used with *it* as sbj; note especially the half-slangy *go it, come it* = 'act vigorously, furiously, excessively': Kipling L 36 I ran it fine, awfully fine | Di D 79 I say, young Copperfield, You're going it! | Shaw 1.212 Go it, little missie, go it | Hope In 49 you seem to be going it | Di P 479 it's my 'pinion that you're a comin' it a great deal too strong | Galsw P 11.64 he never comes it over [= is angry with] you | Wells JP 173 to let young W come it over him | Hardy F 390 Oak is coming it quite the dand [i. e. dandy].

Other idiomatic uses of *it:* Stevenson MB 207 he and Sermaise had it out alone [= fought] | Kennedy CN 132 I meant to tease you a little before I had it out with you | Priestley B 75 I'll bet you had it pretty rough, didn't you? | Pinero Iris 174 I desire to make it up to you — desire to make amends | Caine P 191 But I'll give it her | Carry it off well 'make a brave show' | Carry it high | beat it (orig. U.S.) = cut it 'get away'.

4.6₁₁. Unspecified *it* is found after a prep. in many idiomatic phrases:

of it: Goldsm V 1.111 I think we have made an excellent day's work of it | Sterne M 1.73 he had but a very uneasy task of it | Sheridan 285 and a very comfortable living I had of it | make a day, a bolt of it (both 18th c., NED) | GE S 33 the rich were entirely in the right of it to lead a jolly life | Stevenson T 107 Silver was the captain and a mighty rebellious crew he had of it | ib [p.?] we had a good enough place of it in this cabin | ib [p.?] what a supper I had of it that night | id B 85 they made but poor speed of it now | Pinero Iris 171 I make a clean breast of it (also Allen S 194) | Caine C [p.?] she started the cheering again, and said she meant to make a dead heat of it with Tennyson's brook | Haggard S 165 one might think from the look of you that you had been having a night of it | make a night of it | have a nice time of it.

for it: There is nothing else for it but to submit | Defoe M 185 I ran for it | Carlyle S 59 thou hadst nothing for it but to leave | Stevenson T 178 I made a bolt for it over the stockade | James S 49 Why didn't she make a bold personal dash for it? | Wells T 24 Ride for it | Bennett B 72 Now I am fairly in for it.

in it: (pun:) He never opens his mouth but he puts his foot in it.

to it: Locke CA 229 he had been greatly put to it to satisfy Amos's omnivoracity | Maugham FPS 254 the publishers ... were hard put to it to fulfil the pressing orders of the booksellers.

The Generic Person

4.7₁. English has no pronoun for the generic person exactly corresponding to Scand. and G *man*, F *on*. ME had *man* and the weakened form *men*, which was not the pl as shown by the vb being in the sg (see Skeat's note on Ch MP 5.22).

The notion of a generic person is in ModE expressed by

(1) a passive construction,
(2) *we,*

(3) *you*,
(4) *they* (4.7₃),
(5) *one* (4.7₄), *oneself*, etc (4.7₅),
(6) a substantive denoting a person preceded by the indefinite article (4.7₆).

These possibilities will be exemplified and discussed in what follows.

(1) a passive construction: He is said to be very rich | French spoken here | An old deed has been found.

In this way one avoids mentioning who the acting person is.

(2) *we:* the speaker includes himself, often with a certain humility: we are but human | we live to learn.

(3) *you:* this appeal to the second person as an ideal person is found in many languages (see e.g. Wackernagel, *Vorles. über syntax* 1.109). In ME we find *thou* (Ch E 265 Ther maystow seen) and poet. in Byron 2.364 I felt as on a plank at sea, When all the waves that dash on thee, At the same time upheave and whelm, And hurl thee towards a desert realm.

4.7₂. Generic *you* is distinctly colloquial in tone, though very frequent in literature, also outside of conversations. The original purport of the pronoun is never entirely forgotten, and *you* cannot be used except when there is a possibility of applying what is said to the hearer (or reader). Thus in speaking of a remote past, it would be impossible to translate *on a vu* by "you have seen", though in hypothetical expressions it is, of course, possible to say, for instance, "In 1604, you might have seen Shakespeare play the ghost in Hamlet." In Jack London's Martin Eden, p. 65, Miss Ruth asks Martin: "By the way, Mr. Eden, what is *booze*? You used it several times, you know." "Oh, booze," he laughed. "It's slang. It means whisky and beer —

anything that will make you drunk." — This makes her say: "Don't use 'you' when you are impersonal. 'You' is very personal, and your use of it just now was not precisely what you meant." "I don't just see that." "Why, you said just now to me, 'whisky and beer — anything that will make you drunk' — make *me* drunk, don't you see?" "Well, it would, wouldn't it?" "Yes, of course," she smiled, "but it would be nicer not to bring me into it. Substitute 'one' for 'you,' and see how much better it sounds." — As a general rule, it may be said that *one* is preferred for the generic person if referring to the speaker himself — *you* if referring to the hearer — and *they* if neither is uppermost in the mind of the speaker.

Therefore, *you* could not very well be used with *ought to* or *should:* "You ought never to be cruel to animals" would be felt as too personal.

This use of *you* does not seem to have been at all frequent in ElE; at any rate Al. Schmidt in his Sh-lex. has only one instance, Wiv II. 1.233 In these times you stand on distance. Cf, however, *your* below.

In this quotation *you* is first generic, then = the person addressed: Cronin H 109 You would think you were starved to hear you.

A few modern examples: Quincey 20 the memory strengthens as you lay burdens upon it | Di D 16 You mustn't marry more than one person at a time, may you, Peggotty? ... But if you marry a person, and the person dies, why then you may marry another person, mayn't you, Peggotty? — You MAY, if you choose, my dear | Ruskin Sel 2.414 you cannot tell a secret which you don't know.

Parallel to the generic use of *you* = 'one' we have a generic use of the possessive *your* with no reference to the person addressed, very often with an implication of contempt:

Sh Hml IV. 3.22 Your worm is your onely Emperor for diet. ... Your fat King, and your leane begger is but variable service to dishes | ib V. 1.189 your water is a sore decayer of your horson dead body | Alls I. 3.66 your marriage comes by destinie, your cuckow sings by kinde | Oth II. 3.79 ff. | Rehearsal 27 your grave lookers are the dullest of men ... your gravest bird is an owl, and your gravest beast is an ass | Sheridan 224 not like the work of your modern Raphaels who contrive to make your portrait independent of you | Austen PP 316 he may be a little whimsical ... your great men often are | Scott Lockh. 582 your scornful dog will always eat your dirty pudding | Di Do 90 None of your live languages for Miss Blimber | Ru Sel 1.164 your dunce thinks things are standing still, and draws them fixed: your wise man sees the change or changing of them, and draws them so | Meredith E 27 Vernon was one of your men that have no occupation for their money | Stevenson JHF 10 one of your fellows who do what they call good | Ward F 94 some young aristocrat no doubt, one of your idle insolent rich | Doyle S 1.80 it is your commonplace, featureless crimes which are really puzzles | Stephen L 138 a little swearing was thought no blemish in your muscular Christian.

4.7₃. (4) *they:* they say (= people say, it is generally said) | Stevenson M 217 (beginning of story:) They had sent for the doctor | Marett Anthropol. 32 They were digging out a place for a gas-holder in a meadow | Christie in BDS 360 My poor little girl. What have they been doing to you?

They alternating with *people:* Fox 1.75 At all the dissenting chapels they are telling the people that they are sure to go to a very uncomfortable place if they don't vote for you.

Thus as subject only, probably never e.g. I have heard them say.

4.7₄. (5 and 6) A sg form of the third person, either *one* or a sb preceded by the indefinite article. In both cases we have often a disguised first person, the speaker avoiding the direct use of *I*, though thinking chiefly of himself.

(5) *one*—often weakly stressed though keeping the full vowel [ʌ]: she looks at one in a most peculiar way [ət wʌn]; cf Sweet E 62 [-itri maindzwanəv:wanəvmistə ·pikwiksəd ventʃəz]: the first *one* weak, the second half-stressed.

Examples of this *one:* Caxton R 54 One myghte haue luste to see suche a feeste | Sh Ro III. 3.174 May not one [='I'] speake ? | Hml I. 5.108 one may smile, and smile, and be a villaine | One would think he was mad | One must draw the line somewhere | Why, may one ask ?

Alternating with *you:* Keats 4.153 these chasms ... turn one giddy if you choose to give way to it | Montague Rough Justice 274 One does get a sort of pleasure out of it, don't you ?

The gen. of the indefinite *one* is always *one's*, when the nominative is not found in the same sentence, thus twice in Sh, Err IV. 3.72 Some diuels aske but the parings of ones naile | Gent V. 4.67 Who should be trusted, when ones right hand Is periured to the bosome ?

4.7₅. When the indefinite *one* has to be repeated the usual English practice nowadays is to use forms of the pronoun itself: One has to take care of *oneself* and *one's* family if *one* can. But the old practice, which is still frequent in Scottish and U.S., is to use forms of *he:* One has to take care of *himself* and *his* family if *he* can. Further examples (see also some in NED *one* 21): Bacon (q Bøgholm 34) one can scarce draw his breath | Sh Lucr 1393 one would swear he saw them quake and tremble | Sh Gent IV. 1.115 one cannot climb it without danger of his life | As III. 2.24 I know the more one sickens, the worse at ease he is | Goldsm 651 If, indeed, like an Eastern bridgroom, one were to be introduced to a wife he never saw before, it might be endured | Carlyle [?] One does not stickle about his vehicle | Barrie M 269 one can no more drive in tackets properly than take cities unless he gives his whole mind to it | id Echoes 166 down here one knows he has risks to run | Lowell StW 316 many passages which one is rather inclined to like than sure he would be right in liking them | Hawthorne T 48 if one could live a thousand years, he might have time to grow rich | Holmes A 123 How one does tremble with rage at his own intense momentary stupidity about things he knows perfectly well (ib 104, 155, 157) | Washington U 243 I believe that one always does himself and his audience an injustice when he speaks merely for the sake of speaking | Hurst Five 77 One cannot bear to be in the company of the insipid young girls, once he has known you.

Cf also Sh Hml V. 2.147 to know a man wel, were to knowe *himselfe* (no pronoun *one* preceding) — which would now be *oneself*.

English compositors now correct authors on this point, thus Carlyle FR 404 "One must verily stir *oneself*", where the original ed. had *himself*.

I have found the same proverb in three different forms: As one makes his bed, so he must lie in it | As one makes One's bed, so one must lie thereon | As you make your bed, so you must lie upon it.

Some old examples of *one* repeated by the pronoun

she are given ESt 17.394; cf also BJo P IV. 1.35 And how must one behave her selfe amongst 'hem? | New York Teachers' Monographs 1902 p. 88 When one thinks, by contrast, of the English work in our best schools to-day, *she* can but exclaim that times have changed.

An advantage of the British way is seen in such a sentence as "It is absurd to tell a person something about his own will, but it is not absurd to tell him something about one's own will." On the other hand the British repetition of *me* (*oneself*, etc) is sometimes more clumsy than the American *he himself*), as seen if inserted in the following sentence (Cooley, Human Nature 124): "if *one* likes a book, so that *he* feels *himself* inclined to take it down from time to time and linger in the companionship of the author, *he* may be sure *he* is getting something that *he* needs, though it may be long before *he* discovers what it is." But then the Englishman would feel inclined to substitute *someone* for *one*, and then go on with *he*, etc, or else to use the generic *you*.

4.7₆. (6) a designation for a human being in the sg with the indefinite article:

a man: Ch C 513 | Sh H4A I. 2.105 and now I am, if a man should speake truly, little better then one of the wicked | ib 117 'Tis no sin for a man to labour in his vocation | H4B I. 1.257 A man can no more separate age and couetousness, then he can part young limbes and letchery. Cf Err III. 2.91 | Hml III. 2.116 What should a man do but be merry | Cæs V. 1.122 | Rehearsal 79 Must a man be eternally telling you of these things? | Swift J 47 What must a man expect from his enemies? | ib 271 'Tis a plaguy ticklish piece of work, and a man hazards losing both sides | Di Do

The Generic Person: Substantive.

352 an accountable speculation, such as sometimes comes into a man's head | id Ch 75 that's hardly fair upon a man | id D 335 "A man might get on very well here," said Markham — meaning himself.... "Upon my honour," returned Markham, "town seems to sharpen a man's appetite. A man is hungry all day long. A man is perpetually eating." Cf the introduction of Markham: he always spoke of himself indefinitely, as "a man," and seldom or never in the first person | Thack P 2.146 | Brontë V 357 Really it does a man good to see the spirit of that boy | Stevenson JHF 6 I got into that state of mind when a man listens and listens and begins to long for a policeman | Kipling L 46 "A man can't work for ever." "A man might have gone to a pub, and got decently drunk" | ib 132 what is there in that nonsense to make a man restless? | Shaw C 139 what can a man say more than that he has had enough? | ib 137 What do you mean by shoving your elbow into a man's breadbasket for? | Hope R 105 you're always so down on a man.

a fellow, coll., common from the 19th c.: Thack V 227 but hang it, if a pretty woman *will* throw herself into your way, what can a fellow do? | id N 520 Don't make fun of a fellow | ib 521 A fellow can't help letting it be seen | Beaconsfield L 89 If a fellow is obliged to marry, he always likes to marry one of the B family | ib 90 as if a fellow could have too much land | Trollope D 1.50 What the deuce is a fellow to do?

Other examples in Meredith, Stevenson, etc.

a body (cf the use in *nobody*, etc, and in Sh Tit II. 3.103 any mortal body): Found in Bacon according to Bøgholm, but not so frequently as in Sh | Sh As IV. 3.166 a body would thinke this was well counterfeited | Swift P 136 this eating and drinking takes away a body's stomach | ib 170 you plague a body so | id J 13 it is good enough for naughty girls that won't write to a body | Fielding T 4.319 where a body means no harm, what signifies a hasty word? | Hardy T 114 it is wonderful what a body can get used to of that sort in time!

Especially frequent in Sc and Amr: Burns 3.151 Gin a body meet a body Comin' thro' the rye, Gin a body kiss a body, Need a body cry? | Stevenson K 200 where can a body turn to? | id JHF 204 a body would think there was something in this | Twain M 16 I think a body's got his hands full enough if he sticks to just what he knows himself | Aldrich S 10 How was it, Molly? Tell a body, dear! | Cronin H 237 you always offer a body something tasty.

a person (most frequent in the mouth of a woman): Di D 352 but when a person is umble, Master Copperfield, a person treasures such things up | id F 857 it isn't easy for a person to know where to begin, when a person is in this state of delight | id Do 33 it's one thing to give orders, and quite another thing to take 'em. A person may tell a person to dive off a bridgehead foremost into five-and-forty feet of water, but a person may be very far from diving | ib 375 [same speaker:] it turns all the blood in a person's body into pins and needles, with their pints all ways | Trollope O [p. ?] Might a person ask what you are going for? | Twain M 189 There's one thing in this world which a person don't ever try to jew you down on. That's a coffin.

an individual: Di D 495 does an individual place himself beyond the pale of those preferments by entering on such an office? | Mulock H 133 Well done, Phineas — to walk round the garden without one resting! — now I call that grand, after an individual has been ill a month.

a woman, a girl: Meredith H 62 It makes a woman feel cold to think of him | ib 156 mayn't a woman have secrets? || Caine C 34 a medical school containing lots of nice boys, only a girl may not speak to them | ib 153 there must be some explanation, if a girl could only find it out.

In more or less vg or slangy speech *a chap, a cove:* Shaw Me 3 chuck away your silly week-end novel, and talk to a chap | Doyle S 1.231 what d'you want to frighten a chap for? | Wells L 153 Chap ought to fight || *a cove* is used constantly by the boy Rob Grinder in Di Do, but he is taught by Miss Fox to say *an individual* instead.

4.7₇. Finally we must mention the recent, more or less slangy use of *it*, sometimes spelt with a capital It or IT, mentioned by Louise Pound in the Curme Volume 1930, p. 109f. (cf Karpf in *Anglia Beibl.* 1931. 331). It started in children's games, where "He's it" means 'he is the central figure' (also "He's he"); then, e.g. "She thinks she's it" = 'thinks herself of special importance.' But it also comes to mean 'stupid person,' and, on the other hand, (from an Amr film) 'personal magnetism or attractiveness,' whence even the derivatives *itty, itfulness* and *ittishness*.

I add the quotations I have found for these senses: Maxwell HR 212 I couldn't tell you, Jack. I only know he is quite it | Galsw MW 141 endowed with the conviction, invisible, impermeable, of being IT | Mason Ch 106 You're it, you know, in this house, Lydia | ib. I'm going to be it to-night | Crofts Ch 108 you're simply It! | Frankau Dance 245 And take it from us, you're It. You're more than It. You're the type | Lowndes BD 200 "How wonderful, Brookie!" "What a clever idea!" "It's just 'it'! I can't say more" | Maynard Smith F

302 Teddy is just it. He knows everybody. He has been everywhere | ib 363 I have some new plus-fours which are 'it' | ib 643 Ernest, Inspector, is simply 'It' when it comes to eavesdropping in a Night Club | Stacpoole in BDS 161 He is It.

Reflexive

4.8₁. In a reflexive sense, i.e. referring to the subject of the sentence, or at any rate to the subject-part of a dependent nexus, we have both the simple personal pronouns and composed ones with *self*. Let us first consider the development of the latter forms.

The history of the *self*-pronouns is far from simple. Originally *self* was an adj, inflected as other adjs and agreeing in use and number with the sb or pronoun to which it was added, e.g. nom. *ic self*, acc. m. *hine selfne*, dat. f. *hire selfre*, etc. Besides this use, *self* was also made a sb and as such was combined with a genitive (possessive) as in *myself*, and had a pl *selves*. In ModE the result has been an amalgamation of these two functions, and the original case-distinction in the adj has been abolished. *Himself* was to begin with the dative, added to the vb with the meaning 'for (or to) himself', but it came to be regarded as an emphatic apposition to the subject without this notion of interest (he has done it himself, he himself has done it), or as a reflexive object (he washes himself), and finally it is sometimes used as a subject by itself (himself has done it).

We thus get the following forms, in which *a* denotes the adjectival and *b* the substantival construction, while *c* denotes a mixture of both:

a (meself)		himself herself
b myself ourselves yourself yourselves	(hisself)	herself
		(theirselves)
c		themselves.

The forms in ( ) are obs., except in dialects. *Herself* may be taken either as *a* or as *b*; NED takes it only as *a*.

When a person speaks of himself as *we* (*pluralis majestatis*) he may use the form *ourself* (vol II 4.13).

Itself may be taken as either *a* or as *b* with the obs. possessive form *it*.

By the side of *oneself* (*a*) we find *one's self* (*b*).

The *b*-forms were formerly often written in two words: *my self*, etc.

A few quotations may illustrate how dative-forms came to be used as nominatives, and the old usage in general: Oros. 194 þā ongeat Hannibal, & him self sāde | Orrm 2.327 he nass him sellf nohht Crist | AR 258 he him sulf het seið | Lay 1.136 me seolf ich habben inoȝe; B: i-noh ich habbe mi seolue | ib 141 vs selve we habbet cokes; B: hus seolf we habbeþ cocus | ib. vs sulue we habbet bermen; B: hus seolf we habbeþ bermen | VaV 19 god seið him self | Ch B 44 He scholde him-seluen usen it by ryghte | ib 145 hemself (pl) | C 459 though myself be a ful vicious man | B 407 The sowdan comth him-self | ib 2268 as he him-self recordeth | C 742 But sires ... ye may your self wel rede | F 454 For ye yourself upon yourself yow wreke | Caxton 65 can not helpe hem self | ib 74 thenne may they them self correcte fyrst | id R 84 euery thyng by hym self [= by itself] | ib 86 they them seluen ben hurt | Malory 67 yf she saye so her self | ib 60 they maye saue hym self | More U 31 themselfes (but in Arber's reprint of 2nd ed. themselues) | ib 227 if either of them fynde themselfe ...

greued | Bale T 1761 where Christ hys self is. — Cf further NED under each of the forms and under *self*.

An old grammarian's view is seen in Lowth, *Eng. Gramm.* (1762) 39 *Himself, themselves,* seem to be used in the Nominative Case by corruption instead of *his self, their selves:* as "he came *himself,*" "they did it *themselves.*"

Simple Pronouns in a Reflexive Sense

4.8₂. First as objects of verbs. This was found in a great many cases where nowadays the *self*-forms are used, e.g. Marlowe E 2010 I should reuenge me of the wronges | Sh H4B II. 4.390 I feele me much to blame | Ven 3 Adonis hied him to the chase | Ado III. 1.11 there will she hide her | Shrew IV. 4.63 bid Bianca make her ready | Hml III. 1.124 I could accuse me of such things, that it were better my mother had not borne me | ib III. 3.2 prepare you | ib 24 Arme you.

In a great many cases where the earlier language had reflexive pronouns (with or without *self*) as object, the vb is now used intransitively; see vol III 16.2ff. (e.g. repent me of it > repent it; behave, rest, turn, wash).

On *lie : lay* and *sit : set* (e.g. lay me down, sit me down) see ib 16.7.

4.8₃. *Bethink* with the simple object is quite frequent in the 19th c.; Thackeray uses it continually, e.g. N 298 he bethought him that ..., but it is also found in other writers: Doyle M 242 I bethought me of the quiet Miss Williams | Wells N 462 I bethought me of a youngster named C. | Mason R 58 he bethought him of another argument.

But with *-self:* Brontë J 101 I bethought myself to ring the bell | id V 336 he bethought himself, one day, to intrude on her class.

Other isolated instances of reflexive objects: Di N 664 None of your story-book writers will ever make as good a book as this, I warrant me | Shaw P 233 (Sc) I misdoubt me he will not answer | Maxwell G 38 (vg) I fear me, James, you haven't a very strong sense of humour.

The simple pronouns and the *self*-pronouns as indirect objects were treated in vol III 14.4$_1$.

According to Curme CG 232 it is possible in colloquial speech to say "I bought me (or myself) a new hat," but in the third person only "he bought himself a new hat," as *him* would be taken to mean another person.

Reflexive Pronouns as Regimens of Prepositions

4.8₄. After a preposition the simple form is often used in a reflexive sense if the preposition has a perfectly concrete meaning, chiefly local. It seems to be of some importance whether the action indicated is one which one naturally performs with regard to oneself or to others; thus we say: he looked at himself in the mirror, she pointed at herself, she was angry with herself — because as a rule one looks at, points at, and is angry with some one else, not at or with oneself.

4.8₅. Examples of various prepositions with simple and compound pronouns:

above, beneath, over: We looked at the stars above us | they bathed in the sunlight beneath them | he drew the counterpane over him.

about, (a)round: I had no change about me | she looked inquisitively about (around) her | Sh Cæs I. 2.192 Let me haue men about me that are fat | Mi SA 1501 to sit idle with so great a gift ... about him | Spectator 143 As I was walking in my chamber with nothing about me but my night-gown | Defoe R 54 I had nothing about me but a knife | ib 55 I look'd about me again | id G 91 looking round them | Di D 95 Mr. Creakle was laying about him dreadfully | Doyle S 6.53 Lestrade looked about him.

But in a transferred sense: Milne P 98 You've talked about yourself and thought about yourself quite long enough; now I'm going to talk about myself.

besides: Always (?) with *self:* They were quite beside themselves with joy.

before, in front of; behind, after: She drew him after her | Coming events cast their shadows before them | He gazed straight before (in front of) him | He left a large fortune behind him | They burnt their boats behind them | We have a couple of hours' work before us | Bunyan G 31 it made me suddainly look behind me | NED 1766 Goldsm V xxii Next morning I took my daughter behind me | Macaulay H 1.83 Great statesmen who looked far behind them and far before them | Wharton HM 107 Lily and Selden had the whole afternoon before them | Walpole Cp 24 She gazed before her | id DF [?] staring in front of him.

But: he can't look after himself.

in, within: Baily (q Kruisinga) Great art has always, or nearly always, in it a transitory element of contemporary fashion | Mill, Poetry (402) Great poets have found within them one highly delicate and sensitive specimen of human nature.

to, into, for, towards: (Kruisinga) He had the difficulty pointed out to him | Walpole Cp 30 her aunt drew her towards her.

But: He came to himself a few minutes afterwards | he sat, smiling happily to himself | Scott I 249 murmuring to herself a Saxon rhyme | Bennett B 77 he's one

4.8₅.] Reflexive Pronouns as Regimens of Prepositions. 167

of those that keep themselves to themselves | Maugham Alt 6 we should keep ourselves to ourselves | Wharton HM 115 he said to himself that even her weeping was an art | Maxwell G 113 she retired into herself | Wharton HM 107 a girl who has no one to think for her is obliged to think for herself | ib 114 What a miserable future you foresee for me! — Well — have you never foreseen it for yourself? | he is old enough to do for himself.

by: always (?) with *-self:* He lives by himself in an old dilapidated cottage | he woke by himself.

on, upon: Sh Gent IV. 4.13 one that takes vpon him to be a dog indeede | the teacher took it upon him (or himself) to punish the lad (Curme).

with: She took her children with her.

between, among [reciprocal]: They had 5/- between them | a patch of land which they were to divide between them | Mackenzie C 9 We enjoy between us a comfortable little sum of money.

But: Between ourselves = entre nous, unter uns gesagt.

4.8₆. Some vbs are always, or nearly always, used reflexively (with *-self*): avail oneself of | bestir oneself | betake oneself to (cf above) | content oneself with | pride oneself on (e.g. Goldsm V 1.2 She prided herself much also upon being an excellent contriver | Phillpotts GR 89) | in the same sense: pique oneself on.

Thus some vbs with *over-:* I overslept myself, I overrate myself.

Many other vbs can, at any rate occasionally, take a reflexive pronoun as object. I note the following instances in the beginning of Maxwell's Gabrielle: 7 she pulled herself together | 11 she had perhaps too much accustomed herself to swift reactions | 28 So I turned myself into the next best thing | 37 he shook himself free of the spell | 68 all opportunities that presented themselves | 87 Make yourself at home | 107 one had to shout to make oneself heard | ib. Every minute she enjoyed herself more completely | 117 these pretty things showed themselves solid and real | 121 with a lovely lady fanning herself.

Reflexive Possessives

4.9₁. Possessive pronouns are used reflexively in a great many cases where other languages generally prefer the definite article. Thus in objects: More U 71 he shaked his heade | Brontë V 21 by putting her fingers in her ears | Di D 91 he shook his head, and rubbed his hands | ib 676 he cleared his voice | id N 615 the old gentleman snapped his fingers twenty or thirty times | Kingsley Y 53 Lancelot hung down his head | Shaw P 275 shall we just put our heads together | Zangwill G 66 she hung her head (also Austen M 13, Di D 5) | Caine P 199 wipe your eyes and blow your nose | Wells T 120 he bit his nail | Hope R 296 we hung our heads | Doyle S 5.54 He wrung his hands | Parker R 103 the crowd held their breath.

'He licked his hand' — here *his* is reflexive, but not in 'The dog licked his hand.'

In prepositional groups: Sh Gent III. 1.333 she doth talke in her sleepe. It's no matter for that; so shee sleepe not in her talke | Mcb 564 There's one did laugh in's sleep | Fielding 3.495 she fell on her knees | Di D 114 they blow upon their fingers, and tap their feet upon the floor | id N 387 a great many dissuasions uttered by Mr. Crowl with his mouth full | Pinero B 4 she struggles to her feet | Wells TM 77 I turned with my heart in my mouth | Kingsley H 274 the soldiers ran for their lives | Maxwell G 97 Mr T. was on his way home.

On the shortened constructions like 'hat in hand' see vol V 6.7$_6$.

Here we may place combinations like "He walks his four miles before breakfast" in which the possessive pronoun does not indicate possession in a strict sense. Note the inverted commas in the Maugham quotation: Sh Hml II. 1.98 He seem'd to find his way without his eyes | Kipling P 133 Dan had come to grief over his Latin | NP 1925 The author knows his poor because he has sympathy | Dine B 33 Professor Bertrand Dillard was a man in his sixties | Sapper in BDS 13 one of those open-air, clear-eyed men who came over in their thousands to Gallipoli and France | Maugham FPS 95 It will bring on your lumbago. — Miss Porchester had 'her' sick headaches and Mrs. St. Clair had 'her' lumbago.

Cf *work one's hardest* vol III 12.2$_5$.

Note, on the other hand, the following quotations in which the vb has no possessive pronoun before it (in some of them we have two-member combinations, which always tend to brevity): Ruskin S ix a nation ... hardly able to keep soul and body together | id P 1.305 my father lived alone, parting with wife and son at once for the son's sake | ib 314 he instantly took off boot and sock and walked over [the Cherwell] and back | Caine P 160 Helga was standing before him with head down | Wilde L 26 Ten minutes later, with face blanched by terror, and eyes wild with grief, Arthur rushed from Bentinck | Galsw Sw 5 they've got to save face...each wished his face saved at the expense of the other fellow's! | ib 63 she would save face this time — strongest motive in the world | Ridge G 185 I won't give her rest from the moment she puts foot inside the house.

4.9₂. As a subdivision of this class we must reckon those cases in which a contrast to what is done to other people is (as in the following section) especially noticeable. While the reflexives mentioned so far correspond to the simple reflexive pronouns in other languages (Dan. *han ... sig*, G *er ... sich*, F *il se*, etc), other languages have here a double pronoun (Dan. *han ... sig selv*, G *er ... sich selbst*, F *il se ... lui-même*, or *à lui-même*). The following quotations are from Maxwell G: 21 What does he imagine? she asked herself | 36 he interrupted himself | 79 He gave himself away | 87 she wronged herself | 95 never sparing himself | ib. she worked herself to death. She wore herself out by work | 101 heaven helps those who help themselves | 108 Have I disgraced myself?

Most of the examples above (4.8₅) of prepositional uses with *-self* have the same peculiarity.

As a reflexive use of the *self*-forms we must also reckon the predicative in "he is quite himself again" = 'in a normal condition', though NED takes it to be the emphatic, i.e. non-reflexive use. Thus also in Maugham P 11 She did feel more herself now.

The reflexive use does not always refer to the subject itself; see, e.g., We left Jane to herself; cf Jane was left to herself.

Non-Reflexive Use of the *Self*-Pronouns

4.9₃. This use is generally called emphatic or emphasizing (Sonnenschein), but as a matter of fact the essential thing is contrast rather than emphasis (contrast to some one else), though these pronouns have generally strong stress, while the reflexive pronouns as a rule have at most half-strong stress.

These pronouns stand in apposition with some sb (or other primary), whether the subject of the sentence or not. In other languages we find correspondingly the word for *self* (Dan. *selv*, G *selbst*, F (*lui-* etc) *même*, etc) without a reflexive pronoun.

In English the word-order varies considerably. We find both "he himself did it" and "he did it himself." The former position is somewhat more pretentious and perhaps more literary, the latter, in which the pronoun comes as a kind of after-thought, is frequent in colloquial speech.

Sometimes the early position of the *self*-pronoun is chosen because it would otherwise be taken in the reflexive sense: Maxwell G 21 Gabrielle herself had stopped | ib 25 I wouldn't myself mind showing you the house | ib 110 as he himself changes, his past will change.

A third position is between the small vb and the full vb or a predicative: Thack (q Poutsma) He had never himself had the measles | Maxwell G 125 I hope of course that I am myself not mischievous.

The word-order chosen is obviously the only one possible in cases like the following: Maxwell G 53 Talking herself, she at first gave scant attention to what Gabrielle said | ib 77 (vg) the best way would be to inform her so yerself | ib 92 No one goes in there without an invitation from him himself | ib 130 she would have helped him to rise to his highest aims and herself have risen with him.

In a relative clause end-position is necessary after *that*, but the *self*-pronoun may follow immediately after *who*: I heard it from one of the men that had been present himself: I heard it from a man who himself had been present | Hewlett Q 15 Nicolas ... of whom, himself, there will be plenty to say.

An example of the rarer *it itself:* Bradley S 37 the persons are not really something outside the order, so that they can attack it or fail to conform to it; they are within it and a part of it. It itself produces them.

The *self*-pronoun may also stand in apposition with other words than the subject: the consent of the negroes themselves.

"You yourself must set some tasks," or "you must set some tasks yourself": non-reflexive, but in "you must set yourself some tasks" *yourself* is reflexive.

I am mad, he said himself — non-reflexive.

I am mad, he told himself — reflexive.

Sonnenschein § 84 quotes a conversation in which the difference between the two uses of *myself* appears:

A. I had good sport in Scotland this season.

B. I think I shall go and shoot myself there next year — and adds: though not perfectly clear in writing, would be quite clear when spoken.

Sometimes the *self*-pronoun stands by itself; this is especially found in groups with *and*, and after *as*, *like*, and *than:* This will be very convenient to Mrs Brown and myself | Sterne 19 In order to satisfy myself and reader | ib 21 place his rib and self in so many tormenting lights | Maxwell G 99 he spoke of the great love that subsisted between Lady Sarah and himself | ib 116 That person is a friend of my mother and myself || His love of strong drink was stronger than himself | He wanted to have round him people abler than himself | Stevenson K 224 And how is yourself, Cluny? (also Mackenzie C 263) | Wharton HM 286 bothers that a girl like yourself ought never to have known about.

Isolated this is poetical; NED has a quotation from Browning: What am myself?

4.9₄. *Self* is also an independent sb and may be found in combinations like the following, where it serves to introduce an adjunct: Barrie TG 373 she was quite her old self | Maugham P 56 His blue eye sparkled and he was once more his gay and jovial self | Mackenzie C 411 He became his own diligent self | Myers M 177 he was his alert and competent self | Letter of credit: We hereby beg to accredit with your goodselves the bearer of this letter | GE A 415 (vg) with only our two selves and mother.

4.9₅. This *self* is also found in compounds: self-confidence, self-assertion: Brontë P 200 I re-entered my own room, self-deprived of the means of living, self-sentenced to leave my present home | Meredith E 101 the forfeits she had to pay for self-assistance and, if it might be won, the world's | Kipling DW 211 they'll blame everyone except their foolselves | Lawrence L 108 the same ruddy self-contained look on his face, as though he were keeping himself to himself.

As a genitive to *self* we may consider *own:* he cooks his own meals | I like their children better than my own | I like their children because I have none of my own.

4.9₆. We may place here the use (chiefly Sc) of *lone* (*lane*) with preceding possessive as a kind of variant of *self*; in ME we sometimes find *by myn one* (Pearl 243, see Osgood's note; Towneley 117); *lone* < (*a*)*l-one:* Little Book of Sc. Verse 29 walkand your alone / Scott OM 105 if they meet a fraim body their lane in the muirs / Cronin H 360 I want to be quiet and by my lone in the darkness.

Cf the variants: London V 372 All by his lonely out there / Maxwell WF 111 Who are you going with? No one. All by my little lonesome / Ade A 26 if she went runnin' around the street by her lonelies / Mannin W 101 I'd sooner be the cat that walks by its wild lone / Sayers Unn. D 109 (vg) coming all

Chapter V

Sex and Gender

5.1₁. Sex is a natural quality shown primarily in the productive organs; male beings are distinguished from female beings. What is neither, is sexless.

Gender is a grammatical category. Many languages have class distinctions of different characters. Gender in primary words (chiefly substantives) is not always shown by the form of the word itself, but it may influence the form of other words (secondary), and is thus chiefly a syntactic category. Languages vary very much with regard to the number of classes distinguished, also with regard to the correspondence found between these grammatical classes and natural distinctions such as those of sex, between big and small, between living and lifeless, etc. Gender thus cannot be defined as the grammatical expression of sex, but may relate to many other things. — Not infrequently the distribution of words into different genders is so arbitrary that no reason can be discovered. See G. Royen, *Die nominalen Klassificationssysteme in den Sprachen der Erde.* 1929.

Old English, like the other ancient members of the Aryan (Indo-European) family of languages, had three genders, masculine, feminine, and neuter. The distinction to some extent corresponded to the real one between male, female, and sexless, but deviations were very frequent, as when *wīf* 'wife' was neuter, and *wīfmann* 'woman' was masculine. Many animals had a distinctive gender irrespective of the actual sex of the animal spoken of; thus *hund* 'hound', *apa* 'ape', *hara* 'hare' were masculine, and *mūs* 'mouse', *crāwe* 'crow', *nǣdre* 'adder' were feminine.

Besides, an enormous number of words denoting sexless things belonged either to the masculine or to the feminine gender. Thus *stān* 'stone', *dæg* 'day', *dēaþ* 'death', *mōna* 'moon' were masculine, and *bōc* 'book', *hnutu* 'nut', *hand* 'hand', *sāwol* 'soul', and *sunne* 'sun' were feminine, etc, etc.

It will be well to keep apart two sets of terms, thus:

(nature)	(grammar)
sex	gender
male ⎱ beings	masculine ⎱ words
female ⎰	feminine ⎰
sexless things	neuter.

Thus OE *wīf* denotes a female being and is a neuter word, etc. This terminology is clearer than that used by Sweet, who says that OE *wīfmann* is a grammatical masculine, while OE *mann* is a natural masculine (NEG § 146). No, both words are masculines, but *wīfmann* denotes a female being, while *mann* denotes either a male being, or, in many instances, a human being irrespective of sex.

Gender in OE is shown partly by flexion, partly by syntax. The flexion of neuters is characterized by the absence of any distinction between the nominative and accusative, and by the plural in *-u* or without any ending; the genitive in *-es* is peculiar to masculine and neuter; a nominative plural in *-as* is only found in masculines, and one in *-a* is only found in feminines. But such characteristics are not carried through with any degree of consistency. Thus the syntactic criteria are more important; they consist in the use with each gender of separate forms of adjuncts, especially pronominal adjuncts, as e. g. the 'article'. But such distinctions are not found everywhere, and in the plural the distinctions between the three genders are much less strongly marked than in the singular.

The origin of this system (if system it can be called) is lost in the darkness of pre-history, and does not concern us here. It is found in all the members of our family of languages, though it has been modified in some of them. The simplification has been carried out with greatest consistency in Armenian which has no genders, in Modern Persian, in the dialects of West Jutland, and in English. Now, what is the cause of this sweeping change?

With regard to Armenian, A. Meillet without hesitation thinks that the loss is due to a "substratum" which had no grammatical genders: when a foreign population adopted an Aryan tongue, they transferred this negative peculiarity to their newly acquired language. This theory, however, is not universally accepted, thus not by Holger Pedersen.

5.1₂. With regard to English, too, some scholars have thought of influence from foreigners. Van Ginneken and N. J. H. Royen (see *De jongere veranderingen van het indogermaanse nominale drieklassensysteem*, Leiden 1926, p. 87) think that on account of the formidable influence from the Normans, English should be reckoned "more or less" among Creolized languages, i.e. is placed in the same category as Pidgin English, French-Creol of St. Mauritius, Negro-English and Negro-Dutch in the Antilles, etc.

On such languages see Ch. XII of my book *Language*. I characterize these languages as makeshift or minimum languages: the grammar in all of them has been simplified to such an extent that it has reached the vanishing point. They are simply English, French, etc, learnt very imperfectly indeed by natives who have kept practically nothing of their own languages. But the conditions in which such languages come into existence are totally different from those prevailing in England after the Norman conquest; the native English population did not give up their own language in favour of a mutilated French, but kept up their old language with here and there an interspersed word taken from the speech of their superiors. Neither did the Norman lords speak a kind of Pidgin English, or if some of them did occasionally, it did not survive and was not imitated by the great majority of English people. If the loss of genders had been due to influence from the French, we should expect it to have taken place more rapidly in the South than in the North; but the exact opposite is what actually happened: genders for some centuries after the Conquest were kept with much greater fidelity in the southernmost part of the country than in the North, where it had practically been given up before the Normans occupied the country.

The destruction of the genders is not an isolated phenomenon; it is intimately bound up with the whole process of simplification in the flexional system of the language, more particularly in the case system. The beginnings of this movement are as old as the language itself, but the rapidity of the breakdown increased very considerably in the North from about 1000, while the South was much more conservative. I have elsewhere tried to show that the principal cause of this simplification was the inconsistency of the old system, in which the same ending had in various words many different functions, and some endings might in many words be pronounced with indistinct vowels or with no vowel at all without the meaning of the whole sentence being therefore much obscured. The tendency to slur over the flexional endings would be especially strong where there was a strong element of Scandinavian immigrants, who spoke a language that was indeed different from, but yet closely similar to English in most of the vital elements. Therefore, cases and genders were effaced much more rapidly and effectively in the North than in the South, where the Scandinavian influence was not very strong; but even there the old system had eventually to give way to the simpler linguistic structure which characterizes Modern English.

This, however, is only one side of the question; it explains the falling together of the various forms of the article, the disappearance of the difference in e.g. the adj-forms *gōdne gōdum gōdre*, etc. (ModE uniformly *good*), and the genitives such as *þǣre cwēne* and *þæs cyninges* (ModE *the queen's* and *the king's*). This might very well have been combined with the retention of the use of the pronouns *he* and *she* in referring to orig. m. and f. sbs like *stān* (stone) and *bōc* (book). But as a matter of fact this was given up completely. The reason was a strong feeling for natural sex and sexlessness. Very early we find the pronoun *she* referring to such words as OE *wīf* or *mǣgden* (n.) and *wīfmann* (m.) even when these were accompanied by articles and adjs showing the grammatical neuter and masculine gender, respectively; similarly *hē* or *hēo* (she) referring to *cīld* (n.) if a male or female child was spoken of. (Similar phenomena are frequent in German). The use of these pronouns thus is more or less independent of the gender of sbs and depends on notion more than on grammar.

Similarly, we find in OE and still more in ME *hit* (*it*) used in speaking of a thing, irrespective of the grammatical gender of the word. I take some examples from S. Moore's valuable article *Grammatical and Natural Gender in Middle English* (*Publ. Mod. Lang.*

Ass. 1921): hlǣw ... beorhtne ... *sē* scel ... þæt *hit* ...
(Beow.) | anne arc ... *hit* (Ælfric) | ænne calic ... *hit*
(id) | Etað þisne hlāf, *hit* is mīn līchoma (id) | þone
kinedom ... *hit* (AR) | þene drunch ... *hit* (ib). See
full statistics in Moore's paper.

The use of *it* is chiefly found at some distance from
the gender-indicating word.

The old and the modern usages are mixed in Malory
125 the grete *stone*, and *he* was so heuy that an C men
myghte not lyfte *hyt* vp.

This side of the question is not treated in Morsbach's *Grammatisches und psychologisches geschlecht im englischen*. Berlin 1913; here and in Moore's paper further literature; see especially N. v. Glahn, *Zur geschichte des gramm. geschlechts im mittelenglischen (Angl. forschungen* 53, 1918). Hoops, *Engl. sprachkunde* s. 85 ff. gives a summary of Morsbach and v. Glahn. Cf also my own PhilGr 226 ff. — With regard to the following sections see especially A. Knutson, *The Gender of Words Denoting Living Beings in English* (Lund 1905). But my treatment is very different from his.

5.1₃. We shall now see how sex is indicated in English. We may distinguish the following categories:

(1) male sex, e.g. *father, bull; he*
(2) female sex, e.g. *mother, cow; she*
(3) both sexes, e.g. *reader, eagle; who*
(4) no sex, e.g. *glass; it*
(5) indifference to sex or no-sex, e.g. *they.*

To class 5 also belong all adjuncts: *the, no, good,*
etc. Those pronouns which as primaries belong to
class 4: *this, that, what,* may be prefixed to any of the
substantives just mentioned.

In the following pages it will be my task to go more
into detail. It will be seen that though the simplification

sketched in the preceding sections is "one of the most beneficial of all the changes which the English language has undergone" (H. Bradley), no perfectly consistent system has been arrived at.

Substantives

5.2₁. To distinguish the male from the female sex we find various means. Sometimes we find totally different stems, e.g. *father : mother;* sometimes the same stem, but with a derivative ending added to one of the words, e.g. *god : goddess; widow : widower;* and finally composition or an adjunct is resorted to, e.g. *tom-cat, she-eagle, a male frog.*

(A) We shall first consider names for human beings, and among them in the first line those instances in which we have three names, one for both sexes, one for the male, and one for the female. In the following list those words which call for special detailed treatment are marked with a star.

Two-sex- words:	Male:	Female:
man*, person, human	man*	woman
spouse	husband	wife
parent	father (papa, dad)	mother (mummy)
child*, baby	boy	girl
child*	son	daughter
youth*	lad	lass
monarch, sovereign	king	queen.

5.2₂. *Man* is a difficult, and therefore an interesting word, because it is used in three different senses, viz.

(a) as a contrast to beast and God: a human being.

(b) as a contrast to woman: human being of the male sex.

(c) as a contrast to boy: human male grown-up.

Edward Carpenter was conscious of this ambiguity, when he wrote (Art of Creation 171) "the deification of the Babe. It is not likely that Man — the human male — left to himself would have done this ... But to woman it was natural." On the other hand Carlyle, without hesitation, uses *men* in sense (a), even in such a combination as this (FR 301) "atrabiliar old men, especially old women, hint that they know what they know." The effect of the same use is comic in Miss Hitchener's line which according to Medwin (Shelley 118) so much amused Shelley: "All, all are men — women and all!" Compare also Defoe R 2.234 Cromwell ... killing man, woman and child, — where *man* must be taken in sense (c).

In a great many combinations *man* will naturally always be understood in sense (b) only: I saw an old man whom I did not know, etc. In the plural in the same way: Two or three young men made a fearful noise | Sh Tp II 1.157 No occupation, all men idle, all; And women too. Cf also the "Young Men's Christian Association". *People* may function as the plural of *man* in sense (a): A few young people made a fearful noise.

But *everyman* and *no man* ("no man's land") are taken in sense (a). The general ambiguity of *man* is, however, probably the reason why *body* is used in the pronominal words *everybody, anybody, somebody, nobody;* cp. also Burns's "If a body meet a body", etc; see above, 4.7$_6$.

In the generic sense we find
(1) the singular used in sense (a): Pope: The proper

study of mankind is man | Cowper 197 God made the country, and man made the town; cf below, 14.3$_3$ f.

(2) the singular in sense (b): Caine C 352 Man's the head, but woman turns it; it may really be taken in either sense in Shelley 67 Can man be free if woman is a slave?

(3) the plural in sense (a): Mi PL 1.26 justifie the ways of God to men (cf below, 14.3$_4$);

(4) the plural in sense (b): Gissing B 259 I am studying men, she had said. In our days this is the proper study of womankind. (Other quotations vol II. p. 132 and 134).

A male, but hardly a female, can use *a man* in the sense of 'one' (Fr. *on*): It does a man good to see the energy of that boy. (In the same way *a fellow*). Cf. 4.7$_6$.

The verb *man* has really no reference to senses (b) or (c): "A German ship during the war was reported as manned with women" (q McKnight, *English Words* 209) | Bennett LR 2 Two Thames barges, each manned by two men and a boy.

5.2$_3$. This ambiguity is old and common to many languages. It has been obviated in German and Scandinavian by the derivative *mensch, menneske, människa;* in English by the use of *human being* and recently of *human* as a sb with the pl *humans*. Examples of both: Beresford G 117 you must know that women are human beings just as well as men (b) | Wells Ma 2.157 Marriage isn't what it was. It's become a different thing because women have become human beings || Farnol A 307 since humans, of every degree, are only men and women after all | Galsw P 2.74 By Jove, Molly, I sometimes think we humans are a rubbish lot | id TL 256 to humans without ideas (also id Ca 475) | Walpole OL [?] what children these humans were! (also id RH 48) | Carpenter Ad 178 devotion to other humans | Locke BV 294 we poor humans (very frequent in Locke). Cf for the adjunct Harraden F 56 a book on the marriage question, which is neither a woman's book nor a man's book, but a human book.

5.2₄. The old collective *mankind* (now stressed on the second syllable) comprises all human beings, but the younger compound *mankind* (stressed on the first syllable) is opposed to *womankind*. (The stress-difference, as made in NED and by Dan. Jones, is not, however, recognized by everybody). Note the quotation Di D 181 [girls] "whom my aunt had taken into her service expressly to educate in a renouncement of mankind, and who had generally completed their abjuration by marrying the baker." The ambiguity is sometimes avoided by a new formation with *human:* Tennyson L 1.12 for universal humankind.

5.2₅. Among derivatives *manly*, *mannish* and *manful* refer to male man (b), but *manlike* generally to both sexes (a). *Manhood* according to NED has the meanings: human nature (a), the state of being a man, as opposed to childhood (c) or as opposed to womanhood (b), the qualities eminently belonging to man, manliness (b), the adult male population (c).

In compounds preposed *man* is always used in sense (b): *man-servant*, *man-milliner* | Sterne M 1.92 Dr. Slop, the *man-widwife*'s house | Allen A 118 On her lap was a *man child*. | Waugh W 169 I doubt if a man often makes a *man friend* after boyhood. Thus also in the plural: Kipling DW 331 *men-visitors* | ib 359 her *men-folk*.

With regard to compounds containing *man* as the second element, we have various classes. *Man* is used in the sense (a) in the two old compounds to denote the two sexes: OE *wǣpnedman* or *wǣpman*, ME *weop-*

monn, and OE *wīfman*, whence modern *woman*. In modern usage, some compounds may be applied to both sexes: she is a good *horseman* | Norris O 312 Mrs. C. was a fashionable woman, the president or *chairman* of a score of clubs | Wells JP 445 That's all I have to say, Mr. Chairman (or 'My Lord,' or 'Mrs. Chairman,' as the case might be) | Elizabeth was a great *statesman* | Mrs. N was the *spokesman* of her sisters | Mottram EM 7 she prided herself on being a *sportsman* (as she called it, never a sportswoman) | Cather Lost Lady 116 Mrs. Forester is a fine *penman*. — But the forms *horsewoman*, *chairwoman*, *stateswoman*, *spokeswoman* are also in use and would be preferred in these cases by many; Wells H 244 writes "the very first task of our *Women Statesmen*" | Galsw SS 271 she noted the one *lady juryman*. — On *leman* see below, 5.3$_6$.

In another group of compounds *-man* is used exclusively of the male, and if a female is referred to, *-woman* is used: *kinswoman, madwoman, noblewoman, policewoman, postwoman, saleswoman, sportswoman*. Poutsma has an interesting quotation from Mrs. Gaskell, illustrating the difference between vocation-feminines and marriage-feminines: "The *post-woman* brought two letters. I say *post-woman*, but I should say *the postman's wife*." Cf also Di Do 109 Mrs. Pipchin was but an indifferent *pen-woman* | Stephen L 206 to hear a *female clergyman* or *clergywoman* (cf *lady juryman*, Galsw SS 271, above).

Some national denominations: *Englishman, Scotsman*, or *Scotchman, Irishman, Welshman, Frenchman, Dutchman* — are in the singular used of a male, in the plural also of both sexes (cf also *the English*, etc, generically, see vol II 11.5), while in the singular *Englishwoman, Scotchwoman* (hardly *Scotswoman*), etc, are said of a female. Similarly *Chinaman*, but also *a Chinese man*, if the male sex is emphasized, pl of both sexes *Chinamen* (and *Chinese*). I find both a *Bushman woman* (Westermarck M 366) and a *Bushwoman*.

Finally there are some compounds which are always used of males and have no corresponding forms in *-woman: alderman, footman, journeyman, yeoman*. To *gentleman* in one sense of the word *lady* is the corresponding female word: note Gissing H 55 She is a lady — *my* idea of a lady. Christopherson's a gentleman, too, there's no denying it — where the word *too* shows that there is one common notion underlying the two words, though there is no two-sex word to express it. *Gentlewoman* means 'woman of good birth or breeding' (NED).

Some compounds with *man* are now used to denote sexless things; thus *Indiaman, merchantman* = ships. *Man-of-war* was formerly = 'warrior' (thus Sh R2 II. 2.286, AV Luke 23.1 Herod with his men of war); now it is no longer applicable to a male being, but only to a ship.

The phrase *to a man*, in the sense 'without exception, unanimously,' may be used even when women only are concerned: NP 1906 [half jocularly] every woman, to a man, became a fierce advocate of admitting women to the suffrage. — Cf also Maxwell BY 124 She [an artist] told us of a grand one-man show that she was going to have next month.

Poutsma quotes from the Review of Reviews: "The lawyers have decided for us that the word 'man' always includes 'woman' where there is a penalty to be incurred, and never includes 'woman' when there is a privilege to be conferred."

5.2₆. *Spouse:* this word is literary and not much used. As a synonym *consort* is used of royal personages, often in compounds: *queen-consort, prince-consort*.

Child, it will be seen, has two significations, one in relation to age, and one in relation to the parents.

Youth as applied to a single young person should naturally be a two-sex word, and is sometimes found as such: NED has some examples (1580 *vertuous youthes of both sexes*, and 1881 *Before she was twenty she wrote verses like other youths*). But as a matter of fact it is most often used of young males, as in NED's quotations from Sh (He that hath a beard, is more then a youth: and he that hath no beard, is lesse then a man) and Milton (To many a youth, and many a maid). I may add one quotation: Locke W 3 large classes of tradesmen's children, both youths and maidens. (In Dan. *et ungt menneske*, though containing the two-sex word *menneske* is always understood of a young male). — Other quotations for *youth* in various senses are found in vol II 4.94.

5.3₁. (B) Next, we come to those cases in which we have only two, not three words.

Male:	Female:
bridegroom	bride
widower	widow
bachelor	spinster, old maid
brother	sister
uncle	aunt
nephew	niece
lover*	love, lady love, mistress*
gentleman	lady* (gentlewoman)
lord*	lady*
landlord*	landlady
sir*	lady*, madam
master*	mistress
mister (Mr.)	missis (Mrs.) and miss

schoolmaster	schoolmistress
monk (friar)	nun
wizard	witch
merman	(merwoman,) mermaid*
sloven*	slut, slattern

Note the transference of names of animals in the colloquial American *stag-party* and *hen-party* for parties consisting of respectively men and women only.

Lover: though the plural naturally refers to both sexes (*a pair of lovers*, etc) the sg is almost exclusively applied to the male (though NED has some old examples of the contrary use from old writers). Thus it is quite natural to say with Sh: *There was a lover and his lass*, but it would not be possible to say: *There was a lover and her lad*. In the predicative, it is possible to use the word of a woman in a somewhat different sense: *she is a great lover of music*. — As given above, *lover* for the man and *love* (*lady love*) for the woman, the words apply only to the mutual relation of a pair of lovers (*her lover, his love*). *Love* is used of a male in Sh Wiv III. 5.79 to search his house for his wiues loue. Differently in Quiller Couch T 86, where an Admiral is addressed by his wife: You are wet, my love.

Mistress is given above in two senses, cf also 5.3_3.

Sir is generally used only in speaking to or of a man; but sometimes, especially in Scotland, it is applied to a woman (NED from 1578 to 1818); *sirs* in adressing women twice in Sh (LL IV. 3.211, Ant IV. 15.85) and Scott A 1.230.

Note that *landlord* has two significations, (1) male host, with *landlady* as the corresponding feminine word; (2) owner of land, used of both sexes, as in Shaw 1.23 Lady Roxdale is one of the head landlords. — In a similar way *lord* and *master* have sometimes been used in speaking of women: Sh Merch III. 2.169 I [Portia] was the *Lord* of this faire mansion, *master* of my servants, Queene ore my selfe | Caine C 24 he was a poor curate in the country, where the *lord* of the manor chanced to be a lady.

Mermaid is perhaps preferred to *merwoman* on account of the alliteration.

It is not quite correct to say, as many grammars do, that *sloven* is exclusively used of males; as a matter of fact it is applied to either sex; see quotation in NED: she came in — a dirty sloven.

Witch was formerly applied to men as well as to women, now only to the latter, cf below, 5.3$_6$.

5.3$_2$. Here we have to consider those cases in which the name for one sex is derived from the other by means of an ending. Only in one case is it the name for the man that is formed from that of the corresponding feminine word, namely *widower* from *widow;* the social reason for this exception is obvious. In all other cases it is inversely the name for the female that is the derived one, chiefly by means of the ending *-ess*, as in *goddess*, see vol VI 19.1. When Shelley, according to Medwin 273, "used to say that every city had its Devil or its Diavolesse — we have no word in our language for the fiend feminine," he is not right, see NED *deviless* with quotations 1693, 1761, 1881.

"There is a derogatory touch in it [the ending *-ess*] which makes it unsuitable when we desire to show respect," says Curme (CG 228), and on the same assumption Fowler (MEU: Feminine designations) puts in a plea for an intenser use of this suffix concluding by three short selections of (A) established feminine titles, (B) recent or impugned ones, and (C) words unfortunately not provided with feminines, among them *artist, clerk, cook, cyclist, singer, teacher, typist*.

Other feminine endings are the learned *-(t)rix* as in *victrix*, see vol VI 15.9$_4$, *-ine* as in *heroine*, ib 21.4$_2$, and *-ina* as in *czarina*, ib 21.4$_4$.

On *-ette* in *suffragette* see vol VI 24.6$_3$. I might there have mentioned Trollope B 374 a leash of *baronets* and their *baronnettes* (neither correct French nor English).

In very few cases the French feminine *-e* has been used in English as an ending for women. *Confidant* for the man and *confidante* for the woman are sometimes found in E writing, though the sound is the same [kɔnfi'dænt]. Similarly *figurant, -ante*, further *protégé* and *protégée* (Di D 181), *fiancé* and *fiancée:* these words are generally marked in print as French by italics. *Coquet* is an adj for both sexes, but *coquette* is a sb used of a woman. Ruskin (Sel 1. 197) writes "the *lionne* of a ball-room" (cf below *lioness* of the animal). On *pianiste* of a woman player see vol VI 19.9$_2$. Sometimes *comédienne* and *tragédienne* are used as feminines to *comedian* and *tragedian*.

In two cases we have words from F with the ending *-eur* for the man and *-euse* for the woman: *accoucheur, -euse, masseur, -euse;* further *danseuse* corresponding to the two-sex word *dancer*.

5.3$_3$. The word from which a derivative in *-ess* is formed may in itself sometimes be used for the man (exclusively or generally), e.g. *governor, prince, shepherd*, sometimes for both sexes indiscriminately, e. g. *quaker, ancestor*. Some examples will illustrate these differences in concrete details.

When we speak of a *poetess*, we are thinking at the same time both of her quality as a poet and of her sex, as when we say "Mrs. Browning is one of the greatest English poetesses;" but as this splits the attention, it is a much greater praise to say "Mrs. B. was a real poet" than it would be to say "she was a real poetess." Thus Stedman has (NED): She [Miss Rossetti] is a poet of a profound and serious cast.

"We may speak of a woman as a successful *actor* (rather than *actress*), or as a brilliant or beautiful *actress* (rather than *actor*), according as the distinctive qualities of sex are ignored or emphasized" (Carpenter, Princ. E. Gr. 51). *Actress* was (see NED) originally used only = 'a female doer', not in the dramatic sense; now inversely, for we would say "The female prisoner appears to have been the chief actor in the tragic scene." Note the difference in the two substantives in Goldsm. 416 "Signora Mattei is at once both a perfect actress and a very fine singer." In the pl we find "actors and actresses" (Salt Joy 13), but also *actors* embracing both sexes; cf OHenry B 129 Actor people never stay long anywhere.

Doctor, in the sense 'medical practitioner', is used of both sexes; a woman is often specified as *woman-doctor*, *lady doctor* in the sense 'one who has taken a doctoral degree', *doctor* is a two-sex word. *Doctress* or *doctoress* is used only when the sex is emphasized: Brontë M 166 my mother herself is something of a doctress.

In the following quotation the pl *Jews* is first taken of males only, but later evidently of both sexes: Caine C 189 the audience consisted largely of lively German Jews and Jewesses in evening dress, some Polish Jews, and a sprinkling of other foreigners.

Mistress in some cases corresponds to *master*, e.g. *mistress of the house*, *mistress of her own fate;* placed before a name (written *Mrs.*) it corresponds to *Mister* (*Mr.*), but in the sense of 'female lover' it has no masculine correlative.

5.3₄. Where we have a separate word for the woman, it sometimes means 'having such and such a position or occupation', sometimes 'married to a man of such and such a position'. *Queen* has the former meaning in Queen Elisabeth, the latter in the case of the present Queen of England. An emperor's wife is an *empress*, but a murderer's wife is not a *murderess*. *Farmeress* in NED is defined (1) a woman who farms, (2) a farmer's wife.

Here is a list of marriage-nouns. With the exception of the two first they are used also in the first-named meaning. They refer chiefly to the higher social ranks. There are no such words corresponding to *author*, *negro*, etc.

Male:	Female:
Husband	wife
Mr.	Mrs.
emperor	empress
king	queen
viceroy	vicereine (rare)
prince	princess
duke	duchess
marquis	marchioness
earl, count	countess
viscount	viscountess
baron	baroness
lord, etc.	lady
mayor	mayoress
elector	electress
ambassador	ambassadress
landgrave	landgravine
margrave	margravine.

Further *bishopess* (nonce-word?, Philips L 96), *bank-cress* (nonce-word, Thack N 275).

Priestess generally designates a female priest, but may be used for a priest's wife, thus e.g. Trollope B 408, in Trollope B 164 we further find the unusual *prelatess* (prelate and prelatess) in the same sense. Cf also *knightess* in NED.

A woman may rank with a count or earl in her own right, or be married to a count or earl; in both cases she is a *countess*. *Lady*, besides corresponding in the ordinary way to gentleman, is a marriage-word to *Sir* and the titles above knights in rank. A Lord Mayor's wife is a *Lady Mayoress* (e.g. Ritchie M 86). *Electress* generally means the wife of a (German) Elector (of the Empire), rarely a woman having a vote.

5.3₅. (C.) We now come to the very comprehensive class of words for human beings which have no separate names for one of the sexes.

Cousin, relative, friend, guest, enemy, comrade, servant, slave, outlaw, fool, criminal, prisoner, thief, dwarf, neighbour, stranger, foreigner.

Agent-nouns like *thinker, writer, conqueror, interpreter, possessor, successor, intruder, liar; student, agent, inhabitant, copyist; musician, violinist, novelist, librarian; drunkard.*

European, American, Norwegian, Dane, Londoner, Oxonian.

Christian, Lutheran, methodist, Mohammedan, heathen, atheist.

Republican, democrat, socialist, partisan, candidate. member, etc.

An interesting case is seen in the Bible, Luke 15.6 and 9, the parable of the lost sheep and the lost piece of silver. In the Greek, and likewise in the Latin, Gothic, German, and Danish versions, the sex of those he or she calls together, is expressly indicated, because it can easily be done by means of an ending:

sugkalei tous philous kai tous geitonas ... sugkalei tas philas kai tas geitonas | convocat amicos et vicinos ... convocans amicas et vicinas | galaþoþ frijonds jah garaznans ... gahaitiþ frijondjos jah garaznons | ruffet er seinen freunden und nachbarn ... ruffet sie jren freundinnen und nachbarinnen | sammenkalder han venner og naboer ... sammenkalder hun veninder og naboersker. In the English versions the difference is not indicated: Wycl.: clepith togidir hise freendis and neiȝboris ... clepith togidir freendis and neiȝboris | AV: calleth together his friends and neighbours... calleth her friends and her neighbours together (thus also the OE versions, though Lindisf. has ðā wīf-frīondas & nēhebȳrildas, and Rushw. ðā wīf-frīondas & ðā nēhgibūras).

Cousin is one of the words applicable to both sexes, the French forms *cousin* and *cousine* have fallen together in English: Mary is John's cousin | John is Mary's cousin | GE M 1.336 Lucy's pitying questions about her poor cousins [i.e. Tom and Maggie] | Doyle G 46 [they were not lovers] It was cousin and cousin, she said.

On account of social conditions many words which properly belong to the two-sex class C have been and are practically always used of men only:

Shoemaker, baker, merchant, lawyer, soldier, general, bishop, etc. Nowadays this is being changed with regard to words like *professor, doctor, member of Parliament* and *mayor* (cf *Lady Mayoress* 5.3₄).

Some male words may in certain applications be used of women. *Captain* is so distinctly male that NED has no example of it being applied to a woman, but a girl may be captain of the school hockey team or a *guide captain*. Cp. also "she is a good *sailor*."

5.3₆. Some words which were formerly used of both sexes, have now been restricted to the female sex. Thus some expressions for contemptible women: *leman*, OE *lēof-man* 'dear man' (*man* = 'human being'), Ch

B 917 he sholde Hir lemman be (cf ib A 4247, H 204, 205, 238; female: H 220), Maundev. 25 he wolde ben hire limman; Sh Wiv IV. 2.172 his wiues lemman, but fem. Tw II. 3.26, H4B V. 3.49; now only used of females, but obsolete in ordinary language. *Harlot* till the middle of 17th c. was used of both sexes, now only of a female. *Bawd* formerly very often used of a male 'go-between', from ab. 1700 only of females. *Witch* used of both sexes in Sh and BJo, now only of a woman; *witch* is combined with *wizard* to denote the two sexes in Hawthorne Sn 77, Kipling J 2.70 father and mother .. confess they were witch and wizard; but ib 77 *witches* is used in the pl of both sexes: "she and I are witches" [said the man]. *Shrew* now only of a woman; thus also generally *slut* and *slattern*, though NED has the latter word used of a man in Thackeray, and Bennett writes A 47 his puffed, heavy face ... gave the idea of a vast and torpid male slattern.

In the same way, *nurse*, *dressmaker*, and *milliner* are chiefly, if not exclusively, used of women. The bedmaker (in slang *bedder*) in English colleges, is a woman.

It is natural that changed social conditions may influence the use of a word; thus it has been said pointedly, though inexactly, that in the sixties, the word *teacher* in the United States changed gender, as most teachers before the Civil War were men while now most are woman.

Girl was formerly applied to either sex (hence we sometimes in early texts find *a knave girl* = 'a boy'), but since 15th c. only to female children. Similarly *wench*.

The substantives *prude*, *jilt* (and *coquette*) are nearly always applied to women; occasionally we may find *a male jilt*, etc.

Child, of course, is a two-sex word, but the NED remarks: "It has been pointed out that *child* or *my child* is by parents used more frequently (and longer) of, and to, a girl than a boy. Shakspere nowhere uses 'my child' of or to a son, but frequently of or to a daughter"; it quotes Wint III. 3.7 A very pretty barne: A boy, or a childe I wonder? — and from Notes & Q. 1876: a country woman (in Shropshire) said to me, apropos of a baby, 'Is it a lad or a child?'

Gossip is thus defined in NED 1. a godfather or godmother 2. friend, chum. Formerly applied to both sexes, now only (somewhat arch.) to women ... 3. a person, mostly a woman ... who delights in idle talk. According to Al. Schmidt senses 2 and 3 are in Sh found only of women, but I have found a modern example of *gossip* applied to a loquacious man (Pinero S 2).

Gipsy, too, though naturally a two-sex word, is used contemptuously with the special meaning of 'a cunning or deceitful woman', but not correspondingly of a man.

But I have never found a single instance of words originally designating female beings being made into names for either both sexes or specifically for males, still less of an ending used at first to derive feminines being later used to form masculines. It cannot be called an exception when *maid*, *maiden*, and *virgin* are (or were) sometimes used to denote sexual purity and thus applied to men as well as to women, for these words cannot properly be said then to denote *male* beings. Examples:

Malory 723 thou [Galahad] hast ben a clene mayden as I [Ioseph] have ben and am | Sh Tw V. 1. 270 You [Olivia] are betroth'd both to a maid and man. Hence Ben Jonson (q NED) speaks of "two noble maids of either sexe, to union sacrificed."

Virgin: AV Rev 14.4 These are they which were not defiled with women: for they are virgines (20th C. V. they are as pure as virgins).

Still less have I been able to find an example in any language of a derivative ending used first to form feminines, later to form common-sex words or masculines. This, however, has often been asserted of the ending *-ster*, see now vol VI 15.1.

5.3₇. Language is often capricious in the way in which some words are provided with feminine derivatives, and others not, as seen, for instance in the following collocations: Shaw StJ 14 that she was a *liar* and *impostor*, that she was a *sorceress* | ib 33 she was tried, not as a *traitress*, but as a *heretic, blasphemer, sorceress* and *idolater* | Bennett Cd 135 the Countess of Chell ... that great *aristocrat ... Mayoress ... witch ... benefactor ... patroness* | Walpole OL 198 then you will be a *murderess* as well as a *thief*.

In the predicative, it is often possible to use a distinctly male word of a woman, the sex being sufficiently indicated in the subject: she was *master* of the situation | Tracy P 189 At any rate, she was *victor* in a struggle of which she had not the slightest knowledge | She is a very good *judge* of character | Shaw Ms 141 (Queen Elizabeth speaking) it is well that I am a merciful *prince* (NED has some examples from 1560 to 1650 of *prince* applied to a female sovereign, but this is different). Cp. the examples of *lover* 5.3_1 and *Satan* below. In the same way a German would say "Die frau war sein feind", although the word *feindin* exists, and a Dane: "Hun er en ven av tyskerne", not "en veninde".

Servant is a two-sex word, as used, e.g. in signing a letter "Your humble servant." The word, however, in consequence of social conditions is chiefly used of female domestic servants.

Cook, which in OE was masculine (gen. *cōces*, pl *cōcas*), is now used of a man in ships, and colleges, cf also *pastrycook*, but in ordinary houses of a woman. — *Housekeeper* is a woman, but *householder* is a two-sex word.

Fellow is a two-sex word in *school-fellow, fellow sufferer* and other combinations, where it means 'companion'; but used by itself it is chiefly a familiar synonym of 'male person'. The synonym *chap* is generally male; cf, however, Macdonald Rasp 176 My dear chap! You poor child! — to a girl.

5.3s. The predominance of the male sex is shown in the fact that when a two-sex word is used without any qualifying word, it will in many combinations naturally be understood to refer to a man. Thus with some words indicating nationality: when I say "The other day an Italian told me ..." it will be taken to have been a man — if it had been a woman, it would be necessary to say *an Italian lady* (or *woman*), though in the plural *Italians* refers to both sexes: *there are a great many Italians in France;* thus also *every Italian* knows that | *no Italian* would ever do that, etc. Similarly with *Spaniard, Jew, negro,* etc.

Heir is a two-sex word in spite of the existence of the derivative *heiress*, which is generally used with the specific sense of a rich marriageable lady; therefore we have e.g. AV Prov 30.23 an handmayd that is heire to her mistresse | Victoria was heir to the throne | the only heir was Miss Mary, etc.

Hero to some extent is a two-sex word in spite of the existence of *heroine*. Prof. Campbell writes of Meredith (*Univ. of Wisconsin Studies* 1918. 325), "All his heroes are heroines" — the same idea could have been expressed in a less pointed way: all his principal characters are women.

Though *angels* are generally imagined as male beings, (Gr. *aggelos*, Lat. *angelus*), there is no objection to using it in a transferred sense of a woman, as when Romeo (II. 2.26) says to Juliet: "Oh speake againe bright angell". In a similar way: She is a little *Satan*.

5.3₉. How to specify sex with two-sex words? Compounds with *man* were mentioned above, 5.2₅. Cf *gentleman friend, boy friend, girl friend*. We say *women doctors*, but *beggar women*. The adjs *male* and *female* are always handy: I expect to see my oldest male friend there, etc.

Note *buck:* Bell Prec. Porc. 205 Until that night he had been, in the quaint colloquialism, a buck virgin. In U.S. slang *buck nigger* = 'negro man'.

Girl may be preposed: Gosse F 86 my girl-cousins | Ru S 12 some girl readers | ib 32 my girl friends | girl graduates.

With inverted order: *servant-girl*. In the same sense *maid-servant* is used; the corresponding male is either *man-servant* or *servant-man*. Cf also *bachelor girl* (Waugh W 82, Lowndes Ivy 68). *Maid child* (Sh Per V. 3.6).

Lady is often preposed and then has lost its specific sense and has become more or less a mere mark of sex: Ru F 185 my young lady readers | Brontë V 64 the lady-chief of an English school | lady friend | lady acquaintance (Kaye-Smith GA 80).

But *tom-boy* means a romping girl: Aumonier OB 145 Motlie, in spite of her delicate appearance was a regular tomboy.

Preposed *he* or *she* are not very often applied to names of persons. Marlowe F 417 a hee diuell and a shee diuell ... all hee diuels ... all shee diuels | Sh Wint IV. 4.211 a shee-angell | H4B V. 4. 25 you shee-knight-errant | Swift 1.248 she-companions | Lamb letter (in Campbell's Coleridge 111) the She-Coleridges | Wilkins

P 60 by the hee bawds ... the she bawd (cf 5.3₆) |
Wells T 104 she-creatures. Note the Amr *a he-man*
= 'a very masculine man': Plunket Greene 28 a dim
collection of he-men. Facetiously *a Shebrew* = 'Jewish
girl' (Frankau My Unsent. Journey 262).

The adjectives *male* and *female* are naturally much
used. Sh A5 I. 2.54 sole heir male | Per Prol: female
heir | Sh John III 4.79, AV Mat 1.16 male child.

The adjectives *fair, gentle,* and *lovely* are in old-
fashioned novels added to the word *reader*, as in Thack
N 137 I think of a lovely reader laying down the page
and looking over at her unconscious husband. But ib
638 he uses the words *gentle reader* of both sexes: If
my gentle reader has had sentimental disappointments,
he or she is aware that the friends who have given
him most sympathy, have had dismal histories of their
own — where we note also the substitution of *him* in
the second place for *him or her.* — Cf also Sh Wint IV.
4.503 my faire belou'd H.

Note these two quotations: By L 248 English women
wear better than their continental neighbours of the
same sex | Christie LE 224 People discussing their
friends of the opposite sex.

Finally I may mention the legal Act for shortening the
language used in acts of Parliament (13 &14 Victoria
cap. 21, June 16, 1850): That in all acts words import-
ing the masculine gender shall be deemed and taken to
include females, and the singular to include the plural,
and the plural the singular, unless the contrary as to
gender and number is expressly provided.

Animals

5.4₁. (A) Here we sometimes find three distinct
names, showing that the interest is greater in the
diversity than in the underlying common notion.

Both sexes:	Male:	Female:
horse	stallion	mare
foal	(colt)	filly
ox (collective: cattle)	bull	cow (heifer)
sheep	ram (wether)	ewe
swine, pig, hog	boar	sow
(red) deer	stag, hart	hind
fallow deer	buck	doe
fowl	cock, rooster	hen
bee	drone	queen-bee.

Colt is generally a two-sex word. *Wether* is generally a castrated ram. *Bullock* or *ox* is a castrated bull. *Fowl* is often a collective, or else used in reference to the meat. *Rooster* is chiefly dial. and U. S.

5.4₂. (B) In the following cases we have two distinct words, sometimes the word for the male used also for either sex:

dog (hound)	bitch (brach)
ruff	reeve.

But in other cases the name for the female is used (chiefly in the pl) for both sexes:

gander	goose
t(i)ercel	falcon
drake	duck
cob(-swan)	swan.

Only with some feline animals are there derivatives in *-ess*, while the word without that ending is used both as a two-sex word and for the male: *lion: lioness*, *tiger: tigress*, and the rarer *leopardess* and *pantheress*. *Doggess* is very rare and chiefly used of women (Huxley L 2.239 the anti-vivisection pack-dogs and doggesses).

Note the use in Freeman Th 138 a beautiful American widow was the lion (or should we say lioness?) of the season: Cf above *lionne*, 5.3$_2$.

The ending *-ine* (cf vol VI 21.4$_2$) is found in *wolverine* (Wells Ma 2.216).

5.4₃. (C) To indicate sex with regard to all other animals we must have recourse either to the adjs *male* or *female*, or else to compounds. In some cases we have Christian names, in others names of such animals as distinguish sex. Thus we have:

Both sexes:	Male:	Female:
otter	dog-otter	bitch-otter
fox	dog-fox	bitch-fox
cat	tom-cat	tabby-cat, tib-cat
donkey, ass	jackass	jenny-ass
goat	billy-goat	nanny-goat
roe, roe-deer	roe-buck	roe-doe
hare	buck-, jack-hare	doe-hare?
rabbit	buck-rabbit	doe-rabbit
rat	buck-rat	she-rat
ape	jack-ape	she-ape
peafowl	peacock	peahen
robin	cock-robin	jenny-robin
heathbird	heathcock	heathhen
black grouse	blackcock	grey-hen
pheasant	cock-pheasant	hen-pheasant
pigeon	cock-pigeon	hen-pigeon
sparrow	cock-sparrow, jack-sparrow	hen-sparrow

Tom cat dates from a book "Life and Adventures of a Cat" (1760).

Note that *buck* has lost its old special signification

'male of the goat' and is now used only in the combinations mentioned above.

The OE *fyxen* 'she-fox' is continued in ModE as *vixen*, generally applied to a quarrelsome woman, see vol I 2.538. I find in Kingsley H 144 the old vixen-fox took care to get her profit out of the bargain. *Bitchfox* is applied to a woman in Gammer 138. Cf Huxley L 2.11 two foxes ... a fine dog fox and his vixen wife, Sh Tro II. 1.11 bitch-wolf. To *heathbird* there is a collective *heathgame*, and to *black grouse* a collective *black game*.

Other compounds are *tom lion, cow rhinoceros, turkey cock, jack merlin* (see NED: *merlin*).

A motley collection of quotations to illustrate these and similar names: Caxton R 73 the she ape | Marlowe J 409 shee asses | Sh Lr III. 6.25 [Q] you shee foxes (his daughters) | As IV. 1.161 cock pigeon | ib III. 2.86 she lamb | Merch II. 1.29 she bear | Tro II. 1.11 bitch-wolf | Walton A 43 bitch otter | ib 91 the female trout ... the male trout | ib 147 a he and a she pike | Merriman S 129 he would be afraid of a cock pheasant, though he would be plucky enough among the hens | Stevenson B 34 jack-sparrow | Hewlett Q 131 hen-sparrow | London W 85 ptarmigan hens | Lawrence L 124 a lovely dog-fox | ib 135 the she-fox | Rose Macaulay T 13 a cock canary | London M 265 the bull-seal | Masefield S 197 the toms [i. e. wild cats] are as bad as the shes | Butler W 79 if his father does not know a cock from a hen lobster ... till that moment I had not so much as known that there were cocks and hens among lobsters.

Plants

5.4₄. With plants, the discovery of sex has not left any mark in language, with the sole exception of *carl* *hemp*, which should etymologically denote the male plants, but is really used of the female plant because it is bigger; the other sex is called *fimble hemp* (through Low German from F *femelle*). Botanists of course speak of male and female plants.

Pronouns

5.5₁. Many pronouns are absolutely indifferent to sex, thus *I*, *you; they; mine, yours, theirs*, the interrogative *which*, and finally (cf 5.1₃) all the adjunctal pronouns.

A distinction between a two-sex word and a no-sex word is made with

Interrogative	*who*	—	*what*
Relative	*who*	—	*which*
Indefinite	*someone, somebody*	—	*something*,

and similarly the corresponding forms with *any*, *no*, *every*.

It is quite natural that *I* and *you* have no separate sex-forms, as the sex will practically always appear from the situation (at any rate when *you* is addressed to one person).

It is similarly natural that we should have common-sex interrogative pronouns, *who* and *which* (*of you*), as it happens very often that in asking such a question as "Who bought it?" we do not know whether the buyer was a he or a she.

On the distinction in the *wh*-pronouns (relative and interrogative) see vol III ch VI, on *whose* below, Case.

A triple division is only found in the third person sg: *he* of male beings, *she* of female beings, and *it* of sexless things.

The ordinary use of *he* and *she* as applied to human beings naturally presents no difficulty.

But we have two opposite tendencies in the use of these three pronouns. One may be termed desexualizing, when *it* is applied to beings really provided with sex, and the other sexualizing, when *he* or *she* is applied to sexless things.

5.5$_2$. The want of a both-sex pronoun in the third person sg is often felt; it is remedied by

(1) the clumsy: *he or she*, as in Fielding T 1.174 the reader's heart (if he or she have any) | Thack P 3.294 every woman and man in this kingdom who has sold her or himself | Mulock H 2.128 each one made his or her comment | Doyle St 66 the murderer has written with his or her own blood.

(2) *he* alone, thus especially before a relative clause, as in AV Mark 4.9 he that hath eares to heare, let him heare | Luke 11.23 he that is not with me, is against me. This was legalized by the Act 13 & 14 Vict. Cap. 21.4, see above, 5.3$_{10}$. Further Maugham FPS 170 [lady speaking:] And we've decided that if either of us wants his liberty the other will place no obstacles in the way of his getting it | Canfield Her Son's Wife 120 She looks to me like a person that's walking in his sleep.

(3) *they*, as the plural makes no distinction as to sex: nobody prevents you, do they? See vol II 5.56, with many quotations from Sh, Thackeray, Austen, Ruskin, etc. An English friend writes that *they* may also be used in other cases, e.g. I can hear someone talking in the hall. I don't know their name | Yes, I had a friend with me. I didn't bring them in because I didn't know if you'd care to see them.

(4) a preposed *thou* has not been successful, see Murray D 186, Progr. §§ 24 and 204.

On *it* see below.

5.5₃. *It* is a sexless pronoun for things that have no natural sex (the sun, a star, earth, stone, door, space, time, argument, etc, etc). Other less concrete uses were treated in more detail in the chapter on Person, ch 4.

But *it* may also be used about such beings as have really a sex, thus not only plants, but also animals, especially lower ones, whose sex is not obvious, or in which the speaker takes no particular interest, and even about a child to avoid the clumsy *his or her:* a child does not always love its parents of its own accord. *It* is not infrequently said of a baby (though parents, nurse, etc, will naturally use *he* or *she* instead). Thus Sh Ro I. 3.30 [nurse speaking of Juliet:] when it did tast the worme-wood on the nipple of my dugge ... to see it teachie [i.e. tetchy] | Fielding T 1.10 She must take care of the child, and in the morning he would give orders to provide it a nurse ... the hussy its mother | By DJ 2.148 Hushed as a babe upon its mother's breast | Bennett HM 50 your two-year-old babe may defy you by the instinctive force of its personality. This desexualizing use of *it* is similar to the use of the word *thing* about a human being: Poor little thing!

It is used of the [male] ghost in Hml I. 1.40 Looke where it comes againe ... Speake to it, Horatio. Lookes it not like the King?, etc.

5.5₄. As *God* is referred to as *he* (most often with capital letter: *He*) and *who*, so are also often veiled expressions for God: Sh John V. 7.60 heauen he knowes how we shall answer him | Cowper L 1.134 the intention of *Providence* when *he* endued them with the faculty of speech | Bennett W 1.60 in those days *Providence* was still busying *himself* with everybody's affairs | Compton-Burnett, Brothers and Sisters

99 "Providence might have kept it back altogether, if *it* had kept it back as long as that." — "Is Providence 'it'?" said Tilly | Rose Macaulay O 7 Strange indeed are the ways of Providence, *which* had thought fit, in *its* inscrutable wisdom to save the doctor. — Cf, on the other hand, with the Latin gender of *providentia* Bridges, Bradley 12 Nor was his good Providence deserting him. *She* was holding a trump up *her* sleeve | McKenna Sh 15 Poor providence! Sometimes I think *she* has punished the English in advance. — Cf further By DJ 3.104 all that springs from the great *Whole*, *Who* hath produced, and will receive the soul. — It is rare to find *which* referring to *God:* Froude C 4.260 I could only believe in a *God which* did something. — *Fate* is made feminine (like *Nature*) in spite of Lat. *fatum:* Browning 1.205 let *fate* reach me how *she* likes | Galsw Car 908 Fate would turn *her* thumb down on them.

5.5₅. A predicative is, at any rate often, felt as a neuter, i.e. it is referred to by means of the sexless pronouns (see vol II 16.344 and PhilGr 242). This is true not only of the predicative after a finite vb, but also in a dependent nexus.

Thus *it:* She is a witch, and she looks it | Carlyle FR 490 long years ago it was borne on his mind that he was to be Finance-Minister; and now he was it | Benson C 6 "Be good, sweet maid, and in course of time you will become stupid and ugly." They now, most of then, become it.

That: Gissing R 107 All men my brothers? Nay, thank Heaven, that they are not | id G 288 Narrow-minded? You admit they are that? | Kipling S 64 I thought he was only a beast. — He's that, too, of course, but he's worse | Hope D 91 And what an angel Mrs. Musgrave is! — Well, I should hardly call her that.

This: Brontë J 188 she assured me she would not stir till I was ready. This I quickly was.

Interrogative *what.* Nowadays *What is he?* generally asks about a man's profession, but also about his general qualities. In ElE the same question was often used where PE would employ *Who is he?* (where we may doubt which of the words is subject, which predicative) in asking about a person's name or identity: Sh Oth I. 1.95 what are you? My name is Roderigo | John I. 1.35 What art thou? The son and heire to that same Faulconbridge (cf Franz[3] p. 304 f.). Note that ElE has not *what* for *who* in other positions.

Examples of *what* in the modern sense: Sh Merch I. 3.162 O father Abram, what these Christians are! (exclamation) | R3 I. 3.132 if you forget What you haue beene ere this | Hope D 7 You're so very elliptical. So very what? | ib 53 When you were young, were you ever — ? he paused. — Was I ever what, George? — In love || NED q 1854 Who or what he was ... no one ever cared to inquire.

Relative *which:* Di F 261 I propose to be of some use to somebody — which I never was in this world | Stephen L 139 he could be impatient which no clergyman ought to be | Gissing G 179 they would talk like gods — which indeed they are.

A few other neutral predicatives (note the pl): Di X 21 the arms were very long and muscular; the hands the same | Doyle S 6.151 He was noble, unselfish, loving — all that my husband was not | Kaye-Smith HA 201 She had always been friendly, interested, sympathetic; but he had felt that if she loved him she would not have been quite all these — not quite so kind or friendly or patient.

5.5₆. The neuter idea may also be expressed by *thing,*

not only in the ordinary pronouns: Hope D 6 He was everything he shouldn't be | James A 1.168 I did not say she was too fond! She is not too anything! | Locke FS 187 He is good and kind, and noble, and everything that is right | Galsw T 79 I'm quite serious. Never knew you anything else | to earn his living as a clerk or something of the kind | Walpole DF 129 Nikitin was an idealist, a mystic, a dreamer — everything that Semyonov was not | ib 159 she was honest, impetuous, pure, if ever woman was those things | Walker L 833 Macaulay entered the House of Commons as member for Calne, and as that thing which he had been certain he would never be, a Whig | Gissing G 387 Edwin and Harold seem to you inert, flabby, weakly envious, foolishly obstinate, impiously mutinous, and many other things | Bromfield ModHero 193 men ... who were engineers and business managers and a dozen other things || Byron DJ 3.51 He enter'd in the house no more his home, A thing to human feelings the most trying.

5.5₇. A (comprehensive) neutral idea is often expressed by the pl *things* or *matters:* Quincey 88 things had not yet come to Sinbad's state of desperation | Di D 650 you won't mind things going a tiny morsel wrong, sometimes | id Do 188 let me know how things are going | Shaw P 281 Saylors always understand things | Kipling L 68 you know things and the ways of doing things | ib. let things stay as they are | id J 1.13 if things came to fighting || Marlowe F (1616) 772 there be of vs here, that haue waded as deep into matters as other men | Austen M 297 how matters stand between you | Di D 227 Mr. M. tried to be talkative, but was not at his ease, and made matters worse | Kipling J 2.128 that made matters rather worse.

A verbal idea is similarly referred to by a neutral

pronoun: He never complains, but that is what she does every day | I go there whenever I have time, which isn't often.

5.6₁. With regard to animals the only general rule that can be established is that when a speaker takes a special interest in a particular animal he will specify the sex by using *he* or *she*. Where there is no such personal interest or sympathy, *it* will generally be used. Still there is a strong tendency to 'sexualize' the names of animals, i.e. to use *he* or *she* without regard to the actual sex. Sweet says that "*dog, horse, fish, canary* are generally masc., while *cat, hare, parrot* are generally feminine." Elsewhere he says: "children will even speak of their *silkworms* as *she*" (Storm EPh 1018).

5.6₂. Wheeler says (*Journal of Germ. Philol.* 2.536): "The pronoun *he* is commonly used of a horse, when no reference whatever to sex is intended, but simply to express a slightly increased degree of sympathy with the animal as compared with what would be expressed by *it*. In speaking of a cat we should use *she* for the same purpose. The use of *he* would involve a somewhat offensive allusion to sex, not contained in the use of *she*."

5.6₃. According to the overwhelming number of quotations collected by W. Sattler (Anglia 14. 193 ff.), the prevailing tendency in ordinary modern prose is to refer to any animal, whether a mammal, a bird, a reptile, or an insect, etc, as *he*, if *it* is not used. The rule sometimes given that *he* is used in reference to strong or big animals and *she* in reference to weak or small animals, is absolutely wrong. Even such a name as *goose* may be mentioned as *he* when the individual sex is taken no account of: "Not a bird is visible. Yes, one! — a goose — he is swimming straight this way." When a bird is mentioned in connexion with its *young* *ones*, *brood*, or *nest*, *she* is very often said; but when there is no such inducement to think of the female sex, *he* is nearly always preferred.

In the old language there was a greater tendency to use the pronoun *she;* thus the Bible has: They are like the deafe *adder* that stoppeth *her* eare (Ps 58.4) | the *storke* in the heauen knoweth *her* appointed times (Jer. 8.7). This usage has been kept up by poets who will often refer to birds especially as *she*, where the ordinary language of prose would have *he*. Similarly sportsmen will often speak of a *hare* as *she*, especially in the phrase, "the hare in her form", and of a *fish* as *she;* similarly whalers speak of a *whale* as *she*.

5.6₄. Very often *he* or *she* and *it* may be used in the same sentence, e.g. A *doe* was brought up from a little fawn with a dairy of cows; with them *it* goes a-field. The dogs of the house take no notice of this deer, being used to *her* | This young *leopard* was about to try *his* teeth on the dead body of a gazelle, which *its* mother had just captured | Do not hurt the *mole*. *He* is continually destroying grubs. No trace of vegetation is ever found in *its* stomach | A *rat*, though living in and among garbage, is always clean in *its* person, and *his* teeth are always beautifully clean | A *swan* ... *him* ... *he* ... *it* ... *its* | The *frog* was evidently much alarmed. *It* repeatedly shook off the enemy by jumping, and then threw *himself* out of pursuit.

5.6₅. I now give some quotations from my own collections: Sh Ado III. 3.74 the ewe that will not heare her *lambe* when *it* baes, will neuer answere a *calfe* when *he* bleates | As IV. 1.54 a *snaile* for though *he* comes slowly, hee carries his house on his head | AV Prov 6.6 Goe to the *ant*, thou sluggard, consider *her* wayes, and be wise. 7 Which [the ant] ... *her*

meat | Walton A 22 *cuttle-fish* .. *her* .. *she* | 41 *otter* ..
her, she, she, him, his, he | 48 *chub* .. *him* | 59 *chevin* ..
him | 89 *trout* .. *he,* thus also 94 of *brandling,* 96 of
minnow, 132 of *salmon,* 179 of *pearch,* 193 of *eele* | 145
pike .. *he* never eats a venemous *frog* till *he* hath first
killed *her* (frog, she, also 88) | 190 *lamprey, her* | 207
hare, her | Defoe R 100 the *Turtle* ... I found in *her*
threescore Eggs | Fielding 6,59 a poor *hare, which* is
certain, whenever *it* ventures abroad, to meet *its*
enemies | Cowper L 1.47 my *linnet;* I keep *him* in a
cage | Wordsw 481 *linnet* ... *his* music .. *throstle* ..
He, too, is no mean preacher | ib 195 The *hare* is running
races in *her* mirth; also 490 | Shelley 403 *spider* .. *she;
silkworm* ... *his* | Quincey O 421 a *crocodile* ... *him* |
Peacock M 183 a *frog* ... *him* | Di B 1.131 he supposed
the *Bee* liked to make honey, or *he* wouldn't do it |
Kinglake E 164 the *camel* kneels to receive *her*
load ... *she* ... | Holmes A 95 a *Canary-bird* ... hung
him up in a cage | Ruskin Sel 2.248 the *fly* ... there is
no courtesy in *him;* the *earthworm* has *his* diggings;
the *bee her* gatherings and building; the *spider her*
cunning network; the *ant her* treasury | Hardy R 255
a *sparrow* ... *he* | Wilde L 195 the howling *swan,*
which, still looking down, waileth *her* end | Kipling
L 3 the *goat* ... *he* | Fludyer 102 *cat* ... *him* (N.B.
mentioned as a she-cat) | Stevenson M 180 the big
and foul *fly,* that lives on carrion, had set up *his* nest
in the rotten woodwork | id T 110 I saw *snakes,* and
one raised *his* head | Caine E 423 the *cat* took *his* place
on the gravel path | Benson N 9 a *cat* or two stretches
himself on the grass | ib 181 a *grouse* ... *he* | Butler
Ess 219 *penguin* ... *he* | Bennett A 32 the Persian
cat ... *he;* also ib 37, but 207 *it* | Mackenzie S 1.82 he
felt as the ugly *duckling* must have felt when *he* saw

himself to be a radiant swan | Hemingway Sun Also R 124 the first *trout* ... *He* ... *his* ... *him*.

Knutson, *Gender of Words*, etc, p. 74 ff. gives many quotations for the use of pronouns in speaking of animals.

5.7. As stated in vol III 6.3$_5$ the relative pronoun *who* is generally used in reference to animals, where *he* or *she* would be used, and *which* corresponding to *it*. To the examples there given, also of inconsistencies, the following may be added: Southey L 32 the *bulls* ... were quiet, harmless *animals*, *whom* a child might safely have played with ... The fiercest of the whole was one of the four *who* were only tormented | Kinglake E 219 the *dromedary which* fell to his lot ... *he* (but ib 222 my poor *dromedary* ... *she*) | Benson D 2.45 a *thrush*, perhaps the same *which* had called Dodo to the window. *He* ... *his* ... *he* ... | Pennell L 17 With the *cat itself* I had no fault to find. *It* was a charming creature to *whom* I gladly would have given shelter | Galsw SS 141 everything [was] removed, except the *cats*, *who* lay replete before the fire | Wells ScL 255 Our *amphibian* ancestor, *which* certainly had no more brains than a frog, could give rise to descendants with the brains of men.

Of plants: Shelley 655 *lily* of the vale, *whom* ... its tremulous bells. Cf Tennyson 248, where the *yew*, though addressed in the second person, yet has *which:* Old Yew, which graspest ... Thy fibres ... Thy roots.

Relative *who* or *which* as referring to human beings depends chiefly on the corresponding use of *he*, *she*, or *it;* thus after *child:* she had only one child, which was still-born | She has only one child, who is now in Australia.

Bank = *bankers* in Plunket Greene E 47 The Southern Bank, who were financing the transaction.

5.81. The use of the pronouns *he* or *she* in speaking of inanimate things always implies a strong personal feeling of affection.

The usage in sailors' language (in many counries) to sexualize a ship as *she* is often attributed to the fact that most names of ships are feminine; cf, however, Morsbach, *Gramm. und psych. Geschlecht im Engl.* p. 27 on OF influence.

Examples: Sh Tp I. 2.7 a braue *vessell* (Who had no doubt some noble creature in *her*) (but once *him* about a ship in the (spurious) Pericles V prol. 18) | Franklin A 185 another *packet* arrived, *she* too was detained | Doyle G 33 an old *merchantman* ... *her* yards were square, and *she* was running with all sails set. — Note Archer Am 8 The Lucania has no individuality as a ship. It — I instinctively say "it," not "she" — is merely a rather low-roofed hotel.

This even applies to ships with a masculine name, e.g. BBC 1944 The *Tirpitz* ... *she*.

This sexualization is extended by railwaymen and others to trains and engines: Anstey V 286 she will be in in another minute | Buchanan F 11 when an Irish train steamed out of Euston, I was one of her passengers | Freeman Th 27 [railwayman:] a goods train takes some stopping; before they could bring her up, the engine had gone over the poor beggar | Brett Young PC 474 The Scotch express was fifty late at Durby, and they've got to get her clear before they think of locals. Ay, here she comes | Rolt, Sleep No More 92 he caught the sound of the 'Mountaineer' [train] beating it up the bank ... well up to her time.

A motor-car is constantly spoken of as *she* (quotations Kaye-Smith HA 149, Williamson L 29, Bennett LR 12, Galsw TL 53, MW 232, Frat 90, Locke GP 13, Oppenheim Laxw 201, Lewis B 36, MS 54).

Professor O. Vočadlo heard the following assertion in BBC: The tank is the queen of the battlefield.

See also a long article by T. H. Svartengren in AmSp 5.85 ff. on the increasing colloquial use in U.S. of *she* referring to things, actions, etc: it is chiefly found in men's talk and has a strongly marked emotional character and shows a feeling of companionship between a man and his tools. *It* mentions the fact, more or less coldly and indifferently.

5.8$_2$. On the other hand many men will use *he* in speaking of their pipe, watch, etc. (But note Meredith E 248 she [his watch] was four minutes in arrear). Cf also Bentley T 117 a little leaden bullet ... Is that the one ? — That's him — Lodged in the bone at the back of the skull | Galsw Escape 51 Do you know the turnip in a state of nature, Sir ? He's a homely fellow | ib 54 cigar ... I shall down him next time | McKenna M 36 [a pearl necklace] Isn't he a ripper? I got him in Paris for Dina | Childers R 218 anchor ... the rusty monster himself | Pascoe PS 254 [Charterhouse] Any cake is called a *he*, but a cold plum-pudding of a more "stodgy" nature is termed a *she*.

Two old quotations for *he:* Swift 3.94 we reeft the foresail and set him | Sterne M 1.116 ... sees no ... prison opening his gates upon him.

In dialects the usage varies (Wright, *Rustic Sp.* 144): "In Sc., Irel. and the dialects of the northern counties the feminine pronoun is used [of inanimate objects], while in the Midlands, the e.s. and sw. counties, the use is variable."

5.8$_3$. While the sexualization so far considered is popular and colloquial, we have in other cases a purely literary attribution of sex to objects of nature and to abstract notions, which are otherwise always spoken of as *it*. The choice of *he* or *she* depends chiefly on the Latin gender (and French, which agrees with Latin), but often also on the writer's imagination, which represents something to him as masculine or feminine. It is characteristic of Shakespeare and Ben Jonson that when they differ in the "sex" which they attribute to the same thing, we see the free play of the imagination in the case of the former, and strict adherence to classical gender in the latter. For Sh, see Franz p. 203 ff, for Tennyson see Dyboski p. 334; also E Ausbüttel, *Das persönl. geschlecht unpersönl. subst.* (Halle 1904) and Knutson, *Gender of words denoting living beings* (Lund 1905).

The personification or animation shown in the use of pronouns like *he* or *she* is essentially the same that leads us to expressions like "Fortune smiled on him" and that led the King in Sh H4B IV. 5.92 to say "Thy wish was father, Harry, to that thought" (which in Galsw FM 173 becomes "Your wish is mother to your thought" and in McKenna, While I Remember 149 to "The wish being parent to the thought"). On differences in this respect in different languages and difficulties in translations on that account see PhilGr 236.

Nature of course is *she* (e.g. Lytton K 54). So is *the world* in spite of Latin and French: Mackenzie S 1.82 The world was opening *her* arms and calling to Michael.

Soul, mind, etc: Sterne M 1.132 that part where the *soul* principally took up *her* residence | similarly Spectator 143 and Brontë V 156 | Sterne M 1.111 the *mind* ... within *herself* | Bennett LR 122 to restore ordinary British *common sense* to *her* throne | Butler Er 285 Common Sense ... *he* could not mistrust *her*.

Natural objects (cf. vol III 6.3$_8$). *The sun* is *he* as in Latin (different from OE): Sh often | Swift 3.207 |

Cowper L 1.135, 248 | Byron 640 the *Sun's* gorgeous coming — *His* setting indescribable ... as I behold *Him* sink | Macaulay WH 65 the next morning, before the *sun* was in *his* power | O'Rell JB 82 when the *sun* makes *his* appearance *he* is photographed, that folks may not forget what *he* is like | Thack N 5, etc. See Storm EPh 1008.

The moon is *she* as in Latin (but in OE m.): Sh Tp II. 1.183 | Lamb R 18 | Stevenson JHF 72 | Galsw P 2.74 Haven't seen such a *moon* for years, *she's* like a great, great lamp | ib 92, etc.

The river ... *he:* Byron 589 (but immediately before *it*); thus generally also individual names of rivers: Wordsw P 10.7 *Loire* ... *his;* but Phillpotts M 83 *Walla* ... *she*, on account of the ending -a. Cf. also Wordsw P 4.51 The famous *brook*, who, soon as *he* was boxed within our garden, found *himself* ... Stripped of *his* voice.

The sea, according to Moon, *Eccles. Engl.* 1886, 30, is in the revised Old Testament, both m., f., and n. It would be vain to search for psychological reasons where we have arbitrary personifications of this kind. Shelley West Wind III Thou who didst waken from his summer dreams The blue *Mediterranean*, where *he* lay, Lulled ... In Sh *the sea* is *it* (except Tro I. 3.34 boates dare saile Vpon *her* patient brest). Kinglake E 116 There *she* lay, the *Sea* of Galilee.

5.8$_4$. Names of countries and nations are very often referred to as *she*, particularly when their actions (politics, etc.) are mentioned. Many examples are given in vol III 6.3$_7$ in connexion with the use of relative *who*. Note also Mi A 49 a noble and puissant *nation* rousing *herself*. — An exception which is easily accounted for, occurs in Mi SA 240 *Israel* still serves with all *his* sons.

5.8₅. Names of *towns* are treated in the same way as countries: Ru P 2.27 *Oxford* taught me as much Greek and Latin as *she* could, | Mackenzie S 607 *Paris* was *herself* again. — *It*, of course, may also be said, thus in spite of the mention of *hand*, etc, in Quiller Couch T 85 *Troy* saw the joke, and, hand on hip, laughed with all *its* lungs.

Time, etc: GE S 221 in spite of Time, *who* has laid *his* heavy hand on them all | Stevenson M 180 | Hope C 120 would Time have arrested *his* march (note the capital letter) | Wordsw P 1. 476 the *year* ... in his delightful round || Mi PL 5.1 *Morn*, *her* rosy steps ... Advancing | Brontë J 80 *Spring* drew on: *she* was indeed already come (immediately after this: winter ... its: winter is not so poetical!) | Mackenzie S 571 *April* went *her* course || Masefield M 197 The *wind* ceased from *her* whirling about continually. *She* blew steady (seems very unnatural).

5.8₆. *Abstract notions* are often referred to as *she* (on ME personifications of vices as *he* on account of the Moralities, see Morsbach, 1. c. 16 ff.): Sh Ro IV. 5. 130 *Musicke* with *her* siluer sound | Sh H4B IV. 4.87 *Peace* puts forth *her* oliue euery where | Mi A 18 *vice* with all *her* baits ... *vertue*, *her* adversary | Sterne M 1.19 *Humility herself* | By DJ 6.63 I love *Wisdom* more than *she* loves me | ib 8.62 *Crime* .. *she* is not the child of Solitude; *Health* .. *Her* home is in the rarely trodden wild | Brontë P 173 *solitude* .. he will find *her* brooding still and blank over the wide fields | Trollope W 2 here probably *Scandal* lies, as *she* so often does | Carpenter C 52 *Science* has failed because *she* has attempted an impossible task | Wilde In 11 Maupassant strips *life* of the few poor rags that still cover *her* | ib 17 | Wells M 76 it is a pleasant superstition that *Nature* (who in such connections becomes feminine and assumes a capital N) is to be trusted in these matters. — Thus also *philosophy, poetry, literature, the church* (Macaulay H 1.171), *the University*, etc. But *Love* is very often made *he* (after Eros, Amor), and so is *Death* (cf Shelley 29: Ruin calls His brother Death | ib 1 Death and his brother Sleep). *Sleep* is *she* in Brontë V 151, but *he* ib 434. — Further examples below, $16.5_1(3)$.

Animate and Inanimate

5.9_1. In connexion with the chapter about sex and sexless we must mention the distinction between animate (living) and inanimate (lifeless), which is not exactly the same thing; some of the pronouns considered (*it, this, what*) refer not only to lifeless, but in certain circumstances also to living beings.

A distinction between animate and inanimate plays a certain role in various departments of syntax.

With names for inanimate there is a marked disinclination to use the genitive of nouns and the possessive pronouns, cf e.g. *the man's body*, but *the roof of the house;* with names of countries we say e.g. *France's policy*, but *the mountains of France*. This distinction, however, is not neat, for we may in many instances use *of* instead of the genitive even with living beings, and we say e.g. *out of harm's way*.

5.9_2. In vol II we have already mentioned several cases in which the distinction between animate and inanimate appears: Collectives denoting persons may take the vb in the pl (my family are early risers), while those denoting things require the vb in the sg (my library is rich in Oriental books). An adj may be used as primary in the sg for something inanimate (What's the good of it ?); but referring to living beings this is only possible in the pl (the dead do not rise again), while in the sg we must have an addition (a good man, a good one). *The good ones* when not anaphoric (referring to what has just been mentioned) will be understood of persons; but anaphorically it may refer to things just as well as to living beings. A distinction is shown in such dictionary definitions as *creeper = one who creeps, or that which creeps. Those who* referring to persons is opposed to *those that* about things: the distinction, however, is not strictly carried through, see vol III 5.1$_5$. The pronominal advs *therewith, wherewith, thereat*, etc, never refer to animate beings.

5.9$_3$. There is in the south-western dialects a curious distinction between (1) full shapen things, and (2) unshapen quantities; (1) is referred to as *he, en* (< OE *hine*) and takes the pronominal adjuncts *theäse* and *thir*, (2) is referred to as *it* and takes *this* and *that:* Come under theäse tree by this water | goo under thir tree, an' zit on that grass (Barnes, Dorset Gr. 20, Ellis EEP 5.85, Wright, *Dial. Gr.* § 393, 416 f.) This seems to some extent to coincide with the distinction between thing-words and mass-words, which has been shown to have grammatical importance in other respects (see vol II. 5.2 and 10.91). — Examples of *en* as applied to 'full shapen things' may be found in Hardy's novels, e.g. R 25 a black cross ... in en .. I zid [saw] en | ib 52 beaker ... pass 'en round. Cf also Wright, *Rustic Sp* 144 f.

Chapter VI

Case

6.1$_1$. Case is defined in NED as "one of the varied forms of a substantive, adjective, or pronoun, which express the varied relations in which it may stand to some other word in the sentence." I know no better definition than this. There is really no definition in the latest comprehensive treatment of the subject, L. Hjelmslev, *La Catégorie des Cas*, I, Aarhus 1935, II 1937. In my chapter on Case in PhilGr 173-187 I discuss at length the number of English cases and decide in favour of a purely formal standard; but on p. 185-6 I give a survey of the notions which cases may stand for in general.

In Present English we distinguish two cases in substantives, a 'common case' and a genitive, three in pronouns, a nominative, an oblique case, and a genitive; the genitive is generally reckoned as a separate class of pronouns (possessive); on the difference in rank between *my* (secondary) and *mine* (primary), etc, see vol II 16.2 ff. (Cf on *no* and *none* ib 16.6). In adjectives there is no longer any case distinctions, except when they are used as primaries and may take a genitive inflexion — see vol II 9.5.

Case in Pronouns

6.1$_2$. This chapter is to a great extent based on the one entitled "Case-shiftings in the pronouns" in *Progress in Language* (1894), reprinted as Ch. 2 in *Chapters on English* (1918). But here it appears in a somewhat different shape, with omissions, additions, and transpositions, caused partly by my studies in the intervening years, and partly by its now being part of an English grammar, while originally it was written chiefly to illustrate progressive tendencies in the development of language in general. It is possible that too many traces are left of the original composition.

6.1$_3$. In OE pronouns we find the nom., acc., and dat. cases distinct both with regard to morphology and syntax, although in a few pronouns there is no formal difference between the nom. and acc. (in the plurals of the third person: *hīe;* in the neuter: *hit, hwæt,* etc.; in the fem. form *hēo* or *hīe*).

The first step in the simplification of this system is the abandonment of the forms *mec, þec, ūsic, ēowic, uncit, incit,* which were used in the very oldest texts only, as accusatives distinct from the datives *mē, þē, ūs, ēow, unc, inc,* and were soon ousted by the latter forms. By parallel developments occurring somewhat later, the old datives *hire (hir, her), him* and *hwām (whom)* supplanted the accusatives *hēo, hine* and *hwone.* In some of the southern counties *hine* has, however, been preserved down to our times in the form of [ən], see EEP 5.43, EDG § 405; in the literary transcription of these dialects this is written '*un*, e.g. in Fielding T (Squire Western, etc) and Thack P (1.62 Show Mr. Pendennis up to 'un). In the plural also the dative form has ousted the old acc.; *hem* (OE *him, heom;* preserved in coll. and vg speech: I know 'em) and the later *them* are originally datives; the neuter sg, on the other hand, has preserved the old acc. forms *hit (it), þæt (that), hwæt (what),* at the expense of the old datives.

The reason for this constant preference for the dat. forms in the person-indicating pronouns is no doubt the fact that these pronouns are used as indirect objects more often than either sbs or adjs; at any rate it is a phenomenon very frequently found in various languages.

6.1₄. In what follows I shall discuss at some length those tendencies towards further modifications of the pronominal case-system which have been and still are at work after the establishment of one oblique case. The forms concerning us are in modern spelling:

Nom.	Obl.
I; we	*me; us*

Nom.	Obl.
thou; ye	*thee; you*
he, she, it; they	*him, her, it; them*
who	*whom.*

By the side of *them* there is a colloquial form *'em*, from OE *hem*, which was the regular form before the adoption of *them* from Scandinavian.

Some of the modifying tendencies are of a more universal character and may be found more or less in other languages as well; others are peculiar to English, and even to some parts of the English system. Here and there they have already brought about comprehensive changes in the system, but elsewhere the result has only been a good deal of natural hesitation in the right use of the forms, which, indeed, is one of the knottiest points in English grammar.

It should be noted that in many of the sentences quoted below two or even more causes of shiftings have operated concurrently.

6.1₅. The principal rules for the syntactic use of these forms may be briefly stated as follows:

The forms before the semicolon are singulars; those after the semicolon are plurals. This, even traditionally, applied to *thou, thee* in addressing one person, and *ye, you* in addressing more than one. With *who* there is no distinction between the two numbers.

The nominative is used as the subject and the oblique case at the object:

I (we, he, she, they) loved him (her, them), etc.

The obl. case is further used as indirect object and as regimen of a preposition:

He gave me (us, him, her, them) a shilling.

He spoke to me (us, him, her, them).

In the same way originally with *thou, ye,* and *thee, you.*

6.1₆. On the cases when the pronoun is turned into a sb, see vol II 8.22 (quotation sbs) and 8.4 (others).

To the examples in the latter place may be added: Di Do 11 [vg] You have a son, I believe? said Mr. Dombey. — Four on 'em, sir. Four hims and a her | Ridge S 70 Show them up. — It isn't a them, sir, it is only a bit of a lad | Zangwill G 389 can't you put her second for once? — I didn't say it was a her. — A she, corrected the governess | Galsw TL 256 compared with him or her whose fixed idea is the possession of some her or him | Lewis MA 75 somebody ... It isn't a Him, it's a Her | Maugham P 233 But it wasn't me, it wasn't the real me.

Extraposition

6.2₁. On this term see vol III 17.1, AnalSynt Ch. 12 and EEG 9.6₅.

A speaker begins a sentence with some word which takes a prominent place in his thought, but has not yet made up his mind with regard to its syntactical connexion; if it is a word inflected in the cases he provisionally puts it in the nom., but is then often obliged by an after-correction to insert a pronoun indicating the case in which the word should have been. This phenomenon is extremely frequent in the colloquial forms of all languages, but in literary language it is often avoided. I shall first give some examples where the case employed is correct or the fault at any rate is not visible:

Ch B 4267 oon of hem, in sleping as he lay, Him mette a wonder dreem | Sh As IV. 1.77 verie good orators when they are out, they will spit | ib IV. 1.177

that woman that cannot make her fault her husbands occasion, let her neuer nurse her childe.

6.2₂. Next I quote some instances in which the nom. might also be caused by relative attraction (cf below, 6.2₅):

Ch B 4621 For he that winketh, whan he sholde see, Al wilfully, God lat him never thee! | B 2505 for certes he that ... hath to gret presumpcioun, him schal evyl bitide (also ib B 3045) | Malory 150 ye that be soo wel borne a man ..., there is no lady in the world to good for yow | Sh R3 III. 2.58 that they which brought me in my masters hate, I liue to looke vpon their tragedie (cf for the genitive below, Ch IX) | H4A V. 4.167 Hee that rewards me, heauen reward him | Ado I. 1.260 | H5 IV. 3.35 | ib II. 1.104 | Cor I. 4.28 He that retires, Ile take him for a Volce (also Hml III. 2.252) | AV Matt. 19.12 He that is able to receiue it, let him receiue it | John 8.7 Hee that is without sinne among you, let him first cast a stone at her (cf on *let* 6.4₁) | Matt 19.12 | Luke 3.11 | Carlyle H 9 He that can discern the loveliness of things, we call him Poet | Mrs Browning A 42 But we indeed who call things good and fair, The evil is upon us while we speak.

There is no relative attraction in the following sentences: Sh Meas V. 134 But yesternight my lord, she and that fryer I saw them at the prison.

6.2₃. Sometimes no corrective pronoun follows: Marlowe F 594 She whom thine eie shall like, thy heart shal haue | Sh Wiv IV. 4.87 and he my husband best of all affects | Meas V. 531 She Claudio that you wrong'd, looke you restore | Austen P 475 He, who had always inspired in herself a respect which almost overcame her affection, she now saw the object of open pleasantry | Di D 775 She in whom I might have inspired a dearer

love, I had taught to be my sister | Browning [Tauchn.]
1.235 She, men would have to be your mother once,
Old Gandolf envied me, so fair she was! | Brontë V 378
She, who had been the bane of his life ... he treated
with the respect a good son might offer a kind mother |
Stevenson V 31 She, whose happiness you most desire,
you choose to be your victim.

Apposition

6.2₄. Related to the phenomena just dealt with is
the fact that when two or more words are in *apposition*
to each other it often happens that the appositum
does not follow the case of the first word; the speaker
forgets the case he has just employed and places the
appositum loosely without any connexion with what
precedes. This is frequent in OE, where it is extremely common with participles (*gehāten*, etc). In more recent
periods it is found in many other cases as well: Ch B
1877 prey eek for us, we sinful folk unstable | id D
1912 I speke of us, we mendinants, we freres | id MP
5.421 Beseching her of mercy and of grace, As she that
is my lady sovereyne | Sh LLL IV. 3.7 this loue ...
kils sheep; it kils mee, I a sheep | H4A I. 2.16 by Phoebus, hee, that wand'ring knight | Wint II. 4.114 I am
not yet of Percies mind, the Hotspurre of the North,
he that killes me some sixe or seauen dozen of Scots |
ib V. 1.86 Prince Florizell ... with his princesse (she
The fairest I haue yet beheld) | Swift J 129 did you
never hear of Dryden Leach, he that prints the Postman?
| Wordsw P 11.107 the auxiliaries which then stood Upon
our side, us who were strong in love! | Shelley 227 Know
yet not me, The Titan? he who made his agony the
barrier to your else all-conquering foe? | Brontë V 386
I heard one of my examiners — he of the braided

surtout — whisper to his co-professor | Kipling B 69 I'd ha' left it for 'is sake — 'Im that left me by the ford | Gosse F 147 go in and waken Mary, whom, however, they found awake, praying, she too, for the conversion of Bess.

Relative attraction may of course have also been at work in some of these sentences.

Relative Attraction

6.2₅. A pronoun in the main sentence is often put in the case which the corresponding relative pronoun has or ought to have. This is particularly easy to explain in relative contact-clauses; cf vol III ch 7. Examples abound, both where the relative pronoun is expressed and where it is not:

Sh Cor V. 6.5 Him I accuse [:] the city port by this has entered | Ant III. 1.15 him we serues [i.e. serve's] away | Ro II. 3.86 her I loue now Doth grace for grace, and loue for loue allow [the oldest quarto *she whom*] | Hml II. 1.42 him you would sound ... be assured he closes ... | As I. 1.47 better than him I am before knowes mee | Tp V. 1.15 | H6A IV. 7.75 | Shelley PW 1.96 [Zastrozzi] Before her, in the arms of death, lay him on whom her hopes of happiness seemed to have formed so firm a basis | Tennyson 370 Our noble Arthur, him Ye scarce can overpraise, will hear and know | Trollope D 1.161 [lady writing] I have come to be known as her whom your uncle trusted and loved, as her whom your wife trusted | Haggard S 246 thou didst say that Kallikrates — him whom thou sawest dead — was thine ancestor.

Very often with *it is:* Marlowe J 1034 'Tis not thy wealth, but her that I esteeme [= I esteeme her] | Sh H6B IV. 1.117 it is thee I feare | Sonn 62 'Tis thee (my self) that for my self I praise | Thack P 1.269 it's not me I'm anxious about | ib 3.301 it is not him I want | Trollope O 121 It is her you should consult on such a matter | Dickinson C 23 him it is that I wish to characterize, for he it is that is the natural and inevitable outcome of your civilization | Bennett LR 252 it's him you've got to settle things with.

On *it is I* caused by relative attraction see 6.7$_5$.

6.2$_6$. A nom. instead of the oblique case is rarer in the instance of relative attraction: Fulg 52 He that hathe moste nobles in store Hym call I the most noble | Sh Ven 109 thus he that overrul'd I overswayed |Tro II. 3.252 Praise him that got thee, shee that gaue thee sucke | Hml I. 2.105 | H6B III. 2.89 | R3 IV. 4.101 | Hardy L 187 This from His Car'line, she who had been dead to him | Stevenson B 361 I will tell a secret to my Lady Shelton — she that is to be | Steel F 81 their worship alike of sex and He who made it, seemed incomprehensible | Allingham P 17 you would be rendering your eternal debtor he who begs always to remain, my dear fellow, Your devoted, M.F.

Preposition and Conjunction

6.3$_1$. A good deal of confusion arises from some words being both prepositions and conjunctions. A characteristic example is *but*; cf NED with examples, especially under the heads C. 3 and 4. It should, however, be noted that the confusion in the use of *but* is not, as said in NED, a consequence of the want of distinct case-endings in the nouns and the use of the obl. case instead of the nom. in other connexions. In my opinion, on the contrary, the existence of such two-sided words as *but*, etc, is one of the primary causes of mistakes of *me* for *I* or *vice versa*, and careless uses of the cases generally. Even in such a language as German, where the cases are generally kept neatly apart, we find such combinations as "niemand kommt mir entgegen ausser ein unverschämter" (Lessing); "wo ist ein gott ohne der herr" (Luther); "kein gott ist ohne ich," etc. See Paul, *Principien*[4] 372; in Danish similar examples abound (ingen uden jeg, etc).

If we use in one place the term preposition and in another conjunction in speaking of such words, the real meaning is that in one case the word concerned is definitely felt as part of the (main) sentence (no one but me), and in the other as loosely connected with it, whence a stronger feeling of its virtually being the subject of a latent verb (no one but I).

6.3₂. In some of the following examples (which have been starred) the nom. is used, although both the preposition and the conjunction would require the obl. case:

AR 408 no þing ne con luuien ariht bute he one | Ch MP 2.30 no wight woot [it] but I | id C 282 no man woot ther-of but God and he (rimes with *be*) | E 476 no wight ... but we tweye | D 1936 But we | E 2050 no wight but they two (ib 2136, 2160, 2412) | id (q Brusendorff Chaucer Tradition 280) That euery wight but I haþe sume solas [N.B. *haþe* 3rd person] | Towneley 27 bot ye | ib 32 bot oonely we | Malory 42 but he | Redford W 712 who sent it but I? | More U 206 what man wakynge feleth not hymselfe in health, but *he that is not? | Marlowe J 1576 I neuer heard of any man but *he Malign'd the order of the Iacobines [*he* felt as sbj of *maligned*] | Sh H4A V. 2.50 that no man might draw short breath to day But I and Harry Monmouth | John IV. 1.14 no body should be sad but I | Cymb I. 1.24 but hee | ib II. 3.153 That I kisse aught but *he |

As I. 2.18 my father had no childe but *I | Mcb III. 1.54 but he | Ro I. 2.14 Earth hath swallowed all my hopes but *she | R3 II. 2.76 What stayes had I but *they? | H6B I. 2.69 here's none but thee, and I | Tp III. 2.109 I neuer saw a woman But onely Sycorax my dam, and *she | Defoe G 68 education was for no body but *they that were to trade with it | Di T 1.112 There were no other passengers that night, but we four | Brontë W 42 Nobody but I even did him the kindness to call him a dirty boy | ib 245 | Hope Q 86 who but he was responsible.

Obl. case after *but:* Bunyan P 7 since there is none but us two here | Defoe R 2.178 there is no God but him | By DJ 2.106 So nobody arrived on shore but him | Thack V 521 how pretty she looked. So do you! Everybody but me who am wretched | Stevenson Child's Garden 17 So there was no one left but me | Galsw T 29 Nobody comes here but him for a long time now | Maugham Pl 4.107 I suppose everybody knows but us.

Save (formerly also *sauf*) presents similar phenomena of confusion, although it is not very often found as a preposition (with the obl. case) as in Tennyson 319 Who should be King save him who makes us free? | Arnold P 1.159 For the race of Gods is no one there, save me alone | Macaulay E 4.332 All who stood at that bar save him alone, are gone | Conway C 268 Who could be her husband save me? | London M 100 there was no woman who would not have guessed — save her.

In Chaucer *sauf* (*save*) is very common with the nom., e.g. B 473 Ther every wight save he ... was with the leoun frete | E 2045 he wol no wight suffren bere the keye Save he himself (also B 627, G 1355, I 25, LGW 1633, T 887, etc.). Later examples: Fulg 30 There is neuer a knaue in the house saue I | Gammer 147 Yet shal ye find no other wight saue *she | Sh Tw III. 1.172 nor neuer none Shall mistris be of it, saue I alone | Cæs III. 2.66 | AV Matt. 19.11 All men cannot receiue this saying, saue they to whom it is giuen | Byron DJ 3.86 Where nothing, save the waves and I, May hear (also By 4.332) | Mary Shelley F 143 All, save I, were at rest | Di D 105 I believed there was nothing real in all I remembered, save my mother, Peggotty, and I | McCarthy King 103 None must know who he is save you and I and Tristan | Bennett C 1.293 No one heard save she | Walpole GM 389 he dreamt that all were drowned save he.

An example of an abnormal use of the nom. is Sh Sonn 109.14 For nothing in this wide uniuerse I call, saue *thou, my rose.

With *except*, and *excepting*, too, we find both nom. and obl. case, as in Defoe M 39 [this] amazed the whole family, except he that knew the reason of it | Mary Shelley F 78 Did any one indeed exist, except I, the creater who would believe | Ru P 2.74 the horror which neither he nor any other Englishman, except Byron and I, saw | Meredith T 28 And everybody is to know him except I? | Wilde P 103 every one is worthy of love, except he who thinks that he is | Sutton Vane, Outw. Bound 64 There's no one at all on board this ship, excepting we five — and those two || Mrs. Browning Letter in Orr 232 Nobody exactly understands him except me who am in the inside of him and hear him breathe | Mulock H 2.22 No one ever knew of this night's episode, except us three | Hardy T 101 Perhaps any woman would, except me.

Except with the nom. not mentioned in NED.

Note the exceptional nom. in Di P 2.398 upon which

every man (including he of the mottled countenance) drew a long breath.

Ere as a preposition with obl. case is rare. NED has one example with pron. 1649 Lovelace Poems 22 Could you ascend yon Chaire of State e're him? I have further noted Arnold P 1.140 three kings, ere thee, Have I seen reigning in this place.

6.3₃. The conjunctions *as* and *than*, used in comparisons, give rise to similar phenomena. As it is possible to say both "I never saw anybody stronger than he" (viz. *is*), and "than him" (obl. case agreeing with *anybody*), and "I never saw anybody so strong as he," and "as him," the feeling for the correct use of the cases is here easily obscured, and *he* is used where the rules of grammar would lead us to expect *him*, and inversely.

In what follows I shall first give some examples of *as* before the nom.: Ch T 4.948 he fond him allone, As he that of his lyf no lenger roughte | Marlowe E 1384 things of more waight Then fits a prince so young as I to bear | Greene F 12.66 I do love the lord, As he that's second to thyself in love | Sh Ro I 2.3 For men so old as we | As II. 5.58 Heere shall he see grosse fooles as he | Bunyan P 154 lest heedlessness makes them, as we, to fare | Swift 3.370 to a creature so inferior as I | Di N 642 she will be married to a man as bad as he | Meredith E 192 What was the right of so miserable a creature as she to excite disturbances? | ib 244 because of finding no one so charitable as she | Trollope A 4 Harrow School was disgraced by so disreputably dirty a boy as I | Bridges E 95 [dost thou think] I cannot bear another son As good as thou | Wells Cl 86 [it] does seem to so amateurish a reader as I a straightforward story.

Obl. case after *as*: Sh Ant III. 3.14 is shee as tall as me? | Fielding T 2.115 you are not so good as me |

Thomson Rule Britannia: The nations not so blest as thee Must in their turn to tyrants fall | Scott A 1.247 [Sc] he now really looks as auld as me, that might be his mother | Austen E 30 they are quite as well educated as me | id S 133 you do not know him as well as me [i.e. as I do] | Shelley in Ingpen, Shelley in England 323 No son can be so dutiful so respectful as me | Hazlitt A 57 Who is there so low as me? | Di Do 60 [boy:] when Florence was as little as me | Trollope D 3.31 [young lord writing:] the Carbottle people were quite as badly off as us, only they are poorer than us | Childers R 108 every steamer that goes in would see as much as me | Bennett P 222 There must be quite a few others in the same fix as me in London | id W 2.24 you ate about five times as much as me | Maugham Pl 3.98 Duchess: I shall be obliged if you will not get in the same carriage as me.

6.3₄. After *such as* (*such ... as*) we have generally the nom.: Ch A 243 For un-to swich a worthy man as he ... | Marlowe E 713 laugh at such as we | Greene J4 416 Exile, torment and punish such as they | Bunyan G 35 pray to nothing else but to these, or such as they ... on such as he [.. not for such as thee] | Swift 3.127 mimicked by such diminutive insects as I | Goldsm V 1.128 she shall chuse better company than such low-lived fellows as he | Scott I 101 it is not fit for such as we to sit with the rulers (ib 249, 257) | Tennyson 256 what then were God to such as I (also ib 430) | Browning [Tauchn.] 3.78 The land has none such left as he on the bier (ib 1.280, 282) | Mrs Browning Sonn. f. the Port. 8 who hast ... laid them on the outside of the wall, for such as I to take (after prep. also id A 185, 210, 219, 241, 304) | GE A 11 We want such fellows as he to lick the French | after vb Lowell St

49 | Fox 2.141 Can He love such an one as I? | Di Do 388 to such as he | Brontë J 307 Death was not for such as I (after prep. also Brontë P 258, V 56, 369) | Whittier 440 of such as he Shall Freedom's young apostles be.

Many other instances found, but not noted here.

But the obl. case after *such as* may be found: Swift J 487 while such as her die | Di Do 299 what's a torn foot to such as me | Wells L 7 Did ever man have such a bother with himself as me? | Rose Macaulay P 35 they were not bad, for such as her | id K 50 The Folyot's household was no place for such as her | Pennell L 137 Men — even such as me — are much too needed out here.

6.3₅. Even after *as well as* the confusion may be found, at any rate in earlier authors, though in the mouths of vulgar persons: Sh Meas II. 1.75 I will detest my selfe also, as well as she | Fielding T 3.121 Dost fancy I don't know that as well as thee?

The same phenomena are known from other languages as well, thus in Italian with *come*, and in Spanish with *como*, e.g. Serao Fant. 75 egli è, come me, una vittima della fatalità || Calderon AZ 3.556 Con un hombre como yo, Y en servicio del Rey, no Se puede hacer.

6.3₆. As *like*, which as a rule is combined with the oblique case, means the same thing as *as*, we sometimes find a nom. after it:

Sh Ro III. 5.83 And yet no man like he doth greeue my heart | Burns 1.177 Frae onie unregenerate heathen, Like you or I | Shelley 577 To think that a most unambitious slave, Like thou, shouldst dance and revel on the grave Of Liberty | Huxley L 1.289 men, who like you and I stand pretty much alone | Stevenson T 64 a pair of old bachelors like you and I may be excused | Vizetelly, With Zola in England 211 They, like we, were waiting for the verdict | Deeping 3R 326 Hard-working people like you and I have to be punctual | Loos Gent. Marry Brunettes 147 the kind of a gentleman that appeals to a girl like she. Cf *Am. Speech* 1.103.

6.3₇. With *than* we have the same confusion. According to the strict grammatical rule we should expect the same case of the pronoun after *than* as its antecedent (if *than* is not followed by a whole clause), which is sometimes the nom., sometimes the obl. case. Hence the possibility of interpreting *than* now as a conjunction, now as a preposition, and if a speaker or writer more or less consistently uses the word in one of these functions only, we may get "ungrammatical" constructions like the following. Note that in most of the examples with the obl. case as against the strict rule there is in the preceding sentence no verb with an object, but generally a verb with a predicative.

Nominative after *than:* Ch LGW 446 To me ne fond I better noon than ye | Sh Cor IV. 5.170 but a greater soldier then he, you wot one | As I. 1.172 my soule ... hates nothing more then he (cf Tro II. 3.199; Cymb V. 3.72 then we (obj.; relative attraction) | Osborne 14 I have knowne better men then hee, lye | Defoe R 347 it was enough to have terrify'd a bolder man than I | Scott A 1.283 under protection of a much Greater than he | Di T 2.173 Carton, who was a mystery to wiser and honester men than he | Brontë W 230 I thought Heathcliff himself less guilty than I | Carlyle H 93 the care of Another than he | GE M 1.186 I have known much more highly-instructed persons than he make inferences quite as wide | Tennyson Becket 1 But we must have a mightier man than he for his successor |

Lowell St 64 To a thinner man than I, or from a stouter man than he, the question might have been offensive | Meredith E 141 if I could see you with a worthier than I | Doyle S 1.53 I love and am loved by a better man than he | Philips L 189 you will have no bitterer enemy than I! | Zangwill G 194 May you always be happy, and find a worthier wife than I | Walpole Cp 85 he did not believe himself better than they because he had not yielded to their temptations | Galsw Frat 29 it required a greater psychologist than he to describe | Maugham Pl 3.283 Forget me and live happily with a better man than I.

Obl. case after *than:* More U 63 seing that man that is condempned for thefte in no lesse ieopardie ... then hym that is convict of manslaughter | Otway 169 There's not a wretch ... But's happier than me | Fielding T 1.49 My sister, though many years younger than me, is at least old enough | ib 3.129 you are younger than me | Bosw 2.87 A woman does not complain that her brother, who is younger than her, gets their common father's estate | Goldsm V 2.3 our cousin, who was himself in little better circumstances than me | Lamb E 1.185 he was good bit older than me | Byron 434 none Can less have said or more have done Than thee, Mazeppa! | ib 628 he seems mightier far than them | (and elsewhere in Byron) | Shelley 262 I am ... mightier than thee | Keats 1.51 But what is higher beyond thought than thee | Di Do 23 (said the boy) the swordbearer's better than him | Thack N 41 Ethel's younger than me | ib 101 | Brontë V 104 flowers ... the sweetest that blow — yet less sweet than thee, my Peri. Cf the dialectal GE A 173 There's One above knows better *nor* us.

Any number of further examples might be adduced.

The construction with the obl. case is now so universal as to be considered the normal one. Nevertheless, many grammarians reject this natural use of the obl. case; and the nominatives in some, at least, of the above examples have certainly been called forth by an artificial reaction against the natural tendencies of the language.

Than is clearly a conjunction in Allingham P 16 it [is] more likely that you would ... consult me ... than I you.

The obl. case is always used in *than whom*, see vol III 10.4$_2$.

Notional Subject

6.4$_1$. In the preceding section it was indicated how the feeling that a word was virtually the subject (of a latent verb) gave rise to the use of a nom. instead of an obl. form after *but*, etc. Now we are going to consider a similar preference for the nom. in other cases in which traditional grammar requires the obl. The combination *let us (let's) go* has taken the place of older *go we;* the formula is V O(S I). Hence we find a nominative

(1) in apposition to *us:*

Pinero B 212 let's you and I go together | Sutro F 96 let us not be ashamed, we two, but only very proud | Bennett Cd 250 Let's halve the cost, you and I | Bentley T 138 Let's you and I hope we never see anything nearer hell.

(2) when the S itself is composed of two members, joined by means of *and:*

Bunyan P 185 let thee and I go on | Farquhar B 375 let my dear and I talk the matter over | Defoe Rox 111 let you and I go into the next room | Shelley P 297 Let you and I try if we cannot be as punctual and businesslike as the best of them | Di Do 304 don't let you and I talk of being dutiful | id N 366 let he and I say good night together | Meredith R 180 So let you and I come to an understanding | Hughes T 1.3 let you and I cry quits | Maxwell WF 84 Now Mr Charles, let you and I have a quiet chat about it | Stevenson B 176 let thou and I go round about the garden.

(3) outside these combinations:

Sh Merch III. 2.21 Let Fortune goe to hell for it, not I | Byron Cain II. 2.88 (ed. London 1831: 3.316) Let He who made thee answer that (relative attraction, corrected into Let him ... by later editors) | Tennyson 322 Let love be blamed for it, not she, nor I.

The feeling for the pronoun as virtual subject is seen clearly in Maugham Pl 2.224 Herbert, let's go and lunch at Prince's, you and I, shall we.

Cf vol V 24.1$_5$ and NED *let* 14 b, Storm EPh 678, who also quotes Dickens: Leave Nell and I to toil and work.

The same phenomenon is found colloquially in Danish-Norwegian *lad vi det* for *lad os det*. In the corresponding Dutch construction both the nom. and the obl. case are allowed: *laat mij nu toonen* as well as *laat ik nu toonen* 'let me now show'; similarly *laat hem [hij] nu toonen, laat ons [laten wij] nu toonen, lat hem [laten ze] nu toonen*.

6.4₂. A similar confusion after the vbs *make*, etc, is found in Sh Tp IV. 1.217 mischeefe which may make this island Thine owne for ever, and I thy Caliban for aye thy foote-licker. — Here Caliban forgets the first part of his sentence and goes on as if the beginning had been 'this island shall become'. So also R2 IV. 1.216 [God] Make me, that nothing haue, with nothing grieu'd, And thou with all pleas'd, that hast all achieu'd | Bunyan P 85 Christians fall makes Faithful and he go lovingly together | Fielding T 4.130 I would have both you and she know it is not for her fortune that he follows her | Rose Macaulay K 126 it made Dad and I laugh | Oppenheim Pawns Count 88 I want us three to meet, you and she and I.

Cf also Beresford Mount. Moon 6 to persuade Richard to let us go alone — we three, you know | Brontë W 186 he is willing to let us be friends, at least, Linton and I (*let us* different from above).

6.4₃. The combination is also a virtual S in an infinitival nexus with *for:* Defoe G 135 those we have every week for the parson and I to talk over | Huxley L 1.133 I see nothing for it but for you and I to constitute ourselves into a permanent committee | Herrick M 324 it's no more use for you and I to kick.

We have also a notional subject before a gerund (cf vol V 9.76): Walpole SC 176 and behind it I saw... Nikitin and I sitting on the bench outside the stinking hut | Bertram Atkey in BDS 270 to advance him ten thousand pounds on the strength of Gene and I signing a — a — promissory note | Mannin W 202 But there was no harm, surely, in she and Richard having a friendly drink together.

And in a predicative nexus: Deloney 14 I verily thought, that you were inuited by the Widow to make her and I sure together [i.e. engaged] | Norris S 176 she [the ship] comes back with you and I aboard | Jerome T [Brockhaus ed.] 59 with Harris at the sculls and I at the tiller-lines.

When we find in the middle of the 16th c. such sentences as these: Roister 38 And let me see you play me such a part againe | ib 76 I would see you aske pardon — we may be pretty sure that the author meant *you* as the obl. case and the verbs *play* and *aske* as infinitives; but to a later generation neither the form of the pron. nor that of the vb would exclude the possibility of *you* being the subject of finite vbs (= let me see (that) you ...).

Loosely Connected Nexus

6.4₄. We must here mention some forms of sentences in which no finite verb is used. The most important class is the nexus of deprecation (PhilGr 129, Negation 23 f., with predicative vol III 17.8₃ ff., with infinitive vol V 20.3₂ ff.). In exclamations of scorn or similar feelings an idea is, as it were, brushed aside as impossible or absurd.

The use of a nom. here need not surprise us: Austen P 333 She a beauty! I should as soon call her mother a wit || Sh LLL III. 191 What? I loue! I sue! I seeke a wife! | ib 202 And I to sigh for her, to watch for her ... | Greene J4 410 What, I take a reward at your hands, maister? Faith, sir, no! | Thack P 2.130 Why! they don't come here to dine you know, they only make believe to dine. They dine here, Law bless you!

When the subject is put in the obl. case, this need not be an instance of the 'absolute' case mentioned below (7.2₁ ff., 7.5₃). Examples vol III p. 374 and further: Mackenzie C 264 Me married? I don't think (on this phrase see vol V 23.7₉) || Thack N 171 did you dance with her? — Me dance! says Mr. Barnes | Kipling J 2.72 Me to sing to naked men! | Bennett A 175 What! And me be left all afternoon by myself? | Shaw StJ 110 ... admitted the said Joan to the ranks of Venerable and Blessed. — Me venerable! | Bennett P 241 Were you begging or what? — Me begging, sir!

In a different kind of loosely connected nexus there is no negative meaning, but generally a contrast to what precedes, introduced by means of *and;* these combinations form a transition to the nexus-tertiaries which were treated in vol V ch VI.

Sh R2 IV. 1.129 And shall the figure of God's Maiestie ... Be iudg'd by subiect, and inferior breathe,

And he himself not present? | H5 IV. 1.205 when our throats are cut, hee may be ransom'd, and wee ne're the wiser | Tim III. 1.50 Is't possible the world should so much differ, And we aliue that liued? | Mi SA 1480 Much rather I shall choose To live the poorest in my tribe, than richest, And he in that calamitous prison left | Stevenson K [T] 199 there might have been twenty squadron of dragoons there, and we none the wiser | Rose Macaulay T 94 he writes essays like a polished gentleman of the world, and he a round-faced cherub barely out of school.

The nom. may be found here even though it is in fact parallel to the object or the regimen of a preposition in the preceding sentence: Marlowe T 244 Me thinks I see kings kneeling at his feet, And he with frowning browes and fiery lookes Spurning their crownes | Sh Ro I 5.5 good manners shall lie all in one or two mens hands and they vnwasht too | Mrs. Browning A 154 I fail to hold and move One man — and he my cousin, and he my friend | Ward D 3.133 It made her mad to see their money chucked away to other people, and they getting no good of it | Maugham Pl 4.289 to bolt with the daughter of an old friend and she only just out of the schoolroom.

In some of these sentences the construction might be called a kind of apposition.

Position

6.4₅. Word-order is a very important formal element (see PhilGr 44, cf ib 147 and 174), and has to no small extent been instrumental in bringing about shiftings of the original relation between the two cases. In OE prose the subject is already placed before the verb in nearly every sentence; the exceptions are almost the same as in Modern German and Danish; thus inversion is the rule after adverbs such as *þā* (while, curiously enough, the subject precedes the vb where the clause is introduced by *hwæt þā* or *efne þā*). Gradually these exceptions disappear or are reduced to a minimum, so that in ModE the order subject — verb — object is practically invariable. (On *do* in interrogative sentences see PhilGr 26 and vol V 25.6$_1$ ff., especially 25.7$_2$).

On the percentage of this order S - V - O in some modern authors see above, 2.1$_8$.

Cooper in his *Gramm. Linguæ Anglicanæ* (1685) 121 defines the difference between the nom. and obl. case of pronouns in the following manner: "*I, thou, he, she, we, ye, they,* verbis anteponuntur, *me, thee, him, her, us, you, them,* postponuntur verbis & præpositionibus." However naïve the modern grammarian may find this definition, it contains a good deal of truth: this is the popular perception which often overrides the older rule according to which the use of *I* and *me* was independent of position.

Before the Verb

6.5₁. Before a vb the nom. comes to be used in many cases where the obl. case was required by the rules of the old language. This is in the first place the case with *who*, as the natural position of this pronoun is always at the beginning of the sentence (or clause), the vb as a rule following immediately after it. It would be an easy matter to find hundreds of examples of *who* as an object or regimen of a preposition placed last from the ME period on. I shall here print only a few selected from my own collections to supplement the numerous examples adduced by Storm EPh 680, and those given in vol V 25.1₃—1₅, where I refer to the chapter in Progress that is taken up again in this volume.

Marlowe T 4190 UUho haue ye there, my Lordes? | Greene F 1.143 Espy her loves, and who she liketh best | BJo 1.17 now I see who he laughed at | Spectator 266 who should I see there but the most artful procuress? | Goldsm 668 Who does it come from? | ib. Do you know who it is from? | Sheridan 39 who can he take after? | ib 48 who can he mean by that? | Thack V 74 Who, I exclaimed, can we consult but Miss P? | Ward R 2.141 [Lady Helen:] Who does this dreadful place belong to? | Shaw 2.84 how can he tell who it was intended for?

6.5₂. As regards Sh's use of *who* in the obl. case, it must suffice to refer to Sh-lex. Under the interrogative pronoun we find there 15 quotations for the use in question, and then an *etc.* is added, which is certain proof that examples abound. Finally Schmidt names 19 places where the old editions do not agree. It is well worth noting that where such variations of reading are found it is nearly always the earliest edition that has *who* and the later editions that find fault with this and replace it by *whom*. Most modern editors and reprinters add the *-m* everywhere in accordance with the rules of 'orthodox' grammar.

6.5₃. The reaction of school-grammar is seen, e.g. in Jerome Tommy & Co. 71 "... that gaby Mary Ramsbotham has got herself engaged." ... "Who to?" demanded Tommy. "You mean 'to whom'. The preeposition governs the objective case," corrected her James Douglas McTear ... who himself wrote English better than he spoke it.

Whom is required after a preposition: *To whom did you give it*? But the natural expression is *Who did you give it to?* Most people will also use the form *whom* after the vb in the form *I saw him. You saw whom?* | Stevenson T 171 Some one was close behind, I knew not whom.

Under the influence of schools *whom* is found here and there, but very rarely, in literature.

6.5₄. As to the relative pronoun the tendency to replace *whom* by *who* is strong, though not quite so strong as with the interrogative pronoun, the reason being that *who(m)* is not here followed immediately by the vb. In Sh-lex. Al. Schmidt under the relative pronoun adduces 12 quotations for *who* as the obl. case, followed again by an *etc.*, and by 11 references to passages in which the oldest editions give different readings.

6.5₅. Examples of relative *who* as object and regimen of preposition from other authors: Spectator 583 a gentleman who of all others I could wish my friend | Defoe Rox 12 a poor woman that had .. and who I had often ... been very kind to | id R 25 the boy, who they called Xury | ib 321 The other two who I had kept till now [very frequent in Defoe, but ib 321 the two prisoners, to whom ... I had given their liberty, — and 324 from whom] | Keats 4.10 to Fanny who I hope you will soon see | Di N 566 She is the daughter of a lady, who, when she was a beautiful girl herself, and I was very many years younger, I loved very dearly | Thack N 38 the servants, who she never would allow to sit up for her | Stevenson D 23 with one who, in spite of all, he could not quite deny to be a lady | Butler W 353 the writer of the Odyssey (who, by the way, I suspect strongly of having been a clergyman) | Merriman S 21 the man who we last saw on the platform.

On relative *who(m)* and *who(m)ever*, etc, see vol III 3.3₁ ff.

6.5₆. The last refuge of the form *whom* is the combination *than whom*, where originally it had nothing to do, and in concatenated relative clauses, in which *whom* is natural, though criticized by grammarians (we feed children whom we think are hungry); see vol III 10.4_2 and 10.7_3, and PhilGr p. 349. Note that in neither of these cases is the pronoun followed by the vb. But as these combinations belong more to literary than to everyday language, *who* is now to be considered almost as a common case. Compare what Sweet wrote to Storm (EPh 680): "I think many educated people never use *whom* at all; always *who*."

6.5_7. A great many vbs (often, but not very felicitously termed impersonal) have shifted what was once the object (generally at first a dative) into a subject. This change was dealt with succinctly in vol III 11.2, where it was attributed to three causes: (1) the greater interest taken in persons than in things, which caused the name of the person to be placed before the vb, (2) the identity in form of the nom. and the obl. case in sbs (adjs) and some pronouns, and (3) the impossibility of distinguishing the cases in certain constructions, thus with an infinitive.

6.5_8. Here I shall supplement the quotations given in vol III, partly from what is already found in Progr; the arrangement as in Progr, not as in vol III.

(1) the original construction O V S; S of course may be an infinitive: AR 238 me luste slepen | Ch B 1048 hir liste nat to daunce (also MP 3.878 and 1019) | MP 4.39 when he deyned caste on him her yë | B 4371 Him deyned not to sette his foote to grounde | Malory 100 I shold fynde yow a damoysel ... that shold lyke yow & plese yow [the two vbs are synonymous] | AR 214 ou schal euer hungren | Ch B 3229 so thursted him | AR 330 þet us scheome | Ch B 101 To asken help thee

shameth in thyn herte | MP 1.76 him thar not drede in soule to be lame || Ch HF 119 me mette ['I dreamt'] I was | MP 3.276 me mette so inly swete a sweven (frequent in Ch) | B 4578 hem thoughte hir herte breke | Malory 65 (four times) hym thoughte | Latimer (Skeat's Spec. 21.91) me thynketh I heare | methinks, methought(s).

6.5₉. The old constructions with a different word-order: Ch B 4456 Nothing ne liste him thanne for to crowe | Bale T 1264 And maye do what him lust | AR 338 hit mei lutel liken God [dative], and misliken ofte | Ch MP 5.397 as hit best lyketh me | ib 22.63 al that hir list and lyketh | Greene F 4.55 this motion likes me well | Sh Hml II. 2.80 It likes vs well | Oth II. 3.49 it dislikes me | Tro. V. 2.102 I doe not like this fooling ... But that that likes not you pleases me best | Mi Pr [p.?] much better would it like him to be the messenger of gladness | Scott I 189 my poor monastic fare likes thee not | Thack V 89 Some [women] are made to scheme, and some to love: and I wish any respected bachelor ... may take the sort that best likes him || AR 136 hit schal þunche þe swete | Ch MP 4.150 And what his compleynt was, remembreth me ['I remember what ... '].

Sometimes with *to:* Ch E 345 It lyketh to your fader and to me, That I yow wedde. — With *unto* MP 1.139.

6.6₁. (2) O/S V S/O. In many cases it is impossible to decide whether the vb is used with one or the other construction, as, e.g., when it stands with a sb or with one of the pronouns that do not distinguish cases. It goes without saying that the frequency of such combinations has largely assisted in bringing about the change to modern usage. A few examples will suffice: AR 286 hwon þe heorte likeð wel, þeonne cumeð up a deuocioun | Ch MP 1.172 Right so thy sone list, as a lamb, to deye | B 477 God list to shewe his wonderful miracle | HF 517 Eleanor Ne mette swich a dreem | B 4302 how Kenelm mette a thing | Malory 65 Thenne the kyng dremed a merueillous dreme.

6.6₂. The construction similarly is not evident in the infinitive nexus: Ch MP 5.108 That made me to mete | ib 115 [thou] madest me this sweven for to mete.

(3) The transition to the new construction is shown by the possibility of joining two synonyms, such as: Prov. of Alfred (Specimens 1.148) þat ye alle a-drede vre dryhten crist, luuyen hine and lykyen | VaV 69 wele, ðe ȝie michel ȝitsið, and luuieð and likeð, and dradeð to forliesen | Malory 35 the kynge lyked and loued this lady wel.

6.6₃. As early as Ch we find passages in which a nom. is understood from a differently constructed vb to a following vb of personal construction: B 3731 For drede of this, him thoughte that he deyde, And [he] ran into a gardin, him to hyde | MP 7.200 her liste him 'dere herte' calle And [she] was so meek | ib 5.165 Yit lyketh him at the wrastling for to be, And [he] demeth yit wher he do bet or he.

Sometimes both constructions are used almost in a breath: Ch LGW 1985 me is as wo For him as ever I was for any man | Malory 74 Arthur loked on the swerd, and lyked it passynge wel; whether lyketh yow better, said Merlyn, the suerd or the scaubard? Me lyketh better the swerd, sayd Arthur | Greene F 6.138 Peggy, how like you this? — What likes my lord is pleasing unto me | Sh Tro V. 2.102 above, 6.5₉.

6.6₄. In Ch MP 5.114 [thou] dauntest whom *thee* lest, — some of the MSS read *thou*, probably in order to avoid the two oblique cases after each other.

Sometimes an expression with the obl. form is followed by a connexion of words that is strictly appropriate only after a nom.: AR 332 Ase ofte ase ich am ischriuen, euer me þuncheð me unschriuen (videor mihi non esse confessus) | ib 196 swetest him þuncheð ham [the nuns: they appear to him [God] most lovely] | Ch E 106 For certes, lord, so wel vs lyketh yow And all your werk and ever han doon.

The last quotation is of particular interest as showing a sort of blending of no less than three constructions: *us lyketh* as a third personal sg with no object, the old construction, where *like* means 'to please', *us lyken ye*, and finally the modern use, *we lyken yow;* the continuation "and ever han doon" (= 'and we have always liked you') shows that the last construction was at least half present in Chaucer's mind.

6.6₅. Other blendings of a similar nature are found with *think; me thinks* (OE *mē þynceth*) and *I think* (OE *ic þence*) are confused in *me thinke*, found, e.g. in one of Latimer's sermons (Skeat's Specimens 21.176); *thinks thee?* and *thinkst thou?* give *thinkst thee* in Sh Hml V. 2.63 (folio; the old quartos have *thinke thee;* some modern editors write *thinks't thee*, as if contracted for *thinks it thee;* but this is hardly correct, as this vb is very rarely used with *it*, at least when a personal pronoun is added).

6.6₆. Note particularly *who* in the following sentences: AR 38 hwo se þuncheð to longe lete þe psalmes [whoever thinks (them) too long may omit the ps.] | Ch B 3509 Hir batailes, who-so list hem for to rede ... Let him vnto my maister Petrark go | T 1.398 and who-so liste it here.

These we may consider either the oldest examples of *who* as the obl. case (centuries before any hitherto pointed out), or else the oldest examples of OE *þyncan* and *lystan* used personally. I suppose, however, that the correct way of viewing these sentences is to say that the two tendencies, neither of which was strong enough to operate at that time by itself, here combined could bring about a visible result.

6.6₇. (4) the modern construction S V O: Ch B 2230 to hem that listen nat heren his wordes | Sh Rom I. 1.47 as they list | Mi PL 4.804 as he list | Gesta Rom. (q Kellner) þou shalt like it | Redford W 68 I lyke not that waye (in ElE also *like of*) | Greene F 10.45 if thou please | Sh Shrew IV. 3.70 as I please | Ch B 3930 and eek a sweuen vpon a nyghte he mette | ib 4117 this dreem, which ye han met to-nyght | ib 4223 his dremes, that he mette.

On *ail*, etc, see vol III 11.2₂ ff., on *seem* ib 11.3₃.

6.6₈. I must here mention the history of some peculiar phrases. When the above-mentioned tendency to have a personal subject seized upon the idiom *me were liever* (or *me were as lief*), the resulting personal construction came in contact with the synonymous phrase *I had liever* (or *I had as lief*), and a considerable amount of confusion arose in this as well as in the kindred combinations with *as good, better, best, rather*. A further confusion arose from the fact that the weak forms of *I would* and *I had* fell together in *I'd*. I give a few examples:

(1) the original dative with *was, were:* Oros 220.26 him lēofre wæs þæt ... | AR 230 ham was leoure uorte adrenchen ham sulf þen uorte beren ham | Sirith 382 Me were levere then ani fe That he hevede enes leien bi me | Ch MP 5.511 him were as good be stille | T 4.84 to teche in this how yow was best to done.

(2) nom. with *had:* Ch F 572 Ne never hadde I thing

so leef, ne lever | Malory 87 he had leuer kyng Lotte
had been slayne than kynge Arthur | ib 92 I had leuer
mete with that knyght | Marlowe J 147 Rather had I
a Jew be hated thus, Then pittied | Sh Meas III. 1.190
I had rather my brother die by the law, then my sonne
should be vnlawfullie borne | Cor IV. 5.186 I had as
liue be a condemn'd man | Fielding T 2.110 Your
La'ship had almost as good be alone | Smollett Roderick
Random 19 I had as lief stand | By T 5.198 That she
had better woven within her palace | Thack P 3.131
you had much best not talk to him.

(3) with case-confusion: Ch B 1027 she hadde [var.
l. *Hire hadde*] lever a knyf Thurghout hir brest, than
ben a womman wikke | C 760 if that yow be so leef
To fynde deeth [two MSS *ye be*, others *to you be*] | R
1646 Me hadde bet ben elleswhere | Bale T 889 Thu
were moch better to kepe thy pacience | Roister 46 ye
were best sir for a while to reuiue againe | Deloney 57
if shee come any more in my house, she were as good
no | Marlowe J 1798 he were best to send it | Sh Meas
III. 2.38 he were as good go a mile | As III. 3.92 I were
better to bee married | R2 III. 3.192 Me rather had,
my heart might feele your loue | R3 IV. 4.337 What
were I best to say? (also Shrew V. 1.108, Cymb III.
6.19).

6.6₉. Many examples may be found in vol IV 9.4
(2,3) on account of the use of the preterit of imagination, but without special regard to case; cf ib 19.9(1)
on the confusion of *would* and *had*. Cf also vol V 11.2.

See on the whole question C. Stoffel in Taalstudie
8.216, Lounsbury SU 150, 269 ff., van der Gaaf ESt
45.381 ff., McKnight MnE 511.

Finally I shall here refer to the phenomenon so
frequent in English that what in the active is an in-

direct object or the regimen of a preposition may in the *passive* become the subject (he was given a watch, she was taken no notice of). See the full treatment in vol III 15.2—15.6.

After the Verb. Predicative

6.7₁. Having dealt with the substitution of the nom. for an original obl. case before the vb, we shall now proceed to the corresponding tendency to use the obl. case after the vb, where a nom. would be used in the old language. This is of course due to the preponderance of the instances in which the word immediately following the vb is its object. Thus, when Trollope writes (D 2.227) There might be somebody, though I think not her, — *her* is viewed as a sort of object of *I think*.

6.7₂. I have already had occasion to mention a few connexions in which the obl. case will naturally come to be used after *it is* (see 6.2₅); to these might be added infinitival nexuses ("acc. with inf."), as in Greene F 10.57 Let it be me, cf Curme CG 40 A noun or pronoun which is predicated of an accusative subject is in the accusative ... He thought Richard to be me | I supposed it to be him | ib 108 A boy whom I believed to be him just passed | Whom do you suppose them to be.

But even where there is no inducement of that kind to use *me*, this form will occur after *it is* by the same linguistic process that has led in Danish to the exclusive use of *det er mig*, and which is seen also in the French *c'est* used in OF with the obl. form of nouns and then also of pronouns, *c'est moi*, etc (see L. Foulet, *Comment on est passé de ce suis je à c'est moi*, in *Romania* 46 (1920) p. 46 ff.).

6.7₃. In OE we have *ic hit eom* (cf German *ich bin es*), which in Ch has developed into *it am I* (A 3766, B 1109, MP 3.186, T 3.752), and *it is I:* Ch R 4365 For it is I that am come down | Malory 38 it was I myself that cam | Caxton R 88 yf ony hier shold haue a reward it shold be I by ryght | Towneley 127 it had neuer bene I | ib 129 it is I | Gammer 142 was it I that it broke? | ib 143 it was not I | Roister 21 that shall not be I | ib 58 it was I that did offende | Marlowe J 656 'tis I | Eastw 561 it is I | Swift T 2 it must be I | Galsw TL 247 It's only I, Jon dear (but 245 Yes, it's me).

Similarly in the 2nd and 3rd persons: Ch B 1054 it was she | ib T 3.1354 It were ye that wroughte me swich wo | Malory 713 they sayd alle, O my lord sir launcelot, be that ye, and he sayd Truly I am he | Towneley 131 I wold say it were he | Caxton R 88 I am he | Fulg 34 Am not I he that ye wolde haue? | Roister 26 this is not she | Sh R2 IV. 1.174 God saue the king! although I be not hee; And yet, Amen, if Heauen doe think him mee | Mcb (three times) tis hee.

6.7₄. The nom. accordingly seems to have been the natural idiom, just as *det är jag* is still in Sweden; but now it is otherwise, just as *det er mig* is good Danish. In Sh (besides the passages accounted for above) we find the obl. case used in three passages, and it is well worth noting that two of them are pronounced by vulgar people, viz. Gent II. 3.25 [the clown Launce:] the dogge is me | Lr I. 4.204 [the fool:] I would not be thee (cf Per II. 1.68 [the fisherman:] here's them in our country of Greece gets more); — the third time it is the angry Timon who says (Tim IV. 3.277) [I am proud] that I am not thee. Nowadays even to the most refined speakers *it's me* is certainly more natural than *it's I*. And Shelley has consecrated the construction as serviceable in the highest poetic style by writing in his Ode to the West Wind (Shelley 642) Be thou, Spirit fierce, My spirit! Be thou me, impetuous one! (the poet may have used the obl. case to avoid two nominatives following one another immediately, and 'Be thou I' would have been phonetically infelicitous and difficult to understand).

I shall now give some examples of the modern usage (from about 1700 on), nearly all from very good authors.

(1) *it is (was,* etc) *me, that is me:* Defoe R 2.41 he had no notion of its being me | Austen M 293 it is me | Keats 4.158 If it was me, I did it in a dream | Hunt A 204 I know it is no more me | Di D 282 are you sure it was me? | Whitman L 111 how often I question and doubt whether that is truly me ... oh I never doubt whether that is really me | Hope D 12 I'm glad it's not me, you know | Kipling L 209 it is only me | Shaw P 227 [Scotchman:] That was me, sir | id M 27 it might have been me | id C 158 if either of us goes, it must be me | Caine C 34 that is me | ib 40 it is me — I know it is me | Benson D 283 it isn't me a bit | Galsw P 10.80 [clergyman:] It's me ... only me! ... It was me | Bennett LM 103 But it's not me that's teaching you | Maugham P 233 It wasn't me that lay on that bed | ONeill Strange Interlude 51 It's me — I, I mean.

(2) Other sentences with predicative *me:* Di F 871 you should have been me | Brontë V 137 And what would you give to be ME? | Collins M 477 if you were me | Stevenson A 86 Willoughby is me! | James S 20 He was already me | Benson D 2.33 The result is me | Locke GP 27 everything I can think of as being me | Shaw StJ 111 Is that meant to be me? ... Is that funny little thing me too? | id TT 271 but the robbed

victim is me — ME! | Kaye-Smith HA 304 the last person he recognized was me | Bennett Imp Pal 404 I'm me | Galsw D 261 That nymph is you; and this man is me | id WM 16 if you were me, wouldn't you tell Frederic | OHenry B 20 I'm me without my hair, ain't I?

6.7₅. *It is I* is often caused by relative attraction (cf 6.2₅): Thack P 876 It is I am in fault, is it? | Caine M 143 It was I that promised myself to Pete | Benson J 213 Don't you see it is I who stand there on that easel? This thing which you think is me, is nearly dead | Galsw MW 304 it's I who have to trust them.

But *it is me* is naturally found before relative clauses in which the pronoun is the object: Brontë V 371 it was me he wanted — me he was seeking | Collins W 101 I wish it was me you had frightened, and not her | Flecker Hassan 134 It is not me you want but my shame!

6.7₆. (3) Obl. case 1st pers. pl: Austen E 162 it is us | Thack V 453 It's you are thrashed, and not us | Benson D 2.330 since we are us | Wells L 129 how sweet it was to forget it all, to be just us two together for a little while | id PF 229 they aren't us ... it isn't us, Stephen, really. It can't be us | Galsw P 12.103 It's only us!

(4) Obl. case 3rd pers. sg: Goldsm 176 "Who's there?" My conductor answered that it was him | Austen P 284 If I was her, I would not have put up with it | Keats 5.23 in doubt whether it was him or his brother | Brontë W 51 if I were her | Swinburne L 46 "That's her," said Redgie, using a grammatical construction which, occurring in a Latin theme, would have brought down birch on his bare skin to a certainty | Shaw 2.16 thats him | Hope F 106 What a pity it's Eugene, and not him |

James S 146 Oh, it isn't really you. I mean it's *her* | Ridge B 5 this is him | Pinero Q 9 This is her | Wells U 250 I'm certain it was her | id V 124 That's *him*, said Ann in sound idiomatic English | Norris P 312 this is him | Locke St 139 "That's him," cried Miss Bunter, in suppressed and ungrammatical excitement | Galsw FM 16 I think that's her (often in Galsw) | Walpole W 103 Rosalind declared that were it her she would be terrified | Kennedy R 331 It turned out that the person they heard was him | Garnett Go 27 if it had not been him it might have been me.

6.7₇. In the following examples the obl. case is due to relative attraction: Marlowe E 1129 ist him you seek | Thack P 794 I like the Captain. But it is not him I want | Rose Macaulay K 267 And, anyhow, it's not her you're engaged to, it's me.

We may even find the obl. case in a sentence where the pron. is in subject relation to an immediately following finite verb: Cronin H 380 It was him tried to kill me.

6.7₈. A predicative in initial position will always be in the nom.: He it is who ...

Thus also if the pron. is immediately followed by *who* as subj. of a relative clause: Kaye-Smith HA 308 it was not he who had failed the spirit of life | ib 312 it was she who had killed him | Wells TM 85 it was they who had taken it.

6.7₉. (5) Obl. case 3rd pers. pl: Austen S 108 it never entered my head that it could be them | Norris O 514 That's not them | Wells T 26 it is not them | Bridges New Verse 13 it was them or nothing | Bennett Acc 178 he entered into their souls. He became them | Galsw FM 93 That's them, I expect ... It *is* them | Ballard Thought & L 38 it cannot *be* them.

6.7₁₀. In sentences where the predicative is the same pron. as the subject, we must necessarily have the nom.: Bennett W 2.50 the axiom that he was he.

In Sh Cor I. 1.236 And were I any thing but what I am, I would wish me onely he, — *he* is the only natural form for the predicative, as *him* would only obscure the meaning of the sentence.

6.7₁₁. If the personal pron. is followed by a corresponding reflexive pron. we shall probably always have the nom. in order to avoid collocations like *him himself*, *her herself* even in cases where relative attraction might suggest the use of the obl. case: It was she herself he wanted to see | It was he himself she wanted to see.

6.7₁₂. Palmer Gr.² writes § 107: "In the normal and spontaneous speech of everyday life, especially between friends and in the conversation of men-folk, the forms [miː], [him], [həː], [ʌs], and [ðem] are usually heard: ... In careful and deliberate speech, especially between strangers and women-folk, when one is on one's guard against possible criticism, the forms [ai], [hiː], [ʃiː], [wiː], and [ðei] are generally heard. Those who have cultivated a bookish or formal style of speaking almost invariably use this form." — Weekley in *Saxo Grammaticus* 79 ff. unreservedly accepts *That's me*, but would "hesitate at 'That's him (or her)' and draw the line at 'Between you and I, him and her drink too much'." (Cf below, 7.4₃, 7.5₄, and 7.5₆). According to Mr. Walt Arneson, Americans are inclined to use *It is I*, etc, much more than English people.

In some of my quotations the construction with obl. case is expressly characterized as "ungrammatical" or the like, and it is sometimes used with a certain diffidence.

After the Verb. Subject

6.8₁. The obl. case may even be found in the subject, thus in the first place in sentences introduced by the preparatory *there:* Thack V 278 [Oxf. undergraduate:] there was me and Ringwood of Christchurch | Hardy R 71 there are only you and me now to think of | Kipling K 217 There is none but me can doctor a sick pearl ... for a sick pearl there is only me | Bennett LR 149 there are others, for instance me, who can't quite afford ... | McKenna M 120 There was Bertie and me and a third man.

Both cases in Di N 665 There'll only be she and me.

Thus also with the 1st pers. pl: Di P 483 there was only us two | Kipling L 107 there are only us two in the world | Norris S 231 that there was just us — you and I — in the world | Locke FS 170 there will be only us two.

The obl. case is rarer after *here* BJo 1.10 here be them can perceive it | ib 1.101 here be them have been... | Shaw Ms 175 Heres the boy in gaol and me disgraced for ever.

6.8₂. Next in cases like the following with *us*, which occur at any rate from the 15th cent.: Towneley 31 hens must vs fle | 103 ffyrst must vs crepe and sythen go (also ib 33) | Devil E 532 Shall's in to breakfast? | Eastw 426 when shal's be married? | Beaumont 1.139 Shall's geld him. — *Shall's* for *shall we* is found six times in Sh. As in four of the quotations it means pretty much the same thing as *let us* (Cor IV. 6.148 Shal's to the Capitoll | Wint I. 2.178 | Cymb V. 5.228 | Per IV. 5.7) it is probable that this idiom is originally due to a blending of *let us* and *shall we* (compare the corresponding use of a nom. after *let*, 6.4₁). But it has been extended to other cases as well: Tim IV.

3.408 How shal's get it? | Cymb IV. 2.233 Where shall's lay him?

6.8₃. Towards the end of the 18th cent. *shall us* was common in vulgar speech according to Pegge († 1800) Anecd 1803 p. 159, who adds: The Londoner also will say — "Can us," "May us," and "Have us." — Storm EPh 676 quotes some instances of vg *shall us*? etc, from Dickens and Trollope, and on p. 831 he quotes from a rendering of children's language: What shall us do first? To which I may add Kipling L 161 [child speaking] Shall us take some liver pills? | Hardy F 438 [dial.] Let's look into Warren's, shall us, neighbours? | id Under the Greenw. Tree 70 They [tunes] move his soul; don't 'em, father? — Cf also Matthews, *Cockney* p. 39. — This usage is decidedly substandard.

6.8₄. I find a further trace of the influence of position in Sh Mcb V. 8.34 And damn'd be him that first cries hold, enough! (*him* of course "emended" to *he* by Pope and most later editors) — *Damn'd be* is here taken as one whole meaning the same thing as, and therefore governing the same case as (*God*) *damn*. Cf. also Otway 227 Curst be him that doubts Thy virtue! | Morris E 48 Curst be the King, and thee also.

The person that should properly be the subject of the vb is in later English practically always governed by *to:* Fielding 1.449 you a rogue, and be damn'd to you, without a penny in your pocket (also id T 1.297, 2.118, 4.87) | id T 50 be rotted to'n | Byron Corresp. 1.29 be damned to them (ib 67, 71) | ib 2.238 Murray showed (and be d—d to him) a letter ... | Thack V 158 be hanged to them | Darwin L 3.76 I went to Lubbock's, partly in hopes of seeing you, and, be hanged to you, you were not there | Meredith H 117 Be off, and be blowed to you | Ward D 1.220 be d—d to your Christian brotherhood! | Stevenson C 136 It's a bad business and be damned to it. *Be damned (hanged, dashed) to* ... in innumerable other passages in recent novels.

Here the phrase *be damned* or *hanged*, etc, has become an exclamation, and *to you* is added as if "I say" was understood; compare also *Hail to thee* (ME *heil be þow*); *farewell to you; welcome to you, good-bye to you* (properly containing two *yous*). Cf Stevenson T 256 I've got my piece o' news, and thanky (< thank ye) to him for that.

6.8₅. An earlier form of the phrase *Would to God* is *Would God*, where *God* is the subject: Ch MP 3.814 God wolde I coude clepe her wers | Malory 66 so wold god I had another | ib 81 wolde god she had not comen in to thys courte | Greene F 6.40 would God the lovely earl had that. — But when people lost the habit of placing a subject after the vb, they came to take *would* as an aphetic form for *I would* and *God* as the obl. case (dative); and the analogy of the corresponding phrase *I wish to God* (or, *I pray to God*) would of course facilitate the change of *God* into *to God*.

6.9₁. The position after the vb has probably had no small share in rendering the use of *thee* (and *you*) so frequent after an *imperative*, especially in early ModE; the usage is still seen in the poetical phrase "Fare thee well." Here we have, however, a concurrent influence in the use of a reflexive pronoun (without the addition of *self*) which was extremely common in all the early periods of the language, and which did not perceptibly alter the meaning of the vb to which it was added (See Voges, *Der reflexive dativ im englischen* in Anglia 6.317 ff.). This reflexive pronoun was sometimes originally added in the accusative, e.g., after *restan* (see Voges 333), but generally in the dative, a distinction which, however, obviously had no significance for any but the very earliest stages of the language. As now it made no difference whatever whether the speaker said *I fear* or *I fear me* (cp. e.g. Marlowe J 876 with ib 1110), the imperative would be indifferently *fear* or *fear thee* (*fear yow*) (cf e. g. Ch L 1742 dreed thee noght | Malory 61 and 85 drede yow not); but it was equally possible with the same meaning to say *fear thou* (*fear ye*), with the usual addition of the nom. of the pronoun to indicate the subject, e.g. Malory 73 go ye | ib 74 telle thow | ib 75 doubte ye not, etc, etc. Voges even quotes (p. 336) an example of both cases used in the same sentence: Judas: Slep thou the anon. — In other words, after an imperative a nom. and an obl. case would very often be used indiscriminately.

6.9₂. Examples (the vbs alphabetically):

(1) nom. or obl. case with the same vb:

care: Malory 72 Care ye not : ib 135 care not yow.

fare (well) : Sh Merch I. 1.58 and 103 fare ye well | Tp V. 318 fare thou well : Mcb IV. 3.34 Far thee well | Tw III. 4.183 fartheewell | ib III. 4.236 far-thee-well | Merch II. 7.773 and Cor I. 5.18 fare you well | Tim I. 1.164 Well fare you (rare).

get: Redford W 8 and 282 get ye foorth | Marlowe J 1226 get ye gon : get thee gone (common, Sh) | Mcb V. 8.5 get thee back | Greene F 11.20 get thee from Bacon's sight.

sit: Sh H4B IV. 5.182 sit thou by my bedde | Di Do 77 sit ye down, girls, sit ye down | GE A 192 sit ye down : Sh Mids IV. 1.1 sit thee downe vpon this flowry bed | Dryden 5.404 Sit thee down (also Congreve 270, Scott I 192). Also with the transitive vb *set:* Sh LLL IV. 3.4 set thee down (in some editions emended to *sit*).

stand: Sh Alls V. 3.35 stand thou forth : Ado IV. 1.24 stand thee by.

stay: Sh Cæs V. 5.44 stay thou : H6C III. 2.58 stay thee.

turn: AV Ps 69.16 turn vnto mee | Ezek. 33.11 turne ye from your euill wayes : Ps 25.16 turne thee vnto me | Prov. 1.23 turne you, at my reproofe | Marlowe T 801 bid him turne him back to war with vs | Swinburne A 109 Turn back now, turn thee, As who turns him to wake.

(2) the obl. case:

cheer: Greene F 13.99 cheer thee [= cheer up].

haste: Ch B 1347 hasteth yow (also id I 72) | id B 2240 ne haste yow noght too faste | Marlowe T 805 Haste thee | Greene F 12.77 haste thee post to Fressingfield.

hie: Marlowe T 934 Hie thee | Greene F 12.57 hie thee to Fressingfield | Sh Mcb III. 1.35 Hye you to horse.

hold: Marlowe J 1130 Hold thee, wench | ib 2299 here, hold thee, Barabas | Sh Mcb III. 2.54 hold thee still.

remember: Ch MP 3.717 Remembre yow of Socrates.
rest: Marlowe T 2577 Reste thee.
run: Sh Ado III. 1.1 runne thee to the parlour.
take: Sh Mcb II. 1.5 take thee that too.

On the transitive and intransitive use of various vbs including some of the above see vol III ch 16.

6.9₃. It will now be easily understood that *thee* or *you* would be freely added to imperatives where the thought of a reflexive pronoun would not be very appropriate. In *hear thee, hark thee, look thee* and similar cases, Voges finds a reflexive dative, whereas Al. Schmidt quotes them under the heading "*thee* for *thou;*" it is difficult to draw a line here. When Troilus says (Sh Tro IV. 5.115) Hector, thou sleep'st, awake thee, — no less then three grammatical explanations are applicable: *awake* may be intransitive, and *thee* the subject (Al. Schmidt), *awake* is intransitive, but *thee* is a reflexive dative (Voges 372), and finally, *awake* may be a transitive vb having *thee* as its object (cf NED); but whichever way the grammatical construction is explained, the meaning remains the same.

It is evident that all this must have contributed very much to impair the feeling for the case-distinction, and it should be noted that we have here a cause of confusion that is peculiar to the pronouns of the second person.

When in PE a pronoun is added to an imperative it is generally placed before it. See examples vol III 11.8$_3$ ff.

In ModE examples may be found everywhere, so I shall only state the fact that in the modern use of *himself* and *themselves* we have an obl. case used as a nom. (or rather as a common case), and that this was formerly the case with *me self* (still in vg) and *us self* (or *us selue, seluen*), which have now been ousted by *myself* and *ourselves*. *Her* in *herself* may be the obl. case or the possessive.

Note Butler in SPE Handwriting Plate 23 it suggests a writer who has him or herself suffered much from some great overwhelming misfortune.

6.9$_4$. Sometimes we come across isolated uses of the obl. for the nom. case, which are probably to be ascribed to analogical influence exercised by the *self*-combinations. Abbott Sh-Gr 214 quotes Sh John IV. 2.50 Your safety, for the which my selfe and them Bend their best studies — and says, "Perhaps *them* is attracted by myself," which naturally suggests the objective "myself and (they) them(selves)."

That this is the correct explanation seems to be rendered more likely by the parallel passage Marlowe T 433 Thy selfe and them shall neuer part from me — and perhaps it is also applicable to the following two sentences: Sh Wint I. 2.410 Or both your selfe and me Cry lost | Cæs I 3.76 No mightier then thy selfe, or me [N.B. *than*!], and to the one modern example I have noted: Hewlett Q 446 when yourself and him are in danger.

Chapter VII
Case in Pronouns (Continued)
Phonetic Influences

7.1. I now come to the last but by no means the least important of the agencies that have brought about changes in the original relations between the cases of the pronouns. I mean the influence of sound upon sense.

A glance at the list of pronominal forms printed above, 6.1_4, will show that six of them rime together: the nominatives *we, ye, he, she,* and the oblique forms *me, thee.* After the old case-rules had been shaken off in different ways, instinctive feeling seized upon this similarity; and likeness in form has in part led to likeness in function.

As evidence of this tendency I shall first mention Malory's use of those vbs in which an exchange of object and subject was going on in his times (above, 6.7_7ff.). He has a manifest predilection for the *e*-forms without any regard to their original case-values. I note all the instances found in some hundred pages:

Malory 115 now *me* lacketh an hors | 127 *ye* shalle lacke none | 71, 90, 148 *me* lyst(e) | 61, 114, 146 *ye* lyst | 76 *ye* nede not to pulle half so hard | 115 *ye* shalle not nede | 153 *he* shalle repente ... *me* sore repenteth | 59, 82, 83, 84, 96, 106, 107, 117, 133 *me* repenteth | 78, 80 *ye* shalle repente hit | 117 *ye* ouȝt sore to repente it | 79, 82, 118 *me* forthynketh [= I repent] | 121 it were *me* leuer | 46 *ye* were better for to stynte | 62 *ye* were better to gyue | 87 whether is *me* better to treate | 69 that is *me* loth to doo | 90 that were *me* loth to doo | 100 *he* wylle be lothe to returne | 105 *we* wolde be loth to haue adoo with yow | 115 *he* is ful loth to do wronge.

The following are the only exceptions: 131 though *I* lacke wepen, *I* shalle lacke no worship | 101 *hym* nedeth none | 82 els wold *I* haue ben lothe | 112, 131 *I* am loth. (*Thynke* and *lyke* are always 'impersonal' in Malory, cf above, 6.5$_8$ and 6.6$_3$).

A century later the same holds good of the vb *lust* in Roister: *ye* (pp. 12 and 51), *me* (12), *he* (42), *she* (87); there are two exceptions: *hym* (43), *I* (44).

The phonetic similarity is used to mark the contrast in Sh Mcb III. 4.14 'Tis better *thee* without then *he* within.

We now see the reason why *me* is very often used as a nom. even by educated speakers, who in the same positions would never think of using *him* or *her*. Thus after *it is*, see above, 6.7$_2$ff.

7.2$_1$. Sweet, *Words, Log. and Gr.* says on p. 26: "The real difference between 'I' and 'me' is that 'I' is an inseparable prefix used to form finite verbs, while 'me' is an independent or absolute pronoun, which can be used without a verb to follow. These distinctions are carried out in vulgar English as strictly as in French, where the distinction between the conjoint 'je' and the absolute 'moi' is rigidly enforced." And in the *Primer of Spoken English* 36: "The nom. *I* is only used in immediate agreement with a verb; when used absolutely, *me* is substituted for it by the formal analogy of *he, we, she,* which are used absolutely as well as dependently: *it's he, it's me; who's there? me.*"

7.2₂. The common answer which was formerly always *Not I!* (thus in Sh, see Sh-lex. p. 565 *a* at the bottom) is now often heard as *Not me!* (Di D 253) Also *only me*, as in Di Do 131 "Wal'r!" cried the Captain. "Ay, ay, Captain Cuttle," returned Walter, "only me." Cf also Scott A 1.225 "the letter that ye opened." "Me opened! ye ken yoursel, it just cam open o' free will in my hand."

The corresponding form in the third person does not seem to be *Not him!* even in vulgar speech, but always *Not he!* At least I find in Thenks 82 Not 'e!

To avoid the natural use of *me*, branded as incorrect in educational institutions, and the unnatural use of *I* standing alone, English people add a superfluous vb more frequently than people of other nations in such sentences as "He is older than I am."

7.2₃. *Me*, then, to some extent has become a common case under the influence of *he*, etc, and we find some traces of a development in the same direction beginning in the case of the other pronouns in [i·], only that it is here the nom. that has been generalized: Sh Wiv III. 2.26 There is such a league betweene my goodman and he | Wint II. 3.6 But shee, I can hooke to me (cf 6.2₃) | Oth IV. 2.3 You haue seene Cassio and she together | LLL IV. 2.30 Those parts that doe fructifie in vs more then he [= in him] | Fielding T 1.200 [Squire Western:] It will do'n ['do him'] no harm with he | ib 2.50 [id:] Between your nephew and she (cf *between you and I* below, 7.4₃) | Cowper John Gilpin: On horseback after we | Goldsm 658 She'd [Betty] make two of she [Miss Neville].

Professor Moore Smith wrote to me: "I do not feel convinced that there is a difference between the vulgar (or natural) English, 'It's me — it's him'; 'not me — and not him'. I think the chief reason of *him* being less common is that while *me* is distinctive, in the third person it is generally necessary to mention the name. It seems to me very familiar English, 'Is he going'? 'Not *him*.' Of course such usages may differ in different parts of the country."

7.3₁. Phonetic influences may have been at work in various other ways. If the vowel of the nom. *þu* were weakened when the word was unstressed the result would be *þe* [ðə], exactly like a weakened form of the obl. form *þē*. This, I take it, is the explanation of the nom. *þe* found frequently in certain combinations in the Ayenbite of Inwit, *þe wylt*, etc, cf *Huannes comste* 'whence comest thou' (cf *to* > *te*). As, however, this use of *þe* for *þu* is only found in a few texts, we cannot ascribe to it any great influence on the later development.

7.3₂. Similarly a *you* pronounced with weak sentence-stress will be reduced to *ye* or even to the short vowel [i], written *y*, e.g. Kipling L 197 yet y' know | ib 266 take it as a loan y' know. — This is especially the case in stock phrases like *thank you* (*thanky*), *God be with you* (Congreve 223 Good b'w'ye > *Goodbye:* the *oo*-vowel is probably introduced from the other forms of salutation: *good-morrow*, *good-night*, etc, the naming of *God* being thus avoided; in Sh it is also written *God buy you*), *God give you good even* (in Sh *Godgigoden, God-igoden, God dig you den*).

Harky (*hark'ee*) and *look'ee* may contain *ye*, weakened for *you*, or the nom. *ye*. I am inclined to think that this phonetic weakening of *you* is the cause of the unstressed *ye* after vbs, which is found so very frequently from the beginning of the 16th cent., although it is impossible in each single instance to distinguish the *ye* which originates in this way from *ye*'s called forth by other circumstances dealt with in this chapter.

In Redford W we generally find *ye*, both as the nom. and the obl. case, though *you*, too, is frequently found in both cases. *Ye* after a vb was probably pronounced as a weakly stressed [i]; cf e.g. the rime 597 plentye : sent ye.

See also the weakened *ye* in Ch T 1.5 er that I parte fro ye : joye, the earliest example of *ye* as obl. case?

7.3₃. Further we have here to take into account the elision of a final unstressed vowel before a word beginning with a vowel, which was formerly extremely common in English (see vol I 6.13 and 9.82). But these phonetic tendencies cannot have any influence on the case-relations of most pronouns; weaken the vowel of *me* as you like or drop it altogether, the remaining *m'* is not brought one bit the nearer to the nom. *I*. But the pronouns of the 2nd pers. have this peculiarity that the cases are distinguished by the vowel only; if the vowel is left out it becomes impossible to tell whether the nom. or the obl. case is meant — one more reason for the old distinction to become forgotten.

In Ch the vowel of *thee* is elided, e.g. B 1660 the goost that in th'alighte. In Greene F 12.78 For ere thou hast fitted all things for her state — we must certainly read *th'hast* (see also ib 13.37). In countless passages, where modern editions of Sh read *you're* the old folio has *y'are*, which should no doubt be interpreted *ye are* (*y'are* also e.g. Dryden V. 137, Rehearsal 35). But when we find *th'art*, e.g. Sh H4B III. 2.189 do'st thou roare before th'art prickt | ib III. 2.233 and 268 [Q] th'art (Fol. thou art, Cambr. ed. thou'rt) | Cor IV. 5.17 and 100 th'art, mod. edd. thou'rt | Tim I. 2.25, II. 2.58, IV. 3.45 and 481, — is this to be explained as *thou art* (*thu art*) or as *thee art*? (*Thou'rt* is found in the fol. Mcb I. 5.29 | John IV. 3.121 | Meas III. 1.15 and 25, Wint I. 2.211).

Similarly Sh *th'hast* (mod. edd. *thou'st*), *th'hadst* (mod. edd. *thou hadst;* Dekker F 2072 th'adst). In Mcb IV. 1.62 Say if th'hadst rather heare it from our mouthes — it is especially difficult to decide in favour of one or the other form on account of the peculiar constructions of *had rather* (see above, 6.6$_8$, and vol IV 9.4(3) and 19.9).

7.3₄. There is one more thing to be noticed. Where the pronouns are combined with the verbal forms commencing with *w*, those forms are preferred that contain rounded vowels. The past subjunctive of *y'are* is in Sh *you're* (Cymb III. 2.79 Madam, you're best consider); the 2nd pers., corresponding to *I'le* for *I will*, is not *ye'le*, but *you'le* (Marlowe J 708; acc. to Sh-lex. *ye'le* is found only once, in the 1st quarto of LLL I. 2.54, where, however, the 2nd quarto and the folios have *you'll*), or more frequently *you'll*. Now I take it to be highly probable that these forms were heard in the spoken language at a much earlier period than they are recorded in literature, that is, at a time when *you* was not yet used as a nom., and that they are contracted not from *you were*, but from *ye were, ye will* (? *ye wol*), the vowel *u* being thus a representative of the *w* of the vb. If this is so, we have here yet another reason for the confusion of *ye* and *you*, as the contracted forms *you'll* and *you're* would be felt instinctively as compounds of *you* and *will* or *were*. For *thou wert* we find *thou'rt*; for *thou wilt* similarly *thou'lt* (e.g. Marlowe J 1144; often in Sh, who also, though rarely, writes *thou't*).

7.3₅. The pronouns in question were pronounced by Chaucer and his contemporaries as follows:

Nom.	ðu· (ðu)	je· (je)
Obl. case	ðe· (ðe)	ju· (ju),

the forms in ( ) being used whenever the pronouns were unstressed or half-stressed. A regular phonetic development of these pronunciations would have given the following modern forms:

Nom.	ðau (ðu)	ji· (ji)
Obl. case	ði· (ði)	jau (ju).

The forms [ðu] and [jau] are no longer heard, but their former existence is directly evidenced by the works of the old phoneticians, thus Bullokar *(Booke at large* 1580, and *Æsopus* 1585) transcribes *thou* with the same sign as that used in *full, suffer, but, us, put,* etc, i.e. short [u] as in ModE *full*. The spelling *thu* is by no means rare in the 16th cent.; it is used consistently, e.g. in Bale T. And Gil, *Logonomia* 41, states that a pronunciation of *you* rhyming with *how* and *now* was found in his times.

It is in accord with this that in Roister (printed 1566) *you* rimes with *thou* (pp. 31 and 32), with *now* (15, 43, 48, 53, 60, 63, and 70), and with *inowe* (18). Cf Dekker Sh III. 3.36 *vow : you*.

Now the [au]-form of *you* is extinct; the current pronunciation [ju·] or [juw] must be due to a natural lengthening of the originally unstressed form [ju], when it was used with stress. The existence of the form [juˑ] at the time of Sh may be concluded from the pun in LLL V. 1.60 on the pronoun and the fifth vowel.

7.3₆. In *thou*, on the other hand, it is the fuller form with [au] that is now heard solely. This is quite natural because the word is now never found in colloquial language, so that only the emphatic pronunciation of solemn or ceremonial speech has survived. But when the two pronouns *thou* and *you* were used side by side in ordinary conversation, their sounds were alike; *you* and *thou* formed correct rimes, exactly as *thee* and *ye* did. The feeling of *you* and *thou* as parallel forms is manifest in the rimed dialogue in Roister 31: I would take a gay riche husbande, and I were you. — In good sooth, Madge, e'en so would I, if I were thou. — But to the formal likeness corresponded a functional unlikeness: *you* is not the same case as *thou*, but as *thee*, and *ye* has the same case function as *thou*. Are not these cross-associations between sound and sense likely to have exerted some influence on the mutual relations of the forms?

7.3₇. This supposition becomes the more probable when it is remembered that the pronouns of the 2nd pers. are different from the other pronouns in that the sg and pl to a great extent are synonymous. *I* and *we* cannot be used in the same signification, except in the case of the "royal" and "editorial" *we;* but in the second person the pl *ye, you* begins very early in imitation of French politeness to be used in addressing one person. See further vol. II 2.82 ff.

For curiosity's sake I may mention that Chaucer's Melibee addresses his wife as *thou*, but she him as *ye*, and that in Sh's VA Venus says *thou* and Adonis *you* (not *ye*).

If I am not mistaken, then, *thou* had some share in the rise of the *you* nom.; and I find a corroboration of this theory in the fact that, as far as I know, the earliest known instances of *you* as a nom. (15th c.) are found in addressing single individuals. This is the case of the four certain instances pointed out by Zupitza in the Romance of Guy of Warwick, where *you* is not yet found as a nom. pl. Some of the old grammarians expressly call attention to the use of *you* for *thou*, *thee* and *ye* as its plural in colloquial speech (Wallis 1653, Cooper 1685).

But that distinction could not remain stable; even before the utterances just mentioned were written, *you* had in the spoken language found its way to the nom. pl; Latimer (1549) uses *you* in addressing those whom he has just called *ye lords*, and Sh and Marlowe use *you* and *ye* indiscriminately without any distinction of case or number. If any difference is made it is that of using *you* in emphasis, and *ye* as an unstressed form (cf above, 7.3$_1$): Marlowe T 3988 you, ye slaves | ib 687 you will not sell it, will ye? | Carlyle FR 383 And you, ye Friends of Royalty. — Perhaps also Mi A 50 We can grow ignorant again ...; but you then must first become that which ye cannot be. Mason. *Engl. Gr.* 49 states: In Spenser *you*, as a nominative, is emphatic, *ye* is unemphatic.

See also Abbott § 236, who gives some instances of the use of *you* and *ye* being sometimes the directly opposite of the original one, e.g. Cæs III. 1.157 I do beseech yee, if you beare me hard. Also Gent IV. 1.3.

To return to the original sg of the 2nd pers. As an early instance of vacillation between *thou* and *thee* I shall mention: Ch MP 1.107 O tresorere of bounte to mankynde, The whom God chees to moder for humblesse!

— where the *the* is probably caused by relative attraction (cf above, 6.2$_5$); but one MS has *yee*, and another *þou*.

In Elizabethan literature *thee* is not rare as a nom. though it is on the other hand far less frequent than *you;* we have already seen the explanation of some instances of *thee*, among others H6B I. 2.69 here's none but thee, and I (cf above, 6.3$_2$) | Hml V. 2.63 Thinkst thee — and several instances of *thee* after *it is* (6.2$_5$). But these explanations do not hold good in the following quotations: Marlowe J 1056 What hast thee done? | Sh H4A I. 2.127 How agrees the diuell and thee about thy soule, that thou soldest him? | Dryden Poems 2.220 Scotland and Thee did each in other live | Lewis Morris Poet. Works 74 What I worship is not wholly thee.

To supplement what is said in vol. II 2.83 (and in *Progress* p. 268-9) on the Quakers (*thee has*, etc) I may refer to AmSp 4. 359-363.

7.3$_8$. As the upshot of all these varying influences we may give the following paradigm of the pronoun for the second person in Standard English:

Everyday use	Poetical
nom. sg. *you*	*thou*
obl. sg. *you*	*thee*
nom. pl. *you*	*ye*
obl. pl. *you*	*ye*

On the use of *you people, you girls, you all*, etc, in addressing several people see vol II 2.87 f.

7.4$_1$. I place here a few instances of what might be called anomalous case usage which it has not been possible to class among the previous sections.

We is sometimes found as a preposed unchanged adjunct (cf. Dan. *med vi andre*, common particularly in Jutland). In English perhaps in imitation of *you Americans*, etc, with *you* unchanged. Examples: Pinero B 12 I'm the only single one out of we three musketeers | Rosebery Fight to a Finish (1914) 8 the position of we elderly ones, who have to dwell among the sheepfolds | Loos, Gentlemen Marry Brunettes, three times 112 and 173 we Americans, as object or after a preposition.

Contrast this with *us two*, etc, as subject, below, 7.5$_3$ (2).

On the other hand we may find the obl. case in the subject of a content-clause, e.g. Swift P 116 You think us old fellows are fools; cf: you think us fools.

7.4₂. In the section on Notional Subject (above, 6.4₁ff.) we noticed several examples of groups ... *and I* where traditional grammar would require ... *and me*. It is possibly from such occurrences that the type has become so firmly rooted in the language as to be used even as an ordinary direct or indirect object: Greene J4 339 Nor earth nor heauen shall part my loue and I [: die] | Osborne 24 She that was borne to persecute you and I | Defoe R 259 ask why God does not kill you and I | id M 24 as it respects you and I | Goldsm 645 Won't you give papa and I a little of your company? — In apposition to the object: Walpole Cp 177 God will come and He will find us both together — you and I.

And as regimen of a preposition: BJo 1.103 he has been with my cousin Edward and I, all the day | Defoe Rox 276 she came up to Amy and I | Burns 1.121 This life has joys for you and I | Pegge Anecd 307 To you and I, Sir, who have seen half a hundred years, it is refunding | Keats 4.137 the pleasure of such romantic chaps as Brown and I | Bennett PL 32 [vg] a point that is appreciated by both Braiding and I | Walpole

GM 360 You're settled — all of you — but with Millie and Henry and I everything's to come.

With *or:* Fox 2.10 different to you or I.

Cf above, 6.3$_6$, *like you and (or) I*.

7.4$_3$. Though *between you and me* may be found (Spectator 181, Congreve Double Dealer 212, Fielding 1.205, etc) the combination *between you and I* has been frequent from ElE to the present day: Sh Merch III. 2.321 all debts are cleerd betweene you and I | Deloney 7 | Congreve 118 | Defoe M 34 there was nothing between Mr. Robert and I | id Rox 40 So far had this innocent girl gone in jesting between her and I | Fielding 1.508 | Di P 104 | Maxwell G 202 between two such people as Gabrielle and I | Wilder H 83 | Maugham Pl 4.237 between you and I and the gatepost.

Sweet NEG 341 explains the modern use of the construction thus: "The result of this reaction against *me* in *it is me*, etc., is that the *me* in such constructions as *between John and me, he saw John and me* sounds vulgar and ungrammatical, and is consequently corrected into *I* occasionally in speech, but oftenest in writing." Similarly Fowler MEU p. 50 says that *between you and I* "perhaps results from a hazy remembrance of hearing *you & me* corrected in the subjective." But this reaction ('hyper-correct') does not explain everything.

Final Remarks

7.5$_1$. Here I end my survey of the various case-shifting agencies and of their operations. It happens extremely often that in the same sentence two or more causes co-operate to make the speaker use a different case from what the grammar of an earlier stage of the language would require. The more frequently such concurrences occur, the greater the vitality of the new manner of using the case in question. We saw in 6.5$_7$ that two separate tendencies, whose effects do not appear properly till some two hundred years late, were powerful enough when co-operating to bring about a result. And in the quotations used to illustrate the first sections of this chapter it will be noticed that the forms in *e* supply a comparatively greater contingent than the other forms, showing thus the concurrence of the associations treated in 7.1 ff. It will also be clear that with the pronouns of the second person, more shifting agencies were at work than with the rest (7.3$_1$ ff.), the result being that the original case-relations have been completely revolutionized in these pronouns. In the case of *I* and *me*, too, some special causes of changes in the case-relations have been pointed out (7.1 ff. and 7.4$_2$ f.), but they are much less powerful than those seen in the second person, and operated besides in opposite directions, so that the same simplicity as that found in *you* was here impossible. Finally, we have seen that the invariable position of *who* before the verb has caused it to become a common case, *whom* being relegated to a very limited province which did not properly belong to it.

7.5$_2$. There is one factor I have not taken into account, though it is by many grammarians given as explaining the majority of case-shiftings in a great many languages, — I mean the *tendency to let the oblique (object) case prevail over the nominative (subject) case*. My reason is simply that this tendency cannot be considered as a *cause* of case-shiftings, but merely *indicates the direction of change and the final result, but not its why and wherefore*. Indeed, in English, at least, it does not even exhaustively indicate the direction of change as the nominative carries the day in the nexus tertiary, in *who* and in the combination *between you and I;* note also *I like* for *me likes*, etc. Still, it must be granted that the nominative generally has the worst of it, the majority of the case-shifting agencies operating in the favour of the oblique case. Thus, while it is only the position immediately before the verb that supports the nominative, the oblique case is always the most natural case in any other position; see, e.g., the treatment of *than* as a preposition.

7.5₃. Here I give some quotations for the use of more or less loose or 'absolute' pronouns as used when not directly joined to a vb.

(1) as notional subject of a vb understood from the previous context: Austen M 24 What could I do with Fanny? Me! a poor helpless widow | ib 131 "You must be Cottager's wife." "Me!" cried Fanny | Di D 218 I suppose you are quite a great lawyer? "Me, Master Copperfield," said Uriah | id N 161 It's Mr. Noggs that's wanted. Me! | Thack N 347 I don't know what the world is coming to, or me either | Ru P 3.76 there was no one in the cabin but ourselves (that is to say, papa, mamma, old Anne, and me) | Vachell H 64 "who was in your room?" Without waiting for Lovell to answer, the other boys, each in turn, said, "I, sir," or "Me, sir." | Galsw Ca 452 what would you have done? Me? Let her stew in her own juice | Bennett RS 159 She does get an afternoon off. But me? When? || id P 142 who are the guests? Oh! Nobody! Only us and Charlie, of course || id LR 20 I believe he wants to make you a minister. — Him! He'd lose the war first | id Acc 199 He told me you weren't hurt, nor him either | Galsw P 8.38 [educated lady:] They're hopeless, all three — especially her | Hart BT 161 [vg] Other men might, but not them.

(2) as the subject of a vb which does not follow immediately after the pronoun: Defoe Rox 211 when I

plainly saw that the farthest of the two, him whose face looked towards the coach, was my friend the Dutch merchant | Thack N 157 I don't know how his mother — her who wrote the hymns, you know, ... comes to be Rebecca | Stevenson T 38 [the author himself:] another fellow, probably him who had remained below ... came to the door | Bennett P 305 what about that wife of yours? — Oh! Her! She's dead | Priestley G 551 That tall one — no, the very long thin man, him with the eyebrows — he plays the banjo || GE S 157 us old fellows may wish ourselves young to-night | Ridge G 138 Us two will lead the way | Butler W 351 [vg] What us poor girls wants | Priestley G 584 us girls must stick together | ib 322 but us dressmakers we can't help noticing, you know | NJacob Lie 303 Only Angela and I are left, just us two.

(3) the pronoun in question is not the only subject: Bunyan P 15 both he, and them that are with him shoot arrows | Defoe R 287 that the two which appear'd (viz.) Friday and me, were two heavenly spirits | Goldsm V 2.83 [gentleman:] we shall shortly see which is the fittest object of scorn, you or me | Austen P 276 Kitty and me drew up all the blinds (also ib 275) | id S 150 Anne and me are to go | Thack V 56 [vg] him and his fam'ly has been cheating me | ib 179 [city man:] me and George shouldn't part in anger | id N 37 for which you and me between us paid the purchase-money | Di F 848 [Police Inspector:] now that we meet, him and me, you'll say | Stevenson JH 70 [servant:] "Who is going to do it?" "Why, you and me, sir." | Henley B 35 Me and the Bantam went out and finished the evening on hot gin | Kipling S 268 out we went — forty Pathans, Tertius, and me | ib 277 him and thirty Sikhs went down | Hope Ch 183 You and

me and the recorder 'ud drive up in the coach | Ridge
L 188 me and you will go down to Epping Forest |
Bennett LR 70 [Lord Raingo:] We've had our differ-
ences, you and me | id RS 238 but you and her under-
stand each other | id Imp Pal 376 Can my husband or
me do anything? the bar-woman amiably enquired |
Galsw Ca 453 Now baby and me'll get no holiday |
Wells H 213 [Sir Isaac Harman:] me and you can
have a bit of a talk | Mackenzie SA 248 [vg] But now
him and me has never been such friends | Oppenheim
in BDS 62 Him and his young lady typist, they left
together somewhere about seven | Lewis MA 37 Either
he or me has got to get out | id MS 140 But her and I
have worked our fingers to the bone ... Mama and me
are planning to go ...

7.5₄. In vulgar speech *me* is very common in *and*-
combinations, also with *me* immediately before the vb:
Di D 241 we are too 'umble, sir, said Mrs. Heep, my
son and me, to be friends of Master Copperfield | ib
356 [Uriah Heep:] Mother and me will have to work
our way upwards | ib 535 [id:] Father and me was
brought up at a foundation school | ib 538 [id:]
you and me know what we do | Ridge Mord Em'ly
92 Me and you ain't. Me and you like a certain
amount of liberty | Shaw Getting Married 211 Me and
the beadle have been all over the place in a couple of
taxis, maam | id A 137 You and me is men of the
world, aint we? | Sherriff J 103 my old lady and me
used to walk.

7.5₅. (4) totally disconnected from any vb. — The
first quotations may be in imitation of Lat. *me mise-
rum!* — : Dekker F 204 Oh miserable me! | ib 1990
wretched mee | Sh Sonn 37.14 then ten times happy
me! | Mi PL 4.73 Me miserable | Fox 2.147 Poor Druids!

and Poor Us! | Barrie M 189 Merry me! | Sayers NT 225 'The French haven't any of our inhibitions about dealing with witnesses.' 'Lucky them, my lord.' | Bennett P 112 More fool him! || Priestley G 450 [lady in letter:] Isn't it fantastic — you out there, and me here? | Black P 2.141 I am not going to be talked out of my common-sense, and me on my death-bed!

Cf above, 6.4$_4$.

With *poor me*! compare the use of *me* in other exclamations: O me! Woe me! Ay me! (Mi PL 4.86, etc), O me accurst! (Devil E 529), Aye me detested! (Sh Tw V. 142), Alas me! (Keats 2.70), The use of *me* in *dear me*! *gracious me*! and other apologies for oaths is probably due to analogy with the corresponding use of the pronoun as an object after a vb, as in *bless me*! etc. So perhaps also in Sh H4A II. 3.97 Gods me, my horse.

7.5₆. This will afford an explanation of the fact that wherever we see the development of special emphatic or "absolute" pronouns as against conjoint pronouns (used in direct conjunction with the verb), the former will as a rule be taken from the originally oblique cases, while the nominative is restricted to some sort of unstressed affix to the verb.

Such a development is not carried through in Standard English, which has formed the principal subject of our investigations. But in the dialects now existing in England, we find this *distinction of absolute and conjoint pronouns* made very frequently, see Murray D and Elworthy, *Dial. of West Somerset*, see also Joseph Wright, *Engl. Dial. Gr.* § 402, but the remarks on syntax in the following sections are unsatisfactory.

In the vulgar dialects of the town populations (especially of the London Cockney) the oblique case has been victorious, except when the pronoun is used in immediate conjunction with the verb as its subject;

a point of special interest is the use of *them* as an adjunct before a sb. As examples abound everywhere, I shall give only a few of which the first and third are peculiarly instructive for the distinction of absolute and conjoint forms: Di M 352 Don't they expect you then? inquired the driver. — Who? said Tom. — Why, them, returned the driver | Orig. Engl. 140 Him and mother and baby and me could all go with him | ib 123 Them paddling steamers is the ones for goin'. They just begin to puff a bit first. — Compare, however, ib 90 Them's the two I see.

On *them* used in vg speech as an adjunct see vol. II 16.13.

7.5₇. To return to Standard English. We see that the phenomena dealt with in this chapter bear on morphology (*you, who*), on syntax (*himself* as the subject, the nom. in nexus tertiary, the subject of passive vbs, etc.), and finally on the sense of words (the meaning of some of the old 'impersonal' vbs now being changed: the old *like* = 'be pleasant', the modern *like* = 'be pleased with'). I shall here call special attention to the latent though complete change which has taken place in the grammatical construction of more than one phrase while seemingly handed down unchanged from generation to generation. I am thinking of such phrases as:

if *you*	*like*
if *you*	*please*,

formerly: dat.(pl) 3rd pers. sg subjunctive;
now: nom. (sg or pl) 2nd pers. (sg or pl) indicative.

7.5₈. Compare also *you were better do it*, where *you* was a dative and is now the subject in the common case, and where simultaneously *were* has changed imperceptibly from the 3rd person singular (*it* being understood) to the 2nd person pl or sg. In handing something to someone you will often say *"Here you are!"* meaning, 'Here is something for you, here is what you want', e.g. Sh Hml I. 5.11 So Unckle there you are | Di D 80 he laid it out on my bed, saying: there you are, Copperfield | Caine M 14 Pete, where's your hand? — Here you are. — I think this phrase, too, contains an old dative; and perhaps, some centuries ago, in handing only one thing, people would say, "Here you is!"

7.5₉. A scheme of the pronominal forms treated in the present chapter according to their values in the everyday language of the beginning of the 20th cent. would look something like this:

Subject, joined to the vb:	Subject, when not joined to the vb:	Everywhere else:
I, we	me, we	me, us
you	you	you
he, she, they	he, she, they	him, her, them
(himself, herself, themselves)	himself, herself, themselves	himself, herself, themselves
who	whom, who	who.

If now finally we ask: Are the changes described in this chapter on the whole progressive? — the answer must be in the affirmative. Although for obvious reasons pronouns are more apt to preserve old irregularities than other classes of words, we find instead of the old four irregular forms, *thou, thee, ye* and *you*, one form carried through uniformly. The same uniformity is, as far as case is concerned, observable in the *self*-forms as compared with the old *he self, hine self,* etc, and *who* shows almost the same indifference to cases. Then there is some progress in syntax which does not appear from the scheme just given. Many of the uncertainties in the choice of case exemplified in the early sections of this chapter are due to a want of correspondence between notional and grammatical categories; for instance, when a word might be notionally, but not grammatically, the subject. Here logic has completely conquered the old grammar. The rule which is entirely incompatible with the old state of things, that the word immediately preceding the vb is notionally and grammatically the subject of the sentence, has been carried through on the whole with great consistency. And in the great facility which the English have now acquired of making the real psychological subject grammatically the subject of a passive sentence, the language has gained a decided advantage over the kindred languages. Thus we see that many phenomena, which by grammarians of the old school would be considered as more or less gross blunders or "bad grammar", but which are rather to be taken as natural reactions against the imperfections of traditional language, are really, when viewed in their historical connexion, conducive to progress in language.

Chapter VIII
Case in Nouns

8.1₁. In nouns (sbs and adjs) ModE distinguishes only two cases, a common case and a genitive, the latter always ending in *s* with the three phonetic values [z, s, iz] according to the final sound of the stem (see vol VI ch 16).

The name 'common case' has been objected to by Sonnenschein, who asks, "common to what?" It has, however, been widely accepted (Sweet, etc) for want of a better name. Non-genitive would be appropriate, but clumsy.

8.1₂. OE distinguished four cases in nouns: nominative, accusative, dative, and genitive, but the distinction between the three first-named has gradually been given up, and so have the various ways of forming the genitive, with the sole exception of the *s*-ending.

I have elsewhere (*Phil Gr* 173 ff., *System of Grammar* § 14) shown that it is wrong in ModE to speak of an accusative and dative as distinct cases. I am surprised to find Hjelmslev (*La Catégorie des Cas* 1.118) speaking of three cases in a sentence like *the boy* (subjectif) *sent his mother* (datif) *a letter* (translatif). These sbs are all in the same common case though their syntactic functions are different.

Use of the Common Case

8.2. The easiest formula for the use of the common case would be that it is used wherever the genitive is not used.

What is said here of nouns applies equally well to those pronouns which have no distinct nominative, e.g. *somebody*, *neither*, *either*, and nowadays also to *you*.

It will be expedient here to give a list of these various employments:

(1) as subject, object (direct or indirect) or predicative of a finite vb: John gave Mary a kiss. He was a man.

On objects see vol III chs 12—15; on predicatives see ib chs 17 and 18. On object with passive vbs ('retained obj.') ib 15.2—15.6.

(2) as subject, object, and predicative in a dependent nexus; see vol V chs 2 and 3.

Here a pronoun is put in the oblique case.

(3) as subject, object, and predicative in a gerundial nexus; see vol V chs 8 and 9.

As subject of a gerund the common case has to a great extent superseded the genitive.

(4) as subject, object, or predicative of an infinitive; see vol V chs 11—13.

(5) as subject, object, or predicative in a nexus-tertiary; see vol V ch 6.

(6) as apposition, not only to the common case, but also to some extent to a genitive; see above, 6.2$_4$.

(7) as regimen of a preposition, e.g., to John, of John, between John and Mary, etc.

(8) as what may be termed recipient (or regimen) of a few adjectives, thus

like: he is like his brother.

worth: worth our admiration | Goldsm V 2.201 all that I ever thought worth the acceptance. Cf below on *worth* with a tertiary of measure below, 8.4$_7$

(*un*)*worthy* generally takes *of:* worthy of our admiration. But sometimes, like *worth*, it is combined with a substantive without a preposition: Gay BP 182 you are unworthy your profession | Cowper L 2.397 The house itself is not unworthy some commendation | Shaw TT 32 he forfeits his command unless he can convince the court that he is still worthy it | ib 114 the man who would raise his hand to a woman .. is unworthy the name of Briton.

(9) as a secondary: as first (or second) part of a compound; see vol VI 8.2 ff.

On the relation of a first component to an adjective,

and in some cases transition to an adjective; see vol II ch 13.

(10) as a tertiary; see the following sections.

Common Case as Tertiary

8.3₁. The common case is *very* often used as a tertiary (subjunct in a junction, or more often subnex in a nexus). A sb is not often used in this way by itself, but is generally accompanied by an adjunct.

On the distinction of such tertiaries from objects, see vol III 12.1₅, where I wrongly imagined them to be placed in vol IV. (Corrected in the edition of 1949).

An obvious division of these tertiaries will be in tertiaries of time, tertiaries of space, tertiaries of manner, etc. This, however, is no strictly grammatical division, as it depends chiefly on the lexical meaning of the word employed. In Latin it is customary to speak of ablative of time, ablative of place, etc, but this is rightly objected to by E. P. Morris, *Principles and Methods of Latin Syntax* (N.Y. 1902) p. 69. In some of the following sections I have placed together words indicating time and space, etc.

Very often we find such tertiaries entering into competition with prepositional groups without any clear distinction.

Tertiaries of Measure

8.3₂. First we shall deal with tertiaries indicating the measure of a difference, thus with comparatives and (not so often) with superlatives, with *too*, with *late* = 'too late', and other similar expressions. In most cases it is possible to use also the preposition *by*, generally with a different word-order: an hour too early = too early by an hour: GE M 1.79 Maggie, taller by her head, though scarcely a year older | Doyle M 174 my opponent was two inches the shorter man | Thack P 1.319 a large man, that weighs three stone more than me, and stands six inches higher | id V 92 you're five years my senior | id N 40 being six years the junior of his present biographer | Finnemore Soc. Life in Engl 4 his wages were a penny a day less than the sums given above | Tennyson was a long way the most popular poet | Aldrich S 227 he was head and shoulders the best of the new lot | NP 1926 men who stood head and shoulders above their fellows | Darwin L 1.354 if it [the variety] were a good deal the commonest | Stevenson D 97 a soft felt hat seven sizes too small | Smedley F 1.232 it's too bad a great deal | you are five minutes late | Meredith E 248 she [the watch] was four minutes in arrear | ib 202 Crossjay darted up to her a nose ahead of the colonel | Sheridan 270 a fortnight previous to the performance | Meredith H 109 Mr. J. R. stood about a head under Evan | Kipling L 108 I shall always be threepence short in my accounts | Swift 3.96 our men had the start of him half a league | Galsw P 6.4 we're a clerk short as it is | Scott Iv 306 they had several hours the start of him | Locke GP 187 He was three months overdue | NP 1922 the date was three months wrong | Meredith H 428 Eva sat three chairs distant from her | Di P 440 the two parties are kept the carpet's length apart | Huxley L 1.178 opinions lay poles asunder.

Cf further: so much the better | Ruskin F 33 they are deadly, and all the deadlier because .. On *one two many* see vol II 6.211.

8.3₃. A comparative idea is also latent in expressions like the following: Osborne 76 you are some letters in my debt | Cowper L 1.11 I was debtor to Bensley seven pounds, or nine | ib 2.197 or he will die a promise in my debt | Burke Am 56 the colonies were then in debt two millions six hundred thousand pounds sterling money | Di P 342 You haven't made me out that little list of fees that I'm in your debt, have you? | Thack H 100 I was in debt nearly a hundred pounds to tradesmen | id N 37 we are many, many hundred pounds debtors to you | Austen P 414 you are quite a visit in my debt [= you owe me ...] | Marlowe F (1616) 1559 I am eighteen pence on the score | Sh Shrew Ind. 2.22 if she say I am not 14 d. on the score for sheere ale | GE Mm 215 he would be fifty-five pounds in pocket | Austen P 379 ten pounds a year the loser | Allen First 46 I came out 15 pounds a loser by this venture | Shaw A 197 [clothes] without the least regard to their being many months out of fashion | id IW 218 from the point of view of the employee there is not a penny to choose between Conservatives and Liberals | Galsw T 53 he would "cut up" a good fifteen thousand pounds to the bad.

Cf further the gaming or sporting expression *up:* Wells Par 69 he was one up on Sir Bussy | Oppenheim Prod. Monte C 270 At the present moment I must admit that you are one up | Galsw TL 70 he saw that he had gone up one in his host's estimation.

8.3₄. Tertiaries frequently indicate extent in time (duration) or space: he lived there several years [= for several years] | I slept an hour or two | he was half an hour dressing | Walpole Cp 119 Your aunt's a long time. I've been waiting half an hour | Benson D 108 What an age you have been | Sh Meas IV. 2.16 I haue beene an vnlawfull bawd, time out of minde || Maxwell WF 277 she's expecting — she's six months gone | Cronin H 170 She was ... seven and a half months pregnant || we walked seven miles | go great lengths [object ?] | Hankin 3.69 I'm prepared to go any lengths | Scott A 2.207 he was far from carrying his detestation so great a length | Di D 543 as if the streets had been strown that depth with feathers | Maugham Pl 3.8 I have kept the wolf some distance from the door | NP 1925 the wheel has come full circle | Walpole F 486 full circle he had come | Keats 2.130 By her in stature the tall Amazon Had stood a pigmy's height | Tennyson 173 she rose her height | ib 196 all her fair length upon the grass she lay | ib 373 there lay she all her length and kissed his face | Stevenson T 278 he fell all his length upon his side | ib 143 he stumbled and fell his length on the ground | Bennett B 127 I lay down full length in it [the dinghy].

We have a tertiary rather than an object in Brett Young PC 49 none of them can see a yard in front of their noses.

The extent is very frequently indicated in this way with *care, mind,* and *matter:* I don't care a bit, a button, a morsel, a pin (and many other fanciful expressions) | Austen P 274 he never cared three straws about her | Byron DJ 10.60 Juan, who cared not a tobacco-stopper About philosophy | Ruskin Sel 1.391 the old Venetian cared not a whit whether his edges were sharp or not | Sterne 21 he did not mind it a rush | Wilde P 125 I should not mind a bit | GE A 360 I don't value her a rotten nut.

8.3₅. This leads us to other tertiaries of measure, as in: I am not a bit tired | he is every bit as good a gentleman as you | Meredith E 40 How women despise their sex! — Not a bit | Benson D 9 I didn't expect it one little bit | Kipling J 2.127 not a bit impressed | Hamerton F 1.169 Anglicanism is every whit as strong in England as the older Church is in France |

Hardy L 32 she was not an atom to blame | Galsworthy C 13 her lips were the least thing parted.

Here we may place Sh Lr IV 6.109 every inch a king | Swift 3.103 I trembled every limb (also Brontë W 90) | He used to laugh a good deal || Sh Alls I. 1.112 Thinke him a great way foole.

On the border-line between object and tertiary we place: That speaks volumes for her innocence | he thinks worlds of you | Prokosch A 60 I might have wept a tear or two | Walpole Cp 158 She'd been crying buckets.

8.3₆. *No end* is a frequent colloquial tertiary with the signification 'very much': Hughes T 1.246 We'll be no end quiet | Wells L 243 If a man is well off they will truckle to him no end | Gissing B 444 it'll make you laugh no end | Gissing G 197 she blames herself no end | Hardy F 197 I have assisted your uncle in these fields no end of times | Shaw Ms 22 Between the lot of them Joey got cultivated no end | Carpenter Ad 74 he chats away to Pedri and the crew no end | Galsw EC 16 It's no end good of you, Dinny || Swinnerton Three Lovers 215 Patricia thinks no end of herself | Galsw EC 845 I think no end of you for coming.

Cf for the sense (not for the grammar) Kipling S 239 you're no end of a fine chap.

8.3₇. Words denoting fractions are very often used thus as tertiaries of measure: [this is not half bad] | Stevenson JHF 120 my life had been nine-tenths a life of effort | Philips L 308 before the day is two-thirds gone | Swinburne L 70 he would be three-quarters murdered | Doyle S 3.199 the box was already a third full of bundles of paper | ib 5.276 I found him three-parts drunk | Sterne 109 in a tone two parts jest and one part earnest | Stevenson D 46 emotions, part religious . .

but part human | Shaw P 298 Lady C., part pleased, part amused, part sympathetic | Trollope D 63 a feeling which he had no time to analyse, but of which he was part aware.

Here *by* can also be used, especially when the name of the fraction is separated from the word it belongs to: McCarthy 2.361 the checks and balances were too cleverly arranged by half.

A tertiary of extent is also found in phrases like *go halves* (= 'share the expenses equally'): Thack N 606 I'll go you halves | Defoe R 2.30 he went share and share alike with them | Bellamy L 87 the rich went share and share with the poor | Darwin L 1.201 he offers me to go share in everything | go shares (common).

8.4₁. In combination with another time indication a tertiary often denotes the distance in time reckoned from the first-mentioned point. This may either refer to the future or to the past. First, examples referring to the future:

Ch A 1850 And this day fifty wykes.. Everich of yow shal bringe an hundred knightes | Bacon A 32 he will be here this day seven-night | Sterne 87 I shall be back at Strasburg this day month | Darwin L 1.209 I can hardly think there will be a coronation this time fifty years | Gissing H 145 A week to-day I leave.

8.4₂. Referring to a past time: BJo A V. 1.38 I heard it too, iust this day three weekes | Swift J 164 Mrs E set out last Monday se'ennight | Cowper L 1.256 Last Saturday se'nnight ... we were alarmed by a cry of fire | Goldsm V 1.172 that day month was fixed upon | Sterne M 1.254 I am this month one whole year older than I was this time twelve-month | Di N xxiv he remembers being waited on, last January twelve-month, by two gentlemen | Hardy W 219 She had never had a moment's illness since the previous January twelvemonth | Thack V 436 he was a better man than I was, this day twenty years | Wells TM 19 the trick we had witnessed that day week.

Note the omission of *a* or *one* in these combinations.

Cf with *ago:* Darwin L 1.181 I left Shrewsbury this day fortnight ago.

We say *this day week*, but hardly *this month year*.

8.4₃. A measure is very often added to such adjectives as *high*, *thick*, etc: five feet high | two inches thick and four broad | four months old | a three weeks long vacation, etc. — More or less peculiar expressions of this kind are: Sh Hml V. 1.214 let her paint an inch thicke | Conway C 17 the door, which she had left an inch or two ajar | Hope Z 287 Black Michael's banner hung there half-mast high | Steel F 64 children carried shoulder high to see the show | Defoe R 11 the sea went mountains high | Di Do 320 to heap mortification, mountains high, on the head of Mrs. S || Carlyle FR 466 they rush to the attack, thousands strong | Butler W 119 the table was loaded with books many deep | Wells N 187 we had come in the motor four strong | Merriman LH 236 he looked round the peering faces, two and three deep round the table | the books stand two deep on the shelves || Macaulay H 2.202 the executioner stood ankle deep in blood | Quiller-Couch M 288 his feet at every step sinking ankle-deep in the fine shingle (frequent) | Macaulay H 1.178 they were yet ready to fight knee deep in blood for her cathedrals | Locke FS 172 They waded in ... until they were waist deep | Wordsw 99 I have seen him, mid-leg deep | Sherriff F 194 the two stood up together breast high in the sea.

8.4₄. Thus also in the predicative without the adjective: he is twenty [= twenty years = twenty years old] | Sh Shrew IV. 1.29 Am I but three inches? Why, thy horne is a foot, and so long am I at the least | Shaw C 83 he stood five feet ten in his stockings | Kipling J 1.188 Kala Nag stood ten fair feet at the shoulders.

8.4₅. *Fill* may be the object in combinations like Mi PL 9.594 to pluck and eat my fill; but from this it approaches insensibly to being a tertiary of measure as in: Sh Shrew I. 1.73 gaze your fill | Mi Il P 128 When the gust hath blown his fill | Conway C 52 we gaze our fill | Shaw P 234 have you stared your fill at me?

8.4₆. Such expressions of measure cannot be separated from indications of price, as in: I bought it sixpence [= for s.] | they sell it one and threepence [= at 1/3] a dozen | Sh Hml II. 2.281 my thanks are too deare a halfepeny | Fielding 1.371 Tho' rack, in punch, eight shillings be a quart | Goldsm V 1.119 I had them a dead bargain | Sheridan 222 you shall have 'em a bargain || the judge fined him six shillings | I bet you a shilling | Maugham MS 73 You can bet your boots I'd have routed her out fast enough (*bet your boots* is a set phrase).

8.4₇. Note also the construction of *worth:* a gold medal worth twenty pounds; cf above, 8.2.

Measures of weight: he weighs ten stone | Thack P 1.148 he rides sixteen stone.

As a measure we may also reckon *times* in multiplication: four times five is twenty | Di Ch 76 I'd carry twenty times her weight.

Tertiaries of Time

8.5₁. Tertiaries also frequently indicate a definite point of time, especially with words like *this* or *last:* he came this morning | he died last night | he will be back to-morrow or the day after | I shall come again the year after next | Sh Ro III. 5.113 early next Thursday morne | he does that every week | what time will you be back ? | Hope Ch 43 I'll come some day this week | Maugham HB 576 I haven't got money to throw away these days | Wilde L 160 he became a member of the A.D.C. his first term | Defoe M 260 I expect to be cast for my life the very next sessions | Kaye-Smith HA 9 I missed him last leave.

The following combinations are a little rarer: Defoe Rox 133 my wife died the beginning of September last | Swift J 145 I this minute sent Patrick to Sterne | Ward E 170 I thought you were due at home, beginning of June | Tennyson L 1.115 [Hallam:] Gaskell is in the ninth heaven of happiness, going to be married the end of May | Ward E 4 He was at Chicago just those days | Mackenzie C 237 You can go home tea-time | Lewis MS 240 each twilight she was afraid || Di DC 139 [vg] you shall find it as if I expected you here directly minute (also in a child's mouth Dane FB 22).

"He has been here *many times*." The corresponding combination *some times* is now written *sometimes* as one word, which grammars and dictionaries term an adverb. The original feeling that there are two words is shown in such a passage as Austen M 186 the memory is sometimes so retentive, so obedient; at others, so bewildered and so weak. — The same combination *sometimes ... at others* also Locke HB 150, Maugham HB 272, but Lewis MA 51 writes *other times* without a preposition. Note *at times* without *some*.

Cf Galsw D 123 had noticed it in horses, time and again (frequent): *time* in itself is here a tertiary, as if it were an adverb.

A point in time may be denoted indirectly by a

word belonging to some other sphere: Swift J 57 I writ to him last post | Scott A 2.293 letters arrived every post | Shelley L 946 Mary will write next post | Kipling M 232 I wrote that to H next mail | Ch C 679 He hath a thousand slayn this pestilence | Sh H5 IV. 1.100 men wrackt ... that looke to be washt off the next tyde (also Defoe R 300) | By DJ 13.53 last war the News abounded | Wells T 53 I found it that trip | Brontë V 48 You will scarcely make many friends this voyage | Maugham MS 243 The purser ... told me last journey that he hadn't met a nicer girl in the islands | Mitford OV 77 she [a dog] is five years old this grass [= summer] | Fielding 3.487 I will satisfy you the first opportunity | Austen S 134 I am determined to sit for it [my portrait] the very first opportunity (ib 363) | Page J 239 I determined to unmask Peck the first chance I should have (also Caine S 1.91); cf *first thing* 8.9$_7$ | Defoe R 352 looking behind him every step | Masterman OT 35 The scout thought that he had found out, first guess, what Fothergill really liked for breakfast | Swift J 148 How do you pass your time this ugly weather? | Di N 42 you are going all the way down into Yorkshire this cold winter's weather | ib 73 it's a long journey this weather | Shaw 2.97 Ow do you find yoreself this weather (very often *weather* with or without an adjective) | Herrick M 21 Good weather I used to drive to Euraka (U.S.) || Walpole C 365 This house will collapse, the first gale.

8.5$_2$. In U.S. it is customary to use words denoting indefinite time in the plural, where Britishers generally say *in the night*, etc: Twain S 59 their cats were pretty sociable around her nights | Lewis MA 464 He wanted to work nights, every night | ib 465 I've got to work evenings! | Wilder H 18 It's a wonder your depositors can really sleep nights | ib 33 Summers I used to cover Missouri... | Hemingway FA 104 I went over there afternoons.

Cf below, 8.6$_6$, *places*.

In the sg: Hemingway FA 17 to wake with it sometimes morning and all that had been there gone.

8.5₃. *Time enough* = 'in time' (obsolete): Sh Err IV. 1.41 lest I come not time enough | H4A II. 1.48 | Swift J 123 if I have it [a letter] time enough to answer here, 'tis well enough | Thack N 302 if he hadn't got out time enough (also ib 124).

8.5₄. The conjunction *while* has developed from the use of (*all*) *the while* = 'during the time' as in "Won't you like some lollipops to eat the while?" (NED) with the addition of a clause with or without *that* (see vol V 21.2$_2$ and 2$_7$). Examples of the transition: Osborne 4 what you have done all this while you have bin away | Defoe M 295 [it] fetched tears from me, almost all the while he talked with me. Cf also Kennedy CN 56 Jacob came the same time Tony did.

Many examples are adduced by Ellinger in EStn 71.73 ff.

In the same way indirect indications of time (cf above, 8.5₁) may sometimes serve to introduce a clause tertiary: Williamson L 174 the first shadow of proof I get that he's breaking his half of the bargain he shall learn ... [U.S. = when I get a shadow].

We may have both kinds of time indication (point and duration) together as in Merriman S 126 you have been doing that any time these twenty years.

Tertiaries of Space

8.6₁. Tertiaries of space are not so frequently expressed by a common case, because spatial relations (with their three dimensions) are more complex than temporal relations; consequently the exact indication by means of a preposition is generally preferred.

8.6₂. *Way* is used frequently in tertiaries with *this*, *that*, etc: Sh Lr III. 4.21 That way madnesse lies | Hope Z 115 evil lay both ways | Did you come the same way as yesterday? — No, today I came a different way | which way shall we go?

With possessive pronouns, *way* often stands in a transferred sense: Ritchie M 59 she used to walk off with those of her pupils who lived her way | Kipling J2 40 he had taken honour when it came his way | Doyle S 6.48 a real piece of news has come my own way | when he passed me in the street, he wouldn't look my way | he went his way. Cf the obsolete: Caxton R 55 tho wente he his strete.

Way is often used with a place name before it (as a kind of adjunct): Thack N 56 if ever you come Bernard Street way on a Sunday | ib 295 a chap out Hampstead way | Doyle S 4.170 an ironmaster up Northumberland way.

8.6₃. *Side* (with an adjunct) is also frequent as a tertiary, followed sometimes by a regimen without prep., and sometimes by *of*: Ward E 4 English people are so ungrateful this side of the water | Hope Z 310 this side the grave, I will live as becomes the man whom she loves | ib 235 I made out a window two yards my side of it | Trollope D 2.79 Somebody seems to have got out of bed at the wrong side ... You accuse me of getting out of bed the wrong side | Kipling S 158 You'll laugh the other side of your mouth before you've done | Meredith E 196 the blackbird ... dangling the worm each side his orange beak | Phillips P 18 Stand either side of me you whom I love.

8.6₄. *Pair of stairs* (= 'floor, story') is obsolete in tertiaries as used in Defoe M 92 I now had but one room two pair of stairs | Swift J 462 I am got into an ordinary room two pair of stairs | ib 465 I stole into a room up two pair of stairs | Fielding TJ 2.128 she broke out at a window two pair of stairs.

8.6₅. *Next door* (also metaphorically): Thack P 3.283 Bows lived in the house next door to Captain Strong | Defoe R 2.19 next door to starving | Stevenson M 274 It might have been worth nothing, or next door.

8.6₆. In U.S. it is customary to say *go places*, where in England a preposition would be used; similarly in the sg with a pronominal adjunct: Lewis MA 232 the habit of social ease, of dressing, of going places without nervous anticipation | Wilder H 94 Let's go out and go places | Waugh W 222 [British] You want to be able to go places and do things | ib 83 She'd take him all the places he had never been to; the places she had got bored with | ib 137 He hasn't been places yet | ib 303 she had wished she could take him places and give him things | Hammett Th 162 I've seen her places with Harrison Quinn || Bromfield Mod. Hero 7 We've been every place | Dreiser AT 2.39 Please come and take me away some place, anywhere, so I can get out of here | Hemingway FA 134 "Let's go some place," I said | ib 219 I'll go any place any time you wish.

8.6₇. A movement *to* a place is exceptionally indicated by the mere common case in *home:* go, come home. *Home* is here often termed an adv.

From this is derived the use of *home* after *be*, when this means *be (have) come*, especially for a short stay (holiday, etc): Sh Merch IV. 2.3 wee'll away to night, And be a day before our husbands home (cf Sh-lex *home* 548a) | Defoe R 283 he had been quite home for an earthen jugg | Di P 121 The large man was always home precisely at ten o'clock | Di D 76 I was informed that Mr. Creakle would be home that evening | id N 749 how glad I am to see you home again | Stevenson U 43 Home is the sailor, home from the sea, And the hunter home from the hill | Sweet E 39 he is never home before half past six | Bennett ECh 205 when he was home from school for the holidays | Galsw IPh 136 'I should like to get married while I'm home,' said the Indian civilian | Rose Macaulay P 36 Gideon was home, wounded | Maxwell EG 63 He was home on leave in London | Hardy L 16 You'd like to be home again? | Doyle Sh 5.147 two gentlemen who were home on a visit from South Africa | Shaw 1.176 I shant be home to tea | Maugham P 96 He told them what pieces he had seen when he was last home on leave.

The implied motion is evident in Caine C 392 Gloria isn't home from the races yet | Doyle Sh 6.279 Is Mr. Holmes at home? — He will be home, sir, at a quarter to one | Merriman Last Hope 293 to tell me that you were home again. Yes. Home again to the old place | Wells TB 1.106 Don't say anything home yet [= don't go home and say ...].

8.6₈. Americans extend this usage and often use *home* (with *stay*, etc) where people in England would say *at home*, thus in Dreiser, Lewis, Hammett, McCoy (Booktitle: I should have stayed home), etc. This seems now to be spreading to England: Mannin RS 128 If you stop home for the rest of the term | id W 193 the continuance of this romantic love could best be secured by staying home.

The corresponding use of *back* is not quite parallel; *back* must be considered strictly an adv. Originally it was an aphetic form of *aback* from OE *on bæc*. U.S. *back of* = 'behind'.

8.6₉. The names of the 'four quarters of the world'

are often used to indicate a direction, in U.S. also to indicate the 'place where': I shall go South in July | Austen P 433 the windows are full west | Bennett C 1.8 the canal ran north and south || Herrick M 198 while I was East | Page J 95 they had lived East. Note the colloquial phrase *go west* = 'die'.

Tertiaries of Manner

8.7₁. As tertiaries of manner we have first frequent combinations with *way*, which, incidentally, loses its spatial meaning: Couldn't you do it some other way? | he wants things his own way | Sh H4B IV. 5.127 commit The oldest sinnes the newest kinde of wayes | Defoe M 205 it was the first money I had gained that way | Hamerton F 2.146 he would not take such a sum into consideration, one way or the other | Kipling M 220 we used to heliograph, and they used to give us orders same way.

When *way* means 'manner', it is now generally used with *in:* in the same way.

With a following clause: Maugham HB 350 I might have been a thief the way she talked.

Cf *ways* (which reminds one of *wise*) in Scott Iv 179 and, falcon-ways, we swoop on them | Cronin H 429 What way [= why] not call it after me and be done wi' it? (often in Cronin; Sc?). Differently in Irish-English: Synge 26 And what way [= 'how'] will yourself live from this day ... ? Scotch *gate* in the same sense as *way:* Scott A 1.94 dinna speak that gate o' the gentlemen.

8.7₂. With *fashion* we have corresponding expressions: Sh H4A III. 3.104 Must we all march? Yes, two and two, Newgate fashion | Di D 451 we had tea, with the kettle boiling gipsy-fashion | Swinburne T 77 shone lion-fashion forth with his eyes alight, And lion-wise leapt on that kinsman knight | Shaw C x some of its characters appear, Trollope fashion, in the later novels | Kipling J 2.101 native fashion, they delayed their departure | ib 263 he threw up his hands monkey-fashion | Stevenson T 64 things shall go man-of-war-fashion on board the good ship | Doyle S 5.271 he saluted and stood sailor-fashion | Hewlett Q 158 he gave him his hand afterwards, English fashion.

Fashion here approaches the function of an adverbial suffix, and has completely become so in dialects (see Elworthy, *Gramm. of West Somerset* 225).

8.7₃. The same transition is seen even more clearly with *wise*, which is generally written together with the preceding word: More U 31 the shyppes ... were made .. flatte, and broade in the botome, troughewyse | ib 277 Contrarye wise | Sh Mids III. 2.171 My heart to her but as guest-wise sojourn'd | GE V 226 he's got nothing but uncles — leastwise, one | Twain M 222 respected the day religiouswise | Buchanan J 17 the great black River crept Snakewise.

Otherwise is generally called an adverb (one word); but the original feeling of it as adjective + substantive (two words) is shown by the combination *no otherwise* (cf vol II 16.783), as in Bunyan G 119 I confessed myself guilty no otherwise | Dickinson S 57 all ought to have happened just so and no otherwise.

8.7₄. Tertiaries are often found with vbs of motion. Instead of the usual *go (come) for a walk* we may say *a walk* without the preposition: Swift 1.246 when their husbands are gone a journey | Defoe R 2.217 I was gone a wild goose chase indeed | id Rox 273 Then you'll never go the voyage at all | Cowper L 1.369 before Mrs. N. went her journey | Lamb E 172 when we go out a day's pleasuring | Ward M 20 she heard him flying upstairs three steps at a time | Ridge G 73 she ran upstairs two steps at a time to change | Galsw D 16 he came downstairs two at a time | id IC 22 he ran upstairs three at a time, and came down four | Ward M 46 Will you come a walk with me to-morrow? | Wilde Im 17 she goes long walks | Meredith R 261 Mrs. B. left the room tiptoe | Benson D 269 I'm going to go a ride this morning | ib 2.85 he was perfectly happy to go a motor drive with aunts and grandmothers | id N 211 he had run full tilt against the doctor's theories | Romanes Mental Evolution 96 larvæ, crawling Indian file | Kaye-Smith T 32 The Town Committee walked single file | travel third class (also *third*, without class) | Bennett Cd 249 those people are actually going steerage | Galsw MP 320 everyone to-day went Underground | Aumonier Q 120 they rambled together and went picnics | Hammett Th 106 it [the letter] had had come airmail || Collins W 20 a bachelor who had once taken me a cruise in his yacht | Maxwell BY 26 Send him a voyage | Stevenson T 94 The Hispaniola now sailed a course that would just clear the island on the east.

Similarly with *be* in the perfect or pluperfect (but not in other tenses; cf *I have been to London*, but not *I was to London last year*): Defoe R 29 as I had been one voyage to this coast before | Keats 5.180 I have been a walk this morning.

Post in *ride post* may be originally the object, but it is now rather a tertiary; cf also *post-haste:* Greene F 12. 77 haste thee post to Fressingfield | Sh All IV. 5.85 His highnesse comes post | Mi SA 1538 For evil news rides post, while good news baits | Tennyson 62 ride post-haste (also Meredith E 257).

8.7₅. In *come a walk* we might at a pinch speak of

'cognate object'. In the following idiomatic expressions one would rather think of the instrumental object, if object it be: Kipling L 52 he'll come a cropper if he tries that sort of thing | Wells T 54 my helmet came a whack, fit to split, against the nigger's canoe | id Ma 2.84 That's where all these Socialists come a howler | id H 419 Don't come that over me | go it.

With Doyle in NP 1895 when we kissed good-bye — compare vol III. 14.9$_6$ *kiss him good-night*, etc.

8.7₆. Manner is also denoted in *walk barefoot;* on the relation between this and *barefooted* see vol VI 24.1$_{11}$. Rarer combinations are: Mandeville 116 upon that see went oure Lord drye feet | Maxwell WF 157 Mr. Lake was sent off hot foot to make a preliminary tour of the scholastic agencies || Wilde in Sel. Short Stories 2.365 sitting down cross-legs in a circle, [they] began to play (not in NED or Suppl.).

8.8₁. *Name*, too, must be called a tertiary in the frequent combination: I call him *that name* (while *Tom* in "I call him Tom" is the predicative part of a nexus-object). Examples: Sh R3 I. 3.236 thou hadst call'd me all these bitter names | R2 IV. 1.259 and knowe not how, what name to call my selfe | Byron 630 The Maker—call him Which name thou will | Keats 2.102 called him [Death] soft names in many a mused rhyme | Hardy R 80 she would have christened her boys such names as Saul and Sisera. Also *call names* without an adj = 'abuse'. Cf vol III 14.9$_6$.

The transition between the two constructions of *call* can be seen in Swift T 66 he called them damned sons of whores, rogues, traitors, and the rest of the vile names he could muster up | Huxley L 1.221 they would call me atheist, infidel, and all the other usual hard names.

Name is used differently in Farnol A 252 There was a fellow in the Eighty-eighth, name of Crichton (frequent, rather vg).

8.8₂. Where the tertiary consists of one word only, it is generally reckoned as an adverb, thus *cheap* (I bought it *cheap*, formerly: *good cheap* (e.g. Heywood P 140), *best cheap*; cf vol II 13.71), *zigzag* (Di D 735 blown ashore out of their courses in trying to get *zigzag* back), *bodkin* in "to ride bodkin" (e.g. Thack H 28), i.e. to sit wedged in between two others. This especially applies to a great many short words with expressive sounds; in many cases it is impossible to decide whether the starting-point is a substantive or a verb; but the tertiary ('adverbial') use is very characteristic. Such are: Swift T 26 fall plum into the jaws of certain critics | Morley M 1.200. The famous diatribe against Jesuitism... points plumb in the same direction | Shaw 1.165 I said, plump out, that I couldn't stand any more of it | Galsw D 21 the boy felt his heart go thump | Sterne 75 she fell backwards soss against the bridge | ib 27 slap dash | Kipling S 287 I stumbled slap on Stalky in a Sikh village | Holmes A 327 going smack through the crown [of the hat] | Kipling S 277 He'd been hit smack in the middle of the hand | stand bolt upright *(bolt upright* already Ch A 4266) | Masefield W 54 the gate went clack | ib 80 his teeth went clack | Bennett C 1.163 that infernal kid was right bang off her head | Spencer F 25 a fact that goes slick through a great generalisation | come pat | fall crash.

8.8₃. A frequent way of using such echoic tertiaries is by placing them first, followed by some verb like *came, went:* Sterne 17 till at length, in some evil hour, pop comes the creditor | NP 1914 when crash came catastrophe | Hawthorne Sn 52 Ting-a-ting-ting! goes the bell | Doyle B 85 Snap goes our third thread | Wells T 31 Bump he went against the ceiling | Hardy R 215 then jerk went the rope, whizz went the wheel | Masefield W 11 Clash go the crockeries ... Baa go the sheep, thud goes the waxwork's drum || Benson D 2. 247 what a bang I came.

Pairs of Words

8.9₁. The tendency to use sbs as tertiaries is particularly strong when they go in pairs. English like many other languages, favours formless combinations; especially in set phrases. Many of these combinations resemble the condensed constructions dealt with in vol V 6.7₆.

8.9₂. *Time*, e.g., is indicated by such examples as: year in and year out (frequent at least from Chaucer's time) | (rarer:) month in and month out (Twain M 47) | Galsw Sw 318 he'd suffered, night in, day out | day by day (Sh and frequent) | Virginia Woolf Mrs. Dalloway 194 sitting hour after hour silent | Defoe R 358 they were obliged to keep guard night and day, but especially in the night | Merriman VG 220 Below all, summer and winter, at evening and at dawn, night and day, growls the Wolf [a river] | Maugham Pl 2.35 you've loved him morning, noon and night.

8.9₃. *Manner*, as denoted by two words connected with *and:* Malory 145 [they] bound hym hand and foote (frequent till our own day) | Fielding T 1.252 a soldier who is tied neck and heels | Thack V 51 the chairs are turned up heads and tails along the corner | Di M 412 falling on the supper tooth and nail | Darwin L 3.82 we always fight tooth and nail | Ridge G 47 we went at it hammer and tongs (common).

The two words connected with a preposition: Browning [Every man ed.] 261 Let's sit and set things straight now, hip to haunch | Jerome T 51 I'm making money hand over fist | Sackville West E 209 one walks round with everybody else, nose to tail like a string of caterpillars | Maugham TL 193 Shacks are cheek by jowl with stone mansions.

8.9₄. *Measure and extent:* NP: the Irish administration will have to be reformed root and branch | Doyle F 241 I am with you heart and soul | Hughes T 2.68 they are ruining themselves body and soul | Stevenson A 66 an ill thing poorly done is an ill thing top and bottom || Huxley L 1.381 I was sound, wind and limb.

8.9₅. A tertiary is often made up of two identical words connected with a preposition: they walked arm in arm (frequent; already Ch) | Greene F 6.142 I see the lovers hand in hand | Ward M 362 she and Elizabeth sat, hand in hand | Sh Mcb V. 5.6 We might haue met them darefull, beard to beard | Gissing B 140 see his name side by side with those of the leaders of thought | Quiller-Couch M 42 their houses stood side by side | Masefield M 194 So they stood shoulder to shoulder | Gissing B 21 you and he will work though life shoulder to shoulder | We are face to face with a great change | Di Do 364 face to face with him, Rob had no doubt that ... | Meredith E 219 talking not simply face to face, but face in face. | Walker O 190 he saw eye to eye with him in most things | Bennett C 1.206 houses were constructed brick by brick, beam by beam, lath by lath, tile by tile | Maxwell F 73 Why the devil couldn't he come and ask me man to man? | Hope M 106 it was true word for word | Butler Er 210 each age should take it turn in turn about, week by week | Freeman Th 176 promenaders who walked foot to foot (more often: foot by foot) | Maugham Alt 393 In the distance stretched blue mountains, range upon range, as far as the eye could see | A Huxley Eyeless in G. 207 a marmot with its female, crowded fur to fur in their subterranean burrow.

Or two identical words may be joined by *and:* Bennett ECh 282 The two great rivals in the illustrated daily press were running neck and neck after him (frequent) | Dreiser AT 1.178 he had left the bulk of his property ... to these two elder brothers, share and share alike. — More examples in the last section of 8.3$_7$, above.

8.9$_6$. Cf such alternatives as: we should set out, *rain or no rain* (see vol II 16.824 ff) | Brontë J 266 fair or foul, she went to church | ib. 397 rain or fair, he would take his hat and go out | Maugham TL 248 rain or fine.

Combinations like Sh Ado III. 1.68 So turnes she euery man the wrong side out | Brett Young PC 186 I know her inside out — belong to nexus-tertiaries (vol V ch 6).

First thing

8.9$_7$. In "I shall do it the first thing to-morrow morning," *the first thing* might be called an appositum to the object, but the same expression is used (also without the article) in a looser way as a tertiary joined even with intransitive vbs, and might be termed an appositum to the whole sentence: Sh H4A III. 3.206 Rob me the exchequer the first thing thou do'st | Brontë V 174 The first thing this morning I went to the Rue Fossette | GE M 1.38 he promised himself that he would begin to fish the first thing to-morrow morning | ib 305 you must pay him first thing | id Life 1.273 I am writing to you the last thing | id A 272 the letter should be written the first thing | Di D 518 we resolved that she should go to Dora the first thing in the morning | Kipling J 1.157 they came in, the last thing, to look at their boy | Maxwell BY 49 he used to go into her room for a word or two the last thing at night | Gissing in NP 1896 the next thing you'll be turning on her || Doyle M 99 he guessed the price first shot.

Defoe has a fuller form of the phrase: R 2.136 he made them every one a shirt the first thing he did. Similarly ib 310 and 340.

"Sixpence an ounce"

8.9s. As a final general note to this chapter we may remark that in the extremely frequent combinations like: he earns 400 pounds a year, but spends 50 a month | they got five shillings a head | it costs 5 s. a pound | the price is sixpence an ounce | he is paid one pound a line | he passes the house twenty times a day | once a month, etc, what is now apprehended as the indefinite article before a substantival tertiary denoting rate or proportion, was originally the shortened form of the preposition *on*. See NED *a* 4, *a* prp.¹ 8b, and below, 12.5_7.

Chapter IX

Case (Continued)

Possessive, Genitive, and Use of *Of*
Possessive of Third Person Plural

9.1₁. The possessive of the 3rd person pl was OE *heora*, ME *her*, but *their* (*theirs*) prevailed, chiefly on account of the confusion of *her* with the feminine pronoun. Examples of the old form: Malory 448 and bare the two knyghtes out of her sadels to the erthe, and so lefte hem lyeng and rode her wayes | ib 50 kepe theire castels and her countreyes | Sh Oth III. 3.66 the warres must make example out of her best | H6A I. 1.83 Were our teares wanting to this funerall, these tidings would call forth her flowing tides | Lucr 1588 these water-galls in her dim element.

Possessive of *it*

9.1₂. As a genitive (possessive) corresponding to *it* OE had *his*, which remained in use throughout the ME period (Ch, e.g. LGW 125 referring to *erthe*) and in the beginning of the ModE period: Lyly E 41 Though yron be made soft with fire, it returneth to his hardnes | the usual form in Sh, e.g. Sonn 95.14 The hardest knife ill used doth lose his edge | Ven 756 the lampe that burnes by night, Dries vp his oyl, to lend the world his light | BJo 3.63 Is this curl in his right place? | AV Mark 9.50 if the salt haue lost his saltnesse | Walton A 131 every thing is beautifull in his season | Mi PL 6.782 the uprooted hills retir'd Each to his place | ib 8.97 the sun ... his beams.

As a possessive *it* is found in the ME allitterative poems from Lancashire (Cleanness 1021, etc) and became tolerably common about 1600, thus in Sh Hml I. 2.216 it [the ghost] lifted up it head [Q *his*, the other early editions *it*] | ib V. 1.244 The Coarse they follow, did with disperate hand fore do it owne life | Ro I. 3.52 it brow [the child's; some early editions *its*] ib I. 5.54 Did my hart loue till now, forsweare it sight | Lear I. 4.236, etc.

But alongside of *it* the new form *its* appeared about 1600 and rapidly spread on account of its clearness and the analogy of other genitives, though at first it was not considered elegant. It is neither found in Spenser nor in AV, and is not recognized in Alex. Gil's *Logonomia* 1621. The oldest quotation in NED is from

1598. In Sh it is found in comparatively few places, in Mi PL only twice (1.254 and 4.813, and in Nativity 108, each time with a special reason for not using *his*). From the end of the 17th c. *its* must be considered the only form in use.

Its as a primary is very rare; the only quotation in NED is Sh H8 I. 1.18 (authorship doubtful); I am able to add some modern examples: London C 187 they will have attained their maximum development, before the whole world, in the same direction, has attained its | Dickinson Ch 12 the State demands their sacrifice to itself. They must have no conscience but its, no belief but its, no cause but its.

9.1₃. On the distinction between *my*, *thy* as secondary and *mine*, *thine* as primary see vol II 16.21 ff.; on the corresponding distinction between *her*, *their* — and *hers*, *theirs* ib 16.27.

Use of the Genitive and of Possessive Pronouns

9.2₁. In OE the genitive was used much as e.g. in Latin and German. Besides possessive, subjective, objective, partitive, descriptive genitives, etc, we find genitives governed by various verbs and adjectives (e.g. bidan norþanwindes | þundes weorþ); but in the course of time this extensive use has become much more restricted, and nowadays the genitive is chiefly used as the adjunct (secondary) of a primary, which is now always placed after the genitive, while the opposite order was frequent in OE, as it still is in German.

9.2₂. The form, too, of the genitive has undergone considerable change since OE times. Then it changed according to gender and stem-class and ended in some words in -*s* (sometimes with changes in the stem: *meares* from *mearh*, *engles* from *engel*, *heriges* from *here*, *bearwes* from *bearu*), in others in *-e* (*giefe* from *giefu*, *sāwle* from *sāwol*, *mǣdwe* from *mǣd*), in others in *-a* (*suna* from *sunu*, *handa* from *hand*), in others again in *-n* (*guman* from *guma*, *tungan* from *tunge*); in some words it had no ending (*dohtor*). The gen pl ended in *-a* (*daga*) or *-ena* (*gumena* from *guma*).

All this has been regularized, the genitive ends always in *-s*, whether sg or pl, and irrespective of gender. This has been an enormous gain to all users of the language, though it entails the inconvenience that in the vast majority of words the form is identical with the common case in the pl, and that there is no difference between the gen. sg and the gen. pl. Hence the vacillation found sometimes in spelling between *-'s* and *-s'*.

For details in ModE (sound, spelling) see vol VI ch 16, for group-genitives see ib ch 17. On the rarity of the gen. pl see ib 16.8$_7$.

Corresponding to the genitive of sbs we have in the pronouns the so-called possessive forms (my, mine; our, ours; your, yours; his; her, hers; its; their, theirs; whose). The use of these two groups is nearly, but not exactly, the same.

9.2₃. In competition with the genitives and possessives we have the combinations with the preposition *of;* very often these are used with the same meaning as the genitive or possessive, but in other cases there is a difference: sometimes one of the two (genitive-possessive and *of*-groups) is preferable to the other or even obligatory.

The extensive use of the *of*-combination, which first appeared in the 12th c., is to some extent due to French influence though this influence should not be exaggerated; see particularly Trampe Bødtker, *Crit. Contribu-*

tions io Early Eng. Syntax (Christiania Vidsk. Selsk. 1908). Anyhow, "the fact that modern English possesses both [constructions] enables us to express shades of meaning which cannot be rendered which equal precision in French or Latin" (Bradley M 60).

9.2₄. We have, in fact, to distinguish four constructions:

(1) John's friend; his friend
(2) friend of John; friend of him
(3) friend of John's; friend of his
(4) [this is] John's; his.

If we call *John* (or *he*) the subordinate and *friend* the superior member of these combinations, we see that in

(1) the subordinate member is put in the genitive (or possessive) as an adjunct (secondary) to the following superior member as a primary, — that in

(2) the subordinate member is made the regimen of the preposition *of;* the prepositional group follows the superior member as its secondary; — in

(3) the subordinate member is put in the genitive (possessive), but in this form is made the regimen of the preposition *of;* the whole combination is a secondary placed after the superior member as its primary, — and in

(4) the superior member is latent; the genitive (possessive) of the subordinate member is made a primary.

No. (3) is often termed the prepositional genitive or the phrasal genitive (Bradley); but it is much better to reserve the name genitive for the formal case and to stress the parallelism between this form and the possessive forms of the pronouns. Nor is Kruisinga's term post-genitive for no. (3) felicitous, as it consists of the preposition and an ordinary genitive.

No. (3) was dealt with in vol III 1.5.

No. (4) was treated in vol III 1.4; on the difference between *my*, *her*, *their* as secondaries, and *mine*, *hers*, *theirs* as primaries see vol II chs 16 and 17.

The choice between the four possibilities is determined partly by the character of the subordinate member (whether denoting an animate being or an inanimate thing, and on the other hand whether we have to do with a sb or with a pronoun), partly by the mutual relation of the two members.

9.2₅. The meaning of the genitive and of possessive pronouns is first and foremost 'possessive', — in a wide sense of this word, indicating any kind of intimate relation:

John's (his) house, wife, son, servants, father, uncle, master, work, books (not only those he owns, but those he has written), pictures (which he has bought or painted), enemies, life, opinions, portrait (one representing him), etc.

How easy the transition is between different employments of the genitive, and how natural the use of 'subjective' and 'objective' genitives is, can be shown by such series as:

[possessive > subjective] a girl's (*or* her) heart, mind, will, illness, feeling, admiration.

[possessive > objective] a man's (*or* his) sons, friends, heirs, pupils, successors, followers, admirers.

The subjective and objective genitives have been treated in vol V in connexion with

(1) nexus-substantives (ch 7): the doctor's (his) arrival (S) | our (S) pursuit of happiness (O) | their (O) perusal by me (S) | his (S) decision | its (O) discovery. Cf also AnalSynt ch 20;

(2) gerunds (ings, ch 8): eager after his (O) undoing |

his (S) killing of the king (O) | no chance of Frank's (S) dropping in | who would have thought of its (S) being you?

(3) agent-nouns (ch 22): our (O) well-wishers | John's (O) supporters.

The combination of a genitive and a substantive denotes something definite: *John's son* means his only son or the one we have been speaking about. Similarly *Dr. Arnold's pupils* means all his pupils or those indicated by the context. If this meaning is not to be implied, the *of*-construction must be used instead of the genitive: *We were pupils of Dr. Arnold* (= some of of Dr. A.'s pupils).

This agrees with the use of the definite article before the superior member in the synonymous *of*-combination: the son of John | the pupils of Dr. Arnold.

There are very few cases where a genitive cannot be supplanted by a prepositional group with *of*, thus *in the opinion of John = in J.'s opinion. The young wife of this clergyman = this clergyman's young wife.*

Still there is a strong tendency to employ the genitive where the strict sense of 'possession' is implied: *my neighbour's garden;* especially if the genitival adjunct is a proper name: *John's stick*, or a pronoun: *his stick.*

It is in accordance with this preponderance of the possessive notion that the genitive is mainly used of names for human beings and secondarily for other living beings.

With *love* as the primary we have also *of* before *God* and names of (fictive) saints:

Ch G 1351 for love of god (*for the love of God* common) | Lewis B 28 For the love o' Pete | for the love of Mike (common Amr; AmSp 1.94).

9.2₆. The genitive is chiefly used with the names of

Genitive and Possessive Pronouns.

human beings, God, and the devil; thus also with such transferred designations as:

Thack H 30 the poor thing's eyes filled with tears | Ru Sel 1.491 an entire understanding of Heaven's ways [H. = God] | ib 492 Heaven's kindness.

Names of supernatural beings and notions, of (fictive) saints, etc, in the genitive are often used in terms of imprecation. Thus in the combinations with *God* and modifications of this word frequently used in earlier times. Cf Swaen, *Figures of Imprecation*. EStn 24. 16 and 195, where i. a. lists of various forms of genitives are given. A few examples:

Ch A 1084 For Goddes love (very common in Ch) | A 4270 by goddes dignitee | D 385 by goddes swete pyne! | A 3743 By goddes corpus | B 1166 for goddes bones | A 3767 for Cristes swete tree | A 3716 For Jesus love and for the love of me | G 1089 by the hevenes quene | Skelton Magnyfycence 399 By Goddys body | ib 768 By Goddes fote | Sh Hml II. 2.554 Gods bodykins || Ch H 9 for cokkes bones | Skelton M 512 For Cockys harte (ib also Cockes woundes, armes, body) | Ford 163 'Ud's pity | Wycherley Plain Dealer 99 Odds my life! | Congreve Old Batchelor 53 Adsheart | Sheridan 201 Gad's life, etc.

Combinations of a genitive and *name* or *sake* in terms of imprecation are very common:

Ch: on (in, a) goddes name (C 250, 386, D 1276) | in God's name (frequent till the present day) | Galsw Sw 80 in heaven's name | in the Devil's name | Graves Goodbye 180 Why in hell's name ... || Ch: for goddes sake | id C 81 for Cristes sake | Freeman Th 403 for the Lord's sake (all these frequent) | ib 351 for mercy's sake | Biggers Chinese Parrot 150 for Pete's sake (U.S.).

Extremely often the genitival *s* only is left, which then is written together with the primary:

Arden III. 6.5 Zounds (for *God's wounds*; frequent in dramatists as late as Sheridan, also written Zoons) | Sh Hml III. 2.386 'Sblood (not in the Fol. 1623) | Ford 161 'Sfoot | Rehearsal 53 'Sdeath (frequent here and in other dramatists of the 17th c.) | ib 75 'Sheart | Congreve Old Batchelor 5 s'life | Kipling Many Inventions 45 [Mulvaney:] "'Strewth," I sez (also Graves Goodbye to All That 121; common in earlier times).

And even that may be dropped as in Congreve Old Batchelor 58 Oons (cf *Zoons* above) | ib 28 Death (frequent).

In the following few recent examples other words in the genitive are used in terms of imprecation:

Stevenson T 284 you have the Davy Jones's [i.e. the devil's] insolence to up and stand for cap'n over me | Masefield W 43 What did it cost ye ? — What did what cost ? — It. Your devil's penny for the devil's bit | Macdonell E 55 'Hell's eggs!' cried Mr. Huggins | Sayers UD 240 Hell's bells, there's somebody at the door.

But periphrasis with *of* is used also in this type of phrases if the subordinate member is the name of a lifeless 'thing', see the following modern examples:

Ward M 209 What in the name of fortune are you doing, Kitty ? | Doyle B 200 But how in the name of wonder did you come here | Chesterton Man Who was Thursday [Tauchn.] 24 And now, in the name of Colney Hatch, what is it ? | id Wisd. of Father Brown [Tauchn.] 28 Well, what in the name of Bedlam do you mean ? | Freeman Th 48 How in the name of goodness did you know ...

9.2₇. Alongside of the frequent genitive *God's* we very often — and now perhaps more frequently than formerly — find *of God* without any appreciable difference: the will of God = God's will | It was a sin in the eyes of God | Phillpotts GR 90 All men receive death from the hand of God ... when God's hand falls | Shaw StJ 84 you have shut it [the door] in our faces and in the face of God.

The Lord's is always used in some fixed combinations: *the Lord's Day* (= Sunday), but *the Day of the Lord* = Judgment Day, *the Lord's Supper*, *the Lord's Prayer*.

Other synonyms: *of Providence*, never *Providence's* | Maugham Alt 32 the Temple of the Most High | Ruskin Sel 2.319 Judas could not make out the worth of Him [Christ], or meaning of Him.

9.2₈. A special sense of the genitive-possessive which is not so easily derived from the possessive meaning, is found with some comparatives: the genitive (possessive) is virtually the second member of the comparison. This is true of *elder*, *better*, and some of the Latin comparatives. In this sense an *of*-combination is rare: Deloney 62 I am her elder | Swift T 56 he was their elder | Hardy L 44 she watched with inquisitive eyes their effect upon her elder || Sh As II. 4.68 Who cals? Your betters, sir | Kingsley (q NED) She will grow as proud as her betters || Caxton 100 [he] was your better and wyser (not used now) | Kipling J 2.93 they do not kill their weaker for food, but for sport || Macaulay E 2.248 In reply Fox was as decidedly superior to Pitt, as in declamation he was Pitt's inferior | Ridge S 43 boys who were all some years his junior || Wells V 39 he was the junior of both his sisters.

9.2₉. Collectives indicating persons are found in the genitive as well as with *of;* thus *Philological Society's Transactions* and *Transactions of the Philological Society* (on back of cover and on title page respectively). Some examples of the genitive:

Kipling K 200 without the Railway's knowledge [= the R. Company's] | Wells V 214 his sex's freedom | id N 206 she was entirely unfitted for her sex's sphere | Galsw SS [Tauchn.] 115 I must beg the House's pardon | Lucas Rose and Rose 36 the medical profession's best friends | NP 1923 in spite of Labour's weakness [= the weakness of the L. party].

But *of* must be reckoned the usual form with collectives: the policy of the Conservative Party | the endeavours of the police | the feelings of the crowd, etc.

9.3₁. *The world* is frequently used in the genitive;

some examples among many: Carlyle E 251 the world's movements | Tennyson 341 The world's loud whisper | Merriman VG 74 the world's arena.

When a country or town is thought of as a political agent, the genitive is frequently used:

Trollope D 2.68 all his country's pluck and pride | Stevenson T 56 he lost it [a leg] in his country's service | Benson Dawn of All 79 the country's welfare | Galsw MP 103 his country's life | Seeley E 290 to question Russia's power or her will to make distant conquests | Waugh W 4 Oil was the fountain of Trinidad's prosperity | Maugham C 161 the wise person who said that he did not care who made a nation's laws so long as he wrote its songs | the town's finances | on Oxford's part.

But *of* is used if the country or town is looked upon from a geographical point of view: the boundaries of Switzerland, etc.

(Compare with this the use of pronouns referring to the names of countries; see under Sex and Gender ch V).

9.3$_2$. Apart from the cases already mentioned in which *of* is used, the *of*-group is very frequently employed with names of human beings. First, of course, where no genitive is available: Lyly C 278 the opinion of vs both | Hope Z 146 And the eyes of both of us were wet | Austen M 92 there was gloom on the face of each | Thack V 360 Money has only a different value in the eyes of each | Caine C 293 a childlike creature, and of such are the kingdoms of Heaven (biblical).

With adjectives as primaries periphrasis with *of* is always used in natural language: the views of the learned | talk of rope in the house of the hanged | AV Job 6.23 deliuer me from the enemies hand, or redeeme me from the hand of the mighty | Ward D

59 With the usual imperfect sympathy of the young | Thack V 260 the Father of all.

On rare cases of genitives of adjectives see vol II 9.5 (juridical: the accused's identity) and 9.9 (for evil's sake).

Of is also preferred where a group-genitive (see on these vol VI ch 17) would be too long and clumsy; see, e.g., He is the son of the well-known politician whose death was announced the other day | Spectator 106 the character and quality of the gentleman who sent them .. | ib 107 the conversation of so much good company, who were as silent as myself | ib 108 Will Wimble's is the case of many a younger brother of a great family | Thack: the wife of a clergyman of the Church of England | Stevenson JHF 43 This was the home of Henry Jekyll's favourite; of a man who was heir to a quarter of a million sterling | ib 106 I come here at the instance of your colleague, Dr. H. J. Henry Jekyll.

A group-genitive would be specially awkward with clauses like the following: More U 236 the hole lyfe of them that be occupied | ib 188 the opinion of them whiche defende pleasure | Sh LLL V. 2.871 A jest's prosperity lies in the ear Of him that hears it; never in the tongue Of him that makes it | AV Job 12.5 in the thought of him that is at ease | ib John 4.34 to doe the will of him that sent mee | Bosw 1.432 the future happiness of him who is the immediate subject of correction | Trollope B 4 But by no means easy were the emotions of him who sat there watching | Walpole Cp 210 His whole carriage was that of a boy who was entering life for the first time | Stevenson B 73 for the lives' sake of many men that hurt you not.

9.3₃. Similarly with long combinations with conjunctions: More U 30 did beare the changes of him and his fyue companions | Marlowe E 983 cursing the name of thee and Gaueston | Swift 3.2 by the assistance of him and my uncle John, and some other relations | ib 3.377 at the very smell of him and his men | Byron L 28 I rode out on the vizier's horses, and saw the palaces of himself and grandsons | ib 153 all the activity of myself, and some vigorous friends | Maxwell G 293 working for the daily bread of herself and the child | Locke HB 240 the story of her disastrous marriage; of the far separated lives of her husband and herself | Wells N 269 she refused to be teased in spite of the taunts of either him or her father | Tarkington, Guest of Quesnay 53 I was receiving, every evening at dinner, a detailed report of the day's doings of Professor Keredec and his companion | Galsw IC 67 the house which was to have been the home of him and her from whom he was now going to seek release | id Car 179 some inkling haunted me of the dignity of himself and brother | Dowden Shelley 308 [it] became the joint property of himself and Byron.

Eve's daughters would be those born to Eve; *the daughters of Eve* = all women.

9.3₄. *The King's English* is a fixed phrase = 'correct English'; cf Lounsbury SU 30 [George III] his published correspondence has made us aware that the English of the king varied widely at times from the king's English.

9.3₅. There seems to be a disinclination to use the genitive of a word qualified by the indefinite article. Wells has the book-title "The Soul of a Bishop" — *a Bishop's soul* would rather be taken as a compound (Dan. *en biskopssjæl*, G *eine bischoffsseele*); *a cat's tail* is Dan. *en kattehale*, G *ein katzenschwanz* rather than *en kats hale*, *der schwanz einer katze*.

Examples: Jane's eyes were the eyes of a child | Defoe Rox 150 an affection equal to that of a wife | Cowper L 2.294 he has in him the soul of a gentleman | Mackenzie S 1.469 Not even was his personality strong enough to retain the love of a girl for six weeks | Masterman WL 86 he made her live the life of a nun | Shaw 2.147 That foolish boy can speak with the inspiration of a child and the cunning of a serpent | Wells JP 475 unsocial as the will of a criminal | Maugham P 91 That would be the act of a madman | Stevenson T 65 I have this confounded son of a Dutchman sitting in my own house.

A trapper's story would be = a story of the kind told by trappers; *the story of a trapper* = a story about a trapper.

9.3₆. We may here also remind of the combination *of man*, in which *man* is taken in the generic sense, related to the use of by *man* with the indefinite article or the pl *men* (cf 9.3₅, 12.5₆, 12.6₈ and 14.3₃): AV Job 10.5 Are thy day as the dayes of man? are thy yeares as mans dayes? | ib 14.19 thou destroyest the hope of man | Mason R 165 the faults and vanities of men | Maugham P 194 A little smoke lost in the air, that was the life of man | Haggard S 183 behold the lot of man! | Wilde SM 100 Men may have women's minds just as women may have the minds of men.

Cf, however, Mi PL 1.1 Of Mans first disobedience ... Sing Heav'nly Muse.

9.3₇. When an adj precedes a genitival combination, it may qualify the genitive (*the naughty boy's hat*) or the primary (*a shrill child's voice*); if the adj might be taken to go with either, it is generally felt to belong to the primary, as in *the stout Major's wife;*

if *stout* is to go with *Major*, *of* is preferred: *the wife of the stout Major*. — See vol II 12.331 and Appendix.

Where there are adjectives to both nouns, *of* is required: Spectator 106 versed in all the little handicrafts of an idle man.

9.3₈. The combination of two or more successive genitives is not very frequent as in Di D 211 could she be Dr. Strong's son's wife? | Mrs Browning A 162 all the hoofs of King Saul's father's asses. — In such cases *of* is preferred. Most people will tolerate a long series of *of*'s, as in "On the occasion of the coming of age of the youngest son of a wealthy member of Parliament", or "that sublime conception of the Holy Father of a spiritual kingdom on earth under the sovereignty of the Vicar of Jesus Christ himself" (Hall Caine) | Thack V 50 the wife of a clergymen of the Church of England | Locke HB 202 He had no idea of the state of mind of the Rosaline-rejected young Romeo of a son of his, — whereas they will resent the iteration of *s*'s in Pinero M 124 He is my wife's first husband's only child's godfather.

9.3₉. *Of* is practically always used in a number of combinations which may be considered composite prepositions: on account of (18th cent. *upon a. of*) | for the benefit of (in the interests of) his family | at the instance of his brother | on the part of Mr. Brown.

Cf Dreiser AT 2.287 Then you really went up there on her account. — Yes, sir, only on account of her.

In (on) the king's behalf alternates with *in (on) behalf of the king*, "the choice being determined by considerations of euphony and perspicuity" (NED).

9.4₁. In newspapers the *of*-combination is often necessitated by the addition of information on supplementary circumstances in the mention of a person's death: NP 1903 The death in his sixty-fifth year is announced from Rome of the Deputy Giovanni Mestica, a distinguished writer on literary history ... | NP 1924 The death has occurred in London, after a short illness, of Sir William Goschen, British Ambassador in Berlin in 1914.

9.4₂. It is quite natural that with pronouns the possessive form (= genitive) is generally preferred to the less handy *of*-combination. Sometimes a distinction may be made: *his thought* is the thought he has (subjective), while *the thought of him* is objective. Some approach to an 'objective' conception is seen in the following string of quotations: Marlowe E 1011 your loue to Gaueston Will be the ruine of the realme and you | Osborne 118 't has bin the ruine of us both | Thack P 517 I must give it up, or it'll be the ruin of me | Sh H4A II. 1.15 it was the death of him [= what killed him] Thack N 287 a lively woman would be the death of me | Di M 391 Don't question me, or I shall be the death of you, or some one else | Plunket Greene E 49 It's the end of Foster & Co. — And it's the end of me as well.

Just as we have *the death of* (*me*), we have the opposite idea: *the life of* (*me*); this is chiefly used in imprecations; I add some other imprecations: Marlowe E 885 the life of thee shall salue this foule disgrace [= 886 thy life] | Sh R3 IV. 1.76 by the life of thee | Di M 377 For the life and soul of him Tom could get no further in his writing | Harraden F 121 for the very life of her, she could not help being sorry for him | Swift J 465 I could not finish my letter last post for the soul of me | Sterne M 1.98 for the soul of me I cannot see what connection there can be | Goldsm 650 I can't help laughing for the soul of me | Byron DJ 4.117 I could not for the muse of me put less in that [in the canto].

Combinations like "I hate the sight of him" (O) may

have led to the frequent use of "the look of him" = his appearance: Stevenson JHF 23 and the look of him went somehow strongly against the watcher's inclination | ib 31 black secrets, by the look of him | Haggard S 165 from the look of you | Mason Ch 23 If he had a touch of George Brymer, for instance, the look of him, the easy way and cheek of him.

In the same sense a possessive pronoun may be used, but then with the pl *looks:* Stevenson JHF [p. ?] When Utterson remarked on his ill-looks | Hamerton F 2.144 asked in marriage for her looks.

But *his look* = 'the way in which he looks at this.'

9.4₃. The combination *of* + personal pronoun is found in a great many other cases, chiefly with words denoting personal appearance or qualities, in some cases with a tinge of contempt. I have noted the following instances: pate (Sh H4A II. 1.33 the pate of thee), heart (Carlyle H 84, Ward D 2.306), air (Benson N 69), face (the poor face, James RH 225), back (Kipling L 118), figure (Wells H 177), body and mind (London A 130), flesh (Hewlett Q 9), size and ugliness (Mackenzie S 1.35), nature (Swinburne L 142), easy way (Collins M 16), will (London A 34), power (Dreiser AT 2.178), pride (Tarkington F 81), gait (Hardy R 135), honesty (Barrie TG 99), pathos (Bennett ECh 151), price (Stevenson JHF 217), cheek (Wells JP 382), charm (Maxwell F 21), chief sin (Wells N 76).

I place in a class of its own *the like of* — (= those like): Kipling L 219 you might be going to be hanged by the like of you | Black F 88 it isn't for the like of me to try to take Linn's place | Shaw P 149 I do not need to be told what to do by the like of you.

Of it is of course so natural that it calls for no further remark: Sh Cæs I. 2.235 Tell vs the manner of it | Congreve 126 the impiety of it startles me | Kingsley

H 297 people began to murmur at the cruelty and the heathenry of it | Shaw Ms 177 The disgrace of it will kill me | id F 84 a measure which, on the face of it, would fortify the private drink trade | id TT 178 All this was cruelty for its own sake, for the pleasure of it | on the top of it | in the middle of it | at the bottom of it.

9.4₄. With names of animals the *of*-construction must be considered the normal one. The gen., however, is not infrequent, chiefly of the names of higher animals and in combinations which may be considered compounds. The use in Sh is as follows: the gen. of *calf* is only found in compounds:

Ado V. 1.156 a calues head | Err IV. 3.18 calues-skin | John III. 1.129 and 220 a calues skin | ib III. 1.299 a calues-skin (cp Hml V. 1.124 calue-skinnes) | Cy II 3.34 horse-haires and calues-guts.

The only genitive of *cow* is also part of a compound: As II. 4.50 the cowes dugs.

There is only one genitive proper of *dog*, but several compounds:

Ro II. 4.223 A mocker that's the dogs name || Tim II. 2.91 Thou shalt famish a dogges death | H6B IV. 2.26 dogges leather | Err V. 1.70 a mad dogges tooth.

There are, however, several instances of the actual genitive of *horse:* H6A I. 4.108 with my horses heeles | Tro V. 10.4 at the murtherers horses taile | Lr III. 6.20 He's mad that trusts in the tameness of a wolfe, a horse's health | R2 III. 2.7 their horses hoofes | Cor III. 2.2 Present me Death on the wheel or at wilde horses heeles.

In the main, the genitive is restricted to the higher spheres of the animal kingdom, but, especially in compounds, it may also be found with the lower species (some examples in vol II 7.43):

I saw something white with long ears like a cat's

[to avoid the clumsy: those of a cat] | Butler Er 281 put temptation in the dog's way | Galsw SS 65 His [baby's] kicks and crows and splashings had the joy of a gnat's dance, or a jackdaw's gambols in the air | Shaw C 214 he pulled the white horse's head || Ru F 153 a jewel of gold in a swine's snout [from Prov. 11.22] | Hardy W 39 a boy, who was creeping on at a snail's pace | Mackenzie S 1.48 a woman with ... little pig's eyes | Maugham P 79 Unless we can hush this up I don't stand a dog's chance.

9.5₁. With names of inanimate things an *of*-construction must be looked on as the normal expression: the environs of London | the foot of the mountain | the legs of that table | the walls of our house | the colour of the wall | the doors of the room | the roof of the church | in the middle of the night | the beginning of this novel | the head of the statue | other parts of the garden | on the other side of the door | the cause of the accident, etc.

Exceptional uses of the genitive are collected in the following sections.

9.5₂. The genitive is often used before *sake:*

Ford 110 For pity's sake (frequent) | Di D 727 Mr. Micawber did right, for right's sake | Thack P 310 it was only for form's sake (and Seeley E 3) | Stevenson JHF 18 for old sake's sake as they say (and Kipling S 170) | Seeley E 260 let this be granted for argument's sake | Kipling P 87 for shame's sake | Doyle S 5.184 to work for work's sake |Rose Macaulay T 24 for honesty's sake | Galsw Car 233 I'd like to have a look at the little chap, just for old times' sake (and Maugham Alt 266; but id MS 239 for old time's sake).

The genitive alternating with *of* is seen in:

Ward M 72 it would not be for the lie's sake, but

for the sake of some romantic impulse or imagination | Caine C 7 for economy's sake — for the sake of general tidiness | Galsw TL 128 Art for Art's sake — Science for the sake of science.

Cf with the latter Wilde In 137 emotion for the sake of emotion is the aim of art, and emotion for the sake of action is the aim of life | Merriman S 150 Even for her sake, even for the sake of her own vanity.

On the omission of the genitive ending before *sake* see vol VI 16.8$_8$.

9.5₃. The gen. is used in a certain number of more or less fixed phrases, thus: at (from, to) death's door (extremely frequent).

Similarly Butler Er 182 rushing into death's arms | J. J. Bell in BDS 232 the decided step in death's direction.

Other set phrases: *my (his, the, etc) mind's eye*, from Sh Hml I. 2.185 | *to my (his, etc) heart's content* (Di, Jerome, Bennett B 29, etc) | they were at *their wits' end* (e.g. AV Psalm 107.27 | know at *one's fingers' ends* (also *finger ends*).

And *in pity's name* (Stevenson D 91 | James RH 352).

Out of (from) harm's way (e.g. Spect 10 | Defoe G 66 | Thack N 269 | Kipling J 1.189) || Hope In 181 he did not seem to be in luck's way to-night | Bennett W 1.60 in misfortune's way.

The genitive of *ship*, *boat*, and *vessel* is pretty frequent, where we should rather expect *of*; some of the combinations quoted may be considered compounds (*like two ship's doctors*, where *two* qualifies the whole. Cf on such compounds vol VI 16.9₄).

Defoe R 56 all the ship's provisions | ib I went down the ship's side (also Brontë V 46) | ib 2.134 the ship's cook ... the ship's mate (similarly ib 139, 220) |

ib 241 the boat's crew | Kingsley H 30 he kept the boat's head continually towards the monster (also Haggard S 53, etc) | Browning 1.531 our ship's condition | Masefield C 261 all the ship's company | ib 267 a bad effect upon the ship's discipline | Williamson S 106 on the boat's gangway | Priestley F 224 the ship's old doctor | Freeman A Cert. Dr. Thorndyke 128 The vessel's keel.

9.5₄. In poetry and in higher literary style the gen. of lifeless things is used in many cases where *of* would be used in ordinary speech; the gen. here conveys more or less a notion of personification:

Sh R3 IV. 3.8 in their deaths sad story | id R3 IV. 2.74 my sweet sleeps disturbers | id Hml II. 2.265 the shadow of a dreame ... (268) it is but a shadowes shadow | Wordsw 76 His limbs are cast in beauty's mould | Shelley 67 Fraud [would] rebuild religion's tottering dome | Browning 1.531 we stumble at truth's very test | Mrs Browning A 33 at poetry's divine first finger-touch | Stevenson JHF 42 terror of the law and the law's officers | Butler Er 70 remember pity's kinsman [i.e. love] | Maugham Pl 2.39 Those five minutes that a man stays against his will are the nails in love's coffin | Maxwell WF 99 from childhood's days.

9.5₅. The genitive is pretty frequent before *end:*

Deloney 13 the Tables end (and ib 16) | Sh Err IV. 4.17 a ropes end (also Stevenson K 49) | Meas IV. 3.187 to the lanes end | As II. 6.10 hold death a while at the armes end | Tw V. 1.292 He holds Beelzebub at the staues end (Scott A 1.253 at staff's end) | AV Psalms 107.27 at their wits end (cf 9.5₃; frequent) | Goldsm 632 from year's end to year's end | Sterne M 1.7 [he] had got to his journey's end (also Wordsw 12,

Di Do 97, Di C 433, etc, and the title of Sherriff's play) | Austen M 71 she had it at her tongue's end (also Brontë P 147, GE SM 160) | ib 387 at about the week's end from his return | ib 398 I'd give her the rope's end (also Di Do 340) | Di T 1.18 to my life's end | Browning 1.529 at my tether's end | Kipling P 126 his father came the summer's end | Wells V 309 at the session's end | Benson Dawn of All 39 Of course Manners has it all at his fingers' ends (cf 9.5$_3$, common) | Tarkington Pl 348 even as he came to this dream's end | Waugh W 168 There was no dividing of the sexes at the meal's end.

Note the difference between *from week's end to week's end* and *week end* (*weekend*) = Saturday, Sunday (Monday).

Thus also with some related notions, especially with *edge:*

Wordsw 133 by the chimney's edge (similarly ib 135) | Kipling S 17 to the cliff's edge | Maugham Alt 3 the water's edge (frequent) | Waugh W 38 at the pavement's edge | Rose Macaulay O 106 the wood's edge || Bunyan G 38 out of the grave's mouth (also Ruskin F 122; from Psalm 141.7) | Di D 121 she sat by my bed's head | Rose Macaulay O 106 from the table's head | ib 108 at the table's foot | ib 295 over the hill's top | Kinglake E 268 on the mountain's side | Galsw MW 241 he vanished over the hill's shoulder.

With these may also be compared Brontë V 439 near the park's centre | Di Do 213 the river's bank (also Jerome 62) | Allen W 143 a dry torrent's bed | J. J. Bell in BDS 236 the knife's haft.

During the last few decades the genitive of lifeless things has been gaining ground in writing (especially among journalists); in instances like the following the *of*-construction would be more natural and colloquially the only one possible:

Ruskin S 69 the sailor wrestling with the sea's rage | Ellis M 225 the rapidity of the heart's action | Bennett Cd 142 a glass knob was the door's sole fitting | Wells H 27 that picture's completeness | Galsw IC 28 to change the room's atmosphere | id TL 241 nothing so soft as a rose-leaf's velvet | Hewlett Q 72 the needle's eye | Henderson Shaw[1] 384 The play's greatest faults | Walpole ST 106 to affect a book's good or evil fortunes | Brett Young PC 85 Rather some ghostly visitant stood and mocked her from the mirror's shining oval | ib 234 Clare should watch each moment of her trousseau's manufacture | ib 275 she seemed a bodily emanation of all the house's light and comfort.

(Hope R 62 in time's fullness, cf AV Gal 4.4 when the fulness of time was come.)

9.5₆. The genitive of lifeless things is idiomatic in indications of measure of space; some of the cases may, however, be regarded as compounds:

Marlowe E 2374 At euery ten miles end | Tennyson 526 one hair's-breadth | Di DC 16 with her needle drawn out to its thread's length | Kingsley H 68 Philamon followed, sulkily and unwillingly, at a foot's pace (also Butler ER 306) | Meredith E 73 a small speck, a pin's head | Stevenson M 207 she has not a hair's resemblance to what her mother was at the same age | Ward F 414 she would only be a stone's throw from the house [also *a stone throw*] | Kipling Diversity of Creat. 45 one could scarcely see a cow's length across a field | Hawthorne 1.470 a thumb's bigness of evil | Myers M 210 Not until she was within arm's length could I realise that she didn't know I was there.

With these should be compared Di F 631 I'll have
my money's worth out of him (also e.g. Stevenson MB
177, Rose Macaulay T 200) | Di P 492 a wery good one
and nine's worth || James RH 364 Her affection has
not a shadow's weight with Mr. Hudson!

Note *a shilling's worth*, but *three-penny worth* (cf vol
II 7.3).

Cp also Austen M 60 at a foot's pace.

9.5₇. The genitive is especially frequent in indications
of a measure of time, as in

Roister 61 at minutes warning | Sh Rom Prol 12 the
two houres trafficque of our stage | Sh Ant IV. 14.35
the long dayes taske is done [here *long* may qualify
day or *dayes taske*] | Sh R3 II. 1.1 a good daies work
[the adj belongs to the compound] | Kipling J2 227 here
is this season's kill | Parker R 73 fresh from an all-night's
drowse | Wells V 173 she reflected upon her half-day's
employment | Quiller-Couch T 164 There was a second's
pause | A good hour's work (= work that will take
rather more than an hour).

Note that time-indications are rendered vague by the
use of the genitive followed by *time: an hour's time;
three weeks' time*, etc.

The gen. pl of time-indications is sometimes found
without the apostrophe: Shaw 2 220 I owe six weeks
rent. — The spelling wavers especially in compounds;
see vol II 7.28.

A possessive pronoun before the genitive of time-indications will often belong to the whole combination,
or rather to the latter part of it:

Sh Ro III. 2.100 I thy three houres wife | id Mcb
I. 7.61 his dayes hard iourney [= his hard day's journey]
| Marlowe T 1929 thy solemn evenings walk | Mi PL
5.115 of our last evening's talk | Greene F 11.36 my

seven years' task | Swift J 195 our this day's company | Di P 574 Having delivered this manifesto (which formed a portion of his last week's leader) ... the editor paused to take breath | Thack P 1.176 he might spoil her night's rest | Spencer A 1.280 a lover whose to-morrow's bride has been drowned | Wells V 148 her last winter's jacket | Locke CA 260 Had he not proved it by his year's silence? | Priestley G 579 Dear Sir, I have communicated your yesterday's wire to Mr. Mortimer.

A different type of genitive of words denoting time is seen in the following examples, where no measure of time is indicated:

Sh Meas III 2.240 this newes is old enough, yet it is eurie daies newes | Anstey V 61 you have this evening's paper, I see | Thack P 1.81 it arrived in the Wednesday's bag | Hawthorne S 228 it was a last year's nut | GE A 1.165 everything was looking lovelier for the yesterday's rain | Hope In 30 taking up the loaf. "I told Mrs. Stryver I wouldn't have a yesterday's" | Beswick OD 336 the to-morrow's test would be very successful.

Here the prepositional group has acquired a substantival character.

For examples of similar genitives of *to-day*, etc, without any article, as in Gissing G 116 to-morrow morning's chapter, — see vol II 8.71, and cf vol III 1.2 on prep. + object (i.e. regimen) as primary.

While genitival compounds as in Ward D 2.263 "she would hardly be persuaded to give her bandaged foot the *afternoon's rest*" denote some measure of time, compounds like *afternoon walk* | take *afternoon tea* | an *after-dinner nap* denote points of time. Still Sh has an *after-dinners sleepe* (Meas III 1.33).

Genitives as Primaries

9.5₈. The ordinary function of the genitive is that of an adjunct (a secondary), as in *His wife's fortune*. But it may also stand as a primary:

AV Matt. 22.21 Render therefore unto Cesar, the things which are Cesars; and unto God the things that are Gods| Maugham Alt 754 His yellow skin had the smoothness of a woman's || St. Paul's is one of the principal sights of London || he is a friend of John's | this is no fault of Frank's.

These phenomena (with "that long nose of his") were dealt with at some length in vol III 1.4 and 5.

9.5₉. Instead of a genitive as primary it is often preferable to use *of* preceded by *that* or *those:*

Di N 744 a gentleman who had run through his own fortune, and wanted to squander away that of his sister | James RH 168 And then her divine mouth — it might really be that of a goddess! | Russell Ed 113 Correct Latin is fixed once for all: it is that of Vergil and Cicero || Spectator 107 rising to greater estates than those of their elder brothers | her eyes were darker than those of her sisters.

Other Employments of *Of*

9.6₁. In the preceding parts of this chapter we have considered uses of *of*-combinations more or less equivalents of a genitive. We shall now take up other employments of this preposition which may still be considered grammatical, leaving out of account all the more concrete significations of the preposition found in the dictionaries (come of a good family | die of pneumonia | to be had of all the booksellers | made of steel | he did it of himself | speak of the war | I am sick of him, etc).

9.6₂. First, we shall mention the repetition of the same word in the pl after *of* to denote excellence in its kind, a usage that is ultimately derived from Hebrew, as in *the holy of holies*. Examples: Sh Hml III. 2.78 in my heart of hearts (common, cf Thack below) | Austen M 71 the place of all places | Mitford OV 179 that rarity of rarities, a fine day | Thack N 100 I remember you a buck of bucks | ib 148 every lad has a friend of friends, a crony of cronies, whom he cherishes in his heart of hearts | Lecky D 1.21 the evil of evils in our present politics | James TM 60 the woman is a horror of horrors | Sully, Study of Childh. 71 that mystery of mysteries, the beginning of things | Ward E 265 she is a modern of moderns | Caine C 443 love like yours is the pearl of pearls, and he who wins it is prince of princes | Barrie TG 6 chemistry had been the study of studies for T. Sandys | NP (q Wendt) a dog of dogs.

Compare also Kipling J 2.160 I am sorrowful to my tail's tail.

It will be found that in the following sections we have not infrequently cases in which *of* may, or may not, be used, so that the combination may often be considered a kind of apposition.

9.6₃. Some prepositional phrases are found with and without *of:* on this (or that) side (of) the river. Quotations without *of:* BJo: I lov'd the man [Shakespeare], and doe honour his memory (on this side idolatry) as much as any | Defoe R 216 on my side the island (also ib 238) | ib 163 on the other side the island | ib 164 as the current was on both sides the island | Swift 3.134 on each the river | Fielding 1.232 on the other side the river | Quincey 349 he would reach the bottom on the wrong side the Cordilleras | Brontë V 100 parallel with the very high wall on that side the garden | Di N 386 she had put her head out of the coach-window a mile or two this side Kingston | Walker L 25 In the vernacular there was, this side the Middle Ages, little literature.

Nowadays *of* would be generally used in *on the other side of* and *on both sides of*. Always *by the side of*.

Alongside is used as an adv with *of* and as a preposition without *of*.

Similarly *on board (of) the steamer:* Defoe M 257 I was put on board of a ship | ib 258 my going on board the ship | Scott OM 12 on board of slave ships | Byron DJ 4.50 on board of one of these [galliots] | Doyle S 1.213 on board of a ship.

Atop as a prep. is American (Lewis MA 38, Ferber S 78) = Brit. *on the top of*, though *on top* as a prep. may be found: Mannin ChE 50 'Tis likely too many children, one on top t'other.

Sh Err I. 1.86 at either end the most — now with *of*.

In U.S. *of* is left out after *out:* London M 336 the cub passed out the door | Hemingway FA 148 Don't throw the cognac out the window (frequent in modern U. S. authors.

Partitive

9.7₁. Next, we have the partitive sense: one of his daughters | the rest of the party | the best of men | one part of the soldiers | the beginning (middle, end) of the story | at the bottom (top) of the page | his head only was visible, the rest of him was hidden | the best of poetry (but: poetry at its best). | first of all.

Partitive *of* may be used without any preceding sb: He gave us of his best.

Fractions: one half or two thirds of the population. But *half* is also used without *of:* half an hour | the half-hour | half the lands of Europe. — Even before a relative clause: Di T 1.222 you don't mean half you say | Maugham Pl 3.140 I don't suppose he means half he says | Cather P 94 I always tell people you don't mean half you say | Graves IC 289 a commission of half whatever they succeeded in making out of their appointments should be paid to him.

9.7₂. On the use of *half* partly as an adj, partly as a sb, and partly as a hybrid of both (one half the world), see vol II 12.58. Before *it*, *of* cannot be omitted.

With other fractions we have similar hesitations: The effects were sold at a fourth their value, or at one fourth (of) their value — equally good, says one English professor. Examples with *quarter* and other fractions without *of* were given in vol II 12.59 *A quarter-hour* seems to be universal in U.S., where in England *a quarter of an hour* is usually said.

Plenty is in its origin a sb and takes *of:* plenty of money, of people. But in recent usage it is constructed without the prep. and may even be considered an adj, which it resembles in form; this seems to be especially frequent in Sc and Amr: NP 1922 if there are plenty such people among the English artisans | Marshall Sorry Sch 144 There are plenty middle-aged women who have their night-out | Sayers NT 219 there's plenty farms now with the big brewing coppers still standing | Cronin H 124 There's plenty time — plenty o' time.

In Sc the two sbs are also in other cases placed together without the preposition: Sc A 1.241 a hantle [= handful] letters he has written | ib 2.74 A wheen poor drudges ye are | ib 225 a wheen blackguards (see EDD) | Barrie W 77 in a bit paper | Scott A 1.30 the deil a drap punch ye'se get here | Douglas House w. Green Shutters 27 a drop milk.

9.7₃. Closely akin to the partitive *of* is the use of that prep. after a quantitative or numeral word, as in: a bottle of rum, lots of people (of money), a distance of two miles, a reward of £ 10, a couple of days, a pair of stockings.

But in U.S. *couple* is very often used without *of:* Lewis MA 188 a couple months in Italy | Hammett Th 173 she touched me for a couple hundred to blow town.

The numeral sbs *dozen, score, hundred, thousand, million, myriad* are used without *of* as a kind of numeral adjs, even when preceded by *a* or a numeral: a dozen bottles, a hundred years, two thousand pounds, five million inhabitants, etc.

A few quotations: Shelley 250 see those million worlds | Darwin L 2.43 I have been collecting facts for these dozen years | Brontë P 185 when she had gone through some half dozen pages | Zangwill G 309 Two and a half million dollars are an awful lot of money | Stevenson D 306 I am now a private person like yourself and many million others | Doyle M 42 the man who observes the myriad stars | James RH 352 Rowland took the note and glanced at its half-dozen lines | Bennett Cd 135 a list of several score shops | id Imp Pal 625 they were girls among a couple of score men | Golding SD 84 we must buy another dozen and a half machines.

On the use of such words in the pl without any ending see vol II 3.52.

Exceptionally *of*, in the last quotation occasioned by *or so:* Thack N 19 to do a thousand of secret kindnesses | ib 20 half a dozen of religious edifices | ib 66 a dozen of little children | ib. a score, at least, of adopted children | ib 206 a half-dozen of theatre tickets | Ruskin F 191 a girl worth anything ought to have always half a dozen or so of suitors under vow for her.

But when these words are used with the pl ending, chiefly in indefinite indications, they require *of:* dozens of instances | Marlowe T 1447 thousands of lamps (but ib 508 Our army will be forty thousand strong) | Seeley E 241 there are not less than fifty millions of Mussulmen | Doyle M 179 at the end of a hundred millions of years || Exceptionally: Tennyson Demeter 41 in the gleam of a million million of suns.

9.7₄. When one of the quantitative words which otherwise require *of* is accompanied by *more*, the latter word influences the construction so that no prep. is used: Defoe M 68 I had a great deal more money than I ever pretended to have | id G 20 there were abundance more classes | Hunt A 47 There is a good deal more wood in the map than is now to be found | Di D 353 asking for a cup more coffee | Trollope B 417 Give me half a glass more champagne | Darwin L 1.245 I have just received a bundle more letters | Shaw IW 409 shove a couple more passengers into it [the boat] | id 1.168 shall I get a couple more chairs | Bennett W 1.320 a lot more money | Gibbs Heirs App 32 "No more adventure!" "Heaps more adventure" | Myers M 213 We need a bit more proof | Maugham Pl 2.311 I don't mean to do a stroke more work than I'm obliged to | Stephen L 458 I had taken for granted that he was to have a year or two more life | Housman J 224 with a good deal more concern | Walpole F 196 There are a lot more photographs | Mackenzie RR 239 I've got a lot more years to live before I die.

Cf also NP 1936 One doubts if a drop more or a

drop less praise can ... move one so solidly entrenched | Beswick OD 84 They get a lot too much prestige out of workmen's compensation, the unions.

Specializing *of*

9.8. *Of* is sometimes used between a more general and a more special designation; in many of such cases a simple apposition is found. Thus with *name, word, title:* Congreve 173 brand me with the name of villain | Defoe M 184 the name of Moll Flanders | Di D 202 my adopted name of Trotwood [different from the use in: What is the name of your brother-in-law?] | Byron DJ 5.4 I have a passion for the name of "Mary" | Stevenson M 230 Madame Desprez, who answered to the Christian name of Anastasie | Galsw SS 60 There's a man to see you, sir, by the name of Bugfill || Spencer A 1.381 no one to whom the name philosopher is applicable | Roberts M 145 he did not love her in any sense of the word love | the title (of) Cardinal.

Analogous cases: Quincey 323 I detest your ridiculous and most pedantic neologism of firstly | Goldsm 651 to blurt out the broad staring question of, (")Madam, will you marry me?(") | Ridge G 133 the cemetery gates, with its warnings of "No Smoking Allowed" | Carlyle FR 444 the old story of Vive le Roi | Wells Cl 536 the new game of bridge | Bennett LR 322 technical articles on the disease of pneumonia.

This leads to the next employment of *of*.

Appositional *of*

9.9₁. I use this term in cases when the two words connected by *of* are coextensive and in which, therefore, the term partitive is not applicable, though NED (*of* 42c) says, "Under the partitive form the whole may be included." The combination *all of* was, if not directly produced, at any rate helped on by such instances as: this is found in some, but not in all, of the books on the subject | Spencer A 1.398 I saw in her many, if not all of the needful qualifications | Henderson Sc Lit 323 he shared in some, though not in all, of the superstitions of the ecclesiastic | Wells T 32 slip off some or all of your clothes | Galsw Sw 261 If anything should happen to either or both of us, things would soon be in Queer Street.

9.9₂. According to Baldwin § 86, neither *all of them* nor *both of them* is found in Malory; but from Elizabethan times these expressions become frequent. Examples with *all:* Sh R2 III. Yes, all of them at Bristow lost their heads | R3 III. 3.5 God keep the prince from all the pack of you | Bacon A 4.19 if yee will sweare, (all of you) | Ruskin P 3.11 we all of us became acquainted with the curé | Hope M 25 all of us men in Aureataland were at her feet.

With the noun in the sg: Lang T 60 Tennyson had all of Keats's sentiment for Burns | Lowndes Ivy 116 Lexton had been something of a wastrel and all of a fool | Lowell 313 collect all of its force.

Examples with *both:* Sh Err V. 291 I am sure you both of you remember me | Di D 12 I lay claim to both of these characteristics | ib 475 both of these expressions Mrs. Crupp considered actionable | ib 394 for both of these songs | Lang T 46 Probably both of these young writers did not share the undergraduate enthusiasm.

9.9₃. Analogous expressions with numerals, etc: Defoe P 171 we are only three poor men of us | Di D 145 there were three or four of us [= we were three or four] | Thack V 194 the three of us will lay siege to old Mr.

Osborne | Ruskin P 3.42 all the three of them | Doyle S 6.162 he said a few words to the man, and the two of them went off together | Oppenheim Laxw 274 The three of them had risen to their feet together | Maugham HB 359 He had ordered dinner for the two of them | Pinero S 3 You two fellows ... the three of you | Wells TB 1.25 They were, all three of them, pensioned-off servants | Caine E 122 and all four of them got into the carriage | Jerome T 93 Confound the stuck-up pair of them | Priestley F 386 I think the pair of you are acting the goat | Shaw StJ 21 She may strike the lot of us dead if we cross her | Wilde W 13 the whole of London knows it.

9.9₄. In all such cases we have coextension of the two terms: the three of us = the three who are we = we, who are three. Now, the same is the case with *the City of Rome* = the City which is Rome (while *the City of London* is partitive). Other geographical instances of appositional *of* are the Isle of Wight | the Isle of Man | the kingdom of Denmark | Mandv 45 the lond of Egipte, unto the cytee of Alisandre ... the ryvere of Nyle | Scott I 86 the town of Sheffield | Doyle S 1.155 the pretty little country town of Ross | Merriman S 52 the village of Osterno.

In similarly parallel instances of geographical names a simple apposition is used: Cape York | Lake Agnes | River Hudson or Hudson River — thus without the article — and with the article: the river Thames (or the Thames river). Cf below, 16.1₄.

9.9₅. In vol III 1.5 I have applied the same explanation to the well-known phenomenon found in *a friend of mine* (= a friend who is mine), no money of mine, that long nose of his, etc. But I must here take up the full treatment of a category there (p. 19) dealt

with very briefly, viz. *a stripling of a page* (Byron 437.
= a stripling who is a page, a page who is a stripling);
see also PhilGr 98-99 with parallels from other languages
and references, to which might be added Curme, *Germ.
Gr.*[2] 109, 127, Einenkel in *Furnival Miscellany* 68, Joyce
Ir 42, A. Lombard in *Studier i modern språkvetenskap*
XI (1931).

These combinations are chiefly used in a depreciatory
sense as equivalents of a contemptuous adj. Some of
my quotations are from the 18th c., but the majority
from the 19th and 20th centuries, when the colloquial
style has been more prominent in literature than in
former centuries. It should be noted that in some
quotations the indefinite article occurs before a proper
name.

First we have examples of the indefinite article or an
indefinite pronoun: Sterne 13 a lean, sorry, jackass of
a horse | Quincey 317 [a baby] such a love of a plaything | Brontë V 98 a Methuselah of a pear-tree |
Thack P 71 his eldest son was a little scamp of a choirboy | id S 94 Ponto's house is a perfect Paradise of a
place | Di H 7 a plain, bare, monotonous vault of a
schoolroom ... the speaker's square wall of a forehead |
Locke FS 140 It's going to be a beast of a journey |
Doyle M 31 I told you what a lamb of a temper he
has | Hope D 13 he sends me a love of a bracelet |
Galsw Car 467 this was a very kitten of a woman |
Shaw 1.167 a fairly presentable old blackguard of a
woman | Wells L 58 Monday dawned coldly and clearly
— a Herbert Spencer of a day | Locke W 10 England
is a beast of a place | Maxwell F 176 Isn't that a duck
of a kitchen? || Di D 184 any dog of a fellow | Browning 1.518 And nip each softling of a wee white
mouse.

Examples of the definite article or with *this* or *that:*
Swift J 53 I went to see the Ladies Butler, and the
son of a whore of a porter denied them | Thack P 745
She pays the debts of that scamp of a husband of hers |
id V 260 that clever little wretch of a Rebecca | Di D
255 that poor dear baby of a mother of yours | Thack V
3 that pompous old Minerva of a woman | id S 101
this earthquake of a piece of music | Di D 532 as she
worked away with those Chinese chopsticks of knitting-
needles | Locke HB 15 bringing him into this silly fool
of a world | Meredith RF 148 Hang that confounded
old ass of Benson! | Wells Fm 82 Well? said Vacor in
the ghost of a voice | Bennett RS 214 Something has
to be done about that thief of an Elsie | Galsw D 93
this old wild tangle of a park | Locke GP 187 You're
the most exasperating proud cat of a woman I know |
Maugham PV 191 He gave the ghost of a chuckle.

There are many examples with the possessive pronoun: Swift J 367 her brute of brother would not
advance it [the money] | Spectator 530 § 4 Had not
my dog of a steward run away | Sheridan 320 my cox-
comb of a brother | Thack V 180 her old sharper of
a father | Collins W 158 make my idle beasts of servant
give you a good lunch! | Locke HB 10 it was my
scoundrel of a father | Galsw Car 1 My fool of a doctor
told me to make my will.

This figure of speech is particularly frequent with
swear-words: Swift J 518 she is the devil of a teaser |
Di M 350 leading a devil of a life [= a devilish life] |
Thack H 9 I walked down the village at a deuce of a
pace | id V 333 Posting will cost a dooce of a lot of
money | Huxley L 1.215 we have the devil of a lot to
do in the way of smiting the Amalekites | Benson D
11 he's got the devil of a temper | Hope C 18 he's had

the deuce of a facer | Galsw FM 123 It'll make the devil of a scandal | Hutchinson Clean Heart 94 This is the most devil of a predicament that ever a man was in | Kennedy CN 24 you've been the hell of a time fetching it | Maugham PV 15 you seem in a devil of a hurry to get rid of me | Bennett Pl 184 it took me a dickens of a time | Shaw 2.11 I promise you a fight — a devil of a fight | Maugham PL 3.79 Oh, she's been making me a hell of a scene | Merriman S 67 these poor devils of peasants of yours ‖ Note the Amr spelling in Quentin P 37 A few words ... made me feel a helluva fellow | Dreiser F 171 You think you're a helluva fellow, dontcha?

I place here the following constructions, which bear a certain resemblance to the preceding ones: *a passion of crying* = a passionate [fit of] crying, just as *the devil of a temper* = a devilish temper: Defoe M 31 I burst out into such a passion of crying that ... | Thack V 4 she was in such a passion of tears | Rose Macaulay P 114 She broke suddenly into the most terrible passion of tears | Kingsley H 168 she burst into an agony of weeping | London W 80 he was in a panic of terror | Kaye Smith GA 251 Mabel burst into a storm of crying | Wells TM 57 In another moment I was in a passion of fear | ib 90 I was in an agony of discomfort.

Chapter X

Comparison

10.1$_1$. The morphology of comparison in English was not treated in vol VI (see vol VI 14.1, 19.9), apart from that of compound adjectives in *-ed* (vol VI

24.1$_8$), partly for reasons of space, partly because morphology and syntax (the question of comparison by means of the endings -*er* and -*est* or by means of *more* and *most*) are closely interwoven.

In the following chapters on comparison I shall first discuss some phonological features of the endings in question, next regular comparison, then irregular comparison, and finally various syntactical and semantic questions.

10.1₂. The ending -*er* [-ə] is used to denote the comparative and -*est* [-ist] to denote the superlative.

These are direct continuations of the ordinary Gothonic suffixes, in OE -*ra*, corresponding both to Goth. -*iza* and Goth. -*ōza*, and -*ost* and -*est*, corresponding to Goth. -*ōst*- and -*ist*-. The forms corresponding to Goth. -*i*- have *i*-mutation, still preserved in a few cases (see below, 11.1$_3$ ff.) but even in OE the two endings are no longer clearly differentiated.

10.1₃. We should expect the *e* in -*est* to be lost in the superlative (as it is in the 2nd sing. of the vb), and as a matter of fact forms with dropped *e* are frequent in ElE, e.g. Gascoigne Steele Glasse (Arber) 78 guilefulst | Marlowe F 1283 the beautifulst | id T 1210 loveliest (two syllables) | ib 1789 cruelst | Sh H4B I. 1.151 ragged'st | Mcb II. 1.24 kind'st | ib II. 2.4 stern'st | Cymb V. 5.349 sweet'st | R2 III. 3.201 strong'st (but *longest* always two syllables) | Cor IV. 6.68 yong'st (but elsewhere two syllables). See also some examples in Franz[3] p. 205. — According to König, *Der Vers in Shaksperes Iramen*, p. 18, syncope does not occur at all in Sh's earliest plays, but is most frequent in his latest. Further: Habington C 115 the spreadingst Laurell | ib 132 the slenderst atome | Drayton (Ormond Poets) 47 powerful'st | Earle M 81 nakedst | ib 56 the modern'st man | Otway 24 the dismalst story | ib 259 wretchedst. — A few more examples below, 10.2_8, 10.3_3, 10.3_4, 10.3_7.

But all these examples are exceptions used for rhythmical reasons.

Haplology occurs in Malory *perylloust* for *peryllousest* (Baldwin, *Inflections and Syntax of the Morte Darthur.* Boston 1894. Sect. 36), and Sh Tim V. 1.185 *The reuerends throat* for *reuerendest*.

Milton seems to have always *-est* (*sweetest*, *loudest*, etc) with *e* pronounced, except for *midst* = 'midmost', e.g. PL 2.508, 5.165.

10.1₄. The common pronunciation of *-est* is [-ist], thus written by most phoneticians (Sweet, Jones, Palmer, etc), still I find Fuhrken 37 hæpiəst and Edwards 29 haiəst, 41 rʌfəst, 44 faˑstəst, laudəst, 51 fʌniəst, 52 bigəst, etc.

10.1₅. Changes of the final sound(s) in the comparison are found in the following cases:

(1) Mute *r* regains its consonantal value:
dear [diə] — *dearer* [diərə] — *dearest* [diərist]
poor [puə] — *poorer* [puərə] — *poorest* [puərist].

(2) Syllabic [l] becomes non-syllabic:
simple [simpl̩] — *simpler* [simplə] — *simplest* [simplist]
gentle [dʒentl̩] — *gentler* [dʒentlə] — *gentlest* [dʒentlist].

But [britl̩-ə, britl̩-ist] retains its syllabic [l̩].

Similarly, *i* may become non-syllabic, as in the frequent pronounciations *happier* [hæpjə], *wealthier* [welþjə]; *happiest* [hæpjist], *wealthiest* [welþjist], even occasionally [-ist] instead of [-jist]. Poets use the syncopated forms freely for the sake of the metre.

(3) The sound of [g] appears after [ŋ], written *ng*:

long [lɔŋ] — *longer* [lɔŋgə] — *longest* [lɔŋgist] —thus in *long*, *strong*, and *young*, the only adjectives of that form, whose degrees of comparison are in common use today.

Shaw's writing: 2.88 *young-er* indicates a vulgar pronunciation [jʌŋə].

There seems to be some uncertainty with regard to the pronunciation of the form *wronger* (Walpole C 90 [you were] Never wronger in your life). The form is very rare; comparison with *more* and *most* is preferred (e.g. Wilde SM 156 Such a view would be still more wrong now).

In occasional new-formations from participial adjectives like *cunninger*, *cunningest* (see below 10.3₃) [ŋ] only is sounded.

10.1₆. The OE alternation between voiceless fricative in final and voiced fricative in medial position also occurs in the comparison, thus

leof [f] — *leofra* [v] — *leofost* [v]
lāþ [þ] — *lāþra* [ð] — *lāþost* [ð]
wīs [s] — *wīsra* [z] — *wīsost* [z].

But in most cases a levelling took place at an early stage, so that e.g. *smooth*, *wise* get [ð, z] in the positive, and others get the voiceless sound in all positions, e.g. *deaf*, *loath*.

Traces of this alternation may now be seen in one word only, viz. *lief* (OE *leof*), archaic in British English, but common in Irish English (Joyce Ir 286, Synge) and Amr. (e.g. Day, Life with Father 45 he would as lief go around in a wheelbarrow | Hammett Th 78 I'd just as lief ask you).

Ch has in the positive sing. *leef*, pl. *leve*, comp. generally *lever*, but LGW A 75 *leefer*.

Spencer has *f* in all forms.

Sh has H6B I. 1.28 alderliefest | ib III. 1.164 liefest.

Tennyson has 333 *liefer*, but elsewhere *liever*.

The positive occurs especially in the phrase *had as lief* or *lieve*, in early editions of Sh both *-f* and *-ve*. *As lieve* in Sheridan and Dickens.

Other examples:

Swift T 127 I had as lieve he may ... | Defoe Rox 230 I had as lieu he had been dead | GE SM 115 I'd as lieve you married | ib 247 | Lang Lett. on Lit. 50 we would lief see | Wells Mr Polly 146 I'd liefer 'ave a lump-about like that other girl | Ridge Mord Em'ly 165 just as lief.

Some examples are quoted vol IV 9.4(2).

Orthographical Changes

10.1$_7$. (1) Mute *e* is dropped: *safer — safest; freer — freest; politer — politest*.

(2) *Y* after a consonant is changed into *i: happier — happiest* (but preserved after a vowel: *gayer — gayest*).

In monosyllables *y* may be preserved: *drier driest* commoner than *dryer dryest*, thus also *slier sliest* : *slyer slyest*. In comparatively rare words like *shy* (*shyer* Mitford, Meredith, Walpole, Ward; *shier* Stephen) and *spry* (*spryer* Galsw, *spryest* Bennett) the *y*-forms seem to be preferred. Hesitation between *i* and *y* is avoided through the periphrasis in Bennett W 2.108 most wry | Mackenzie S 1.252 & 1.384 more shy (Dan. Jones has *wryer wryest* alongside of *wrier wriest*).

(3) Gemination after a short stressed vowel (written single): *bigger biggest, thinner thinnest* (but *cleverer* and *deafer*).

But *l* is doubled even after an unstressed vowel: *painfuller*; see below, 10.2$_8$.

10.2₁. The two degrees of comparison, the comparative and the superlative, are expressed partly by means of the endings -*er* and -*est*, partly by periphrasis with *more* and *most*.

In the following classification I have not thought it necessary to indicate the exact source of each form found in my very full collection, but have only indicated vaguely the period in which each form is found, by means of the following abbreviations:

ElE = Elizabethan English.
Mn = Modern English writers up to about 1850.
P = Present English writers from about 1850.
J = forms registered in Daniel Jones, *An English Pronouncing Dictionary*. 4th ed. London 1937. These may be considered normal in PE.
* = forms not registered by Daniel Jones.
r = rare.
fq = frequent.

The use of -*er* and -*est* in ModE is subject to certain restrictions, which, however, are not quite fixed. Euphony and the want of shortness and clarity are often decisive for the choice of the endings or the periphrasis, but a good deal is left to the taste of the individual speaker or writer. The rules given in ordinary grammars are often too dogmatic.

Monosyllables

10.2₂. Monosyllabic adjs generally take -*er*, -*est*.

Though *higher* and *highest* are extremely frequent, *the Most High* is generally preferred as a name for God. Carlyle in this sense also writes *the Highest*.

Some monosyllabic adjs, however, rarely take the endings, thus *own*, which because of its meaning is rarely compared at all. Still Tennyson 298 my ownest own (also Kipling, Sayers).

strange: the superlative *strangest* is common enough, but *-er* is not frequent in the comparative because of *stranger* sb, thus *more* is used in Sh Mcb III. 4.82 more strange Than such a murther is | Ruskin P 2.315 something more strange | id S 18 Galsw M 261 a room, lighter, warmer, more strange than any.

Examples of *-er:* Di Do 352 nothing can make us stranger to each other than we are henceforth | ib 403 we are stranger to each other than we were | Holmes A 48 Stranger things have happened | Meredith E 587 Surely there is nothing stranger in mortal experience | Hope R 103 if the King's delay seemed strange at six, it was stranger at seven, and by eight most strange. — Further examples of *stranger* in Byron, Carlyle, Raleigh, Saintsbury, and others.

full: periphrasis seems commoner than comparison with *-er, -est* especially in a figurative sense and when *full* is followed by a prepositional phrase, e.g. Scott Iv 23 in a more full detail | Wells H 399 full of such notions; much more full even our refreshment girls | Jerome Novel Notes (T) 108 a world that was much bigger than this world — more full of joy and of grief.

free : the comparative with *more* is frequent when the word is used predicatively, more especially when followed by some complement, e.g. Sh As II. 1.4 Are not these woods More free from perill then the enuious court? [but freer 5 times in Sh] | Richardson G 19 she was a good deal more free when ... than when ... | By DJ 5.109 more free from specks | Di D 332 still fresher, and more free | Butler W 200 having got his head more free.

just: juster, justest J, as against NED, but not very common.

like with periphrastic forms occurs in Kingsley H 40 I've found out what he is most like | GE Mill 1.69 she used to be more like me. *Liker* is rare: Keats 2.157 Most like the struggle at the gate of death; Or liker still to one who ... [N.B. in verse] | Ru P 3.115 paint flowers which were a great deal liker the flowers themselves than my own studies | Tennyson 214 in long years liker must they grow [Masefield M 15 John looked liker an author than his friend [by one Englishman labelled 'not English', by another 'affectation'] | Wells JP 150 to make his pictures ... liker every time. Boswell corrects *much liker* as a Scotticism into *much more like* (see I.xxxiii). Both *liker* and *more like* in Browning 1.520 Why can't a painter ... Make his flesh liker and his soul more like. — *Likest* is found in Sh LLL IV. 2.78 likest to a hoggshead; also P.

right if compared at all would take *more* and *most*; *-er* and *-est* are not recognized by NED and J; still *rightest* is found in More A 144, Bunyan G 32.

drunk is felt as a participle and hence will rarely take the endings. Still I have found *drunker* in five recent authors, *drunkest* in one.

Monosyllables in *-d* and *-t* regularly take *-er*, *-est*, e.g. bold, glad, kind, loud, mad, rude, sad, wide, wild, etc; fit (Spencer: survival of the fittest), flat, soft, tight, etc.

But a few words belonging here rarely take the endings: dead: deader, -est Mn P * | chaste: chaster Mn, chastest ElE, both * | staid: staider ElE (Sh), P *. For *just* and *right* see above.

Words in *-r* (*-re*) generally take *-(e)r*, *-(e)st*, e.g. *clear*, *dear*, *pure*, etc.

There is, however, a marked tendency to avoid *-rer*,

thus I have quotations of *more* with *bare* P, *clear* Mn P, *dear* Mn, *pure* (AV), *rare* P, *sure* ElE (Sh), Mn.

Forms in -(*e*)*st* are very frequent with all these.

Adjectives denoting nationality or language, such as French, Welsh, Scotch, etc, would rarely be compared, but if so, practically only by means of *more* and *most* (Note Maxwell F 215 all in the very Frenchest style).

More than One Syllable

10.2₃. Adjectives of more than one syllable with end-stress generally take -*er* and -*est*. Exceptions are some that are only used as predicatives (*afraid, alive, alone, aware*), and some characteristic foreign words, such as *antique, bizarre, burlesque* (Fowler MEU 145).

10.2₄. Words in -*ct:* correcter r *, correctest Mn P, J | directer Mn *, directest M P J | distincter Mn P *, distinctest Mn P J | exacter J, exactest Mn P J | selectest Mn *.

The following disyllables with end-stress all may take -(*e*)*r*, -(*e*)*st* according to Daniel Jones: *austere, devout, divine, intense* (*most intense* P), *obscure, profane, profound, profuse, severe*, and *sublime*.

But others require special mention: abstruser Mn * | absurdest J | completest Mn P J | discreetest Mn J | expertest J | extremer P *, extremest P J | forlorner, -est P * | genteelest Mn * | humaner (from *humane*) P J (generally avoided in writing, because it cannot be distinguished from the comp. of *human*, e.g. McCarthy: the healthier and more humane spirit) | maturer Mn * | minuter Mn *, minutest Mn J | remoter, -est Mn P * | robuster, -est P * | serener Mn *, serenest Mn J.

10.2₅. Among adjs in -*ly* those in two syllables regularly take -*er*, -*est*, thus *costly, deadly* (but Quincey predicatively: none is more deadly), *early, holy, kindly,* *likely, lively, lonely, lovely, manly* (Meredith: nothing manlier nothing more gentlemanly), *surly, ugly*, all J.

Other examples of words in *-ly*, all *: beggarliest Mn, cowardliest Mn, friendliest P, heavenlier P.

Other disyllabic words in *-y* also normally take *-er*, *-est*, thus: angry, bloody, clumsy, easy, gloomy, guilty, happy, hasty, haughty, healthy, heavy, hungry, loftly, lucky (unluckiest, Carlyle), mighty, murky, petty, ready, ruddy, shabby, sultry, thrifty, wealthy, worthy, all J.

Some rarer forms from words in *-y:* fierier Mn, ordinariest Mn, praiseworthiest P, skyiest P, and veriest Mn, all *.

10.2₆. Words in *-er* may be compared in both ways; comp. with ending rarer than the superlative: bitterer, -est Mn P J (but Wilde, etc, more bitter) | cleverer P J, cleverest Mn P J (periphrasis r: Trollope; more clever) | properer ElE (Sh), Mn P * (Sh: more proper), properest Mn P * (Spectator: most proper) | slenderer J (Di: more slender), slenderest Mn P J | somberer P *, sombrest J | tenderer, -est Mn P J.

Eager apparently only takes *more, most* (Seeley, Wells: *more eager*).

A nonce-form characteristic of Sh occurs LLL IV. 2.16 (spoken by Holofernes:) untrained, or, rather, unlettered, or, ratherest, unconfirmed fashion.

Words in *-ar: vulgarer, vulgarest* J are probably the only ordinary forms, though GE has *partic'larest* (vg) and Browne RM *singularest*.

Words in *-ow* normally take *er, -est*, thus *hollow, mellow, narrow, shallow* J. Walton has *yellowest*, Cronin *yellower*.

10.2₇. Disyllables in *-le* take endings, e.g. the following all found in J: able, ample, feeble, gentle, humble, noble, simple (Scott: most simple), and subtle (Kipling: more subtle).

Note *idlest* Mn * (*idler* avoided because of *idler* sb).

Words in -*l:* civiller ElE Mn P *, civillest Mn * | crueller J, cruellest Mn P J (Trollope: most cruel).

For *evilest, littler, littlest* see below, 10.5$_1$.

Words in -*al*, all *: comicallest P | dismal(l)est Mn P | fatallest Mn | loyalest Mn P | realest P (Butler, etc: more real) | royaller (Chaucer), royalest Mn | substantialler P, substantiallest ElE.

10.2$_8$. Words in -*ful*. Note that there are very few examples from recent literature. Jones has *joyfullest, wilfullest*, the rest are *: awfuller Mn, awfullest P | beautifullest ElE Mn, fairly fq (see Storm EPh 684 *gracefullest* erlaubt, aber *beautifullest* vulgär) | cheerfuller, -est Mn | delightfullest Mn P | dreadfuller P | faithfullest Mn | fancifullest Mn | fearefuller Mn, fearfullest Mn P, not r | gracefullest P | gratefuller Mn | guilefulst ElE | hatefullest Mn | heedefull'st ElE (Sh) | unhopefullest (ib) | joyfullest P J | mournful(le)st ElE P | needfullest Mn | peacefullest P | pitifullest Mn | playfullest Mn | powerful'st, -fullest Mn P | respectfuller Mn | shamefuller Mn | skilfullest Mn] sorrowfullest Mn | spitefullest Mn | usefullest Mn | wakefullest Mn | wilfuller P, wilfullest J | woefullest Mn (Ch: wofullere) | wonderfullest Mn.

10.2$_9$. Words in -*able*, -*ible*, all *: admirablest ElE | advisablest Mn | comfortablest Mn P | considerablest Mn | damnablest Mn | fashionablest Mn | honerablest (More U) | horriblest Mn | indispensablest Mn | ineffablest Mn | lamentablest Mn | lovablest Mn | miserablest Mn P | notablest Mn | peaceablest Mn | profitablest Mn | respectablest Mn | seasonablest Mn | sociabler P (N.B. the only comparative in the list), sociablest P.

Eight of the above words are found in Carlyle, six in Ruskin.

10.3₁. Words in *-some:* handsomer, -est fq J (Thack: most handsome) | loathsomest Mn * | lonesomer, -est P * | toothsomest Mn * | troublesomest Mn P * | wholesomer Mn *, (not r), wholesomest Mn P J, not r.

Note also: welcomer (ME Sirith: welcomore) Mn P *, welcomest Mn *.

10.3₂. Words in *-n* (*-en*, *-on*, *-rn*): barrenest P J (-er *) | commoner, -est J, very fq (but Lord Brougham, Doyle: most common) | drunknest P r * | goldenest Mn r * | modernest Mn P * (Byron: more modern) | opener, -est J fq (Stevenson, Doyle: more open) | rottener P *, rottenest Mn J | solemnest (Mi) * | wantoner Mn *, wantonest ElE P *.

10.3₃. In spite of Sweet NEG section 1309: "those in *-ed* and *-ing* ... are not inflected because they have the form of verbals, although some of them, such as *wretched* and *cunning* are of different origin" [*cunning* actually the pres. pple of *cunnan*. O.J.] forms of such adjs are not at all rare, though perhaps not recognized by everybody.

I have found the following words derived from *-ing*, all *: bafflingest P | bitingest Mn | blindingest Mn | charminger (vg) P | charmingest Mn P, cunninger, -est Mn P, not r | daringest P (Sh: daring'st) | darlingest P | drivinger P | "knowingest" (GE) | lovingest Mn | lyingest ElE | piercingest Mn | pleasinger Mn | provokingest Mn | railingest ElE | ramblingest Mn | rippingest P | soothingest P | stunningest P | swingingest Mn | willinger (three early quotations) | willing'st (Sh), unwillingest (Mi).

It is worth noticing that all the forms in *-inger*, *-ingest* ascribed to Sh occur in plays or parts of plays that Sh probably did not write (H8, Shr Ind, H6B); cf from the undoubtedly genuine Shakespearean plays *most lying* (Tp), *more daring* (H4A), *most daring* (Merch), *more willing* (Tim), *most willing* (Cymb).

10.3₄. Words in *-ed*. The word most apt to take a termination is *damned* with its synonyms and antonyms: damneder P r, damnedest ElE, Mn P, especially in the modern expression *do (make) one's damnedest* | darnedest (Amr darndest) P | confoundedest (Amr) P (Fielding: -dedst) | cursedest (corsedest, cursed'st, curstest) ME ElE Mn | doggonedest (Amr) P | goddamdest (Amr) P | blesseder (Di, vg), blessedest Mn, not r | sacredest P.
All these *.

Other pples in *-ed:* belovedest P | devotedest (Di, vg) | learneder, -est (many examples in NED from 1562 to 1870 Emerson. 'Now archaic') | paddeder P | tireder P.
These, too, *.

Adjectives in *-ed:* crookeder, -est Mn P J | doggeder P * r | naked(e)st Mn P * | raggedest Mn P J, fairly fq | ruggedest Mn * | wickeder Mn P * fq, wickedest Mn P J fq | wretcheder P * | wretchedest Mn P * fq.

Adjectives in *-id:* fervider Mn * | horrider J, horridest P J fq | insipidest (Di, vg) | placider Mn *, placidest Mn P * | solider Mn *, solidest Mn J | sordidest P * | splendider Mn *, splendidest P * | squalidest P J | stupider *, fairly fq, stupidest J fq | validest Mn r * | vivider P *, vividest P J.

Words in [-əd]: awkwardest Mn J | backwarder Mn *, backwardest Mn * | forwarder Mn J, forrader (from vg *for'ard* 'forward', fq in coll. style) P *, forwardest Mn J | straight-forwardest Mn (Meredith) *.

Words ending in [-t] after a vowel (even after several weak syllables): accuratest Mn * | delicatest ElE Mn P *, fq | exquisitest (Mi) r * | fortunat'st (BJo) r * | infinitest P r * | quieter, -est J fq | secreter Mn *, secretest ElE P *.

Sibilants, etc

10.3₅. With words ending in sibilants periphrasis is the rule. Sweet says "so as to avoid the repetition of the hiss-consonant in the superlative;" as a matter of fact, however, the use of ending is more frequent in the superlative than in the comparative.

Words in *-ous;* beauteousest Mn | curiouser, Lewis Carroll: curiouser and curiouser, and hence fq in other recent writers, cf Fowler MEU 146 a product of Wonderland | deliciousest P | famousest (Mi) | generousest Mn | mischievouser (GE, vg) | nervouser P | sagaciousest Mn | strenuousest Mn | treacherou'st (BJo) | virtuousest Mn. All *, and, except curiouser, r.

Words in *-ish*, all *: churlisher Mn | devilishest Mn | foolisher Mn P, not r, foolishest comparatively fq.

10.3₆. Words in *-st*. The reason given by Sweet for avoiding *-est* in the superlative is recognized e.g. by Daniel Jones, in spite of superlatives of monosyllables like *fastest, justest, moistest, vastest:* earnester Mn, earnestest P | honester, -est fq. dishonester P | manifester Mn | modester Mn, modestest Mn fq.

Words in *-ive* rarely take the endings: activest Mn * | inventiuest (Ascham) *.

In words in *-ic* end-comparison is avoided because of difficulties of spelling (see my only example: *tragic-est* Dobson).

10.3₇. Words in *-nt* (*-ant, -ent):* auncienter Mn * (More: aun-), ancientest Mn P J fq (More: aun-) | arrantest (BJo: -nt'st) Mn * | brilliantest Mn * r | constantest (Mi) * r | decenter Mn *, decentest P * | diligentest(e) ElE Mn * | gallanter Mn, gallant'st (BJo), both * | imprudentest Mn * | impudentest Mn (BJo: -nt'st) * | patienter P * r, patientest Mn * r | pleasanter, -est J, very fq, unpleasantest Sh Mn * | prudenter, -est Mn r * | silenter, -est P * r | sufficienter Mn * r | valianter Mn * r.

Outside the above groups: difficultest Mn * r | perfecter ElE * r, perfectest ElE (Sh, etc.) Mn P *, not r | solemnest Mn P * | uncouther Mn * r.

If a word ends in several weak syllables, comparison with *-er*, *-est* is generally avoided, thus with words like *complimentary, elementary, contemptuous, natural, tyrannical*. See, however, several examples above.

A form like *ordinariest* (Wells) is exceptional.

10.3₈. Endings — especially in the superlative and in longer words — are generally felt as more vigorous, more emphatic than *more* and *most*, cf above *damnedest* and synonyms. (Deviations from the rule are apt to be more emphatic). A characteristic example is Twain M 227 the confoundedest, brazenest, ingeniousest piece of fraud.

As vulgar speech makes a more extended use of the endings than standard language (see Storm EPh 778), words with end-comparison may often also get a vulgar stamp, as in Di Do 42 the peaceablest, patientest, best temperedest [N.B. double superlative] soul.

Adverbs

10.4₁. In the cases where adverbs are not formally distinct from adjs, i.e. are either identical in form with adjs, or have no corresponding adj form, they follow the same rules with regard to the use of *-er* and *-est* as adjs: closer | deeper in thought (Di), sleep deepest (Carlyle) | earlier, -est | work harder, -est | higher (Di: As the lark rose higher, he sank deeper in thought) | livelier P | longer, -est | oftener, oftenest (Cf Carlyle: the oftenest laughter) | seldomer, -est Mn * | sooner, -est | wider awake (Stevenson VP 132).

With adverbs formed from adjectives by adding *-ly* periphrasis with *more* or *most* is the rule: more freely, most easily.

But other ways of comparison occur.

In some cases, esp. in colloquial speech the adjective form with *-er*, *-est* is used, especially in set phrases:

easier said than done (but: that is easily said | he can do it more easily than I can) | they could easier do without his service than they can tolerate his fractious spirits (Stevenson); *easier* occurs three (or five?) times in Sh, who has no examples of *more easily* | cheaper, gentler (Sh).

10.4₂. Adverbs in *-ly* with *-er* or *-est* added are by no means rare, as will be seen from the following chronological list: witerluker 'more plainly' (Juliana) | gladlyest (Mandv), also in Malory, see Baldwin § 40 | craftelyer (Caxton) | gladliest (Ascham) | spedelier, wyselyere, gladlier (More, but ib more holily, certes more wisely) | deadlier (Peele) | easiliest, freelier, proudlier, quicklier, wiselier (Sh) | eagerliest, the fineliest, the heartilier, (the) safelier, softlier, trulier (BJo) | calmeliest, quicklier, trulyer (Earle) | firmlier, gladlier, likeliest (Mi) | kindliest, stranglyest (Osborne) | closelier (Wordsw) | finelier, harshlier, kindlier, proudlier (Lamb) | freshlier (Byron) | ablier, darklier, deeplier, faintlier, gladlier, lightlier, looselier, plainlier, safelier, strictlier, vainlier (Tennyson) | sparelier (Browning) | directlier, lightlier, surelier (Mrs Browning) | closelier (Rossetti) | proudliest (Carlyle) | hotlier (Arnold) | clearlier, surelier, trulier (Lowell) | neatliest (George Eliot) | princelier (Meredith) | chiefliest, slowlier, surelier (Swinburne) | clearliest (Watson) | clearlier, deeplier, rarelier, thickliest, widelier (Stevenson) | darklier (Shaw; but ib. more quickly) | closelier, quicklier (we learn quicklier and mature more rapidly), slowlier, wiselier (and more tenderly; Wells) | divinelier (Quiller Couch) | gentlier Bennett) | loudlier, safeliest, wiselier (Hewlett).

In a very few cases *-ly* is added to a comparative: *formerly, latterly, utterly,* and from a modern point of view this seems quite natural or even necessary, as *former* has no positive form, *latter* is very loosely connected with *late*, and *utter*, at any rate, is not felt as related to *out*; — I generally term such forms ex-comparatives.

10.4₃. The OE comparative corresponding to the adj *long* was *leng*. In later ME and Early ModE this came to be considered as a positive, hence the analogical form *lenger* arose (frequent in Malory, Caxton, also found in More U and Spenser FQ).

Group-Comparatives, etc

10.4₄. Sometimes a comparative or superlative ending added to the latter of two adjs is also meant to modify the former. Thus we get a kind of group-comparative or superlative (cf group-genitive and group-plural vol VI 17.1ff. and ib 17.8, respectively):

Sh Meas IV. 6.13 the generous and grauest citizens | Lr I. 4.285 choice and rarest | Tro IV. 4.7 a weak and colder palate | BJo A II. 1 the pure and gravest of divines.

Several cases may be doubtful, thus some of those from Sh quoted in Sh-Lex and some quoted in Abbott § 398 from other Eliz. poets; further Sh Wint III. 2.178 What old, or newer torture must I receiue?

Modern examples: in the free and easiest manner possible (quoted in Flügel s.v. *easy; free-and-easy* is felt as one unity). Here perhaps belongs also Tennyson 98 Then her cheek was pale and thinner than should be for one so old.

Finally, the ending may be added to the first adjective(s) only, but is obviously meant to modify the following adjs as well:

Marlowe J 1196 I haue the rarest, grauest, secret, subtil, bottle-nos'd knaue to my master, that euer Gentleman had | Wells H 284 one has felt that they were ever so much stronger and cruel and hard than one is — a slipshod construction as if the writer had begun: much more strong.

On *deep and deeper, near and nearer,* etc, see below, 11.5$_4$.

10.4$_5$. It is not always easy to see why writers prefer one or the other method of comparing adjs. In poetry rhythm or rime is often decisive, or even the mere desire for variety, as in:

Wordsw 172 meek infant! Among all forlornest things The most forlorn | Rossetti 149 He framed a sweeter song, More sweet than ever a poet's heart Gave yet to the English tongue | Dobson P 110 Mine is a soul whose deeper feelings lie More deep than words.

What is the difference intended in the following sentence? Tarkington MA 175 I tell you, I never have been more calm or calmer in my life!

10.4$_6$. When several adjs in close juxtaposition are to be compared, different methods may be employed. The most regular method is that of treating each adj on its own merit: this may lead to alternations like the following:

Mandv 221 more noble and more excellent and ricchere and more merveyllous | Sh H4A V. 1.89 a brauer gentleman, More active, valiant, or more valiant yong, More daring, or more bold | Defoe G 70 the strongest and most durable ... the most early and timely hints | Macaulay E 4.7 softer and more pensive | Di D 80 he was the sternest and most severe of masters | ib 365 the pleasantest and most fascinating little ways | Thack V 35 the handsomest, the bravest, the most active, the cleverest, the most generous of created boys | GE SM 128 the sadder and more serious elements of life | Ru S 1.171 the commonest, closest, most familiar thing | id T 28 foolishest and most monstrous of conceivable human words | Hawthorne T 46 people always grow more and more foolish, unless they take care to grow wiser and wiser | ib 121 Never was there a prettier or more fruitful valley | Trollope B 167 in the most placid and gentlest of humours | Hay B 293 she was sweeter and more tender than he had ever seen her before | Swinburne L 122 more liberal, fresher, clearer altogether | Stevenson MP 14 something at once rougher and more tender | Gissing R 226 nothing could be simpler, yet nothing more right and reasonable | Chesterton F 233 greyer, paler, and more insignificant.

Sometimes the alternation seems to be due simply to a desire for variety: Di X 25 the room became a little darker and more dirty (does *a little* belong to both?) | Kingsley H 268 a happier and more healthy slumber.

10.4₇. Not infrequently *more* and *most* are used for the sake of emphasis with all the parallel adjectives, even if some of them would have admitted endings. In some passages *more* is repeated: Wilde P 19 the poor are more charitable, more kind, more sensitive than we are | Kaye-Smith HA 242 It had made her more receptive, more warm, more eager | Trollope A 236 a world more glorious, more rich, more witty, more enterprising, than their own.

10.4₈. But more often one *more* or *most* does duty for two or more adjectives:

Spectator 133 a more low and servile condition | Goldsm 655 the more grave and sensible part of the sex | Gibbon M 50 the most idle and unprofitable [months] of my whole life | Lamb R 14 more dear and choice | Wordsw Lit 7 to render their feelings more sane, pure and permanent, in short, more consonant to nature | Kinglake E 126 my attempt to sleep was more new and strange than I had fancied it | ib 242 a race more brave and beautiful than Jacob's descendants | Ru P 2.315 the most smooth and soft sward | Froude C 2.394 Johnson himself was not more rude, disdainful, and imperious | Stevenson JHF 1 more often and loudly | Swinburne L 216 a face ten times more beautiful and lovable | Carpenter Ad 213 they make the most wild and unjustifiable statements | Gosse P 119 It would be impossible to conceive a more gentle, innocent, or delicate life than his was or a more happy one.

This is even found where the second adjective is *good* (thus: most ... good = best): Thack N [?] the most honest and good old gentleman.

And *most* is repeated also before *good* in Jerome Idle Thoughts (q Poutsma) the most beautiful, the most good, the most charming, the most divine, the most perfect human creature that ever trod this earth.

For other instances of periphrastic comparison of *good*, see below, 10.5$_1$.

10.4$_9$. The ending *-est* is occasionally added to sbs: Hardy Under the Greenwood Tree 122 [dial.] The parishioners about here ... be the laziest, gossipest, poachest, jailest set of any ever I come among | Shaw Devil's Disciple [Notes] 141 Here you have the man [General Burgoyne] at his Burgoynest | Henderson Shaw[1] 322 the joker Shaw at his Shawest | Rosamond Lehmann Dusty Answer 30 'Three great gawps, that's what we are, three great gawps.' He looked at Mariella's back. 'And Mariella's easily the gawpest' | NP: The most earnest student of the fourpenny-halfpennyest of magazines barely believes in him (q from Wendt Syntax).

On *chief* and *choice*, etc, as adjs with their common superlatives *chiefest* and *choicest*, etc, see vol II 13.71. On superlatives of sbs in other languages see PhilGr 80.

Regular instead of Irregular Comparison

10.5₁. Instead of the forms taken from a different stem we find occasionally regularly formed comparatives and superlatives. Many such forms are found in dialects, see EDG § 398.

From *ill* (= 'in bad health'): Mc Kenna SM 279 I did really feel iller than I can tell you | Arden Green Hat 168 [she's ill] Can't really, you see, be iller if she tried | Galsw Car 256 (vg:) gettin' iller and iller | Graves IC 117 When I was well again, or no iller than usual || Caine P 237 looking more ill and weak than ever | [naturally in a compound:] Hay B 14 she is more ill-bred than I suspected.

From *evil:* Sutton Vane Outw. Bound 97 the evilest thoughts of the human mind. — Cf *more evil* below, 11.3₈.

From *little:* Sh Hml III. 2.181 where loue is great, the littlest doubts are feare | Di D 678 [vg] she fell into the weakness of the littlest child | ib 808 [Mr Peggotty:] the littlest of these | Thack P 1.301 her own sex, who prefer littler women | Hardy T 497 he will not love me the littlest bit any more | Kipling J 2.127 the littlest streams | ib 173 each littlest leaf-rib | Wells Br 152 I'd just die for your littlest wish | Galsw MP 96 these littler things.

From *bad.* NED has *badder, baddest* from 14th to 18th c.; from the 19th c.: Wells PF 13 [child:] I didn't seem able now to go on being badder and badder | Egerton Castle K 16 [woman:] perhaps if you were badder and I were gooder we'd meet half-way.

From *good:* Ridge G 40 Baby's going to be the nicest, goodest, goodest boy ... He's going to be the bestest, bestest — oh, wicked little man || Kingsley H 313 Will God not forgive me, then? You have forgiven me. He? — He must be more good even than you | Galsw D 114 he looked more good than ever [*better* would be taken to mean 'in better health'].

From *well;* Pennell L 80 I am awfully 'bucked' you are feeling happier and weller.

10.5₂. From compounds, such comparatives and superlatives are formed as:

well-known   better-known   best-known
hard-working harder-working hardest-working.

On compound adjs in *-ed* see vol. VI. 24.1₈, and add: Thack P 445 Sir Hugh is the best-natured fellow in the world. Cf ib 475 one of the most good-natured of women | His most well-to-do parishioners (Sweet) | More far-reaching conclusions.

Comparatives from Prepositions, and Superlatives in *most*

10.5₃. As in other languages we have comparative adjs and advs formed from prepositions or prepositional advs: *inner, outer* and *utter, upper;* further *hinder* from *hind,* which only survives in compounds like *hindleg,* and in *behind* (Kipling J 2.24 he went upon his hind legs ... he walked upon his hinder legs). *Former* was formed from the old superlative *forma.* That these are not real comparatives is seen by the impossiblity of using *than* with them; nor can they be used predicatively. But real superlatives with the ending *-most* are formed from them.

10.5₄. The ending *-most,* is from OE *-mest,* orig. a compound suffix, Old Gothonic *-mo-* (OE *-ma* as in *forma* 'first', cf L *primus*) + *-isto-*, etym. identical with *-est.*

Already in OE the suffix was interpreted as identical with *mǣst* 'most', hence the frequent spelling *-mǣst,* later *-most,* cf below, 10.5₉. However, as the suffix was unstressed and the vowel hence frequently pronounced [ə] the spelling *-mest* may be found as late as the 16th c.

In OE the suffix was chiefly added to adverbial (or prepositional) stems, thus in the following surviving words; *fyrmest* > *foremost*, *innemest* > *inmost*, and *ȳtemest* > *utmost*. Exceptions are *midmest* > *midmost*, and *eastmest*, *westmest*, *norþmest*, and *suþmest* from the names of the points of the sky.

Benmost is Sc. for *inmost* (Burns 2.4 the benmost bore 'the inmost hole').

From OE times it has been a rule to add *-most* (*-mest*) only to words denoting position in place, time, or serial order; and in ME and especially ModE a number of superlatives in *-most* have been coined from such adjs, e.g. *backmost* (Hope Z 257 in the backmost rank), *deepmost*, *highmost* (Sh Sonn 7 high-most pich; now obs. or dial.), *leewardmost* (sea term), *lowmost*, *midmost* (Tennyson 355, 437, Bridges E 106 in midmost night), *nearmost* (dial. acc. to NED, but note Bennett PL 237 the nearmost gun, and an example in NED Suppl.), *rearmost*.

Falling outside this semantic group are a few noncewords: *happy-most* (q NED), *longmost* (Tarkington F 70 these flannels are yours, and though I may not fill them to the utmost, I do to the longmost), *secretmost* (NP 1910), and even *hiddenmost* (q NED).

10.5₅. From early ModE it has been possible to form superlatives in *-most* from substantives, mostly denoting position: *bottommost* (Kipling J 2.200), *centremost* (Hardy F 420 in the centremost parts of her heart), *devilmost* (Ingoldsby 75 bid him "do his devilmost"), *endmost* (Browning T 4.214 The endmost snow), *headmost*, *sternmost*, *tipmost* and *topmost* (Tennyson 439 to tipmost lance and topmost helm | Shaw A 201 from his topmost hair to his tipmost toe), *vanmost* (Carlyle), *weathermost* (nautical).

10.5₆. In ME a tendency developed to add *-most* to comparatives in *-r*, or change the root in existing words to comparative form. This development is probably due to several factors.

The word in which *r* first appears seems to be *eftermest* (NED 1160), levelled after the preposition *efter*. Of importance in the later adjustment or coinage of other words are probably the existence of comparatives in *-er* corresponding to the superlatives in *most*, and combinations of comparatives and *more*, like *farthermore, furthermore, innermore, outermore*, etc (prob. developed under the influence of Scand.; see NED *-more*).

Thus we get semantically identical pairs like the following: *aftmost* (sea term) : *aftermost, farmost* (obs.) : *farthermost* (Ridge G 201, Parker R 339, London M 110) and *furthermost, hindmost* : *hindermost* (both of which may be used in the common phrase: the devil take the hind(er)most) (Galsw MW 308 hindmost, R.Bennett P 10 hindermost), *inmost* : *innermost* (Mrs Browning A 285 But innermost Of the inmost ... | Ruskin S 131 | Wells Br 397 Necessity is the uttermost thing, but God is the innermost thing), *lowmost* (see above) : *lowermost* (the lowermost hell, common), *outmost* : *outermost* (Swift 3.214 the innermost ... the outermost | Defoe R 159), *upmost* : *uppermost* (Swift 3.385), *utmost* : *uttermost*.

10.5₇. *Utter* is an old formation from *out* (with the vowel shortened as in *latter*); it has lost its local meaning and now denotes degree (utter darkness, an utter scoundrel). *Utmost* has kept more of its local meaning (the utmost edge, etc), but is also chiefly used of degree (with the utmost care), etc. *Out(er)most* is used in a local sense only.

In a few cases we have only forms derived from comparatives, thus *bettermost* (frequent, e.g. Lytton K 376, GE M 2.18, Meredith E 34, Hawthorne 1.410 in their faded bettermost, to go to church, Phillpotts M 154, Quiller Couch M 248, Hardy R 156), (note the exceptional *bestmost* mentioned in Farmer, *Americanisms*), and *nethermost* (Benson D 2.211 the nethermost pit | Bennett GS 196 the nethermost hell). Further from advs *hithermost* (e.g. Cooper Dict.) and *undermost* (Kingsley H 37, Stevenson B 113).

10.5₈. There are three types of words in -*most* added to names of the points of the sky, thus *eastmost* (now only poet.), *eastermost* (Defoe R 2.107 the Easter-most side of the island; obs.), and *easternmost* (now the only current form).

Similarly *westmost, westermost, westernmost, northmost* (Shaw Pur 171 the southernmost column ... the northmost of the two columns), *northermost, northernmost, southmost* (Mi PL 1.408), *southermost* (Defoe R 295), *southernmost*.

The words in -*most* are not always used to denote the highest degree; they may also denote only a very high degree, as in the following quotations: Washington Irving Sketch Book 37 He was a foremost man at all country frolics ... | Sweet, Trans. of Phil. Soc. 1877-79 405 Noreen, a foremost Swedish dialectologist | Quiller Couch M 132 a bettermost person | id T 218 a bettermost body. — Cf below, 13.3₃.

10.5₉. In accordance with the supposed identity of -*most* and the independent word *most*, the pronunciation [-moust] is common, but in accordance with its actual origin (OE -*mest*) and its want of stress, the suffix is also frequently pronounced [-məst]. For the limited number of words in *-most* in Daniel Jones's *Pron. Dic.* [-moust] is given as the primary or only form, and [-məst] as a secondary form. But Fowler MEU *-most* recommends [-məst] in the commoner words — *foremost, innermost, uppermost, topmost, inmost, upmost, hindermost.*

Chapter XI
Comparison (Continued)
Double Comparison

11.1₁. A double comparative or superlative may be formed in two ways:

(1) by adding *-er* or *-est* to a comparative or superlative; this is found in *worser* and *lesser*; see below, 11.3₂.

In dialects we have such forms as *betterer, betterest, bestest, leastest,* etc; see EDG § 398. Jocularly in Shaw Geneva 53 My ownest and bestest, you are the Dame of the Empire.

According to Sayce, *Introd.* 1.403 children will talk of *more-er* and *most-est*.

Note Fielding T 2.108 [vg] one had lieverer touch a toad.

(2) by placing *more* or *most* before a comparative or superlative. Examples (more or less colloquial or vg); first with *more;*

Ch M 3.196 more esyere | Malory 142 I am more weyker than ye | Mandv 29 that lond is meche more hottere than it is here | Lyly E 35 more fitter for Paris then Hector | ib 47 more easier | common in Sh, e.g. Mids III. 1.21 more better | LLL IV. 1.62 More fairer | Oth V. 2.110 She [the moon] comes more nearer earth than she was wont (see Sh-lex. 739) | Greene F 10.61 more finer stuff | AV 12.24 How much more are yee better then the foules | Fielding T 2.31 [Mrs. Honour:] more properer ... most handsomest | Di N 557 Nature, said Squeers, solemnly, is more easier conceived than described | GE Mm 190 this made him look all the more dimmer and faded | Caine M 51 more surer ... more aisier | Mackenzie S 1.74 [child:] every time you ask me not to hum, I'll hum more louder.

With *most:* Ch M 3.186 the moste grettest | Malory 144 moost weykest ... moost leuest | ib 148 most shamefullest | LondE 67 in the most best wyse | Lyly E 39 The Pestilence doth most rifest infect the clearest complection | AV Acts 26.5 after the most straitest sect of our religion | Fielding 4.477 [Mrs Slipslop:] the handsomest, most properest man I ever saw | Goldsm V. 1.105 the most lowest stuff in nature | Tennyson 617 But if ... in the rich vocabulary of Love 'Most dearest' be a true superlative — I think I likewise love your Edith best | Swinburne A 35 the most dimmest height of trembling heaven | Smedley F 2.37 [vg] he was one of the most virtuousest of men.

Examples from U.S. of various kinds of double comparatives and superlatives in Mencken AL⁴ 463.

In a different way *furthermore* (Ch: forther-more), e.g. More U 63, Sh three times.

Sh has once *less* + the comparative: R2 II. 1.49 less happier.

Parallel Increase

11.1₂. In OE the instrumental *þy* of the demonstrative pronoun was used to indicate a difference in connexion with a comparative. A remnant of this is ModE *the* used especially in two connected sentences to denote parallel increase: the more, the better. See vol V. 21.7₂ ff. and below, 14 6. Cf also Christophersen, *The Articles* p. 115 ff.

We have a corresponding use of *the* before a comparative in cases like: I like him all the better on account of his shyness | "He won't come." — "So much the better. The more fool he." | The young people were plainly the worse for drink.

Change of Vowel, etc

11.1₃. Change of vowel is sometimes found in the formation of the comparative and superlative. In OE and ME a certain number of adjectives had mutation in these forms (*lenger, strenger* still in Malory), but PE has only preserved this change in one instance: *old — elder — eldest*, beside the new formations *older* and *oldest*.

These levelled comparative and superlative forms date from ME, but the present distinction between the two sets of forms is of later origin. PE would have the form with *o* in Gascoigne 51 This Galant ... woed my sister, for she elder was | Sh Ro I. 5.40 his sonne is elder sir; His sonne is thirty | H5 V. 2.247 the elder I wax, the better I shall appeare | R3 III. 2.62 ere a fortnight make me elder (F, but Q older) | Dekker F 1366 Ere he be two howres elder | Massinger N II. 2.30 were you two years elder.

Down to the 19th c. *elder* and *eldest* appear in cases where *older* and *oldest* would now be employed in natural style: Nares Elem. of Orthoepy 324 I have not regarded the practice of poets elder than Spenser | Quincey Sel 1 My two eldest sisters — eldest of three then living, and also elder than myself | Hawthorne 1.296 as an elder customer than himself would have been likely to do.

11.1₄. The *e*-forms now have a limited range. They are primarily used about family relations; they do not refer to age or duration but to date of birth: A firstborn who died an infant was yet the eldest son. (Alford).

Thus *elder* forms a contrast not to *old* but to *younger:* Austen M 18 the younger brother must help to pay for the pleasures of the elder | Hope Z 27 if a man will be a younger son, why he must take what the elder leaves | Macaulay E 4.5 the younger clerks ... the elder enriched themselves | Thack P 1.142 the younger gentleman promising the elder not to leave Chatteries without a further conversation.

See also Fowler MEU with some nice distinctions, which do not seem to be generally carried through.

The *e*-forms are secondarily used to express seniority and priority of rank, chiefly referring to a fairly permanent and established relation, rarely to an accidental one: the elder partner of a firm | one of the elder captains | Carlyle SR 17 our Hofrath, being the elder, richer ... of the two.

Thus also about earlier authors, artists, scholars, etc: Pliny the Elder | Wordsw Lit 17 The invaluable works of our elder writers | Ruskin Sel 2.405 the elder artists = ib 1.274 the masters of elder times | Fox 1.195 the elder Mill | Dobson F 101 with the elder essayists.

11.1₅. *Elder* and *eldest* are chiefly used preceded by some determining word (genitive, possessive pronoun, or article). *Elder* thus (like *latter* and *near*) may be termed an ex-comparative. Cf the sb *elder* with the pl *elders*. The *o*-forms are used in cases of actual comparison, in fact now always when *than* follows or can easily be supplied, as in *he is old, but she is older still*.

11.1₆. Examples with both *e*- and *o*-forms: Austen M 12 William, the eldest [of her brothers], a year older than herself | Trollope D 1.35 The elder brother, who was considerably older than Frank | id O 162 He was older. Yes: it was a pity that he should be so much the elder | Ward R 1.277 the older man suddenly caught him by the arm. "Elsmere, let me — I am the elder by so many years — let me speak to you" | id E 386 You who are older, ought you not to feel towards her as a tender elder sister | Phillpotts M 11 while she listened to her older companion ... while the elder talked.

The difference between the old and the new forms is sometimes slight. Speaking of two friends, Sir Rider Haggard uses *older* and *elder* alternately of one and the same person: S 2 the older man ... the expression of the elder man. Neither *elder* nor *eldest* can be used predicatively except as a primary preceded by the definite article (he is older than me | he is the elder of the two).

Eldest is even rarer than *elder;* it is now archaic except of family relations: Austen M 3 Her eldest [child] was a boy of ten years old | Shaw Ms 3 There was twelve years between me and the next eldest || Masterman WL 76 my oldest male friend.

The application of *e*-forms to non-personal relations, as in the following examples, is decidedly archaic: Hawth S 112 in the streets of our elder towns | Carpenter C 13 According then to the elder conception, and perhaps according to an elder experience, man to be really healthy must be a unit.

According to Krüger § 216, Scotch commonly uses *elder* and *eldest*, e.g. the eldest houses (W. Scott). On the other hand, in popular American there appears to be a tendency to make *older* and *oldest* the universal forms; see Storm EPh 904 & 1036.

11.1₇. Shortening of vowels in closed syllables before

the comparative ending *-re* was a frequent phenomenon in ME (cf vol I 4.323). The change was often indicated orthographically by a double consonant: AR 290 luddure ('louder') | ib 328 deoppre ('deeper'). Cf Ferd. Brück, *Die consonantendoppelung in den me. comparativen und superlativen* (dissertation, Bonn 1886). A few of these forms were still to be met with in early ModE (Malory: gretter (grettest) | Caxton R 24 gretter | ib 84 derrer 'dearer'), but PE remnants of this phenomenon are very scarce. Incidentally, the comparative has influenced and modified the vowel of the positive degree as well: *great* and *hot*, but these cases do not concern us in this connexion (see vol I 4.323). A form with long vowel beside one with short in the short comparative of is still found in some dialects, but StE has only preserved one example:

11.1₈. *utter*, derived from *out* (< OE *ūt*). Neither *utter* nor the new form *outer* are pure comparatives, as seen by the impossibility of using *than* with them. *Outer* has now taken over the original sense of *utter*, while the latter word has acquired the sense 'complete, absolute, unqualified': an utter scoundrel | Furness (ed. of Sh's Merch. 277) the obscurity which envelops it is as utter and impenetrable as ever. — The last example clearly shows that *utter* may now be regarded as a pure positive form, and this is further corroborated by the fact that *utter* = 'absolute' has a special superlative form (cf *uttermost* above, 10.5₆): Mrs Browning A 319 the most utter wretch | McCarthy 2.29 the most utter delusion | Butler Er 209 in a spirit of the most utter reverence | Haggard S 93 a look of the most utter tenderness that I ever saw | Deeping 3R 104 You would make the most utter mess of it || Dine B 13 the utterest nonsense. — The old local meaning of *utter* survives, for instance, in Mi PL 6.716 the utter Deep.

Similarly the superlative *outermost* (*outmost* is rare) has a stronger suggestion of local sense than *ut(ter)most*, which is often used figuratively: *with the utmost care*. Note, however, that *uttermost* is not a superlative corresponding to *utter* in its usual PE sense; see above. Caxton uses *utterest* where we should now say *uttermost:* R 109 the vtterist of my myght. — Cf above, 10.5$_7$.

11.2$_1$. While the vowel of OE *læt* was lengthened in ME to *late*, the short vowel was retained in the comparative *latter* and the superlative *last*, which furthermore suffered contraction to a single syllable and consequent loss of the first *t* in *tst* (cf. *best* < OE *bet(e)st*). A new, regular comparative and superlative *later — latest* came into use in ME and Early ModE, but the old forms survive in special senses.

Latter is now used chiefly in contrast to *former;* cf Bradley S 18 If we compare the earlier tragedies with the *later*, we find that it is in the *latter* .. that this inward struggle is most emphasized. The same sense ('second') is also recognizable in a phrase like "the latter half of the year", but sometimes *latter* merely refers vaguely to the part towards the end, without there being any division into just two parts: Austen M 338 the little cottage in which he and Fanny were to pass all their middle and latter life | Gissing H 88 his daughter, who had the look of the latter twenties | the latter part of the book (century). The word means 'recent, present' in *these latter days* and *Latter-day Saints, the latter Platonists*, and 'final' in the one phrase *the latter end*, i.e. 'death'.

Later regularly means 'following after (in time)'. The present distinction between *latter* and *later* appears to be a fairly late development; it was not observed by

Bacon, who occasionally has *later* corresponding to *former* and also sometimes *latter* where we should now use *later* (see Bøgholm 67-8).

11.2₂. *Last* very often is not a true superlative; it has reference to a series of items arranged in a definite order (without special regard to time). It is the only form that may be used in a local sense: the last house on the right.

Latest indicates only a relative finality: it refers to 'the last (one) so far', i.e. the most recent, out of a series that may go on for a long time yet. This difference between the two forms is seen in: Macaulay E 3.58 they saw each other for the last time | ib 3.56 all the latest scandal of the court.

The two forms are often pitted against each other: NP 1912 The latest Irish Home Rule Bill is now in the last stage of its struggle in the House of Commons | NP 1913 I hope that Mr. Harrison's latest book is not going to be his last | Dobson (Poem in NP 1913) But who of men shall so forecast His latest as to call it last ? | NP 1917 Germany is the latest but not the last Carthage in the history of war | NP 1925 This is only the latest, not the last phase of the case.

The difference is not always obvious: Mi PL 5.18 my latest found, Heaven's last, best gift | By DJ 17.13 The guests dropped in — the last but one, Her Grace, The latest, Juan, with his virgin face | London M 68 their conversation turned on other themes — the last poetry he had read, the latest poet he had studied | NP 1908 [advertisement:] The works of Oscar Wilde ... reprinted from the latest editions issued under the superintendence of the Author, and in many cases they contain his last corrections. — In some of these quotations the use of both forms may be for the sake of stylistic variation.

Conversely, we have *last* where, according to the definition above, we should expect *latest* in: Maugham Alt 449 taking the last ones [i.e. papers] first [they] glance at the latest news from home. — Fijn van Draat *(Anglia* 24.51 ff.) thinks that several cases of *latest* for *last* may be explained as due to the requirements of rhythm.

Last often indicates a valuation, almost like *least:* great is the last adjective I should apply to him | this is the last and least consideration. — It naturally may come to mean 'conclusive, definitive', as in: the last word has not yet been said.

11.2₃. Besides the above-mentioned meaning of *last*, the word has a different sense, closely related to that of *latest*. In a series of everyday phrases *last* is used of the period, etc, immediately preceding the one in which we are now or of which we are now speaking: last Christmas, summer, Tuesday, week, year, time, etc | the last century | the last few years | as I said in my last [letter]. In this sense *last* often forms a contrast to *next*. Sometimes, however, the word is almost synonymous with *latest:* Galsw WM 151 she took up Nazing's last [i.e. latest book] | Have you heard Mr N's last [latest joke] | the last thing in hats. — In cases where the spheres of use of *latest* and *last* overlap, the former carries a stronger suggestion of lateness, while on the other hand it has not the same element of finality as *last;* it is opposed to all the earlier members of the series, while *last* is opposed to the *first*.

11.2₄. Historically, these irregularities may perhaps be regarded as remnants of earlier usage. In early ModE, where *latest* makes its first appearance (NED earliest

Sh, but see below Marlowe), the present distinction between *last* and *latest* appears to have been unknown: Sh H4B IV. 5.185 heare .. the very latest counsell That euer I shall breath [thus several times in Sh] | Marlowe T 4615 Now eies inioy your latest benefite. — In the following passage from Marlowe the difference is probably due merely to the requirements of the metre: E2 2043 So shall my eyes receive their *last* content, My head, the *latest* honor dew to it.

11.2₅. *At last* = 'finally', *at (the) latest* = 'not later than': at last he died | you must be here at the latest at five | Stevenson D 46 Then, at the latest, you must ride with me | Bennett HL 123 At latest she should have caught the evening train.

Always *to the last:* McCarthy 2.207 the Prince Consort died. He knew the Queen to the last. His latest look was turned to her.

Latest (but not *last*) may refer to the future: Macaulay E 3.78 Plutarch and Diodorus have handed down to the latest ages the respectable name of Anytus.

11.2₆. *Last* (but not *latest*) can be used as an adv: when last I saw the place.

Adverbs in *-ly* may be formed both from *last* (see vol VI 22.9₆) and *latter:* Mitford OV 40 Latterly the taste had been renewed and quickened | ib 42.

11.2₇. A strange kind of irregularity is found in the word *near*. OE had *nēah, nēarra, nēxt* (WS *nīehst*). all three forms have been preserved down to ModE, but the relation between them has changed. The positive form became ME *niȝ* > ModE *nigh*, while the OE comparative became *near*, found as a true comparative in Ch G 7201 of his science am I neuer the neer | [Sh?] E3 I. 2.125 I will come no neare | Mcb II. 3.146 The neere in blood, the neerer bloody. Perhaps also in R2

III. 2.64 and V. 1.88, in connexion with which Wright quotes Drayton: ne'er a whit the near | T. Churchyard: Your time is lost, and you are never the near. In PE *near* is used only as a positive form. The transition probably took place through such expressions as: Come near! | Lyly C 296 will you draw neere? And the development was supported by the opposition to *far* (Ch T 1.451 fer or neer) and other advs of place, *here* and *there*, of the same form. From the new positive form then the new comparative and superlative *nearer* and *nearest* were formed: Caxton R 49 in gretter paryl ne nerrer my deth | Lyly C 321 neerer to my court | Sh Mcb II. 3.146 above. — On *near* = 'no nearer' see above, 3.3_7.

Conversely, the relation of *nigh* to *near* having become obscure, the new forms *nigher* and *nighest* were developed: Gammer 114 nyer | Bunyan G 47 this came nighest to mine | Defoe R 2.208 the nighest boat | Byron DJ 3.42 the nighest guest | ib 8.20 nigher | Morris E 113 she drew yet nigher. — *Nigh* (*nigher*, *nighest*) is now archaic or poetic, but *well-nigh* may still be used in prose: Doyle S 1.204 I was well-nigh certain that some foul plot had been woven round him.

Like *last*, the form *next* in its most frequent sense is no longer a superlative; it is used with reference to a series of items, to pick out the item immediately succeeding (in space, time, value, etc) the one under consideration: *the next house* | *his next letter rather surprised me*. Cf Galsw Car 260 All that day and the next and the next she saw the bright side of things. *Next* here means 'following', not 'nearest'. The difference is clearly brought out in Krüger U 46: At 12.10 the nearest full hour is twelve, but the next full hour is one. — In certain of its applications, however, the old superlative meaning of next (= 'nearest') is still evident: the next of kin | the person next to him in rank | she sat next to me at table | the chair next the fire | the Sunday next before (after) Easter. Cf *next to* = 'almost': this will be next to impossible | next to nothing.

An obsolete superlative of *high* is found in the proverb When bale is hext, boot is next (Heywood Prov 46).

11.3₁. In a series of paradigms we have different stems supplementing each other. In some cases this is still obvious (*good — better — best | bad, ill, evil — worse — worst*); in others the similarity is so great that the various forms may now be generally supposed to be of the same root:

much, many — more — most. Historically, the two positive stems (mutually unrelated) are different from that of the comparative and superlative. On the distinction formerly made between *mo* as a pl and *more* as a sg (and adv) see vol II 2.74.

little — less (lesser) — least. The positive is of a different root from the other two forms.

Worse may be considered not only as the comparative of *bad, evil* and *ill*, but also of other synonymous adjectives, such as *vile, wretched, wrong* — the essential thing is that it is the opposite of *better*. See e.g. Swinburne L 157 I cannot think how things can be as dreadful as they are. I suppose, if I can live through this, I shall live to see them become worse.

11.3₂. *Worse* and *less* are the only comparatives in the language that do not end in *-r;* therefore the popular instinct seized on them and added the usual ending *-(e)r. Worser*, which was formerly frequent (for instance in Sh, also as an adv; other examples are Lyly C 279 worser fortune | Bunyan P (2) from worser thoughts | Coleridge

11.3₂.] *Worse, worser, less, lesser.*

Letter 1816 (Campb xcvii) my worser self | Carlyle SR 78 the worser sort | Orig. Engl. 18 worser than the first | 25 makes me feel worser | Jocularly in Kipling L 82 But the worst of it is, no man can save his brother. — No, and the worser of it is, there is no discharge in this war || And in Lytton K 100 when a man once parts with his money, whether to his betters or to his worsers) has passed out of use.

Lesser has survived, and a differentiation has taken place, so that *less* generally refers to quantity and is opposite to *more* (Ruskin Sel 2.195 the less or more capacity | more or less), or to *greater* (Spencer E 2.338 a greater or less likeness | Sayce Introd 1.170 a greater or less influence) while *lesser* refers to size and especially to value or importance; *lesser* is more literary than *less*.

Examples: The later you come the less time will there be for discussion | Mi PL 4.853 More glory will be won, Or less be lost || The Lesser Antilles | The Lesser Bear | The Lesser Prophets | Conway was one of the lesser poets of the period | Tennyson 102 Woman is the lesser man.

Though Earle (EProse 153) would admit *lesser* in poetry only, it is by no means rare in prose, not only in older authors (Marlowe E 1141, Defoe R 117, Swift 3.214, Scott Iv 71, 254, Austen M 379, id S 308, Mrs Browning A 329, Di D 114, GE Mm 216), but also in recent writers (Benson D 2.64 frequency, Archer A 35 the lesser of two evils, Wells A 101 degree, ib 244 probability, Wilde In 136 perfection, Kipling J 2.153 kings, id L 139 battle, Stevenson A 53, id MB 183 count, Harraden D 9, etc).

Less as an adj is found, e.g., in Caine E 48 the less of two evils, Hardy L 186 request, Darvin E 70 to a greater or less extent, Macaulay H 2.158 a less disaster, Ruskin T 12 the greater or less convenience, Galsw WM [p?] the less of two evils; in the sense 'smaller' of a boy Mitford OV 166.

Cf also Fijn v. Draat in *Anglia* 24.53.

Least is comparatively rare in the sense of 'smallest': Di D 31 she was sitting by my side upon the lowest and least of the lockers | ib 307 said this least of women.

Less as a pl was formerly frequent; it is found, e.g., in Marlowe F 686. Now *fewer* is preferred, it is found from the 14th c., *fewest* from the 15th c. Sh has *fewer* H4A II. 4.111, *fewest* AV Deut. 7.7. Ballard in *Thought and Lang.* 217 defends against pedantic critics Less than a hundred people were present.

Lesser as an adv is found in Sh Cymb V. 5.187; both forms together in Cor I. 4.16 Nor a man that feares you lesse than he, That's lesser then a little. *Lesser* as an adj and *less* as an adv is also found in Stevenson MP 14 endowed with a lesser and a less romantic sense of life | Hope Q 77 blindness to Quisanté's lesser, but not less galling faults.

Less as an adj is always used in *no less a man (person, thing) than* (Mi A 8, Quincey 279, Meredith EH 496, Caine C 421, Hope R 166).

11.3₃. A kind of emphatic superlative is *the least little:* Tennyson 289 Or the least little delicate aquiline curve in a sensitive nose, From which I escaped heat-free, with the least little touch of spleen (also Hope C 104, Norris P 84).

A vg variant is *the leastest* (Ridge G 305 and other places).

[But the best good fortune (Mrs Browning A 118) is different: *good fortune* forms one idea].

11.3₄. *far — farther (further) — farthest (furthest).*

According to NED, *further* (< OE *furðor*) is from the root of the adv *fore* + the comparative ending found also in *o-ther* and *af-ter*. A different theory explains *further* as being from the stem of *forth*. *Farther* goes back to ME *ferþer*, which is probably due to the vb *ferþran* < OE *fyrþrian*, formed by mutation from *furðor*. Owing to the great similarity both in meaning and form, *farther* and *further* came to be used as the comparative of *far*, thus displacing the regular form *farrar*. The superlatives *farthest* and *furthest* are later formations.

As for the use of the *a*-forms as compared with the *u*-forms only the vaguest rules can be given. "The fact is surely that hardly anyone uses the two words for different occasions; most people prefer one or the other for all purposes, & the preference of the majority is for *further*," says Fowler (MEU) in protest against the distinction attempted in the NED. — Sh has *further* about seven times as frequently as *farther*. Milton always has the comparative form in *u: further* or rarely *furder* (thus apparently always in Mi A), but the superlative *farthest* (not so frequently *fardest*). Among authors who nearly always use *farther* are Swift (3.242 receive farther information | ib 289 after two or three farther trials | ib 306 I said farther that ...), Scott, Carlyle, and Ruskin, but of course only *further* as a vb, from which *furtherance* (Ru Sel 2.201; cf vol VI 21.6$_3$).

Generally, however, *farther* is rare in the sense 'additional, extra'. The tendency seems to be in this case to use almost exclusively *further*, while where distance is in question, whether real or figurative, the two forms compete: Fielding T 3.138 abandoning all farther thoughts | Sheridan 209 farther instructions | ib 220 without farther ceremony || Di Do 72 reaching over further yet, to shake his uncle by the hand | Stevenson

JHF 48 at the further end, a flight of stairs mounted | Sweet E 1.5 as she gets further and further away | Swinburne T 110 the furthest star || Mannin CI 91 With every fresh device of our intellectuality we get farther away from fundamental satisfaction, still further clutter up our lives with inessentials.

According to Stoffel S 190 vg has developed a positive form *fur* on the analogy of the comparative and superlative in *u*. On the other hand, a superlative *furtherest* is found in U.S. (Dreiser AT 1.34).

11.3₅. The periphrastic comparatives and superlatives with preposed *more* and *most* are found not only in those cases in which the endings *-er* and *-est* cannot be used for phonetic reasons, but also extensively in other cases.

Sometimes it is possible to see a reason why *more* and *most* are preferred, thus when the adj enters into a more or less fixed combination with what follows, e.g. Sh As II. 4.77 [I wish] My fortunes were more able to releeue her | Maugham HB 302 the noisy merriment made his own misery more hard to bear.

Still we find Carlyle R 1.73 people apter to do than to speak — where we should expect *more apt*: Carlyle on the whole favours the endings, see Schmeding.

11.3₆. Further, when *more* or *most* belongs at the same time to two or more successive adjs: Greene J4 374 since you are growne greater and your garments more fine and gaye | BJo III. 1.287 More pure, or free ... more rich, Or this more learned | Sterne M 1.207 the most candid and scholar-like examination | Thack P 524 Had he been a Crown Prince, he could not have been more weak, useless, dissolute, or ungrateful | Galsw FS 701 son who ... could ... become more rich and cultured than himself | Wells Cl 27 I find most of the worlds that other people describe much more hard and clear and definite than mine is || Sheridan 362 he has not been more false to you than faithless to me.

Somewhat similarly in Black Ph 367 It is good deal more proper; and a great deal more dull | Hazlitt A 50 No footsteps ever fell more slow, more sad than mine.

In Byron DJ 13.9 [Quixote] Of all tales 'tis the saddest — and more sad, Because it makes us smile — the clause gives the reason for *more*, not for *sad*.

11.3₇. There is further a decided tendency to use the periphrasis with *more* when the comparison is not between two persons or things, but between the same person or thing at two different times; very often there is no *than* expressed, but it would have been possible to supply "than before, than ever":

Sh Merch III. 2.156 A thousand times more faire, ten thousand times More rich [than I am now] | Goldsm V. 1. 202 [to] make the opulent still more rich | Poe 342 Her voice grew more gentle — more low | Kipling K 185 Every month I become a year more old | Hope R 274 her eyes grew more calm | Mackenzie S 1.68 more grim every day | ib 73 Nurse, looking more old and wrinkled and monkeylike than ever | ib 109 he felt more sorry than ever | Walpole DF 161 His pockets were more full than ever of knives and string and buttons. — Sweet NEG § 217 does not give this rule, but has the example: I said nothing, which made him still more angry.

The *-er* form will, however, be used in such familiar cases as: The patient feels better, though the temperature is higher than yesterday.

11.3₈. When two qualities of the same person or thing are compared, the rule is to use *more:* He is more proud than conceited [= proud rather than conceited] | His mother was more kind than intelligent.

But in speaking of two dimensions, we may say, e.g., Hardy Greenwood T 39 The upper windows were much wider than they were high | Mason House Arrow 161 [the room] was longer than it was broad | Priestley AP 106 all the rooms seemed higher than they were long or broad | Shaw TT 94 the rough path through the gap is taller than it is broad | *oblong* is defined in some dictionaries as *longer than broad*.

Cf also Sh Meas IV. 3.85 your company is fairer than honest | Tarkington Pl 152 his hair was yet darker than it was grey | NP 1920 a few personal attendants, all of whom are kinder than they are wise [generally *more kind than wise*] | Golding SD 436 He had been a better soldier than he was now a business-man.

Flatter may be avoided on account of the vb *flatter:* Bennett L 205 his face was more flat and milder.

More evil is used because of the special meaning of *evil*, which is not covered by *worse:* Haggard S 76 I had never seen more evil faces | Franklin 235 fraught with the most evil consequences | Wells N 59 It was the most evil thing that ever came into the house | Sherriff F 130 a smaller, and more evil boy. — Cf *evilest* above, 10.5_1.

Versification accounts for Sh As II. 1.2 Hath not old custome made this life more sweete Then that of painted pompe?

And a desire for variety for Priestley A 181 He's ... had the most weird adventures and met the weirdest people.

But in a great many other instances of periphrasis it does not seem possible to discover any reason for not using the ending.

Meaning

11.4₁. After these considerations (mostly of a formal character) we shall now look into the meaning of these degrees of comparison.

If we compare two persons or things in regard to some quality, we find three possibilities:

(1) Superiority: more dangerous than, better than
(2) Equality: as dangerous as, as good as
(3) Inferiority: less dangerous than, less good than.

Obviously (1) and (3) are closely connected as indicating inequality and requiring *than*, while (2) requires *as*, before the second member of comparison.

Comparisons with *less* are not very frequent; instead of *less dangerous than*, we often say *not as dangerous as* (or *not so dangerous as*), and whenever there are two adjs of opposite meaning, we say, for instance, *weaker than* rather than *less strong than*.

11.4₂. Some adjs and advs are incapable of comparison on account of their meaning, e.g. *several, other, divers, half, daily, future, previous, triangular, mutual.* Others, which strictly speaking should seem incapable of being put in the comparative or superlative, are used thus in a slightly modified meaning: *more perfect* and *most perfect* really mean 'nearer and nearest to perfection'. Similarly *fuller, fullest*, and cf *ownest* above, 10.2₂ (and Shaw in 11.1₁(1)).

Soon in the absolute meaning of OE *sōna* 'at once' did not admit of degrees of comparison, but now *sooner* and *soonest* are all right.

In dialects *nor* is frequently used instead of 'than', see EDD.

11.4₃. Not infrequently we find hesitation between a comparison of equality and one of inequality with a resulting uncertainty as to the particle. The following examples will probably be considered slipshod by purists: Bridges HBradley 43 he had perhaps as much or more trouble in the cracking of nuts as in the forging of iron | Galsw IC 152 Soames' position was as bad or worse than her own | id SS His daughter was as good or better than any of them | Wells TB 1.51 he could box as well or better than I || Sh LLL III. 180 A domineering pedant ore the boy, Then whom no mortall so magnificent (sentence begun as if to continue with *more*).

11.4₄. Note. *Than* is also used after *other* (which etymologically is formed like a comparative) and then occasionally after *else* (= other) and *elsewhere* (= otherwhere, at another place): Ruskin Sel 2.58 this is nothing else than a large ... vase | Norris S 269 how could his behaviour seem else than ridiculous | Carlyle H 155 Strong men are born there, who ought to stand elsewhere than there | Matthews A 51 distrust of those who dwell elsewhere than where we do | Morgan S 363 there is corresponding ecstasy to be found elsewhere on earth than in the idea of death.

11.4₅. *Than* is by no means rare after *different;* Fitzedward Hall has it from Addison, Steele, etc. Cf from more recent writers: Thack P 10 she had hoped for a different lot than to be wedded to ... | Trollope B 523 things were conducted very differently now than in former times | Wilde P 41 things will be made different for me than for others | Lawrence SL 71 you used to 'ave a different nose than that | Wells Cl 204 a different sort of strategy than the disorganisation of political parties | Maugham Pl 4.192 It's different for a man than for a woman | Cronin H 463 Things were different for me than they are for you, Nessie!, etc.

Cf Ericson in *Anglia* 56. 111—12 and AmSp 1.128.

11.4₆. Through a blending of *scarcely (hardly) when* and *no sooner than* we find in vg or half-vg speech constructions like the following, which according to Fowler MEU 229 are surprisingly common: Frankau Dance 96 and hardly had I had time to recognize her, than she was inside (also ib 229, 274, etc) | ib 307 And scarcely had we finished our muffins, than she said to me … | Plunket Greene E 28 Hardly has he delivered himself … than he again hears footsteps behind him.

11.4₇. Popular speech avoids a combination of *than* with a finite vb and inserts a clause with *what:* Sterne M 1.38 This, by the way, was no more than what was reasonable | ib 102 he would feel more pain … than what he ever gave (also ib 1.14, 1.47) | Maugham C 257 No woman could want a better husband than what he made me | Sayers NT 249 he must have struck him harder than what he meant (Cf vol III 9.6₂).

Instead of the comparative some dialects use the 'positive' with the preposition *by:* she is young by you = 'younger than you' (Elworthy WSomerset 166); cf Stevenson K 60 His wife (who was "young by him," as he often told me). In U.S. frequently *young by the side of you*.

11.4₈. A comparative may sometimes be used though the idea of comparison is not very prominent: *the lower classes, the younger generation, the higher criticism, the higher schools, Longer Poems* (as a book-title). In such cases there is no indication of the second member of comparison, and the implication is only 'lower than some other classes', etc. Similarly in: You had better stay.

Two old quotations: Sh Hml II. 1.114 it is common for the younger sort To lacke discretion | LLL I. 1.275 Iaquenetta (so is the weaker vessell called).

11.4₉. The idea of comparison is often particularly weak in *rather:* It's rather warm today | Does it rain? Rather. — It is, however, a real comparative when supplemented by the frequent addition *than otherwise;* as well as when two verbs are compared:

Sh Merch III. 2.105 thou meager lead, Which rather threatenest then dost promise ought | Wells H 369 they displayed rather than concealed their opinion | Bennett ECh 244 She felt, rather than knew, that the two great men were ... | Locke W 127 she sought rather than avoided opportunities || Butler W 235 he did not know any woman whom he would not rather die than marry.

The positive *rathe* 'early' as in Mi Lycidas 142 the rathe primrose — is now obsolete.

11.5₁. It is very important to keep in mind that the comparative does not necessarily mean a higher degree of the quality in question than the positive does itself: "Peter is older than John" does not imply that Peter is old, and the comparative may therefore really indicate a lesser degree than the positive would in "Peter is old". Nor does it, of course, say anything about John's being old — if this is meant, we say "Peter is still older than John."

11.5₂. On the other hand, such a combination as *more than kind* means that *kind* is an inadequate expression and thus criticizes the use of the simple term *kind:* She was more than old-fashioned; she was antediluvian | You're worse than unfair. You're ungenerous — you're mean | Marlowe T 1812 These more than dangerous warrants | Mi PR 2.137 With more than human gifts from Heav'n adorn'd | Byron 437 The Count was something more than wroth | Di T 2.100 by being more than ready and willing to cut his throat | Tracy P 44 Furneaux seems more than anxious that nothing should appear in the Press | Maugham FPS 250 his more than feminine sensitiveness | Gibbs Heirs A 227 single women of more than doubtful character | Bennett RS 81 She was more than intimidated — she was frightened | Crofts Ch 19 It's more than good of you both || Sayce Reminiscences 66 the food was more than indifferent [indifferent = not particularly good] ||

Di F 888 he had struck the worse than useless blows. — Cf vol II 15.28 *passing, exceeding*.

Compare also: Caxton R 84 thenne shal thou be richer than riche | Hart BT 178 Do you feel better? Better than best | Walpole W 116 they are all kinder than kind (also 181) | ib 16 they are poorer than poor | id GM 224 Aunt Sarah, deafer than deaf | RBennett P 268 He can't be madder than mad, poor chap.

11.5₃. A similar use is found with substantives, e.g. Haggard S 101 my dear friend — my more than father | Lowndes Ivy 225 when I told him of my more than suspicion, of my absolute conviction, that Mrs. Lexton had had some all-powerful motive.

The last example leads to the corresponding use with a vb: Scott OM 179 K. more than answered the expectations of Burley | Di Do 335 whatever good I may be fortunate to do the children, you will more than pay back to me | Macaulay H. 1.112 one advantage which would have more than compensated for the want of stores and money | Swinburne L 102 she is, I more than suspect, touched more deeply than we fancied | Butler W 8 the boy more than justified the favourable opinion which Mr F had formed | Stevenson B 183 Dick more than made it up by his greater agility | id V 222 What we lose in generous impulse, we more than gain in the habit of generously watching others | Hope Z 232 to double the party more than doubled the risk | Beresford G 90 the reality more than confirmed his anticipations | Raleigh Sh 21 When Sh describes anything you more than see it, you feel it too | Housman J 181 before you have much more than begun | Locke SJ 170 I more than expected to find the dwarf on the quay | Dane FB 131 Florence more than kept her promises.

The following quotations are somewhat different: Brontë V 361 while I read, my heart did more than throb — it trembled fast | Mason R 14 Thus their eyes met, and did more than meet | Darwin L 1.48 my time was sadly wasted at Cambridge, and worse than wasted.

Gradual Increase

11.5₄. To indicate a gradual increase we use two comparatives connected with *and:* Conditions are getting worse and worse every day | He became more and more eloquent towards the end of his speech | Lamb E 1.171 I confess a less and less relish daily for those cates | McCarthy 2. 391 it made them feel more and more safe in their enterprises.

In literary style some variants of this figure are found: Mi PL 10.844 from deep to deeper plunged | Burns 442 The dancers quick and quicker flew | Shelley 54 And swift and swifter grew the vessel's motion | Byron 4.230 it grows small and smaller | ib 236 the clouds still open wide and wider | Tennyson 106 The music in his heart Beats quick and quicker | ib 101 And at night along the dusky highway near and nearer drawn | Browning 3.176 all sin ... would drop down, low and lower, to the earth | Stevenson T 223 the hill ... loomed faint and fainter (cp Fijn v. Draat in *Anglia* 24.56) || Byron DJ 4.35 till each trace More like and like to Lambro's aspect grew | Tennyson 106 More close and close his footsteps wind || Shelley 161 drawn nearer and more near | ib 716 I grow bolder and still more bold | ib 728 The strong fantasy Had made her accents weaker and more weak | Di X 186 Caleb's scanty hairs were turning greyer and more grey | Ruskin P 1.40 the visits became rarer and more rare |

Kingsley H 62 the screams grew fainter and more faint || Byron 4.230 And as it waxes little, and then less | Archer A 158 such errors will become, in the future, rarer and ever rarer | Bromfield ModHero 153 He grew steadily more gaunt and yellow and ugly | Beresford G 154 her position was becoming daily more insecure | Maxwell G 107 Every minute she enjoyed herself more completely.

Latent Comparatives

11.5₅. We have what might be termed a latent comparative in the word *too*, which means 'in a higher degree than enough or than is allowable or advisable': I am afraid that we shall be too late for dinner | This is too good to be true (with Shaw's variant Too True to be Good — book-title) | Too much and too little of a good thing spoils it.

The comparative meaning is weakened in the colloquial: I am only too glad (too delighted) to do this for you | Maugham Pl 4.158 it's only too natural | ib 167 I was only too anxious to do anything in the world for you | Russell FO 302 All of them were only too anxious to make use of the bank.

11.5₆. Another latent comparative is contained in the vb *prefer* (= 'like better'). This is normally followed by *to* (as the Latin comparatives, see below, 11.7₇): I prefer claret to sherry.

But occasionally the character of a comparative may induce the use of *than* after *prefer*, thus to avoid clashing with another *to* in: Thack Sk 138 preferring a solitude, and to be a bachelor, than to put up with one of these for a companion | Galsw FCh 96 And you preferred to go to a money-lender than to come to me? | Maugham TL 237 He preferred to be over-charged than to haggle. — Further: Priestley F 387 preferring that the young man should play the fool for a year or two in Tahiti than in Paris (*to* would not do before *in*) || Brontë W 151 it is preferable to be hated than loved by him | NP 1940 it is deemed greatly preferable to kill an innocent person than miss a would-be assasin.

Or *than* may be expanded: Benson D 58 I'd prefer you hit me ... than that you should hit anyone who can't hit back | Maugham MS 262 who preferred to live with a native woman rather than work for his living | Sherriff J 114 he preferred being up with the men better than down here.

The Three Degrees

11.6₁. The way in which the three degrees are generally given makes us imagine that they represent a graduated scale, as if *old : older : oldest* formed a progression like, say, the numbers 1 : 2 : 3 (arithmetical progression) or 1 : 2 : 4 (geometrical progression). But this is only rarely the case, as in Sh LLL IV. 3.17 the clowne bore it [my sonnet], the foole sent it, and the lady hath it: sweete clowne, sweeter foole, sweetest lady | Keats 4.126 We dined yesterday on dirty bacon, dirtier eggs, and dirtiest potatoes | Brontë V. 369 I, too, was happy — happy with the bright day, happier with his presence, happiest with his kindness. — This way of placing the three forms together, in which the superlative denotes what is otherwise indicated by *still* (still sweeter, still dirtier), may really be due to the teaching of grammar; but it is important to insist on the fact that in ordinary usage the superlative does not indicate a higher degree than the comparative, but really states the same degree, only looked at from a different point of view. If we compare the ages of four boys, A, B, C, and D, we may state the same fact in two different ways:

A is older than the other boys, or
A is the oldest boy.

In both cases A is compared with B, C, and D; but the result is in the former case given with regard to these three (the other boys), in the latter with regard to all the boys, including A.

11.6₂. The comparative must be supplemented by a member expressed by means of *than* or understood. The superlative, on the other hand, is often followed by *of* or *among all*. But as both forms really express the same idea, we should not be surprised to find a confusion (frequent in older writers), resulting in such blendings as Bacon A 20.17 a king, whose memory of all others we most adore | BJo A 2.162 They will doe it best. Best of all others | Mi A 54 the worst and newest opinion of all others | Swift 3.318 the trade of a soldier is held the most honourable of all others | Sterne M 1.285 of all others he stood most interested to watch accidents | Austen S 231 the very person whom of all others they would have been most anxious to mortify | Quincey 25 that spectacle which of all others is the most touching | Carlyle P 179 and you, first of all others, I think, were wise to take note of that! | Thack N 609 Isn't he the mortal of all others the most to be envied. Examples may still be found in recent journalese.

11.6₃. Another blending occurs when the singular is used where we should expect the plural after *of:* as *the best temper* and *the best of tempers* mean practically the same thing, many people will say and write: He was evidently not in the best of temper (or health) | People taking the gentlest of exercise.

This is particularly frequent with words that are seldom or never used in the plural number.

11.6₄. When there is no direct comparison (with *than*), some grammarians — in accordance with Latin syntax — insist on the use of the comparative if two, and the superlative if more than two are referred to. Many quotations both for the comparative and the superlative in speaking of two were given in vol II 7.77 (771, 772, 773). Always: Put one's best leg foremost.

11.6₅. It is a natural consequence of the nature of the superlative that it is generally used preceded by a defining word: The richest man in the town | My youngest boy | Thackeray's best novel | Wordsw 206 That best portion of a good man's life, His little, nameless, unremembered acts Of kindness and of love | There you may see England at its best — and in its best.

Still, a superlative may be used after *any* or *no:* On any smallest occasion (= any, even the smallest) | Ruskin Sel 2.308 Football, or any roughest sport | Thack P 876 it frightened Blanche much more than any the most serious exhibition | Gissing H 99 She knew his face better than that of any oldest acquaintaince || Carlyle SR 99 Rightly viewed no meanest object is insignificant. — Cf below 13.3₂.

11.6₆. The superlative may be limited by some addition like: The next best (= better than all the others with the exception of one) | Thack P 197 the next best thing to being amused at a pantomime one's self is to see one's children enjoy it | Ruskin U 14 the next clearest and simplest example [= ... but one] | Di F 149 the most desirable of his neighbours ... the next most desirable | Collins W 308 Mr. Gilmore's partner is our next best friend to Mr. Gilmore himself || Bennett

T 157 the next to the last unmarried daughter | Lewis EG 284 favoured by the next-to-the-best surgeons || Shaw P 216 dressed in somebody else's very second best | Roosevelt A xi to accept the second best if what he considers the first best is not attainable | Doyle S 5.240 It is the second most interesting object that I have seen in the North | Wilder Bridge 84 is the second most delightful man in the world | St. Paul's is the third longest cathedral in Christendom || The largest but one (but two, three, etc) | OHenry B 100 next door but one to McGary's Family Café.

A Very High Degree

11.7₁. In consequence of the almost universal tendency to exaggerate, people will often use the superlative where they mean only a very high degree, as in: I should do it with the greatest pleasure.

A superlative without the article is not infrequently used to denote a very high degree; this, however, is found in literary style more frequently than in conversation: Mi A 5 it is of greatest concernment | ib 44 Writers of good antiquity and ablest judgement | Brontë V 338 these feelings were known to me but by briefest flashes | Di (q Poutsma) From earliest spring to latest autumn | Tennyson 20 in stillest evenings | I acknowledge, with sincerest thanks, your generous gift | With best wishes, Yours ...

Here belongs the colloquial *not best pleased* (e.g. Keats 4.142, Di N 161, id P 293 by no means best pleased).

11.7₂. This leads to the use of *most* as a strengthened *very* before an adjective. Here *most* is no longer a real superlative and is distinguished from real superlatives by being used (1) with the indefinite article, (2) in the predicative without an article, and (3) after *this*, because this is determined, not determining: Sh Lr IV. 2.26 My most deere Gloster | Mcb V. 1.8 in a most fast sleepe | H8 II. 4.15 am a most poor woman | Shrew II. 1.152 with a most impatient diuellish spirit | Fielding 3.523 what made for the advancing their most noble projects (different from *noblest*) | Thack N 299 the Fleet Prison would be a most wholesome retreat for this most reckless divine | Haggard S 53 this most perilous coast | Advertisement: Most desirable appartments.

Similarly with advs: Sh Hml II. 2.217 I will most humbly take my leaue of you | Shelley Prom III. 3.173 thou hast borne it most triumphantly | Maugham HB 182 It's most awfully good of you | most frequently = very frequently. — The true superlative must be expressed: more frequently than not.

11.7₃. Curme calls attention to the difference in stress (and tone) between

This girl is the ˈmost beautiful (relatively)

This girl is most ˈbeautiful (= very)

He was ˈmost eloquent at the close of his speech (more than before)

He was most ˈeloquent at the close of his speech (= very).

11.7₄. *More* may mean 'a greater number of (people)', and *most* 'the greatest number of (people)', e.g. More people go to London than to any other place in Europe | Most young Englishmen are fond of outdoor sports.

11.7₅. Note in consequence of this, the following expressions:

(1) I got to know most respectable people in the town (= the greatest number of respectable people).

(2) I got to know the most respectable people in the town (superlative of *respectable*).

(3) I got to know some most respectable people in the town (= some highly respectable).

With a shorter adj this would correspond to

(1) I got to know most (of the) kind people in the town.

(2) I got to know the kindest people in the town.

(3) I got to know some most kind people in the town.

11.7₆. In a few cases ambiguity may arise: He had known more attractive women than Annie | The house where he had entertained his most distinguished guests | Most valuable things are found under the surface of the earth.

But the ambiguity will generally be avoided by saying e. g. "a greater number (or quantity) of furious faces (or palatable food)". Note the difference between "I never saw kinder faces" and "more kind faces", "I never had better food" and "more good food". In the following examples *more* will naturally be understood in the latter sense, because otherwise the comparative in *-er* would have been used:

Austen P 462 you may have more fine clothes than Jane | GE A 273 it's no use meeting to say more hard words | Swinburne L 122 capable of far more hard work | Wells JP 490 Perhaps there were rather more dark types, perhaps more high cheekbones.

In connexion with this use of *most* may be mentioned the dialectal (also U.S.) *most* = 'almost'. NED *most* 4, Mencken AL⁴ 468.

Latin Comparatives and Superlatives

11.7₇. Some adjs are taken from Latin comparatives: *anterior, interior, inferior, superior, major, minor*. When they are used as virtual comparatives, they do not take *than*, but *to:* prior to the war, inferior to other brands, etc.

Note the advs *much*, if the comparative meaning is clear, and *very*, if not. Cf Swift 3.370 a creature so inferior as I | Bennett C 1.229 smiling a little superiorly.

When used as substantives, they are combined with the genitive: John's superiors = 'those that are higher (in office) than John'. Cf above, 9.2$_8$.

Many Latin forms are in English no real comparatives and superlatives, e. g. *interior, exterior;* see also Kipling S 257 fellows as senior as you are can easily see why | Macdonell E 169 and the more senior of the critics went moodily out for drinks | Waugh BM 162 a man at least ninety years of age, greatly my own senior | Di N 708 [Mrs Squeers; would-be educated] the juniorest Palmer | Priestley AP 8 This was the office boy or very junior clerk | Sayers GN 96 She was the most junior of the dons | Seeley E 151 a very minor question | Archer in Fortn. Rev. Oct. 1906. 621 That is a very minor matter.

Extreme (Latin superlative) is capable of degrees of comparison: Sh Merch I. 1.138 extremest | McCarthy 2.481 the extremest need (also *extremer* in Meredith) | McCarthy 2.327 the more extreme Reformers | Strachey EV 31 Every day his arguments became more extreme.

Strengthening

11.8$_1$. Cf Stoffel, *Intensives and Down-Toners* (Heidelberg 1901) and E. Borst, *Die gradadverbien im englischen* (ib 1902).

The most general ways of intensifying adjs and advs are by *very* with the positive degree and the superlative and *much* with the comparative.

Very is originally, and to some extent still, an adj meaning 'true' (OF *verai* < L *veracus*), but has been used extensively from the 15th c. as in *very great*, etc, where formerly *much* was used. — Cf *full* above, 1.5$_5$.

Examples of the old *much*, where now *very* would be the rule: Caxton R 27 [they] were moche fatte | Sh H4B IV. 4.111 I am much ill | Cymb II. 3.109 I am much sorry (very frequent in Sh) | Ado I. 1.18 [he] wil be very much glad of it | Mi PR 2.173 in much uneven scale || Scott A 1.210 my loss is not much worth speaking about (on account of *worth*, cf *worth much*) | id OM 120 she would have been much averse to exert this influence | Ruskin P 1.3 ideas which I find for the present much obsolete (perhaps because *obsolete* = 'antiquated') | Trollope D 37 Lord Silverbridge was ... much subject to the influence of his friend (on account of the verbal character of *subject*).

It seems superfluous here to give quotations for *very* before adjs and advs. It seems to be found once only in Mi: Ps 6.4. A peculiar use is Fielding 3.578 he thought proper to put the matter very home to Fireblood. — *Very* may be used alone with the adj understood: Swift J 54 [the fit] went off, leaving me sickish, but not very | Austen M 225 Are you fond of dancing? — Yes, very | Hope Ch 131 Have you seen him lately? — No, not very: I passed him in the street the other day.

Very cannot be used with the adv *so* when this replaces a previous adj; in reply to the question "Is he ill?" we must say "Not (very) much so" or "Not as much so as yesterday." But "Not very" without *so* is all right.

With second participles *very* is used more and more instead of the older *much*, which was required on account of the verbal character, see for details vol V 22.5$_7$.

With *like* both *much* and *very* are found, the former perhaps because *like* does not denote perfect identity, but implies some difference. *Very much like* is also used. One English friend would establish a difference: very like in face, etc, very much like in character.

Malory 102 al were shapen moche lyke the poure man | Walton A 204 much like the pearch | Cowper L 1.163 effects much like those it had produced before | Shelley 384 Hell is a city much like London | Hawthorne Sn 18 wondering how a little girl could look so much like a flowing snow-drift, or how a snow-drift could look so very like a little girl | Benson D 7 one crowd looks much like another crowd.

Cowper L 1.93 an attachment that looks very like a friendship | Di N 49 it tasted very like toast and water | Trollope B 99 she looked very like an angel | Di T 1.117 Did you ever see anybody very like the prisoner? ... Are they very like each other? | Bennett W 2.250 he was very like you | Shaw M 7 Thats very like Jack | Galsw M 79 a little girl of ten, very like her mother | Benson N 68 she was very like Jenny, and very unlike ‖ in a different sense Maugham Alt 1498 I felt very like crying.

After a negative, *much like* is generally preferred: Benson N 153 the figure ... was not much like Frank | Masefield M 140 a tsetse is not much like a cleg to look at ... | ib 141 They are very like common house-flies | id C 236 The colonials aren't much like Athenians. — I think they're very like ... They're very like Athenians. — Cf Di T 1.131 we are not much alike ‖ Wells N 163 not very like my mother.

11.8₂. *Much* = 'nearly', before *the same* and synonyms: McCarthy 2.231 much the same thing | Butler E 221 it kept pretty much to the same pane | Cowper L 1.219 yet sometimes much such a part act I | Austen E 157 every thing was relapsing much into its usual state | Harrison R 156 St. Ursula became to Ruskin much what Beatrice was to Dante | Lowndes Ivy 97 a young married woman of much her own age | Tarkington Guest of Quesnay 166 He seems to me much of a type with these others |

Lecky D 1.88 the managers of the machine can usually do much what they please | Scott A 2.129 much such a sort of earthen jar as that | Hope D 42 the history of the affair is much as follows | Wells F 190 he is younger than myself, but much my sort of man.

11.8₃. Note the gradation in honorary titles: Very Reverend — of deans, Right Reverend — of bishops, Most Reverend — of archbishops. Honourable — of children of some peers, members of the Government, etc, Right Honourable — of peers below the rank of Marquess, etc, Most Honourable — of marquesses, etc.

11.8₄. Among other intensives used with the positive degree may be mentioned *so* (*ever so*), *entirely*, (*most*) *awfully*, *too* (cf above, 11.5₅), *pretty*, *quite:* Di D 762 She, who so gloried in my fame, and so looked forward to its augmentation | Ward F 428 I was so glad to help Mr. Fenwick — he interested me so | Walpole Cp 176 they'd be most awfully pleased if you were to retire / Philips L 104 Oh, how too kind of you! | Collingwood R 373 such an entirely good workman.

With comparatives the most usual intensive is *much*, sometimes the synonyms *a good* (*a great*) *deal*, *considerably*, *far*, and *quite* (apparently only in *quite better*); on *any* and *no* see vol II 17.16 and 16.83: much better | Payn in NP 1915[?] a friend who was much my senior | Walpole RH 42 Cards, a man a good deal the elder of Francis, lived now at Seddon | engaged to a man considerably her senior | Caine C 51 I've grown older, of course. — Oh, terribly older | Fielding 3.406 far the greater number are of the mixt kind | Stevenson D 28 the streams were very far better | Masefield M 189 Are you quite better now? | Bennett C 2.52 Are you quite better?

Very is exceptional (*younger sons* is felt like a compound): Hankin 3.13 The Bar is a good enough profession, of course. But only for very younger sons.

11.8₅. As remarked above (11.4₅) *different* is felt as a kind of comparative, hence we have, e. g. (Sh Err V. 46 much different from the man he was) | Tarkington MA 161 He isn't much different from the way he's looked all his life | Campbell Shl 156 we may ask, is he any happier? — is he any different? | Maugham Alt 325 It's no different from suborning a witness.

11.8₆. *Only less* = 'a little less, nearly as much' (not mentioned in NED?): Shelley 642 only less free Than thou, O uncontrollable! | Tennyson L 2.213 the "Idylls", which Kingsley admired only less than "In Memoriam" | Thack N 421 the cathedral [of Milan] ... only less magnificent than the imperial dome of Rome | Gissing R 20 the air affected me only less than at a later time did the atmosphere of Italy | Chesterton B 51 In Pippa passes he has the only less easy task of giving an account of humanity | Raleigh Sh 100 only less famous than Kemp were Cowley, Armin, and many others | Stopford Brooke, Milton 167 the great Singer whose name shines only less brightly than Shakespeare's | Bennett C 2.118 he was extremely sad, only less sad than his father | Roosevelt A 335 A foolish optimist is only less noxious than an utter pessimist.

Similarly, but rarer, *only more:* Philips M 299 I'm only more sorry for her than I am for myself | Huxley L 2.404 the lie from interested motives was only more hateful to him than the lie from self-delusion.

11.8₇. A superlative may be strengthened in various ways. The old *aller-, alder-* (OE gen pl *ealra*) died out in the 16th c.; Sh has it only once: alderliefest H6B I. 1.28. Other expressions: the very best (NED from 1567 on) | Fielding T 4.240 he had been much the greatest part of the time employed in his service | Austen M 193 the subject was so much uppermost in Lady B's mind, that she ... | Hope Ch 115 The others were wisest. — Much wisest | Collingwood R 217 he played Home, sweet Home — quite the most wonderful thing I have ever heard | Doyle S 6.78 This set of rooms is quite the oldest in the college | Carlyle R 1. 287 I was far the richest of the sect | Carpenter P 58 it is far best and wisest to abandon the idea | Maugham P 41 He's far and away the best bridge player at the Club | NP: Out and away the best book on the subject | Priestley G 406 Tewborough ... was easily the most depressed and depressing [town] | Roberts M 196 He had come at last, and long last, to recognise ...

In recent use (originally U.S.?) we find the elliptical *ever:* Bennett Imp Pal 464 This brioche is the finest ever | Harris Shaw 377 that the play was his best ever and no journalist should miss it for anything | Ade A 81 I thought she was the best ever | Bertram Atkey in BDS 281 you're the best little humanizer ever.

Chapter XII

Determination and Indetermination (The Articles)

12.1. We are here in the first line concerned with the articles, the definite (or better: defining) article and the indefinite article, as well as with the use of words without either of them (zero or the zero article).

[*Note by Niels Haislund.* Otto Jespersen did not intend to use the term *zero*, but would have spoken about "the bare word". But in accordance with the usage and theory set forth in many modern linguistic works I prefer to retain the zero-term. Cf Roman Jakobson, *Das Nullzeichen* in the *Bulletin du Cercle Linguistique de Copenhague V* (Copenhagen 1940) pp. 12—14. Professor Jakobson first quotes F. de Saussure: "La langue peut se contenter de l'opposition de quelque chose avec rien," and then goes on as follows: "Soweit ein Nichtvorhandensein zum entsprechenden Vorhandensein in einer binaren Opposition steht, wird es dadurch zu einem wahren semiologischen Bestandteil. Es erweist sich immer deutlicher, dass dieser "Nullwert" eine der wesentlichsten und reichhaltigsten sprachlichen Kategorien darbietet. Ein Komplex wird einem gleichartigen Komplex mit einem fehlenden Element (Nullelement) entgegengesetzt." Thus we should speak about zero only in cases where the form in question is in opposition to others with some "positive" criterion, and zero should not be confused with omission of one of the other articles (see e. g. below 12.8$_4$ ff., 12.9$_1$).]

I treat the three articles together, following in that respect Paul Christophersen's very valuable book *The Articles. A Study of their Theory and Use in English* (Copenhagen & London 1939), in these chapters denoted by the name Christophersen.

The use of the articles presents a great many intricate problems, and it is impossible to give a small number of settled rules available for all cases; idiomatic usage very often runs counter to logic or fixed rules. It will, therefore, be impossible in this book to cover the whole ground, and I must refer for further details to Christophersen's fuller treatment and the previous literature quoted by him. For the theory of the articles in general, see also E. Seidel, *Zu den funktionen des artikels* in the Rumanian *Bulletin Linguistique* VIII (1940), with examples from the best-known languages and from Rumanian, and id, *Der gegenwärtige Stand der rumänischen and allgemeinen Artikelprobleme* in the same periodical vol IX (1941).

It is very important from the outset to insist on the fact that the articles are not the only means of making a word definite or indefinite. *My hat, John's hat, this hat* are just as definite as *the hat;* and *some hat, one hat, any hat* just as indefinite as *a hat*. This has often been overlooked by grammarians.

Before dealing with the functions of the articles it will be necessary to treat of their forms.

Forms of the Articles

12.2₁. The definite article is now invariably written *the*. The complicated OE flexion, with *s* in *se* and *sēo* and with its full case system in the sg and pl gave way in the ME period to complete simplicity — in writing, at any rate. In pronunciation we have two forms: [ðə] before a consonant and [ði] before a vowel: [ðə mæn], [ði eg]. The distinction of course is made according to the sound, not to the spelling; we have thus [ði] before words with mute *h*, e. g. *heir, honour*, and [ðə] before words like *one:* [ðə wʌn], etc. *The M.A.* is read [ði ˡem ˡei]. It should, however, be noted that some people pronounce [ði] before the sound [j], as in *the year, the university*, etc (Miss Soames). And instead of the vowel [i] one may very often hear the consonant [j] before a vowel: [ðj aˑt, ðjəˡraivl], etc.

There is also a weak form with elision of the vowel, chiefly, but not exclusively, before a vowel; this was very frequent in earlier times, see vol I 6.13: Elphinston 1765 still thinks *th'Omnipotent* less stiff than [ðj] *Omnipotent*. Milton elides before a strong vowel, Pope only before weak vowels. Now the elided form is only found archaically in poetry, where one may also see *i'th'* = *in the*, but not in coll. speech, except perhaps vulgarly.

The [þ] or [ð] sound was formerly often assimilated to a preceding [t]: *at the* became *atte*, and when weak *e* disappeared, this was indistinguishable from *at* without the article. This explains *at* in combinations like *at last* (ME *atte laste*), *at least*, *at best*, vol I 6.36; *the* is reintroduced in *at the very root*, where Sh had *at very root*. Perhaps this *at(te) church* has been a contributory factor in making *church* and similar words be used in the bare form, cf below, 12.8₁ f., and note Maxwell G 99 at sight of her, at the touch of her hand ... he felt at peace.

12.2₂. There is an emphatic form [ˈðiˑ] used in contrast: I didn't say *a* [ei] man, but *the* [ˈðiˑ] man | he was one of the first (pl), if not *the* first (sg) to use a typewriter | Fox used to say, "*I* never want *a* word, but Pitt never wants *the* word" (q Byron 745 note).

This emphatic form may be used to mean 'the real, the best', etc, as in Huxley L 1.119 to stop in London. It is *the* place, the centre of the world (cf below, 14.2).

But in *that's the thing* (see below, 14.2₈), where *the* has the same meaning, the pronunciation is weak: [ðə].

12.2₃. Finally must be mentioned the variant *t*, due to the old neuter OE *þæt*, ME *that*, used before a vowel (without regard to gender) and eventually metanalyzed, *that* being taken with the following vowel. This was especially the case before *one* (at that time pronounced without the initial [w]) and *other* in contrasts: Gen. & Ex. c 1230 ðe ton, ðe tother | Wyclif Matt 6.24 he shal susteyn the toon, and dispise the tothir.

Examples with (*the*) *tother:* Ywaine 2300 on the tother syde | Sh Hml II. 1.56 I saw him yesterday, or tother day | Cor I. 1.246 I'll lean upon one crutch and fight with tother | BJo 3.171 with the t'other youth | ib 194 t'other day | Walton A 218 the tother cup.

Dryden uses *t'other* in the highest tragical style: Dryden 5.372 I could pull out an eye, and bid it go, And t'other should not weep, — and it is frequent in Defoe, Swift, Fielding.

In the 19th. c. it is found in more or less vg speech: Austen S 135 t'other day (also ib 272) | Di P [Ch & H] 729 [Sam Weller:] the t'other madman | id Do 47 by the t'other gate | Thack P 1.273 he heard it openly talked of in the Club by So and so and T'other who were present at the business | Pinero B 210 t'other side of the Channel.

Note the Sc: Scott A 1.147 the ghaist gae Rab a kick wi' the tae foot, and a kick wi' the tother.

12.2₄. The indefinite article has two forms: [ən] before a vowel, and [ə] before a consonant. Both are continuations of OE *ān*, on the later forms of which see vol I 11.21 and below, 17.1₃ ff.

We have *a* regularly before such words as *man, hair, ewer, university;* an before e. g. *heir, M. P.*, etc.

A is pronounced [ei], not only when emphatic in contrast (above, 12.2₂), but also now and then in England and very frequently in U. S.

12.2₅. Before *h* matters are not quite simple. Chaucer and Caxton have *an* not only before a vowel, but also before *h* (similarly *mine*), and remnants of this practice are found much later, though not carried through as in these writers. Marlowe has *an* before *hart, herd, hundred,* Cooper Dict. before *high, hill, hole, holy, horrible;* Sh often has examples like *an hair, an happy end, an hospital, an household, an hundred;* Bacon *an halfe, an heavenly.* In the AV Dawson has shown that the translators, wherever they follow Tyndale, preserved his *an* before *h*, but otherwise wrote *a*. Ford has *an high, an harbinger,* Milton *an host,* Bunyan *an* before *hair hard, hedge, helmet, help, high, hungry,* etc, Defoe before *half, horn,* Addison before *heart, heathen,* Swift before *harbour, harmless,* Smollett before *hackney, hale, hammock,* Goldsmith before *halfpenny, harvest, horse, house,* *husband*, and Sterne has *an Hobby-Horse* (also *a H.*) and *an high*.

An hundred is especially tenacious; I have found it in Defoe, Swift, Addison, Sam. Johnson, Smollett, Goldsmith, Gibbon, Scott, and even towards the end of the 19th c. in a few Amr writers (Norris, Page); even Kipling P 124.

I subjoin some later examples of *an* before a pronounced *h* in stressed syllable: Burke Am 69 an House of Commons | Keats 5.75 an half-fledged brain | Byron DJ 16.29 an hair's breadth | Shelley 121 an home | Ruskin CWO 21 an hospital.

It is not to be wondered at that *an* is found frequently before those words (with *h* from French) in which the pronunciation without [h] was long prevalent: *humble* (Byron, Kingsley, Hazlitt, Browning, Collins), *herb* (Hawthorne), *hotel* (Di, Collins, Gissing, Black, Ridge, Jerome, Merriman, Wells, Bennett, Belloc, Chesterton, Galsw, Priestley, Hemingway, and others).

12.2₆. Before *h* in unstressed syllables, which is dropped even by the educated who otherwise do not drop their aitches (vol I 13.67), *an* must be said to be the all but universal rule; cf Ellis EEP IV 1137. A great many examples from modern authors have been collected by Louis N. Feipel in his paper *"A" and "An" before "H" and Certain Vowels*. AmSp IV 444 ff.

For some years I took the harmless trouble of noting down all the examples I came across of *an* before *h*, without the exact indication of the passages. But it must be confessed that I probably left out many of the instances I found in which *a* was used before *h*.

Examples: *habitual(ly)* (Austen, Keats, Mill, Shaw, Wells, Bennett; Twain, Hawthorne, James, Norris; but *a* in Thackeray). — *hallucinated* (Caine), *hallucination*

(Hardy, Shaw, London, Graves). — *Hannoverian* (Benson). — *harmonic* (Thackeray). — *harmonious* (Galsw). — *Harrovian* (Vachell). — *Hegelian* (Wells). — *hereditary* (Macaulay, Mill, Merriman, Wells; but *a h.* Macaulay, Lawrence; Hawthorne). — *hermaphrodite* (Darwin). — *heroic* (Sheridan, GE, Ruskin, Stevenson; Twain; but *a h.* Stevenson). — *historian* (Goldsm, Gibbon, Coleridge, McCarthy, Birrell). Graves IC has *an historian* p. 15, but *a historian* p. 19 and 494. — *historic(al)* (Gibbon, Lamb, McCarthy, Archer, Bennett, Wyld; Twain; but *a historical* Thackeray, Lang, Shaw, Lawrence, Maugham). — *homeric* (Priestley). — *horizon* (Gissing, Mackenzie). — *humiliating* (McKenna). — *hydrangic* (Galsw). — *hypothesis* (Brontë, Kittredge). — *hypothetical* (Mill). — *hysteric(al)* (Brontë, Kipling, Wells, Maugham).

On the use of *an* before *h* Fowler says (MEU: *a, an* 1.): "now that the h in such words is pronounced the distinction has become pedantic, & *a historical* should be said & written; similarly *an humble* is now meaningless & undesirable."

12.2₇. Before initial [ju], spelt *u* or *eu*, the rule is now to use the form *a*, but *an* is or was by no means rare, especially if [ju] is (was) weakly stressed. This may be due to the less marked consonantal character of the [j]-sound, but may partly be a survival of the practice before [u·] was diphthongized into [iu·, ju·]

I have noted *an* before *unanimous* (Goldsm, Macaulay, Mackenzie), *uniform* (Byron, Browning, Huxley), *union* (Sh, but also *a* in the Folio, Goldsm, Macaulay), *unique* (Brontë, Ruskin, Wilde, Galsw *a* and *an*, Stevenson *a*), *unison* (Ford), *unit* (Gibbon, Browning), *Unitarian* (Chesterton), *united* (Macaulay), *vnity, -tie* (Deloney, Puttenham), *universal* (Sh, Smollett, Gibbon,

Johnson, Shelley, Mill, Dickens, Macaulay; Swift *a* and *an*, Mi *a*), *University* (Smollett), *Vrinall* (Earle), *useful* (Sterne, Brontë, Macaulay), *useless* (Cowper, Mary Shelley, Dickens), *usurer* (Sh, AV, Byron), *usurper* (Sh, Macaulay, Henley), and *usual* (Fielding).

An before *eu*: *eunuch* (Sh, AV, Shelley), *European* (Gay, Defoe, Swift, Brontë, Kinglake, Macaulay, McCarthy), and *eucalyptus* (Galsw).

12.2₈. *Such an one* when found in the 19th c. may be due to unchanged literary tradition from the time when *one* had not developed the sound [w]. It is found in Cowper, Pater, Jerome, Kipling, Caine, Mason, sometimes with a tinge of contempt. Sh has not only *such a one* as a rule (but twice *such an one*), but also *never a one, not a one, many a one*.

The indefinite article is often written together with the sb in *awhile*, which is perhaps felt to be an adv like *aside*, etc. Cf below, 12.5₇.

Border Cases

12.3. As such we may denote those cases in which *the* and *a* are not completely 'articles' as used in the functions to be dealt with in the rest of this chapter, but retain much of the demonstrative and numerative quality inherent in *that* or *this* and *one*, respectively.

12.3₁. *The* is a weaker demonstrative in a series of temporal indications: I am (was) occupied for the moment (thus also for the day, for the time; at the time or moment, upon the instant) | NP 1934 Nearly all the characters [of "Ulysses"] are recognizable to anyone who knew the Dublin of the time | Sayers NT 17 Lord Peter will be staying the night.

Further: Lend you money? No, I shall do nothing of the kind | Mrs Browning A 187 she loved him ... as the sort of woman can.

Perhaps we may place here the Sc and Irish *the day* 'today', *the morn*, *the year*, which according to Joyce Ir 83 is a translation of Irish *andiu* (*an* is the def. article). *The day* is found in Scott A 1.327 and 2.31; cf further Stevenson C 139 I haenae seen nae horse the day | Cronin H 460 You're too early the day, Brodie | Strong B 134 Five weeks to the day from the Rowing, Hector was seated on the knoll || Scott A 1.132 ye wad maybe be rueing it the morn | Stevenson C 268 he micht come here the morn | id K 37 I'll tell ye the morn || Cronin H 24 You're lookin' a bit tired the night.

Cf also Sc *the now*, frequent in Barrie, also Stevenson C 229 adieu to your David-Balfourship for the now | Hewlett Q 117 Our affair the now is to get her fast wedded.

12.3₂. Numerical *a*, *an*.

Proverbs: a stitch in time saves nine | Bunyan P 23 a bird in the hand is worth two in the bush | Goldsm V 1.211 Acting was not learned in a day | Di H 194 Rome wasn't built in a day | id Do 77 we mustn't leave a stone unturned.

Set phrases: *at a word:* Ch MP 3.306 at oo word(e) | Ch B 428 Cbr MS at on word; Petw. at oon word; El. and Lansd. at o word(e); Heng. at a word. ModE always *at a word:* Sh Cor I. 3.122, Mi A 27, Defoe G 40 | *in a word:* Ford 196, Spectator 57, 147, Sterne 21, Di D, T 191, Ruskin S 1.4 | Tennyson 332 at a leap | Scott A 2.23 we should go in a body | Stevenson JHF 9 we went in a body to the bank | Hawthorne Sn 52 You perceive, at a glance, that this is ... | Bridges E 68 at a bound | at a blow.

A and *one* together: Sh Cor III. 1.215 Heare me one word, 'beseech you tribunes: heare me but a word | Thack N 364 She does not care a fig for him — not one fig | Meredith T 97 there is but a step to the realization of it. One step | Doyle S 6.106 I never said a word — never one word.

A contrasted with *two:* for a day or two = 'one or two days' | a mile or two | Defoe P 21 once in a day, or in two days.

To a man; cf ch V on Sex and Gender: Spectator 6 the Lacedæmonians rose up all to a man | Doyle S 1.31 so say the Serpentine mews, to a man | NP 1894 the younger generation are to a man evolutionists | NP: here are the Tories declaring to a man for Protection.

To with other words: Congreve 253 punctually at ten. To a minute, to a second | Swift J 396 not to come, which they have all resolved to a woman | Di Do 128 they all, to a boy, doated on Florence | Ruskin P 2.121 the people pious, learned, and busy, to a man, to a woman — to a boy, to a girl | Barrie MO 155 four shillings to a penny! | NP 1925 Lord Grey had held the post of Secretary of State for exactly eleven years to a day.

12.3₃. *A* = 'one and the same': Birds of a feather flock together | three at a time | Sh Ro II. 4.220 doth not Rosemarie and Romeo begin both with a letter? | Alls I. 3.244 he and his phisitions Are of a minde | Sheridan 214 we are of a mind once more | Ruskin P 3.74 we were all of a mind | Sh Hml V. 2.277 these foyles haue all a length | Tw II. 1.20 both borne in an houre | As I. 3.86 we rose at an instant | Lr I. 4.316 fiftie of my followers at a clap | Beaumont 232 two children at a birth | Bunyan P 222 the waters were all of a depth | Swift T 40 the coats were so nearly sown, you would swear they were all of a piece | Sterne 14 both of a piece | Pinero Iris 86 I know I'm cruel. But it's of a piece with the rest of my behaviour | Sheridan 200 a table d'hôte where no two guests are of a nation | Phillpotts M 37 they might have been near of an age.

[*The rest of the book written by Niels Haislund after Otto Jespersen's death, cf Preface*]

Prosiopesis

12.3₄. Above, 3.3, under the headline Abbreviated Sentences, there is a brief mention of what has elsewhere been termed prosiopesis (see *Language* 273, *PhilGr* 142, 310), i e. omission of the first part of a sentence. In 3.3₅ and 3.3₆ omission of *the* is briefly exemplified. It may not be out of place to offer some further remarks on this phenomenon as far as the articles are concerned.

A is dropped by prosiopesis e. g. in Di P 55 [A] Bottle of wine to the gentleman on the box | ib 191 [A] 'Queer sort of thing, this,' said Tom Smart | Wells K 380 [A] Penny for your thoughts, Artie | Priestley F 241 [A] Lot of damned nonsense talked and written about these islands. Life here's too slack. [The] French are too slack | King O 85 [a] hell of a lot of good he is to me now.

This is particularly frequent before *quarter* in *a quarter of an hour* (*mile*, etc), *a quarter before* or *past*, etc: Stevenson K 165 [A] Quarter of an hour later, Alan stopped | Jerome TB 72 [A] Quarter of a mile from the station I overtook George and Harris | Crofts Ch 184 [A] Quarter of an hour later they passed once more... | Waugh BM 91 [A] Quarter of a mile distant lay the low sea-front of Matodi || Jerome TB 188 [A] Quarter to eight | Priestley F 111 "What is it now?" said Mr.

Ramsbottom. "[A] Quarter-past nine" | Lehmann DA 353 [A] Quarter to five.

This use, no doubt also under the influence of *half* used without the indef. article, has led to omission of *a* before *quarter* within a sentence: Jerome T 49 It's [a] quarter to ten | Lawrence SL 162 you wouldn't have gone before [a] quarter-past ten | Galsw TL 55 I'll come along in about [a] quarter of an hour | id MW 68 it's only [a] quarter of a mile | Cronin H 56 Suddenly he observed that it was [a] quarter past eight | Waugh BM 199 for [a] quarter of an hour the place was in an uproar.

Often one or more words + *a* are dropped: Mackenzie C 192 [it is a] Shame after the glorious weather we've been having | Galsw SS 62 [it is a] pleasure to see you | Priestley F 241 [As a] Matter of fact, it's a pity... | Cole W 214 What's up? ... [There is a] Body over there.

Omission of *it's a* is frequent before *fact* and *pity*: Di P [Ch&H] 163 [It's a] Fact, my dear sir, fact | ib 302 "Fact, sir," said Mr. Weller | Fletcher CB 226 I nodded solemnly. "Fact." said I || Jerome TC 42 [It's a] Pity he's dead and can't thank you | Kipling DC 72 You've no imagination. — 'Pity you haven't a little | Myers M 111 Pity you didn't confide in Dolliver | Waugh BM 131 'Pity,' remarked Sir Samson Courteney.

12.3₅. *The* seems to be more frequently dropped by prosiopesis than *a:* Di P 130 [The] Coach is ready, sir | Jerome T [Brockhaus] 84 [The] Bank be blowed! What good was he at the bank? | Pennell L 68 [The] Weather is ghastly | ib 145 [The] Poor Woman was almost demented | Galsw Sw 99 [The] River's still high | Malloch in BDS 476 [The] Body lay here | ib 478 [The] Bird's flown, it seems.

Thus particularly with the following words:

Lord: Collins M 9 in search of Lord knows what, Lord knows where | Thomas Burke in BDS 333 We get our minds from lord-knows-where | Myers M 165 I may be all wrong. Lord knows, I hope I am. — Of course there is influence from *God knows* with zero.

fact: Fact is is very common (Twain, Matthews F 4, Wells, Galsw, Bennett, Maugham, Sayers, and many others).

question: Kipling S [MM] 48 But, look here — question is, are our characters good enough just now ...? | Connington TT 272 Question arose: Was there anyone else ...? | Crofts Ch 31 Question still is ...

thing: Myers M 64 Thing to do is find out | McClure DG 136 Thing that puzzled me was ... | King OR 38 Thing to do is inflate credit.

trouble is (various modern novels).

truth is: Osborne 204 all this is nothing to your Mares & truth is my deare I can give you but a slender accounte of them | Congreve OB 12 Truth on't is she fits his Temper best | Keats 4.18 and 4.20.

same: Beresford 1D 5 Same with Percival, I fancy | Walpole CN 23 No, not mad...Religious. — Same thing | Shaw TT 145 Same everywhere, I expect | Maugham AK 227 How old was he? — Same age as me | Maynard Smith F 498 Too much tummy, eh? Same here (*Same here* common).

The following examples of omission of *the* before *day* have not prosiopesis, but may be due to analogy with *quarter past*, etc: OHenry Sixes and Sevens 208 Come back day after to-morrow | Lewis B 42 I had Allen up on the carpet day before yesterday | Loos GPB [T] 16 Mr. Eisman would not be in town until day after to-morrow | Allen A 17 not until day after to-morrow | Steinbeck LV 238 This [letter] was mailed day before yesterday.

Horwill MAU 96 says: "An Am. idiom is the omission of *the* before *day after, day before.*" — Cf below, 15.3$_9$.

Headlinese

12.3$_6$. "In headlinese the treatment of the article is arbitrary, i. e. a matter of mere typographical caprice", says Heinrich Straumann in *Newspaper Headlines* p. 51 (cf ib 35 and above, 3.6$_5$). This applies to both the definite and the indefinite article.

I shall give just a few examples of headlines from daily papers of 1947: Jews Likely To Reject New Plan | Labour Will Fail If Crisis Is Not Beaten | Breakdown Expected In Midlands | Ten Boys Charged With Murder Of Master | Palestine is Awaiting Next Move | Headmaster Killed = Felsted Head Dies After Road Crash | Long Time Before Demand Is Met | India Budget May Hasten Show-down.

This habit of concentration in headlines may give rise to ambiguity. Is the def. art. left out in the sentence "Poles Seeking British Trade"? Or is the sentence complete?

Such ambiguity is liable to occur in connexion with any plural or massword in a headline.

Syntax

12.4$_1$. Many functions have been attributed to the articles as essential ones, such as definiteness, determination, defining, familiarizing, concretizing, substantiation, realization, individualization, etc, see Christophersen, p. 50-51 (§ 20).

If Otto Jespersen had lived to finish the present chapter himself, he would probably more or less briefly have discussed the various theories. He has in fact nowhere else attempted any exhaustive discussion of the problem, thus neither in the *Philosophy of Grammar* nor in the *System of Grammar*.

In EEG he only offers a fairly traditional exposition of the theory of articles in English.

During his last illness he dictated a plan for the arrangement of the material to be discussed in the following chapters according to a "theory of stages of familiarity, i. e. knowledge of what item of the class denoted by the word is meant in the case concerned."

He expressly stated that he wanted to lay special stress on this theory.

Stages of Familiarity

12.4₂. Stage I. Complete unfamiliarity (or ignorance).

(1) Unit-word: indefinite article: an apple.

(2) Mass-word: zero: he drinks milk every morning (quantity left indefinite).

(3) Unit-word plural: zero: he eats apples every morning.

12.4₃. Stage II. Nearly complete familiarity. The word in question still requires *the*.

The necessary determination given

(1) either by the context: Once there lived an old tailor in the village. The tailor was generally known in the village as the crook.

(2) or by the whole situation: the government [of the time, of the country concerned] | The King is dead — long live the King! | the school [i. e. that one to which he was sent] was an old and famous one | the sun [that one among many suns of which it is most natural to speak] | the devil.

12.4₄. Stage III. Familiarity so complete that no

article (determinative) is needed. The most important classes:

(1) direct address (vocative): God, forgive us our sins | come along, boy, but quick | what do you say to this, doctor?, etc.

(2) proper name (cf below).

(3) God,

(4) father, uncle, baby, nurse, and other members of the family circle,

(5) dinner and other regular meals,

(6) church, prison, town, etc (chiefly in prepositional phrases denoting "professional tours," — further *go to college, to sea*, etc).

A separate section is to be given to proper names. "Uniques" not separately treated.

[Unfortunately I had no opportunity of discussing the theory of stages of familiarity with Professor Jespersen in detail, especially as distinct from other theories of the articles. As I have undertaken to treat the subject according to the plan sketched above, which indeed offers a workable basis and frame for treatment of the subject and involves new points of view, I shall leave out any discussion of the theory of articles in general. But within the various sections I shall of course have to offer general remarks again and again. N. H.]

Stage I
Complete Unfamiliarity (or Ignorance)
(1) The Indefinite Article

12.5₁. The indefinite article may be used to modify all kinds of sbs (and some words belonging to other parts of speech), i. e. to indicate that the word it precedes denotes an individual member of a class. Many words refer to something naturally conceived as such, while others denote something naturally thought of as an unlimited mass or quantity, and hence grammarians formerly divided concrete common names into class-nouns and material nouns (the former group being subdivided into individual and collective nouns, thus Sweet NEG § 150). Besides concrete nouns a group of abstract nouns was set up, a distinction, which, however, is linguistically irrelevant.

It is Otto Jespersen's merit that he included "abstract nouns" in the group of mass-words (most of them he also characterized as nexus-words). The modern grammarian holds that the existing substantive-forms may function now as unit-words (countables), now as mass-words (uncountables), and hence a word (i. e. a word-form) cannot once for all be reckoned as belonging to any of the two groups. The meaning of a word preceded by the indefinite article is different from that of a word with the zero article. In other words, a difference on the plane of expression is accompanied by a difference on the plane of contents.

12.5₂. According to the above definition of familiarity as "knowledge of what item of the class denoted by the word is meant in the case concerned" all combinations of the indefinite article *a* with some word or word-group must belong to Stage I.

A denotes one member of the class or species concerned, but it does not indicate which member. It specifies the class, while *one* (as a numeral) denotes quantity (number). — Cf below, 17.1₃.

Compare the following two sentences:

(1) There came a soldier marching along the high road (Hans Andersen, The Tinder Box);

(2) There came one soldier marching along the high road.

In (1) we are referred to the class of soldiers and told something about a member of this class, we do not know which.

Thus also in (2), only that here the number of members in question is emphasized (not two or more).

Compare, further, the following two pairs of questions and answers:

(1) Can a boy carry that plank? — No, but a man can.
(2) Can one boy carry that plank? — No, but two boys can.

In (1) the article (unstressed) is retained, while another substantive (stressed) is substituted in the answer. In (2) the numeral, which is stressed, is replaced by another (stressed) numeral.

12.5₃. The term "indefinite article" is not very felicitous, as this article actually refers to a definite item, even if it is not made known which member of the class is mentioned. The indefinite article thus is different from *any*, which does not refer to a definite item (known or unknown), but to some one among all items within its class, no matter which.

Compare the following questions and answers:

(1) Can a boy do that? No, but a man can.
(2) Can any boy do that? No, but some boys can.
(See further *any* below, 17.5₃ ff.).

Finally we shall mention the difference between *a* (*an*) and *some*.

The difference has been explained as follows by Professor Collinson in *Indication* (Lang. Monogr. No. 17) p. 30: "In reply to the question 'Which (boy)?' we may not have a particular boy in mind, but we are anxious to secure one — and we do not mind whom — provided that he is such as to fulfil certain conditions. We are not indicating on the ground of the known qualities as when we said '*a* negro'. We are laying down a condition for indication and it is possible that no member of the set fulfils it. Thus we may ask that *someone* be indicated within the set 'who has had experience' or '*someone* not too old', or restricting the possibilities still further: '*some* negro who has had experience'. It is for the moment immaterial that in English we can use 'the classifying indefinite' *a* and say '*an* experienced negro'. The point is that when in the given set we said '*a* negro' we knew that negroes were included in the set, but we may not know whether any negro who is experienced is included in it. We will call an indicater like *some* as used above a 'conditional (or contingent) indefinite indicater', which may be defined as an expression which indefinitely indicates an item or items in a given plurality by reference to a condition. — The condition need not be explicitly stated...."

On *some* see further below, 17.6$_1$. The essential thing is here that *a* is classifying, which *some* is not, e.g. Day, Life with Father 140 She could make him an offer, surely, *some* offer; let it be what it might.

In what follows I shall give examples of the use of *a* in the context and of its use with some semantic groups of words.

Meaning of Substantives with the Indefinite Article

12.5₄. In the above illustrative sentences we may distinguish various shades of meaning of the sb with the indefinite article.

These shades naturally fall into three groups:

(1) The sb refers to one definite, though unknown, member of a class, as in: I met a man in the street yesterday.

The so-called introductory use, which has been given

great prominence in many grammatical works, I consider as a secondary function: NP 1929 A day or two ago I had a letter from McLaren. ... When I read the letter to Her whom I honour and obey, she said, "Poor darling angel!" | ib. "I'll write a cheque." "There is no hurry," he said, "take a day to think over it." "All right," I said, "I'll write the cheque to-morrow".

Here the sb, after being introduced by means of the indefinite article, is taken to denote something familiar, and hence in what follows it takes the definite article or a definite pronoun (There came a soldier marching along the high road — *right, left! right, left!* He had his knapsack on his back ...). The essential thing, however, seems to be the degree of concreteness and individuality of the meaning of the word in question.

A in Book-Titles

A book is often introduced to its readers by a title with *a:* A Study in Scarlet (Doyle) | A Diversity of Creatures (Kipling) | A Family Man (Galsw) | A Motley (id) | An American Tragedy (Dreiser), etc.

This especially applies to scientific and educational works, manuals, readers, etc: A Classical Dictionary of the Vulgar Tongue (Grose) | A Practical Study of Languages (Sweet) | A History of Our Own Times (McCarthy) | A New English Dictionary | An Advanced English Syntax (Onions) | A Modern English Grammar | A Course of Book-keeping | A Primer of Foreign Exchange, etc.

If the title of a book is (considered as) familiar to the reader or listener, the *a* is often replaced by *the* (cf Conflict between Articles below, 12.9$_1$), e. g. Collinson, Indication 15 the author found especially useful the [*A*] *New English Dictionary* | Sweet, Coll. Papers 367 note

2 In the [*A*] *Handbook of Phonetics* I have assumed (*i*) and (*y*) as the sounds.

A genitive similarly suppresses *a*, e. g. Partridge Slang 43 Harman's Caveat for Common Cursetours [A Caueat ..] | ib 75 Grose's [A] Classical Dictionary of the Vulgar Tongue.

Other Uses of *A*

12.5₅. (2) the sb vaguely refers to a member of a class especially indicating the typical qualities of the person or thing in question: Hughes T 2.1 he had never spent an autumn away from school till now | Ruskin F 27 You think that there ought to be no such differences in habitation: that nobody should live in a palace, and nobody under a heap of turf? | Mackenzie C 44 She had never yet been inside a theatre | Kipling K 33 Kim was the one soul in the world who had never told him a lie | Hammett Th 16 [He] Usually needs a haircut | NP 1933 The very thought of going in a boat made him sick.

Predicatives belong to this group. In relation to the subject the predicative has a more comprehensive (general) character (cf *System of Grammar* p. 21 ff. = *Linguistica* p. 320 ff.), the typical qualities of the class in which the subject is to be ranged being emphasized. Note that a substantival predicative may often, without this making much difference in sense, be replaced by an adjective: He is a fool : he is foolish. — Examples: Ruskin F 7 Every man's heart on sea and shore says that — if he isn't at heart a rascal | ib 20 I beheld, and, lo, the fruitful place was a wilderness | Cambr St 81 We voted that Hayling must be a fool | Mackenzie C 29 However on earth can you be a boy when you've been made a girl? | NP 1930

King Edward [VII.] was simply a Tory | NP 1933 That she was a lady all might know by the way she held her little bag when she went to church.

Here also belong appositives with the indefinite article: Introd. to Chatterton, Poet. Works 9-10 There must also be noted his acquaintance with Mr. Barret, a surgeon and antiquarian.

It seems impossible to draw a fixed line between (2) and (3).

12.5₆. (3) This is often called the generic use of the indefinite article, but perhaps it would be best to reserve the term *generic* for the use with the definite and zero articles. With *a* the sb refers to all members (or any member) of the class or species it denotes, but only as a representative of the members. It does not denote the class or species in itself. I propose the term *all-representative use*. The meaning of *a* here approaches that of *any*.

Examples: Shelley PW 1.285 A man has a right to think as his reason directs | ib 287 A Christian, a Deist, a Turk, and a Jew, have equal rights: they are men and brethren | Quincey [World's Class.] 98 no person whatever answering to the idea of a Philistine | Ruskin F 8 A fool, or a corpse, can do any quantity of mischief | Carroll A 34 You're enough to try the patience of an oyster! | ib 67 "To begin with," said the Cat, "a dog's not mad" | ib. a dog growls when it's angry | Stevenson K [T] 241 But Robin .. struck into the slow measure of a pibroch | Rose Macaulay T 169 A crowd is queer | Mason Ch 8 he had the strong teeth of a rodent | Shaw in NP 1934 I hate a fool | id TT 257 it's no use giving tracts to a missionary.

This use of *a* is frequently found in dictionary definitions, where it was formerly the rule: Grose: *Con-*

venient. A mistress... *Coquet.* A jilt. *Corinth.* A bawdy-house | Slang Dic. (Hotten): *Blower*, a girl... *Bob*, a shilling | Annandale: *Daggle-tail.* A slattern... *Dastard.* A coward; a poltroon | Bowen, Sea Slang: *Jinny Spinner.* A cockroach... *Mudhook.* An anchor | Ruskin F 8 Clava means a club. Clavis, a key. Clavus, a nail, or a rudder.

Here also belongs the use in comparisons, as in Carroll A 16 I must be shutting up like a telescope | ib 42 something comes at me like a Jack-in-the box and up I goes like a sky-rocket! | Kipling K 17 Kim followed like a shadow | ib 33 Kim could lie like an Oriental Mackenzie C 255 "I don't think it's much else, I don't," said Elsie. "How like a girl. How exactly like every other girl."

Also in a number of more or less established comparisons such as: as sound as a bell | as jumpy (or nervous) as a cat | as bald (or mad) as a coot | as straight (or square) as a die | drink like a fish | as close as an oyster (or a clam) | as proud as a peacock | as plain as a pikestaff, etc.

Distributive A

12.5₇. *A* is occasionally used distributively, with the meaning 'each', as in "sixpence a pound," etc. This *a* was orignally the preposition *an, on* as used before words denoting time, e. g. "once a day", and then was extended to words denoting weights and measure, etc. The connexion between prep. and sb was felt as being pretty close. Cf the fact that *a* sometimes was merged with the sb, as in *abed, aback, afoot*, etc, and this close connexion of the distributive *a* with the following sb formerly was sometimes indicated by a hyphen: Quincey [World's Class.] 128 About half-a-guinea a-day

| ib 116 five shillings a-mile | Di P [Ch&H] 151 a shilling a-piece | Gaskell Cranford 78 three times a-week | Carlyle FR 343 some three gold louis a-man.

The fact that the distributive *a* is now generally interpreted as the indefinite article appears from the occasional use of a prep. before it as in Sh LLL I. 1.36 But there are other strickt obseruances: ... one day in a weeke to touch no foode | Sterne M 1.26 the brisk gale of his spirits ... ran him foul ten times in a day | NP 1925 A joke to a paragraph appears to be his motto.

Ordinary examples: Greene J4 389 A smile a day, is all I will require | Goldsm V 294 easy journies of ten miles a day | Carlyle P 157 selling manufactured cotton at a farthing an ell cheaper than any other people | Tennyson 246 Love will come but once a life | Jerome T 40 the cheeses had cost him eight-and-sixpence a pound | Locke GS 163 [a car] would do its fifty miles a gallon | Shaw TT 271 These pirates think nothing of extorting a million an acre for land in the city. — See more examples above, 8.9$_8$.

Cf distributive use of *the* below, 14.5.

The Indefinite Article before Words Generally Used as Proper Names

12.5₈. *A*, as said above, denotes an indefinite member of a class. Therefore, if we find the indefinite article before a word ordinarily used as a proper name, this must have lost its function as a mere non-denotative label of some individual (person or thing), and must have acquired some class-noun quality.

Often such a word is used with the indefinite article to denote a member of a class of which the bearer of the name is a typical representative, e. g. Sh Merch

IV. 1.223 A Daniel [i. e. a just and wise judge] come to iudgement, yea a Daniel [stock example of English grammars!] | Wordsw 17 An Orpheus! An Orpheus! ... | Benson Daisy's Aunt [Nelson] 17 Daisy ... was a George Washington for truth | Galsw Sw 5 I wish we had a Mussolini | A Huxley Little Mexican 316 He was not a Mozart.

Sometimes the word may refer to the bearer of the name himself, but then with special reference to his characteristic qualities: Pater R 189 When professional education confers nothing but irritation on a Schiller, no one ought to be surprised; for Schiller, and such as he, are primarily spiritual adventurers | Belloc Em. Barden 15 the infamous shorthand notes of a Pepys | Hadow Chaucer 201 when he lives at a court like that of Edward III and is intimate with a John of Gaunt | Jeans MU 30 The mind of a Newton, a Bach, or a Michelangelo, it was said, differed only in complexity from a printing press, a whistle or a steam saw.

We frequently find *a* before a family-name to denote a member of a family: Lamb E [World's Class]. 107 My grandmother was a Bruton, married to a Field | Gaskell Cranford 95 she was born a Tyrrell .. | Smith Cowper 2 His mother was a Donne.

The family name is often supposed to indicate something excellent, thus in Wordsw 54 above the Board Where sits in state our rightful Lord, A Clifford to his own restored! | Stevenson New Arab. Nights 120 by that action she did as much as anybody could to derogate from her position; but to me she is still a Pendragon | Bentley TI 7 he ... had married a Schuyler. Trent, though not sure what a Schuyler was, gathered that it was an excellent thing to marry.

12.5₉. Finally we may find *a* before a proper name

preceded by a title of some sort, which gives the combination the character of an appellative. *A* might here be replaced by *a certain*. *A Mr. Smith* means 'a certain person (presumedly unknown to the hearer), namely Mr. Smith,' and *a certain* is 'an allusive indicater' (Collinson, *Indication* p. 29). Examples: Broughton Rem. 1.117 On board also was with us a Captain Milnes | Byron Corresp. 2.54 Two years ago a Mr. Wilson offered eighty thousand pounds for Newstead | Sackville West E 248 "A Mrs. Spedding," they said; "wife of a doctor" | NP 1935 The owner of the yacht, said to be a Mr. Hicks, was one of the victims.

As a transition to the following group we may consider actors' parts, as in Lamb E 189 Few now remember Dodd. What an Aguecheek the stage lost in him!

Many unit-words denoting "things" are often primarily proper names (personal and place-names), e. g. names of products of various kinds, of works of art, of units of measure as used in physics, etc, also some names of animals and plants. This use may be due to ellipsis, as in *gladstone* for *Gladstone bag*, but this is not the commoner group.

On Jespersen's view of proper names and their transition to common names see PhilGr p. 64 ff.

12.5$_{10}$. A few examples of the use of *a* before thing-words derived from proper names will suffice:

(1) Books named by their author, and of works named by the artist: Lamb E 223 To expect a Steele or a Farquhar, and find — Adam Smith | ib. A Shakespeare or a Milton (unless the first editions), it were mere foppery to trick out in gay apparel || Wilde In [Brockhaus] 35 It was very second-rate Turner, a Turner of a bad period | ib. A false Vautrin might be delightful. A doubtful Cuyp is unbearable.

(2) Names of works of art named by the person they represent: Ch A 115 A Cristofre on his brest of silver shene | Lamb E 310 a Polypheme, by Poussin | Browning 1.522 I painted a Saint Laurence six months since.

(3) Various: a Ford (car) | a tilbury (gig) | a landau (carriage) | an albert (chain) | a watt, an ampere (units of measure) | a jenny (ass) | a victoria (plum) | Goldsm V 1.161 drest in a green joseph, — and many others. — See E. G. Withycombe, *The Oxford Dictionary of English Christian Names* (1945) pp. 131-36: Some Common Words Derived from Christian Names.

In many of the words in Group 3 the transition from proper name to common name is complete, the sense of the origin of the word being lost.

Indefinite Article with Quantifiers

12.5₁₁. Some quantifiers are often found in connexion with the indefinite article, thus *many*, *few*, *little*, and cardinal numbers.

Few

Few preceded by the indefinite article and followed by a plural substantive or used in absolute position is recorded from ME, and has several functions in common with ordinary substantives, thus it may take adjectival adjuncts: *a good few*, etc. See examples vol II. 4.972.

Examples with *a few* used absolutely: Sh Alls I. 1.73 Loue all, trust a few, Doe wrong to none | Swift (NED) Party is the madness of many, for the gain of a few | Morley (NED) A level which had ... been reached only by a few.

According to Fowler MEU s. v. *a, an* 2. *a good few* is now illiterate or facetious or colloquial; *a very few* is permissible. S. v. *few* he brands *a comparatively few* as an "ugly combination".

Many

Many before a sb in Early English was used with zero, cf vol II 2.73. The latest example in NED with this construction is from 1583. Note also Sh H6B II. 1.93 And many time and oft my selfe haue heard a Voyce.

In PE *many* always precedes *a* before a sg sb (with or without a qualifying adj). The first example in NED of this construction is from Layamon, cf vol II 2.73.

A few examples, especially from early texts: Ch A 212 He hadde maad ful many a marriage Of yonge wommen at his owene cost | ib 464 She hadde passed many a straunge strem | Skelton Magnyfycence 52 Lyberte makyth many a man blynde | Abr. and Isaak 6 many a þing made I for his ioy and daliaunce | Spenser FQ I. 1.1 The cruell markes of many' a bloudy fielde | Wordsw 6 And many a hill did Lucy climb | Keats 4.110 The leaves have been out here for many a day | Pater R 38 brought to Florence by many a needy Greek scholar | Lawrence SL 252 Many a sketch is dedicated to you.

Many is often redoubled, as in Sh John I. 183 But many a many foot of Land the worse — but especially in the form *many and many a:* Keats Endym. 1.49 Many and many a verse I hope to write | Crofts Cask 75 Many and many a thorny problem he had solved with far less to go on.

On *many a one* see vol II 2.73.

That *many a* before a sb is conceived as a unit seems to appear from the use of the definite determinative *this* before *many:* Hml III. 1.91 How does your Honor for this many a day ? | Byron Corresp 2.27 I am indebted to her for the pleasantest month I can reckon this many a day | Barrie MO 215 I've had it this many a year.

A many, which according to NED is not a development of the OE sb, but has developed spontaneously in Early ModE, was formerly ordinary English. Now it is considered vg, see vol II 4.971. The following use must be considered an archaism or provincialism: Tennyson 39 They have not shed a many tears | Barrie MO 204 There will be a many errands for her to run.

Now this substantival *many* in standard language is necessarily preceded by an adj (in connexion with *a* generally *great* or *good*); see vol II 4.971. It is hardly necessary to give any more examples here.

Little

In the sense of 'small quantity of' *little* takes the indefinite article before sg mass-words, cf vol II 2.71, 2.72, and 5.212.

Cardinals

12.5₁₂. A cardinal may denote a higher unit, i.e. a whole consisting of the number of units indicated by the numeral. In this sense cardinals are regular sbs, and hence may take all the three articles. Here belong the words *hundred, thousand, million*, etc, but also special uses as in *an eight* 'a crew of a rowing boat' (NED 1847 I rowed in a fairish 'eight'), *a four* 'a set of bridge-players' (Maugham AK 7 he ... asked me if I would make up a four), *an eleven* 'a 'side' in cricket or football', a Rugby *fifteen*, etc.

Other words denote things that have something to do with the number in question, e. g. *a four* 'a card with four pips', *a five* 'a five pound note', *a six* (in dicing, domino, cricket), etc. These likewise may take all the articles, though in some cases they chiefly occur in connexion with e. g. the definite article or zero.

This 'unification of plurals' is discussed in vol II 5.11 ff.

A special case is offered by *one*, which has developed its special function as a 'prop-word', see vol II ch 10, where a great many examples of *a* + an adj + *one* are given. We also find *a one*, see ib 10.57. To the examples given there a few may be added: Wells K 55 You *are* a one for being roundabout | Maugham FPS 74 I'm not much of a one for novels | id Pl 2.178 I'm not much of a one for talking, miss | Myers M 88 There isn't a one of 'em you can trust | Cabot Pebbles 219 she was a one for taxis, nearly as bad as Miss Diana | Sayers UD 56 "Go on! You are a one, aren't you?" said Parker, jeeringly | Lawrence SL 84 what a one he is!

On *a oner, a fiver, forty-niner*, etc, see vol VI 14.3_5.

Unification

12.6. In vol II Jespersen distinguished between *material* and *immaterial mass-words*, and the same distinction is utilized by Birger Palm in his paper *Obestämda artikeln vid ämnesnamn och abstrakta i engelskan* (Malmö 1916), but this is grammatically irrelevant, see below, 12.6_3. Some of Palm's differentiations, however, may be utilized in a classification of instances of unification.

A is frequently used to denote unification of something uncountable. The words in question are generally used as mass-words, cf vol II 5.211 ff. and below.

12.6₁. The indefinite article thus is found before

(1) Words denoting a unified or individualized part of something uncountable (*a piece of*, says Birger Palm). Instead of this type we often find phrases with *a piece* (*bit*, etc) *of*.

Examples: Bunyan P 32 it put me into an Agony | Browning 1.518 It's not your chance to have a bit of chalk, A wood-coal or the like? | Meredith Sel. Poems

104 Like a smoke melted thinner than air | Doyle S 330 A curry was exactly the medium which would disguise his taste | Galsw Forsyte Interludes 26 perhaps you could get a snooze | Maugham Alt 974 He was ready to do anyone a kindness | Lawrence SL 187 She had a fire in the parlour | Beat somebody to a jelly.

Here belong words denoting a spell or fit of illness or some bodily or mentally abnormal state, thus frequently the word *ache* and compounds with it: Galsw FCh 271 Soames watched it with an ache | Jerrold C 132 and you tell me there's nothing like being still for a headache | Stevenson N 323 swollen by a blow or a toothache | Ward M 82 I'll go and see if she has a headache | Caine C 299 her mother, whose weak heart and a headache kept her upstairs | Benson Da 65 I didn't like them to know I had a heartache.

Formerly words with *-ache* generally took the definite article; see below, 14.4$_6$.

Other examples: Sh H4A II. 3.9 'Tis dangerous to take a Colde [in Sh generally *catch cold*] | LLL IV. 3.95 a Feuer she Raignes in my bloud | Ado V. 4.97 I was told, you were in a consumption | Pope [Headline of an epitaph:] On Mrs. Corbet, who died of a Cancer in her Breast | Swift J 155 he [Mr. Prior] has generally a cough, which he only calls a cold | Johnson Lives [Morley] 133 He [Pope] had for at least five years been afflicted with an asthma ... Thomson declared his distemper to be a dropsy | Byron Corresp. 1.60 being partly confined with a cough | Jerrold C 19 the wet's sure to give me a cold | Sherwood Anderson WO 134 Her body shook as with a chill.

Professor Collinson distinguishes between *catch cold* 'incur a cold' and *catch a cold* 'catch it from somebody else'.

On *a pox* see vol II 5.76.

Various bodily or mental states: Skelton M 1617 I am all in a swete | Sh Hml II. 2.147 [He] Fell into a Sadnesse, then into a Fast, Thence to a Watch, thence into a Weaknesse, Thence to a Lightness, and by this declension Into the Madnesse whereon now he raues | Byron Corresp. 1.56 they are all ... in a pucker | Keats 5.132 my mind is in a tremble | Broughton Rem 1.2 Somerset, who was thrown into a fidget and a fright | Kipling S [M] 205 after a bit I got in no end of a bait | Galsw FCh 64 she was all of a flutter | Bentley O 65 he was in too much of a dither | RBennett P 79 Is he still in a paddy, then? | Lindsay CA 31 Don't put yourself in a lather now | Wodehouse, Code of the Woosters 104 she was a good deal stirred up — all of a doodah would perhaps express it better | go into a huddle.

Words denoting 'a portion of something uncountable' form a subdivision. Birger Palm treats these words as a special group, which seems uncalled for. The essential thing is that we have to do with a unified quantity of something. The words in question (exclusively?) denote portions of food and drink (including medicine) and 'beatings'.

A few examples: Sh All's II. 2.58 you would answere very well to a whipping if you were but bound too't | Mrs. Wood, The Channings (Palm) I got a caning from old Pye | Meredith E 312 He very properly received a wigging from Mr. Whitford, I have no doubt | Wilde, Lady Winderm. (Palm) Cecil, you'll have a whisky and soda | Boys' Stories 187 he just gave Bromfield minor a welting on his own and let it go at that | ib 516 I think a thrashing would do him good | Hammett Th 21 I shut off the radio and poured myself a cocktail | ib 167 Sit down and have a drink | (Palm) I have no objection to an ice | Will you have an aspirin? — Cf orders given at restaurants: a beer, a coffee (also, of course, with *one*).

12.6₂. (2) Words denoting 'a kind of something generally conceived as uncountable'. The indefinite article thus has a typical classifying function. This use when the word refers to something concrete (chemical substances) is mostly more or less technical. To most people *gas* is *gas*, i. e. 'gas for fuel or light', and there an end, but the chemist and other scientists naturally talk about *a gas* and *gases*, i. e. chemical substances, e. g. Jeans MU 28 Waterston, Maxwell and others had explained the properties of a gas as machine-like properties with great success | ib. When sound was transmitted through a gas ...

Other examples: Mi PL 1.650 Space may produce new worlds; whereof so rife There went a fame ['a rumour'] in Heaven that ... | Bunyan P (Palm) Unto each of these things a righteousness belongeth | Defoe R (Palm) The shore on that side being a soft oozy sand, almost like a quicksand | Swift PC 72 'Tis a Folly to cry for spilt Milk | Sheridan [World's Class.] 98 there is a beauty in Lauretta's simplicity | Sterne Sent. Journey [P] 115 I think there is a fatality in it | Di P [Ch&H] 277 his coming had evidently cast a damp upon the party | Stevenson T 252 I ... did not draw a breath till I was seated on the cross-trees | Meredith Sel. Poems 112 perceiving him weak Before Gods, and to shepherds a fear, A holiness ... | Lawrence SL 385 there was a hostility between them | Doren Swift 16 Swift's reading was always an experience | Brit. Encyc. (*s. v. alkali*) they turn litmus, reddened by an acid, into blue | (Palm) Green vitriol is a salt.

In some cases it may be difficult to decide whether the example in question belongs to (1) or (2), but it is evident that we have to do with unification.

Many words generally take no article when used without a determinative, but when such a word enters as primary in a junction, this frequently takes the indefinite (or the definite) article.

A case in point is the word *silence*, which often occurs with zero (and perhaps just as often with *a*), when used without any determinative, but if the word takes an adjective we practically always have the indefinite (or def.) article: Di P [Ch&H] 628 There was a short silence | OHenry B 653 Then there was a little silence | Sherriff J [Novel] 156 Soon a long silence fell | AHuxley EG 55 There was a long silence | Christie ABC 67 Another silence fell | the cliché: a silence which could be felt, etc.

The only examples I have noted of zero with adj before *silence* are: AHuxley BNW [Albatross] 115 there was absolute silence | OHenry B 639 And then during absolute silence, ... Sam tenderly and carefully tied his guitar across his saddle.

Other examples of *a* before unified words entering in various kinds of junctions: Milton SA 1724 ... what may quiet us in a death so noble | Congreve DD 197 'Tis only an inhancing the Price of the Commodity | Swift P 97 If you are sick, you shall have a Caudle of Calf's Eggs | Fielding JA 112 I am mightily deceived if this lady has not a violent desire to get your worship a good drubbing | Shelley 662 First there came down a thawing rain ... Then there steamed up a freezing dew | Dickinson MS 113 Well, that is a heresy of mine | Mason Ch 146 he nudged Mr. Ricardo in the ribs with his elbow, a familiarity which Ricardo had never found to his liking | Lindsay CA 38 No one bothered to question a rationality like that | Allen A 86 Opera was a pet aversion of the marquis' | AHuxley MC 89 Imagine a shyness more powerful than curiosity or desire, a paralysis of all the faculties.

Mass-Words

12.6₃. The term *mass-word* as used in grammar only refers to a certain function of substantives. A substantival form may function as a unit-word and as a mass-word, perhaps even as a proper name as well. Mass-words are formally characterized by the use of the zero and the definite article. They are distinguished from proper names by these (except in some specially defined cases) being unable to take any article, and from unit-words by these being unable to take zero, see the below diagram.

	Indef.	Def.	Zero
Unit-word	×	×	
Mass-word		×	×
Proper name			×

In vol II 5.211 the term *countables* is used about unit-words and *uncountables* about mass-words; and the various constructions with the latter are treated there as regards the category of number. In 5.212 it is stated that countables can be qualified by such words as *one, two, many, (a) few*, and uncountables by words like *much* and *(a) little*.

I should not, as in vol II 5.221, apply the name of massword (or mass-name) to *wine* in sentences like the following: *this wine* is different from the *one* we had yesterday | *many different wines* grow in France. — In both cases *wine* is a countable. By definition a mass-word = an uncountable cannot be put in the plural, a fact which does not exclude some vacillation in the construction of e. g. names of sciences, etc, in *-ics* (vol II 5.775) and other words (ib 5.7).

The distinction between material and immaterial mass-words (vol II) seems linguistically irrelevant. "Immaterial" mass-words take the same quantifiers as "material" ones, e.g. *much* (proverb: Much coin, much care), *a piece of* (a piece of bread : a piece of information), *a good deal of* (a good deal of money : a good deal of trouble), etc. They may leave the category of mass-words and take the plural form just as other mass-words (kindnesses).

Mass-words take either zero or the definite article. As unit-words may also take the definite article, we may come across instances in which it is difficult to decide whether we have to do with a unit-word or a mass-word. Such cases will be discussed in a later section. In this one we shall deal only with mass-words connected with the zero article.

Shades of Meaning of Mass-Words with the Zero Article

12.6₄. Mass-words connected with zero may denote

(1) an indefinite (undefined) quantity (part) of the 'thing-meant' (Christophersen p. 33 the *parti-generic sense*): Luke 22.19 And he took bread, and gave thanks, and brake it | Butler Er [Penguin] 48 Solitude had unmanned me already | Jerome T [Brockhaus] 205 Sailing is a thing that wants knowledge and practice too | Dickinson S [L 1915] 6 Cantiloupe at first objected

strongly, but yielded to pressure | Mason Ch 251 Darkness had hidden the slope of the garden | Huxley EG 77 Daylight shone pale between the curtains | Waugh W 38 There was rain in the wind | Borden AS 11 And since it is a game of continual risk, you must have nerve.

Note the difference between *he has nerve* 'he is courageous' and *he has a nerve* 'he has cheek enough' (hence: he has the nerve to come).

The same with junctions of various kinds: Sh Tw III. 4.61 Why this is verie Midsommer madnesse | Hml I. 1.9 Haue you had quiet Guard? | Walton A 49 I warrant it good meat | Fielding JA 97-98 the good humour which it indicates being often mistaken for good nature, and the vivacity for true understanding | Shelley 655 The snowdrop, and then the violet, Arose from the ground with warm rain wet, And their breath was mixed with fresh odour ... | Lamb E [World's Class.] 74 He is boy-rid, sick of perpetual boy | Carlyle H 19 Let us forget that it is erroneous Religion; let us look at it as old Thought | Burnett F 94 a rabbit ... scudded away with a twinkle of short white tail behind it | Maugham Alt 967 She had delicate health | Shaw TT 293 I am nigger. I am bad imitation of that eater of unclean foods.

12.6₅. (2) the whole genus (Christophersen: *totogeneric sense*). Statements with mass-words in this sense have a general character, hence they are particularly frequent in scientific, proverbial, and other abstract styles: AV Gen. 4.7 if thou doest not well, sinne lieth at the doore | Quincey [World's Class.] 130 No matter: won in whatsoever way, success *is* success | Di P [Ch&H] 590 What a rum thing Time is, ain't it, Neddy? | Browning 1.518 Take away love, and our earth is a tomb! | Wilde P [T] 19 Prosperity, pleasure and success, may be rough of grain and common of fibre | Shaw 1.126 Marriage suits a good many people | Jerome TB 207 instinct is liable to error | Dickinson S 52 government means compulsion, exclusion, distinction, separation; while anarchy is freedom, union and love | Maugham Pl 4.276 He knew I hated shop | id AK 115 Tact is the subterfuge the lax avail themselves of to avoid doing their duty | Brit. Enc. 2.420 Charcoal is a black, brittle, light, inodorous substance | ib 6.43 Hydrogen combines with some elements directly.

This type is very common in proverbs. I take a few at random from Everyman's *Dic. of Quotations and Proverbs:* Haste makes waste, and waste makes want, and want makes strife between the goodman and his wife | Might overcomes right | Mirth and motion prolong life | Money begets money | Necessity hath no law | Opportunity makes the thief.

And with junctions: Ch A 126 For Frensh of Paris was to hir unknowe | Sh Mids I. 1.134 The course of true loue neuer did run smooth | Wordsw 214 Plain living and high thinking are no more | Carlyle H 10 the best attitude for us ... is awe, devout prostration and humility of soul | ib 13 Worship of a Hero is transcendent admiration of a Great Man | ib 13 what therefore is loyalty proper ...? | Tennyson 49 simple faith [is more] than Norman blood | Lawrence SPW 44 Turkish rule was gendarme rule, and Turkish political theory as crude as its practice | AHuxley EG 140 Matter, analysed, consists of empty space and electric charges.

12.6₆. To these Christophersen p. 34 adds

(3) Nothing of the genus (*nulli-generic sense;* in negative sentences): I have not tasted food for three days | they never get rain in summer.

But it may be doubted if it is necessary to set up a nulli-generic group. In the above two sentences I should say that the words *food* and *rain* are used in a parti-generic sense, representing in thought some positive quantity, the existence of which then, it is true, is negatived by means of *not* and *never*. I am inclined to think that in most "nulli-generic" sentences we may rather speak of a parti-generic sense (rarely toto-generic).

Some forms because of their meaning are generally used as unit-words, but we may find contexts in which they are used both as unit-words and, in a shifted sense, as mass-words, generally in the parti-generic sense; e. g. Byron DJ 1.133 'Tis pity though, in this sublime world, that Pleasure's a sin, and sometimes sin a pleasure | Gore-Browne, Murder of an M.P. 16 When he [the artist] is a genius, he has the television of genius.

The sb preceded by a secondary: Ruskin F 94 A good law is one that holds ... a bad law is one that cannot hold ... Read your Carlyle ... and you will learn from him first, the eternity of good law, and ...

12.6₇. Names of diseases are generally considered as uncountables; see, however, plural names below, 12.6$_{11}$, and names with the indef. article (especially *-ache*) above, 12.6$_1$. In former times many names of diseases which are now generally used with zero, regularly took the def. article; see below, 14.4$_6$.

Learned names (of Greek and Latin origin) practically always take zero, thus many words in *-itis:* appendicitis, bronchitis, parotitis (Brit. Enc. 8.34 Epidemic parotitis is mumps). Further: anæmia, apoplexy, asthma, cancer (on *a cancer* see 12.6$_1$), catarrh, cholera (on *the cholera*, etc, see 14.4$_6$), colic, dysentery, elephantiasis, enteric, hydrophobia, hysteria (and the pl or sg *hysterics:* Sayers DC 88 had an attack of hysterics), influenza, leprosy, lumbago, neuralgia, neurasthenia, pleurisy, pneumonia, psittacosis, rheumatism (previously also *the rheumatism*), scarlatina, sciatica, silicosis, typhoid, typhus, and zymosis. I have quotations with this usage for practically all the words enumerated.

Many examples of more popular names of diseases might be given, e. g. of words in *-ache* (on *a headache*, etc, see 12.6_1). Further: blackwater, croup, 'flu, goitre, gout (formerly also *the gout*), heart-disease, -failure, -trouble (but: an affection of the heart, a heart malady), jaundice, scarlet-fever, small-pox, and summer-fag.

Plurals

12.6s. Plurals are semantically related to mass-words. Both of these in themselves denote an indefinite quantity, the difference being that mass-words denote uncountable, plurals countable quantities.

Plurals with the zero article belong to Stage One, complete unfamiliarity: the number of items denoted by the plural word is left indefinite and thus there can be no "knowledge of what items of the class denoted by the word is meant" (above, 12.4_1).

The use of plurals may be divided into toto-generic and parti-generic use like the use of mass-words. Cf above and Christophersen 35 f., where it is said that "interest centres round the generic qualities; hence the indefiniteness of the quantitative delimitation."

The term toto-generic in connexion with plurals should not be taken to mean 'denoting the genus' in a strict sense such as the sg with the def. article; see below, 14.3. The plural has rather a general than a generic sense. It rather denotes all members of the genus than the genus as a whole.

The toto-generic sense of plurals is generally found

in scientific and literary (often proverbial) statements.

Examples of the toto-generic use, various groups being kept apart both here and with examples of the parti-generic use:

Marlowe Jew 457 For euils are apt to happen euery day | Sh Ado II. 3.65 Men were deceiuers euer | ib III. 5.19 Comparisons are odorous | Merch I. 3.22 ships are but boards, Saylers but men, there be land rats, and water rats, water theues and land theues, I meane Pyrats, and then there is the perill of waters, windes, and rocks | Tp IV. 1.156 we are such stuffe As dreames are made on | Mi PL 1.423 For Spirits, when they please, can either sex assume, or both | Byron Ch 1.9 Maidens, like moths, are ever caught by glare, And Mammon wins his way where Seraphs might despair | Shelley 480 As long as skies are blue, and fields are green, Evening must usher night | Galsw SS 272 counsel, parsons, policemen, they all suffer from it | Chesterton Ch 31 Theories soon grow stale | Shaw TT 103 fathers are not so easily killed | Brit. Enc. 7.365 Many mammals also are nest-builders, notably mice, moles, dormice, squirrels, foxes, weasels, badgers, rabbits, etc. || Proverbs (from Everyman's Dic. of Quotations and Proverbs): Affirmations are apter to be believed than negations | Beggars must not be choosers | Children are poor men's riches | Wishers and woulders are never good householders, etc.

Examples of toto-generic use of junctions with plural primaries and secondaries of various kinds (adjs, clauses, prepositional phrases, etc):

ShHml III. 1.101 Rich gifts wax poore, when guiers proue vnkinde | Byron Ch 3.42 quiet to quick bosoms is a hell | Carlyle H 180 Men of letters are a perpetual Priesthood | AHuxley, Antic Hay 206 fish suppers will make a man hop like a flea | Russell, Sceptical Essays 105 since I came to know China, I have regarded laziness as one of the best qualities of which men in the mass are capable | Jeans MU 20 Radio-activity provides a third instance, being confined ... to atoms having from 83 to 92 electrons | Brit. Enc. 7.362 Impressions (or stimuli) conveyed to the central nervous system ... give rise to sensations of smell, taste, touch, or sight, etc. | Proverbs (from Everyman): Evil communications corrupt good manners | Fetters of gold are still fetters, and silken cords pinch | High-flying hawks are fit for princes, etc.

12.6₉. The parti-generic use is particularly found in ordinary narrative (oral or written statements): Mi PL 1.410 The flowery dale of Sibma clad with vines | Herrick: Gather ye rosebuds while ye may | Defoe R 152 I had Tortoise or Turtles enough | Di P [Ch&H] 162 Volumes could not have said more | Tennyson 304 Half the night I waste in sighs | Dickinson MS [1915] 7 Remenham has principles, and I have only prejudices | Strachey QV 15 Funds were lacking for the journey | Lawrence SL 242 *Why* can't you come with me to places? (cf the common American phrase *to go places* above, 8.6₆) | Pennell L 67 Aircraft are flying about | Advertisement: Businesses for Sale.

Examples of parti-generic use of junctions of plurals as primaries and secondaries of various kinds: Sh Mids II. 1.88 Therefore the Windes ... haue suck'd vp from the sea Contagious fogges | ib II. 1.110 An odorous Chaplet of sweet Sommer buds | Mcb I. 3.109 Why doe you dresse me in borrowed Robes? | ib I. 3.51 Good Sir, why doe you start, and seem to feare Things that doe sound so faire? | Mi PL 6.93 wont to meet So oft in festivals of joy and love Unanimous, as sons of one great Sire ... | ib 6.82 Bristled with upright beams innumerable Of rigid spears | Smollett R 49 a circle of peasants armed with pitchforks | ib 52 he enriched us with advices how to behave in the world | Shelley PW 1.242 this leads them ... to commit acts which justly excite displeasure | Ruskin F 46 so far as you have hearts capable of understanding them | GE A 244 That simple dancing of well-covered matrons ... that holiday sprightliness of portly husbands paying little compliments to their wives | Kipling K 215 he wore Sahib's clothes | ib 212 a collection of Tibetan devil-dance masks | ib 216 dull copper incense-burners neither Chinese nor Persian ... | AHuxley EG 234 there were uncomfortable silences.

12.6₁₀. Plurals are often found after a collective term, a quantifier, or the name of anything having component parts followed by *of* (cf NED *of* 22). In these cases I also interpret the plural as parti-generic, and *of* as generally meaning 'consisting of (some)', e. g. Mi PL 1.338 As when the potent rod Of Amram's son ... up called a pitchy cloud Of locusts | Adam Smith: A nation of shopkeepers | Shelley 205 a bare strand of hillocks | Byron Corresp 2.116 If Mr. Murray plays me those kind of tricks he will run himself into a puddle | Di P [Ch&H] 6 as if he were catalogued in some collection of rarities | ib 136 among a variety of papers | Jenkins B 24 a riot of antimacassars, stools, furniture, photograph-frames, pictures, ornaments ... | Forster P 166 Aziz paid a herd of natives to suffocate her in a cave | Nichols Twenty-five 192 an apparently inexhaustible stream of reminiscences.

This use is common with quantifiers such as *pair(s)*, *brace*, *dozen*, *score*, etc; see vol II 3.51 ff with examples, cf ib 4.73 *a pair of trousers*, etc, and 4.15 on the meaning of some plurals after *pair*.

We have also parti-generic use in some combinations

of vb and object, e. g. in set phrases like: make (or pull) faces | crack jokes | exchange greetings | draw lots | compare notes | throw stones | ask questions | cry quits | tell tales out of school | play ducks and drakes with.

12.6₁₁. Some names of diseases and bodily disorders occur in the plural only, among them some generally or occasionally used with zero. In scientific language and other references to the disease in general we have toto-generic use; when concrete cases are referred to, parti-generic use. I have noted such words as: collywobbles, hysterics, measles, megrims (generally, it seems, with *the;* NED: s. v. 4: The poor mare was suddenly seized with megrims, or mad staggers), mulligrubs (generally with *the*, NED one ex. with zero), mumps (according to NED now construed as sg), shingles, sniffles (Morley TL 141 And you've got sniffles already; NED: The sniffles).

Names of Languages

12.6₁₂. Names of languages generally have zero. This is due to their being considered mass-words, as in Ben Jonson's poem to the memory of Shakespeare: ... though thou hadst small Latine, and lesse Greeke | I have no Irish | he knows French: he knows a little French, — as well as the frequent quasi-tertiary use in *talk French*, etc. Thus also if the word is the subject of a sentence: Russian is not so very difficult after all.

The definite article, however, is found sometimes: Sh Merch I. 2.77 I haue a poore pennie-worth in the *English* (cf immediately before this: he hath neither Latine, French, nor Italian) | Byron Letters (Sel.) 35 I speak the Romaic, or modern Greek, tolerably. — If this has become the rule in speaking of translations *from the*

German, etc, the reason probably is the frequent addition as in *from the German of Goethe, from the French of George Sand*, where the *of*-group necessitates the article. — Cf also: What is the French for cauliflower?

A Scotchman may say: Have you the Gaelic?

Zero with Substantives in Certain Grammatical Functions

12.7. Substantives often have zero in the position as predicatives, objects, and regimens of prepositions, e. g. in many set phrases.

From the point of view of our theory of familiarity we may state the reason to be that in these cases the question of familiarity (which involves use of the definite article) is of no interest, the sb being used in a general sense without reference to a particular known individual or quantity.

The late Professor Brøndal in his work on the parts of speech (*Ordklasserne*, København 1928; with a summary in French of 50 pages) operated with the fundamental categories of substance, quality, quantity and relation; according to his definitions proper names denote pure substance, while sbs and adjs denote both substance and quality, the stress being laid on substance in sbs and on quality in adjs. In the above-mentioned cases the stress is shifted more towards quality in the sbs in question, and only substance requires the definite article (cf Christophersen's theory of substantiation).

Object with Zero

12.7₁. In combinations of a verb and its object with zero — frequently set phrases — there is a statement of unfamiliarity with some individual or quantity; or, if there is actually some familiarity with the individual or quantity in question, this is not expressed linguistically; the chief thing is a general reference to the quality of the individual or to an indefinite quantity.

It is worth noting that the vbs most frequently used in these combinations are such more less vaguely defined words (frequently in idiomatic phrases) as *do*, *get*, *have*, *keep*, *make*, and *take* (the last word being perhaps the most frequent vb in this connexion).

Examples (alphabetically according to the verbs).

(1) Mass-words used in a parti-generic sense: Benson D 33 Don't bear me malice | Sterne M 1.8 I ... must beg pardon for going on a little further (now with a possessive: I beg your pardon; cf also this example: Marlowe F 876 it may be some ghost ... come to begge a pardon of your holinesse) | break silence | break surface (about a submarine) | break cloud (aircraft) | change colour | declare war | do penance | give battle | Galsw WM 209 suddenly he gave chase | Di P [Ch&H] 494 I am proud of her. I have reason | lose patience, courage | Maugham A 477 he found it difficult to make conversation | make haste | put on flesh | Brontë V 24 I thought she ran risk of incurring such a ... repulse (now with *the*) | say truth (also: truth to tell, e.g. Ingoldsby 108 still, truth to tell, some of the old leaven was even yet supposed to be at work; but commonest with different word-order: to tell the truth) | screw up courage | take care | take counsel | Austen P 3 You take delight in vexing me | take heart | take hold (of) | take revenge | take silk | talk sense | Chesterton B 84 Browning could not merely talk art with artists — he could talk shop with them.

In connexion with *play* it depends on the character of the object whether we have zero or *the*. If the object denotes a game, we have zero: play football, cricket, chess (and pl: play billiards). — Note the idiomatic Amr phrase *play ball* 'cooperate': Maugham Razor's

Edge (Pocket) 176 She was prepared to play ball with him as long as it suited her convenience. — If the object denotes an instrument it takes *the* (see below, 14.3$_9$). On *play the fool* see below, 14.2$_1$.

We have zero with plurals as obj, denoting indefinite quantity or unknown number: Benson D 33 She never gave herself airs | Golding SD 19 They ... held hands for about an hour | shake hands | take orders.

Finally class-nouns, the quality of the individual denoted being emphasized, while familiarity with it is left out of consideration: BBC 16. 1.41 it became necessary to abandon ship | Sayers NT 125 [he] made a brutal attack on a warder and broke prison | cast (weigh) anchor | Stevenson K [T] 11 no man more plausibly conducted school | Scott Iv 61 he shall draw bowstring no more | Kipling PP 76 He turned and bade them hoist sail | Mi PL 5.395 A while discourse they hold | ib 5.733 To whom the Son ... Made answer | pitch camp | Wells V 77 he pulled rein at the sight of her | Selden T 54 Put case I bow to the Altar, why am I guilty of Idolatry? (obs., now with *the*) | Di D 101 when I set foot in the hall (hence: Bennett W 1.170 the dog had never put paw into that house) | Stevenson N 230 he never so much as showed face at a window | Broughton Reminiscences 1.132 They took boat at Cairo (also Strong B 285) | Locke CA 294 They took cab to the hotel | take horse (common; but literary; thus also *take ship* (common in early literature) and *take train* | Wordsw 58 He hath kenned them taking wing (also Southey L 185) | turn tail.

Zero with Predicatives

12.7$_2$. Predicatives have been dealt with at length in vol III chs 17 and 18. The question as to which verbs take a predicative, the distinctions between predicatives of being and becoming, and quasi-predicatives are discussed in detail and will not be considered here. Our subject is chiefly connected with that summarily treated in vol III 18.4—18.5 under the heading *What can be a Predicative?*, but reference will be made here and there to other sections, mainly for illustrative examples.

On the relation between subject and predicative see *PhilGr* p. 150 ff.

In general it may be said that in predicatives with zero prominence is given to the quality inherent in the sb in question, while familiarity and reference to a definite individual is left out of consideration, cf on objects with zero 12.7_1 and regimens of prepositions with zero 12.8_1. This tallies with the fact that adjectives, in which the element of quality is predominant, are very frequently used as predicatives. Sometimes it is difficult to decide whether the word in question is a sb or an adj, e. g. Bennett Acc 74 he'll be communist next | Barton & Sitwell 44 One of the disciples declared he would turn Unitarian.

Note also the frequent occurrence of advs to denote degree of quality in connexion with predicatives, as seen in examples of the types: I am not philosopher enough | I am more coxcomb than fool — vol III 18.4_4, and the following instances: Stevenson N 352 it was so dashing, so florid and so cavalier (cf ib 345 a white handkerchief cavalierly knotted at his neck) | Chesterton Di 68 As our world advances ... it becomes more specialist, less democratic | id B 120 Browning was never more thoroughly Browning than in this splendid and unselfish plagiarism | ib 150 the way in which Browning, when he was most Browning, regarded physical nature | AHuxley BL 75 "What an innocent!"

mocked Mrs. Aldwinkle, still very Congreve | Sayers HH 91 I'm glad they didn't make themselves too Lewis Carroll.

12.7₃. In the arrangement of the following examples we shall distinguish between predicatives denoting persons and predicatives denoting "things".

It is a well-known rule that a predicative denoting the holder of an office, a profession, etc, has the indefinite article if the position in question may be held by more than one person: He is a bishop (one among the class of bishops); but generally has zero if the position may be held by one person only: He is Bishop of Durham. (Also: He is the Bp. of D.).

But this only applies to names of persons. If the subject is a place-name the predicative takes the definite article: Paris is the capital of France.

The predicative with zero here forms a kind of framework to be filled out by the subject.

I shall first give a few examples of the indefinite article and zero used in close connexion: Sh R2 V. 5.32 Sometimes am I King [i. e. King of England]; Then treason makes me wish my self a beggar, And so I am. Then crushing penurie, Perswades me, I was better when a king | Butler W 1 Mr Pontifex was a carpenter by trade; he was also at one time parish clerk | NP 1919 I became a director. I became Managing Director | Maynard Smith F 52 a grocer in Cheapside, who made money and became Lord Mayor and a baronet.

When there is no reference to a definite office or position, we have the definite article: she was the widow of one John Simpson | he is the owner of several millions. See below, 13.1₂.

On "typical *the*" and some other cases of use of the definite article see below, 14.2.

Next, examples of single words with zero: Jerome TB 253 The man who bangs his perfectly finished glass upon the table first is victor | Caine D 24 Kerry, the midwife, who was nurse as well, carried the child to church | Burnett Fauntl 10 if the eldest son died the next one would be heir | Salt Joy 118 Never let a woman know she is top dog. They despise you for that | Walpole OL 22 she had acted hostess bravely | Sapper in BDS 15 his wife, who had been doing cook, was a rather timorous-looking little woman | Maugham F 16 He had office duties, he was judge and tax collector | Nicolson SP 234 The Colonel was doing host. For *go cabin-boy, stand sentinel*, etc, see vol III 17.2_2 and 17.4_2.

12.7₄. Examples of such predicatives followed by *of* are very frequent: Marlowe F 302 How comes it then that he is prince of diuels? | Sh H4A II. 4.10 though I be but Prince of Wales, yet I am the King of Curtesie | Mcb II. 3.2 If a man were porter of hell gate, hee should haue old turning the key | Swift 3.192 he appointed me master of the sloop ... although he were not commander of either ship | Goldsm 10 he was owner of the estate | Burns 3.272 The honest man, tho' e'er sae poor, Is king o' men for a' that | Cowper L 2.159 Our lacquey is also clerk of the parish | Jerrold C 123 I suppose I'm to be mistress of my own house? | London W 141 when Lip-lip was leader of the pack. But Lip-lip was no longer leader | Doyle Sh 5.234 In his view he should himself have been heir of all my estates | Galsw D 134 the meeting of which he had been witness | Strong B 174 You are head of the family | Cronin H 19 You're still top of the class, aren't ye?

Note Sh Tp I. 2.54 ff. Twelue yere since (Miranda) twelue yere since, Thy father was the Duke of Millaine and A prince of power. — Sir, are not you my father? — Thy mother was a peece of vertue, and She said thou wast my daughter; and thy father was Duke of Millaine.

Is this vacillation due solely to rhythmic reasons? If we had not the continuation in the former place "and a prince of power", we might here take *the Duke of Millaine* as the subject, and *thy father* as the predicative, but this seems now excluded.

Examples of predicatives followed by *to:* Sh. As I. 2.236 I would thou hadst beene son to some man else | ib II. 4.78 I am shepheard to another man | Ado V. 1.299 she alone is heire to both of vs | Tp V. 192 she is daughter to this Duke (frequent in Sh, see Sh-lex s. v. *to* 1237[b]) | Goldsm V 2.29 his guardians had bound him apprentice to an attorney | Hunt A 75 I never was fag to anybody | Kingsley Y 84 I am playing traitor to myself every hour in the day | Butler W 380 Joey was now ordained, and was curate to Theobald | id Er 121 rewarded for having been son to a millionaire ... having been the son of a rich father | Campbell Shl 118 Eliza, who had hitherto been Banker and General Manager to the household, seems now to have become also Head Nurse | Maxwell G 230 he had been godfather to their children | cf fall an easy prey to, fall heir to — vol III 18.2$_4$.

Predicatives with *in* (*into*): Ch A 314 Justice he was ful often in assise | Osborne 15 my Lord Lisle was to goe Ambassador into Sweden | Swift 3.3 I was surgeon successively in two ships | Di MutFr 37 He was clerk in the drug-house of Chicksey, V., & St. | Gissing H 36 Up to the age of five-and-twenty I was clerk in a drug warehouse | Tracy P 189 she was victor in a struggle of which she had not the slightest knowledge | Bennett ECh 291 He was senior warehouse-man in an earthenware manufactory | id P 194 He was master in his own house.

Other prepositions: Ch A 355 At sessiouns ther was he lord and sire | Goldsm V 2.3 my first scheme was to be usher at an academy | Trollope B 25 he became preacher at a new district church | Locke S 246 He was leading man at the theatre || Lawrence SL 144 She could not be princess by wealth or standing || Cowper L 2.207 before I commenced writer for the press | Lawrence SL 186 her husband, Baxter Dawes, was smith for the factory || Wilde P 26 I ceased to be lord over myself | Kipling S [MM] 246 his mother stood guard over him.

12.7₅. The secondary may also be an adj, as in the following established collocations: Caine P 110 he'll be best man (i. e. 'groomsman'; *he'll be the best man* would be taken in a non-technical sense) | Collins M 447 If an order comes to me, which is own brother to an order come from Bedlam, it don't matter (cf vol III 17.5₅: Wells F 141 he would have looked own brother to Mr. Kenna) | Sh H4A II. 4.7 I am sworn brother to a leash of drawers | Butler ER 250 I will be sworn brother to them.

Cf Congreve OB 113 Bluffe turns arrant traitor | Scott I 297 I will be true prisoner.

12.7₆. But we may also have zero with names of persons not denoting an only holder of an office, etc. This particularly applies to words denoting and emphasizing moral quality. See examples vol III 18.2₁ (he went Berserk; go Bolshevik), 18.2₅ (turn traitor), 18.2₈ (commence author), and the following: Sh Hml II. 2.599 Who calles me Villaine? | Congreve DD 155 I'd as lieve you call'd me Fool | Goldsm V. 2.4 What do you think of commencing author? | Byron L 25 I promise to turn Mussulman | Brontë W 97 What possessed him to turn listener? | O'Brien, Lord Russell 181 Afterwards Carey turned informer | Wells LL 285 She was drudge, she was toy | Mackenzie C 278 I've turned suffragette | Maugham A 772 He is god, he is devil | Wallace Green Archer passim: he is crook | Doren Swift 103 Swift would not admit that he was partisan | Mannin ChE 29 Marie was nineteen and virgin, but she was essentially woman | Beswick OD 21 Ensnared by rhythm she was no longer woman but automaton | ElSmith Tz 46 Now she was gypsy, pure gypsy.

12.7₇. As in other grammatical functions mass-words with zero denoting indefinite quantity are frequent as predicatives. A few examples will suffice: Ecclesiastes 1.2 Vanity of vanities, saith the Preacher, vanity of vanities; all is vanity | Locke D 223 Every caress I gave you would be sin | Birmingham IS 62 which makes me think that science is rather rot | Galsw MW 10 In a word, she was background. — Cf vol III 18.4₃.

This may also be found in sentences with words denoting persons as subjects. The predicative then denotes the sphere within which the person denoted by the subject belongs: Moore EW 151 another place that would have suited her was lost through answering that she was chapel | Maugham Pl 4.214 I'm labour | id FPS 213 she liked her servants to be Church of England | Connington TI 32 He was Science and I was Arts, so we didn't see much of each other.

Thus often with junctions of adjectives and ordinary masswords: Earle M 22 hee is best company with it when hee can but prattle | Mason R 112 He could be good company when he chose | Maugham FPS 195 he was a sportsman and he was good company | Meredith

E 546 Lady Busshe would have it was a screen, and she was deemed high wisdom | Birmingham IS 12 He ... decided that he was, if not an actual "bounder", at all events "bad form" | Porlock X 167 Nicholas looked polite inquiry.

Cf vol III 18.4$_3$ (He is great fun | he's very good company).

With non-personal subjects such junctions as predicatives are of course common. A few examples: Trollope B 149 it might be good policy | Swinburne L 209 it is poor comfort to reflect that ... | Carpenter D 47 Boating ... It was healthy exercise | Dickinson MS [1915] What the sword shall be called ... is small matter | Rose Macaulay T 7 I dare say it's low class | Lawrence SL 168 It was great excitement to Miriam to catch a train at Sethley Bridge.

12.7s. *Pity* as a predicative now takes the indefinite article, but formerly it was used with zero: Ch MP 3.1266 And pite were I shulde sterve, Sith that I wilned noon harm, y-wis | Lyly C 280 it is pitie | Sh Merch II. 2.209 No that were pittie (for more examples in Sh see Sh-lex) | John Ford [title of play:] 'Tis Pity she's a Whore | Eastw 438 tis pittie any trade should dull that quicke brain of yours (ib 480 it is great pity) | Smollett R 261 it was pity such idle disputes ... should create any misunderstanding ... | *it is pity* also Lyly C 280, Behn 312, Congreve 128, Farquhar B 358, Spectator 156, Defoe G 109, Richardson G 63, Cowper L 2.124.

Shame and some other words which now generally take the indefinite article in a predicative position, formerly frequently took zero: [Ch A 446 she was somdel deef, and that was scathe] | Ch A 503 And shame it is ... | Sh R2 II. 1.238 'tis shame such wrongs are borne | Scott I 391 It were shame to our profession were we to suffer it | Tennyson 260 She ... holds it sin and shame to draw The deepest measure from the chords || Sh Lr IV. 7.41 'Tis wonder that thy life ... Had not conluded all | R2 I. 4.20 He is our Cosin (Cosin) but 'tis doubt, When time shall call him home from banishment | Sterne M 1.9 My father ... was, I believe, one of the most regular men in everything he did, whether 'twas matter of business, or matter of amusement, that ever lived | Dickinson C 11 It is matter of life and death to you | Fielding 5.435 every syllable of what I have said is fact (cf Gissing R 189 it is plain fact that ...).

12.7₉. There are some cases in which the definite and indefinite article alternate with zero.

It is natural to have the indefinite article in the predicative: There was a time when ... | It is a fact that ... ; but when the same words are placed first we have *the:* The time was when ... | The fact is that ... (also extended, and then we clearly see the reason for the use of the definite article: The fact of the matter is that ..., i. e. the whole truth about that particular matter). But in the latter case we get through prosiopesis a third form beginning with *time* and *fact* (cf above, 12.3₄). Finally, the frequency of *The fact is* ... leads people to use the definite article also after *It is*.

Quotations for the various forms with *the* and zero are: Sh Alls IV. 4.5 Time was I did him a desired office | R2 III. 3.11 The time hath beene, Would you haue beene so briefe with him, he would Haue beene so brief with you | Di D 643 But the time was, when she believed in that man most entirely (also ib 631) | id T 1.246 Time was, when a poet sat upon a stool in a public place | Hardy W 65 Time had been when she would have shown disappointment at the loss | Caine E 170 Time was when nobody saw the corruptions || Macaulay E 1.5 The fact is, that common observers reason from the progress of the experimental science | Ruskin U 31 | Bennett W 1.92 The fact was that Mr. Baines had wakened up | Hope F 85 "Fact is, I don't show up over well". — "You don't: that is the fact" | id M 54 Fact is, I wanted him (also ib 104, Zangwill G 243, Bennett T 424) | Kipling [?] 193 Fact was, I'd heard the firing | Ridge L 289 Fact of it is, we're both beginning | Bennett A 49 it was the fact that at school all the boys had combined to tease him | id T 97 It was not the fact that she had often thought of the plan. But in her eagerness she imagined it to be the fact | id W 1.77 | Carpenter Civ 2 it seems to be the fact that we are actually less capable of taking care of ourselves than the animals are.

Time has zero when not referring to a definite period: as time went on, we became better acquainted | Time will show [here nearly generic].

But *the time* is used of the definite period of which we expect to hear: Sh Hml I. 5.189 The time is out of ioynt: Oh cursed spite, That euer I was borne to set it right | Di D 162 ... during the remaining term of our residence under the same roof; and I think we became fonder of one another as the time went on.

On *all the time* see below, 14.8$_6$.

12.7$_{10}$. Proper names in their full sense are not used as predicatives, but we may find sentences like the following, in which originally place-names are used in a derived sense as a kind of mass-words in which, as in other zero predicatives, their inherent quality is emphasized: Brooke SP [The Soldier] 75 If I should die, think only this of me: That there's some corner of a foreign field that is for ever England | Rose Macaulay I 62 Embittered by English injustice he had gone Highland, gone Hebrides, gone Skye.

Among predicatives we must reckon also instances like the following (on *as* with a predicative see vol 1V 23.1): McCarthy 2.245 the King of Denmark sat as Duke of Holstein in the old Germanic Diet | his power as President is practically unrestricted | Henry the Fifth, when Prince of Wales, was committed to prison for a gross contempt of court.

As we shall see (12.8_4 f.), fixed collocations of two words and enumerations have zero. Thus also when these are used as predicatives: He is hand and glove with my brother (e.g. Trollope B 19).

Zero in Prepositional Phrases

12.8₁. Zero is frequent in prepositional phrases. Many instances of this use call for no comment, because the sb would also in other positions in the sentence have zero, e.g. proper names in a wide sense (personal names and place-names): Brethren in Christ | pray to God | write to Peter | go up to London.

River-names, which normally have the definite article, have zero after a preposition in town or village names: Newcastle upon Tyne (cf below, 16.1_5).

Differently: Stow on the Wold | Moreton in the Marsh | Lee on the Solent.

Further we have zero in double expressions of the types *from end to end, from beginning to end, day by day*, etc; see below, 12.8_6.

In many *at*-phrases *at* is a development of *atte* from *at the*, thus *at last, at least*, see above, 12.2_1.

In a few cases such prepositional phrases even have developed into adverbs, e.g. *away, beside, indeed, today*, and others.

12.8₂. It is worth noting that the prepositions most frequently followed by zero are those oftenest used in a transferred, more abstract, non-local sense, thus *at, by, in, of, on,* and *to*.

I shall first give some examples of zero in connexion with these six prepositions, and then a group of examples with others.

At

With mass-words: have something at call | Spenser FQ I. 1.11 At length it brought them to a hollow caue | Sh LLL III. 1.124 I meane, setting thee at libertie | Smollett R 333 At sight of me she startled (very frequent) | Barrie MO 165 At thought of him her face would become almost hard | AHuxley CY 30 Parallel straight lines ... meet only at infinity.

Plurals: be out at elbows | Doyle B 178 Dr. Mortimer remained with him at cards | Galsw MW 171 some queer desire to be at grips with Life | be at loggerheads, at odds, at daggers drawn.

Class-nouns: at night (cf 15.3_7) | at school, at home, at court, at church (cf 15.2_3) | at dinner, at breakfast, at table (cf 15.2_1) | Sh Hml I. 1.9 I am sicke at heart | Lawrence SL 61 "Let him not be killed at pit," he prayed (institution, cf 15.2_3) | Chesterton B 15 The French Revolution was at root a thoroughly optimistic thing | Maugham MS 195 I was more at sea than ever.

By

Mass-words: Sh Tp I. 2.497 of a better nature (Sir) Then he appeares by speech | Mids I. 1.30 by Moone-light | by day, by night | by land, by sea, by air | Spectator 2 It is said he keeps himself a Batchelor by reason he was crossed in Love | Doyle B 181 he preferred to do good by stealth.

Class-nouns: Sh LLL III. 1.36 Negligent student, learne her by heart. — By heart, and in heart Boy. — And out of heart Master | Mi PL 4.867 and now by glimpse discern Ithuriel and Zephon | ib 9.420 By fountain or by shady rivulet He sought them both | by name | by steamer, by train | AHuxley CY 252 That is why I always travel by Tube, never by bus f I can possibly help it.

In

Mass-words: In time | in fact, in effect, in reality | in secret | The covetous man is always in want | Spenser FQ I. 1.27 His Ladie seeing all ... Approcht in hast | Sh LLL I. 1.11 Our late edict shall strongly stand in force | ib I. 1.54 I swore in iest | ib I. 2.60 I am in loue | Hml I. 2.232 A countenance more in sorrow then in anger | Galsw SS 76 I suppose you'll have no use for me in future | Crofts G 31 a very nice gentleman of whom she was somewhat in awe.

Plurals: Sheridan 24 I am not in spirits to be of such a party | Maugham Pl 3.141 I knew he had to be in chambers early.

Class-nouns: in court, in town (cf 15.2_3, 15.2_5) | Sh Hml I. 1.165 So haue I heard, and do in part beleeue it | Mi PL 9.494 So spake the Enemy of mankind, enclosed in serpent, inmate bad (but ib 10.3 He, in the Serpent, had perverted Eve) | Maugham F 19 when ... they are once again in harness.

Of

Mass-words: Abr. & Isaak 17 Isaac ful feyre of hewe | Sh LLL I. 1.148 We must of force dispence with this Decree | Jackson S 29 the modern reformer is of necessity an iconoclast first and a builder afterwards.

Plurals: Doyle S 442 The married officers live out of barracks | Woolf D 9 Evelyn was good deal out of sorts.

Class-nouns: laugh someone out of court | Sh LLL III. 1.192 A woman that is like a Germane Cloake ... euer out of frame | Di P [Ch&H] 591 he was leaning out of window (obsolete) | Dickinson MS [1915] 106 we are out of court | Maugham P 185 as though he had just jumped out of bed.

On

Mass-words: on land | set on fire | on purpose | on business | on arrival | Mi PL 11.850 The ark no more now floats, but seems on ground | Benson D 22 she had felt she was on trial.

Cf *afire, aground*, etc (see vol VI 27.3).

For *on -ing* see vol. IV 12.2, 12.3, 12.5.

Plural: be on tenterhooks.

Class-nouns: on hand | stand on end | set on edge | Ch A 271 hye on horse he sat | Doyle B 238 I must request you to walk on tiptoe | MacCoy N 121 Where's the Major? — On stage somewhere, I guess.

To

Mass-words: Skelton M 222 all men laugh at Lyberte to scorn | Sh Ant III. 2.55 he cried almost to roaring | Tp II. 2.158 I shall laugh my selfe to death | Gent III. 2.8 Dissolues to water | Oth II. 3.197 I am hurt to danger.

Plurals: go to pieces | set to rights (Sterne M 1.7).

Class-nouns: go to school, to church, to press (cf

15.2₃) | Sh LLL I. 2.163 thou shalt to prison | Hml I. 2.100 Take it to heart | Byron Ch 1.28 To horse! to horse! | Kipling MI 62 Now to hospital you go | Lawrence SL 201 Mrs. Morel went upstairs, and the three men came to table | Galsw Fors. Interludes 69 all had gone according to programme | according to plan.

Various Prepositions

12.8₃. Mass-words: across country | off colour (but: off his stroke) | Sherwood Anderson DL 41 when you caught them off guard (also: off his guard) | Goldsm V 193 I extolled her prudence, economy, and obedience till death.

Plurals: Burnett Fauntleroy 78 people were kept below decks | Earle M 42 The waiting women Spectators are ouer-eares in loue with him.

Class-nouns: go up (down) stream, up (down) hill | Maugham P 9 They know I always sleep after tiffin | Sherwood Anderson DL 73 Bruce Dudley had just come down river | Maugham F 16 was brought into court | Sherwood Anderson DL 108 he was a boy taking a trip up river with his father and mother | Mi PL 6.435 though pierced with wound | Di Do 257 You to marry a second time without family! You to marry without beauty! | Pennell L 54 Both letters were written late in September, but without date.

Here also belongs such frequent phrases as the following: at sight of | by way of | for fear of | in act to | in face of (Galsw TL 33 In face of these proffered allurements) | in order to | in place of (in lieu of) | on purpose to | on top of.

Zero in Enumerations and Pairs of Words

12.8₄. As in many other languages it is very frequent in English to use zero (generally instead of the definite article) with words found in pairs, often forming an antithesis. This use of zero is apt to lend a certain epigrammatical force to the phrase in question, while the element of familiarity inherent in the definite article and that of individuality or classification inherent in the indefinite article are left out of consideration.

A frequent type is a combination of two different words by means of a conjunction, *and, or, but*, etc.

Examples with *and:* Ch B 4292 And ship and man under water wente | Spenser FQ I. 1.2 Right faithfull true he was in deede and word | Earle M 22 he runnes wildly ouer hill and dale | Scott Iv 227 cup and horn was filled to the Norwegian | Di D 168 I can't be buyer and seller too | Stevenson M 74 for three days horse and foot, cannon and tumbril, drum and standard, kept pouring downward past the mill | Ward M 285 Kitty hurriedly gathered up gloves and fan | Wells V 92 Niece and aunt regarded each other | Shaw 1.79 unfortunate creatures that have hardly enough to keep body and soul together (common) | Bennett C 2.209 Brother and sister were at breakfast | McKenna M 18 twirling the stem of a wine-glass between thumb and first finger, etc.

Alliterative phrases of this type are not infrequent: Skelton M 1771 Spare for no cost to gyue them pounde and peny | Abr. & Isaak 265 in wele and wo | Bale T 146 at market and at myll, Of corne and cattell, they shall haue non increase | Di P [Ch&H] 230 that anyone ... should ... have dared to aspire to the hand and heart of the only daughter of the fiery old Lobbs | ib 723 master and man separated | Ruskin On Painting 38 I can not at the same time do homage to power and pettiness | Wilde R 157 For oak and elm have pleasant leaves ... | Drinkwater P 76 And blood is warm in man and maid | Bennett RS 121 She alone had seen Mrs. E.

as a bride and Mr. E. as a bridegroom, and the magic of her belief compelled the partners also to see themselves as bride and bridegroom | Sherwood Anderson WM 222 he had agreed that such lives were without point and purpose | Waugh BM 199 eating me out of house and home (common).

12.8₅. Thus also with two adjs used as primaries: high and low, rich and poor, through thick and thin, see examples vol II 11.2.

To the examples of agent-nouns contrasted with past participles found there may be added: Jerome I 205 war in the future is going to be rendered equally satisfactory to victor and to vanquished | Brett Young PC 696 In the African bush I've been hunter and hunted at once | Cholmondeley Red P. 4 Had he been tempter or tempted? | Christie Big Four 5 Pursuers and pursued vanished into the night.

Or we may have the same word-form repeated, each time referring to a different person as in Earle M 39 Hee is the ordinarie Embassadour betweene Friend and Friend | Drinkwater P 90 rare Of beauty as thoughts between friend and friend | Chesterton Di 121 Dickens could find in any street divergences between man and man deeper than the divisions of nations.

Further some examples with *or* and *nor:* Bale T 1074 Father nor mother, Syster nor brother, I spare not in my moode | Wordsw 44 There's neither dog nor heifer, horse nor sheep, Will wet his lip within that Cup of stone | Lamb E [World's Class.] 91 Dear little T. H., ... who was never allowed to hear of goblin or apparition | Kingsley H 249 the drama died a natural death; and when that happens to man or thing, you may weep over it | Hawthorne T 118 as sweet a day as the heart of man or child could wish | Collins W 159 I am an obscure, unnoticed man, without patron or friend to help me | Galsw Car 664 so that whether he was moth or candle was becoming a moot point | Lawrence SL 80 Neither wife nor husband spoke.

Thus also with alliteration: Mitford OV [3rd ed.] 2 how much we dread ... any fresh importation of savage or sailor | Brontë V 30 For many days and nights neither sun nor stars appeared | Stevenson T 176 some time in the following night, without sign or sound, he went to his Master.

We have the same use of zero in antithetical collocations like *family or no famiiy*, cf vol II 16.824.

12.8₆. Very frequently we find two different words connected by a preposition, or two words each preceded by a preposition: from beginning to end | make money hand over fist | from first to last | from right to left | Benson Dawn of All 194 As he stood himself on the platform at Thurles, bag in hand ... | Dickinson MS [1915] 14 it has to grow, and to be handed down from father to son | Sackville West E 209 one walks round with everybody else, nose to tail like a string of caterpillars | Hadow Ch 40 To French erotic poetry we owe the elaborate code of duties owed by husband to wife and lover to mistress | ib 49 Chaucer's range from knight to miller, from aristocratic prioress to bourgeois wife of Bath | Wodehouse, Code of the Woosters 57 I settled myself in my chair and, putting match to gasper, awaited the inside story.

Thus also with alliteration: from stem to stern | Cowper L 2.190 had I been painter instead of poet | Browning 1.409 His queer long coat from heel to head Was half of yellow and half of red | ib 518 Let's sit and set things straight now, hip to haunch.

Still more frequent is repetition of the same wordform in connexion with preposition(s): step by step |

from end to end | from side to side | hour after hour | day by day | from generation to generation | Wordsw 54 From Town to Town, from Tower to Tower, The Red Rose is a gladsome Flower | Shelley L 788 a violation of what is due from man to man | Browning 1.410 From street to street he piped advancing, And step for step they followed dancing | Ru P 1.351 And day followed on day, and month to month | Ridge G 55 the consideration always due from girl to girl | Bennett B 118 Let me tell you, as man to man | Galsw FCh 66 Crinoline by crinoline they sat | Woolf D 204 he could feel her mind, like a bird, falling from branch to branch, etc.

Such a repeated sb with zero may be modified by an adj, but frequently the adj is only added to one of the two identical forms, practically always the second: Drinkwater P 24 From age to unconfessing age | Brooke Selected Poems 26 He does not tell you how white Helen bears Child on legitimate child | Freeman Certain Thorndyke 32 So hour after weary hour passed | Bullett Modern Fiction 57 moving from mystery to dark mystery | Lehmann DA 53 night after sleepless night he jumped out of the kitchen window into the garden | ib 101 as if giving him secret for delightful secret || Drinkwater P 100 From hidden crest to crest.

12.8₇. Further, we may have zero in sentences, chiefly of a sententious character, before the same word-form found both as subject and object or predicative: like cures like | diamond cut diamond | Carlyle SR [Univ. Libr.] 49 Fantastic garbs ... succeed each other, ... like monster devouring monster in a Dream | Kipling P 179 well I know tribe never helps tribe except for one price | Phillpotts K 99 'Tis funny how rogue knows rogue | Walpole OL 56 dog succeeded dog, and apartment succeeded apartment | AHuxley BL 26 And as marquess succeeded marquess and prince prince, an expression of ever profounder imbecility made itself apparent | id EG 29 Let dog eat dog (cf Nevinson The

English 34 one member of the class will not swindle another, just as dog will not eat dog | McCoy No Pockets 163 It's a game of dog eat dog) || Lawrence L 54 But prison is prison, even if it were heaven itself.

Here, too, we may find an adj connected with the repeated word-form only: Drinkwater P 26 Yet I have felt the quickening breath As peril heavy peril kissed —.

12.8₈. In enumerations with or without conjunctions it is customary for shortness' sake to use zero: Ch A 603 Ther nas baillif, ne hierde, nor oother hyne | Bale T 1484 Pope, Cardynall, byshop, monke, chanon prest and fryre, Not one of ye all, but a woman wyll desyre | Skelton M 1883 I plucke downe kynge, prynce, lorde, and knyght | Mi SA 609 With maladies innumerable In heart, head, breast, and reins | Wordsw 54 They came with banner, spear, and shield | Di D 766 an old house which had stood untouched by painter, carpenter, or bricklayer, for a century | Ward M 62 she had lost youth, fortune, child, and husband | Drinkwater P 16 Till my proud flesh again is thrown To sea and wind and flame.

Conflict between Articles

12.9₁. A word or word-group which regularly takes the definite or indefinite article, would often syntactically require an extra article. In such cases the article regularly used with the word is dropped, as appears from the following examples:

(1) *the* + *a* (*an*) > *the:* Macaulay H 1.13 During the [a] century and a half which followed the Conquest | Thack P 1.76 the [an] hour and a quarter which poor Pen could afford to allow himself | Smedley F 2.33 the [a] year and a half which had elapsed | Wells Short Hist. [P] 97 The [a] century and a half that followed the defeat of Persia | Lehmann DA 22 All around grew

flags and forget-me-nots, and the [a] hundred other rare enchanting trivialities | Maugham Pl 2.11 The cocktail takes the place of the [a] cake and a glass of wine | Waugh BM 64 It made very little impression on the [a] million or so Londoners ...

(2) *the* + *the* > *the:* Ridge ME 7 At the [the] Paragon end of New Kent Road she stopped to take breath [*the* end near *the* Paragon] | Sayers WB 245 any sleepers on the [the] Prince of Wales Road side of the house [*the* side near *the* P. of W. Road] | Woolf D 35 dun-coloured animals stretched long necks over the [the] Zoo palings [*the* palings of *the* Zoo] | NP 1923 The [the] Ruhr industrialists [*the* i. in *the* Ruhr].

(3) *a* + *the* > *a:* Collins W 24 I sat silent, and looked at a [the] Madonna and Child by Raphael [*a* picture of *the* M. and Ch.] | Harrison Introd. Sh [P] 33 some of his former associates ... established a new [the] Lord Chamberlain's Company | Grierson MS 210 she took an Edgware Road bus to Praed Street [E. R. generally takes *the*; see below, 16.2₅].

(4) *an* + *a* > *a:* Di X 58 I wish it was a[n a] little heavier one [*a* one *a* little heavier] | Jerrold C 97 A[n a] month old baby would have eaten more [*a* baby *a* month old] | Freeman TI 16 This looked like a[n a] good deal bigger affair than he had anticipated [*an* affair *a* good deal bigger] | Lewis B 31 Our little bunch has a[n a] lot liver time than all those plutes [*a* time *a* lot liver] | Priestley G 428 We can give them a[n a] jolly sight better show even now than they can appreciate [*a* show *a* jolly sight better] | dos Passos P [T] 74 They took a[n a] dollar and a half room between them [*a* room at *a* dollar and a half].

The determinative suppressing the article may be a preceding pronoun: Butler W 375 His [a] year and a half of peace had effaced all the ill effects | Doyle S 4.30 during the whole of that [an] hour and a half.

12.9₂. An *a* preceded by *half* is protected by this word, and so we may find two articles in connexion with *half*. In this case there would be a semantic difference if *a* was omitted: *a half-crown* is a coin, and *(a) half a crown* is an amount of money. Cf vol II 15.121.

(1) Examples with *the half a:* Twain H 1.116 for the next half an hour (*"The next half-hour* is the usual English use." Professor Bruce Dickins) | Hawthorne 1.327 her face, with ... the half a dozen freckles | Oppenheim People's Man 170 You will get the half a crown a week which your leaders demand | NP 1912 if we turn to the half-a-dozen lines which are so translated | NP 1913 so did the half a dozen fellows who ... ("With *the* I prefer *half-dozen*." Professor Collinson).

(2) Examples with *a half a:* Twain M 168 as I've told you a half a dozen times before | Black P 2.36: a half-a-dozen | Wells N 476 we should meet for a half a day.

In a review in the New Statesman and Nation, July 27, 1937, of Horwill MAU, Ralph Partridge says: He does not discuss the universal American habit of saying and writing "a half an hour," "a half a dollar." Professor Collinson commented: "*A half an hour* is quite common and has not struck me as American."

(3) The conflicting determinative may be a genitive or a pronoun: Hawthorne S 35 the old Surveyor's half a dozen sheets of foolscap | Congreve DD 206 we'll read over those half a Score Lines again | Oppenheim People's Man 171 That half a crown a week will come to you | Sterne SJ [P] 54 an inventory of my half a dozen shirts and silk pair of breeches | Hawthorne 1.514 other Pyncheons, the whole tribe, in their half a dozen generations | Wilkins P 28 some halfe a dayes iourney | Con-

greve OB 9 the Pleasure of enjoying some half a score of Mistresses | Di OT 412 some half an hour before.

In the following example *the* also belongs to *a dozen:* NP 1919 the ten or a dozen Europeans who have crossed the Sahara.

Chapter XIII

Articles before Junctions

13.1₁. In EEG 16.8₁ ff. Jespersen deals with what he terms "the article of incomplete determination", i. e. "those cases in which the definite article is not in itself sufficient to determine what we are speaking about," and then he gives examples of various kinds of junctions preceded by the definite article.

It is regrettable that Jespersen did not consider the articles in his analyses in *Analytic Syntax*, for then he would have been forced to decide whether the articles should be considered as belonging to the primary of a junction or to the junction as a whole. The former view would in some cases lead to awkward consequences, not least with articles before compounds, e. g. *a first-nighter*, where *first* is actually a secondary to *night*, not to *nighter*, which is non-existent as an independent word. To which word does the article belong in such "equipollent compounds" (AnalSynt 6.2) as *sun-god*, *queen-dowager*, and *subject-matter*, which are symbolized by Jespersen as 1-1? In elliptical forms such as *a cabinet* for *a cabinet photograph* and *a return* for *a return ticket*, also in the so-called bahuvrihi compounds (AnalSynt 6.6) such as *redcoat*, which is symbolized as 2(21)1°, it is at least awkward to be obliged to consider a preceding article as belonging to the omitted primary. It should finally be noted that in many cases we may substitute one word for a junction (preceded by an article) without any semantic change worth mentioning, as in *a grig* for *a small eel, a groom* for *a servant having care of horses* (according to COD).

13.1₂. If we consider an article connected with a junction as belonging to this as a whole, all these difficulties disappear.

Junctions denoting countables, if preceded by the indefinite article, belong under Stage I, e. g. *a grey cat. A grey cat* is more restricted in sense than *a cat*, it is true, but this has nothing to do with the function of the indefinite article, which in both cases denotes "complete unfamiliarity".

Junctions denoting countables, if preceded by the definite article, belong under Stage II, "greater familiarity", as in *the grey cat*.

Junctions denoting uncountables, if used with zero, belong under Stage I, "complete unfamiliarity", e. g. *cold water*.

Junctions denoting uncountables, if preceded by the definite article, belong under Stage II, as in *the cold water*.

13.1₃. If words generally used as proper names enter into junctions we must distinguish between restrictive and non-restrictive secondaries. If the secondary is non-restrictive, the proper name retains its character as a genuine proper name, and as a rule the junction in question is treated as a simplex proper name, i. e. takes zero, as in *Old England*. But if the secondary is restrictive, i. e. is used to distinguish the person or thing in question from others bearing the same name, the proper name like simplex proper names applied to several specimens loses some of its character as a genuine proper name and hence takes the definite article, as in *the younger Pitt*. See further vol III 4.3₄ and below, 16.6.

Junctions and the relation between their primaries (principals) and secondaries (adjuncts) have been dealt with in vol II chs 12—15, and vol III chs 4—10, and examples of the various types of junctions may be found throughout these chapters.

As apparently all the various types of junctions can take all the three articles, it would serve no purpose to go into detail here and adduce a great many examples. So in what follows I shall only enumerate the various main types with reference to the chapter or section where such junctions are treated adducing one example of use with the indefinite or definite article (before junction with a countable) and one with zero (with uncountables):

13.2₁. The secondary may be

(1) A prepositive or postpositive adjective: a/the young lady. For examples and discussion of the various types, direct, indirect adjuncts, etc, see vol II chs 12 and 14. — A battle royal | the Church Militant || issue male | proof positive (vol II 15.4 ff.; we can also say *positive proof* and *male issue*).

(2) A substantive in the common form: a/the gold chain | gold dust. For examples and discussion of the problem whether the secondary is to be termed a sb or an adj see vol II ch 13.

(3) A participle or participial group: an/the interrupted conversation | a well-known author || home-made jam | intoxicating drink (vol II 14.31 ff.) || a man more sinned against than sinning (vol II 15.52).

(4) Another word-group (often descriptive): a cat and dog life (vol II 14.51 ff.) | a/the catch-cold weather (vol II 14.71 ff.) | a hole the size of a wafer | a face the colour of a peony (vol II 15.71) || hearsay evidence (vol II 14.73) | at breakneck speed (ib 14.74) | mock-turtle soup (14.78).

(5) A prepositive or postpositive infinitive: an/the impossible-to-be-realized wish (vol II 14.41 ff.) | a house

to let (vol II 15.8 ff. and vol V ch 15) || in time to come (vol II 15.8₁).

(6) An adverb or adverbial group, pre- or postpositive: an/the after sadness | an/the out-and-out failure (vol II 14.9 f.) | an afternoon out | a/the valet out of employment (vol II 15.73) || in after life (vol II 14.92).

(7) A prepositional phrase, pre- or postpositive: an/the after-dinner speech | an/the out-of-doors party (vol II 14.61 ff.) | a/the man-of-war (vol II 15.76) || afternoon tea | his supply of after-dinner whisky-and-water (vol II 14.61) | plenty of money (ib 15.76).

(8) A clause: a/the man who knows nothing | a vexation they are better without || wine which had to be drunk at once (vol III chs 4—10).

Junctions with several (different) secondaries are common: An/the English man-of-war.

13.2₂. If a designation for a person consists of a title with *of* and a place-name, the definite article is required, as the designation is on a par with such combinations as *the King of England*, *the Archbishop of Canterbury*, etc, thus: the Duke of Westminster | the Prince of Wales | the Earl of Rosebery.

13.2₃. When a proper name is connected with a secondary, a clause, a restrictive (contrasting) adjective, an adverb, or a prepositional phrase, it loses its character of being a proper name in the strict sense; it becomes a class-noun and hence must have *the*, e. g. this is not the Smith I was speaking of | GE A 371 Adam stood upright again, and looked more like the Adam Bede of former days | Lowell St 280 these passages might have been written by the Dryden whom we learn to know some fifteen years later | Parker R 314 it was the old Charley Steele, the Charley Steele of the court-room | NP 1922 Walter Raleigh was hailed on the strength of this book as a wit and the Mercutio of professors || Lecky D 1.102 the America Tocqueville described was, in some respects, very unlike that of our own day | Henley Burns 235 the Scotland he loved so well, and took such pride in honouring, could scarce have been the Scotland she is, had he not been | Stevenson MB 205 Paris now is not so different from the Paris of then | Archer A 87 How different is the impression produced by the Chicago of to-day!

13.2₄. This also applies to such quasi-proper names as *God, Providence,* and *Hell:* The God of Israel | Carlyle H 119 the providence presiding over him | Dickinson MS 38 The Providence whose purposes he so readily divines is dark to me || Mi PL 4.20 horror and doubt... from the bottom stirr The Hell within him, for within him Hell He brings | ib 78 a lower deep, To which the Hell I suffer seems a Heav'n.

13.2₅. When mass-words take a determinative, they may lose their character of mass-words. The whole junction, as it were, forms a class-noun, and as such may take the definite article: Sheridan 290 when history, and particularly the history of our own country, furnishes a case in point | Pattison Mi 89 Milton's paraphrase of the Psalms belongs to history, but to the history of psalmody, not that of poetry | Stevenson A 19 we must not take from those that have little the little that they have.

Superlatives and Ordinals as Secondaries

13.3₁. Superlatives used as secondaries are generally preceded by the definite article. A superlative with its primary denotes something of the highest degree of the quality in question. To decide that the thing belongs here one must have some knowledge of it and this is generally sufficient for the word to require the definite article: *the longest way*. It is hardly necessary to offer more examples here.

On *the* + superlative + primary as post-adjunct of a substantive preceded by *a* (Carlyle: born in an age the most prosaic) see vol II 15.68.

The same holds good with Ordinals. An ordinal together with a primary denotes something belonging in a certain place in a series, but to decide which place it is necessary to have some knowledge of the thing in relation to the other things in the series, and this, again, is sufficient for the junction to require *the*: *the fifth time*. Nor is it necessary to cite more examples here.

Since superlatives and ordinals on the whole are on the same plane with regard to the use of articles, they will be treated together in what follows.

13.3₂. Frequently, however, we find junctions with superlatives and ordinals with the indefinite or the zero article.

The indefinite article may occur in some more or less established phrases, such as *a best man* 'groomsman', *best dress, best seller* (book), *first night* 'first performance of play', *second nature, there will not be a second time* (*sitting, innings*, etc), etc. These junctions each denote one of several items belonging to the highest degree or to a certain place in several series (every performed play has its first night, etc.).

Examples: Macaulay Addison (q Poutsma) He fully expected to play a first part in Parliament | NED 1861 ... whether there was a best man | GE Mill 2.173 I'd a best suit that lasted me six years | Gissing B 34 An eldest Miss Lumb had been fortunate enough to marry ... Mr. Job Whitelaw | Galsw SS [T] 93 After that she ... went to a first night | Bennett RS 119 it was obviously not a new frock ... But it was unquestionably a best dress |

Lawrence SPW 33 A first difficulty of the Arab movement was to say who the Arabs were | Mansion E-F Dic. It's a best-seller | ib. A second Attila | ib. To stay in a form for a second year.

Note the following quotation with a Latin superlative: Byron Corresp 2.41 he is a very superior if not a *supreme* man.

There is nothing remarkable about *the third time;* but *a third time* means 'once more' (after trying, etc. 'twice'), see Christophersen p. 141.

13.3₃. Superlatives formed with *most* may denote not the highest degree, but a very high degree, and then they will naturally take the indefinite article, as in Sh Tp I. 2.181 I finde my *Zenith* doth depend vpon A most auspitious starre | ib II. 2. 93 a most delicate Monster | NED 1720 A most vile, stinking Whigg | He is a most dangerous man.

Foremost may be used in the same way: Meredith E 18 His duty to his House was a foremost thought with him | Adv. 1911 (q Poutsma) won ... a foremost place. Cf above, 10.5₈.

Zero with junctions of superlatives or ordinals and their primaries are less common. It may occur with such established collocations as *best man* and *second watch:* Meredith E 527 I refused the office of best man | Galsw EC 354 You were best man, if you remember | Maugham HB 403 he was to be best man at a wedding | Rose Macaulay T 91 your wife ... has first claim | Eberhart, Patient in Room 18. 278 Second watch, however, passed quite as usual.

13.3₄. Further we find zero with junctions of masswords and superlatives denoting a very high, not the highest, degree. Such junctions, found more frequently in early than in modern authors, are particularly common as regimens of prepositions. It is now decidedly literary. Examples: Sh Hml I. 3.43 be wary then, best safety lies in feare | Kyd (q Ritzenfeldt) First, we are plac'd upon extremest height | Mi PL 8.253 As new-waked from soundest sleep . . . | id SA 1147 With solemnest devotion | Swift G 3 the late Queen Anne, of most pious and glorious memory | Brontë V [Everyman] 268 pity, goodness, sweet sympathy, blessed it with divinest light | Dreiser F 70 Others were singly engaged in fiercest battle with large groups | Huxley EG 20 the face was a mask of extremest grief.

13.3_5. The same construction with plurals as primaries: Kyd (q Ritzenfeldt) For deepest cares break never into tears | Mi PL 2.114 to perplex and dash Maturest counsels | ib 4.641 With charm of earliest birds | id SA 210 wisest men have erred | By Ch 1.61 in feeblest accents | Carlyle E 226 so complex as to puzzle strongest heads.— Note the following junction with *all:* Shelley 600 All loathliest weeds began to grow.

13.3_6. This type of junction may also occur in other functions in the sentence. Particularly in early authors we also find countables as primaries. Examples: Sh H6B I. 3.163 York is meetest man to be your Regent in the Realme of France | R2 V. 1.90 So longest Way shall haue the longest Moanes | Hml I. 2.110 with no lesse Nobility of Loue, Then that which deerest Father beares his Sonne | Mi PL 9.85 . . . and found The serpent subtlest beast of all the field.

13.3_7. The use of zero with the superlative is of a decidedly literary character. In Milton's poetical works it abounds.

Fowler in MEU *s. v. Superlatives* quotes a selection of examples of zero with the superlative, apparently all of them from newspapers, and then says "that such superlatives are, for better or worse, departures from custom." He concludes, "The writers have no sense of congruity, & are barbarically adorning contexts of straightforward businesslike matter with detached scraps of poetry or exalted feeling; the impression on sensitive readers is merely that of a queer simulated emotionalism."

13.3s. Sometimes the superlative or ordinal asserts itself and causes the use of *the* where a construction with *a* might have been expected: Mary Shelley F 72 I did not conceive the hundredth part of the anguish I was destined to endure | Collins W 6 are we just the least trifle in the world too well brought up | Hope Z 39 the oval of its contour was the least trifle more pronounced.

Chapter XIV

Stage Two

The Definite Article

14.1₁. The definite article plus a substantive in the singular denotes one individual (supposed to be) more or less familiar to the speaker or writer: Some image or notion of the thing or person denoted by the substantive is (supposed to be) already found in the consciousness of the speaker or writer before he makes the statement.

Sometimes such pre-knowledge is given in the context (*Explicit contextual basis*, Christophersen p. 29), the thing or person is introduced to the listener or reader in some way, often by means of the indefinite article, cf above, 12.5₄, e. g. Once upon a time there lived an old tailor in a small village. The tailor was known all over the village as "Old Harry" (EEG 162).

This method of opening a tale is frequently found in fairy-tales and other old-fashioned literary forms. Nowadays the technique in which the author carefully introduces the person or thing he wants to tell the reader about is not very common. Instead he simply uses the definite article (or a name, or even a pronoun) at once and then the reader must try in what follows to find out about the person or thing in question.

As pointed out by Christophersen p. 29 there is a tendency to use *this* or *that* instead of *the* immediately after the word introduced: Wyclif-Purvey John 1.6—7 A man was sent fro God, to whom the name was Joon. This man cam in to witnessyng, that he schulde bere witnessing of the liȝt | AV Job 1.1 There was a man in the land of Vz, whose name was Iob; and that man was perfect and upright.

14.1₂. We often have what Christophersen terms *implicit contextual basis*. A thing is mentioned, and then we simply use the definite article when talking about something else connected with it, e. g. speaking about a university, we may go on to speak about the professors, the terms, the colleges, the library, etc. Examples: Southey L 202 [nibble: fish] See what a nibble I had, though Stanier Clarke caught the fish | Shelley PW 1.333 [village: villagers] we arrived at Hermance, a beautiful little village, containing a ruined tower, built, the villagers say, by Julius Cæsar | Kipling K 5 [museum: curator] The Museum was given up to Indian arts and manufactures, and anybody who sought wisdom could ask the curator to explain | Locke Ordeyne 3—4 [school: class-room, lesson, etc.] The post used to arrive just before first school. I opened the letter in the class-room ... The lesson over, I passed along the cloister ...

But if the word used first denotes a person, we generally use possessive pronouns with the following words: a man ... his hat, his wife, his feelings | Shelley PW 1.286 A man has not only a right to express his thoughts, but it is his duty to do so.

Note, however, an example like Trollope BT 5 [bishop: breath] Bishop Grantly died as he had lived, peaceably, slowly, without pain and without excitement. The breath ebbed from him almost imperceptibly.

14.1₃. Often the whole situation is sufficient to show what the sb refers to (*situational basis*, Christophersen p. 30).

This basis may change from the smallest to the greatest. If the scene is staged in a room, we may speak about *the housemaid, the door, the table, the keyhole*. In the open we may speak about *the wind, the wood, the ground;* in a town about *the mayor, the street, the church, the gasworks, the pavement*, etc.

"While *king* in itself may be applied to hundreds of individuals, living and dead, *the king* is as definite as a proper name: if we are in the middle of a story or a conversation about some particular king, then it is he that is meant, otherwise it means 'our king', the present king of the country in which we are living. But the situation may change, and then the value of the definition contained in the article changes automatically. "The king is dead. Long live the King!" In the second sentence the same two words refer to the legal successor of the man who was mentioned in the first." (EEG 16.4₃).

As will be seen, implicit contextual basis and situational basis are closely related, the only difference being that with situational basis the word denoting the basis is not found in the context as with the implicit contextual basis.

Examples of ordinary situational basis: Di P [Ch & H] 408 The Prince remained to hear no more. He fled the spot | Gissing R [1921] 207 See how friendly together are the fire and the shaded lamp .... Another sound, blending with both, is the gentle ticking of the clock | ib 210 I woke this morning to find the land covered with a dense mist ... no light save a pale, sad glimmer at the window | ib 216 The mere chink of cups and saucers tunes the mind to happy repose | Galsw FCh 45 All these [papers] were committed to the fire | McKenna S 29 O'Rane propped Sinclair's book against the window-ledge and began writing | Russell Scept. Ess. 11 I wish to propose for the reader's favourable consideration a doctrine which may, I fear, appear wildly paradoxical and subversive | James Stephens in GP 182 Lie closer to the ground, The shade is deep ...

14.1₄. Some grammarians operate with the concept of *uniques*, i. e. classes containing one member only. But human thought may assume as many members as it likes of any class it may feel inclined to set up. NED even has two quotations with *universe* in the plural. At any rate, in connexion with the use of the definite article this notion of uniques would seem to be irrelevant, as all singulars with the definite article are uniques in so far as only one member of the class in question is considered in the context. Hence, I shall not here use the term *unique*, but it may be said that some words (in this connexion, English words) have a *constant situational basis*, i. e. they may be used with the definite article in any situation, or, in other words, the conceptions they represent are (supposed to be) once for all existing in the minds of all English-speaking people, and thus these words may be used in any situation in the same meaning (however vaguely this may be defined).

NED *s. v. The* 3 says that the definite article is used "before the name of a unique object or one so considered, or of which there is only one at a time."

Examples of constant situational basis:

air: Jerome TB 128 In Germany one breathes in love of order with the air.

beyond: Doyle S 1102 How a beast-man could have laid his vile paws upon such a being of the beyond I cannot imagine.

Commonwealth: Bailey Milton 61 Milton's chief occupation during the Commonwealth.

Creation (now with zero): Goldsm V 221 a fine girl is worth all the priestcraft in the Creation.

Creator: Benson DA 110 there was nothing alien to God — no line of division between the Creator and the creature.

devil: Bale T 616 Marry thu art the deuyll hymselfe.

the earth, the Heaven: AV Gen 1.1 In the beginning God created the Heauen and the Earth. — In poetry we may find *Earth* with zero: Sh Oth V. 2.110 She [the moon] comes more nearer Earth then she was wont. — Further when personified: Mi PL 7.501 Earth in her rich attire Consummate lovely smiled. — It is frequent in connexion with *heaven* as in other cases of double expressions: Mi PL 7.124 To none communicable in Earth or Heaven. — Thus also after prepositions (cf 12.8): Mi PL 11.780 When violence was ceased and war on Earth (but ib 11.824 on the Earth) | Shaw 2.104 every spot on earth | Note: go to earth (about a fox). — Finally the word may be used as a mass-word, and in this function takes zero. — On *heaven* and *the heavens* see below, 16.7$_2$.

enemy: James G 122 he ... had sold his soul to the enemy.

Fiend: Quincey [World's Class.] 77 clearly it must come from the Fiend.

King: Drinkwater P 107 They wouldn't let him in to see The drowning of the King.

Lord: AV and RV passim: the LORD, the LORD God.

Messiah: Belloc EB 15 He ... declared himself the Messiah.

millennium: Shaw TT 241 that does not mean that I have taken it on myself to bring about the millenium.

moon: Marlowe F 646 are there many heauens aboue the Moone?

Pope: Sh John III. 1.135 Heere comes the holy Legat of the Pope.

Saviour: Browning 2.527 The Saviour at his sermon on the mount.

Scripture: Selden T 20 therefore we must all, Men, Women and Children, read and interpret the Scripture (in the same chapter three times with zero, which is now the commonest form) | Cowper L (1827) 9 the scripture must be the word of God (also ib 14) | Scott I 216 'If thou readest the Scripture,' said the Jewess, '... only to justify thine own license ...' ("*Scriptures* must have *the* in the Christian sense, but we say e. g. *Buddhist scriptures.*" Professor Collinson).

Sun: Sh Mids III. 2.50 The Sunne was not so true vnto the day, As he to me.

universe: Bullett IC 195 He personifies the universe in order to give it a piece of his mind.

world, Zodiac: Marlowe F 658 All ioyntly moue from East to West in 24. houres vpon the poles of the world, but differ in their motion vpon the poles of the Zodiake.

Sun, world, and *universe* have not zero in an ordinary connected context.

Typical *the*

14.2₁. The article in *he plays the fool* seems to originate in the old drama with its standing types, where it was usual for one actor to be constantly representing the same character in any play (the lover, the villain, etc). The sb here denotes the typical or characteristic or particularly excellent specimen.

Examples with verbs like *play, act,* and synonyms: Skelton M 1177 In a cote thou can play well the dyser ['the fool'], Ye, but thou can play the fole without a vyser ['visor'] | Cooper Dic.: *Accissare,* to play the ydiot | Sh Merch II. 3.11 if a Christian doe not play the knaue | Hml III. 1.135 Let the doores be shut vpon him, that he may play the Foole no way [i. e. nowhere] but in's owne house | Bunyan G 105 had I been minded to have played the coward | Goldsm V 283—4 Olivia, on her side, acted the coquet to perfection | Brontë J 265 you acted the spy and informer | Doyle B 139 to act the spy upon a friend was a hateful task | Gissing B 361 he is acting the hypocrite | Hope Z 290 the fear that I had counterfeited the lover as I had acted the King | Connington DT 11 He had the gift of playing the fool in season without looking like a fool.

A few more examples are found in vol III 17.4₃.

Without and with the article in Ward R 2.42 you could act dragon splendidly ... she had already played the dragon hard. — *To play truant* is now more common than *to play the truant*, which was formerly frequent; Sh has the phrase without the article in Wiv V. 1.27 and LLL II. 74.

This use of *the* to denote the typical specimen then is extended to other constructions, particularly ordinary predicatives: he is quite the gentleman (the typical or perfect gentleman).

> Sweet had not seen this connexion, when he said (NEG § 2028) that the article is used with a single class-noun to suggest the idea of belonging to or representing a class, and places *he looks quite the gentleman* on a par with *the man in the street* (where we simply have a junction, cf above, 13.2_1 (7)) and *the lion is the king of beasts* (where *the lion* is generic, and *the* with *king* is due to the addition of *beasts*).

14.2₂. Examples of predicatives: Cowper L 1.176 whether you are perfectly the man of sense, and the gentleman, is a question | ib 2.129 he is so much the gentleman, that it is impossible to be more so | Bosw 2.75 he should never play any more, but be entirely the gentleman, and not partly the player | Austen S 299 she found him perfectly the gentleman in his behaviour to all his visitors | id P 7 His brother-in-law, Mr. Hurst, merely looked the gentleman | ib 146 Colonel Fitzwilliam ... was ... most truly the gentleman | Stevenson M 273 he was the man of business | Hardy R 245 Eustacia was no longer the goddess but the woman to him, a being to fight for, support | McCarthy 2.645 Mr. Lecky is always the historian, and never the partisan | Bennett BL 104 she was the child again | London A 78 she was so slenderly and prettily the woman — the girl, rather.

Quite the gentleman comes near to being a set phrase: Doyle S 950 Very smartly dressed, sir — quite the gentleman | Shaw 1.91 | Galsw WM 217 | Christie 3A 86.

The sb is sometimes modified by *some(thing) of, a touch of:* Doyle S 541 He is clean-shaven, pale, and ascetic-looking, retaining some of the professor in his features | ib 359 a ... man, with a touch of the sheeny about his nose | Barrie MO 30 There was always something of the child in her | Lucas RR 58 Lady Ferguson was an ordinary motherly woman ... with a touch of the snob | Maugham MS 199 It may be that in order to realise the romance of life you must have something of the actor in you.

14.2₃. Often an adj like *typical* or *perfect* is added to emphasize the inherent quality of the sb: Doyle S 1173 She was, of course, the celebrated beauty | Kipling S 17 we look the complete Bug-hunters | Benson D 53 he looked the model of the typical English gentleman | Chesterton Flying Inn 121 the beast typical, the beast of beasts | Hope Z 157 I played my part, and made shift to look the happy lover | id M 105 he really looked the happy bridegroom as he said this | O'Neill SI 195 Pooh! Aren't you the superior bachelor! | Locke FS 119 She was the perfect companion | Woolf D 219 There he was, ... the perfect gentleman, the fascinating, the distinguished | Rose Macaulay P 151 Jane was the perfect egotist | Mason 3G 78 But his host that night was the perfect host.

Of course the adj may be an ordinary restrictive one: Massinger N I. 1.67 your land gone ... You grew the common borrower | Locke GP 238 his attire was that of the rich man | Priestley F 218 He was very much the stiff little Englishman in his speech | Waugh W

156 He was very much the big brother in all their dealings | Shaw TT 261 He was the popular man, the safe man.

And the secondary may be a prepositional phrase or a clause: Lang T 10 Tennyson looked the poet that he was | NP 1912 Southey was essentially the man of letters | Mason Ch 247 Thus he, Scott Carruthers, like the strategist of mark, had been able to adapt his tactics to an emergency | Maugham Alt 243 an elegance that suggested the woman of fashion.

The following quotations show the definite and the indefinite article together: Austen S 285 he is undoubtedly a sensible man, and in his manners perfectly the gentleman | Bennett W 2.164 she was a landlady. She was the landlady: efficient, stylish ... | id C 2.149 she was a wondrous girl! She was the perfect girl!

14.2₄. I have noted a few modern examples of personal names with the "typical *the*," most of them from modern detective stories. In most of the quotations the article is italicized, i. e. it is the emphatic form [ðiˑ], see above, 12.2₂. It should also be noted that in some quotations the emphatic form is contrasted with a zero form.

Examples: Byron Corresp. 1.281 On Friday, Lord H., Douglas, *Kean* (*the Kean*), and myself, dined together | Di P [Ch&H] 367 I wish I was *the* Weller as owns you, mother-in-law | McCarthy 2.622 Sir Bartle Frere seems to have had in him something of the Cromwell, combined with a good deal of the William Penn | Carpenter C 85 In history, the Rousseau precedes the Voltaire | Dane L 7 "And of course Kent Rehan." "Kent Rehan?" "*The* Kent Rehan," said the Baxter girl | Plunket Greene E 42—43 A telephone call was put through to me in his absence from Mr. David. *The* Mr. David, the biscuit manufacturer, in fact | Holt AS 43 Gloria! *The* Gloria! And her murderer had got away | Muir Silent Partner 136 Not *the* John Prior? Not John Prior the big financier? | Bird W 12 I'm Danby — not *the* Danby, but the understudy, as it were | London Opinion 1927 *Niece:* Auntie, let me introduce Mr. Daventry — you know, *the* Mr. Daventry. *Auntie:* Oh, yes, of course. ... I've so often heard you on the wireless | [Signboards in London (1934):] Lawrence & Lawrence *The* [underlined] Jewellers | Harry Hall "The" Tailor | BBC 1942 Quisling, *the* Quisling, the original Quisling.

14.2₅. From names of persons the use of *the* to denote the typical or preeminent specimen has been transferred to words denoting inanimate things, chiefly of an abstract character: Austen P 279 But slyness seems the fashion | Rose Macaulay T 104 It was quite the fashion to have a few exiled Russians at your parties (common) | ib 103 That summer Russian refugees were greatly the mode | Cowper L 1.301 Balloons are so much the mode, that ... | NP 1936 New film companies seem to be the craze just now | Allen A 22 They told me that you were quite the rage at the Petit Trianon | Masefield Sh V These are sad things; for art is the life | Bird S 209 they felt that this was the life! | Morley HB 235 Just one period ... of which he may say Those Were the Days | Galsw SS 53 "Good!" said Michael; "that's the spirit" | Ridge ME 14 "It — it 'urts,", gurgled Mord Em'ly piteously. "That's the idea," said the Bermondsey girl | Maugham Pl 2.234 I suppose she was very inconsiderate. — Inconsiderate isn't the word, Miss | Wodehouse, My Man Jeeves [P] 26 Absent treatment seemed the touch | Huxley LM 201 The female infidel symbolised ... all that was exotic, irregular, undomestic; all that was not the family.

14.2_6. Examples of italicized *the* [ði·] to denote the typical or perfect specimen: Butler Er [P] 124 One of these [mercantile codes] ... was supposed to be *the* system | Vachell H 17 After all, the Manor had been *the* house once, and it might be *the* house again | Cambr St 114 the third [boat] was of quite *the* typical scratch description | Bentley T 117 Is that *the* one? | Christie ABC 65 "They're quite sure that this is *the* crime?" I asked.

14.2_7. Substantives with italicized *the* as opposed to those with other determinatives: Kipling P 163 "Is it just *a* Wall? ..." said Dan. "No, no! It's *the* Wall ..." | Ward M 28 Henri actually gave me a puppy of the great breed — *the* breed, you know | Lawrence SL 298 Their eight years of friendship and love, *the* eight years of his life, were nullified | Freeman Th 229 "The only other point that I notice is ..." "Yes," agreed Thorndyke, "and that is *the* point" | Shaw IW 120 Now the trade in drink is extremely profitable: so much so that in England it is called *The* Trade, which is short for The Trade of Trades | AmSp 3.237 Miss Hadida's [*Pitfalls in English*] isn't, to be sure, *the* bible. But it is *a* bible, one of many guides to righteousness | Sayers HC 216 And the scream I heard may not have been *the* scream | Macdonald Rasp 192 A woman, of course. *The* woman! — Cf Fox above, 12.2$_2$.

14.2_8. The word *thing* is often used to denote the 'real' or 'good' or 'correct' thing (cf above. 12.2$_2$), as explicitly expressed, e. g. in Gosse F 269 it was not exciting art, but it was, so far as it went, the real thing | Benson

DA 103 But what we've seen to-day seems somehow the real thing | Borden AS 138 perhaps that was the noble thing to do, the decent thing. — Referring to a person it means 'fit,' 'up to the mark.' Other examples: NED 1762 Goldsm. [The silk] is at once rich, tasty, and quite the thing | Browning 1.524 It is the thing, Love! | Di P [Ch&H] 17 The stranger took Mr. Winkle's measure with his eye; and that feature glistened with satisfaction as he said — "just the thing" | ib 19 [Mr. Jingle] *incog.* the thing | Stevenson C 319 his descent is not the thing | Galsw SS 71 It was the thing to be "catty" || id Forsyte Interludes 59 "I'm not feeling the thing" (*the thing* frequent in Galsw).

A special ironical use of *the Thing*, which may have been derived from the above-mentioned use, is mentioned by Uno Philipson in *Political Slang* 1750—1850 (*Lund Stud. in Engl.* IX. 1941) p. 303, but not by NED. "A term invented by Cobbett and often repeated in the *Rural Rides* and in the *Register*, meaning the system of the English Government," e. g. 1830 Cobbett Rur. Rides 2.259 There can be no interruption but *war:* and war the Thing dares not have. — Also called *the great Thing of things*.

Further *the stuff* (*the stuff to give 'em* or *give the troops;* a catch-phrase from the first World War; *stuff* with zero = 'nonsense'), and, applied to persons, *the goods:* Macdonell E 57 'By the sun of Austerlitz!' he cried, 'but that is the stuff' | Christie LE 139 I will say — you're the goods, M. Poirot. (Very frequent).

Generic Use of *the*

14.3₁. In vol II 5.4ff. five ways of expressing generic singular and plural are discussed. Cf PhilGr. p. 203. In what follows we shall deal with (1), (3), and (5).

The commonest way of expressing a generic sense

is by means of (3), the singular with the definite article, and this is perhaps in a strict sense the only way. Thus plurals may denote all members of the species, but they do not denote the species itself as (3) does (cf above, 12.6₈).

The problem of general ideas has been discussed by English psychologists from Hobbes (*Elements of Law*) to Russell (*Analysis of Mind* Ch. XI, see further Christophersen p. 31). For our purpose it seems sufficient to state that in the speaker's or writer's mind there is a more less vague image of one member of the species in question and this is somehow taken as representing the whole species. As the species is presupposed to be known to the speaker or writer, we must have the definite article when using the singular to denote it.

I should prefer to put it like this: the generic sg, as denoting one member of the class, offers a sufficient *delimitation* of the concept or image to allow the definite article, as distinct from generic use of mass-words with zero (see above, 12.6₅).

14.3₂. From a grammatical point of view there is no difference between the generic use with names of persons and with names of things, but for practical reasons it may be useful to subdivide the examples.

Examples of generic use of *the* before names of persons in the sg: Wyclif-Purvey Matt 10.24 The disciple is not aboue the maistir, ne the seruant aboue hys lord | Sidney AP 24—25 So doth the Astronomer looke vpon the starres ... So doe the Geometrician, and Arithmetician, in their diuerse sorts of quantities. So doth the Musitian in times ... The Lawyer sayth what men haue determined. The Historian what men haue done. The Grammarian speaketh onely of the rules of speech ... | Goldsm V 202 He early began to aim at the qualifications of the soldier and scholar | Dickinson MS 29 The policeman is a permanent public defiance of Nature | Jerome NN 73 What is it consoles the tradesman when the actor, earning eighty pounds a week, cannot pay his debts? | Galsw SS 44 The farther North we go in the States, the more idealistic we get about the negro | Maugham MS 213 The rogue, like the artist and perhaps the gentleman, belongs to no class | Shaw MS 279 The Anarchist, the Fabian, the Salvationist, the Vegetarian, the doctor, the lawyer, the parson ... all have some prescription for bettering us.

Man

14.3₃. *Man* generally takes the zero article when referring to human beings in general, but referring to the male, whether individually or generically, it usually takes *the*. No definitive explanation of this extraordinary English use of *man* with zero seems to have been given so far. It does not belong to colloquial speech; in fact, most general statements, including statements with generic use of words, have a decidedly literary character. Perhaps the biblical use of *man*, which is found both in Wyclif-Purvey and the AV may have been influential in the development, and the use in the versions of the Bible may be due to influence from the Latin text. Further, the usefulness of the differentiation between *man* 'human being in general' and *the man* 'the male person (generically or individually)' at any rate may have favoured the development. In practice this distinction, however, is not strictly observed. — Cf above, 5.2_2 f.

The assertion that *man* should have developed into a kind of generic pronoun, like e. g. F *on* and German *man*, is not correct, as clearly appears in translations from these languages into English or *vice versa*.

Examples of *man* used generically about the human species: Towneley 6 now make we man to oure liknes | Bale T 250 God sent me vnto Man | ib 1961 [Deus pater:] Man is our people, hys God we are agayne | More U 191 if it be a poynte of humanitie for man to bryng health to man | Sh Mids IV 1.211 Man is but an Asse, if he goe about to expound this dreame | AV Gen 2.7 And the LORD God formed man of the dust of the ground | ib NT: the Son of man | Cowper L 2.369 Fruit ripens only a short time before it rots; and man, in general, arrives not at maturity of mental powers at a much earlier period | Di P [Ch&H] 49 Man is but mortal | Stevenson C 158 I would ... tell myself that ... the opinion of the rest of man was but moonshine and spilled water | Jerome I 116 Man has been described as an animal with aspirations reaching up to heaven and instincts rooted — elsewhere | Dickinson MS 20 the stubborn and rebellious members of this growing creature Man | Brit. Enc.: *Man*. The most highly organized member of the animal world. ... One system expressing a vast gap between the Quadrumana and man, classifies man in the order of Bimana ...

The following two quotations may probably both be taken as examples of the obsolete generic use of *the man:* Bale T 870—71 thu shalt not kyll, Lawe is the reuenger, the man maye do no yll | Lyly E 41 Perfumes doth refresh the Doue, and kill the Betill, and the nature of the man disposeth that consent of the manners.

A few examples of *man* contrasted with *men*, *a man*, and *one man:* Browning 2.530 But one, a man, who is man and nothing | NED 1859 Lowell: Men are weak, but Man is strong | Dickinson MS 158 But is it men who attain? Or Man? | id 155 Paganism speaks for the men in Man, Christianity for the Man in men | Chesterton Shaw 238 they appealed to man, not to particular men | Rose Macaulay I 178 You know, what's the matter with that tiresome girl is that she's in love with Man. Not one man ... but just Man.

In quasi-generic use we also find *men:* Wyclif-Purvey Matt 6.1 Takith hede, that ȝe do not youre riȝtwisnesse bifor men | Earle M 35 men doe with him as they would with Hebrew letter, spell him backwards | Ruskin On Painting 39 But the lesson which men receive as individuals they do not learn as nations | Dickinson MS 75 Men think the life of reason cold.

The man is used generically of the male (in contrast to the female) part of mankind, or of the grown man (in contrast to the child): Wordsw 115 The Child is Father of the Man (frequently quoted) | Lamb E (World's Class.) 90 Credulity is the man's weakness, but the child's strength.

Woman.

14.3₄. On the analogy of *man, woman* has come to be used generically with zero. too (cf vol II 5.411): Ford 202 There is no faith in woman | Congreve 210 I never exposed a woman since I knew what woman was | Ingoldsby 86 But woman. wakeful woman, 's never weary | Kaye-Smith T 226 He saw clearly that is was woman he wanted | Galsw MW 170 if I was woman as a whole, I'd show 'em | Strong B 109 The rôle of each was clear; man the pursuer, woman the victim.

But in a general (quasi-generic) sense we may find the pl with (1) zero or (2) *the:*

(1) Woolf D 217 It was this that made him attractive to women | Cabot P 276 women were the devil | Shaw TT 118 a man should have one woman to prevent

him from thinking too much about women in general.

(2) Gosse C 17 ... having been read to pieces by the women | Mannin ChE 28 not a one for ... running after the women | Caldwell G 12 The women will wear Shaw to a frazzle | Hammett Th 232 I'm hell with the women.

Names of Animals and Plants

14.3₅. Animal names in generic use with *the* are fairly frequent, e. g. Ch A 191 Of prikyng and of huntyng for the hare | Sh Tit II. 3.142 When did the Tigers young-ones teach the dam ? | ib 149 'Tis true, The Rauen doth noth hatch a Larke | Walton A 3 my purpose is to bestow a day or two in hunting the *Otter* | Jerome TB 243 English huntsmen regard the fox as an animal to be envied | Brit. Enc.: *Halcyon*, an old or poetical name for the kingfisher.

Particularly in poetry there is a special kind of generic use of names of animals. Perhaps it would be more correct simply to term this a *representative use*. The animal is mentioned as an individual, and in a statement may act as an individual, but still it is to be considered a representative of the species. The animal fable is the most typical example of this use.

Examples: Sh LLL III. 1.90 The Foxe, the Ape, and the Humble-Bee, Were still at oddes, being but three. — Vntill the Goose came out of doore, Staying the oddes by adding foure | Mids II. 1.232 the story shall be chang'd: ... The Doue pursues the Griffin, the milde Hinde Makes speed to catch the Tyger | H4A V. 2.9 Treason is but trusted like the Foxe (to Group One above ? This use is common in Sh's metaphorical language) | AV Gen 3.1 Now the serpent was more subtill then any beast of the field | Wordsw 57 The Eagle, lord of land and sea, Stooped down to pay him fealty | Thomas Hood in CP 16 The squirrel gloats on his accomplished hoard | Drinkwater P 100 The rock-bird chattered shrilly to its kind.

14.3₆. In the same way with names of plants. Examples of toto-generic use: Spenser FQ I. 1.8—9 Much can they prayse the trees so straight and hy, The sayling pine, the cedar proud and tall ... the Poplar neuer dry ... The Laurell, meed of mightie Conquerours ... the Firre ... The Willow ... | Jerome TB 130 Among trees, your German's favourite is the poplar | Brit. Enc.: *Elm:* ... The wahoo ... is a small tree | ib. *Fingers and Toes* ... a disease or malformation in the bulb of the turnip.

And the representative use (the "fable type" is not so frequent as with names of animals): Ch LGW 182 for to loke upon the dayeseye, That wel by reson men it calle may The 'dayeseye' or elles the 'ye of day' | Browning 1.508 That day the daisy had an eye indeed — Colloquised with the cowslip on such themes | Sydney Dobell in CP 77 [A Chanted Calendar] First came the primrose. ... Then came the wind-flower. ... Then came the cowslip.

Names of 'Things'

14.3₇. Various examples of names of 'things' used in a generic or general sense: Byron Ch 1.46 The feast, the song, the revel here abounds | Quincey [World's Class.] 223 As to the opium, I have no objection to see a picture of *that* | Browning 1.520 Paint the soul, never mind the legs and arms | Jerrold C 138 There's a tipsiness of the pocket as well as of the stomach | Stevenson T 192 It was as good as the play to see them | Wilde P 118 We are no longer in art concerned with the type. It is with the exception that we have to do |

Merriman VG 52 It was afternoon and the hour of the siesta | Drinkwater P 89 For the carol and the colour, Lord, we bring What things may be of thanks | Lawrence SL 71 You should tell him to keep off the drink | Connington TI 173 All this stuff about splitting the atom, and so forth | Rose Macaulay T 6 He was not ... like Stanley, an ardent hunter of the Idea.

14.3₈. For practical reasons some words and wordgroups will be treated apart, thus some names of institutions may be used generically with *the:* Shaw 1.173 You! Ruined! How? The turf? | Merriman VG 76 The older man's presence suggested the Court, while Marcos was clearly intended for the Camp | Jerome I 35—36 One of the first things I should take in hand, were European affairs handed over to my control would be a rearrangement of the Carnival | Galsw TL 33 there seemed to Jolyon nothing in the meantime, for Jon, but University, travel, and perhaps the eating of dinners for the Bar.

This leads to names of mechanical devices, some of which may also be termed institutions: Swift P 11 there is hardly a polite Sentence in the following Dialogues which doth not absolutely require some peculiar graceful Motion ...; and in Ladies, the whole Exercise of the Fan | Doyle S 71 I think of writing another little monograph some of these days on the typewriter and its relation to crime | Bennett RS 296 I hear he's got the telephone now | Maugham AK 106 the seine cannot be used with any effect; but there is a fish which may be taken on a rod | Graves Goodbye 174 At this time the British inclined more to the 'cosh', a loaded stick | Russell W 22 Many a man has borne himself proudly on the scaffold | NP 1936 a murderer who has met his death in the chair | break a condemned man on the wheel | NP 1936

A calm defence of the theatre and a vigorous denial of the idea that the cinema or the television could be an adequate substitute.

14.3₉. Names of musical instruments form a subdivision: AV Gen 4.21 Jubal: hee was the father of all such as handle the harpe and organ | Smollett R 222 Narcissa, who played perfectly well on the harpsichord | Keats 4.198 she plays the Music [i. e. the piano] without one sensation but the feel of the ivory at her fingers | Kipling S 103 You can't teach a cow the violin | Benson D 49 Then Maud would ... take to playing the piano | OHenry B 652 whenever a troubadour lays down the guitar and takes up the sword trouble is sure to follow | Cronin C 119 Can ye play the fiddle?

In spite of this, and in spite of the tendency to have the article with ordinals, we generally say *play second fiddle*. This is used both in a literal and a figurative sense, while *play the second fiddle* is generally used only literally. — Note, however: Lancaster Pageant 143 It would be good for my Lady Berry to play the second fiddle (another example in NED).

(On names of games as obj of *play* see above, 12.7₁).

14.4₁. We often find a symbolic use of names of concrete inanimate things to denote persons or abstract notions generically, e. g. *the bridge* 'the captain, the authorities': Shaw TT 283 The lower deck doesnt want to give orders, it looks to the bridge for them | *the gas* 'suicide': Galsw WM 89 If he didn't get a job within a week or two, there would be nothing for it but the workhouse, or the gas | *the gown* 'the University' (of Cambridge): Byron Corresp 1.51 we met Dr. Clarke and others of the gown | *the gutter* 'proletarians': Shaw TT 310 Our breed needs to be crossed with the gutter or the soil once in every three or four generations | *the knife* 'violence, the end': War to the knife (common) | Wells

K 98 this was the knife. This was final | *the pen* 'words, literature', *the sword* 'force': The pen is mightier than the sword (NED 1839 Lytton; ridiculed by Logan Pearsall Smith in All Trivia 12) | *the platform* 'professional oratory': Jackson S 66 his speaking possesses none of the usual trappings of the platform | *the revolver* 'suicide': AHuxley MC 83 A few youthful follies, a mountain of debts, and no way out except the revolver | *the spade* 'archaeology': Times Lit. Sup. 1936 his uncovering of Ur has been one of the outstanding achievements of the spade.

14.4₂. Names of grammatical and related terms are often used generically with *the:* Sweet NEG 2.55 Hence a noun in the plural without any article corresponds grammatically to a noun in the singular with an indefinite article | Fowler MEU 24 after every item . . . the comma should be used | ib 244 the hyphen is an ornament | Grattan & Gurrey 197 The Vocative may perhaps . . . be included among the Cases.

14.4₃. With names of branches of learning, arts, and trades used generically *the* is now archaic (or dial.), except for a few words: NED *s. v. The* B. 5. has early quotations with *the dressmaking, the millinery, the Roman history, the currying, the joinering*. The plural *mathematics* also took the definite article: Sidney AP 29 some an admirable delight drew to Musicke: and some, the certainty of demonstration, to the Mathematickes | Cooper Dic.: *Asclepiodorus* . . . ; Also one of Alexandria, which was excellent in the mathematicalles | Walton A 12 the knowledge of the Mathematicks, Musick and the rest of those precious Arts | Defoe R 18 I got a competent Knowledge of the Mathematicks | Smollett R 27 | [Book-title:] English Grammar . . . by J. Bell, Late Teacher of Grammar and the Mathematics. Glasgow 1769.

14.4₄. The word *drama* in contradistinction to other kinds of literature often takes *the:* Bell Ess. 3 the various kinds of composition, in prose, poetry and the drama |

Dickinson MS 141 So with the drama, so with architecture, so with every art | Raleigh Sh 213 his historical plays observe no certain laws, either of history or of the drama | Parker R 303 she read with avidity history, poetry, romance, fiction, and the drama.

This may be due to the fact that the word is frequently used in the concrete sense of *play*, and thus is felt as denoting a unit in contradistinction to other words denoting arts. When referring to dramatic literature and study collectively it will take zero.

Names of indoor games formerly took the definite article in generic use, as still dialectally: NED 1474 Caxton: Vnder this kyng was this game and playe of the chesse founden | Cronin H 265 what disgrace lay in ... a game of the dambrod [i. e. draughts] or even whist?

14.4₅. Names of dances used generically take the definite article: Goldsm V 237 the Miss Flamboroughs ... understood the jig and the round-about to perfection | Barton and Sitwell ST 128 [1846] In the King's presence he executed an original dance, which was neither the polka, nor the mazurka, nor indeed anything known | Galsw Sw 140 What is the most pitiable sight in the world ... next to seeing two people dance the Charleston? | Reed, Limerick Book 80 Her grace in the tango, The waltz and fandango, Was only excelled by her skill.

14.4₆. Some words denoting general ideas occasionally take the definite article when used generically, e. g.

the life (now archaic): Luke 12.23 The life is more than meat, and the body is more than raiment.

the sex (= the fair sex): Sterne SJ [P] 37 he abandoned the sword and the sex together | Ingoldsby 134 But little he recks of the fear of the sex | Bennett GS 77 They do no wrong in the eyes of the sex | Shaw MS 13 the sex is aggressive, powerful.

the democracy: Chesterton Di 58 Dickens was destined to show with inspired symbolism all the immense virtues of the democracy ... The democracy has a hundred exuberant good qualities; the democracy has only one outstanding sin — it is not democratic. (According to Professor Collinson this usage is most unusual. But in U.S.A. *the Democracy* according to Horwill MAU (s.v.) may be used in a special sense as a synonym for *the Democratic party*).

the shade, the sun: to sit in the shade, the sun.

the vote: Mackenzie C 292 we women who want the vote (ib. I don't want a vote) | Russell W 81 this demonstration was essential in winning them the vote | Shaw TT 242 That's all the use they could make of the vote when they got it.

14.4₇. Some names of diseases and bodily disorders formerly were regularly used with the definite article, some of them still being so in popular (rather low-class) language, e. g. the flu, the itch, the pip, etc. The generic use of these words may be found, though not very frequently: Ingoldsby 111 Hath your master ever a charm for the tooth-ache (thus others with *-ache*) | Bale T 415 She can ... helpe men of the ague and pox | Stevenson N 363 A little more serenading, and it was clear he would be better acquainted with the apoplexy | Maugham P 139 You do not know what the cholera is | Sh Tp IV. 230 The dropsie drowne this foole | Bale T 539 wholesom for the pyppe | Broughton R 1.161 The plague is much worse in autumn.

Such more or less popular plural names of diseases and bodily disorders as the following take *the:* blues, collywobbles, creeps, fantods, fidgets, heaves, heebie-jeebies (Sayers NT 257, etc), jitters, shivers, snuffles, twitters (cf *be in a twitter*), the willies. These are mostly used in a parti-generic sense.

It is sometimes difficult to decide whether we have the generic use in a strict sense, but the question is of little practical importance, as these words have *the* whether referring to a particular case or used in general statements.

Distributive Use

14.5. The distributive use of the definite article is a kind of generic use. A certain unit of measurement is mentioned, often in connexion with the quantity to be measured or valued, and this unit is conceived generically.

The indefinite article may also be used distributively, see above, 12.5$_7$.

14.5₁. The unit mentioned is used with or without a preposition.

Examples with *the* only: Southey 1796 (q NED) They are very dear, ten reales the couple | Lancaster P 85 he could savour brandy at eight shillings the gallon | It sold at ten shillings the bushel.

Examples with prepositions: RV Luke 17.4 seven times in the day (but AV: seuen times in a day, and 20th C. Version: seven times a day) | Brontë J 4 He bullied and punished me; not two or three times in the week, nor once or twice in a day, but continually | Barrie MO 29 she could bake twenty-four bannocks in the hour | Strachey EV 124 For many months, the average of deaths during these voyages was 74 in the thousand | Shaw TT 285 Five shillings in the pound!! || AHuxley Little Mexican 174 Fabio disdained to travel at anything less than fifty kilometres to the hour | (q) The average yield of the district is 30 bushels to the acre || Wells H 139 a taxi will take us there under the hour.

[Professor Collinson remarks: "*Under an hour* is merely an expression of duration. *Under the hour* gives me the idea of a definitely measured period in relation to fare or speed."]

The preposition *per* requires zero: 50 per cent. | per annum (and other Latin phrases) | a shilling per man.

When only the standard is mentioned, *by* is generally used: More U 67 so he cometh into the markette place, and there hiereth some of them for meate and drynke, and a certeyne limityd wayges by the daye | Sh H4A II. 4.398 wee shall buy maiden-heads as they buy hobnayles, by the hundreds | H8 V. 4.33 What should you doe, But knock 'em downe by th' dozens? (now only the sg) | Scott Iv 414 Mendicants were, of course, assembled by the score | Butler Er [P] 119 he was one of those valuable men who are paid, not by the year, month, week, or day, but by the minute | Stevenson K 35 he would . . . drink down the raw spirits by the mouthful | Swinburne L 14 Cheyne would hold forth by the hour on divorce | OHenry B 656 you should have taken the rooms by the month | Bentley O 53 any other way of getting rid of money by the cartload | Priestley F 88 spawning lives by the million million.

Sometimes we find *by . . . together:* Di Do 337 he would sit by the half-hour together | Stevenson T 54 I brooded by the hour together over the map | Jerome T 42 He would . . . watch me doing things by the hour together.

Familiar *the*

14.5₂. In colloquial language we may find a use of *the* instead of a possessive pronoun before words denoting members of the family, thus *dad*, *wife*, and the Latin words *mater* and *pater*. In the family a boy will mention his father as *dad* (complete familiarity, Stage III), but among his school-fellows he will say *the dad*.

Examples: (1) Appellations applied to men; Jerome NN 49 The dad thought the mater absurdly sentimental, and the mater thought the dad unnecessarily vindictive | Galsw IC 57 you are just what the dad would have admired | id FCh 96 That brute Davids? Or — the Dad? Which was worse? Oh! Dad was worse! | ib 178 I hope he'll tell the Pater so | Rose Macaulay T 103 He did think it a little comic of the pater.

(2) Appellations applied to women: Galsw IC 316 [Doctor about his patient's mother:] When does the mother come | Lucas RR 189 There's talk of the mater setting me up as a chicken-farmer | Pennell L 114 I received a long letter from the Mater (but 121 Love to Mater | 135 Please also give my new address to Mater) | Crofts Cask 184 The mater's shocked | Twain S 174 the madam shut herself up with her candle | Connington TT 147 Well, that was a nice talk to take home to the wife | Cronin H 202 I'm beginning to wish I had taken the wife's advice | Bentley T 66 I happened to be on leave with the missis at Halvey. — M.V.P.Yeaman's statement in AmSp 1.95 "For a man to call his wife "the Missis" I take to indicate that he is of foreign birth" is not true of Great Britain.

The in Exclamations

14.5₃. *The* is often used in exclamations in the sense of 'what (a)', i. e. the speaker as it were emotionally holds out the person or thing in question for particular denunciation. This practice is closely related to the use of *that* in sentences of the same type. The article may be used before both laudatory, neutral, and depreciatory words, before words denoting persons and things, and before phrases. The essential thing is that there is an emotional element in the statement.

Examples of *the* before single words denoting persons: Goldsm V 290 The villain! The perfidious villain! | Di P [Ch&H] 225 "Oh, he says we're dear," cried the oldest and ugliest [lady] teacher. "Oh, the wretch!" | Browning 1.203 His own fault, the simpleton! | Doyle B 247 "The brute!" cried Holmes | Lawrence SL 182 The *fool!* — the young fool! | Galsw SS 239 Soames went out again. The French! Well, she had a good taste in dress | Rose Macaulay T 96 The darlings, they're all so troublesome just now | Maugham Alt 467 Warburton had made life a hell for him from the start. The snob | Hemingway F 187 "The bastards," he said.

Examples of words denoting "things": Di P [Ch&H] 348 "The idea!" said Miss Nupkins [common] | Lawrence SL 23 she murmured to herself over and over again: "The nuisance! the nuisance!" | Lancaster P 139 The scandal! The scandal! I must have been mad, she thought | Lehmann DA 200 I'm going to Scotland. Oh the moors! | Cronin H 437 The language — and the behaviour! | Maugham Pl 3.176 They're putting me through to Sir Henry. Oh, the suspense | Shaw TT 46 How dare you touch my pillow? The audacity! | ib 145 Pretty places, of course; but the heat! and the mosquitoes! and the smells!

14.5₄. Finally some examples of phrases, viz. (1) prepositional phrases and (2) junctions with contact-clauses:

(1) the idea of it! [common] | Cowper L [1827] 3 You know, by experience, how pleasant it is to feel the first approaches of the health [i. e. the healthy feeling] after a fever; but, Oh the fever of the brain! | Austen P 21

The insipidity, and yet the noise — the nothingness, and yet the self-importance of all those people! | Di P [Ch&H] 153 'Oh, the deception and villainy of man!' said the widow | Benson Daisy's Aunt 94 The pity of it! [common] The hopeless, helpless sorrow of it! | Woolf D 239 Lord, lord, the snobbery of the English! | Lancaster P 277 The music of her voice! he thought. The fineness, sweetness of her! | Lehmann DA 319 The monotony of faces in a crowd! | Cronin H 178 Oh! the wickedness of ye to get us into such trouble.

(2) Goldsm V 374 the monster! the child that was next my heart! | Jerrold C 12 There's the girls, too — the things they want! | Bennett GS 267 The way he grumbled about his feet being cold! | Lucas RR 7 The things that child wants to know! | Maugham Pl 2.250 The humiliation I've endured!

14.5₅. A related use of *the* is found in cases of address. The speaker says e. g. *the man* instead of *you*, thus contemptuously keeping the person addressed at a distance by mentioning him the third person: Swift P 86 *Col.* Wish in one Hand, — *Miss.* Out upon you: Lord, what can the man mean? | Jerrold C 95 Caudle, have you looked under the bed? *What for?* Bless the man! Why, for thieves to be sure | Jerome TB 75 God bless the woman! Do you think I should be standing here at five minutes to nine ... if I had it in my pocket?

14.5₆. Similarly when mentioning someone under stress of emotion, where instead of a personal pronoun the speaker uses a substantive, generally a term of abuse: Congreve OB 10 in my Conscience I believe the Baggage loves me | Browning 1.522 [Fra Lippo Lippi after quoting the monks] Hang the fools! | Jerome T 233 "Oh, drat the man!" she would exclaim | Galsw SS 92 "That may be very unpleasant for you," he muttered, "unless the brute settles out of Court" | Strong B 36 Why couldn't the fool have explained that seals always sank if one shot them? | Ernest Bramah in BDS 465 Dead just when she would have been free of the brute.

14.5₇. But it is not necessary to use *the* or *that* in exclamations or other emotionally coloured expressions as stated above. Often zero is used in address (cf below, 15.1), where however, we frequently find the sb denoting the person addressed in appositional connexion with *you* (you darling! | you brute!), but also in other cases. This is a less articulate mode of expression than that mentioned above. The speaker here gives vent to his feelings in one expressive word.

Examples with words denoting persons: Galsw FCh 89 Well, I *have* been and gone and done it. Women! | ib 129 Children! What things they thought of! | Bennett BA 191 Priam was astonished at the man's exactitude. Scoundrel! | Maugham AK 288 She spared him no details. "Brutes," he said | AHuxley LM 231 Idiot! Why couldn't she take a hint?

Examples of zero with words denoting "things," chiefly words meaning 'nonsense': Bunk! Tosh! Bilge! Poppycock! (U.S.) Hooey!, etc. | Shaw 1.53 Bosh! Dont be moral! | ib 230 Stuff! Politics are not a woman's business | Galsw IC 46 "He's gone bankrupt." — "Fiddle!" | id Sw 7 "Blasphemy!" said Mr. Blythe | id FCh 276 Bunkum! The whole thing's weak-minded! | Hammett Th 172 "Boloney!" she said again | Farjeon O 16 "Sanity!" he said, and threw a belly-band into the bag. "Lunacy!" he said, and took it out again.

Here we may perhaps include the common expression "Good riddance!"

The before Comparatives

14.6. *The* is frequently found in connexion with the comparative. Sometimes there are two *the*'s, which in origin are different, one being a development of *þȳ*, the OE instrumental of *that*, thus meaning 'by how much', while the other originates from the relative *þe*. Neither is a development of the old definite article.

On the historical development of double *the* see Christophersen p. 115 ff. with reference to O. Johnsen in EStn 44 p. 212 ff. Cf vol II 16.42 (*the* as tertiary), vol V 6.8$_5$ (*the* in nexus as tertiary), vol V 21.7$_2$, and above, 2.4$_7$, 11.1$_2$.

14.6₁. In modern usage *the* with comparatives has a distinctly adverbial function. The double *the* causes no difficulty: *the . . . the* means 'by how much ... by so much,' i. e. they indicate a parallel increase in two interdependent cases. The determinant is generally placed before the determined part: Lyly E 39 Alas Euphues by how much the more I loue the high clymbing of thy capacitie, by so much the more I feare thy fall | ib 46 though the Camomill the more it is troden and pressed downe, the more it spreadeth, yet the Violet the oftner it is handeled and touched, the sooner it withereth and decayeth | ib 52 Faire Lady, seeing the shade doth often shield your beautie from the parching Sunne, I hope you will the better esteeme of the shadow, and by so much the lesse it ought to be offensiue, by how much the lesse it is able to offende you, and by so much the more you ought to lyke it, by how much the more you vse to lye in it [this type of parallelism is a characteristic feature of Euphuism] | Goldsm V 188 the poorer the guest, the better pleased he ever is with being treated | Ruskin On Painting 27 for the more powerful the intellect, the less will its works resemble those of other men

| Stevenson M 39 this theory grew ever the longer the less welcome | Lawrence SPW 136 The smaller the unit the better its performance.

But the opposite word-order may be found: (NED) One wants the more, the more one has.

Formerly it was not necessary in such sentences to have *the* in both parts: Earle M 22 The elder he growes, hee is a stayer [i. e. stair] lower from God | Goldsm V [p. ?] they liked the book better the more it made them cry.

14.6₂. Single *the* before a comparative has the primary meaning 'in or by that,' 'in or by so much,' and enters in many set phrases: nevertheless | none the less | not the less (e. g. Quincey [World's Class.] 31 not the less he held himself to be a layman | Carlyle E 174 the fact of their existence is not the less certain and regretable | Lucas RR 155 a consuming longing — which was not the less because each had to hide it from the other) | be the worse for drink | be the worse for wear | the more fool he (Jerrold C 128 the more fool I for my pains | Brontë P 24 "It was my serious intention." - "Humph! the more fool you"; *more fool he!* is used, too, especially in speech) | the more is the pity (often with *the* dropped by prosiopesis: Gissing H 233 my good wife died long ago, more's the pity), etc.

Other examples: More A 87 it may the spedelier rise | Daniel DR 39 let this make vs looke the better to our feete | Campion O 16 that it may thereby the neerer imitate our common talke | Sh Ven 207 What were thy lips the worse for one poor kiss? | H5 IV. 1.2 we are in great danger, The greater therefore should our courage be | Byron Corresp 2.48 if it were so, I should not conceal it the more on that account | Di Do 30 so much the worse for me | Ingoldsby 173 Nobody seem'd one

penny the worse! (but always: for better or worse) |
Hope Z 191 a taste of heaven, the sweeter for the inevitable doom that was to follow | Caine S 1.101 she was the more drawn to him from some scarce explicable sense of his weakness | Benson DA 48 not a soul will be any the wiser | Saintsbury 768 it changed critical habits in England for the better | Shaw StJ 103 I hope men will be the better for remembering me.

14.6₃. Often *the* is preceded by some quantifier (see above the examples from Di Do, Ingoldsby, Benson). Very often we find *all*, apparently with little actual meaning, but sometimes serving the purpose of showing that *the* is here used as a tertiary, not as the definite article proper: Winter put an end to their meetings, but their correspondence became all the more frequent.

Other examples: Hardy W 68 she hastily repudiated any such wish, all the more from a curious creeping feeling | Harraden F 75 silent flattery, all the more eloquent because of its silence | ElSmith Tz 27 Our honeymoon will be all the sweeter | Russell Soc. Reconstr. 90 the old primitive passions surge up all the stronger for repression | Macdonell E 199 in Spain they're white and that makes it all the funnier.

Note that the comparative may be both an adjective and an adverb.

14.6₄. In some cases there is a possibility of interpreting *the* before the comparative as an ordinary article, but only if the comparative refers to one of two: GE A 135 They were nearly of the same height; Dinah evidently a little the taller as she put her arm round Hetty's waist | Stevenson M 59 At each repeated mark of the man's uneasiness I grew the more confident | Campbell Shl 32 [. . Byron . .] Shelley's intellect was far the keener, and his culture much deeper | Russell On Educ. 114 it was hard to say whether the Platonists or the Bolsheviks were the more shocked.

14.6₅. Many people have a difficulty in grasping the meaning and function of the "adverbial" single *the*, and the result is that *the* may come to be apprehended as a kind of emphatic stylistic flourish with which the writer provides more comparatives than required. Fowler, in MEU s.v. *the*. 5, says: "What is here maintained is that good writers do not, & bad writers do, prefix *the* to comparatives when it conveys nothing at all," and then offers a large number of examples of this superfluous use of *the*.

A few examples (not from Fowler): Byron Corresp 2.176 I must one day break with that gentleman, if he is not the civiler | Di D 1.308 I got a little the better | Ward DG 1.277 Lomax fell a victim to one 'ism the more | Bullett Mod. Eng. Fiction 27 in each incarnation he may perhaps have one mistress the more or the less than in another (This construction is probably conditioned by the ambiguity of *more or less*).

14.6₆. In vol II 11.34 and 16.4 it was suggested that *the* in *the like* should be the "adverbial" *the*. But Christophersen p. 117 ff. makes out a strong case for its being a development of OE *þyllic*. Whatever the origin of the phrase, *the* now functions as the definite article, and *the like* means either (a) 'such': Sh Shrew III. 2.244 Of all mad matches neuer was the like; — often in the colloquial form *the like of* 'such as': Synge 75 I never seen anyone the like of you for dreepiness this day, Timmy the smith; — or (b) 'the same': Sh Meas V. 5.6 Goe call at Flauia's house And tell him where I stay: giue the like notice To Valencius, Rowland, and to Crassus.

Articles before Superlatives and Ordinals

14.7. Superlatives and ordinals as a rule require the definite article. The statement of the thing in question being something of the highest degree or belonging in a definite place in the series of numbers necessarily implies some knowledge of the thing and defines the word sufficiently to require *the*. Cf above, 13.3.

14.7₁. We have a superlative or an ordinal as a primary partly (1) in the plural to denote a class, partly (2) in the singular to denote the quality in general, cf for adjectives as primaries vol II ch 11.

A few examples: (1) AV Matt 20.16 So the last shall be first, and the first last | Maugham AK 239 He was one of the best (common) | Shaw TT 239 All goods is alike to that lot provided theyre the cheapest.

(2) Trollope A 221 I do not hesitate to name Thackeray the first.

14.7₂. Thus also in *of*-phrases: Sterne M 1.53 I have imposed this penance upon the lady ... from the best of motives | Ruskin On Painting 84 He is the most dexterous of all our artists in a certain kind of composition | Stevenson N 250 my wife was the bravest as well as the best of women | Doyle B 42 Henry is the last of the Baskervilles | Ridge, ME 99 their conversation had to be carried on in the quietest of whispers | Bailey, Milton 142 Paradise Lost is in several ways one of the most wonderful of the works of man | Shaw TT 228 Dont you know, my love, that you are the best of wives || (with the regimen in the singular:) Cronin H 240 He kept the best of company in Levenford | Bentley T 42 Then you talk about the thing in the coldest of blood | Doren, Swift 188 About the middle of March he was in London, in the best of health ... [common].

When an ordinal is used to denote a fraction, either *the* or *one* may be used: to stop the fifth of a second, or one fifth of a second. From the former we understand the use in Wells V 198 she paused the fraction of a second before her reply came.

14.7₃. Superlatives and ordinals are found in some (set) phrases as regimens of prepositions:

at the best, for the best: Ch A 749 He served us with vitaille at the beste | Browning 1.528 Aha, ELUCESCE-BAT quoth our friend? No Tully, said I, Ulpian at the best! | Benson D 115 Quixotism was doubtful virtue at the best | Bennett BA 58 However, he hoped for the best. The best was a telegram; the second-best a letter | Shaw TT 38 You mustnt think that I ever doubted for a moment that everything you did was for the best.

(*At best* is more prevalent; cf *at worst, at most*.)

at the last: Skelton M 422 Thus at the laste I brynge hym ryght To Tyburne | Bale T 712 He shall be at the last A morsell for the deuyll | Marlowe F 129 your words haue woon me at the last | Doyle S 992 I knew you would not shrink at the last | Walpole OL 64 Death is approaching, and there will be no one to be with you at the last.

in the least: Woolf D 208 no one was in the least to blame | Shaw TT 33 Mr Stalin is not in the least like an Emperor.

Various: Daniel DR 40 . . . which may be easily at the first found out by any shallow conceipt | Priestley F 208 there was a certain amount of gossip about them, as Terry had said from the first there would be | Benson, Dawn of All 238 at the worst, it means that the Socialists will increase enormously throughout Europe | Meynell P 122 He did not like the way things were going in the slightest.

On superlatives and ordinals as secondaries see 13.3.

Superlatives and ordinals may also take *the* as tertiaries, see the following examples.

Examples:

the best: Osborne 55 you tolde mee once that of all my Servants you liked him the best | Carlyle SR 153 those ages are accounted the noblest which can the best recognize symbolical worth, and prize it the highest | Di D 122 that good servant, whom of all the people upon earth I loved the best | Trollope DCh 1.93 I love him the best | Stevenson C 183 Tam'll can deal with them the best | Barrie MO 31 that daughter she loved the best.

the most: Sh Mids II. 2.141 So thou . . . Of all be hated; but the most of me | Fielding 3.591 I told him that I detested him of all mankind the most | Byron 2.356 the being whom I loved the most | Stevenson C 305 you have the character that I respect the most | Wilde P 88 To me one of the things in history the most to be regretted | Masefield C 261 Olivia was the most to be pitied.

Various examples: Osborne 31 my Lady, whome I would the fainest in the world have you acquainted with | Swift 3.31 whoever jumps the highest without falling, succeeds in the office | Cowper L 1.49 the man who coughs the oftenest | Austen M 377 the idea that returned the oftenest was that . . . | Di D 713 three times come the freshest on my mind | Thack N 79 Mr. Newcome asks me the oftenest | Trollope DCh 3.87 the fruit that ripens the soonest is seldom the best | Beaconsfield L 140 The Duke and the Duchess and Lady Corisande came the first | Stevenson JHF 3 those whom he had known the longest | id C 310 which did not interest me the smallest | Mencken BB 16 the doctors say it's the big stout person that goes off the soonest | Cronin H 238 they . . . got rid of her the quickest they could! | Strong B 127 But he had not collapsed the first | Cain S 19 Of all things I hated in Mexico, I think I hated the *meriachis* the worst.

14.7₄. It has been disputed that *the* in such sentences should be the definite article. Poutsma and others term it adverbial. Whether it is interpreted as identical with *the* with comparatives does not appear. Christophersen on the other hand (p. 186) says, "Whatever syntactic rank is assigned to the term [the book I like the best], it is clear, however, that the function of the article is the usual one." A consequence of this view is that we may have the definite article with adverbs. *Best* and *most* may be adverbs; thus also *soonest* and *oftenest*, and we actually find adverbial superlatives ending in *-ly*, with *-est* or prepositive *most*:

Osborne 67 she kist him the kindliest that could be | ib 175 wee made him contradict himselfe the stranglyest that ever you heard || ib 64 to my thinking they talke the most impertinently that Ever People did | Southey L 185 those very subjects which he has handled the most unfairly | Stevenson C 6 what I remember the most clearly | Masefield M 146 Lionel attracted him the most strongly.

On the other hand, we also find superlatives with *the* that are certainly adjectives, thus above *the freshest, the quickest, the smallest. The* in these tertiaries undoubtedly has a distinctive character, which goes very well with the other functions of the definite article.

14.7₅. After *all, any, every* we find superlatives both (a) with zero and (b) with the definite article (but after *no* only zero):

(a) Keats P 49 All tenderest birds there find a pleasant screen | Shelley 139 All lothliest things, even human flesh, was sold || Wordsw P 14.394 in clearer view Than any liveliest sight of yesterday | Carlyle (in Collingwood

Ru 197) I do not recollect to have heard in that place any neatest thing I liked so well as this chaotic one | Henderson Sc. Lit. 152 there is very rarely any faintest glimpse of ... | Ruskin C 31 at football, or any other roughest sport || id F 158 on every visible least thing | id P 2.354 every loveliest scene | Doyle M 179 every tiniest particle of our body || Wells Am 167 no thinnest atmosphere of reflection | Carlyle E 201 No idlest word thou speakest but is a seed cast into Time.

All these examples are literary and somewhat unusual. It would be natural to say e. g. *every particle, even the tiniest* (cf (b)).

(b) Sh Hml I. 2.98 what we know must be, and is as common As any the most vulgar thing to sence | Fielding 3.432 he who had not any the least share in producing | Quincey 57 under any the slightest disturbance (ib 59) | Mi A 44 [?] not beneath the reach of any point the highest that human capacity can soar to | Kingsley H 116 every man who differed from their party on any, the slightest, matter | Carpenter L 99 people assume that any the least loosening of the formal barriers must mean an utter dissolution of all ties || Carlyle S 180 in every the wisest Soul lies a whole world of internal Madness | Brontë P 27 a feeling which was liable to be excited by every the most trifling movement.

14.7₆. Instead of *Book the Third*, some writers prefer the brachylogy *Book Third* as a superscription (from *Book III* —?). Similarly the following rare constructions: Leo Tenth (Carlyle H 122; thus often in Carlyle) | Stevenson MB 195 our Henry Sixth. — In apposition the definite article is (always?) omitted: Ward M 57 Henry, fifth Earl of Blackwater | AHuxley MC 115 Edmund, forty-seventh Baron Badgery. Cf with superlatives: Galsw FCh 77 Nicholas Forsyte — cleverest man in London (but ib 90 the same with *the*).

Most : the Most

14.7₇. There is a clear distinction between *most* and *the most* as secondaries (cf as primaries 14.8₅), *most* meaning 'the greatest number of' and *the most* denoting the highest degree of the adj. By this use of *the* and zero ambiguity is avoided in many combinations: *the most generous men* is parallel to *the best men*, and *most generous men* to *most good men*.

Before plurals there may be some ambiguity: Most horrible things happen in war-time (1) 'some very horrible things ...', (2) 'the greatest number of horrible things ...'

The most part, particularly in *for the most part*, is the ordinary form: More A 35 the moste part of all princes | ib 37 the most part of the world | Maugham AK 112 They were rough fellows, the pearlers, for the most part. — But *most part* with zero (now obsolete) may be found in early texts: Sh H6A II. 1.67 And for my selfe, most part of all this Night ... I was imploy'd in passing to and fro | Oth II. 1.24 On most part of their Fleet | Defoe R 145 all these Things took me up most Part of the third Year of my Abode here | Fielding 4.136 I remained most part of the time behind the curtain | Carlyle SR [Univ. Libr.] 42 For most part, too, we must admit ...

As adjuncts before other sbs we find both *most* and *the most:* (1) Lyly E 45 the Camelion though he haue most guttes draweth least breath | ib 34 some men write and most men beleeue, that ... | Sh H6A I. 4.12 with most aduantage | Mcb II. 2.32 I had most need of blessing | Ant II. 2.169 with most gladnesse | Mi SA 971 Fame ... with contrary blast proclaims most deeds.

(2) Lyly E 49 Who deserued the most blame, in mine opinion, it is doubtful | Sh Cor IV. 3.54 I haue the most cause to be glad of yours | Swift G 4 Have I not the

most reason to complain, when I see these very Yahoos carried by Houyhnhnms in a vehicle ... ? | Ruskin On P 89 those of the Yorkshire series have the most heart in them | id U 40 the officer who has the most direct personal relations with his men, the most care for their interests, and the most value for their lives, ...

When followed by a contact-clause *most* is naturally preceded by the definite article: Sh Wint IV. 4.593 she seemes a Mistresse To the most that teach | Rom IV. 5.71 The most you thought was her promotion | Lehmann DA 275 The most you can hope for was a little false security.

On *(the) most* as a tertiary see above, 14.7$_3$.

Last : the Last, etc

14.7s. With the superlative *last* a distinction is made, *last Tuesday* or *Tuesday last* meaning 'the Tuesday next before now,' and *the last Tuesday* referring to some other date: the last Sunday [sc. of his vacation, etc] he spent at home | the last month of the war. Examples with zero: Sh Merch I. 3.127 you spet on me on Wednesday last | ib II. 5.22 it was not for nothing that my nose fell a bleeding on blacke monday last | Thack P 25 They never used to do so last holidays | Jerome I 15 A newspaper man came up to me last Ninth of November at the Mansion House | Masterman WL 41 and last time Mr. Eric was here they had words over it.

We find both *first (last) thing* and *the first (last) thing* as a tertiary. Zero seems to be fairly late: Sh H4A III. 3.205 Rob me the Exchequer the first thing thou do'st | Di P [Ch&H] 657 so that we may be there, the first thing in the morning | Collins W 238 The last thing at night, my wife returned to Blackwater | Cambr St 142 Spright ... tucks him in with Milstead's assistance the last thing at night | Twain S 157 Family prayers are said in every house the first thing in the morning | Jerome TB 188 We have been riding steadily since the first thing this morning | Flaherty I 83 The very first thing, the two of you got hold of two women || Ward M 227 expect me first thing to-morrow (and ib 231) | Maxwell ML 36 she often gives me a few words last thing at night | Beswick OD 48 let me have the list back first thing to-morrow | Christie LE 86 she brought it back last thing | ead Cards 259 We always took them [the letters] last thing before shutting up.

Next : the Next, etc

14.7₉. With *next* in connexion with indications of time we find both *the* and, perhaps more frequently, zero. Cf names of dates and periods with zero when preceded by an adjective. Examples: Sh Merch V. 302 Whether till the next night she had rather stay, Or goe to bed | Di P 558 punctually at a quarter before nine next morning | ib [Ch&H] 761 If you have not settled it by the next time I see you, I'll tell you what to do | Stevenson D 213 next day when he returned ... on the next, he had ... 216 the next day Harry consumed ... on the next it rained ... 270 the next day, and the next, his meditations ... 271 the next day he proceeded | Benson D 117 Jack went to see Dodo the next afternoon | Caine P 25 Next day Oscar distributed the presents ... 26 Oscar came the next day also ... || Sh Ado III. 3.171 he was apointed next morning at the Temple | R3 III. 7.60 to visit him to morrow, or next day [i. e. the day after tomorrow] | H6B I. 2.53 Next time Ile keepe my dreames vnto my selfe | Carlyle R 2.234 all next day she lay asleep (cf *all day* below, 14.8₆) | Di P [Ch&H] 760 I fretted and fumed all next day | id Do [p. ?] next moment the lady opened her eyes | Meredith E 236 annoyed that Colonel De Craye should talk of going to-morrow or next day | Butler Er [P] 32 Next morning it was fine | Stevenson T 35 Next moment we were both groping down-stairs ...; and the next we had opened the door | James G 40 I'm twelve years old next birthday, sir.

When *next* follows a name of one of the days of the week we have zero: Sh Shrew II 394 On sonday next, you know My daughter Katherine is to be married.

Thus also in *next door:* the people next door.

14.7₁₀. Before superlatives we occasionally find *this the*, but practically never *that the* (one example from Carlyle). It is difficult to decide on the reason for this distinction, but it is worth noting that as a rule *this* refers to what is near and hence perhaps more familiar, which goes very well with *the* as denoting familiarity, while *that* refers to what is at some distance, — something remote.

Examples: Coleridge Sh 220 imagination ... this the greatest faculty of the human mind | Black Ph 345 on this the last night of his being with us | Galsw SS 9 This the first private house he had ever proposed to enter || Di Do 310 how did you find that delightfullest of cities, Paris ? | Ritchie M 232 my father was that best of all audiences, a born critic and yet an enthusiast | Meredith R 84 things which are smilingly endured by that greatest of voluntary martyrs — a mother with a daughter to marry || Carlyle S 39 on that the first gala-day of thy existence.

There is no article when the superlative follows *some* or its synonym *certain:* GE Mm 54 a stronger lens reveals to you certain tiniest hairlets.

Adjectives as Primaries

14.8. In vol. II ch 11 under the heading Adjectives as Principals there is a treatment of what Jespersen would now have called Adjectives as Primaries.

Such adjs as a rule have the definite article, and mostly they have a generic sense, see vol II 11.31: "The chief use of the adjective as a principal is with the definite article to denote a whole class (cf 5.4), either in the sg., in which case it is neuter, or in the pl, in which case it denotes living beings: *the known* = 'everything known' or 'the thing that is known' (We shall now go from the known to the unknown); *the poor* = 'all poor people'. The former is especially found with abstract notions, and is, consequently, more literary than colloquial."

14.8₁. In what follows I shall first add a few notes and examples to some of the sections of ch 11 in vol II, and then offer some remarks on a few features not treated there.

Additions to vol II 11.31. A few extra examples: Fielding JA (Everyman) xl Aristotle ... hath not thought proper to define the Ridiculous | Di P [Ch&H] 35 There is nothing of the marvellous in what I am going to relate | Doyle S 923 there is but one step from the grotesque to the horrible | Maugham MS 11 the subconscious had few secrets from him.

14.8₂. Additions to vol II 11.36. Some more examples: Spectator no. 2 he thinks the World is in the wrong | Ainsworth JS 251 We're all on the square here | Browning 1.518 You snap me of the sudden (generally *of a sudden* as in vol II) | Galsw MW 341 she wanted ... to breathe home air to the full | Benson D 43 ... I swear I shall go to the bad altogether | Maugham P 56 That's all to the good as far as we're concerned |

Galsw MW 187 as if nothing was out of the ordinary | Garnett L 101 Whether in this conclusion Mr. Tebrick was in the right or not... | Gibbs BR 281 The guards were on the alert | Doren, Swift 217 Once more the misanthrope had run against mankind in the abstract | Cabot P 166 Don't want more members, specially if they want to do it on the cheap | Beresford in BDS 258 And that ... seems to have got her on the raw.

As will be noted, many of these phrases are of a colloquial character, and we may add further ones in which the adj is the object of a vb: Maugham Pl 4.293 now you're doing the dirty on us | Fletcher, Ravenswood Mystery 12 Let's hope he will do the handsome to his nephew | NED s. v. *polite:* 'Doing the polite'. — But in these the adj has a more concrete sense than the examples in vol II 11.31; perhaps it approaches the "typical *the*"; see above, 14.2.

14.8₃. Addition to vol II 11.37. *The ready* 'money' is still in colloquial use: Wodehouse IJ 11 Bingo ... has always had a fair amount of the ready. — Cf carry the rifle at the ready.

Other examples of this type: Byron Corresp 2.216 Still I have a due care of the needful | Di P [Ch & H] 534 my friends came down with the needful for this business | Plunket Greene E 50 if I didn't shut my mouth and fork out the necessary ...

14.8₄. In vol II ch 9 Substantivized Adjectives are discussed. Some examples might rather belong to vol II ch 11. Thus *the deceased* (see vol II 9.23 and 9.52) may take the genitive, but often this is avoided, and we find instead an *of*-phrase: Kipling TD 67 the firin' party closes in to guard the remains of the deceased | Christie MA 262 I at once examined the bedroom of the deceased | McDonald D 109 the body of the deceased. — We may also in legal parlance find *deceased* with zero, e. g. Freeman Th 123 and Crofts St 214 and 225. Cf below, 15.1$_6$.

The following synonyms of *God* (cf vol II 9.22 and 9.53) I should term adjs (ptcs) though it is true that *the Almighty* may take the *s*-genitive: Sh Hml I. 2.131 Or that the Euerlasting had not fixt His Cannon 'gainst Selfe-slaughter | Maugham Alt 32 the Temple of the Most High | Bullett IC 18 the flattering delusion that playing chess on Sunday ... sets the Almighty trembling with ill temper.

At any rate it is worth noting that all the examples offered in vol II 9.23, 9.24, and 9.25 have *the* or a possessive pronoun before the adj.

Vol II 11.41 on generic plural. The following examples may be added: Bale T 863 I confort the iust, and the yll I ponnysh with rod | Sh Hml V. 1.137 'tis for the dead, not for the quicke ... | Goldsm V 188 we had the blind, the maimed, and the halt amongst the number | Baring Lost Lectures [T] 50 You will say at once that this phenomenon is not uncommon in the old | Galsw MW 245 His job was with the living | Shaw TT 250 A healer. One who heals the sick.

Adjectives used as primaries do not occur connected with the indefinite article. Words like *dear* (she is a dear), *blue* (a vase of a blue as faint as young hyacinth), *human* (NED: hugging the dog as if he had been a human), *mortal* (a goddess who marries a mortal), *modern* (Ann's a modern), *Radical, natural* 'half-witted person', and *possible*, and also superlatives like *first* (he is a safe first) and *fourth* (be a fourth at bridge), when used with *a* are substantives (see vol II ch 9), which may all take the plural-*s*.

Most : the Most

14.8$_5$. *Most* and *the most* are both used as primaries, the former is, however, the more natural expression, both in the sg and in the pl: Skelton M 801—803 I ne tell can ... whiche of you can do most | Lee G 12 But most found the attempt beyond their strength.

In the sg *the most* chiefly occurs in the phrase *make the most of:* Sh Merch I. 1.130 to you Anthonio I owe the most in money, and in loue | Maugham Pl 4.25 He is a man who makes the most of himself | Hadow Ch 138 she ... is quite prepared to make the most of her attractions; — in the pl, meaning 'the greater number', it is chiefly used by Scottish and American authors: Carlyle E 233 A difficult position, as we said; which accordingly the most did, even in those days, but half defend | Stevenson N 40 The most of my patrons are boys, sir | id T 102 [vg] Now, the most [pl] goes for rum and a good fling | id K 68 The most of the cutlasses were in another place | Mrs. Oliphant [q Bruggencate] You have got a great deal more than the most of your fellow-creatures have | Poe (e. g. S 10, 120, 154 twice).

But *the most* pl may also be found in other authors, generally followed by an *of*-phrase: Sh Tp I. 2.480 To th'most of men, this is a Caliban | H4A IV. 2.45 for indeede, I had the most of them out of Prison | Goldsm V 287 The most of his family ... could sing a good song | Doyle S 1.230 the most lay silent (contrasted with *some* ... *the others*) | Bullett IC 18 the most of mankind continue to cling to the flattering delusion that ... | Sattler EStn 31.344 examples from GE A, Irving Sk, Mulock WTh, Trollope Castle R.

In connexion with *at* we generally have zero: Sh Oth I. 1.182 I may command at most; — but *at the most*, which was formerly frequent, may still be found: Quincey [World's Class.] 128 when having pedestrian exercise to the extent of fifteen miles at the most, and eight to ten miles at the least | At the most she [a motor car] will do thirty miles.

Cf *at last, at least*, etc, above, 12.2_1; on *the most* as a tertiary above, 14.7_3, and on (*the*) *most* as a secondary above, 14.7_7.

All

14.8₆. *All* is often found in connexion with the definite article: Berkeley PM 18 Not only was she doing all the talking, but she was doing it angrily, almost furiously | Mason Ch 154 Her scrutiny ... took all the strut out of him.

The idiomatic phrase *all the difference* is frequent: Collins W [Reader's Libr.] 51 It makes all the difference, though | Pemberton Two Women 37 ... what's the difference — There is all the difference | Mackenzie C 189 "That makes no difference." — " I think it makes all the difference" | Maugham P 45 But there is all the difference between a girl of twenty-five and a married woman of that age.

All the is also found before words denoting time, except before *day* and *night*, where zero is generally used: Wordsw 13 that green corn all day is rustling in thy ears! | Di Do 162 I scarcely slept all last night | id N 620 they had been playing all day and most probably all the day before [*all the* because of the determinative *before*] | Stevenson T 3 All day he hung round the cove ... all evening he sat in a corner of the parlour [generally: all the evening] | Bunyan G 45 all day long, all the week long; yea, all the year long.

But *all the day, all the night* are not rare.

In the United States zero is found with other words than *day* and *night*, too: all summer | Lewis B 322 They and their set worked capably all the week, and all week looked forward to Saturday night. — Cf Horwill MAU *s, v. all*.

All morning and *all afternoon* are modern phrases now becoming popular.

All the time according to Fowler MEU (s. v.) is idiomatic English only when the time in question is a definite period fixed by the context: I did not see you because I was looking at her all the time [that you were present]. But the term is repudiated ("it is slang") when used generically in the sense 'all day and every day': Actors act while they are on the stage, but he acts all the time.

Both

14.8₇. *Both* generally takes zero, but may be found with *the:* More U 116 towardes both the endes | Sh Troil IV. 5.146 There is expectance here from both the sides | Wiv V. 5.126 both the proofes are extant | Spectator 112 Sunday ... puts both the Sexes upon appearing in their most agreeable Forms | Franklin 157 upon both the plans | Thack V 310 both the children.

The word-order with *the* before *both* is exceptional: Steel F 68 he seized him by the both shoulders.

(Of course we also frequently find *both* connected with a possessive pronoun as a determinative parallel to the definite article).

The Which, etc

14.8₈. Formerly *the which* was used rather frequently in English, probably under the influence of F *lequel:* Ch Boeth I Pr. IV 123 Of the noumbir of the whiche accusors oon Basilius ... | Mandv 7 the land of Jude, in the which is Jerusalem | Abr. & Isaak 10 a nodre of his kynd shal plese me a yeyne, þe which haþe euer be my seruaunt | Malory 35 two stronge Castels of his of the whiche the one hyght Tyntagil | Skelton M 2415 Full many thynges there be that lacketh Redresse, The whiche were to longe nowe to expresse | Ascham S 259 for the which cause, I do the more mislike this exercise (frequent in More and Ascham) | Gascoigne 33 maketh that sillable short vpon the which it lighteth | Spenser FQ I. 1.36 Sweet slombring deaw [dew], the which to sleep them biddes | Marlowe F 837 Ouer the which foure stately bridges leane | Merch III. 4.32 I doe desire you Not to denie this imposition, The which my loue and some necessity Now layes vpon you | Tw V. 314 I haue your owne letter, that induced mee to the semblance I put on; with the which I doubt not, but to do my selfe much right, or you much shame | Hml II. 2.426 one faire Daughter, and no more The which he loued passing well (frequent in Sh, see Sh-Lex. s. v. *which*) | AV Gen 1.29 and euery tree, in the which is the fruit of a tree yeelding seed, to you it shall be for meat | Bunyan, Holy War 3.209 (q NED s. v. *Which* 13. b.) He told too, the which I had almost forgot, how Diabolus had put the Town of Mansoul into Arms.

In the first half of the 18th cent. the use of *the which* practically died out, though it may still occasionally be found later, chiefly as a deliberate archaism: Keats P 72 shaping visions ... The which became more strange, and strange, and dim (also ib 73) | Broughton, Reminiscences 1.90 She employed most of her time in quizzing M. A. Taylor, in the which I ... was overheard | Thack V 35 the which tokens | Stevenson C 196 Sherriff Miller gave us the names of several, among the which he was good enough to mention mine (ib 363) | Bridges E 49 the which he did | Hammett Th 248 I can do one of two things, and the which depends on you.

14.8₉. *The who, whose, whom* is very rare. Gower according to Steinhoff has both *the whose* and *the whom*. The latter form is also found in Sh Wint IV. 4.539 your Mistris; from the whom, I see, There's no disiunction to be made.

14.8₁₀. In very rare cases *the* may be put before a whole clause. This seems to be due to the use of *why* and *wherewithal* as sbs (see vol II 8.57, where the frequent phrase *the whys and wherefores* might be added) and cannot be considered part of normal English: Fox 1.145 [we talked] on consumption, and the why [= the reason why] it was so connected with what is beautiful and interesting in nature | Kinglake E 125 the where we should be on the morrow, and the wherewithal we should be fed ... these were questionings not dull nor wearisome | Egerton K 22 few of them have had the insight to find out the key to our seeming contradictions. The why a refined, physically fragile woman will mate with a brute, ... the why strength and beauty appeal more often than the more subtly fine qualities of mind and heart.

Chapter XV
Stage Three. Zero

15.1. Here we have a "familiarity so complete that no article (determinative) is needed" (see above, 12.4₄).

Address

15.1₁. As a rule words used in address (the vocative) have the zero article. Often, perhaps in most cases, the word in question is a proper name, and in many other cases the word has much the same function as a proper name, the mere reference to the person addressed. As Christophersen says (p. 191): "A vocative really takes a unique position among the parts of a sentence: it is in the second person. The article is generally employed in the third person only; it is used for the benefit of the listener, to refer to past experience on his part, but only as regards things outside his personality."

15.1₂. Still, the definite article is found before words of address at all stages of English, though not very often. In ME French influence became active. We may even find the French article as in Noahs Arche 122 hald þe still, le dame. Other examples are: Roister 13 fare well the lustie Maister Roister Doister | Sh Ant V. 2.171 The Gods! it smites me Beneath the fall I haue | Oth III. 3.348 Farewell the Tranquill minde; farewell Content; Farewell the plumed Troopes, and the bigge Warres ... (for other examples in Sh, see Franz[3] 233 § 261) | Scott LL 5.26 What ho! the Captain of our Guard! Give the offender fitting ward — | Stevenson K 210 "Step in by, the both of ye, gentlemen," says Cluny.

In most of these examples *the* seems to be related to the "typical *the*" (see above, 14.2), denoting the excellent specimen.

15.1₃. In quite modern language *the* may still be used in exhortations: Graves Goodbye 150 Their last words were the battalion rallying-cry: Stick it, the Welsh! | ib 351 the signal for the outbreak was the cry: 'Come on, the Bolsheviks.' — Christophersen p. 191 further quotes two examples from the Manchester Guardian.

15.1₄. We find both substantives and adjectives in terms of address, and these may have various functions, the ordinary one being that of attracting a definite person's attention. But they may also express the speaker's feelings towards the hearer(s), feelings of various kinds. Of course the "person" addressed need not be a human being.

A few examples with zero: Deloney 11 Why then Parson sit downe (said the Tanner) | Sh LLL I. 2.187 Adue Valoure, rust Rapier, be still Drum, for your manager is in loue | Hml V. 2.333 Then venome to thy worke | Ford 133 How do you know that, simplicity [i. e. fool] | Sterne SJ [P] 108 Disguise thyself as thou wilt, still, Slavery! | Kəats 47 Ah dismal soul'd! | Merriman VG 15 Little enough, Excellency | Shaw 1.156 Wretch! Now you have lost the last scrap of my regard | id TT 44 Nurse! Mother! Oh, is anyone there? | ib 50 Fathead! Dont be such a coward | ib 231 Very well, dear, very well, very well | Hardy in CP 230 Well, World, you have kept faith with me | Drinkwater P 30 O most blind of heart | Sydney Dobell in CP 79 Yes, Beauty, I see thee ... | Lawrence SL 82 "Mater!" he said. — "My boy!" she cried | Huxley MC 71 AMY. ... I've never met a poet before, you know. DOLPHIN. Fortunate being | Waugh BM 59 'Is all well?' — 'All well, Excellency.' | Steinbeck MM 58 "Hi, Good-lokin'."

Familiar Persons

15.1₅. In use in the family circle some words denoting persons, particularly names of relationship, take zero, and thus are treated like proper names, as at any rate they are to small children when they first hear them. Sweet NEG § 2053 is probably right in supposing that the frequent use of the words denoting relationship as vocatives has something to do with their use with zero. The same rule is found in other languages as well, but in none to the same extent as in English:

Father, mother, papa, mamma: Di P [Ch&H] 359 "Well, young townskip," said Sam, "how's mother?" |

ib 368 "And how's father?" said Sam | Shaw TT 225 I will not stand Mamma any longer.

Pater, mater: Broughton Reminiscences 1.40 [diary] At Newstead; had letters from pater | Lawrence SL 121 We won't keep mater waiting (also ib 174, 210, 319). — As a rule, however, we find *the* with *pater* and *mater;* see above, 14.5$_2$.

Brother, sister (chiefly dial.?): Phillpotts M 99 before brother comes back.

Baby, babe: Shelley L 539 How is sweetest babe? | Caine P 155 I've not seen baby yet (common).

Junior: Chase and Schlink 56 write peacefully in one room while Junior practises the saxophone in the next.

Other words in familiar use:

Boots ('hotel-servant'): Jerome T 53 Boots said it was evident that ...

Coachman (obs.): Austen M 69 Coachman is not very fond of the roads.

Cook: Collins W 109 But cook said that she should take her chair into the cool court-yard (very common).

Doctor: Caine P 169 You were very bad before baby came, and doctor feared you might even do some harm to her.

Master, missis (common among servants): Collins W 155 About that time, master being out, the bell rang hard from the bedroom | James G 42 I know master brought her back with him from his walk one day | Di P [Ch&H] 241 you don't know what harm you may do missis | Lawrence SL 199 "How's missis?" she asked of him. — Cf Fielding JA [Everyman] 17 [Joseph writing:] If madam be mad, I shall not care for staying long in the family.

Matron: Bennett T 456 [Edwin:] "But the matron

seemed to think —" "Matron always fears the worst," said Nurse Faulkner (Note the characteristic difference between the mention of *the matron* by a stranger, and the nurse's familiar mention of her as *matron;* similarly id PL 270).

Nurse: Congreve DD 210 Your Ladyship's Chair is come. — Is Nurse and the Child in it? | Ward M 175 Nurse is not in bed. (Common). — Also *nanny* 'nurse'.

Parson, rector, vicar: Galsw FCh 25 ax parson, 'e may know | ib 26 Vicar 'e may know | Macdonell E 224 Maybe his father taught it to him. Or maybe it was Parson | Sayers NT in rendering of speech always Rector.

Teacher: Mackenzie C 48 I told you yesterday what teacher called Edie | ib 48 Teacher said I sewed well.

Swift J constantly (e. g. p. 234) speaks of his friend the minister as *Lord Treasurer*, and in direct speech in Stevenson T Squire Trelawney is called *Squire* with zero.

Perhaps we may add a word like *Bogy*, which approaches to being a real proper name: Chesterton T 155 Syme remembered those wild woes of yesterday as one remembers being afraid of Bogy in childhood.

Legal Terms, etc

15.1₆. The same usage is found in the court-room:

Applicant: NP 1936 The Bench decided there was insufficient evidence to show that applicant was a single woman.

Counsel: Ridge G 203 Counsel was doing his best | Sayers NT 122 Anyhow, counsel for the defence made a big point of it. (Common).

Debtor: NP 1936 It was necessary for him, said debtor, to visit Berlin ...

Prisoner: Christie MA 252 if prisoner were an innocent man.

Witness: Sayers WB 121 Recovering, witness stated that she had certainly looked into all the rooms | NP 1937 Jones ordered witness to keep back.

Thus also the participle *deceased* (cf above, 14.8$_4$).

And, finally, we may in familiar language use *bow, cox, stroke* with zero about the crew of a rowing-boat: Cambr St 97 ff. cox | Jerome T 77 Bow said, after a while, that he did not ... | ib 201 Bow finds it impossible to keep pace with stroke. Stroke is intensely indignant at this.

Meals

15.2$_1$. Names of regularly recurring meals usually have zero: Deloney 13 Dinner being ended, the Widow with the rest rose from the Table | Sh Gent I. 2.131 Madam: dinner is ready: and your father staies | in Err and Merch often *dinner* after the prepositions *to, for, after* | Farquhar B 334 Ladies, dinner's upon table | Benson D 161 By this time dinner was ready; and after dinner she sat in her room smoking | ib 77 at lunch he had been silent, at tea even more so | ib 107 Besides, you should only drink tea at tea (the first *tea* a massword) | the idiomatic *wait tea, lunch*, etc: Gibbs BR 29 We won't wait tea for them.

But if the food is referred to, or there is some clearly classifying element about the word, we generally have the definite article: Wiv I. 1.270 The dinner is on the table (but cf above, Farquhar) | Scott Iv 24 terriers which waited with impatience the arrival of the supper | Walpole CN 274 The tea was over | Christie 3A 69 There was a doctor present at the dinner [i. e. the dinner previously mentioned].

15.2₂. *Hall* may mean 'dinner at College' and 'College dining-hall'. In both cases we have zero: Cambr St 49 Hall is at six | ib 51 There are some men who consider it beneath their dignity to go to Hall | James G 66 Hall in Mr. Williams's college was at seven | Sayers GN 54 Sunday lunch in Hall was a casual affair | ib 103 Hall was an embarrassed meal at the High Table.

Institutions

15.2₃. Names of public institutions are used with zero when the purpose for which they are meant is thought of rather than the actual building, etc, e. g. go to church | Galsw FCh 12 Of course, *we* all liked Church much better than Chapel | Shaw M 168 as if he were already giving you away to me in church | church [= divine service] commences at eleven | after church | Froude C 3.92 Catholics find Holy Church spoken of without sufficient respect.

Thus also: school is over | Sh Hml I. 2.112 your intent In going backe to Schoole in Wittenberg ... | Stevenson N 212 We had met at College | Lehmann Dusty Answer 140 The weeks drifted on. College became a habit | at court (i. e. at the court of a king) | in court (i. e. before a judge) | it was settled out of court | Di X 3 Scrooge's name was good upon 'Change | he had to go to prison for his offence | Sherriff J 70 I must go into hospital.

This is frequent in military terms: Doyle S 6.156 You are going to headquarters, no doubt? | Kipling MI 29 He wants to live as if he were in barracks all the time | ib 22 I read the book in camp | Masefield M 216 We'll carry these things up to camp | Kipling MI 39 That's the beggar that cut up on parade | ib

42 the gyard [i. e. guard] that came to take me to Clink [i. e. prison] | Gibson, Enemy Coast Ahead 91 So we set course straight to base.

15.2₄. The words *Parliament*, when referring to the English parliament, and *Congress*, used about the congress of the U. S. A. generally have zero: Rose Macaulay T 186 King Edward opened Parliament in state | Shaw TT 242 Parliament, Mr. Hipney, is what the people of England have made it | Sherwood Anderson DL 276 If you ever want to be mayor or to go to Congress ... | BBC 1938 He [the President] will ask Congress for a relief fund.

Dr. Johnson used the definite article before *Parliament:* L. 3.284 some struggle in the parliament | ib 314 two days after the prorogation of the parliament (also in Pepys).

Names of foreign parliaments have *the:* the Dail, the Reichstag, etc. Zero in the following quotation is exceptional (analogy with *Parliament*): Caine P 71 he was to be member of Althing.

Government as a rule takes *the*, but zero may be found: Franklin 137 to offend government | Hogg Shelley (q Poutsma) This he sent up to Government | Emerson (q Poutsma) Government must educate the poor man | Stevenson MB 182 writing reports to Government ... | ib 183 Government by that plan only hastened the spread of new ideas.

With zero also *Congregation* 'general assembly of the members of a university' and *Convocation* 'provincial synod or assembly of the clergy' or 'legislative assembly of the university' (see Poutsma 552).

Town

15.2₅. *Town* has zero when used in speaking of the town which one is somehow connected, the town in which one has one's business or office, etc, e.g. in connexion with certain prepositions, *in, to, from, about,* and others. See a painstaking paper by Emil Låftman, *Om artikelbruket vid det engelska town* in *Årsredogörelsen för högre allmänna läroverket i Borås 1939-1931.* See also NED *s. v. Town* 4 b.

Examples: go to town | live in town | man about town | town is very dreary (i. e. town-life in London) | Austen P 56 When I am in the country, I never wish to leave it; and when I am in town, it is pretty much the same | Sayers GN 222 Town [London] seemed remarkably empty and uninteresting | leave town (only about London). | (U. S.) up town, down town. — But *the* is used anaphorically with *town,* e. g. Doyle S 6.82 the happy chance of your being in the town (i. e. in this town, just mentioned, different from the one in which he has his usual work).

15.2₆. In the same way *bed,* when thought of as the usual place of rest and sleep: go to bed | be in bed | Di X 19 It was so dark, that looking out of bed he could scarcely distinguish the window from the walls.

Names of Periods and Dates

15.3₁. Many names of periods and dates are often used with the zero article, because they are felt as being in the same category as proper names, as indicated by the use in many cases of capitals (*Sunday, May, Christmas*).

It depends on the context whether the names of recurrent periods or dates have zero or *the.* If e. g. *Sunday* or the name of another day of the week refers to a definite date and thus, as it were, denotes a particular individual, it takes zero: Sh Ado II. 1.374 Not till monday, my deare sonne | Austen P 77 On

Sunday, after morning service, the separation took place.

On Sunday generally means 'next Sunday' or 'last Sunday;' *on the Sunday* refers to a remoter period. In fact we have here a case of implicit contextual basis or of situational basis (see above, 14.1₂₋₃), as in: Jerome TB 133 We reached Dresden on the Wednesday evening, and stayed there over the Sunday | We arrived on a Friday and left again on the Sunday, i. e. on the Sunday following that particular Friday. We may also have *the* before *Sunday* (*Monday*, etc), because this is opposed to other days of the week, as in Sh Hml I. 1.75 Ship-wrights, whose sore Taske Do's not diuide the Sunday from the weeke.

The term 'generic' normally applies to class-nouns and mass-words only; in the latter case the word takes zero, but it seems natural to apply the term to a case like the following, too: Sunday is for church, though *Sunday* cannot here be termed a mass-word. Similarly with names of months: March is a cold month. But applied to a particular month there is no difference in the use of article: March was a cold month (this year) | He was married in March.

15.3₂. Names of holidays (periods and special days), whether (1) simplex or (2) composite names, nearly all take the zero article:

(1) Christmas comes but once a year (generic) | Christmas is coming | Sh LLL 1.114 At Christmas | Rom II. 1.30 before Easter | Browning 1.501 Easter may Prove, not impossibly, the time | Beaconsfield L 56 Towards the close of Lent ... they always passed | Mackenzie S 812 [at Oxford] "Don't you realize you are up here for Commem — for Commemoration?" he asked.

(2) Twelfth Night | Holy Week | Palm Sunday | Easter-Day | Lord Mayor's Day (Caine C 112 zero, 123 *the*) | Ascension Day | Armistice Day | Sh As II. 2. 23 [as fit] as a pancake for Shroue-tuesday, a Morris for May-day | John I. 235 Vpon good Friday (but Lawrence SL 163 On the Good Friday he organized a walk to the Hemlock Stone) | Sh H4B II. 1.96 on Wednesday in Whitson week | Browning 1.507 But Easter-Day breaks! | ib 407 Holy-Cross Day | Lawrence SL 79 William was coming on Christmas Eve.

15.3₃. We may add some other names of periods and dates, among them some school and university terms: Black Week: Galsw IC 162 when Black Week came [in the Boer War] | Doomsday: Sh Hml V. 1.66 the Houses that he [a grave-digger] makes, lasts till Doomesday | Judgment Day: Kipling MI 269 we'll never know till Judgment Day; — but often with *the:* ib 174 where he might have lived till the Judgment Day | Browning 1.502 I felt begin the Judgment Day | Maugham AK 52 "I'll tell you what, there is one job I *shouldn't* like," he said. "What's that?" I asked. "God's, at the Judgment Day," said Gaze || Di P [Ch & H] 560 Trinity Term commenced [T.T. is both a law term and a university term] | James G 177 I suppose you will be getting away pretty soon, now Full Term is over | Mackenzie S 552 [Oxf.] Term drew to a close | ib 700 A few days later Michael had an answer from his mother to his invitation for Eights Week | Galsw FCh 179 the school concert at the end of term | Maynard Smith F 133 [schoolboy:] the day before end of leave I went out | Morrah M 159 he liked to cut himself off from the world of term-time directly vacation began | Beckett Iceland Adventure 17 On a lovely day at the end of May Week, 1932.

15.3₄. A few names of holidays and dates have *the* (or *a*, if the context requires it): the Sabbath | Lamb E [World's Class.] 11 Peradventure the Epiphany, ... would, once in six years, merge in a Sabbath. — *Epiphany*, however, is often used with zero. Further dates named by the number of the day of the month: the 1st of January. Thus also the two Roman terms *Kalends* and *Ides:* Sh Cæs I. 2.18 Beware the Ides of March; cf the fictitious term *at the Greek Kalends*, i. e. 'never': Lamb E [World's Class.] 330 somewhere between the Greek Calends and Latter Lammas. Plural names of Roman festivals also have *the:* the Lupercalia | the Saturnalia, etc.

If a name of a holiday, festival, date, etc, is connected with a determinative, or the context otherwise requires it, *the* is used: Browning 1.481 On the Christmas Eve of 'Forty-nine | Everton MP 6 On the Monday of the same week, George received a telegram.

15.3₅. Names of seasons, when used without reference to the particular qualities of this period, thus often with reference to its beginning, or in statements of their mere existence, have zero. This may be due to a more or less pronounced personification: Sh Merch I. 3.82 in the end of autumne | Wiv II. 1.127 ere sommer comes | Shelley 642 If Winter comes, can Spring be far behind | ib 662 When Winter had gone and Spring came back The Sensitive Plant was a leafless wreck | Quincey [World's Class.] 129 As winter drew near ... | Browning 1.518 Here's spring come | Tennyson 264 I dream'd there would be Spring no more | Lawrence SL 216 Now it was spring, and there was battle between him and Miriam.

15.3₆. But if the special characteristics of the sea on

are referred to, we find the definite article. There is, however, much vacillation. Some of the following examples in other authors perhaps would have zero. There seems to be a slight tendency to use *the* more frequently in connexion with *spring* than with the other names of seasons. Sh according to Sh-Lex. s. v. *Spring* has only one instance of zero before *spring* (Tp IV. 114), but plenty with *the* or possessive pronouns. And the other names frequently have zero: Sh LLL I 1. 99 Berowne is like an enuious sneaping Frost, That bites the first borne infants of the Spring | Mids II. 1.111 The Spring, the Sommer, The childing Autumn, angry Winter change Their wonted Liueries | Cæs I. 2.98 we can both Endure the Winters cold | Browne RM 32—33 whether the World was created in Autumn, Summer, or the Spring | Shelley 655 And the Spring arose on the garden fair (also ib 641) | ib 660 Swift Summer into the Autumn flowed | Jerome TB 15 It appeared to me that I was providing for this crew for the winter | Drinkwater P 76 The spring is passing through the land | Rose Macaulay T 71 The Russian country in the summer ... Moscow in the autumn ... And in the winter ... but one cannot think about Russia in the winter at all | Sherwood Anderson WM 281 In the spring he swam in rivers | Allingham P 29 great-aunt, who drives in a victoria in the summer and a brougham in the winter | Lehmann DA 205 Where shall I be, I wonder by the summer | Strong B 264 In the winter, there were jobs to be had too | Howard Spring S 91 The winter was coming on.

Note Merriman S 83 In winter the Neva is a broad silent thoroughfare ...In the winter the rattle of the cobble-stones is at last silent ... (seemingly without any difference between *the* and zero) | Hawthorne T 119 They had done with summer [temporal sense] before the summer [pregnant sense] came.

15.3₇. Names of parts of the day likewise frequently take zero when used in a mere temporal sense and in personification: Spenser FQ I. 1.33 now day is spent | Congreve OB 80 since break of Day | Wordsw 14 at break of day I will come to thee again! | id P 5.435 twilight was coming on | Stevenson K 170 Night fell as we were walking | Doyle S 1261 I expect that we shall see you before morning | Benson D 62 morning found him not only alive, but remarkably well and hearty | Maugham P 194 Dawn was breaking now | Sherwood Anderson WM 99 She had seen him driving at evening through the street (generally *in the evening*) | Lawrence SL 229 Paul did not come till afternoon | Woolf D 224 One might fancy that day, the London day, was just beginning | Sitwell M 266 Dusk came, and he walked up and down along the terrace | Hemingway F 86 Nothing happened until afternoon | Lehmann DA 209 By midday it would be extremely unpleasant in Cambridge | AHuxley BL 18 cataloguing herself among the tranquil charms of evening | Lindsay CA 19 By afternoon they were able to make out its tree shapes.

15.3₈. Here, too, we find *the* when there is a reference to the characteristics of the word. And here, too, there is vacillation in the usage. We say *by day, by night, at night,* but *in the morning, in the evening.* A few examples: Sh Lucr 746 she prays she never may behold the day (rare with *the* in this sense of *day* in Sh) | LLL I. 1.42 to sleepe but three houres in the night, And not be seene to winke of all the day | Merch II. 5.26 [Clown] at six a clocke ith morning, falling out that yeere on ashwensday was foure yeere in th'afternoone | Hml I. 5.9 I am thy Fathers Spirit, Doom'd for a certaine terme to walke the night; And for the day confin'd to fast in Fiers | Matt 8.16 AV: When the euen was come, they brought vnto him many; RV: When evening was come ... | Walton A 2 this fine pleasant fresh May day in the Morning | Byron 586 The day at last has broken | Shelley 655 Like a doe in the noontide | Di P [Ch&H] 23 you shall hear from me in the morning, sir | Benson DA 197 After they had parted for the night | Zangwill G 367 She thought of Reginald the last thing at night and the first thing in the morning | Blunden U 7 Although May had come, the day was dull | Mason Ch 250 The night had fallen.

We always have *the* in the phrase *stay the night:* Galsw T 192 a farm where we could stay the night | id WM 115 | Priestley F 25 I shall stay the night | Sayers NT 16, etc. — This is sometimes parallel in sense to Scottish *the day* 'today'. — Cf above, 12.3_1.

15.3$_9$. In the United States the definite article is often omitted before a composite indication of time, originally probably by prosiopesis: Norris O [p.?] if my carpenters can begin work in here day after to-morrow (also id P 159) | id P 185 year before last | ib 221 only day before yesterday | Matthews F 111 they are going to dine with me day after to-morrow | ib 228 I saw him with Daisy summer before last. | Bromfield Mod. Hero 124 I am coming to Chicago week after next. — Cf above, 12.3_5.

There is an increasing tendency to say *quarter to five*, etc (cf above, 12.3_4).

Chapter XVI

Proper Names

16.1₁. A proper name strictly has a meaning only in connexion with the person or thing it denotes, hence it necessarily involves some degree of familiarity with the "thing-meant" on the part of the speaker.

According to convention, it is true, some names are generally used about certain categories, but this is no fixed rule (only think of the large number of personal names which were originally place-names). In general we may consider a proper name as an arbitrary label used to denote a certain familiar person or thing (or group of persons or things), and according to the theory of the stages of familiarity (see above, 12.4₄) the sb therefore needs no definite article.

On the theory of proper names see Alan Gardiner, *The Theory of Proper Names* (1940) with some references.

We may say that proper names in their ordinary application fall outside the group of words that may be classified or particularized, thus being on a par with certain functions of mass-words, to which they are related in more than one way as regards the use of articles.

Personal Names

16.1₂. In practice personal names when applied to one definite person take the zero article: John, Smith, John Smith, Victoria, etc, but when modified by an adj or a title we sometimes have the definite article; cf below, 16.3₈ ff. and 16.6.

On the use of the indefinite article with words generally used as proper names see above, 12.5₈ ff.

On typical and honorific *the* see above, 14.2, and below, 16.3.

Place-Names

16.1₃. Many place-names regularly take the definite article in English.

For plural names *the* is the rule: the word denotes a plurality of units, and consequently is a kind of class-noun. By definition a proper name denotes familiarity on the part of the speaker, and hence a plural name naturally takes the definite article like (other) class-nouns.

According to vol II 4.74 and 5.742 most place-names with plural forms are now treated syntactically as singulars (The Solomons was no place for a woman).

Use of the definite article with singular names is due to the following reasons:

(1) The name is (supposed to be) an original common name, and *the* denotes familiarity;
(2) Foreign influence;
(3) Ellipsis.

River-Names

16.1₄. In OE river-names had zero, e. g. Cædmon 231 (q Schröter) *þridda is Tigris*, but from early ME we find the definite article with river-names increasingly frequently until about 1720 when this becomes the established usage except in a few definite cases.

A few early examples of *the:* Layamon v. 13790 (vol. II 152) inne þere Temese | Ch E 48 Where as the Poo . . . Taketh his first springing and his sours | Caxton Eneydos (q Pirkhofer EStn 70.96) admyrall of the styge | More A 77 for the length of thirtie miles it filleth all the Anyder with salte water | Lyly E 453 hir maiestie was for hir recreation in hir Barge vpon ye Thames | Sh Wiv III. 5.122 to be throwne into the Thames | Ant II. 7.20 they take the flow o'th' Nyle By certaine scales i'th' Pyramid

| Cymb III. 5.17 Leaue not the worthy *Lucius* ... Till he haue crost the Seuern.

Margarete Schröter in her thesis *Der bestimmte Artikel bei Flussnamen i Neuenglischen* (Halle 1915) has made it probable that the use of the definite article with river-names is due to foreign (i. e. Dutch, French and German) influence, but even so there must in English have developed some susceptibility to this influence, and this is no doubt the familiarity of some river-names. It is worth noting that *Thames*, the name of the best-known English river, seems to be the first name to take *the* regularly, while foreign names more often have zero. In Sh *Nile* takes *the* once only, and *Tiber* does not seem to take it all.

A few early examples of river-names with zero: LondE 127 into Thamise | ib 128 in Themise | Cooper Dic: *Ablacus*, A riuer running into Danubius | Marlowe F 835 Iust through the midst runnes flowing *Tybers* streame | ib 809 Wee sawe the riuer *Maine* fall into *Rhine* | Sh: Tyber; Nile; see Sh-Lex. | AV Gen 2.13 And the name of the second riuer is Gihon (similarly ib 11 and 14).

An influential factor in the development no doubt was the frequent type of collocation *the river Thames* (e. g. Defoe R 47 beyond the river *Amazones;* common to this day: we nearly always say *the river Dee*). Early grammarians explain *the Thames* as short for *the river Thames*, and Sweet NEG § 2037 says, "We have an instinctive feeling that *the Thames* is short for *the river Thames*."

An early type is *the river of Thames*, e. g. More A 77 vntill it come to the ryuer of Anyder | Puttenham 157 any speach vsed beyond the riuer of Trent | Cooper Dic: *Abaortæ*, A people about the riuer of Indus.

16.1₅. In ModE river-names have zero in connexion with town-names, e. g. Newcastle-upon-Tyne, Stratford-(up)on-Avon; still we may find *Frankfurt on the Oder* (from *Frankfurt an der Oder*, thus Brit. Enc. s.v.), *Frankfurt on the Main* (ib s.v. Goethe), but also *F. on Main* (because of monosyllabic *am* in *Frankfurt am Main?*).

Cf above, 12.8, on prepositional groups with zero; the same tendency is also found after *up* (cf *up river, up stream*), e. g. Ruskin P 1.159 up Rhine. — similarly with *Channel:* Austen M 207 written as the ship came up Channel | Kipling MI 3 We're expecting some tea-ships up-Channel | Meredith E 284 our neighbours across Channel — and note Ruskin P 162 across Atlantic.

Further zero with river-names is frequent in modern poetry, e. g. Gray 37 where Mæander's amber waves In ling'ring lab'rinths creep | ib 42 When Severn shall re-echo with affright | Wordsw 47 Wharf shall be to pitying hearts A name more sad than Yarrow | ib 30 And, coming to the banks of Tone, There did she rest | Byron, The Age of Bronze V Like startled giants by Nile's famous flood | Scott LL 2.28 From Yarrow's braes, and banks of Tweed | ib 4.22 were I now where Allan glides | Tennyson 113 But he ... came crowing over Thames | Arnold Poems 184 the low flat strand of Oxus (thus also 193, but 184, 187, 193, 203 the Oxus) | Beddoes in CP 43 'Mongst the reeds and flowers of Styx | Francis Thompson in Anthol. of Mod. Verse 219 And lo, Christ walking on the water, Not of Gennesareth, but Thames | Drinkwater P 101 Where Rotha dreams its way from mere to mere.

Some of these forms with zero in poetry may simply be due to personification, thus, at any rate, when the river is addressed, as in Byron DJ 11.20 Hail! Thamis, hail! Upon thy verge ... | Arnold P 150 Keep fresh the grass upon his grave, O Rotha!

As before other words the definite article may be left out before two or more river-names used in close connexion, e. g. Mitford OV 34 Oh what a watery world to look back upon! Thames, Kennet, Loddon — all overflowed | Drinkwater P 84 The Avon holds as clear a way as Tweed or Thames.

Names of Oceans, Seas, Channels, Straits, and Lakes

16.1₆. Names of oceans and seas have *the:* the Kattegat | the Skagerrack. Most names are composite, and of these an elliptical form is generally used: the Adriatic | the Atlantic | the Baltic | the Mediterranean | the Pacific | Nicolson SP 141 the sad and wintry fringe of the Marmora.

But a full form with *Sea* or *Ocean* is frequently found, *Sea* sometimes being indispensable: The Atlantic Ocean | the Irish Sea | the North Sea.

Names of straits and channels have *the* (foreign influence, originally common names, plurals): the Bosporus | the Channel | the Dardanelles | the Hellespont: Smollett R 219 she demanded to know if I had ever been at the Hellespont (also Byron Corresp 1.80) | the Solent (Ekwall, Dic. of Place-names has *le Soland* 1395) | the Straits (formerly as a rule = the Straits of Gibraltar): Smollett R 224 I had picked up a smattering of Italian during a voyage up the Straits (also Byron Corresp 1.78; now generally about the Straits of Malacca).

Names of lakes have zero: Lake Michigan, Lake Superior, Loch Lomond, Windermere, Derwentwater (Southey L 84 The opposite shore of Derwentwater consists of one long mountain), Lake Leman (e. g. Macaulay E 4.137; = the Lake of Geneva, with *the* before junction), etc.

Names of Countries, etc

16.1₇. Most names of countries in the singular have zero. Plurals always take the definite article (cf above, 16.1₃):

the Americas: Cather D 8 All missionaries from the Americas were inveterate beggars.

the Balkans.

the Brazils (now generally the sg with zero): Defoe R 37 when I came to the *Brasils* (thus ib 85, 115, 147, but 38 at *Brasil*, 144 in *Brasil*) | Byron Corresp 2.39 he means to go to the Brazils with the Danish consul | Pemberton Two Women 226 a party from the Brazils.

the Grisons: Pater R 183 He came home at last, through the Grisons.

the Indies: Osborne 16 'twas brought out of the India's | Sterne SJ [P] 145 had I had both the Indies . . .

all the Russias: Bennett B 12 the feminine equivalent of the Tsar of All the Russias | Conrad Personal Record 122 Alexander I., Autocrat of all the Russias.

the Spains: Macdonell E 25 as if he was King of all the Spains and Emperor of all the Indies.

The same naturally applies to names whose origin from common names is still felt: *the Netherlands, the United States,* etc.

16.1₈. The use of *the* before names of countries in the singular is due to (1) foreign influence, (2) ellipsis, and perhaps in a few cases to the fact that the names were originally river-names:

(1) Foreign influence: the Caucasus | the Crimea | the Dobrudja (Nicolson SP 159 brochures about the Dobrudja and the Eger enclave) | the Engadine | the Friuli (Byron Corresp 1.77) | the Morea (Shelley Corresp 38 to reembark at Leghorn for the Morea; Byron Corresp 1.11 and 12) | the Palatinate | the Punjab (Kipling Kim

1) | the Ruhr | the Saar | the Savoy | the Sudan | the Tyrol (but Tennyson L 1.133 certain parts of Tyrol) | the Ukraine (but Conrad Personal Record 58 and 70 with zero) | the Yemen (Wells OH 319).

A few of these perhaps rather belong to Group Two.

(2) Elliptical names: the Argentine (republic) | the Sahara (desert) | the Transvaal (republic).

(3) From river-names: the Congo (or on the analogy of French?) | the Klondike.

Names of Islands

16.1₉. Names of single islands as a rule have zero, while names of groups of islands like other plural place-names have *the:* Forster P 192 before he goes to the Andamans | Mason Ch 137 in the channels of the Bahamas | Twain S 74 There are no mosquitos in the Bermudas in May (also: in Bermuda) | the Philippines | Belloc EB 84 he saw active service in the Seychelles.

Names of Mountains and Mountain Ranges

16.2₁. British names of mountains have zero, as e.g. all names with *Mount*, but also others: (English:) Scawfell, Helvellyn, Whernside, (Welsh:) Cader Idris, Plymlimmon, (Scottish:) Ben Lomond, Ben Nevis | Southey L 80 Just behind the house rises a fine mountain, by name Latrigg, it joins Skiddaw; (others:) Byron Letters (Selected) 34 We...landed at the foot of Parnassus | ib 35 Mount Ida is still in high feather | NP 1935 Those who read the accounts of the assaults on Everest and Kanchenjunga | ib. The conquest of Kamet was made in 1931.

But in imitation of foreign usage we find e. g. the Rigi | the Jungfrau | the Matterhorn | Ruskin On Painting 157 There are three trees on the Mount Salève.

16.2₂.] Islands. — Mountains. — Towns. 551

The vacillation in Collingwood R 364 I saw Mont Blanc again | ib 367 returning homewards by the Mont Cenis — is no doubt due to *the Mont Cenis* here standing for *the Mont Cenis Tunnel*. "I should use *the* Mont Cenis of the tunnel!" says Prof. Collinson.

Names of mountain ranges seem to have *the* whether plural or singular, the latter perhaps being considered elliptical (omission of *mountains* or *hills*): the Adirondacks | the Alps | Byron Corresp 2.122 possess myself of the pinnacle of the Andes | the Appennines | Shaw TT 56—57 in the Atlas or where you please | the Cheviots | the Grampians | the Dolomites | Woolf D 213 in the Himalayas | the Pennines | A Huxley BL 112 climbing in the Jura | Lawrence SPW 35 In the Lebanon.

Note *Snowdon*, group of mountains in Wales, with zero: Borrow, Wild Wales 199 we set out for Snowdon ... Snowdon or Eryri is no single hill, but a mountainous region...

Names of Towns

16.2₂. Very few names of towns take the definite article: *the Hague* (Dutch *den Haag*, F *la Haye*) and *the Piraeus* (e. g. Byron Corresp 1.16 I am about to take my daily ride to the Piraeus | Maugham Alt 752 He's sailing from the Piræus), both by foreign influence. Further *the Hook* (*of Holland*), an adaptation of *Hoek-van-Holland* (e. g. BBC 1941 a supply ship was sunk off the Hook of Holland), and *the Skaw* (cf Dan. *Skagen* with enclitic article).

Formerly *Bath* had the definite article: Spectator no. 179 a Whistling Match, which, ... I was entertained with ... at the Bath.

Names of Parks

16.2₃. Names of Parks generally have zero.

The Green Park seems to be the commoner form: Bennett P 17 Hyde Park, the Green Park (id PL 4) | Galsw D 210, Sw 66, EC 616 | Walpole W, F 384 | Woolf D 30 in the Green Park . . . in Regent's Park | and others, but Rose Macaulay P 257 walking across Green Park.

Central Park in New York has zero: Dine B 20 Entering Central Park at Fifth Avenue.

Formerly *Hyde Park* had the definite article: Broughton Rem. 1.160 I dined at Cuthbert's, and went with him . . . to the Hyde Park, — and *the Regent's Park* may be found: Di P [Ch&H] 631 [old Weller:] a walk round the Regency Park | Collins W 16 it leads to . . . the Regent's Park (ib 18). Maxwell ML has both *the Regent's Park* and zero. *Regent's Park* is now the normal to Londoners.

Names of Streets and Roads

16.2₄. Names with *Street* as a rule have zero: Oxford Street, etc, but *High Street* in provincial towns generally takes *the:* Di P [Ch&H] 14 the Bull Inn, in the High Street (but ib 435 a wine vaults in High Street) | Browning 1.411 As the Piper turned from the High Street To where the Weser rolled its waters, etc. *High Street* with zero e. g. Bennett BA 147, Galsw IC 125.

The familiar elliptical form of (*the*) *High Street*, Oxford, is necessarily always *the High* (*High* alone perhaps would not be understood): Sayers GN 286 She started up the High. — Similarly *the Broad*.

Names with *Lane* have zero: Park Lane, Petticoat Lane, etc.

16.2₅. Names with *Road* frequently have *the:* this is no doubt due to the fact that many of these are actually roads leading to the place denoted by the first part of the name, e. g. *the Edgware Road* = the road to Edgware. But most frequently we find zero.

Examples with *the*, alphabetically: *the* Banbury Road (AHuxley BL 108) | the Battersea Park Road (Sayers WB 51) | the Bayswater Road (Stevenson N 121, Bennett P 165, Galsw FCh frequently; WLL (= Ward, Lock & Co., London) 140 Oxford Street changes its name to the Bayswater or Uxbridge Road) | the Brompton Road (Wells LL, Lucas RR 87, WLL 128, etc) | the Camberwell Road (Ridge Mord Em'ly 21 Draper's shop in the Kemberwell Road begins selling off a Monday) | the Charing Cross Road (but WLL 113 with zero) | the Cromwell Road (WLL 156 The New Buildings with a frontage to the Cromwell Road of 720 ft. and to Exhibition Road of 275 ft., but ib and elsewhere zero) | the Edgware Road (Hunt A 302 On leaving prison I went to live in the Edgeware Road; Ainsworth Jack Sheppard 380 along the Edgeware Road; Broughton Reminiscences1.190 and in many modern quotations, but perhaps most frequently with zero) | the Euston Road (Wells K 282, Hay KW 153, Galsw Frat, id MW passim, WLL 144, etc) | the Exhibition Road (Wells LL 69, but WLL 156 with zero, see above *the Cromwell Rd*) | the Finchley Road (Hay KW 22,91, Garnett MZ 177; but Hay KW 25 with zero) | the Fulham Road (Hay KW 196, AHuxley EG 311, but Freeman Th 411 along the Brompton Road... down a quiet street between that and Fulham Road) | the Hammersmith Road, etc (Mackenzie S 1.55 up Carlington Road into the Hammersmith Road and along the Kensington Road as far as the Earl's Court Road) | the Hampstead Road (Jerome Tommy & Co. 93) | the Harrow Road (Bentley TI 224, AHuxley BL 171, WLL 140, etc) | the Kennington

Road (Maugham FPS 292) | the Kent Road (Broughton Reminiscences 1.139) | the Marylebone Road (Jerome Tommy & Co. 82 and 86, but elsewhere with zero, Garnett MZ 186, Maugham FPS 32 and 34, WLL 136 The Marylebone Road with its continuation Euston Road runs from Edgware Road to King's Cross) | the Old Kent Road (Ridge Mord Em'ly 6, Chesterton Di 214, etc) | the Tottenham Court Road (Maugham Pl 2.233, Woolf D 210, Sayers GN 12, WLL 142 and 143, but ib 143 with zero; thus also Smollett R 291, Collins W [Reader's Libr.] 17, Sayers DC 24) | the Upper Richmond Road (Bennett BA 147 he returned ... by the Upper Richmond Road to High Street. He was on the south side of Upper Richmond Road) | the Westminster Road (Chaplin, Wonderful Visit 81).

If the *Road* is named after a bridge, the name nearly always takes *the:* Maugham FPS 292 she took the tram that tuns down the Vauxhall Bridge Road (but WLL 101 Vauxhall Bridge Road ... leads to Vauxhall Bridge) | AHuxley EG 56 They ... swung into the Waterloo Bridge Road | Jerome TB 78 drive us to the Westminster Bridge Road (also Maugham MS 239, etc).

Mr. Walt Arneson believes that it is just as often without *the* in U.S.

The King's Road (in Chelsea), which is perhaps less frequent than *King's Road*, should probably be analyzed as *the King's | Road*.

16.2₆. Originally common names generally take *the:* Spectator 1 in the Theatres both of *Drury-Lane* and the *Hay-Market* | Smollett R 62 Isaac Rapine, the moneybroker, in the Minories | the Poultry | the Strand.

Thus also *the Mall:* Swift P 105 Will your Ladyship be on the *Mall* To-morrow Night?

Pall Mall has zero now, but note Swift J 216 [I] then walk up the Pall Mall (and Pepys 13th July, 1663).

American names consisting of an ordinal + *Street* or *Avenue* apparently always take zero, although ordinals normally have *the:* OHenry B 47 on Seventy-first Street | ib 63 where Broadway and Fifth Avenue flow together | Sherwood Anderson DL 24 near Forty Seventh Street | Morley HB 77 across 59th Street to Fifth Avenue | Loos GMB 109 on 44th Street, etc.

The ordinal may be used alone if there is no possibility of misunderstanding: OHenry B 87 They whirled up Forty-second to Broadway | Dreiser AT 1.93 at Eleventh | Morley HB 79 Fifth Avenue between 42nd and 59th | Clarence Day L 2 from Madison Avenue over to Sixth.

16.2₇. Names of streets on the Continent have *the:* Times 1935 the driving power of the Quai d'Orsay | Maugham M 4 They had lunched at a restaurant at the Boulevard Saint Michel | Crofts Cask 80 in the Boule Miche | ib 91 the rue Provence | Rose Macaulay T 78 the Via Babuino | Merriman VG 142 Then master and dog took a walk down the Calle del Pozo Blanco | Jerome I 130 one of the chief restaurants on the Nevsky | Mencken BB 113 one of those big restaurants on the Unter den Linden | Carlyle SR [Univ. Libr.] 23 It was the attic floor of the highest house in the Wahngasse | Gosse D 51 northwards along the Kjöbmagergade (but ib. with zero: Admiralgade).

Mr. Walt Arneson informs me that the tendency in Amr English is to use zero ("On Unter den Linden", etc).

Names of Buildings
(and Groups of Buildings)

16.3₁. Here, again, we find the three types:
(1) Originally common names,
(2) Elliptical forms, and

(3) Forms with *the* due to foreign influence; but it is not easy (or even possible) to keep the three types apart in every case.

Originally common names take the definite article, e. g. *the Tower, the Temple*, and *the Yard*, the familiar name of (*New*) *Scotland Yard*.

Elliptical forms are names of hotels, inns, clubs, theatres, and various other more or less official institutions. If the remaining part is a genitive, then the name has zero: Spectator 1 at *Will's* [coffee-house] | ib. Sometimes I smoak a Pipe at *Child's* | Crofts Ch 214 not one of the great hotels de luxe like the Savoy in London or the de Crillon or Claridge's in Paris | WLL 111 Also on the left are Arthur's, the Cocoa Tree, Brooks's, the New University, and the Devonshire [clubs].

Otherwise we find *the:* Ch A 718 this gentil hostelrye That highte the Tabard, faste by the Belle | Austin P 190 when we got to the George [Inn], I do think we behaved very handsomely | Galsw TL 24 he glanced up at the Iseeum [Club] | id Sw 154 let's go to the Parthenæum! [Club] | Crofts Ch 9 In the Edgecombe: the Edgecombe Hotel, you know, in Plymouth | Gilbert Frankau in BDS 426 that large and lavish hotel, the Tivoli | WLL 111 the Windham, the East India United Service, the Portland, and other clubs | ib 114 the Garrick [Theatre] | the Hippodrome | the Colosseum. — But with zero: go to Drury Lane, — to Covent Garden (probably because of the reference to the place).

16.3₂. This also applies to names of churches and temples. In some cases foreign influence, too, may have been active.

Elliptical genitive with zero: St. Paul's, etc.

Other elliptical names with *the:* Benson DA 92 At nine the procession leaves St. Peter's to go to the Lateran || Harvey Comp. to Class. Lit. 4 On the N. side stood the Erectheum | ib 55 the Areopagus . . . and the Pnyx.

Foreign simplex names of castles and palaces take the definite article: Sterne SJ [P] 106 the Bastile is but another word for a tower | Byron Letters (Sel.) 39 The walls of the Seraglio | Benson DA 82 in the direction of the Trianon | ib 96 a prisoner of the Vatican | the Alhambra | the Louvre.

Elliptical names of colleges take zero: Hughes T 2.3 Oriel at that time alone enjoyed this distinction | Mackenzie S 2.536 a light comedian from Pembroke, a tenor from Corpus, a comic singer from Oriel and a mimic from professional London | Hall, Alma Mater 49 the crocus-fringed paths of Magdalen | ib 53 the Master of Balliol. — On *the House* see 16.3$_3$.

16.3$_3$. Most names of buildings consisting of a common name denoting a building and a preposed determinative (proper name or common name), take the zero article, thus composite names with:

Abbey: Westminster Abbey.

Castle: Windsor Castle.

Cathedral: Westminster Cathedral.

Church: Hampstead Church (WLL 251).

College: Eton College.

Court: Hampton Court.

Hall: Westminster Hall, but often *the* Albert Hall.

Lodge: Pembroke Lodge, but WLL 256 the White Lodge (junction with adj).

Palace: Buckingham Palace, but *the* Crystal Palace.

School: Westminster School. — Note: go to Eton, Harrow, Rugby, etc. (reference to the place).

Yard: (New) Scotland Yard.

British names with *House* as second member as a rule

have zero: Holland House, Mansion House (but WLL 57 the Mansion House), whereas American names of this type have *the* (see Horwill MAU *s.v. house*).

According to Horwill Americans distinguish between names of private houses, with the spelling *house*, as *the Johnson house* (small *h*) 'the house of the Johnson family,' and names of hotels or the like, with the spelling *House*, as *the Johnson House* (capital *H*).
The House at Oxford = Christ Church College, otherwise = the House of Commons.

American names with *Building* as second member also take the definite article: the Woolworth Building, the Flatiron Building, etc (see Horwill MAU *s.v. building*).

16.3₄. Composite names of hotels, inns, restaurants, clubs, theatres, etc, likewise take the definite article: Galsw TL 3 the Knightsbridge Hotel | Mason Ch 75 She ... moved to the Hotel Quirinale in the Via Nationale | Lewis B 40 in the Hotel Thornleigh | WLL 106 the Ritz Hotel || Di P [Ch&H] 14 the Bull Inn | ib 121 the yard of the White Hart Inn || WLL 114 the Trocadero Restaurant || WLL 61 the Union Club || ib 112 the Haymarket Theatre ... the Comedy Theatre | ib 114 the Shaftesbury Theatre ... the Globe Theatre, the Apollo Theatre and the Lyric Theatre.

But if the first member is a genitive, the rule is zero: WLL 123 In this street is Claridge's Hotel || Swift J 2 at St. James's coffee-house || WLL 114 Wyndham's Theatre. — Exceptional instances with *the*: Doren Swift 93 the St. James's coffee-house || WLL 63 the St. Stephen's Club.

16.3₅. Most names of railway stations now have zero: Paddington Station | Edgware Road Station | Liverpool Street Station | Elephant and Castle; but: the Grand Central Station (*the* because of the adj).

But originally they required *the:* Collins W [Reader's Libr.] 178 at the Blackwater station | ib 245 to the Waterloo Bridge station | ib 246 the Limmeridge station (*station* is still felt as an independent common name and hence written with a small *s*) | Payn, Holiday Tasks 215 [q Bruggencate] Starting from the Paddington Station.

And names of foreign stations naturally take *the*: Crofts Cask 99 I took it to the Gare St Lazare | ib 126 the Gare de Lyons | Hemingway TS [L 1933] 56 On our way from the Gare du Nord ... | the Hauptbahnhof.

Double names denoting museums also have the definite article: the British Museum | the London Museum | the Wallace Collection | the Tate Gallery.

Names of arches, arcades, and gates have *the:* the Admiralty Arch | the Wellington Arch | Rose Macaulay T 315 at the Grosvenor Gate | Kipling PT 144 near the Taksali Gate | WLL 117 the Burlington Arcade ... the Royal Arcade ... the Piccadilly Arcade.

The Golden Gate, the name of the channel near San Francisco may have zero. Generally *Marble Arch*.

But names of bridges have zero: Magdalen Bridge (Oxford) | WLL 62 from Westminster Bridge to Blackfriars Bridge | ib 63 below Waterloo Bridge.

The Adelphi and *the Albany* are probably elliptical (Chesterton WFB 77 the steep streets of the Adelphi | Woolf D 27 Little Mr. Bowley, who had rooms in the Albany). *The Kremlin* is no doubt due to foreign influence (Maugham Alt 985 the Kremlin with its pealing bells).

But how about *the Bronx?* (Rice, Imperial City 44 little houses of Manhattan, Brooklyn, Queens and the Bronx). Named after Jonas Broncks (born in the Faroes).

16.3₆. Names of ships practically always have *the* when used by landsmen. This may be due to the fact that these are often originally common names (*The Swan*, etc): Ch A 410 His barge ycleped was the Maudelayne | Sh Mcb I. 3.7 Her Husband's to Aleppo gone, Master o'th' Tiger | Smollett R 146 [I was] put on board of the Thunder, lying at the Nore | Kipling MI 239 The first officer of the Breslau asked me to dinner on board.

I have noted the following two early examples of zero: Mi PL 2.1017 And more endangered when Argo passed through Bosporus | Franklin 42 get yourself ready to go with "Annis"; which was the annual ship.

"The custom in the Royal Navy is to omit *the*. I notice the naval men say *in Warspite* where the landsmen would say *on the Warspite*. Plenty of examples of zero in official reports of naval engagements." (Professor Collinson).

Titles of Books, Newspapers, and Periodicals

16.3$_7$**.** Titles of books when used in a context generally keep their form as printed on the title-page. If there is a definite article this is retained (though not always italicized even though the rest of the title is so): Bailey Milton 120 the author of *Paradise Lost* ... was no morbid sectary | Bullett ModE Fiction 105 the world depicted by Mr. Kipling in *The Jungle Book* | Herford Eng. Lit. (Benn) 47 in *Songs of Innocence* and *Songs of Experience* he reveals the soul of childhood | Amy Cruse, After the Victorians 122 Mary Gladstone pronounced the *Jungle Book* "splendid" | ib 139 In 1868 Collins took another step forward with *The Moonstone*.

However, familiarity with the work in question is often denoted by means of the definite article, which naturally supplants the indefinite article if this is the first word of the proper title (cf 12.9$_1$): Lee, Great Englishmen of the 16th Cent. 28 The prefactory book of the *Utopia* is a vivid piece of fiction | Bailey Mj 102 in the *Prometheus Unbound* | ib 148 the *Paradise Lost* (also 149, 160, but with zero 161,162, 170) | Amy Cruse AV (128 A *Doll's House*) 129 the *Doll's House* should have ended with the husband helping himself to a whisky-and-soda . . .

The indefinite and the definite article in titles are generally left out after a genitive or possessive pronoun: Herford Eng. Lit. (Benn) 42 Goldsmith's *Vicar of Wakefield* | Amy Cruse AV 185 when, in 1896, she published *The Mighty Atom* . . . Her *Mighty Atom*. — But we may find examples of the articles being preserved in this position, e. g. ib 141 Conan Doyle's *A Study in Scarlet* | ib 157 John Oliver Hobbes's *The Dream and the Business*.

Foreign names of books of the Bible, such as *Genesis*, *Leviticus*, *Ecclesiastes*, as a rule do not take the definite article: Bale T 1120 as Genesis diffines | Rose Macaulay T 95 it says so in Genesis. — We generally say *the Apocalypse*, but may find zero as in Chesterton (q Bullett IC 201) the best in Apocalypse. — We have always *the Acts* (in a connected text).

Names of newspapers and periodicals mostly have *the:* The Manchester Guardian | The Daily Mail | The Daily Herald | The Evening News (but: Evening Standard) || The Strand (Magazine) | The Studio | The Bookman | The Physical Review, etc. But orig. mass-words and proper names have zero: Language | Vogue | Life | Time | American Speech | London Opinion || Punch | John Bull. Similarly plurals: Dialect Notes | Publications of the Modern Language Association of America | Tit-bits (but note: The Times).

In a connected text names of foreign papers have *the:* Crofts, Cask 114 the *Figaro* | NP 1935 the *Temps*.

Typical and Honorific *The* before Personal Names

16.3s. *The* is used in five related functions before personal names:

(1) It is used before man's names to indicate the distinction of a certain person: Marlowe J 20 Lawes were then most sure When like the Dracos they were writ in blood | H6A III. 3.31 There goes the Talbot, with his Colours spred | ib III. 3.36 A Parley with the Duke of Burgonie. — Who craues a Parley with the Burgonie? | Cæs II. 1.54 My Ancestors did from the Streetes of Rome The Tarquin driue.

This is no doubt a parallel to the use of the "typical *the*" mentioned above, 14.2.

(2) As a so-called "honorific *the*" it is now used with the surnames of some Irish and Scottish chiefs of clans, viz. *Chisholm* and names beginning with *Mac* or *O'*: Stevenson K [T] 236 a man under so dark a cloud as the Macgregor (and ib 238) | NP 1910 (q NED) Three 'Thes' have sat in the House of Commons in our time — The O'Conor Don, The O'Donoghue of the Glens, and the O'Gorman Mahon. The MacDermott, K.C., .. was an Irish law officer in Liberal Governments.

This use was found among Lowland and Border families at an early stage: the Bruce | Sh H4A V. 1.116 The Dowglas and Hotspurre both together, Are confident against the world in Armes | ib V. 4.26 Go to the Dowglas | Graves Eng. Ballads 65 [The Battle of Otterbourne] And for to meet the Douglas there, He rode right furiously | ib 68 The Percy and Montgomery met | ib. But I would yield to Earl Douglas, Or Sir Hugh the Montgomery, if he were here.

The use was adopted by Scott LL 2.24 Then Roderick from the Douglas broke | ib 2.35 Give our safe-conduct to the Græme | id Rob Roy: the Macgregor, and his use of *the Macgregor* may have given rise to the modern use before names with *Mac* and *O'*.

Cf James Dallas, *The Honorific 'The'* in *The Scott. Hist. Rev.* vol 10 (1913) pp. 39—47, in which this is interpreted as a special distinctive use of *the*, i. e. likewise related to the "typical *the*."

Cf also Herbert Maxwell, ib. pp. 230—31.

(3) In modern language *the* may be used facetiously before man's names, placing them in the category of petnames: Byron Corresp 2.99 Pray remember me to all friends, to the Scrope [i. e. Scrope Davies], and let me hear how you advance | ib 2.111 And the Douglas [i.e. Douglas Kinnaird] has not written to me about "the fee" [deliberate imitation of the above-mentioned Scottish type?] | ib 2.170 I have had a letter from the Dougal [also Kinnaird] | Stevenson N 188 It is the Scrymgeour [a bank clerk]. Very well, Mr. Scrymgeour.

In Kipling's Stalky the following two nicknames are found: S 3 Anyhow, I soothed the Hartoffles [i. e. Mr. Hartopp] | ib 17 The Hefflelinga means well [i. e. Mr. Prout].

(4) *The* may be used before names of some lady artists. This is also a distinctive use, but it may be due to foreign influence (French and Italian): 1796 (q NED) Last night the Siddons and the Kemble, at Drury Lane, acted to vacancy | NP 1933 (q Christophersen) the real farmer's boy of these days is a smart lad with a motor-bicycle and views about the Dietrich and the Garbo.

(5) *The* is sometimes used before a woman's name to confer a depreciatory sense to it. The speaker, as it were, does not want to be in the state of complete familiarity involved in a personal name with zero. Examples: Wells LL 71 It was the Miss Heydinger who had addressed

him | Priestley G 118 He's worried because the Tarvin [Mrs. T.] stopped me on Saturday | Christie Why 33 "It seems to me you're batty," said Frankie crossly, "over a painted-up raddled bitch — yes, I said *bitch* — like the Cayman | Sayers GN 201 Hellup, it's the [Miss] Chilperic | Macdonald N 215 The Carter-Fawcett, what about her?

It may be noted that Byron in his letters often mentions Italian ladies with *the* before their names, no doubt in conscious imitation of Italian practice: Corresp 2.79 I often go to the Benzona's [i. e. the Countess Marina Benzoni] | ib 2.82 The Segati and I have been off these two months | Letters (Selected) 150 I greatly fear that the Guiccioli [i.e. the Countess Guiccoli] is going into a consumption. — Cf Byron Letters 63 The Stael...

Titles and Other Common Names Connected with Personal Names

16.4₁. English royal and noble titles placed before a name generally take zero, because they are felt as being part of the proper name. Thus now always *king, queen, sir:* Sh John I. 1.252 King Richard Cordelion was thy father | Queen Anne is dead (cf Swift P 58 And pray, What News Mr. Neverout? — Why, Madam, Queen Elizabeth's dead) | Sh John I. 1.240 Sir Robert neuer holpe to make this legge.

Prince formerly might take *the:* Sh Wint IV. 2.29 when saw'st thou the Prince Florizel my son. — Thus still when the word refers to a foreign prince: Broughton Rem. 1.154 The Prince Frederick of Prussia and Madame Meerifeldt were in a box opposite to Lord Liverpool | Brit. Enc. 4.259 the German Fifth Army under the Crown Prince Rupprecht of Bavaria — and in court language and similar distinguished style: NP 1934 [From the Court Circular:] It is with the greatest pleasure that the King and Queen announce the betrothal of their dearly beloved son, the Prince George, to the Princess Marina ... | Benson DA 92 The Prince George arrived two days ago. His Highness is in the apartment below.

Princess more often is found with *the*, especially when referring to a foreign princess: Broughton Rem. 1.260 I went to the Princess Jablanowski's | NP 1886 [Berlin:] The Crown Princess was able to go out for a long drive yesterday. Her daughter, the Princess Victoria, has now also quite recovered from her attack of measles | Kipling S 38 The Slave of the Lamp, with the Princess Badroulbadour and the Widow Twankey ... | Strachey QV 189 The Princess Alice ... (but ib 188 Princess Alice played on it) | AHuxley BL 107 Mrs. Cloudesley, who has a profound knowledge of the Royal Family, mentions the Princess Alice | NP 1934 the forthcoming engagement of the Princess Juliana.

Lord formerly often took *the*, thus still in court style: Arden of Feversham I. 32 Yes, the Lord Clifford, he that loves not me | Sh Hml I. 3.89 somthing touching the L. Hamlet | ib 134 [not to] talke with the Lord Hamlet (but more often with zero) | Mi A: yet I for honour's sake ... shall name him, the Lord Brooke | Congreve OB 26 by the Lord Harry he says true (common) | id DD 147 A Gallery in the Lord Touchwood's House | NP 1937 [From the Court Circular:] The King and Queen were received upon arrival at the dais by Field-Marshal the Lord Milne.

On the type *the Right Honourable the Lord M.* see below, 16.6$_6$.

Lady. Here again the female parallel more frequently takes *the* in ModE: Puttenham 36 I haue read that the Lady Cynthia came once downe out of her skye |

Sh Ado II. 1.243 The Lady Beatrice hath a quarrell to you | Bacon always *the* according to Bøgholm BS 131 | Fielding JA [Everyman] 20 the gentle and cultivated mind of the Lady Booby (also ib 25, 27 but more frequently with zero) | Scott Iv (always) the Lady Rowena | Broughton R 2.15 a man recommended by the Lady Bessborough | Di P [Ch&H] 503 That's the Dowager Lady Snuphanuph | Ingoldsby 196 The Lady Odille was quite nervous with fear | Thack P 482 the Countess being occupied with her spaniel, the Lady Lucy's thoughts and eyes being turned upon a volume of sermons, and those of Lady Ann upon a new novel | Stevenson C 103 carried away like the Lady Grange | Jerome Tommy & Co. 99 Tommy can be the Lady Adelaide, your daughter | Belloc EB 85 he took to wife the Lady Arabella Hunt | Hadow Chaucer 58 Here the Lady Fame sits on a throne | Brett Young PC 782 Please tell Steven... to address me as "*The* Lady Wolverbury," not "Lady Wolverbury" | NP 1935 She and her twin sister, the Dowager Lady Lytton ...

On the distinction between *Lady* and *the Lady* see NED *Lady* 6a (small type).

16.4₂. *Viscount* and *Duke* referring to English persons practically always have zero. Poutsma has no examples of *the* before *viscount*. I have noted NP 1937 Donations... should be sent to the Fund's Hon. Treasurer, The Viscount Churchill. Poutsma has two quotations with *the Duke*, to which I may add Masefield Sh 55 The Queen's party, the Duke Humphrey's party. — The foreign titles of *Grand Duke* and *Archduke* always have *the:* Times Lit. Suppl. 1934 we may give his word-portrait of his nephew, the Grand Duke Ludwig III. of Hesse-Darmstadt | Gibbs BR 115 It was when the murder of the Archduke Ferdinand at Serajevo was published ... *Archduchess* and *Grand Duchess* with *the:* Maugham Pl 2.22 What can the *Church Times* have to do with the Archduchess Anastasia? | NP 1934 the marriage of the Grand Duchess Olga to the Archduke Stephen ... in 1845.

Count practically always has zero, but *Countess* often *the*, particularly when referring to foreign countesses: Byron Corresp. 2.39 I saw your correspondent, the Countess Mustani ... | Yeats The Countess Cathleen 59 and 95 with *the* | ib 85 twice with zero | Shaw TT 105 The Countess Valbrioni would like to know | Christie Big Four 71 the Countess Rossakoff.

The following foreign titles mostly have *the: emperor, empress, tsar (czar), tsarina, tsarevitch, elector, electress, comte, graf.* Examples: Puttenham 201 The Emperor Charles the fift was a man of very few words | Deloney 41 The seuenth was the Emperour Probus | Broughton Rem. 1.50 the headquarters of the Emperor Alexander | Mannin CI 280 as lamentable a failure as the Emperor Nero | Broughton Rem. 1.107 The Empress Maria Louisa regrets leaving the Tuileries | Golding SD 35 You might think he was the Tsar Nicholas | NP 1934 In 1841 Prince Alexander's sister was married to the Tsarevitch Alexander, afterwards the Emperor Alexander II. | NP 1934 The Electress Sophia | Chesterton B 22 One friend in particular he made, the Comte de Ripert-Montclar | Gibbs BR 156 The Graf von Arnsberg took her hand and kissed it.

Thus we also find *the* before *Kaiser* in Rose Macaulay T 221 In Tangier, the Kaiser Wilhelm of Germany made a speech; — but during a certain period the Kaiser's name was so familiar in England that he was termed *Kaiser Wilhelm* with zero (as in German).

16.4₃. The general honorific title referring to males has zero. Thus both *Mr.* and foreign titles: I met Mr. Smith in the street | NP 1933 Herr Brunngraber has a passion for figures | NP 1929 M. Briand ... remains at the Ministry of Foreign Affairs | NP 1929 Señor Rubio is certainly a good man of affairs, if the affairs are purely Mexican | Shelley 617 Did you inform his Grace that Signor Pigna Waits with state papers for his signature ? | Byron Letters 303 I am in correspondence with Signor Nicolas Karellas ... || But Lytton (q Poutsma) The Signor Colonna | AHuxley MC 80 so is the Signore Dolphin.

The corresponding female titles *Mrs., Miss, Madame, Mademoiselle, Frau,* and *Fräulein* likewise have zero: Mrs. (Miss) Smith | Madame de Stael (e. g. Byron Letters 61) | Fräulein Schröder (Isherwood).

But *Signora* and *Signorina* seem to require *the:* Shaw 1.113 not the Signora Duse or anyone connected with Ibsen | AHuxley MC 80 Have you seen the Signorina Toomis, Guiseppe ?

16.4₄. Professional names of various kinds, such as *Doctor, General, Professor, Cardinal,* and *Father* before a proper name take zero. Examples superfluous.

Before foreign names of this type we may find *the:* Scott Iv 443 he ... transported her safely to the house of the Rabbi Nathan | Russell, Life of Mezzofanti (1858) The Abbate M. suggests ... | Gosse, Ill. Hist. of Eng. Lit. 3.46 the Cardinal Richelieu.

Names of (existing or dissolved) relationship take zero: Uncle Tom | Sh Tp II. 1.76 Not since widdow Dido's time ... 79 What if he had said Widdower Æneas too ?

Widow may take *the:* Kipling S 38 the widow Twankey | Synge 77 the widow O'Flinn | ib 146 Would

I fetch you the Widow Quin, maybe? — But this is dialectal or archaic; *Widow* is never preposed in Standard Eng. now.

16.4₅. When a common name placed before a person's name cannot be considered part of the name as a title, the definite article is necessary. The common name frequently follows the proper name: Smollett R 41 Damn that son of a bitch, Smack, the coachman | Pater R 115 Cecilia Galerani the poetess | ib 113 So we find him often in intimate relations with men of science, — with Fra Luca Paccioli the mathematician, and the anatomist Marc Antonio della Torre | Sindbad the Sailor | the naturalist Huxley. — Synge even uses this form in address: Synge 73 Of what is it you're speaking, Timmy the smith?

Similarly: William the Conqueror | St. John the Baptist | the Virgin Mary. When Carlyle in such collocations leaves out the article, he is not in accordance with natural English usage.

But *nurse* takes zero: Williamson T 101 The shooting of Nurse Cavell on October 12th roused a storm of indignation | Sayers UD 96 Nurse Forbes primmed up her lips.

And American journalists may use zero in such cases as the following (Time 1945): Critic John Ruskin and Poet William Morris | Author Broch | Lawyer Pellizzari | Translator Samuel Putnam.

16.4₆. When a proper name stands for a statue or picture of a person thus named, it may or may not take the definite article: Gosse D 62 a posthumous statue of Hans Christian Oersted ... some of his pupils ... unwrapped for us, not the Oersted only, but other of the artist's works | Wells L 85 Michael Angelo's horned Moses ... Lewisham regarded Moses ... his eyes went back to the Moses.

Personification

16.5₁. The chief reason why personification is very frequent in English probably is that English has very few traces of grammatical gender left; see further Phil. of Gr. p. 236. — It belongs chiefly to poetic language; a personification is in fact a kind of metaphor. An abstract or collective notion (also occasionally a concrete mass) is conceived as a unit, and this is visualized (poetically) as a person, and the word denoting it is treated to all intents and purposes like a personal name:

(1) It is often written with a capital letter like other proper names: Gray Elegy v. 8 Let not Ambition mock their useful toil ... Nor Grandeur hear with a disdainful smile The short and simple annals of the poor | Cowper L [1827] 13 How mysterious are the ways of Providence! | Pater R 91 Once and again he introduces Love and Death, who dispute concerning him. — More examples in what follows.

(2) It may be constructed with the *s*-genitive: Spenser FQ I. 1.18 God helpe the man so wrapt in *Errours* endlesse traine | Carlyle Essays [Blackie] 209 whether we look at Nature's work with him or Fortune's | Benson Daisy's Aunt 184 And yet I rather like Nature's uneconomical habits | Jerome T 126 Night's heart is full of pity for us | Drinkwater P 87 Earth's little weary peoples fall on peace | Brooke 1914 12 We have built a house that is not for Time's throwing | Woolf D 113 death's enormous sickle had swept those hills.

(3) It may be supplanted by pronouns which only refer to persons: *he, she, his, her, who, himself, herself:* Wm. Johnson Cory in CP 164 For Death, he taketh all away | Dekker Sh II. 2.23 do Fortune what she can, The Gentle Craft is liuing for a man | Trollope W 2 here probably Scandal lied, as she so often does |

16.5₁.] Personification. 571

Bullett IC 145 A philosopher must be faithful to Truth even when she is old and ill-favoured || Spenser FQ I. 1.39 Whiles sad Night ouer him her mantle black doth spred | Daniel DR 30 But it is euer the misfortune of Learning, to be wounded by her owne hand | Byron ChH 1.46 Here Folly still his votaries inthralls; And young-eyed Lewdness walks her midnight rounds | Scott LL 3.31 And Silence claim'd her evening reign | Jerome TB 148 History is fond of her little ironies || Defoe R 174 Nature, who gives Supplies of Food || Byron ChH 4.163 Time himself hath hallow'd it | Browning 1.529 [he] Got touched upon the sleeve familiarly ... By Death himself | Edgar Allan Poe in CP 45 Lo! Death has reared himself a throne | Spenser FQ I. 1.12 Vertue giues her selfe light, through darkenesse for to wade | Sterne M 1.19 as sorry a jade, as Humility herself could have bestrided | Ruskin On Painting 104 But it is a widely different thing when nature herself takes a coloring fit. — Cf above, 5.8₅ f.

Very often *itself* is used in similar collocations, which may also be considered cases of personification: Goldsm V 199 The leaving ... was not without a tear, which scarce fortitude itself could suppress | Galsw FCh 275 the crowd became solidity itself | Jerome Tommy & Co. 27 Curiosity itself paled at contemplation of it | Dickinson MS 115 Time itself works against us | Wilder H 99 Brush's answer was composure itself | Mason Ch 190 Guy Stallard was ease itself.

(4) The notion, etc, may be represented as acting like a human being, thus *death*, as in art, is represented as a reaper with his sickle, etc: Ch C 675 Ther cam a privee theef, men clepeth Deeth, That in this contree al the peple sleeth (*Death* is a character in this tale, the Pardoner's Tale) | Keats 75 Time, that aged nurse,

Rock'd me to patience | Thomas Hood in CP 15 And Morning sings with a warm odorous mouth | Browning 1.528 don't you know, I promised ... We'd see truth dawn together? — truth that peeps Over the glasses' edge when dinner's done, And body gets its sop and holds its noise And leaves soul free a little | Wilde R 182 And Horror stalked before each man, And Terror crept behind | Lindsay CA 13 he gave malice a fair return for playing a rotten trick like this on him.

(5) The word in question, like other proper names, takes the zero article, see examples above.

16.5₂. Sometimes the word *personify* is used in connexion with the abstract word: Ainsworth JS 82 I'm prudence personified | Christie LE 71 Certainly she was neatness and precision personified | id 3A 19 She is virtue and respectability personified | Mannin CI 198 She is personality personified. Cf AHuxley EG 318 the very personification of silence.

And the word *dame* may be used to emphasize the personification: Sterne M 1.12 she had all along trusted little to her own efforts, and a great deal to those of dame Nature | Dame Fortune.

16.5₃. In literature personification is particularly used in allegories, the most famous being *The Pilgrim's Progress* with characters like *Passion* and *Patience* (two little children), *Faith*, and the shepherds *Knowledge, Experience, Watchful*, and *Sincere*. A typical modern example is Rupert Brooke's allegorical poem *The Funeral of Youth: A Threnody*, from which I shall quote the following lines: Old *Wisdom* read, In mumbling tone, the Service for the Dead. There stood *Romance*, The furrowing tears had mark'd her rougèd cheek; Poor old *Conceit*, his wonder unassuag'd; Dead *Innocency's* daughter, *Ignorance;* And shabby ill-dress'd *Generosity;* And *Argument*, too full of woe to speak; *Passion*, grown portly, something middle-aged; And *Friendship* — not a minute older, she; *Impatience*, ever taking out his watch; *Faith*, who was deaf, and had to lean to catch Old *Wisdom's* endless drone. ...

Adjectives before Proper Names

16.6₁. When a proper name has an adjective (secondary) before it, it takes zero in two cases, (1) if the two together form one new proper name: New York | New South Wales | Eastern Africa | British West Africa | Belgian Congo | Wells SH 134 over the high mountain passes of the Pamirs into western Turkestan | ib 161 Nearly every town in northern Gaul was sacked | ib 103 Their return to Asiatic Greece. — On this analogy Stanley called his book "In Darkest Africa."

This applies only to place-names.

In McKenna S 6 the following localities are mentioned: Little End | Big Gateway | Great School | Great Court | (School Library | Cloisters | Chapel).

(2) if the adjective is used in an ornamental or sentimental way, and not to distinguish one person or place from another: Rare Ben Jonson (i. e. B.J., whom everybody knows as rare) | Bale T 1040-41 From me would not go, Cruell Pharao, No more wolde Amalech ... | Sidney AP 20 Let learned Greece ... be able to shew me one booke, before Musæus, Homer, and Hesiodus ... | Spenser FQ I. Introd. 3 Come both, and with you bring triumphant Mart | Marlowe MP 1098 Wicked *Nauarre* will get the crowne of France | Sh Mcb IV. 3.43 from gracious England | ib 52 blacke Macbeth Will seeme as pure as Snow | ib 117 Diuellish Macbeth ... hath sought to win me Into his power | Smollett R 203 honest Brayl ... wept as fast as either of us | Goldsm V 284 I must absolutely insist that honest Mr. Williams shall be rewarded for his fidelity | Byron Ch 1.34 Dark Guadiana rolls his power along | ib 65 Fair is proud Seville | id Corresp 2.152 You may suppose, as pugilistic Jackson says, that I have "a pretty time of it" | Keats P 48 Did ye never cluster round delicious Avon? | Lamb E [World's Class.] 112 situate near the

road-way village of pleasant Puckeridge | Quincey [World's Class.] 94 there remained not quite eighteen miles between myself and venerable Chester | Carlyle R 2.127 in dusty sooty, ever noisy Liverpool | Ruskin S 101 the simple princess-life of happy Nausicaa | Fox 2.177 old rather crabbed-looking Douglas Jerrold | Browning 1.260 Beautiful Evelyn Hope is dead! | Jerome T 60 Great Cæsar crossed the river there | Kipling J 2.48 even in populated India | id P 144 you would have thought Eternal Rome herself was on the edge of destruction | Walpole OL 15 kind Mr. Neilson at the Bank wanted it to stretch | Rose Macaulay T 22 Good-humoured, witty Mr. Spurgeon | Woolf D 18 She advanced ... to be greeted at once by button-faced Miss Pym | Priestley AP 467 in good old Queen Victoria's time | Hall, Alma Mater 50 How does sceptical Oxford write a comment on its own doings? | Harrison, Introducing Sh 101 Dover Cliff whence blinded Gloucester tries to commit suicide | Merry old England | Little Mary.

(Even with a sb as secondary: Carlyle R 2.127 Hebrews have it not [i. e. a sense of the ridiculous], not even blackguard Heine, to any real length).

This is found, too, in cases like *fashionable London* meaning 'the fashionable part of (the population of) London': Ward M 113 fashionable London was talking of nothing else | ib 192 the man whose name all smart London happens to be coupling with that of your wife.

16.6$_2$. Other words that are used with zero as quasi-proper names may take an adj in the same way: Sheridan 9 Why [,] didn't you say you had left young master? | Jerrold C 126 I'll write to-morrow to dear mother | Ingoldsby 105 this had been a great subject of speculation to little Miss | Collingwood R 57 it would only mean fifteen months' absence from home, great part of which deserted papa would spend in travelling [Besides, one would expect *a* before *great part*]| Macaulay E 4.123 the war which degenerate Protestantism had to wage against regenerate Catholicism | Hay KW 156 young hopeful is forced to the inevitable conclusion that he must learn his living ... | Shaw TT 299 not to pretend they know more than God Almighty. — Cf also Di P [Ch & H] 569 when Gracious Majesty honours it [a theatre] with its presence [Would now be *His Gracious Majesty*].

16.6₃. This characterizing use of the zero article + adj is in the first place used with adjs of a general emotional character, such as *dear, honest, great, noble, good, black, devilish, cruel, proud, venerable*, etc, but also with adjs of a more special character, though these adjs may not give any fresh information in the context in question, e. g. *pugilistic* (quot. from Byron), *crabbed-looking* (Fox), *populated* (Kipling), *blinded* (Harrison), etc. What should be particularly noted is the fact that there is a more or less strong emotional colouring about the phrase when zero is used.

16.6₄. But the definite article is also freely used before a characterizing adj. Then there is generally no great emotional colouring or familiarity about the phrase. The speaker in a neutral matter-of-fact statement adds some feature to our knowledge. We have a case of "nearly complete familiarity" (Stage Two). But it must be admitted that not infrequently phrases with *the* may have some emotional colouring inherent in the adj. The difference between phrases with *the* and phrases with zero is one of degree of familiarity.

16.6₅. Examples with *the:* Sh As II. 1.26 the melancholy Jaques grieues at that | Mcb V. 2.2 the good

Macduff | Gibbon M 210 the wretched Travis still smarts under the lash of the merciless Porson | GE A 356 even in the kind-hearted Martin Poyser the younger | Carlyle R 1.233 Procter who for the fair Ann Skepper's sake was very constantly there | Macaulay H 1.5 in the rich and polite Constantinople | Stevenson D 180 to attack the Queen, the sinister Gladstone, the rigid Derby, or the dexterous Granville | Bennett HL 288 the juxtaposition of the young, slim, and virginal Florrie and the large, earth-worn Mr. Boutwood | Hay KW 122 Into this strange vortex the unsuspecting Philip found himself whirled | Sherwood Anderson DL 18 When the Civil War came on, the Middle West got up and fought like the Old Harry [unusual] | Wells SH 130 Against Marius was pitted the aristocratic Sulla | ib 145 Serapis was identified with the Greek Zeus, the Roman Jupiter and the Persian sun-god.

Here also belong honorific adjs like (*Right*) *Honourable* and (*Very*) *Reverend:* the Honourable John Burns | the Reverend Edward Smith.

16.6₆. If instead of a real name we have the name of the office, repetition of *the* is necessary: Nichols, Progresses of Queen Eliz. (1825) 3.90—96 (q Introd. ed. of Sh LL Quarto) She was entertained by "the Right Honourable the Lord Montecute," anno 1591 | Sh Documents 39 ... as it was sundry times acted by the Right Honourable the Earle of Pembroke his seruantes | ib. ... acted by the right honourable the Lord Chamberlaine his servants (also ib 40, 41, 46) | Campion O [dedication:] To the Right Noble and worthily honourd, the Lord Buckhurst | Swift T 104 let the right worshipful the commissioners of inspection give him a regiment | Thack S 26 the most noble the Marquis of Bagwig | id P 153 that refined patron of the arts ... the Most Noble the Marquis of Steyne | Allen W 221 the Very Reverend the Dean of Dunwich | [Shaw TT 233 The worshipful the Mayor of the Isle of Cats].

Note this example with zero and *the* close together before the same words: Carlyle FR 472 Great Burke has raised his great voice long ago ... but the great Burke remains unanswerable.

Quasi-Proper Names

16.7₁. Some words are treated as proper names and have zero, though from a notional point of view they might just as well have been common names. It is natural that *God*, i. e. the one god of Christians, Jews, and Mohammedans, should be looked upon as a proper name, although we have of course *the* when the word is connected with a determinative (junction): the God of Israel | the God he worships | the God of her fathers. — Also: the god of war | the gods of ancient Greece, etc. — And as a class-noun *god* likewise takes the indefinite article: NP 1933 Alexander's tendency to think himself a god or God. — Cf above, 13.2$_4$.

Christ with zero is now the usual form, but formerly *the Christ* was frequent, and may still be found: Sherwood Anderson WM 107 Join in the work of the Christ | id WO 173 On the window ... was a design showing the Christ laying his hand upon the head of a child | Shaw TT 210 [Pilate:] And you are the Christ, the Messiah, eh?

Providence and *Fate* (with or without a capital letter), which like other instances of personification have zero, may to some extent be reckoned as synonyms of *God;* cf above, 16.5.

Satan is usually a proper name and has no article when denoting *the devil*, which like *the fiend* is considered a common name. But *a satan* may be found: Hammett MF 3 He looked rather pleasantly like a blond satan (Now rare according to NED).

Devil with zero may, however, be used in dialectal terms of imprecation: Hardy U 20 "D—l take the hole, the cask, and Sam Lawson too..." | Stevenson C 14 And de'il ha'et! | Devil Stories 189 "Divil doubt him!" as an Irishman would say.

16.7₂. The following "place-names" from Christian terminology also have zero:

Heaven 'the habitation of god and his angels': Ch A 519 To drawen folk to hevene by fairnesse ... this was his bisynesse | Marlowe F 314 tasted the eternal ioyes of heauen. — Also in a transferred sense as in *heaven knows*. In the sense 'state or place of bliss' the word is a class-noun and may take the other articles: Mi PL 1.17 The mind is its own place, and in itself Can make a Heaven of Hell, a Hell of Heaven. Formerly *the heavens* might be used in the religious sense: Marlowe MP 180 The heauens forbid your highnes such mishap | Sh Tp IV. 18 No sweet aspersion shall the heauens let fall (in Sh also *heavens* with zero). But *the heavens* is now the ordinary prose form to denote the visible sky (NED): Marlowe F 548 Under the heauens (ib 603, 612) | Mi PL 1.9 In the beginning how the Heavens and Earth Rose out of Chaos | Ingoldsby 107 The sun rode high in the heavens | James G 116 The sun was declining in the heavens when my cousin walked up to the door. — Cf above, 14.1₄.

Hell 'the infernal regions': Marlowe F 553 Hell has no limits | Mi PL 1.263 Better to reign in Hell than serve in Heaven. — But in the sense 'something resembling hell, gaming-house' the word is a class-noun and may take the other articles (and be used in the plural: Saintsbury NC 41 Only Dante, Beckford, and Scott in *Wandering Willie's Tale* have given us Hells that are worthy the idea of Hell | AHuxley EG 3 she carried her hell about with her. The hell of her grotesque marriage; other hells too, perhaps): Carlyle E 236 a Heaven set against a Hell | Stevenson N 87 the proprietor of a hell | Shaw TT 226 my life here is a hell. — In terms of imprecation like the following, perhaps on the analogy of *the devil, hell* takes *the*: Lehmann DA 104 Where the hell has Roddy got to? | Graves G 171 Why the hell are you wearing your stars on your shoulders ... ? | ElSmith Tz 51 What the hell do I care? | Sayers GN 299 What the hell good does it do anybody these days? | King OF 195 "The hell with it," muttered Michael Lord. — Cf above, 9.9$_5$.

Paradise (1) 'the garden of Eden,' (2) 'heaven' with zero: Mi PL 4.241 Flowers worthy of Paradise, (3) 'any place of bliss' class-noun with *a* or *the:* Sh LLL IV. 3.73 to win a Paradise | Mids I. 1.203 Before the time I did Lysander see, Seem'd Athens like a Paradise to mee.

Eden with zero: the garden of Eden | Mi PL 1.4 with loss of Eden.

Purgatory with zero: Sh Rom III. 3.17 There is no world without Verona walles, But Purgatorie, Torture, hell it selfe | Oth IV. 3.77 I should venture Purgatory for't | Allen A 17 it nearly bumped me into purgatory!

Chapter XVII

Quantifiers

17.1₁. The term Quantifiers is used here as a designation of words denoting quantity, i. e. number (in connexion with countables), amount (with uncountables) and degree (in certain connexions, as tertiaries, etc).

There are many substantival quantifiers. Apart from occasional remarks in the section on numerals they will not be discussed, but see vol II 3.51 ff. on the plurals of such quantifiers as *pair*, *couple*, *dozen*, *score*, *hundred*, etc, and ib 5.11 ff. on unification of plurals of numerals.

Our main subject in this chapter will be numerals and indefinite pronouns.

Numerals

17.1₂. Typical quantifiers to indicate number are the cardinals: *one*, *two*, *three*, *thirteen*, *fourteen*, *twenty*, *thirty*, *a hundred*, etc.

It will be seen that the first numerals up to *twelve* are formed unsystematically, but that there is some system in the words from 13 to 19, which are formed by composition of the numerals *three*, *four*, etc, with *teen*, a modified form of *ten*, the first part of the compound being also in some cases modified; another system comprises the 'tens' formed by means of *-ty:* here, too, some of the first parts are modified: *twenty, thirty, forty, fifty*. *A hundred, a thousand, a million, a milliard, a billion* (Am. *billion* = Brit. *milliard*) are again unsystematic; but otherwise the higher numerals are formed systematically by multiplication and addition, e. g. 2569, two thousand five hundred and sixty-nine.

On *twain* and *seven* see vol VI 20.1₃.

One

17.1₃. On the development of *one* [wʌn] from OE *an* and on vg or familiar *'un* (GE S 125 you're a deep un) see vol I 11.21.

On *one* as a prop-word see vol II ch 10, ib 13.4, and vol V 8.6₁.

One is the lowest cardinal numeral as distinct from *two*, *three*, etc. It is distinct from the classifying indefinite article *a*, which is of the same origin, as seen, e. g., in Stevenson D 32 Is there not a drop for me? — Not one drop | Parker R 77 In a minute, m'sieu' — in one minute | Brett Young PC 11 It was an old man's house, and the spirit of one old man inhabited and informed it. — See further above, 12.5₂.

Before higher composite numerals *a* is hardly so frequent as *one*, as in *one hundred and thirty-five*, etc.

A hundred, a thousand generally mean 'approximately one hundred, one thousand': I have seen her a hundred times | Phillpotts M 275 She is a girl in a thousand.

One third is a fraction ($\frac{1}{3}$); *a third* means 'one more, besides the two already in hand'. Note, however: a third of the distance | a third of the way across the lake, etc.

Like other cardinals *one* is generally used before a sb: One man, one vote. — Thus also before substantival numerals: One hundred, one million.

One (like other cardinals) is frequently used with ellipsis of a sb, as in statements of prices, e. g. one and six (1/6), with *shilling* understood, in statements of the time, with *hour* understood: one o'clock | the train is due at one twenty-five, — and in slangy expressions with some word understood, such as *blow* in: Give him one on the nose.

17.1₄. In additions of 'tens' and 'ones' the 'one' now generally follows the 'ten' (*twenty-one*), but originally it always preceded it: *one-and-twenty*, a word-order which is still used except in numerals above 50.

The only examples I have noticed of the latter word-order in numerals above 50 are the following: Sheridan 197 she's six-and-fifty if she's an hour | Coleridge 452 in Köhln ... I counted two and seventy stenches | Wells TB 163 Fifty-three days I had outward ... three and fifty days of life cooped up | Walpole ST 285 never in all his five-and-fifty years.

17.1₅. We may find both types of word-order in close proximity: Sh H5 1.2.57 Untill foure hundred one and twentie yeeres ... ib 61 Foure hundred twentie six | Defoe R 330 eight and twenty years ... thirty and five years | Thack E 1.147 accepted the Thirty-nine Articles with all his heart, and would have signed and sworn to other nine-and-thirty with an entire obedience | Kipling PT 43 She was two-and-twenty, and he was thirty-three | Caine M 131 you are still so young. Let me see, is it eight-and-twenty? — Twenty-six, said Philip | Jerome T 37 P. was forty-seven ... W. was three-and-twenty | Wells N 142 He was six and twenty, and I twenty-two | ib 199 I grew ... between three and twenty and twenty-seven.

Mr. Walt Arneson states: "Used in U.S. only occasionally, for stylistic effect or facetiously."

17.1₆. Compounds of two numerals denoting a number below one hundred have *and* between the two members if the small numeral precedes: *one-and-twenty*. If it follows the higher numeral, there is generally no connecting word: *twenty-one*. Especially in early authors we may find the type *twenty-and-two*, e. g. Malory 101 xx & viij knyghtes | AV Luke 15.7 ninety and nine iust persons | Swift P 132 there are thirty-and-two good bits in a shoulder of veal | Fielding T 1.17 | Goldsm 645 | Carlyle S 16 | Bennett A 50.

If two neighbouring numerals are to be used, the type with the small number first is commonest, as in this case the higher numeral need not be repeated: Thack E 2.150 though now five or six and forty years | Locke CA 315 Between Nadia and him there was but a separation of two or three years; between Nadia and myself two or three and twenty | Crofts Cask 220 a girl of perhaps two or three-and-twenty.

In the reading of decimal fractions only the type with the higher numeral first is used: 1.25 is read 'one point twenty-five.'

17.1₇. As a numeral *one* may be preceded by the indefinite pronouns *any, some, no* and by the definite article or a possessive pronoun: Scott I 293 do not confine your exertions to any one spot | Stevenson D 258 I no longer expect any one thing more than any other | Dickinson S 47 Nor would I suggest that the socialist community should establish any one form of religion || Dickens N 323 Kate's picture would be in half-a-dozen of the annuals ... Perhaps some one annual ... might even contain a portrait of the mother || Wilde SM 162 There is no one type for man || Seeley E 89 the Mediterranean sea ... the chief, nay almost the one sea of history || Benson Da 34 a man's ... right (he, the one man) to serve the one woman || Kipling MOP 195 they have fifty ponies to our one horse. — Cf vol II 10.22.

And it may be emphasized by adding *only:* Hawthorne S 197 the one only thing for which she had been sent into the world | Henderson Sc Lit 338 he asserted that it might be looked upon as the genuine traditionary version, as if there could be a one and only genuine traditionary version.

17.1₈. The phrase *I for one* probably originates from the use of *I* for 'one' in Roman figures, cf the old nursery rhyme:

X shall stand for playmates ten;
V for five stout stalwart men;
I for one, as I'm alive;
C for a hundred, and D for five;
M for a thousand soldiers true,
And all these figures I've told you.

From this by a kind of popular pun the phrase has become established to denote the pronoun of the first person, and later it has been transferred to use in connexion with names, e. g. Doyle S 4.205 I fancy that Lord Holdhurst, for one, and Mr. Percy Philips for another, would very much rather that the affair never got as far as the police-court.

One or two generally denotes an indefinite small number, cf vol II 5.52 and 6.65.

For *on all fours* see vol II 5.15.

17.1₉. Long compound numerals are often abbreviated, e.g. nineteen forty-six [1946] | Shaw 1.3 in the eighteen-eighties [1880—89] | Mackenzie C 140 the mid-'nineties | Nicolson, Some People 71 The eighteen-nineties [1890—99] and the nineteen-hundreds [1900—09] || Priestley G 313 they had seen Mr. Mitcham before, one in Singapore in Nought Three [1903], the other in Sydney in Nought Eight [1908].

Figures consisting of several digits may for clearness' sake be read one by one, e. g. in the BBC the telephone number Whitehall 1212: one two one two. — Cf 1122 (on the telephone): double one double two.

Foreign Numerals

17.2₁. Some foreign numerals are or have been used in English in certain connexions. Thus the French words *ace, deuce, tray, quatre (cater), cinq, size* have been used in games of dice and cards from early times. A few examples: Ch B 3851 Thy *sys* fortune hath turned into *as* | id C 653 Sevene is my chaunce, and thyn is cynk and treye | Roister 48 I wyll be here with them ere ye can say trey ace | Dryden (q NED 1668) Two sixes and a trey wins it | ib. So, I have a good chance, two caters and a size | Swift J 439 the die is cast . . . and till it settles, I cannot tell whether it be an ace or a sise | Goldsm V 194 I only wanted to fling a quatre, and yet I threw deuce ace five times running | NED 1772 [s.v. *trey*] Tray, ace, or two deuces | NED 1850 Should two quatres be thrown, any of the following moves may be played | NED 1870 [backgammon] Throwing either quatre, cinque or six | Jerome I 65 the score generally is deuce.

On the various uses of these words see further NED.

Cent(.) orig. or direct from Latin *centum* is found in *per cent*. Instead of *100 per cent*. we may find *cent. per cent.*: Gascoigne 71 To gaine no more, but *Cento per cento* | Quincey 348 the horse's value . . . fell cent. per cent. | Di D 476. — Cf Tennyson 139 For lucky rhymes to him were scrip and share, And mellow metres more than cent for cent.

"*Centum* is used in Am. English, though rarely, e. g. Westerfield, *Banking Principles and Practice* (passim)." (Mr. Walt Arneson).

A good number of other foreign numerals and derivatives and derivative elements are used in English, e. g. primary, secondary, tertiary, quaternary, etc | prime, second, tierce | dual | duo, trio | double, treble | triple | duplicate, triplicate |

triad, tetrad | quartet, quintet, sextet, etc | quarto | *bi-* (see vol VI 28.5₁), *tri-*, *quadri-*, etc | *-mo* in *twelvemo* (12mo), *twenty-fourmo*, *forty-eightmo* (see **NED**), and many others.

Uncertainty of Number

17.2₂. Uncertainty with regard to a number may be expressed in various ways. The higher numerals often add the word *odd* to indicate that a number is a little higher than that denoted by the numeral. The compound is generally without any connecting word: Lamb E 1.140 at the age of fifty odd | Spencer F 91 our eighty-odd possessions | Jacobs L 139 two hundred odd pounds || Collier E 311 for seven odd centuries [i. e. for seven hundred (and) odd years].

But *and* may be inserted between the numeral and *odd;* especially when the numeral is *hundred* or *thousand:* Sh H4A IV. 2.15 three hundred and odde pounds | Quincey 88 the fifty and odd hours since my elopement (id Sel 108) | Di N 80 two hundred and odd miles | Haggard S 156 two thousand and odd years (and ib 180) | Vizetelly, With Zola in England 183 throughout the eighty and odd departments of France | Mottram EM 61 the hundred and odd young faces.

Professor Collinson would not use *and* before *odd*.

Instead of *odd* we may have *something:* a pale little woman of forty-something | Gissing R 222 my age is something and twenty | Pinero B 32 during your first season, in eighty-something | Hammett Th 152 a tall scrawny man of fifty-something || Maugham Pl 2.238 They want to catch the four something back to London.

17.2₃. Certain numerals are or have been used to denote approximate number. For the Elizabethan period this question, with special reference to the problem of Hamlet's age, has been thoroughly discussed in the late

V. Osterberg's important paper *Hamlet's Age* (Copenhagen 1924). On p. 20 he says: "Readers of Elizabethan literature know that the numerals 7, 12, 20 and 40 are commonly used as "round" numbers where no definite statement is intended. No doubt 30 should be added to the list." And on p. 30 he says: "Numerals of the "three-and-twenty" type ... are frequently used for the sake of bigness with no claim to exactness." In support of these statements a wealth of examples from the literature of the time is adduced.

Cf further: I have told you a hundred times | to have forty winks | a nine days' wonder | a cat has nine lives [Danish cats only seven!] | W. C. Russel, Master Rockafellar's Voyage 204 [q Brynildsen] with a straw hat on the back of his head — on "nine hairs," as sailors say [three hairs are sufficient for a Dane!].

On *umpteen* and other indefinite numerals that may take *th* see vol VI 24.4_3.

Professor Collinson adds: "Since about 1938 I have noted a growing use of *x*, e.g. x pounds, x students."

17.2₄. Indefiniteness is often expressed by adding to a numeral *or* and the following numeral or *so*, e. g. in a day or two | two or three days ago | a mile or so.

Or two may be added also to a substantive preceded by the definite article (or *this*): within the next hour or two | Meredith EH 517 I engaged to marry you to a Roman prince the very next morning or two | Doyle 248 that is better for you than the patient or two whom you might have seen at home | Maugham Alt 295 You look as though you hadn't had much sleep the last night or two || Di D 211 this century or two.

Or may be left out between two numerals, particularly in dialectal speech and Scottish and American English: Browning T 3.170 fancy us over these letters, two, three times a day | Brontë P 207 After two, three hours' torturing research | GE A 37 I'll set two-three sticks alight in a minute | ib 300 two-three old folks | Kipling P 231 three-four waggons | Barrie TG 56 [Sc] twa three hunder' | Priestley G 486 [Mr. Oakroyd:] There's been a summat i' t'air these two-three week (ib 409) | Bennett T 198 a two-three minutes ago | Lewis MS 13 a big city of two-three hundred thousand | id MA 208 making three-four thousand a year | Dreiser F 301 his trousers four, five times too large for him.

Now always with *or* in normal educated British English speech according to Professor Collinson.

Ordinals — Fractions

17.2₅. Ordinals are not quantifiers, but rather a kind of labels to mark out items in a series; fractions, however, are, and the denominator in an ordinary fraction is an ordinal (apart from *half* and *quarter*).

On the formation of ordinals from cardinals by means of *-(e)th* see vol VI 24.4$_1$. On fractions see ib 24.4$_4$.

Ordinals may also be formed from cardinals of the type *one-and-twenty:* AV Esth 8.9 on the three and twentieth day | Johnson R 47 four and twentieth | Tennyson 125 his one-and-twentieth May. — But such ordinals are not used in fractions.

In decimal fractions only the numerator, not the denominator is read: 19.6 is read as 'nineteen decimal (or 'point') six'; 0.7 is read as 'decimal seven'. .4777... would be read: point four seven recurring.

Distributive Use of Numerals

17.2₆. Distributive use of the numerals is effected either by repeating the numeral in question after *and* or *by* (the latter is the more prevalent), e. g. Tennyson

28 The knights come riding two and two (also: *in twos* or *two abreast*) | Kipling J 1.249 the animals went in two by two — or by means of *by* followed by a plural numeral or a numeral in the singular with *the*, e. g. Maxwell G 7 such girls as you may see by thousands any day of the week | Doyle S 2.136 turning out half-crowns by the thousand.

Cf vol II 5.132.

'Nothing'

17.2₇. 'Nothing' conceived as a number is called *cipher, nought, ought, zero,* or *O (o)*.

Cipher, used particularly in speaking of figures, increases the value of a whole number tenfold when placed on the right side of it: Sh Wint I. 2.6 And therefore, like a Cypher (Yet standing in rich place) I multiply With one we thanke you, many thousands moe, That goe before it | Ruskin CWO 104 But it is not gold that you want to gather! What is it? ... What is it then — is it ciphers after a capital I? ... Write ciphers for an hour every morning, in a big book, and say every evening, I am worth all those noughts more than I was yesterday.

Nought is more generally used in arithmetic: twice nought is nought | nought by two is nought.

Ought "is a vulgar corruption of nought" (NED): Mar. Edgeworth 1801—15 (q NED s.v. *cipher*) It was said .. that all Cambridge scholars call the cipher aught and all Oxford scholars call it nought | Kipling DW 219 fourteen ought ought three; ... seventeen ought twenty-one. — Cf. Sweet NEG § 1147.

Zero denotes the point or line marked *0* on a graduated scale, and 'nought' reckoned as a number.

O [ou] is used in reading figures, particularly on the telephone: Thack V 235 Grigg offered ninety for the mare yesterday, ... and like a fool I wouldn't let her go under the two o's [i. e. 100] | 105 read as: one-o-five. — A brand of tobacco is called: Five-o-eight-one de luxe (on the package marked: 5081 de luxe).

In some games (whist, tennis, etc) *love* is used to denote no score. This obviously originates from the phrase used in negative sentences: (I would not do it) for love or money.

Once, Twice, Thrice

17.3₁. Instead of *one time*, *two times* we say *once*, *twice*. *Thrice* for *three times* is obsolescent.

On the origin of the three words see vol VI 18.1₁.

They may be used as substantives: Di P 430 Bob Sawyer and Ben Allen should be considered at liberty to fill twice to Mr. Winkle's once | Myers M 200 I met her only the once | this once | these twice; the last twice (NED). Cf vol II 8.51.

As an adjunct corresponding to *once*, *one-time* is used, e. g. NP 1924 a one-time disciple of Freud.

At twice, generally in connexion with the very common *at once*, may be found in older authors: Swift J 41 I am afraid my letters are too long: then you must suppose one to be two, and read them at twice | GE M 1.297 Did Mr. Tulliver let you have the money all at once? — No, at twice.

Thrice never succeeded in completely supplanting *three times*, which was often used in early authors, e. g. Ch (tymes thre), Caxton R 28 thryes ... thre tymes, Redford W 640, Sh LLL III. 1.49 H4A I. 3.102, ib III. 1.64 three times ... thrice, Swift J 17, Defoe R 93, etc.

17.3₂. When the two highest numerals are to be mentioned together, there are several possibilities.

We often find *two or three times:* Defoe R 284, ib 2.168 and 206 | ib R 342 not once, but two or three times | Swift J 162 | Austen M 376 | Browning 1.204 two, three times a day | Di D 470 | Thack N 79 | Poe S 83 | Hope Ch 246.

Not so common are *twice (or) three times.* Note the punctuation marks in Di and Jerrold which keep the words apart: Di D 570 once, twice, three times | id F 680 Once! Twice! Three times and away! | Jerrold C 34 I say once, Mr. Caudle; or twice, or three times, at most | Galsw Frat 331 Twice or three times she addressed him timidly.

Twice or thrice: Swift J 221, Di D 575, id N 573 and 578, Kipling L 113. *Twice and thrice:* Stevenson JH 67.

Thrice and four times: Stevenson, Merry Men 103.

Thrice (which is now purely literary) may have the indefinite sense of 'highly': Wordsw [MM] 146 Thrice welcome, darling of the Spring! | Byron DJ 4.11 Thrice fortunate | Meredith RF 376 don't make me thrice ashamed.

17.3₃. Note the use of the adv *again* to denote repetition of quantity: *as long again* means 'twice as long'; *half as much again* means 'this and half as much more'.

Examples: Defoe R 74 every seventh notch was as long again as the rest | Sterne M 1.83 Can'st not thou take my rule, and measure the length and breadth of this table, and then go and bespeak me one as big again | Lamb E 1.54 Then are we as strong again, as valiant again, as wise again, and a great deal taller | Di F 391 looking as old again as she really was || Fielding T 4.167 he speaks all his words distinctly, half as loud again as the other | Di D 500 his chest looked half as broad again

| Norris P 195 the stable was half again as large as her old home.

Pronouns of Totality
All

17.4₁. The primary function of *all* is that of denoting the total number or quantity of what is referred to.

It is used both as a primary, a secondary, and a tertiary (see vol II 17.51 ff.).

On *all* before restrictive relative clauses see vol III 4.8₁, on *all which* see ib 6.4₇, on *all* before contact-clauses ib 7.2₃.

On *all right* see vol II 17.58 and III 17.8₂.

On *all of* in appositional phrases see above, 9.9₂.

Two additional examples to vol II 17.5:

17.54: Austen M 187 take it all and all, I never spent so happy a summer.

17.58: Maugham P 172 She ... had an elegance which made Kitty feel all thumbs.

17.4₂. *All* is frequently, for the sake of emphasis, combined with other quantifying pronouns, such as *sundry, one, any* (formerly also *some*, e. g. Ch A 3135, Ch D 1643, Dryden Abs. & Achit. 2.457 Now stop your noses, readers all and some), *each, several*, and *everything*.

all and sundry: Brontë P 155, Carlyle R 1.225, Hawthorne 1.470, Gissing G 64, Maugham Alt 80.

one and all: Di T 2.93 the foreign ambassadors had one and all left Paris, Brontë J 46, Stevenson T 131, Holmes A 78.

any and all: Holmes A 147, Bennett B 122 he was to keep the vessel at full steam ahead under any and all circumstances. ("*Any and all* is unknown to me." Professor Collinson).

each and all: Brontë P 107, Ruskin P 2.268, James S 47, Hope Ch 241 reports concerning each and all of these incidents.

all and several: Dickinson S 47 I would give encouragement to all and several [forms of religion].

all and everything: Thack N 636 He would believe all and everything a man told him.

A frequent phrase is *every day and all day:* Caine C 383 the church ... open every day and all day.

17.4₃. Appositional use of plural *all* with personal pronouns is frequent: we all | Heywood Prov. (q NED) Euery man for him selfe, and God for us all | Trollope DCh 1.115 He has the choice of us all | Coleridge Anc. Mar. 4.4 And they all dead did lie.

Also in U.S. with interrogative *what:* Dreiser F 53 What had he had? What all had he not missed?

On *you all* see vol II 2.88 and AmSp IV 54—55, 103 (*y'all*), 154 (*you alls*).

On *all our* see vol VI 17.6.

In the proverb "All work and no play makes Jack a dull boy," *all work* is a nexus without a vb ('all being work').

In universally exclusive sentences *all* is used in the meaning 'any whatever.' Now only in such phrases as: beyond all question, doubt, controversy, etc, deny, disclaim, renounce all connexion.

All often precedes a sb with a determinative before it: all the boys | all the world and his wife | we walked all the way | all this day (Sh John III. 1.18) | all those people | all my money | with all my heart | Sh Sonn 112 you are my all the world.

The phrase with the determinative has a more restricted sense than the corresponding phrase without it, as in *all boys* : *all the boys*.

All may mean 'whole' (but as seen above, it precedes a determinative, which *whole* does not): Ruskin 2.399 points which bear intimately on all our subjects | Mackenzie C 318 I've been in your flat all a night.

It may also mean 'the highest degree possible of ...': with all speed | with all respect | Sh R3 IV. 1.57 I in all haste was sent. — And I with all vnwillingnesse will goe.

Here we should perhaps class the common expression *all the difference* and the like: Austen M 150 Then he is your cousin, which makes all the difference | Ruskin P 2.282 there is a vast difference — there is all the difference (id CWO 13) | Gissing G 420 What use should I be? — Oh, all the use in the world | Merriman S 181 I have much to say to you. Besides, we have all the time. Your husband and his German friend are miles away.

All may mean 'every', but this is obs. except in *all kind* and *all manner:* all kind of drollery | all manner of people.

Finally *all* may mean 'everything', thus in the combination *all but* 'everything short of', as a tertiary 'almost', which may also be used attributively: Carlyle SR [Univ. Libr.] 99 the all-but omnipotence of early culture.

17.4₄. Vol II 17.51. In Am. English the phrase *and all* may be used after an adv, at any rate after *still:* Hart BT 104 Still and all, I believe that he was there precisely when he said he was | Dine B 264 'Still and all,' put in Heath, 'you guessed that Robin hadn't been shot with a bow and arrow.'

II 17.58. To the passage about *all* as a subjunct may be added: Williams N 268 The world was assuredly all right ... The world, unquestionably, was getting all righter every moment | Waugh W 37 She was not all sure that she would approve of him.

Both

17.4₅. *Both* (ME *boþe, bothe*, borrowed into ME from ON *baþar;* OE had *bēȝen* m., *bā* f. n.) is related to *all* in its unifying power, only that its sphere of activity is generally a number of two, only.

On ME [-ð] > [-þ] see vol I 6.92.

On the use of the conjunction *both* of more than two see vol II 7.71, on the genitive *both's* see ib 9.55, and on its use as primary, secondary, and tertiary see ib 17.62.

On *both* as subject of the gerund see vol V 9.4₅.

On appositional *both of* see above, 9.9₂.

Both connected with *and*, as in *both he and I*, was originally a primary with the other words in apposition, see Ch MP 1.122 [note the comma!] That I agilt have bothe, him and thee.

Often *both* is placed in apposition after the words to which it belongs: Di D 160 he has kept me in the dark as to his resources and his liabilities, both | id F 31 I knew a little sister that was sister and mother both | Thack N 461 Husbands and wives both will be pleased | Ruskin S 68 you had better get rid of the smoke, and the organ pipes, both | id P 2.37 he and I both liked the fancy | Hardy W 201 she was one of the trimmers who went to church and chapel both | Matthews F 126 you are a bull and a bear both | Norris O 108 prepared .. to denounce it [the scheme] and Osterman both.

Both is frequently found in apposition to a personal pronoun: We are both men of the world | they seem both very obstinate | they both went away.

On *both their*, etc, see vol VI 17.6.

Whole.

17.4₆. *Whole* (ME *hōl, hool*, OE *hāl*) is used before a sg in the sense 'entire, intact, unbroken, all there is of,' but it may be used before a plural, too, in the sense of 'all', e. g. Defoe P 7 and 39, Fielding T 4.187, Sterne M 1.285 his whole thoughts and attention, Lamb R 55, Scott A 1.26, id I 470 the whole brethren, Carlyle SR 135, Thack Hogg. Diam. 68 the whole nine, Kingsley, Hope, Doyle, etc.

As a sb it means 'thing complete in itself, total amount of something.'

On *whole* as homonymous with *hole* see vol I 4.211. On early and dialectal pronunciation of *wh* see ib 11.22.

Each

17.4₇. *Each* (ME *ech*, *euch*, OE *ǣlc*, *ǣghwylc*) meaning 'every (person, thing, or group) out of a certain number of at least two' may be used both as a primary and a secondary — see vol II 17.64.

On *each* as the subject of the gerund see vol V 9.4₅, and on various other functions of it see Index to vol II.

In apposition *each* may stand immediately after the word(s) to which it belongs: Aldrich S 21 they each had a clean story | Philips L 47 we each light a cigarette. — It may follow immediately after the vb: Austen P 56 they have each their advantages | Doyle S 6.61 Mr. L. and Mr. Sherlock Holmes have each come to the conclusion. — And it may follow after a preposition: Rehearsal 123 the general, and lieutenant general, with each of them a lute in his hand | Beaconsfield L 242 The ladies Flora and Grizell entered with each in her hand, a prayer book of purple velvet | Poe S 146 having with us muskets, pistols, and cutlasses, besides each a long kind of seaman's knife.

As *each* refers to one out of a plurality it is often repeated by a personal or possessive pronoun in the pl — cf vol II 5.56.

We may find constructions in which the same sense of plurality is expressed, e. g. in the use of a pl vb after *each:* Ruskin CWO 28 the busy rich people . . . the busy poor people . . . But each look for the faults of the other.

Instead of Christie Big Four 266 They had me under each arm — one would expect: . . . each under one arm.

There is nothing illogical in the following sentence, in which *our* refers back to the subject *we:* Masterman WL 32 We will each carry on with our own line of research. — But in an exactly parallel sentence in the same book the sg is found: 140 Well, we will each keep his own counsel.

The use of *each* after *between* is worth noticing. There is nothing remarkable in the use of *between* before *each* followed by *two* or another numeral, the number being taken as a whole, hence *each*, but actually representing a plurality, hence *between:* Kipling DW 310 Between each five paces he looked at an official telegram | Mason Ch 105 a row of five bedrooms with a bathroom between each two.

As a matter of fact we occasionally find *each* before a word in the sg, where it thus comes to stand for 'each . . . and the following one': Collins W 319 a row of flower-pots were ranged, with wide intervals between each pot | Lowndes Ivy 57 passionate words . . . between each long, trembling, clinging kiss | Kennedy CN 146 staring at her furtively between each mouthful of soup.

Similarly Sackville-West E 50 she counted the sheets in the linen cupboard, putting a bag of lavender between each [two] | Sherriff J 127 Suddenly there comes the faint whistle and thud of falling shells — a few seconds between each.

Each, like *every*, may be preceded by a genitive or a possessive pronoun, but this is rare: Lowell 318 His fingers exploring the prophet's each pocket | Dane FB

261 affected as she must always be by his each unconscious change of tone.

The adv. *eachwhere*, long obsolete (or archaic), is found e. g. in Roister 17 eche where | Spenser Amoretti 78 [I] seeke each where, where last I sawe her face (also id FQ I. 10.54) | BJo A 2.170 each where | Edm. B. Sargant in Georgian Poetry 173 the cuckoo-bird Nowhere seen is eachwhere heard.

Every

17.5₁. *Every* (ME *everich* (generally before vowels), *everi* (before consonants, cf vol I 2.745), from OE *æfre* + *ælc* 'each') may be termed the sg of *all*, i. e. it means 'all taken separately' (cf vol II 17.56 and *each* above). On loss of the middle vowel see vol I 9.76.

Every may mean 'all possible, the utmost degree of': Jerrold C 78 What business had I to take it out of your pocket? — Every business | Barrie M 396 What's the use of keeping it frae her ony langer? — Every use, I said | They showed him every consideration | There is every prospect of success.

Further it may indicate repetition, *every day* meaning 'once (twice, etc) every day': He promised to write every day | NED 1796 The two tides of six hours reappear every day equal.

It is used in connexion with both cardinals and ordinals.

Every four days means 'on the fourth of every group of four days'. According to Professor Collinson it draws attention to the interval as well as the point.

Every other day means 'each alternate day'. This is the usual expression for mere alternation from whatever starting point (Professor Collinson).

Every second day (of the month, the week, the series) according to Professor Collinson implies reference to 1 as starting point.

Professor Moore Smith made a different distinction: 'Every other day', more colloquial than 'every second day', which suggests a doctor's account of a case.

The semantic identity of *every second* with *every other* is seen in Smedley F 2.259 look out of the window between every second mouthful | Shaw M 213 the expense of buying a new horse every second day.

But *every other* need not necessarily denote alternation: *other* may refer to another (different) item, as in James S 50 she had survived the peril, profiting by it indeed as she had profited by every other | Pollard, Sh's Hand 16 [in spite of the similarities] yet the shepherd knows each sheep in his flock from every other | NED 1879 Every particle of matter attracts every other particle.

17.5₂. *Every, everybody, everything, every one,* and *every man* have been discussed in some detail in various places in vol II, see Index.

On *every one, everybody* before restrictive relative clauses see vol III 4.8₂.

Some additions to vol II.

5.166: The type of phrase *every day or two* 'every day or every two days' is common: Darwin L 1.86 every year or two | Stevenson JH 29 pausing every step or two | Maugham Alt 139 Every day or two the administrator rode over | Linklater J 410 Every day or two she reiterated her gratitude.

8.444: *Everything* as a sb in the sg: Bennett ECh 91 You travelled with your own cook, your own bed, your own servants, your books, your everything.

17.63: Here reference is made to two examples in Caxton of *every* as a primary. Bøgholm 57 offers an example from Bacon A 29 this he saith to every of them — and another from NP 1902 each and every of them would.

Like *each* (see 17.4₇) *every* may be preceded by a genitive or a possessive pronoun: Waugh W 94 They would watch each other's every step | Sh Cymb I. 4.48 in my euery action | Ant I. 1.50 whose euery passion | Doyle S (L 1928) 4 To me, who knew his every mood and habit, his attitude and manner told their story | Sherwood Anderson WM 11 with something lazy and care-free in his every movement and impulse | Squire OE 120 his every whim.

The plurality implied in *every* may lead to its being connected with a word or more, ordinarily requiring the plural.

We may have *every* (like *each* — see 17.4$_7$) preceded by *between* and followed by a word in the sg: Di N 695 a certain halting of the breath which made him pause between almost every word like a drunken man bent upon speaking plainly | GE A 201 pausing between every sentence.

The author perhaps would have been hard put to it if asked to analyze the following passage: Stevenson T 8 drawing briskly at his pipe between every word or two (cf *every day or two* above).

The (orig.) Am. phrase *every which way, everywhichaway* 'in all directions' seems to be a variant of *everwhichaway*, from *everwhich = whichever* — see Wentworth, Am. Dial. Dic., though there may be a slight semantic difference between the two forms. — Cf, however, the old form *either which* (in Sh, etc.).

Examples: Twain H 1.88 skipping around every which way | Churchill C 271 the Rebs jumpin' and hollerin' around and shoutin' every which way | Galsw F 113 you may sometimes see a ... boy ... suddenly fling his feet and his head every which way.

Some advs have been formed with *every* as first component, the only one now current being *everywhere*.

Others, some of them obs., are:

† *everydeal* 'in every part'.

everyhow 'in every way'. NED: rare | Di F 728 Any how, and every how, he has been planted here.

† *everylike* 'ever in like fashion'.

everyway 'in every way': Sh Cæs IV. 3.55 you wrong me euery way | Browning 2.547 Certainly it ... *Is* the everyway external stream that now ... Floats it onward.

everywhen 'always': Carlyle PP (1858) 221 Everywhere and everywhen a man has to pay with his life | Cambridge Trifles 111 when ... and when... and when ... and even when they sit down on a hard chair, in fact, everywhen.

everywhence 'from every direction'. NED: rare.

everywhither 'in every direction': 1851 Carlyle. Cf Kipling P 84 many muddy waterways ran all whither into darkness under the trees.

Cf also Stevenson B 328 Every here and there small combats still raged.

Any

17.5₃. *Any* (ME *any*, *eny*, OE *ǣnig*) as a secondary in the sg means 'a (person or thing) no matter which, a (person or thing) of whatever kind or quantity'; in the pl 'some (persons or things) no matter which, of whatever kind or how many', and is used in these senses in interrogative, negative, conditional clauses and clauses of comparison. It may be used in affirmative statements, too, here meaning 'whichever (of all) is chosen'.

Any does not in itself particularize (cf *any* as compared with *some* 17.6₂). This is brought out well in the following example: Bennett in NP 1912 because endeavour — not any particular endeavour, but rather any endeavour! — is a habit that corresponds to a very profound instinct in the plain man.

Any may be used as a primary, a secondary, and a tertiary — see vol II 17.12 ff.

A few additions may be made to some of these sections.

II 17.16: *Any* may be used as a tertiary (subjunct) before *different*, as this latter word is nearly identical with *other*, which also may be preceded by *any* (see the example from Waugh), because it is parallel to comparatives: Swinnerton S 34 Polly could not remember Tom ever to have been any different from what he now was | Waugh W 204 He had no reason to believe that that day was to be any different from any other | Rhode, Pollard Ridge 129 Am I any different from what I was? | Graves IC 235 Germanicus ... could never have behaved any differently from the way he did.

II 17.17: Add the following examples: Crofts in BDS 365 he don't love me any over that lumber deal | ib 379 Don't worry yourself any | Harris, Shaw 40 Such a state of poverty was not helped any by an intolerable landlord system | Hammett Th 24 It wouldn't hurt you any to find out if you can help her | Eberhart 137 I don't see that that helps matters any.

This Americanism is now used in England, but less than the Amr *some;* see below, 17.6_3.

The use of *anything* as a sb was dealt with in vol II 8.445. Add here the following examples: Jerome TB 8 until he ... refuses to eat another anything | Galsw FS 740 as if there were no war, no concentration camps, no feeling on the Continent, no anything unpleasant | ib 1002 the modern woman had no build, no chest, no anything | id Car 879 a fearful wish that had no sense, no end in view, no anything | Rose Macaulay K 195 no intelligence or imagination, and ... no irony or humour, and no anything else worth having.

On *any (one, -body)* before restrictive relative clauses see vol III 4.8_2.

Examples of *any* in affirmative sentences referring to time, in which the possibility of all is implied, though there is no choice on the part of the speaker or hearer: Butler E 32 he began puzzling me, as he has done any time this forty years | Holmes A 114 if you are curious, you shall see it any day | Hergesheimer, Happy End 222 I'm going to die, August, almost any time now | Galsw Sw 129 he'll be here any minute | Allingham P 227 I have a feeling that the really important part of this affair is going to begin at any moment now.

Any may mean 'a very high' (amount or number): Di D 25 I would have given any money to have been allowed to wrap myself up | ib 459 if the broker saw me, he'd ask any price for them! | Ruskin P 2.324 there are any quantity of iron crosses on the Western Alps | Wilde W 22 she has got any amount of explanations for you | Sinclair R 116 there are any number of studies by independent investigators.

17.5₄. *Every* means 'all taken separately' (see above, 17.5₁). It applies to all, but only considers one at a time. *Any* (sg) applies to one only, but the choice of this one is among all. *Some* (sg) applies to one only, too, but it refers to a particular specimen. Sentences in which two or all of these three words (and compounds) are used together are not at all rare:

Any and *every:* Austen M [?] 32 always wanting me to sing before anybody and everybody | Di Do 59 "Money, Paul, can do anything." Paul repeated after a short pause: "Anything, papa?" "Yes, Anything — almost," said Mr. Dombey. "Anything means everything, doesn't it, papa?" asked his son: not observing, or possibly not understanding, the qualifier. "It includes it: yes," said Mr. Dombey | Macaulay H 4.12 It was impossible to make an arrangement that would please every body, and difficult to make an arrangement that would please any body | Kingsley H 346 he plunged eagerly into any and every self-abasement.

Next, some examples with *every*, *any*, and *some* (and compounds): William Temple (q NP 1934) Mathematics tells us something about everything, but very little about anything | Austen M 110 I feel as if I could be anything or everything ... let us be doing something | Proverb: When everybody's somebody, then no one's anybody | Cato: The wise man can learn something from everyone, even from fools. The fool cannot learn anything from anyone, not even from a wise man.

Finally, examples of *any* and *some* (and compounds): You may come any day, but you must come some day | Di Do 412 somewhere, anywhere, to hide her head! somewhere, anywhere, for refuge ... where to go? Somewhere, anywhere! still going on; but where? | Thack P 3.149 I have but to like anybody, and somebody is sure to come and be preferred to me | Carlyle FR 159 ask, why Messeigneurs did not pause, and take some other course, any other course | Twain M 35 I had the strongest impulse to do something, anything to save the vessel | McKenna M 141 will you give me the pleasure of your company at dinner somewhere — anywhere you like? | Phillpotts M 179 If 'twas somebody else — perhaps if 'twas anybody else but me — you wouldn't think twice | Walpole OL 210 She wanted some one to be proud of her. Some one. Any one | Norris S 245 Oh, he cried, turning to the musicians, can't you play something? — anything? | Bellamann, My Husb's Fr 165 What did he mean by that? Was there anything I did not know? Did he know something? Had he seen anything?

17.5₅. Like *every* and *some*, *any* is frequently used as first component of adverbs. *Anyhow*, *anyway*, and particularly *anywhere* are common.

Survey of the various words and their uses:

anyhow; common; (1) 'by any means, in any possible way': Stevenson A 111 Sooner or later, somehow, anyhow, I was bound to write a novel; (2) 'in any case, at least': you won't be late anyhow; (3) 'badly, carelessly, in a happy-go-lucky way': Locke HB 256 I couldn't bear to have things done anyhow when he was dining at the house | id SJ 28 You are also dropping a hairpin. — She hastily secured the dangling thing. I did my hair anyhow to-day, she explained | Galsw D 136 Lennan, whose features were rather anyhow, though pleasant enough | Borden AS 233 the thin young woman who was usually dressed just anyhow.

All anyhow is an emphatic form of the type (3) just exemplified: Farnol A 309 I know my hair is all anyhow — isn't it ? | Galsw IC 21 I can't have him going up to Oxford all anyhow | id EC 830 We meet meaning not to talk about the thing; then it crops up, and we get all anyhow | Williams N 91 Your nerves are all anyhow this evening.

anyway(s); common; 'in any way, at any rate': Ruskin P 1.162 Any way, the roads by land were safe | Ward F 211 you've earned your success anyway | Bennett ECh 121 Who is he, anyway ?

anywhen; not very common; 'at any time': Hardy T 425 I don't trouble you any-when | id W 235 it can't be done anywhen else | Wells L 33 She might leave Whortley anywhen | id V 153 I never ran away from anywhere with anybody anywhen (also id B 123).

† *anywhence;* obs. 'from anywhere'.

anywhere; very common; 'in any place'.

Often *anywhere* is followed by a clause introduced by *where:* Goldsm V 2.102 I am not afraid to lie any where where you are | Tennyson L 2.28 some were written in London, Essex, Gloucestershire, Wales, anywhere where

I happened to be | Merriman S 20 he never is anywhere where the respectable writer is to be found.

But this second *where* may be left out: Hope In 322 Have you anywhere else you want to go? | Hemingway FA 123 Where shall we go? ... Anywhere you want. Anywhere we don't know people.

The *where* in *anywhere* may be treated as if it were an independent sb, thus with an adj before it: Hutchinson, Clean Heart 6 Anywhere, anywhere, any infernal where.

Parallel to *all anyhow* (see above) we may find *all anywhere:* Maxwell S 46 he kept running his hands through his hair till it was all anywhere.

anywhither; archaic; 'in any direction whatever'.

anywise; fairly common; 'in any manner, in any degree, at all, anyhow': Ruskin S 159 | id U [Cassell 1909] 142 if our consumption is to be in anywise unselfish.

17.5₆. Palmer in *Report on Research Activities* 1928—29 gives two sentences which change meaning according as *anybody* is pronounced with (a) a rise-fall-rise tone or with (b) a high-falling tone: I don't lend my books to anybody (a) 'I am very particular as to whom I lend my books' and (b) 'I lend my books to nobody'.

Anybody may have nearly opposite meanings in different contexts. Thus it may mean 'person of some importance': He invited everybody who was anybody (cf vol II. 8.441), — or 'somebody no matter which', which in affirmative sentences has a depreciatory sense 'somebody of no importance': NED 1858 two or three anybodies.

Any may be found before a superlative with the definite article: Sh Hml I. 2.99 as common As any the most vulgar thing | Cymb I. 4.65 lesse attemptible then any, the rarest of our Ladies in Fraunce.

17.5₇. *Not* (...) *any* means the same thing as *no*, though it may be more emphatic than *no:* Di D 205 a gentleman with grey hair (though not by any means an old man) | Masefield S 97 He can make rum ... for not any more than five or seven cents a gallon.

Sweet NEG § 230 mentions the negative *no* corresponding to *some* and *any*, "for which *not any* is substituted in spoken English."

Any and compounds are frequently used in negative sentences with a negative word, such as *not, never:* I do not owe any man a penny | I'm not having any! | I never saw anybody like him.

But they are also used in statements in which a negation is implied, as in connexion with *without, scarcely, hardly, cease, prevent, hinder, doubt, miss, before*, etc: Without doing anything | hardly anything (any one) | we had ceased to pay any particular notice to the song | I shall refrain from any remarks on his conduct | he is forbidden to do any office-work | in his book we miss any attempt to explain ... | Lamb E 1.26 such a blast as set concealment any longer at defiance | Di Do 72 Solomon defied him to find out anything of the kind | ib 105 he had long left off asking any questions | ib 438 in his desire to spare her any wound | ib 163 they passed in before they were observed by anybody.

Any is further used in questions implying the alternative *no (none):* Has he read any Russian books? [or has he read none?] | Is he anybody? | Anything I can do for you? | Can you see it anywhere?

In conditional clauses *any* is used with the meaning 'any at all': Few, if any, will say so | He knows English if any man does | If anybody comes tell them to wait | If he is anything of a gentleman, he will apologize | If he has in anywise offended you, I'll see to it that you get satisfaction.

Temporal clauses with *when* may approach to the sense of conditional clauses: Di Do 72 I am quite sorry when I see you with anything on your mind.

Any in comparisons means 'any possible, any imaginable': He is as hard-hearted as any tyrant | It is as easy as anything.

Compare these two sentences: He is younger than any of his colleagues 'he is the youngest' and He is younger than some of colleagues 'he is not the oldest'.

Like anything denotes a very high degree: To swear like anything 'to swear like a trooper'.

In relative clauses it also means 'any at all': Macaulay H 36 This eminent man deliberately pronounced England to be the best governed country of which he had any knowledge.

In affirmative sentences *any* means 'any whatever, no matter which': Come any day you like | Any doctor will tell you that | Lend me any old book | Anybody will tell you so | Anything will do | Austen P 102 he asserted that I had forfeited all claim to it by extravagance, imprudence, in short, anything or nothing.

Such sentences may be converted into sentences with double negation: Any boy will tell you that: there is no boy who will not tell you that.

Some

17.6₁. *Some* (ME *some*, OE *sum* 'a certain one, some') is the pronoun of unspecified quantity, denoting an unknown or unspecified amount (before masswords), number (before pl), person or thing (before singular countables; cf Defoe R 188 I went home again fill'd with the Belief that some Man or Men had been on Shore there).

Christophersen p. 188 compares *a* and *some:* "*Some* competes with *a* in certain of its uses. It is neither individualizing nor generic; we cannot say, "Once upon a time there was some king who had some daughter," or "some cat has nine lives." *Some* emphasizes the total indefiniteness of the notion. Put the case that a man makes a strange assertion and I ask for his source of information: if he says "I have read it in a book," he may still remember which book it was; if he says "I have read it in some book," he probably cannot recall the title."

17.6₂. Collinson in Appendix A in *Indication* (pp. 101—103) discusses *Some* and *Any* in Modern English Usage. On p. 101 he says: "In general, the sphere of *some* is that of actuality and *any* that of possibility. *Some* particularizes without specifying, it restricts by imposing a condition explicit or implicit. Its psychological tone is thus one of fixation or concentration or recollection. On the other hand *any* does the reverse of particularizing, it encourages random shots as every item is on the same level and none claims preference over another. Its psychological tone is that of freedom from restraint, of sweeping generalization or of sovereign indifference of choice."

Some is the alternative of e. g. *all, much, many, one, any*, or *no (none)*.

On the difference between *some horse* and *some horses* as appearing in translation into German, see PhilGr 198.

17.6₃. The American use of *some* to denote something excellent or a very high degree is now common in England, too. — Cf *any* as a tertiary above, 17.5₃.

Mencken AL[3] 138 says: "Of late *some* has come into wide use as an adjective-adverb of all work, indicating special excellence or high degree, as in *some girl, some sick, going some*, etc. It is still below the salt, but threatens to reach a more respectable position."

In the 4th ed. he says: "The American use of *some* as an adjective indicating the superlative, as in "She is *some* girl," is now common in England, but its employment as an adverb to indicate either moderation or intensification, as in "I play golf *some*" and "That's lying *some*," is still looked upon as an Americanism there. The former usage has respectable English precedents, but the latter seems to be American in origin."

Examples from American writers: Academy Papers 158 the retort of the English officer who, when an American, before we went in [in World War I], watching the battle exclaimed, "Some fight," replied, "Some don't" | London V 372 [He's] some swimmer (ib 373, 374) | Lewis MS 12 they do say he's some doctor (ib 24, 28) | id B 147 I never thought I'd see a thing like that! Some town! | id MA 171 The Young Doc is quite some driver | Dreiser AT 2.127 Gee! Some athlete you are!

Some of the following examples from British authors are conscious Americanisms: Jenkins B 151 She's some dawg, is Lily! | Galsw TL 87 That old boy was 'some' explosive | id SS 59 'Some boy!' he thought; 'as Michael would say' (ib 127) | id Sw 4 'Some' test of the British character! (also id WM 3,129,146) | Crofts Ch 278 "Some morning this, Inspector," Price said (id St 184) | id in BDS 378 [American:] Say, but your railroads want hustling some (ib 363) | Beswick OD 24 My! You're some dancer | Deeping 3R 15 270 It was a day of pearl and of gold ... "Some day!" said the voice from the other corner | Mr. Churchill (when Hitler had threatened to wring England's neck as if she were a chicken): Some neck! Some chicken!

17.6₄. *Some* before a cardinal number means 'approximately' — see vol II 17.151 ff.

On *some few* Collinson in *Gramm. Misc. to Otto Jespersen* (1930) p. 204 says: "As to *few* the addition of *some* in *some few* works against its negative force, but *some few* conveys to me the idea of a smaller number than *quite a few* and could stand in some such context as: *some few villages* are left in this district where the dialect is still spoken i. e. there are such, though not many."

The following examples may be added to vol II 4.972: Austen S 64 To some few of the company it appeared rather a bold undertaking | Di X 19 the air was filled with phantoms ... some few were linked together.

On unstressed *some* [səm] see vol I 9.225.

On *somebody* with weakening of the second *o* ([sʌmbədi]) see ib 9.223.

On stress in *sometimes* see ib 5.42.

On *some* as a primary, a secondary, and a tertiary see vol II 17.1.

In American *English* we may find assimilated forms of *something* with *p* for *th:* Dreiser F 96 Sompin's sure to happen now | ib 171 You think you've pulled off sompin swell | Edgar Wallace, When the Gangs Came to London 198 [Chicago policeman:] Maybe you'll like to say sump'n' before you pop | ib 288 [the same:] What's the matter with me — dead or sump'n'? | Wentworth, Am. Dial. Dic. 577 somepin, sumpm, sumpin, sumpn, somepn, sumpen, etc. — Some of these forms are quoted by Wentworth as negro-dialect. — A form *suthin* is also quoted here.

17.6₅. *Some* (and compounds) is used in negative sentences, though not so frequently as *any* (cf 17.5₇). Its meaning here is the usual one: 'an unknown or unspecified number, amount, person, or thing': Sh H4A II. 4.209 Pray Heauen, you haue not murthered some of them | Defoe P 78 they were yet not so very poor as that they could not furnish themselves with some little conveniences | Fielding 5.489 Did not you find some of the nations ... less troublesome to you than others? | Cowper L 2.200 there is no pleasing some critics | Hazlitt A 24 it is not easy to forget some things! | Di H 61 [a clown to make people laugh] But they wouldn't laugh sometimes, and then father cried | Brontë V 131 I don't object to some of them, but I won't have them all | McCarthy 2.614 He had not for some time taken any active part in public affairs | Norris O 111 you didn't get something for nothing | Bentley T 153 it doesn't really explain some of the oddest facts | NP 1918 He has not spared some of his best friends when he thought that they erred.

Many other examples might be added.

Some may also be used in sentences with two negatives that cancel out (the second negation being implied in *without*): I hope the following statements will not be without some interest.

Similarly in questions: Did you get some letters I sent you from Wales? | May I help you to some jam? | Maugham MS 154 Will you do something for me? ... Will you write to Blanche for me?

Some(thing) is frequent in questions with a negative: Austen M 80 query whether we may not find something to employ us here | ib M 195 am I not certain of seeing or hearing something there to pain me? | Brontë P 239 were you not saying something about my giving up my place? | Caine C 158 Won't you let me do something for you? | Brett Young PC 89 Why don't you say something, Mr. Wilburn?

Finally in conditional clauses: Priestley B 76 Come along, if you want something to eat.

Thus also in conditional clauses with a negative: Walpole OL 15 if she couldn't afford something there and then, she didn't get it.

17.6₆. *Some*, like *every* and *any*, is used as first member of some compound adverbs, the most common of which are *somehow* and *somewhere*.

List of these compound adverbs:

somehow; common; 'in some way or other'.

sometime, sometimes; common; 'now and then, at some time or other, at times'. The former is chiefly used as a secondary: Mr. Smith, my sometime tutor. The latter is used only as a tertiary.

someway, someways; the former rare, except dial., the latter now only dial.

somewhen; common in recent use, especially coupled with *somewhere;* 'at some time, some time or other': Meredith E 173 This afternoon? Somewhen, before the dinner-bell | Ward R 1.285 Where and when and how you will, but somewhen and somehow, God created the heavens and the earth | Wells N 140 Of course he thinks somewhere, somewhen, he will get credit | id L 284 Some day. Somewhen | Wells V 112 it had to happen somewhen ... Somehow (frequent in Wells V; further e. g. id K 92, PF 149, T 6, TB 2.236, OH 204) | Galsw WM 173 Decision waited for him, somewhere, somewhen.

somewhence; rare; 'from some (indefinite) place'.

somewhere (*somewheres* vg: Di Do 211 somewheres or another; Am. (dial.) Norris O 363 he might meet her somewheres; cf Wentworth, Am. Dial. Dic.); 'in or at some place'.

The *-where* (or the whole word) is often treated as a primary, as appears from the following examples: Sh Err II. 1.30 How if your husband start some other where | Ro I. 1.204 This is not Romeo, hee's some other where || Defoe R 28 we were oblig'd to go on Shoar somewhere or other for Water | Maxwell G 205 She asked him the way to somewhere or other | Sayers UD 187 to see the New Zealanders at somewhere or other || Walpole OL 105 she would move from that house in the spring to somewhere brighter | Galsw MW 26 somewhere now submerged beneath the sea | Hemingway FA 124 Where will you be? — ... somewhere splendid | Cabot P 175 They could go somewhere quiet: and cheap | Plunket Greene E 245 Shall we go somewhere more private? || Lehmann DA 270 He had been Governor of somewhere.

Somewhere where is rather frequent: Hope I 118 a desire to go somewhere where he would not be looked at askance | Zangwill G 283 he would take a flat far away, somewhere where nobody knew him | Norris P 351 I wish we could get somewhere where we could see something.

(In Am. Engl. *some place* (*someplace*) is frequently used instead of *somewhere:* Shall we go some place?).

somewhile is now rare; *somewhiles* is dial. or arch.; 'at some time, sometimes'.

somewhither; rare; 'in some direction, to some place': More U 74 I had rather ... that this kind of people were dreuen sumwhether out of my sighte | Sh Tit IV. 1.11 Some whether would she haue thee goe with her | Carlyle FR 448 and R 2.128.

somewhy; rare; 'for some reason(s)': Browning 1.610

the drift of facts, whereby you learn What someone was, somewhere, somewhen, somewhy.

somewise; archaic; 'in some way or manner, somehow'.

Either

17.7. *Either* (ME *either, eyther, ai-,* OE *ǣghwæðer, āh-, ǣgðer*) generally means 'one or other of two, each one', and thus is to *any* as *both* to *all*. It is the pronoun of indifference with regard to two.

On the vowel [ai] see vol I 3.123.

It is used both as a primary, a secondary, and a tertiary — see vol II 17.61.

On *either* with a pl vb see ib 6.44; on *either* used of more than two see ib 7.731 f., and on *either one* ib 10.22.

The ordinary sense of *either* is 'one or other of two': Fielding T 3.162 he was more inclined to eating than to sleeping, and more to drinking than to either | Sheridan 205 before I form my judgment of either of them, I intend to make a trial of their hearts | Dobson F 16 If you have them cheaper at either of the universities, I will give you mine for nothing | May I come to-morrow, or the day after? — Either day will do.

Either 'one or the other' may be used together with — and in contrast to — *both:* Mi PL 1.424 For spirits, when they please, Can either sex assume, or both | Austen P 94 Jane would have defended either or both | Pattison Mi 192 either of these explanations may be true, or both may have concurred to the common effect | Merriman S 148 the Countess stood before her flushed and angry, either or both being the effect of stairs upon emotion.

In some cases *either* may be interpreted as 'one and the other' or 'one or other': Fielding T 1.95 it was always sufficient reason for either of them to be obstinate on any opinion, that the other had previously asserted the contrary | Ruskin 1.264 two little daughters are playing with a great wolf-hound, larger than either of them | Lowell St 281 Burke said of Sheridan's eloquence that it was neither prose nor poetry, but something better than either | Doyle St 192 Stangerson has a son, and Drebber has a son, and either of them would gladly welcome your daughter to their house.

This leads to the use of *either* = 'one and the other', i. e. 'each ... his', as very often in connexion with *side:* Goldsm V 2.149 my son and his mother supported me on either side | Di X 29 Mr and Mrs F. took their stations, one on either side the door | Ritchie M 231 my sister and I sat on either side of our fire | Ward E 191 There were two statues on either side of her, a pair of battered round-limbed nymphs | Walpole F 462 They both waited on either side [of the door] | Beswick OD 80 they ... seated comfortlessly one on either side of the untidy grate.

With other words: Stevenson MB 57 standing one on either bank, [they] held a Bible between them | Grand T 56 a long, low room with a window at either hand | Bridges E 109 from either ear a triple jewel hung.

Either frequently means 'one and the other', and thus might be replaced by *both* (with the plural), though, indeed, *either* generally keeps its element of indifference: Scott I 49 there was a huge fire-place at either end of the hall | Di Do 81 Mr. Dombey, without attending to what he said, was looking impatiently on either side of him ... at some object behind | Thack Hogg 124 he offered her first a five and then a ten-pound note; but she declined either | Kingsley H 29 the great highroads which ran along either bank | Farnol

A 502 the pistols were brought ... 'Good!' nodded Barnabas, and slipping one into either pocket, gathered up his reins | Kipling J 2.261 [61 ?] he caught the throat in either hand | Doyle G 31 he was cocking up his great mustaches at either end | Wells Inv 31 there was certainly a vivid enough dislike on either side [i. e. on both sides, on his and the boys'].

Note NED s. v. *either:* "the disjunctive sense has so far prevailed that in modern English such expressions as *on either side* = 'on both sides' are felt to be somewhat archaic, and must often be avoided on account of their ambiguity."

Either is used as a conjunction followed by *or:* either he or I — see vol II 17.61.

The words following *either* must be considered as originally in apposition: He is either [, viz.] a blackguard or a fool.

Either ... or sometimes comes close to signifying 'both ... and', though here, too, *either* still denotes indifference: Meas III. 1.5 either death or life Shall thereby be the sweeter | H4B V. 1.84 It is certaine, that either wise bearing, or ignorant Carriage is caught, as men take diseases, one of another.

Formerly also *either ... either* (in NED only the 16th c.).

Neither

17.8₁. *Neither* (ME *neither, neyther, nai-* OE *nāhwæðer, nāwðer, nāðor,* from *ne* 'not' *āhwæðer* 'either of two', cf *either*) as a pronoun means 'none of two,' and thus is the negative word corresponding to *either*.

For various references to vols I and II see *either*.

In vol II 10.22 *either one* is mentioned. *Neither one* is found, too, e. g. Stevenson K 248 We're neither one of us to mend the other (ib 310) | id C 251 neither one of us [was] the less pleased.

Neither of either is found in Yorksh. Trag. 1.15 Neither of either, as the Puritan bawde saies | Sh LLL V. 2.459 Neither of either, I remit both twaine.

In early writers we often find *neither* after another negative word instead of an expected (modern) *either*, e.g. Sh Tp III. 2.21 Weel not run Monsieur Monster. — Nor goe neither: but you'l lie like dogs, and yet say nothing neither | Gent III. 1.345 I care not for that neither | Sheridan 255 It isn't fair to laugh at you neither | ib 257 but I don't think we're so totally defeated neither. — Cf further vol V 23.5_4 ff., particularly 23.5_6.

Inversely, we may find *or* instead of *nor* after *neither*, e. g. Defoe R 7 I consulted neither Father or Mother any more (ib 17, 26, 58, 101) | Byron Corresp 1.52 I have lost my appetite, my rest, and can neither read, write, or act in comfort | Rose Macaulay T 188 It could deal neither with education, defences, labour, finance, or poisoned beer | Brock GS 57 Neither phenomenon appeared to interest him or to explain Whitewell's long vigil of the afternoon.

As in the last two examples this usage is especially apt to occur in sentences with a fairly long string of words between *neither* and *or*.

In early authors we find *neither* ... *neither* (or *nor* ... *nor*) instead of modern *neither* ... *nor* — see EStn 18.446.

No, none

17.8₂. On *no, none* (both from OE *nān*, from *ne* 'not' + *ān* 'one'), *nobody, none-so-pretty, no one, nothing* see vol II (Index.) — On *no* (*no one, nobody*) before restrictive relative clauses see vol III 4.8_3. — See also *no, nothing, nowhere* vol V (Index), and ib 23.3_1, $23,5_2$ ff.

No generally denotes complete negation, but it may be used to denote only 'approximation to nullity' (NED), e. g. Di D 151 Mick W. settled him in no time | it is no distance | I shall be back in no (coll. in less than no) time.

No may be used before *different* because of the semantic identity of this word with *other* (cf *any* above, 17.5_3, with reference to vol II 17.16): Maugham Pl 3.124 Pearl at my age was no different from what I am.

17.8₃. Some advs have been formed with *no* as first component (cf *every, any, some*), the most common one being *nowhere*.

Other advs with *no:*

nobbut 'only, merely, just'. NED: now dial.

nohow 'in no manner, by no means, not at all': Cambr Tr 210 There couldn't be any harm nohow | ONeill, Emp. Jones 28 Couldn't see dem now, nohow, if dey was hundred feet away.

noway, noways 'in no manner, by no means, not at all': Tennyson (q NED) I have lived a virgin, and I noway doubt But that with God's grace, I can live so still || NED 1887 The situation ... he was noways loath to accept.

nowhat 'not at all, not in the least' (rare): Trollope (q NED) Many kisses, ... of which she had been nowhat ashamed.

nowhen 'at no time, never'. NED: rare.

nowhence 'from nowhere'. NED: rare | Kingsley H 324 the universe falling from nowhence toward nowhither.

† *no while* 'never'. NED: obs. rare.

no whit 'not at all, not the least': Scott (q NED) But no whit weary did he seem.

nowhither 'nowhere': GE Mm 178 passages which seemed to lead nowhither | Garnett TwG 46 | Wells H 8 this woman has vanished — nowhither (and Kingsley above under *nowhence*).

nowise 'in no manner, not at all'. Common: Carlyle E [Blackie] 170 seems nowise our vocation here.

Adjectives

17.9₁. Some adjectival quantifiers ('half-pronominal adjectives') have been dealt with elsewhere: on *much, many, mo(e), more most, few, little, less, least, enough (enow), several* see vol II Index.

Several, divers (see vol II 2.22), *sundry*, and *various* denote both quantity and difference in quality. *Different*, the chief function of which is that of denoting difference in quality, may be used to denote quantity, too, thus meaning the same as 'various'.

Finally, on p. 621, a survey of pronominal quantifiers.

Explanations to Survey

17.9₂. Explanations to the vertical columns:

A. *All* is the pronoun of collective totality (before the pl) or, like *whole*, a pronoun of entirety (before the sg).

As a pronoun of collective totality it lumps all specimens together as a whole.

Examples: All boys know that | all the world knows that.

B. *Every*, pronoun of totality by units. Like *all* it considers all specimens of an unlimited plurality, but separately.

Example: Every boy knows that.

C. *Each* also considers all the items of plurality taken separately, but the number of items is limited.

Schematic Survey of Pronominal Quantifiers.

	A	B	C	D	E	F
(1)	all	every	each	any	some	no
(2)	all	(every one)	each	any (one)	some (one)	none
(3)	all			any	some	
(4)	all	everybody		anybody	somebody	nobody
		every one		any one	some one	no one
(5)	all	everything		anything	something	nothing
(6)	both			either		neither
(7)		everywhere	(each-where)	anywhere	somewhere	nowhere
(8)		everyway		anyway	(someway(s))	noway(s)
		(everyhow)		anyhow	somehow	nohow
				anywise	somewise	nowise
(9)	always	everywhen		anywhen	somewhen	(nowhen)
					sometimes	(nowhile)
					(somewhile)	
(10)		everywhither		(anywhither)	(somewhither)	(nowhither)
		(everywhence)		(anywhence)	(somewhence)	(nowhence)

Examples: I saw two boys in the street. Each boy had a football under his right arm | each of his children inherited £ 15,000 | we each lit a cigarette.

D. *Any*, pronoun of indifferrence, refers to a plurality within which an indifferent choice of one item or more may be made. Thus it is different from *every*, which clearly includes all, though considering the items separately.

Examples: You may come any day | here is some cheese; will you have any?

E. *Some*, pronoun of unspecified amount or number. This is different from *any*, where the choice is indifferent, while *some* refers to a definite amount or number, although this is not specified.

Examples: Some are wise, some are otherwise | He ate some bread and some grapes.

N.B. *Some* before a countable in the sg is not a quantifier.

F. *No, none*, pronouns of complete negative totality.

Examples: No words can describe my surprise when ... | He had no money || I want none of these things | I sought peace and found none.

17.9₃. Explanations of the horizontal lines:

(1) used as secondaries.

(2) primaries used before *of* and with a sb understood.

(3) used as tertiaries — see vol II Index.

(4) used as primaries in the sg referring to persons.

(5) the same referring to 'things'.

(6) the same as the word above, but referring to two only. *Each*, which also refers to a limited number, though not necessarily two, might be placed below *every*.

The last four groups are adverbs referring to (7) place, (8) manner, (9) time, and (10) direction from (*-whence*) or to (*-whither*).

Chapter XVIII
Mood

18.1₁. A mood, in accordance with PhilGr 313, may be defined as a grammatical form, or the function of such a form, which expresses a certain attitude of the mind of the speaker or writer towards the contents of the sentence, though in some cases the choice of the mood is determined not by the attitude of the actual speaker, but by the clause itself and its relation to the main nexus on which it is dependent.

18.1₂. In English we distinguish three moods, the Indicative, which has been termed 'fact-mood', the Subjunctive, which has been termed 'thought-mood', and the Imperative, termed 'will-mood'. For a general discussion of the functions or meanings of the three moods see PhilGr ch 23.

On the Imperative see vol V ch 24 (p. 467 ff.).

Indicative and Subjunctive

18.2₁. The indicative and the subjunctive will be treated together, mainly because the indicative has for centuries been encroaching upon the function of the subjunctive.

As said above, the indicative has been termed 'fact-mood'. It may be said to be the mood of the most neutral character, as it is the mood most used, the form used when the speaker only wants to state a fact without any special attitude of mind. Though it may be objected that actually the indicative is encroaching upon the sphere of the subjunctive, still the means to express the special attitude of mind generally connected with use of the subjunctive is not now the indicative as such, but generally a combination of a modal vb, without any distinction between indicative and subjunctive, and an infinitive (*may go*, *should go*, etc).

18.2₂. The subjunctive has been termed 'thought-mood', but this seems insufficient. Various grammarians distinguish between the *optative* subjunctive, which represents the utterance as something desired or intended, and the *potential* subjunctive, which represents the statement, not as an actual fact, but only as a conception of the mind. In fact they may be classed together as utterances of something existing in the speaker's mind only. The subjunctive expresses a possibility, perhaps negatived, as in clauses of condition contrary to fact, or as a possibility connected with a an element of feeling, a desire, as in sentences of wish, etc.

Apart from certain stereotyped phrases or types of phrases the subjunctive is now little used in the spoken language, but tradition has kept certain functions of it alive in the literary language, though in most of these cases it is now possible to use the indicative instead.

Webster's remarks in his Introduction (London 1856) p. 52—54 are very much to the point: "Our students are taught in school the subjunctive form: *if thou have, if he come*, etc, and some of them continue in after life to *write* in that manner, but in the course of more than forty years I have not known three men who have ventured to use that form of the verb in conversation. We toil in school to learn a language which we dare not introduce in conversation, but which the force of custom compels us not to abandon. In this respect the present study of grammar is worse than useless." (Quoted here from R. Thum in EStn IV p. 419).

Form

18.2₃. On the endings of the indicative and subjunctive 2nd and 3rd person see vol VI chs 2 and 3.

The OE and ME -*e* of the 1st person like other weak final -*e*'s was lost about 1400 (see vol I 6.15).

In ModE we have the following endings in the singular of the present tense of all vbs except *be*.

	Indicative	Subjunctive
1st pers.	—	—
2nd -	—(*e*)*st*	—
3rd -	—(*e*)*s*, arch. —(*e*)*th*	—

There is no distinction between the two moods in the plural of the present tense, nor in the preterit.

18.2₄. In the conjugation of *be* there are other distinctions (cf vol VI 5.6). In ModE we find the following forms:

	Indicative	Subjunctive
	Present	
Sg 1st pers.	*am*	*be*
2nd -	*art*	*be* (*be'st;* see vol VI 2.6₁)
3rd -	*is*	*be*
Pl	*are* (arch. and dial. *be*, see vol VI 5.6)	*be*

	Preterit	
Sg 1st pers.	*was*	*were*
2nd -	*wert, wast* (vol VI 2.7₂)	*were* (*wert* vol VI 2.7₂)
3rd -	*was*	*were*

No distinction in the plural (*were*).

18.2₅. The word *enter* as used in stage directions may offer some special features. NED in the usual type: *Enter the Ghost* terms it an imperative (3rd person), but in the following quotations, most of them modern, it functions as — or at any rate is parallel to — the indicative: Dryden 5.356 Enter Ventidius, and stands apart | Hankin 1.56 Is just about to go out, when enter Stella | Pinero S 12 just then enter my man with a note | Doyle S 1.(?) 106 then to me enter my housekeeper, with tidings of dismay.

The fact that we have to do with a stereotyped form appears from *enter* being kept in connexion with a preterit and a perf. tense as in Maurier T 92 But enter a freshman or two, and a transformation effected itself immediately | Barrie MO 160 so I have walked to mine [my task] when, enter my mother, looking wistful.

On the question whether *please, suffice,* and the vb *change* should in some cases be interpreted as subjunctives see vol VI 16.8$_9$.

18.2$_6$. I offer a few examples of the archaic present pl indicative: More U 16 one so worthy, as you be | Sh Hml III. 2.111 Be the Players ready? (and ib III. 2.44) | Mi SA 300 Yet more there be who doubt his ways not just | Walton A 64 yonder they be both a milking again | Birrell O 15 This is a terrible temptation to put in the way of a historian, and few there be who are found able to resist it | Maugham Alt 99 you'll thank all the gods there be | the powers that be (from the Bible, Rom. 13.1).

Otherwise only sentences in which the above indicated distinctions are exemplified, will be discussed in what follows.

18.2$_7$. The weakening of the sense for the use of the subjunctive is evident from the frequent occurrence of the indicative and the subjunctive in close proximity. For *was* and *were* close together in conditional clauses see vol IV 10.2(5).

I adduce here some examples of pres. indicative and pres. subjunctive in close proximity, chiefly in conditional clauses, but also in clauses of wish and in indirect speech (and question), — to begin with some examples in which the indicative is used first, then some in which the subjunctive is used first. The reason for the change is not always easy to decide; but this vacillation at any rate clearly proves the uncertainty of the various authors as regards the use of the subjunctive.

Note that in both groups the vacillation is most common in the vb *be*.

Examples with the indicative first: Sh As I. 2.155 if thou dost him any slight disgrace, or if hee doe not mightilie grace himselfe on thee, hee will practise against thee | Wiv I. 1.28 if he ha's a quarter of your coat, there is but three skirts for your selfe ... if Sir John Falstaffe haue committed disparagements vnto you | Swift J 519 If I am cheated, I'll part with it to Lord M.: if it be a bargain, I'll keep it to myself | Fielding 3.606 Provided a hero in his life doth but execute a sufficient quantity of mischief; provided he be but well and heartily cursed by the widow | Austen M 118 something must be fixed on. No matter what, so that something is chosen ... I take any part you choose to give me, so as it be comic | Spencer E 2.13 If, as all know, it is tiresome to listen to an indistinct speaker ... and if, as we cannot doubt the fatigue is a cumulative result ... it follows that ... And if this be true when ... it will also ... | Merriman, Last Hope 383 the part to be played by kings — so easy, if the gift is there; so impossible to acquire, if it be lacking | Jerome T 154 If he loves you — if it be not merely a sense of honour that binds him | Shaw M xx Whether the artist becomes poet or philosopher ... his sexual doctrine is nothing but ... The world shewn us in books, whether the books be confessed epics or professed gospels | Masefield M 222 [practical man:] I believe that the cure (if there is one) will be got by ... [poet:] I believe that the cure (if there be one) will be obtained by the use of sera.

Examples with the subjunctive first: Sh Hml V. 2.245 If Hamlet from himselfe be tane away, And when he's not himselfe, do's wrong Laertes, Then Hamlet does it not | Oth III. 3.384 I thinke my wife be honest, and think she is not: I thinke that thou art iust, and thinke thou art not | AV Lev 25.14 And if thou sell ought vnto thy neighbour, or buyest ought of thy neighbours hand | AV Matth 5.23 if thou bring thy gift to the altar, and there remembrest that thy brother hath ought against thee | Swift J 34 contrive to know whether Mrs. W. be in town, and how she is in health, and whether she stays in town | Defoe G 40 If the lady be a toy, she is happy; if she is a woman of sense and wit, she is ruin'd | Goldsm 4 if what you tell me be true, and if I am to be [*be to be* avoided!] a beggar, it shall never make me a rascal | Brontë V 34 What if my complaint be about to take a turn, and I am yet destined to enjoy health? | Ruskin F 97 But if the mass of good things be inexhaustible, and there are horses for everybody, — why is not every beggar on horseback? | Collingwood R 90 If painting be an expression of the human mind, and if the contents of the mind are Ideas, then the best painting is that which contains the greatest number of the greatest Ideas.

Conditional Clauses

18.3₁. Conditional clauses have been treated in vol V 21.5₃ ff., where examples are given with various conjunctions (*if, unless, and (if)*, etc), prepositions (*except, save, without*), and other introductory words (*suppose, provided, in case*).

Clauses without any conjunction or other introductory word, but with the same word-order as questions (inversion), have been treated in vol V 21.6$_1$ ff.

18.3$_2$. Imaginative use of the preterit (and pluperfect) was discussed in vol IV chs 9 and 10. In conditional clauses, in particular clauses expressing condition contrary to fact (see vol IV 9.1(1)), it was originally the rule to use the preterit subjunctive in this case. The only vb distinguishing between the indicative and subjunctive in the preterit in modern English, the vb *be*, has been treated in vol IV ch 10. The various uses of *was* and *were* in conditional clauses have been treated ib 10.2(1). There is now a tendency towards an emphatic use of *was* referring to the actual past, while *were* refers to something imaginative or unreal, generally with an implication of negation.

18.3$_3$. The present subjunctive is frequent, too, in conditional clauses. These clauses do not refer to conditions contrary to fact (implying a negation).

Some examples with various introductory words: More U 207 yf annye man take | ib 208 yf he lyue | Spenser, Epistle to Shepherd's Cal. if my memory fayle not | Marlowe F 285 vnlesse he vse such meanes ... | id MP 247 And it please your grace (cf vol VI 16.8$_9$) | Kyd ST II. 1.60 If case it lie in me to tell the truth | ib II. 3.18 in case the match go forward | Sh Hml II. 2.626 If he but blench I know my course | Walton A 7 if this satisfie not | Mi SA 274 If he aught begin | Swift P 98 Footman: An please your Honour, there's a man below wants to speak to you (cf vol VI 16.8$_9$) | Di P [Ch&H] 577 if he wish | Kingsley H 247 if I am to see him | Gissing R 28 And — if our conscience mean anything at all — the bitter wrong! | Holmes A 166 unless it differ | Butler Er [P] 157 He must perish if he get that | Jerome I 128 If he like you he does not hesitate to let you know it | Holbrook Jackson, Occasions 187 it means, if it mean anything at all, that we are devoid of that inner richness which is the only true happiness | BBC 1938: unless the storm abate it will be impossible ...

Similar examples with *be* might be adduced from Deloney, Marlowe, Sh, AV, Walton, Rehearsal, Bunyan, Milton, Osborne, Tatler, Swift (P 82 she's on the wrong Side of Thirty, if she be a Day), John Locke, Quincey, Trollope, Stevenson, Gilbert, Lang, Jerome, Chesterton, Shaw, Dreiser, Sherwood Anderson, and others.

18.3₄. But from early times we may also find the present indicative in such conditional clauses:

AR 74 ȝif eni weneþ þet he beo religius, & ne bridleþ noht his tunge, his religiun is fals [translating Lat. si quis putat] | Ch T 4.611 That if Criseyde ... Now loveth thee | ib 615 And if she wilneth | More U 200 if thou haste pleasure therein ... if the hope of slaughter dothe please the | Sh Mcb V. 5.47 If this which he auouches do's appeare | Massinger N III. 2.359 If I am welcome, bid him so | Bunyan G 123 if he hath ... if he doth | Otway 262 if the truth's hid longer | Spectator 558 If the King of France is certainly dead (common in the Spectator) | Defoe G 24 If he has not the virtue, how can he be call'd noble? | Fielding 5.573 if there is really such a person | Goldsm V 1.163 [part of indirect thought] If this was not found sufficient ... it was then fixed upon to terrify him with a rival | Burke Am 57 If these propositions are accepted, everything ... must ... fall | Franklin 114 if he first forms a good plan | Austen S 67 if he is not here by the end of the week, I shall go after him | Quincey 8 if there really is such a person | Ruskin S 112 they must be feelings of delight, if they are to be vital | Kingsley H ix if we are to judge | Stevenson MB xiv If Burns is to be called a bad man | Swinburne L 240 if evil comes of this I shall think we are all born to it | Holmes A 144 if you are a man ... if you are a woman | Doyle Sh 5.83 if my reading of this problem proves to be correct | Hewlett Q 2 if the truth is to be told, let it be there.

"It will hardly be possible to find any example of the subjunctive *be* immediately followed by *to be*, as in "If any such scheme be to be adopted." Here everybody will say and write *is to be*. The reason is not exactly that the phrase is considered cacophonous, but rather the want of clearness involved in the combination *be to be*, which to the hearer would sound as if the speaker stammered or did not know what to say." (O.Jsp.).

18.3₅. *An(d)* and *an(d) if* = *if* also frequently takes the subjunctive (cf vol V 21.5₄). Three examples: Skelton M 1298 A peryllous thynge, to cast a cat Vpon a naked man and yf she scrat | Arden of Feversham I. 120 Nay, and you be so impatient, I'll be gone | ib II. 2.137 Nay, an you be offended, I'll be gone.

18.3₆. *So* = *if* or *if only* often takes the subjunctive. See vol. V 21.5₈ and add on p. 371 the following modern examples with the subjunctive: Yeats CC 98 Let us and ours be lost so she be shriven | Abercrombie in GP 10 Let it be storm or calm, so we be sailing. — And add the following modern instances with *so be:* Chesterton Flying Inn [T] 83 [vg] So be it's the Law, where is it ? | Yeats CC 23 Whatever you are that walk the woods at night So be it that you have not shouldered up Out of a grave ... I welcome you. — But the three authors quoted are apt to use highly literary forms.

18.3$_7$. We may have both condition and comparison in one clause (see vol V 21.7$_9$ f.). — Such clauses are now introduced by *as if* or *as though*, formerly often by *as* alone (Ch A 2041 The statue of Mars up-on a carte stood, Armed, and loked grim as he were wood), as still in the set phrase *as it were* 'as if it were so, so to speak', quoted by NED from Chaucer on (cf vol IV 10.4(8—9)).

In clauses in which condition only — not comparison — is expressed, we frequently find the subjunctive, but the indicative is being used more and more frequently, as in the following quotations:

Bunyan G 33 (see vol V 21.7$_9$) | Defoe M 128 (after repeated *that;* see ib) | Fielding 5.522 she levelled them [her eyes] downwards, as if she was concerned for what she had done | Sterne 34 as if there was no such thing as a critic at table (also twice ib 47) | Southey L 95 he always talks of himself, just as if he was speaking of another person | Keats 5.175 Do not live as if I was not existing | Hazlitt Works 4.235 he smiled ... as if he was already seated in the House (thus often in Hazlitt) | Di F 301 as if you was her proprietor | Collins W frequently | Benson D 19 Jack spoke dreamily as if he was thinking of something else.

18.3$_8$. See further vol IV 10.4(1) ff. on *was, were* after *as if* and *as though* referring to the present time, and ib 4(5) referring to the past. Note the following examples of indicative and subjunctive in close proximity: Chesterton, Wisdom of Father Brown [T] 13 It was rather as if he were thanking a stranger ... than as if he were (as he was) practically thanking the

Curator of Kew Gardens | Walpole C 360 He felt ... as though she was there against her will | ib 361 Mrs. Brandon looked about her as though she were trying to find a way of escape | Beresford R 87 He spoke as if he were on the verge of tears, as if this crowning grievance after all he had borne and sacrificed, was almost too much for him.

In the last example the force of the subjunctive is, as it were, exhausted, hence the indicative in the second clause.

Note the following two sentences: Merriman S 64 I am beginning to feel as if it is a crime | Walpole DW 400 She stopped ... as though, having said what had been in her mind for a long while, she was finished, absolutely, with it all.

In the former sentence the use of the indicative leaves the possibility open that it is a crime, whereas *as if it were* excludes this possibility. In the latter the indicative may be due to the long distance between *as though* and the vb.

Temporal Clauses

18.4₁. Clauses of time introduced by the conjunctions *before, till, until,* and *ere* (*or ever*) (archaic) refer to the future, which actually exists only as a possibility, and hence naturally is put in the "thought-mood". On clauses of time as tertiaries see vol V 21.2.

Some examples of the present subjunctive in clauses with the above-mentioned conjunctions: Ch C 709 Er that he dye, sorwe have he and shame | More U 208 it endeth not vntyll the pleasure dye wyth it | Gascoigne 58 To stop one eare, vntil the poore man speake | Deloney 3 if you have the leasure to stay till the Charme be done | Sh Mcb V. 3.2 Till Byrnane wood remoue to Dunsinane, I cannot taint with Feare | Cymb III. 6.19 yet Famine, Ere cleane it o're-throw Nature, makes it valiant | AV Mk 14.30 euen in this night before the cocke crow twise, thou shalt denie me thrise | Walton A 95 what worms soever you fish with, are the better for being long kept before they be used | Milton SA 176 I hear the sound of words; their sense the air Dissolves unjointed ere it reach my ear | Byron ChH 3.32 The tree will wither long before it fall | Scott Iv [Black] 181 But undo the door to him before he beat it from its hinges | Shelley 466 till to love and live Be one | Carlyle FR 400 The Rustic sits waiting till the river run dry | Mrs Browning (q NED: *or*) That not a letter of the meaning fall Or ere it touch and teach His world's deep heart | Tennyson L 3.208 they must wait till he get some employment | Stevenson V 115 they will forget before the week be out.

18.4₂. We also find clauses with the preterit subjunctive, connected of course with a preterit in the rest of the sentence in relation to which the contents of the clause are in the future, a fact which explains the use of the subjunctive. Here we also find the conjunctions *after* and *once* (see on the latter vol V 21.2$_5$).

Prof. Collinson says: "*Once* as an introductory particle suggests to me *if once*, and *if* often has *were*." Hence he will hesitate less with *once* than with *after*.

A few examples: Bunyan G 127 they clap'd him up before there were any proclamation | Swift 3.346 I durst not come into my master's presence, until I were sufficiently aired | Austen M 193 there was nothing more to be said till Sir Thomas were present | Shelley 63 Cythna by my side, Until the bright and beaming day were spent, Would rest | Holmes A 143

I think I could go to pieces, after my life's work were done, in one of those tranquil places | London, War of Classes 189 Once the crisis were past, the ruling class would proceed to readjust things | Beresford, Pris. Hartl. 76 [he thought] She would look back on the worship of riches with horror once she were away from the influence of this house [subj. because indirect thought?].

Wishes

18.5₁. The present subjunctive is used in sentences expressing wishes for the future. In PE its use is of a distinctly literary character apart from certain (types of) more or less established phrases, such as: God bless you | Long live the King! | Grammar be hanged!

18.5₂. In earlier stages of the language, expressions of wishes that some disease or other unpleasantness should befall the hearer or somebody or something else (see more examples vol III 11.8₆₂): Apollonius of Tyre (Cook, First Book of OE) 181 Swīga ðū. Adl [= disease] ðē fornime, ðæt ðū ne bēo hāl nē gesund | Ch A 4081 Unthank come on his hand that bond him [the horse] so | ib 4172 A wilde fyr up-on their bodyes falle! | id B 4597 A verray pestilens upon yow falle! | Rehearsal 55 the Kings should (a pox take 'em) have pop'd both their heads in at the door | Smollett R 321 Damnation seize me | Goldsm V [Oxf. 1922] 257 A murrain take such trumpery.

18.5₃. Note the archaic phrases with the adv *woe* (in ModE interpreted as the sb?): Skelton M 2103 A, woo worthe the, Lyberte! | Latimer, Ploughers [Arber] 34 Wo worth the, O Deuyll, wo worth the ... Wo worth the Deuyll and all thyne Angelles | Sh Tit IV. 2.56

Now helpe, or woe betide! thee euermore | Keats 187 No utter'd syllable, or, woe betide! | Scott LL 22 Woe worth the chase, woe worth the day, That costs thy life, my gallant grey!

Woe worth is completely obsolete. *Woe betide* is now always followed by a pronoun (*you*, *him*, etc).

18.5₄. Very frequent are sentences in which the speaker expresses a wish that God (*God, the Lord, Christ*, etc, or corruptions of *God*, etc) may do something, bless or punish somebody, forbid or prevent something, etc. The object of the vb is not always stated. Many of these expressions are terms of imprecations. Examples: God bless you | God damn you (God-damn, God damn me) | God forbid | Ch A 3508 Nay, Christ forbede it, for his holy blood! | id B 245 Now, fayre Custance, almyghty god thee gyde! | ib 914 The lordes styward — god yeue him meschaunce! | ib 4621 God let him never the! [i. e. prosper] (such phrases are very frequent in Ch) | Skelton M 1115 That euer thou thryue, God it forfende | Deloney 29 God a [have] mercy good Iack (often spelt in one word, see NED) | Sh Hml I. 5.113 Heauen secure him! | Walton A 45 God keep you all, Gentlemen | Mi SA 1427 the Holy One Of Israel be thy guide | Swift J 61 God send it holds | Wordsw 65 These Tourists, Heaven preserve us! needs must live a profitable life | Scott Iv 317 God assoilzie him (cf vol I 2.312) | Darwin L 1.239 Heaven forefend | Meredith EH 115 Lord forbid, sir! | Jerome T 121 Gor blimy [= God blind me], if she ain't a good' un (ONeill Emp. Jones 5 Gawd blimey!) | Hope C 18 Oh, Lord love you, she did not mean it | Caine M 150 Gough bless me | Chesterton T [T] 80 God blast your impudence! | Merrick MG 211 God grant my opinion's wrong! | A Huxley BL 220 "God rot her!" said the other fervently [conscious archaism] | [vg] Lor' love a duck!

Note the following sentence with the wish expressed in a relative clause: Sh Alls II. 4.11 she's not in heauen, whither God send her quickly.

18.5₅. In ModE the subject in terms of imprecations is generally left out: Sh Wiv III. 3.196 Hang him, dishonest rascal! | Ford 199 Hang 'em! | Rehearsal 85 Bless me! | Congreve OB 106 Damn your morals | ib 119 Hang me, if I pity you | Wycherley PD 39 confound him | Smollett R 64 Damn my blood! what are you afraid of? | ib 197 Curse thee, fellow! | ib 320 damme! | Goldsm 624 rabbit me | id V [Oxf. 1922] 221 strike me ugly | Sterne 21 Rot the hundred and twenty pounds | Austen P 296 Oh! hang Kitty! what has she to do with it? | Keats 4.64 But who's afraid? Aye! Tom! Demme if I am | Browning 1.203 moonstrike him | Di P [Ch & H] 182 'Well, damn my straps and whiskers,' says Tom Smart, '... this isn't pleasant, blow me!' | Thack P 81 dammy, I won't stand it | Stevenson T 79 But dash my buttons! that was a good 'un about my score | Hardy R 25 jown it all | Ridge S 83 jigger me if ... | Kipling MI 137 Blimy [from *God blind me*] if ... | Shaw 2.104 [T] Why, bless my heart and soul | id A [T] 92 Oh, dash it, I forgot | id GM 117 Hang it all | London V 357 [Amr] Doggone it | Wells K 9 Drat and drabbit that young rascal! | OHenry B 74 darn my eyes | Galsw MW 280 Blast my career! | King O 166 'Well, dammit,' complained the latter | Cronin C 174 Dammit to hell, Manson!

The spelling in the last two examples is a further step towards the complete liberation of the vb and its object from its origin, as seen in Waugh W 115 he had dodged it, as near as dammit.

Note similarly the expression *kingdom(-)come* 'heaven' or 'the kingdom of Christ' from *thy kingdom come* in the Lord's Prayer, as in Lancaster, Pageant 303 Some will probably go to Kingdom Come before we're through with this (cf NED *s. v. Kingdom* 6).

The object of the vb may be omitted, too: Damn! | Dash!, etc.

18.5₆. In terms of imprecation *the devil* and synonyms or corruptions are also frequent as subject: Ch B 1408 The devel have part of alle swiche rekeninges! | id D 1544 'The feend,' quod he, 'yow feeche body and bones ...' | Noahs Arche 176 The deuill of hell þe take | Towneley 9. II. 12 The dwill hang hym vp to dry | Marlowe F 766 the diuell choake thee | Congreve OB 10 the Devil take me if I don't love all the Sex | Swift P 92 the Duce take you | Smollett R 86 devil take me if I know ... | Di M 59 Deuce take it | Synge 111 The divil mend you, I'm scalded again! (*the divil mend* .. also Flaherty I 263 and ONeill S 192).

18.5₇. Often the vb is in the passive, and the subject may be a repetition of an immediately preceding word, or of several words: Grammar be hanged! | Ch MP 18.33 Jalousye be hanged by a cable! | Skelton M 1812 A, Syr, thy iarfawcon [i. e. gerfalcon] and thou be hanged togyder! | Jerome T & Co. 64 "... And that if Mr. Grindley would be content with a small salary —" "Small salary be hanged!" snarled Peter | Masefield Odtaa 16 "I hoped, sir, that you would let me go to an engineering works." "Engineering works be damned" | Maugham F [T] 59 "There is such a thing as virtue, you know." "Virtue be damned" | id Pl 2.87 I thought it was so tactful. — Tactful be blowed | Sayers DC 213 "Sit down," I said, ... "Sit down be damned!" | Mannin W 78 He's proud, austere. ... — Proud and austere be damned!

18.5₈. Formerly the present subjunctive was also used in clauses as objects of verbs of wish: Marlowe J 1715 Law wils that each particular be knowne | Sh Meas II. 2.126 Pray heauen she win him | Hml III. 1.38 I do wish That your good Beauties be happy cause Of Hamlets wildenesse | Stevenson JH [N.Y. 1887] 74 God grant that he be not deceived.

The past tense is very frequently used in such clauses after *wish*, etc. On the use of *was* and *were* see vol IV 10.1(1) ff.

18.5₉. Main sentences of wish with inversion are fairly frequent: Ch C 248 Blessed be god, that I shal dye a mayde (a frequent type in Ch) | Goldsm 654 Perish the baubles! | Austen P 277 Far be it from me to depreciate such pleasures | Carlyle SR 35 As exordium to the whole, stand here the following long citation | Doyle M 45 Foul fare the grasping taxman | Merriman S 15 Steinmetz, be it noted, had an infinite capacity for holding his tongue | Galsw P 7.43 if you force me — on your head be it! | Walpole Jeremy 24 how can a man, be he come to three-score and ten and more, ever forget ... that early vision? | Bird R 20 Beaton — to his shame be it spoken — was not a member of the fifteen | Long live the King! | So help me God! | Suffice it to say ... — Cf above, 2.2₂.

Intention or Purpose

18.6₁. The subjunctive is frequently found in clauses of intention or purpose (final clauses), particularly in early authors: Marlowe E 791 See that my coache be readie | Sh R2 V. 3.36 Then giue me leaue, that I may turne the key, That no man enter | Massinger N II. 3.142 Be careful nought be wanting | Sherwood Anderson MM 3 He was ... inclined to have dreams which he tried to crush out of himself in order that he function as a washing machine manufacturer | ib 241 She ... kept putting up the hand that held the stone, first closing it carefully that the precious stone be not lost.

In such sentences the use of *might* or *should* would now be much more frequent.

But in modern authors the indicative is by no means rare in such clauses: Ruskin S 134 see to it that your train is of vassals whom you serve | Kingsley H 316 I will see that no one is listening at the door | GE A 46 His shoes will be dirty, but see that he wipes them | Doyle S 5.164 it is our duty to see that no one molests her | Shaw Pur 101 see to it that no harm comes to her.

On clauses of intention or purpose see further vol V 21.9₃ ff.

18.6₂. After *lest* (*that*) 'in order that ... not' (early spelling also *least*) and *for fear that* or *lest* (in the same sense) the subjunctive is the rule if a modal vb (generally *should*) is not used: NED 1526 Tindale: Take hede lest eny man deceaue you | Spenser FQ III. 4.14 I read thee soone retyre ... Least afterwards it be too late to take thy flight | Kyd ST II. 1.107 Go and attend her ... Lest absence make her think thou dost amiss | Sh Tw III. 4.144 Nay pursue him now, least the deuice take ayre, and taint | Lr IV. 6.235 Hence, Least that [N.B. *that*] th'infection of his fortune take Like hold on thee. Let go his arms | AV Prov. 26.5 Answere a foole according to his folly, lest he bee wise in his owne conceit | Mi SA 951 Let me approach, at least, and touch thy hand. — Not for thy life, lest fierce remembrance wake My sudden rage | Byron, Eng. Bards and Sc. Rev. [p. ?] Beware lest blundering Brougham destroy the sale | Browning 1.469 off with you, Lest of that shrug come what God only knows! | Mason Ch 213 He was a man moved by the very spirit of justice, timid lest anyone should wrong, bold lest the criminal walk unpunished. — Both *lest* and the subjunctive are literary. — See further vol V 21.9_5.

Content-Clauses with *Lest*

18.6₃. The preceding group is related to the group of clauses dependent on vbs of fear and doubt, often introduced by *lest* (*least*) (cf Lat. *timeo ne*). In ordinary, non-literary language we have now *that* in such clauses. Examples with *lest:* Mi PL 9.251 But other doubt possesses me, lest harm Befall thee severed from me | Earle M 26 his scale of Iustice is suspected, least it bee like the Ballances in his Ware-house | Lawrence Seven Pillars 201 he would not be comforted, and afterwards, for fear lest he escape, had to be lashed to his tree again | Sherwood Anderson WO 172 his wife ... worried lest the horse become frightened and run away.

Cf vol V 21.5_3.

Concessive Clauses

18.6₄. On concessive clauses see vol V 21.4_3 ff. — If the clause denotes a possibility, we often find the subjunctive, but also occasionally if the clause denotes a fact. A few examples: Puttenham 80 A staffe of foure verses containeth in it selfe matter sufficient to make a full periode or complement of sence, though it doe not alwayes so | Kyd ST II. 3.3 Although she coy it, as becomes her kind, ... I doubt not, I, but she will stoop in time | Sh ? E3 III. 1.107 claim Edward what he can, And bring he ne'er so plain a pedigree, 'Tis you are in possession of the crown | Mi PL 3.686 And oft, though Wisdom wake, Suspicion sleeps At Wisdom's gate | Swift 3.179 this gave me some faint hopes of relief, although I were not [fact!] able to imagine how it could be brought about | id T 84 what though his head be empty, provided his common-place book be full | Ruskin S 120 whether novels, or poetry, or history be read, they should be chosen for their possession of good | Stevenson MB 62 Burns was always ready to sacrifice an acquaintance to a friend, although the acquaintance were a duke.

Here also belong coordinate sentences like the following. In the sentence with the subjunctive we always have inversion: Ch F 330 And come agayn, be it by day or nyght | Marlowe J 1609 none can heare him, cry he ne're so loud | Defoe R 2.218 Be it, I had business, or no business, away I went | Keats 2.43 it is done — succeed the verse or fail — To honour thee | Quincey 283 Be the artist, however, who he might, the affair remains a durable monument of his genius | Macaulay B 291 be the defence good or bad, it is a defence which cannot avail Barère | Thack S 68 Be it ever so shabby or dismal, nobody ever owns to keeping a shop | Birrell O 67 How then does a man — be he good or bad — big or little ... make his memoirs interesting ?

Indirect Speech

18.7₁. As in many other languages (Latin, German, etc) we may in English find the subjunctive in indirect speech, although the rules for its application are far from being strict, and here as everywhere the indicative is gaining ground at the expense of the subjunctive.

On the shifting of mood in indirect speech see PhilGr 295 ff.

The use of the tenses in indirect speech has been dealt with in vol IV ch 11.

Subjunctival *were* may be used after a preterit referring to the past as well as after the imaginative preterit — see vol IV 11.4(4) (cf ib 11.4(3)).

A few additional examples with *were:* Ch A 691 I trowe he were a geldyng or a mare | Marlowe E 1987 Imagine Killingworth castell were your court | Sh Err II. 2.133 How deerely would it touch you to the quicke, Shouldst thou but heare I were licencious | Meas IV. 3.3 One would think it were Mistris Ouerdons owne house | Bunyan G 15 when I did any thing that I thought were good | Austen P 236 imputing his visit to a wish of hearing that she were well || Carlyle [q Birrell O 19] Who would suppose that Education were a thing which had to be advocated on the ground of local expediency ... ?

And note, with the present after *think:* BJo 3.179 I think this be the gentleman.

On unshifted *if ... were to* see vol IV 11.2(3).

On the unshifted subjunctive in such parenthetical phrases as *blessed be God, thank heaven*, which nearly have the character of tertiaries (cf vol IV 11.7(1) *maybe*); see vol IV 11.7(2).

On unshifted present subjunctive in verbal reports of proposals and motions see ib 11.7(4).

On *be and is hereby* ... in official style see ib 11.7(5), and add the following two examples: Di P 2 The following resolutions ... That the members of the aforesaid Corresponding Society be, and are, hereby informed that their proposal … | NP 1924 At a meeting of the Liberal party … it was moved that "Mr. Lloyd George be and hereby is appointed sessional chairman of the Liberal party."

18.7₂. The pres. subjunctive is common after such vbs as *command, demand, require, suggest, insist,* etc, particularly in American writers, — see examples in vol IV 11.7(6), to which the following early examples may be added: More U 180 I thynk he be [indicative?] some of the Ambassadours fooles | Kyd ST I. 2.124 Hieronimo, it greatly pleaseth us That in our victory thou have a share | Sh Gent II. 3.5 I thinke Crab my dog, be [indicative?] the sowrest natured dogge that liues | Dekker F 1771 he has commaunded that no woodmonger sell you a sticke of wood | Johnson R 63 his character requires that he estimate the happiness and misery of every condition | Austen M 413 what I advise is, that your father be quiet.

Indirect Questions

18.7₃. Questions naturally imply uncertainty and possibility, hence we often find the subjunctive in indirect questions. Examples with pres. subjunctive: Mi SA 337 say if he be here | Spectator 1 'till he knows whether the Writer of it be a black or a fair Man | Goldsm V 1.54 I don't know if this poor man's situation be so bad | Lamb R 47 he has doubted if there be a providence | Di D 48 I wonder if my mother's step be really not so light as I have seen it | Macaulay E 4.34 we doubt whether there be a hundred Bengalees in the whole army | Birrell O 44 But, whether Truth-hunting be ever established or not, no one can doubt that it is a most fashionable pastime.

A few (out of many) examples with subjunctival *were:* Swift 3.191 asking whether I were now settled for life (ib 3.278) | Goldsm V 2.171 he asked me if my son's name were George | Austen P 147 the girls walked to Meryton, to inquire if Mr. W. were returned | ead M 280 he asked if she were there (ead S 161) | Lamb R 69 I could gain no information whether he were dead or living | Di D 286 on my asking now, if that were not so | Thack S 18 What could it matter whether his Reverence were chaplain to his Lordship or not? | GE M 117 he left the room, hardly knowing whether he were more relieved ... or more uneasy | Collins W 437 Strangers might have doubted if she were the Laura Fairlie they had once seen | Hardy L 130 peering in to ascertain if Emily were there alone (id passim) | Stevenson T 115 Whether he were injured much or little, none could ever tell (id M 160 and 161) | Ward F 229 and M 130 | Hope passim | Housman J 47 | Masefield M passim | Walpole DW 18 as though she would see whether it were the truth that she were speaking (N.B. the second *were!*) | Galsw Car 875.

Indefinite Relative Clauses

18.7₄. In indefinite relative clauses (cf vol III 3.1 and 3.6) generally introduced with such words as *whatever, whoever, however, wherever*, we have a hypothetical element, the indifference of a choice, and hence we frequently find the subjunctive in such clauses: Ch A 833 whoso be rebel to my jugement, shal paye ... | Kyd ST II. 1.58 Whate'er it be your lordship shall demand | BJo 3.31 he knows, howe'er his wife affect strange airs, She has not yet the face to be dishonest | ib 3.171 you must keep what servants she please |

Mi A [Arber] 34 there can no greater testimony appear, then when your prudent spirit acknowledges and obeyes the voice of reason from what quarter soever it be heard speaking | id SA 903 In argument with men a woman ever Goes by the worse, whatever be her cause | Dryden Abs. and Achit. l. 99 For priests of all religions are the same. Of whatsoe'er descent their godhead be ... | Spectator 17 However it be, I have been often put out of Countenance by the Shortness of my Face | Richardson G 43 whatever were your subject, I beg you will resume it | Fielding T 1.217 however this be, certain it is that ... | Johnson R 71 whatever be the consequence of my experiment, I am resolved to judge with mine own eyes | Goldsm 636 whatever be our fate, let us not add guilt to our misfortunes | Wordsw 159 Whate'er betide, we'll turn aside, And see the Braes of Yarrow | Austen M 35 he engaged to fetch her away again, at half an hour's notice, whenever she were weary of the place | ead P 169 whichever be the case, her sister's situation remained the same | Byron [T] 4.235 whate'er It seem in those who will replace ye in Mortality | Shelley 405 We'll toss up who died first of drinking tea And cry out "head or tails!" where'er we be | Browning 1.479 Henceforth we are undivided, whatever be our fortune | Tennyson 279 The churl in spirit, howe'er he veil His want in forms for fashion's sake ... | ib 469 King am I whatsoever be their cry | Hewlett Q 16 such a man can hardly be deemed a sinner, whatever he do | Walpole DW 229 whatever she be doing | Bailey, Milton 193 Whatever be the art ... the test is the same.

18.7₅. The indicative, however, is frequent in such sentences, too, thus in Shakespeare (but subjunctive *be* is also common) and in PE. A few examples: Sh Sonn

135 Whoever hath her wish thou hast thy will | Shelley 357 Whatever comes my heart shall sink no more | Browning 2.321 Whatever they are, we seem | Ruskin CWO 44 How many of our present money-seekers would ... hang themselves, whoever was killed | ib 154 the work of the captivity is the same, whatever work we are set upon | Kipling J 2.125 Whatever it is, it is white-face work.

We probably never find the present subjunctive of *happen* after *whatever* (but we may have *whatever may happen*).

18.7₆. On the highly literary imaginative *were* in main sentences like the following see vol IV 10.5 and add: Kyd ST II. 5.40 To know the author were some ease of grief | Gissing R 83 And what were the durability of love without the powerful alliance of habit?

Technical Terms
(mainly syntactical)

Used by
Otto Jespersen
(and *Niels Haislund* in MEG VII chs 12—18).

Abbreviations used in this list: I—VII = Modern English Grammar vols I—VII. — AS = Analytic Syntax. Copenhagen 1937. — ChE = Chapters on English. London 1918. — Eff. = Efficiency in Linguistic Change. Copenhagen 1941. — EEG = Essentials of English Grammar. London 1933. — Lang. = Language, Its Nature, Development and Origin. London 1922. — Ling. = Linguistica, Selected Papers. Copenhagen 1933. — Mankind = Mankind, Nation, and Individual from a Linguistic Point of View. London 1946 (Oslo 1925). — Neg = Negation in English and Other Languages. Copenhagen 1917. — PG = The Philosophy of Grammar. London 1924. — Progr. = Progress in Language. London 1894. — SG = The System of Grammar (1933) in Ling. pp. 304—345 (Reference to sections, which correspond to chapters in EEG. Also published separately). — [= not accepted by O. J. (or N. H.). — † formerly used by O. J., now generally replaced by some other term.

A.

Abbreviated sentences AS 24.9, VII 3.3_1 ff.

[Absolute PG, V 6.1, VII 7.5_3, absolute form of pronoun (> oblique case) III 17.8_2, 'absolute comparative' SG 22, VII 11.4_8.

[Abstract substantive = Nexus-subst. II 12.25. — See also PG.

Accusative SG 14, VII 6.1$_3$. — Cf Case.

Active PG 165 ff., 283, & passim, AS 37.

Activo-passive III 16.8.

Adjective PG, SG 7, II 1.3, VII 1.3, 1.5$_4$, chs 10—11.

Adjective-subjunct PG 99, II 15.2.

Adjunct PG, II 1.2. — Indirect II 12.25, substantival II 13, with compounds AS 6.5 ff., genitival 3.3, prep. phrases 3.4, irregular 3.6, partial II 12.3. — See Rank.

Adled (Dan.) see Rank.

Adverb. PG, II 1.3, VI passim, VII 1.5.

Affirmation SG 28, V 18.2.

After-future, after-past see Time.

Agent-nouns, sb & adj, PG 141 n., 169; tense 283; AS 21, 39.2, V 22, adj V 22.1$_5$, VII 9.2$_5$.

Amorphous sentences AS 26, clauses AS 26.6. — Cf Inarticulate sentences.

Anaphoric II 10.81, 16.32 ff., etc, VII 2.3$_7$, pronouns 4.4$_2$, *it* VII 4.6$_2$.

Animate PG 227, 234, VII 5.8.

Antecedent, e. g. AS 25.5, III passim.

Anticipatory (base) V 12.6$_1$, *it* VII 4.6$_3$ ff., subject (*there*) AS 34.6. — Cf Existential *there*.

Apo koinou III 7.1.

Aposiopesis PG 130, 142, 310 (Lang. 251), VII 3.5.

Apposition, restrictive AS 12.6, a whole idea AS 12.8, with prepositions, *of* AS 4.4, III 1.5, VII 9.9$_1$, with sentences AS 12.3, word-order VII 2.1$_4$, case VII 6.2$_4$.

Articles PG, VII 12—16. — Generic VII 14.3 (cf II 5.4). — Article of complete & incomplete determination EEG 16.4. — Cf Def., Indef., Zero article, Stages of Familiarity.

Attraction PG, II 6.7. — Cf Negative, Relative attraction.

Auxiliaries IV passim, V 12.16, 12.6_5. — Cf Lesser vb.

B.

Back-formation II 5.63, VI 29.3.

Back-shifting (tense in indirect speech) IV 11.

Base SG 7, base-form of vb V 10.1_1.

Before-future, before-past see Time.

Blending Lang. 312 f., in comparison VII 11.4_4 ff., 11.6_2 f.

Bracketing AS 8.1, infinitive AS 15.4.

C.

Case Progr 138 ff., PG (esp. 173 ff.), SG 14, AS 30, VII 6—8. — Cf Common, Genitive, Accusative, Dative, Nominative, Oblique case, Vocative.

Causative PG 287, III 16.7.

Centre of sentence AS 33.4, VII 2.2_1 ff.

Class-noun VII 12.5_1, 12.6_3.

Clause (exclusively of what others call subordinate clause) PG 103, 308, SG 33—35, AS ch 40, primary, adjunct, subjunct PG 103 ff., II 1.8 ff., V 21. — Clause of Time V 21.2_1, Comparison V 21.3, Contrast 21.4_1, Contradiction 21.4_2, 21.5, Restriction V 21.7 (Proportionality 21.7_2), Comparison + Condition 21.7_9, Cause 21.8. — Clause of indifference IV 15.4(7), 19.1, AS 24.8. — Clause of Comparison AS 24.7. — Clause of wonder III 2.6. — See also Relative cl., interrogative cl., etc. — Cf *A System of Clauses*, S. P. E. Tract No. 54 (1940).

Cleft sentences AS 25.4, III 4.6, VII 9.2_9.

Clipped compounds VI 8.9_3 f.

Cognate object III 12.3.

Collective PG 195 f., vb plur. 237, II 4.8, VII 9.2_9, 12.6_{10}.

Common case VII 8.2, number PG 197 f., 208, II 5.5.

Comparison PG 80, 245 ff., 248, SG 22, VII 10—11.

[† Complex object = nexus as obj. II 1.67.

Composite conjunctions AS 24.2.

Compositional adjuncts II 12.4.

Compounds PG, AS 6, equipollent AS 6.2, genitival AS 6.3, dissolved VI 8.9_3 f., appositional II 2.33, phrase comp. II 2.43 ff.

Compound rel. advs, e. g. *whereof* III 10.6.

Concatenated [Rel.] Clause AS 23.7, III 10.7.

Concatenation, rel. III 10.7.

Conceptional neuter (*it*) see Unspecified *it*.

Concord of verb PG, II 6.3.

Condensed construction (in nexus-tertiary) V 6.7_6, (number) II 4.36

Condition(al) PG, IV 9.3, rejected e. g. IV 9.4(2) ff., V 21.5.

Conjunction PG, II 1.86.

Connective, relative PG 85, 90, III 5.6_1.

Contact-clause III 4.3, 7.

Content-clause III 2.

Continuative relative clause PG 113, III 4.3_4, 5.4_1.

Contrast, contradiction V 21.4.

Converted subjects PG 164 (162 n.), III 15.8.

Coordination AS 31.4, PG 90, 97.

Countables VII 12.6_3.

Crude verb-form IV 1.3 = common form = base.

Cumulative Negation V 23.5, Neg ch 7.

D.

Dative PG, SG 14, III 14.1, VII 6.1_3 ff. — See Case.

Definite Article VII 12—16, esp. 12.4 & ch 14.

Degree see Comparison.

Dependent nexus SG 29 ff., simple nexus as obj V 2, 3, AS 14.1, incomplete V 18.5, as regimen after prep. V 5, AS 14.4, as subj V 4.7, as tertiary V 6.1, AS 14.5, incomplete V 6.9, implied V 22.

Dependent infinitival nexus, as obj V, AS 15.1 [acc. w. inf.], after prep. V, AS 15.3, as subj V, AS 15.5, as tertiary V, AS 15.6.

Deprecation PG 129, AS 26.7, V 20.3_2 ff.

Determination see Articles.

Double-faced III 11.5.

Double relative clause III 4.6_6, AS 25.6.

Double restriction III 4.5_1.

Dramatic present PG 258, IV 2.3.

† Duplex object = nexus-obj II 15.4.

E.

Efficiency see Eff.

End-position, e. g. of preposition VII 2.2_9, 2.3_4 ff.

Ellipsis PG, of antecedent III 3.1, — Cf Latent.

Empty *there* see Existential *there*.

Equipollent see Compounds, Rank.

Exclamation PG, AS 13.5, V 25.4_7, VII 14.5.

Ex-comparative VII 10.4_2.

Exhausted relative clauses III 5.5.

Existential *there* PG 155, AS 34.6 with quotations, VII 3.1_1 ff.

Expanded tenses PG 277 ff., IV 1.5, IV 12, 13, 14; Present, Preterit, Perfect, Pluperfect. — Cf S.P.E. Tract No. 36 (1931).

Extraposition AS 12, 25.6, VII 4.6_8, 6.2_1 ff., transition to predicative AS 12.2, III 17.1_2.

F.

Familiarity, stages of, VII 12.4$_2$; Stage I: VII 12.5 ff., Stage II: VII 14, Stage III: VII 15.
Fatal obligation IV 17.2.
Feminine see Gender.
Finite verb PG 87, vol IV. — Cf Nexus.
First-word of compound II 7.1.
Form, Function, Notion PG 33 f, 40 f, 56 f, AS 29.1.
Forward shifting IV 11.8.
Frame, Temporal, IV 12.5 ff.,
Front-position see Word-Order.
Function see above, Form.

G.

Gender PG 55 f., 226 f., SG 19, VII 5.
Generic number (sg & pl) PG 203, SG 20—21, II 5.4.
person PG, AS 34.5 (cf ib *se*, *si*), III 5.1$_1$ f. (*he that*), V 9.8$_8$, 10.1$_3$, VII 4.7, 1.25$_6$, 14.3 f., time V 2.1$_2$, 5.5, 8.2, PG 259, 279 ff.
Genitival adjuncts AS 3.3.
Genitive PG, SG 14, AS 30.5, 31.6, Progr ch 8; VII 9.
Gerund PG 140, 141, SG 31, AS 39.3, V 8—9, case VII 6.4$_3$.
Glottic Ling. 215 f., 218, Eff. ch 7, word-order VII 2.2$_2$ ff.

H.

Half-analyzable sentences AS 26.2. — Cf Amorphous, Inarticulate, Semi-articulate sentences.
Half-pronominal II 11.61 (= Quantifier).
[Historic present PG 257 f., IV 2.3 (= Dramatic present).
Honorific *the* VII 16.3$_8$, adjs 16.6$_5$f.

I.

Imaginative use of tenses IV 9, 10, infin. 10.6, volition 19.2, obligation 20.2(1).

Immediate & mental perception V 18.

Imperative PG, V 24 f., tense IV 7.4, expanded IV 13.5(8).

[Impersonal PG 160, 212, 241, AS 34.4, 34.6, III 11.2, VII 6.5_7 ff.

Implied predicative [in adjuncts] AS 3.7, implied negation PG 336 f., Neg ch IV.

Inanimate PG 227, 234, VII 5.8.

Inarticulate Sentences VII 3.6. — Cf Amorphous sentences.

Inchoative IV 5.9, III 16.7, PG 288.

Inclusive time IV 4.6, 22.4, PG 271 f., plural PG 192.

Indefinite article PG, in predicative III 18.4, VII 12—16, esp. 12.4 ff. — Cf Articles.

Indefinite rel. pron. III 3.6.

Independent neuter II 16.35.

Indetermination see Articles.

Indicative VII 18.1_2 ff. — Cf Mood.

Indirect adjunct II 12.5.

Indirect object see Object.

Indirect speech PG, IV 11, 21, 22.5, pronouns VII 4.4_6, mood VII 18.7_1 f.

Individualization II 5.3.

Infinitive PG, SG 32, AS, tense IV 7.1, passive IV 8.7, imaginative IV 10.6, expanded IV 13.4 f., perf. inf. with *will* IV 16.6. — [Acc. with inf. V 18]. Subj + inf V 18, 19, Isolated V 20.2, Historical V 20.3, Inf of deprecation V 20.3_2, Latent V 20.5. — Bare V 10 ff., Retroactive V 15.2, 15.4, 16.4_9, 17.4. of direction V 16.1, of purpose V 16.4, of result V 16.5_4, of reaction V 17.1, of specification V 17.2.

Ing PG 140 f., 172, tense IV 7.8, gerund or first ptc.
V 8.1. — Cf S.P.E. Tract No. 25 (1926).
Instrumental object III 12.4_1.
Intensives (in comparison) VII 11.8.
Interposition Progr ch 8 = ChE ch 3, V 9.5_1.
Interrogative, word-order PG 26, 297 f., pronoun PG
198, 233, 305; conjunction 297, 305, adverbs V 25.2_7,
clauses AS 22.3, III 2.4. — Cf Question.
Inversion VII 2.2_2 ff.
Introductory (preparatory) *there* AS 34.7, VII 3.1_3. —
Cf Existential *there*.
Irregular adjuncts [symbol 2(3)] AS 3.6.

J.

Junction PG 97, 114 ff., SG 9, VII 13, virtually nexus
AS 14.2, definition also III 11.1 — Cf Rank.

L.

Latent AS 41.1, infinitive AS 18.5, V 20.5, subj of inf
V 10.1_3, primary of genitive III 1.4 f., comparison
PG 248, VII 11.5_5.
Lesser subject AS 8.9.
Lesser verb AS 28.4, V 23.1_4, position VII 2.2. — Cf
Auxiliary.

M.

[Main sentence SG 10. — Cf Sentence.
Masculine see Gender.
Mass-word PG 198 ff., 240, II 5.2, VII 12.4_2, 12.6_3 ff.
Mental parenthesis III 5.7 (Cf S.P.E. Tract No. 48,
Linguistic Self-Criticism, 1937).
Metanalysis PG 94 n., 128, II 5.6, V 11.12_2.
Modified secondaries AS 3.8, subjects VII 3.1_5.
Mood PG 313 ff., SG 27, VII 18.

[Morpheme AS 29.1.
Morphology PG 37 ff., II 1.1, in new sense PG 40 ff.
Morphoseme AS 29.2.

N.

Negation PG, Neg, V 23, nexal V 23, 23.3, special V 23.3, double or cumulative V 23.5. — Negative attraction V 23.4.

Neuter see Gender.

Nexus PG, SG 9, AS 33, etc, predication ib, subj S, predicative P AS 35, of result AS 9.2, after preposition AS 9.5; without verb AS 9.6. — Predicate AS 34.1, S indefinite AS 34.8. — Independent nexus AS 7, dependent nexus V, esp. 1.4_4. — Word-order VII 2.1_3. — Definition also III 11.1.

† Nexus-subjunct (III 17.8_5), now Nexus-tertiary.

Nexus-substantive PG 136 ff., & passim, SG 30, AS 39.4, V 7. — Verbal & predicative V 7.1_1 f.

Nexus-tertiary V 6, esp. 6.8_4.

† Nominal (vol I) = Noun (sb & adj).

Nominative see Case.

Non-anaphoric II 16.33.

Non-reflexive use of *self*-forms VII 4.9_3.

Non-restrictive adjuncts PG 111 f., rel. clauses III 4.3_4.

Notion see Form.

Notional subject VII 6.4_1 ff.

Noun = subst & adj, not subst only.

[Nulli-generic VII 12.6_6.

Number PG 188 ff., & passim, SG 20—21, II 2. ff.

Numerals PG 85, II passim, VII 17.1_2 ff.

Numerical relation II 7.5 ff.

O.

Object PG, SG 10—11, indir. obj, obj of result, obj or tertiary AS 7.4; — AS 36. — Obj of prep. see

Regimen. — Two direct objs III 14.9, 15.5, AS 36.6.
— Object — subject III 11.7. -II 1.6, III 12, indirect only where there is a direct object II 1.66, III 12.1_4, 14.1. — Obj of result III 12.2. — Cognate III 12.3, of instrument or instrumental obj III 12.4_1, [† obj. of adv = prep. II 1.68, see Regimen]. — Word-order VII 2 & passim.

† Objective (case) SG 14, now Oblique case.

Oblique case VII 6.1_4 ff., 7.5_2 ff. — Cf Case.

Omission see III 2.7_1, of subject III 11.8, of object III 16. — Cf Ellipsis, Latent.

[Omnipresent IV 2.1.

Ordinals VII 17.2_6.

Overled (Dan.) see Rank.

P.

Paratactic negation PG 334, Neg 75, V 23.5_8.

Parenthetic clause AS 25, par. adjuncts PG 111 f.

Partial adjuncts II 12.3.

Participial adjectives VII 2.1_5.

Participle PG, tense IV 7.5 f., = inf IV 10.1, expanded IV 13.5(9). — First ptc. V 6.3, 22.2. — Second ptc. V 6.4, 22.5. — Perfect V 6.5. — *Being* with second ptc. (passive) V 6.5_2, *having been* with second ptc. V 6.6. — Loose ptc. V 22.2_7. — Word-order VII 2.7_9.

Particles PG 87 ff., SG 7. — Cf Word-classes.

Parti-generic sense of mass-words VII 12.6_4, of plurals VII 12.6_8 ff.

Partitive PG, AS 32.3, VII 9.7.

Parts of Speech see Word-classes.

Passive PG, SG 12, tense IV 8, of being & becoming IV 8, perfect IV 8.5, pluperfect IV 8.6, expanded IV 13.6, 13.7, AS 37.

Periphrastic comparison VII 11, esp. 11.3_5.

Person PG 212 ff., SG 15, VII 4.

Personification VII, esp. 16.5.

Phrase PG 95, complex verbal phrases AS 8.5, II 1.87.

Plural PG, of verbal idea II 6.9, substitutive II 2.21, unchanged II 3, normal II 4.2, of approximation II 4.5, differentiated II 4.6. — VII passim.

Possessive pronoun II 16.2, etc, VII 9, esp. 9.2_5 ff.

Post-adjunct II 15.4.

Predicative PG, SG 13, II 1.5, VII 2, after particle IV 23, of being III 17, of becoming III 18, without verb III 17.8, case VII 6.7, use of articles with, VII 12.5_5, 12.7_2 ff., 14.2_2 ff.

Preparatory subj or obj, e. g. V 4.3, 8.2_1, *it* III 3.7_6, EEG 16.3_6, *there* see Existential *there*.

Preposition, word-order VII 2.2_9, 2.3_4 ff., case VII 6.3_1 ff.

Prepositional phrases as adjuncts AS 3.4, VII passim.

Primary († Principal) PG, II 1.2. — See Rank.

† Principal (vol II), now Primary.

Pronominal adverb II 1.74, PG 84, with adjuncts PG 100 n.

Pronoun PG 82 ff., SG 16—18, II 1.7, primary, adjunct, subjunct PG 99 f. — Case Progr passim, esp. ch 7, VII 6—7. — EEG 16.1:

  A. Definite indication. 1. Contextual indication (Personal pron.). — 2. Pointing. — 3. Def. article. — 4. Identity. — 5. Similarity. — 6. Connexion (Rel. pron.).

  B. Indefinite indication. 1. Indef. unity. — 2. Indef. article. — 3. Difference (*other*). — 4. Discretion (*certain*). — 5. Unspecified quantity (*some*). — 6. Indifference. — 7. Interrogative.

  C. Totality. — 1. Positive. — 2. Negative.

Proper name PG 64 ff. & passim, II 1.25, VII 16, meaning VII 12.5_8, 16.1_1.

Prop-word II 10.
Prosiopesis PG 310, VII 3.3_2 ff., 12.3_4 f.
Prospective IV 22.3(4).
Providential purpose V 16.7.
Pseudo-active II 16.8.
Pseudo-condition V 21.6_5.
Pseudo-imperative V 24.3.
Pseudo-partitive PG 111.
Pseudo-passive IV 14.9(6).
Pseudo-question V 25.4_8.

Q.

Quantifier PG 85, 113, AS 32, VII 18; in nexus PG 125 f., with mass-words PG 198, AS 5, substantival AS 5.2, genitival AS 5.3, with preposition 5.4.
Quasi-predicative III 17.2.
Quasi-proper name VII 16.6_2, 16.7.
Quasi-subject (*there*) VII 3.1_4.
Quaternary PG 96, AS 10.2, 31.2. — See Rank.
Question PG 302 ff. & passim, SG 28, nexus-question & x-question AS 13.3, V 25, strengthened V 25.2, double V 25.3, incomplete V 25.2, pseudo-questions V 25.4_8.
Quotation-word PG 96 n., II 8.2.

R.

Rank PG 96 ff., SG 8, II 1.2, shifted with nexus-words PG 137. — Rank of predicative AS 35.3. — Primary († Principal) — overled (Dan.) AS 3, 22, 31. — Secondary — adjunct - adled (Dan.) AS 3, 31. — Tertiary — subjunct — underled (Dan.) AS 3, 10, 31, VII passim. — Quaternary — Sub-subjunct — under-underled (Dan.) AS 10.2, 31.2. — Equipollent AS 3.5. — 2/3 secondary or tertiary AS 3.2. — Adjuncts with compounds AS 6.5 ff. — Cf Junction.

v

Recipient AS 11.1, 38.2.
Reciprocal PG 161, 224, AS 8.4.
Reflexive PG, AS 8.2, VII 4.8.
Regimen V 5, AS 38.1.
Relative attraction Progr 154, 162, VII 6.2, 6.7.
Relative pronouns PG 85, clauses PG 103 ff., rel. clause as primary, secondary III 3 ff., as tertiary V 21, double relative clauses III 4.6_6, AS 25.6, contact clause III ch VIII & passim, AS 22.6, 40.2. — Restrictive & non-restrictive PG 112 f., continuative PG 113. — Rel. particle (*as*, etc) III 9.1.
Reported speech IV 11 (= style indirect libre, erlebte rede).
Representative *it* (= preparatory *it*) III 2.1_3, 2.3_6, VII 4.6_3 ff.
Request PG 302 f., 312, AS 13.1, V 24, in form of question AS 13.4.
Restrictive adjuncts PG 108 ff., incomplete PG 110 ff., relative clauses III 4.3_4.
Resumption III 3.7_5.
Resumptive negation PG 334, Neg 72 ff., V 23.5_4.
Retroactive infinitive V 15.2, 15.4, 16.4, 17.4 (cf III 11.6).

S.

Secondary PG 96 ff., number PG 107, comparison PG 252, secondaries that have become predicatives AS 3.9, rank II 1.2. — See Rank.
Semi-articulate sentences VII 3.6.
Semi-predicative II 15.6.
Sentence PG 305 ff., SG 10, built up gradually PG 26 f., various kinds AS ch 13, sentence-structure and word-order VII 2—3.
Sex and gender VII 5.
Sham subject AS 34.6, V 9.7_9, VII 3.1_4.
Situational basis of def. article VII 14.1_3 f.

'Small verbs' V 12.1$_1$, 12.1$_3$. — Cf Lesser, Auxiliary vb.
Speaker's aside AS 25.9, S.P.E. Tract No. 48 (1937).
Speaker's parenthesis V 16.5.
Specializing, specialization PG 75 ff., 96, 108 ff., 150 ff., 158 f., AS 31.3. — Specializing *of* VII 9.8.
Speech/Language Mankind ch 1, Eff. 2.3, cf AS 31.1.
[Split infinitive V 20.4. — Cf S.P.E. Tract No. 54 The 'Split Inf.' (1940).
Split object V 4.4, 18.5, AS 16.3.
Split subject, passive V 4.6$_1$, V 19.3, AS 16.1, active III 11.3, AS 16.2.
Stump-word Lang. 169 ff., Ling. 387, Eff. 3.5, VI 29.
Style-tertiary VII 2.6$_2$ ff. (S.P.E. Tract No. 48).
Subject PG 145 ff. & passim, SG 10—11, definition III 11.1, word-order VII 2.
Subject-part of nexus tertiary (= S) V 11.1$_5$.
Subjunct PG, II 1.2. — See Rank.
Subjunct-adjunct shifted II 12.12, 12.2. — Cf Adjective-subjunct.
Subjunct-predicative III 18.7, AS 9.4.
Subjunctive PG, IV 10.1 ff., 11.7, VII 18.
† Subnex PG 97.
Subordination PG 96 ff., clauses PG 105. — AS 31.5.
Substantival adjuncts (i.e. substantives as adjuncts) II 13.
Substantive PG 72 ff. & passim, SG 7, II 1.3, formation VII 1.2, sex and gender VII 5.2, comparison 10.4$_9$. — See Word-classes.
Substantivized adjective II 9.
Substitutive verb III 12.7.
Sub-subjunct PG 97. — See Rank.
Subtraksjonsdannelse (Dan.) = Back-formation.
Superlative PG 49, 244 f., AS 29.2, VII 10—11, given up PG 245, absolute PG 247.
Syntax PG 45 ff., II 1.1, comparative PG 346 f.

T.

Tense: present tense, preterit, future tense IV 1.2. — Tense/Time PG 254 ff. & passim, SG 23—24. — See also Passive, Infin., Participle, Imperative, etc.

Tense-phrases IV 1.4, perfect IV 5, pluperfect (or antepreterit) IV 6, perfect participle IV 7.7.

Tertiary PG 96 ff., II 1.2, comparison PG 252, word-order VII 2.4 ff., 2.6, common case VII 8.3 ff. — Cf Rank.

Time: Past, present, future time IV 1, before-past, after-past, before-future, after-future IV 1, 19.4(1), 20.1(2). — See esp. IV 22. — Time/Tense PG 254 ff. & passim.— See also Generic, Inclusive time.

Toto-generic sense of mass-words VII 12.6_5, of plurals VII 12.6_8.

Transitive PG 88, 158, AS 38.1, II 1.63, III 16. — See also Object.

Typical *the* VII 14.2, 16.3_8.

U.

Uncountables VII 12.6_1 ff., 13.1_2.

Underled (Dan.) see Rank.

Unification of plural II 5.1, of words PG 93 f., VII 12.6.

[Uniques VII 14.1_4.

Unit-word VII 12.4_2, 12.6_3. — Cf Class-noun.

Unreality, preterit PG 265, infinitive PG 285, unreality & uncertainty IV 22.6.

Unspecified *it* PG 241, AS 34.4, VII 4.6_9 ff.

V.

Veiled Language Ling. 409 ff.

Verb PG, SG 7, 10—11, vb + obj as compound (*pickpocket*) II 1.4, II 8.6, formation VII 1.4, word-order VII 2—3 passim, person VII 4.5.

Verbid PG 87, AS 39.
Verbless sentences PG 120 ff., 311, VII 3.6$_3$ f.
Vocative PG 184, SG 14, AS 12.7 VII 15.1.
Volition, volitional PG 260, future IV 15.5, obligation IV 17.3.

W.

Wish AS 13.6, preterit PG 265, aposiopesis PG 310, mood VII 18.5$_1$ ff.
Word-classes PG 58 ff., SG 7, II 1.3, VII 1.
    Substantive ⎫
                  ⎬ Noun.
    Adjective   ⎭
    Pronoun. — Personal, etc.
    Verb.
    Particle.
        Adverb.
        Preposition; prepositional group AS 10.3.
        Conjunction.
Word-group, primary, adjunct, subjunct PG 101 ff., VII 13.2$_1$. — II 1.8.
Word-order PG, VII 2—3.
Wrong supposition IV 11.4.

Z.

Zero article VII 12—16; see esp. 12.1.

General Index

A.

a see Indef. Article.
Abbreviated Sentences 3.3$_1$ ff.
about 4.8$_5$.
above 4.8$_5$.
'Absolute' pronouns 7.5$_3$.
Abstracts, gender 5.8$_3$, 5.8$_6$.
according to, — *as* 1.5$_6$.
accordingly 1.5$_6$, 2.5$_2$.
Accusative 6.1$_3$ ff.
ache, -ache with *a* 12.6$_1$, with zero 12.6$_7$.
act vb, obj with typical *the* 14.2$_1$.
actor, actress 5.3$_3$.
Actuality 2.1$_2$.
Address, zero 15.1$_1$, 15.1$_4$, *the* 15.1$_2$ f., adj & subst 15.1$_4$.
Adjective, formation 1.3, and advs 1.5$_4$, primaries with *of* 9.3$_2$, in junction 13,2$_1$, primaries 14.8, with *the* 14.8$_1$ ff., before proper names 16.6, quantifiers 17.9$_1$. — Cf Comparative, Comparison, Superlative.
Adjective-subjunct 1.5$_4$(b).
Adjunct, no sex 5.1$_3$.
Adverbs, formation 1.5, word-order 2.4$_1$ ff., style-tertiaries 2.6$_2$ ff., of time, word-order 2.6$_7$, sentence-structure 2.7$_4$, word-order 2.7$_5$, with vb 2.7$_6$, complemental 2.8$_7$, comparison of, 10.4, in *-ly* 10.4$_2$, in junction 13.2$_1$, superlative advs with *the* 14.7$_4$.
after 4.8$_5$, 18.4$_2$.
aftermost, aftmost 10.5$_6$.
again 2.5$_2$, 2.7$_3$, 17.3$_2$.
Agent-noun with genitive 9.2$_5$, & past ptc. (zero) 12.8$_5$.
ago with tertiary 8.4$_2$.
air, the, 14.1$_4$.
alder- 11.8$_7$.
Alford 4.5$_1$.
all 17.4 ff., 17.9$_2$, *all of* 9.9$_1$ f., *all the* before compar. 14.6$_3$, before superl. 14.7$_5$, *all (the), all morning* 14.8$_6$, *all but* 17.4$_3$, *all the difference* 17.4$_3$. — Cf *and*.
Alliterative phrases with zero 12.8$_4$ ff.
All-representative use of *a* 12.5$_6$.
Almighty, the, 14.8$_4$.
alongside (of) 9.6$_3$.
among 4.8$_5$.
an see *and*, Indef. Article.
Anaphoric repetition 2.3$_7$, pronouns 4.4$_2$, *it* 4.6$_2$.
and in numerals 17.1$_4$, *fifty and*

odd 17.2$_2$, *all and* …, … *and all* 17.4$_2$, *(still) and all* 17.4$_4$, *an(d), an(d) if* 18.3$_5$.

and-combinations, notional subj 6.4$_1$, nexus 6.4$_4$, in obj 7.4$_2$, in subj 7.5$_4$, in tertiaries 8.9, gradual increase 11.5$_4$, with zero 12.8$_4$.

angel, gender 5.3.

Animals, names of, gender 5.4, pronoun 5.6 ff., *of* or genitive 9.4$_4$, generic *the* 14.3$_4$.

Animate 5.9.

Answer, inarticulate 3.6$_1$.

Anticipatory *it* 4.6$_3$ ff., *there* 3.1$_3$.

any 17.5$_3$ ff., 17,9$_2$ f., before superl. 11.6$_5$, 14.7$_5$, *any different* 17.5$_3$, compounds (espec.) 17.5$_3$, and *some* 17.6$_2$.

any-, sex 5.5$_1$. — Cf *any*.

Apodosis left out 3.5.

Aposiopesis 3.5.

appear after *there* 3.2$_1$.

applicant 15.1$_6$.

Apposition, word-order 2.1$_4$, *self*-forms 4.9$_3$, case 6.2$_4$, with *a* 12.5$_5$, zero before superl. & ordinals 14.7$_6$, *each* 17.4$_7$.

Appositional *of* 9.9$_1$.

Archduchess, -duke 16.4$_2$.

Arches, names of, 16.3$_5$.

around 4.8$_5$.

Articles chs. XII-XVI, stages of familiarity 12.4$_2$ ff. — Cf Def., Indef., Zero article.

as, word-order 2.4$_6$, *as much as* 2.6$_3$, *soon as* 3,3$_5$, case 6.3$_3$, *as* or *than* 11.4$_3$, *as, as if, as though* 18.3$_7$.

at 2.3$_5$, 12.8$_2$.

atop 9.6$_3$.

Attraction see Relative attr.

awake, case 6.9$_3$.

away, word-order 2.4$_4$.

B.

babe, baby, zero 15.1$_5$.

back (of) 8.6$_8$.

bad, comparison 11.3$_1$ f., 10.5$_1$.

bank (who) 5.7.

barefoot 8.7$_6$.

bawd, gender 5.3$_6$.

be, word-order 2.3$_1$, 2.8$_3$, *(there)* 3.1$_4$, mood 18.2$_4$, 18.2$_6$, 18.2$_7$, 18.3$_2$ ff., *were* in indir. speech, *be and is* 18.7$_1$, indir. questions 18.7$_3$, indef. rel. clauses 18.7$_4$ f., imaginative *were* 18.7$_6$.

bed, zero 15.2$_6$.

bedmaker, gender 5.3$_6$.

before 4.8$_5$, 18.4$_1$.

behind 4.8$_5$.

beneath 4.8$_5$.

benmost (Sc.) 10.5$_4$.

besides 4.8$_5$.

best, best of temper(s) 11.6$_3$, *best man* 13.3$_2$, *at best, at (for) the best* 14.7$_3$, *the best* tertiary 14.7$_3$. — Cf *good*.

bestmost 10.5$_7$.

bethink 4.8$_3$.

bettermost 10.5$_7$.

better(s), with poss. 9.2$_8$.

between 4.8$_5$, *b. you and I* 7.4$_3$, before *each* 17.4$_7$, before *every* 17.5$_2$.

beyond, the, 14.1$_4$.
Blending in comparison 11.4$_4$ ff., 11.6$_2$ f.
board, on b. (of) 9.6$_3$.
boat, genitive 9.5$_3$.
bodkin, ride b. 8.8$_2$.
body, a, generic person 4.7$_6$, 5.2$_2$.
-body 5.2$_2$. — Cf *any, every, no, some*.
Bogy, zero 15,1$_5$.
Book-titles with indef. art. 12.5$_4$, *the* or zero 16.3$_7$.
boots, zero 15.1$_5$.
both 17.4$_5$, *both of* 9.9$_2$, *both (the)* 14.8$_7$, contrasted to *and* = *either* 17.7.
bow, zero 15.1$_6$.
Bridges, names of, 16.3$_5$.
Brøndal on categories 12.7.
brother, zero 15.1$_5$.
buck 5.3$_9$, 5.4$_3$.
Buildings, names of, 16.3$_1$ ff.
bullock 5.4$_1$.
Bullokar on *thou* 7.3$_5$.
but with obl. case, with nom. 6.3$_2$.
by 4.8$_5$, with tertiary 8.3$_7$, *by* for *than* 11.4$_7$, with zero 12.8$_2$, with distrib. *the* 14.5$_1$.

C.

calf, genitive 9.4$_4$.
call with tertiary 8.8$_1$.
captain, gender 5.3$_5$.
Cardinals with indef. art. 12.5$_{12}$. — Cf Numerals.
care, case 6.9$_2$, with tertiary 8.3$_4$.

carl hemp 5.4$_4$.
Case, in pronouns ch VI—VII, in subst. ch VIII.
Castles, names of, 16.3$_2$.
cent(.) 17.2$_1$.
Channels, names of, 16.1$_6$.
chap, gender 5.3$_7$.
cheap, cheaply 1.5$_5$, tertiary 8.8$_2$.
cheer, case 6.9$_2$.
chief, compar. 10.4$_9$.
child, gender 5.2$_1$, 5.2$_6$, 5.3$_6$.
choice, compar. 10.4$_9$.
Christ, (the) 16.7$_1$, 18.5$_4$.
Christophersen on articles 14.1$_1$ ff., vocative 15.1$_1$.
Churches, names of, 16.3$_2$.
cipher 17.2$_8$.
Class-nouns (unit-words) 12.5$_1$, 12.6$_3$, with zero as obj 12.7$_1$, with zero after prep. 12.8$_2$ f.
Clause, secondary 13.2$_1$, in junctions with *the* 14.5$_4$. — Cf Indef. rel. clause.
clean, cleanly 1.5$_5$.
clear, clearly 1.5$_5$.
Cleft sentences 4.6$_8$.
close, closely 1.5$_5$.
coachman with zero 15.1$_5$.
Cohesion 2.1$_4$.
cold, catch (a), 12.6$_1$.
Collective, genitive and *of* 9.2$_9$, coll. term before plural 12.6$_{10}$.
Colleges, names of, 16.3$_2$.
Collinson 12.5$_3$, 12.6$_1$, 18.4$_2$.
colt, gender 5.4$_1$.
come after *there* 3.2$_1$, *a walk* 8.7$_4$, *a cropper* (etc) 8.7$_5$, with echoic tertiary 8.8$_3$.

Common case 8.2.
Commonwealth, the, 14.1$_4$.
Comparison chs X-XI, regular 10.1 ff., classification 10.2$_1$, monosyllables 10.2$_2$, adjs of more than one syllable 10.2$_3$ ff., advs 10.4, in *-ly* 10.4$_2$, *leng(er)* 10.4$_3$, group-comparatives 10.4$_4$, desire for variety 10.4$_5$, several adjs 10.4$_6$, *more* and *most* 10.4$_7$ f., *-est* added to subst. 10.4$_9$, regular for irregular 10.5$_1$ (f.), comparatives from prep. 10.5$_3$, superl. in *-most* 10.5$_4$ ff., comparatives in *-more* 10.5$_6$; double 11.1$_1$, change of vowel 11.1$_3$ ff., *out(er)-most* 11.1$_8$, various irregularities 11.2$_1$ ff., periphrasis or ending 11.3$_5$ f., meaning 11.4 ff., meaning of comparative 11.5$_1$, *more than kind*, etc, 11.5$_2$ ff., gradual increase 11.5$_4$ ff., latent comparatives 11.5$_5$ f. the three degrees 11.6$_1$, blendings 11.6$_2$ f., comparative about two 11.6$_4$, defining word before superl. 11.6$_5$, superl. limited 11.6$_6$, very high degree 11.7 ff. *more, most* 11.7$_2$, Latin comp. and superl. 11.7$_7$, strengthening 11.8.

Complemental advs 2.8$_7$ f.
Composite names of holidays, zero 15.3$_2$.
Compounds, compar. 10.5$_2$.
Comte, the, 16.4$_2$.
Conceptional *it* 4.6$_9$ f.

Concessive clauses 18.6$_4$.
Conditional clauses 18.3$_1$ ff.
Congregation, zero 15.2$_4$.
Congress, zero 15.2$_4$.
Conjunction 2.7$_4$, 6.3$_1$ ff.
consequently, word-order 2.5$_2$.
consort, compounds 5.2$_6$.
Constant situational basis of articles 14.1$_4$.
Content-clause after *it* 4.6$_4$, with *lest* 18.6$_3$.
Contextual basis, explicit 14.1$_1$, implicit 14.1$_2$.
contrary to 1.5$_6$.
Convocation, zero 15.2$_4$.
cook, gender 5.3$_7$, zero 15.1$_5$.
Cooper on case 6.4$_5$.
counsel 15.1$_6$.
Count 16.4$_2$.
Countables 12.6$_3$, 13.1$_2$, 13.3$_6$.
Countess, (the) 16.4$_2$.
Countries, *she* 5.8$_4$, names of, 9.3$_1$, 16.1$_7$ f.
couple (of) 9.7$_3$.
cousin, gender 5.3$_5$.
cow, genitive 9.4$_4$.
cox, zero 15.1$_6$.
Creation, the (or zero) 14.1$_4$.
Creator, the, 14,1$_4$.
Curme on *-ess* 5.3$_2$.
Czar see *tsar*.

D.

dad 5.2$_1$, 14.5$_2$.
dame 16.5$_2$.
damned, compar. 10.3$_4$, *d. be*, case, *be d. to you* 6.8$_4$.
Dative 6.1$_3$ ff.

day 12.3$_5$, *the day* (=*today*) 12.3$_1$, 15.3$_8$.
dead, deadly 1.5$_5$.
dear, dearly 1.5$_5$.
death, d. of 9.4$_1$ f., genitive 9.5$_3$, personified 16.5$_1$(4).
debtor 15.1$_6$.
deceased, (*the*), 14.8$_4$, 15.1$_6$.
deep, deeply 1.5$_5$, 8.4$_3$.
Definite article chs. XII-XVI; 2.4$_7$, 3.2$_4$, omitted 3.3$_3$, before appositional *of* 9.9$_5$, before comparative 11.1$_2$, 14.6; form 12.2, weaker demonstrative 12.3$_1$, syntax 12.4 ff., stage of familiarity II 12.4$_3$, ch. XIV, with names of languages 12.6$_{12}$, conflict between articles 12.9, before junctions ch XIII. - Stage II ch. XIV, meaning, contextual basis 14.1$_1$ f., situational basis 14.1$_3$ f., typical *the* 14.2, generic *the* 14.3, distributive use 14.5, familiar *the* 14.5$_2$, in exclamations 14.5$_3$ ff., in address 14.5$_5$, 15.1$_2$ f., emotional mention 14.5$_6$, before comparative 14.6, with superl. and ordinals 14.7 ff., *this* (*that*) *the* 14.7$_{10}$, before adjs as primaries 14.8, with names of meals 15.2$_1$, indications of time 15.3$_2$ ff., proper names ch XVI, plural names 16.1$_3$, typical and honorific *the* before proper names 16.6, quasi-proper names 16.7.

democracy, the, 14.4$_6$.
Dependent nexus 2.1$_3$.
Determination see Articles.
devil, d. of 9.9$_5$, *the* d. 14.1$_4$, zero 16.7$_1$, in terms of imprecation 18.5$_6$.
different, d. *than* 11.4$_5$, with *much* 11.8$_5$, *no* d. 17.8$_2$.
dinner, zero or *the* 15.2$_1$.
direct, directly 1.5$_5$.
Diseases, names of, 12.6$_1$, 12.6$_7$, 12.6$_{11}$, 14.4$_7$.
Distributive use of *a* 8.9$_8$, 12.5$_7$, of *the* 14.5, of numerals 17.2$_7$.
do, obj with zero 12.7$_1$.
doctor 5.3$_3$, 15.1$_5$.
dog, genitive 9.4$_4$.
down, word-order 2.4$_4$.
drama, the, 14.4$_4$.
drunk, comparison 10.2$_2$.
due, duly 1.5$_5$.
Duke 16.4$_2$.

E.

-*e*, feminine ending 5.3$_2$.
each, eachwhere 17.4$_7$, 17.9$_2$ f.
eager, comparison 10.2$_6$.
earth, the or zero 14.1$_4$.
east, easternmost, easternmost, eastmost 10.5$_8$.
easy, easily 1.5$_5$.
Echoic tertiaries 8.8$_3$.
Eden 16.7$_2$.
edge, with genitive 9.5$_5$.
either 17.7, position 2.2$_3$ f., vb with *either* .. *or* 4.5.
elder, with poss. 9.2$_8$. — *Elder, eldest* see *old*.

General Index.

Elector, Electress 16.4$_2$.

'em, hem 4.4$_1$.

Emperor, Empress, the, 16.4$_2$, *empress* 5.3$_4$.

Empty *there* 3.1$_1$.

end, with genitive 9.5$_5$.

enemy, the, 14.1$_4$.

Engine, she 5.8$_1$.

enough, word-order 2.7$_3$.

enter 2.2$_2$, 18.2$_5$.

Enumerations, zero 12.7$_{10}$, 12.8$_4$ ff., 12.8$_8$. — Cf *and-* combinations.

-er, comparative ending 10.1 ff.

ere, case 6.3$_2$, in clause 18.4$_1$.

-ess, 5.3$_2$ f., names of animals 5.4$_2$.

-est, superl. ending chs X—XI.

-ette 5.3$_2$.

-eur, -euse 5.3$_2$.

even, evenly 1.5$_5$.

ever, elliptical 3.5$_3$, 11.8$_7$.

-ever, compounds with, 3.5$_8$, 18.7$_4$.

every 17.5$_1$ ff., 17.9$_2$ f., before superl. 14.7$_5$, and *any* 17.5$_4$, compounds 17.5$_2$.

every-, sex 5.5$_1$. — Cf *every.*

evil, evilly 1.5$_5$, comparison 10.5$_1$, 11.3$_1$ f., 11.3$_8$.

except(ing), case 6.3$_2$.

Exclamations 14.5$_3$ f., 14.5$_7$.

Ex-comparatives 10.4$_2$.

Existential *there* 3.1$_1$.

Expressive tertiaries 8.8$_2$ f.

Extent, tertiaries of, 8.9$_4$.

Extraposition 4.6$_8$, 6.2$_1$ ff.

extreme, comparison 11.7$_7$.

F.

fact 12.3$_5$, 12.7$_9$.

fain 1.5$_2$.

fair, fairly 1.5$_5$, 2.6$_2$, *fair* feminine 5.3$_9$.

false, falsely 1.5$_5$.

Familiar *the* 14.5$_2$, fam. person (zero) 15.1$_5$.

Familiarity, stages of, 12.4$_2$, Stage I 12.5 ff., Stage II ch XIV, Stage III ch XV.

far, comparison 11.3$_4$.

fare, case 6.9$_2$.

farmeress 5.3$_4$.

farthermore, -most 10.5$_6$.

fashion in tertiary 8.7$_2$.

fast, fastly 1.5$_5$.

fate, she 5.5$_4$, zero 16.7$_1$.

father, (zero) 15.1$_5$.

fear, case 6.9$_1$.

fellow 4.7$_6$, 5.3$_7$.

female 5.3$_9$, 5.4$_3$.

Female see Sex.

Feminine, endings 5.3$_2$. — Cf Sex, Gender.

few, a few 12.5$_{11}$.

fewer, fewest 11.3$_2$.

Fiend, the, 14.1$_4$.

Fijn van Draat 2.1$_6$.

fill, sb, as tertiary 8.4$_5$.

fimble hemp 5.4$_4$.

find it in one's heart 4.6$_6$.

fingers' ends 9.5$_3$.

first, word-order 2.7$_3$, *first night* 13.3$_2$, *first thing,* tertiary 8.9$_7$, *(the) first thing* 14.7$_8$.

fit, fitly 1.5$_5$.

flat, flatly 1.5$_5$, compar. avoided 11.3$_8$.

foggiest, the, 3.5$_5$.

for, word-order 2.3$_5$, *for it* 4.6$_{11}$, with reflexive pron. 4.8$_5$, with notional subj 6.4$_3$.
foremost 10.5$_4$, 10.5$_9$, 13.3$_3$.
former, 4.4$_4$, 10.5$_3$, *formerly* 10.4$_2$.
fowl 5.4$_1$.
Fowler on *-ess* 5.3$_2$, *between you and I* 7.4$_3$, *an* before *h* 12.2$_6$, superlatives 13.3$_7$, adverbial *the* 14.6$_5$.
Fractions 8.3$_7$, 17.2$_6$.
Frau, Fräulein 16.4$_3$.
free, freely 1.5$_5$, comparison 10.2$_2$.
free-and-easy, comparison 10.4$_4$.
Fricative voiced in compar. 10.1$_6$.
full, fully 1.5$_5$, compar. 10.2$_2$.
further, furthest 11.3$_4$.
furthermore 10.5$_6$, 11.1$_1$, *furthermost* 10.5$_6$.

G.

[g] after [ŋ] in comparison 10.1$_5$.
gate (Sc.) 8.7$_1$.
Gemination in comparison 10.1$_7$.
Gender ch V.
generally, word-order 2.7$_3$.
Generic, person 4.7, use of articles 12.5$_6$, 14.3, symbolic use of words 14.4$_1$, grammatical terms 14.4$_2$, names of arts and trades, etc, 14.4$_3$, names of dances 14.4$_5$, general ideas 14.4$_6$, plural (adj) 14.8$_4$.

Genitive ch IX; gen. and poss. 9.2, construction 9.2$_3$ f., meaning 9.2$_5$ ff., with names of human beings 9.2$_6$ ff., after *a* 9.3$_5$, after adj 9.3$_7$, too successive gen.s 9.3$_8$, with composite prep. 9.3$_9$, names of animals 9.4$_4$, inanimate things 9.5$_1$ ff., *sake* 9.5$_2$, set phrases 9.5$_3$, in poetry, etc, 9.5$_4$, before *end, edge*, etc; used by journalists 9.5$_5$, measures of space 9.5$_6$, indications of time 9.5$_7$, as primary 9.5$_8$, *my tail's tail* 9.6$_3$; conflict with def. article 12.9$_2$.
gentle, feminine 5.3$_9$.
gentleman, (quite) the, 14.2$_2$.
Gerund 6.4$_3$, 9.2$_5$.
get 6.9$_2$, 12.7$_1$.
Gil on *you* 7.3$_5$.
van Ginneken, gender 5.1$_2$.
gipsy, gender 5.3$_6$.
girl, gender 5.3$_6$, compounds 5.3$_9$, *a girl* generic person 4.7$_6$.
Glottic word-order 2.2$_2$ ff.
go halves, go shares 8.3$_7$, *go* with echoic tertiary 8.8$_3$.
God, left out 3.3$_3$, *he* 5.5$_4$, avoided 7.3$_2$, in terms of imprecation 9.2$_6$, *God's, of God* 9.2$_7$, primary 13.2$_4$, synonyms 14.8$_4$, quasi-proper name 16.7$_1$, in wishes 18.5$_4$.
good 5.1$_2$, comparison 10.4$_8$, 10.5$_1$, 11.3$_1$.
Goodbye 7.3$_2$.

gossip 5.3₆.
Government, (*the*) 15.2₄.
Graf, the, 16.4₂.
Grand Duchess, Duke, the, 16.4₂.
Green Park, (*the*) 16.2₃.
groggiest, the, 3.5₅.

H.

had; had as good, better, best, rather 6.6₈.
half, style-tertiary 2.6₂, *half (of)* 9.7₁ f., *a (the) half a* 12.9₂.
Hall, zero 15.2₂.
Haplology in superl. 10.1₃.
happen with *there* 3.2₁.
hard, hardly 1.5₅, 2.7₃, *hardly than* 11.4₆.
harky, hark'ee 7.3₂.
harlot, gender 5.3₆.
harm's way 9.5₃.
has to 2.8₅.
haste, case 6.9₂.
have, obj with zero 12.7₁.
he 4.4, 4.7₅, 5.3₉, 5.5 ff., animals 5.6, inanimate 5.8₂, case 6.1₄ f.
Headlinese 3.6₅, 12.3₆.
Hearer's point of view 2.1₇.
heart's content 9.5₃.
heaven, Heaven, he 5.5₄, *the* or zero 14.1₄, 16.7₂, in wishes 18.5₄.
heir, heiress 5.3₈.
Hell, hell of 9.9₅, primary 13.2₄, zero 16.7₂.
hem, 'em 4.4₁.
her obl. case 4.4, 6.1₄ ff., poss. 4.4₂.

here, word-order 2.4₃, 2.6₇, case with, 6.8₁, *here you are!* 7.5₈.
hero, heroine 5.3₈.
hers 4.4₂.
herself 4.8₁.
hext, superl. 11.2₇.
hie, case 6.9₂.
high, highly 1.5₅, with tertiary 8.4₃, *the Most High* 9.2₇, 10.2₂, 14.8₄, compar. 11.2₇.
High Street 16.2₄.
him 4.4, 6.1₄ ff.
himself 4.8₁, generic 4.7₅.
hinder, comp. 10.5₃, *hindermost* 10.5₆, 10.5₉, *hindmost* 10.5₆.
his 4.4₂, poss. of *it* 9.1₂.
hit > it 4.6₁.
hithermost 10.5₇.
Hjelmslev on case 6.1₁, 8.1₂.
hold, case 6.9₂.
home, tertiary 8.6₇.
Honorific *the* 16.3₈, adjs 16.6₅f.
Honorary titles 11.8₃.
horse, genitive 9.4₄.
Hotels, names of, 16.3₁, 16.3₄.
householder, housekeeper 5.3₇.
however 3.5₈.
human (being) 5.2₃, *humankind* 5.2₄, comparison 10.2₄.
humane, comparison 10.2₄.

I.

I 4.2, 5.5₁, 6.1₄ f., *I* for *me* 7.4₂ f., *I for one* 17.1₈.
i non-syllabic in comparison 10.1₅.
[i·], pronouns in, 7.1 ff.
idle, comparison 10.2₇.

if-clauses 2.3_8, 3.5_1 f., *if only* 2.7_3.

ill, comparison 10.5_1, 11.3_1 f.

Imperative, tertiaries with, 2.7_7, case of subj 6.9_1 ff.

"Impersonal" verbs 6.5_7 ff.

Imprecation, terms of, 9.2_6, 9.9_5, 18.5_3 ff.

in, word-order 2.3_5, *in it* 4.6_{11}, *in, in front of* 4.8_5, before zero 12.8_2.

Inanimate things, pronouns 5.9, names of, with *of* 9.5_1 ff., in genitive 9.5_2 ff.

Inarticulate sentences 3.6.

indeed, word-order 2.7_3.

Indefinite article chs XII—XVI; 12.1, *sixpence an ounce* 8.9_8, form 12.2_4 ff., numerical *a, an* 12.3_2, 'one and the same' 12.3_3, syntax 12.4 ff., Stage of familiarity I 12.4_2, 12.5 ff., meaning of *a* 12.5_2 ff., meaning of subst. with *a* 12.5_4, predicatives 12.5_5, all-representative use, dictionary definitions, comparisons 12.5_6, distributive use 12.5_7, before orig.proper names 12.5_8 ff., with quantifiers 12.5_{11} f., unification 12.6, before uncountables 12.6_1, names of diseases 12.6_1, classifying 12.6_2, unit-words 12.6_3, with predicative 12.7_3, *a* or zero 12.7_8, conflict between articles 12.9, junctions ch XIII, *a* and some 17.6_1.

Indefinite pronouns see Pronouns of totality, *any, some, either, neither, no*.

Indefinite relative clause 3.5_7, 18.7_4.

Indetermination see Articles.

Indicative 18.1_2 ff. — Cf Mood.

Indirect speech, pronouns 4.4_6, mood 18.7_1 f., indir. question 18.7_3.

individual, an, generic person 4.7_6.

-ine 5.4_2.

Infinitive 2.3_3, 2.7_8, 13.2_1.

inmost 10.5_4, 10.5_6 f., 10.5_9.

inner 10.5_3, *innermore, innermost* 10.5_6, 10.5_9.

Institutions, names of, with *the* 14.3_8, zero 15.2_3.

Intensives 11.8.

Intention and purpose, clauses of, 18.6_1 f.

Interrogative pronouns 2.7_4.

into 2.3_5, 4.8_5.

Inversion 2.2_2 ff.

irrespective of 1.5_6.

is to 2.8_5.

Islands, names of, 16.1_9.

it 4.4, 4.6, *take it off* 2.1_5, *it for you* 4.3_2, anaphoric 4.6_2, preparatory 4.6_3 ff., cleft sentences 4.6_8, unspecified 4.6_9 ff., *it, It, IT* (slang) 4.7_7, OE gender 5.1_2, no-sex 5.5_1, 5.5_3, case 6.1_4, possess. 9.1_2, *of it* 9.4_3.

it is (was) 4.5_6, 6.2_5, case 6.7_2 ff., *it is him, it is us* 6.7_6.

-itis 12.6_7.

it(s), possessive 9.1.

itself 4.8_1.

General Index.

J.

Jakobson on zero 12.1.
Jew, Jewess 5.3$_3$.
jolly well, style-tertiary 2.6$_2$.
Junction 2.1$_3$, with *a* 12.6$_2$, mass-words 12.6$_4$ f., plurals 12.6$_8$ f., predicatives 12.7$_4$ ff., articles before, ch XIII, with typical *the* 14.2$_3$, in exclamations with *the* 14.5$_4$, proper names ch XVI, titles before proper names 16.4, adjs before proper names 16.6.
Junior, zero 15.1$_5$.
just, justly 1.5$_5$, 2.6$_2$, 2.7$_3$, 10.2$_2$.

K.

Kaiser, (the), 16.4$_2$.
keep, obj with zero 12.7$_1$.
kind of, style-tertiary 2.6$_4$.
King, the, 14.1$_4$, zero 16.4$_1$, *the King's English* 9.3$_4$.

L.

l, (non-)syllabic in comparison 10.1$_5$.
lady 5.3$_1$, 5.3$_4$, compounds 5.3$_9$, *(the) Lady* 16.4$_1$.
Lakes, names of, 16.1$_6$.
landlady, landlord 5.3$_1$.
Languages, names of, 12.6$_{12}$.
last, in tertiary 8.5$_1$, superl. 11.2$_2$ ff., *at the last* 14.7$_3$, *(the) last, (the) last thing* 14.7$_8$.

late, lately 1.5$_5$, comparison 11.2$_1$ ff.
Latent comparatives 11.5$_5$.
Latin comparatives, with possessive 9.2$_8$, and superl. 11.7$_7$.
latter, the, 4.4$_4$, added 4.4$_6$. — Cf *late*.
latterly 10.4$_2$.
least 11.3$_1$ ff., *in the least* 14.7$_3$. — Cf *lest*.
Legal terms with zero 15.1$_6$.
leman, gender 5.3$_6$.
leng(er), adv 10.4$_3$.
leopardess 5.4$_2$.
less 11.1$_1$, 11.3$_1$ f.
-less, advs in, 1.5$_6$.
lesser 11.3$_1$ f.
Lesser verb, position 2.2.
lest (that) 18.6$_2$ f.
let us go 6.4$_1$.
lief, liever 6.6$_8$, 10.1$_6$.
love, gender 5.3$_1$.
lovely, feminine 5.3$_9$.
lover, gender 5.3$_1$.
low, lowly 1.5$_5$.
lowermost, lowmost 10.5$_6$.
Lowth on *self*-forms 4.8$_1$.

M.

Madame, Mademoiselle 16.4$_3$.
maid, maiden 5.3$_6$.
make 6.4$_2$, 12.7$_1$.
male 5.3$_9$.
Male animals 5.4$_3$. — Cf Sex.
Malory, riming pronouns 7.1.
mamma 15.1$_5$ (2).
man, generic 4.7$_1$, 4.7$_6$, 14.3$_3$; gender 5.2$_1$ ff., compounds

with, 5.2_5, *man, men, of* or gen. 9.3_6, *the man* = 'you'.
manhood 5.2_5.
mankind 5.2_4.
Manner, tertiaries 8.9_3.
many, comparison 11.3_1, with *a* 12.5_{11}.
Mass-words 12.4_2, zero 12.6_3 ff., meaning 12.6_4 f., zero after prep. 12.8_2 f., in junction 13.2_5, 13.3_4.
master 5.3_1, 5.3_3, with zero 15.1_5.
mater 14.5_2, 15.1_5.
matron 15.1_5.
matter 8.3_4, *matters* as obj 2.8_8, 'things' 5.5_7.
me 6.1_4, common case 7.1 ff., in exclamations 7.5_5.
Meals, names of, 15.2_1.
Measure, of weight 8.4_7, tertiary 8.9_4.
Meillet on gender 5.1_1.
men (ME, generic) 4.7_1. — Cf *man*.
mermaid 5.3_1.
Messiah, the, 14.1_4.
midmost 10.5_4.
Military terms 15.2_3.
millenium, the, 14.1_4.
mind, she 5.8_3, vb with tertiary 8.3_4, *mind's eye* 9.5_3.
mine 4.2_5.
Miss 16.4_3.
Missis 14.5_2, 15.1_5.
Mister 5.3_3.
mistress 5.3_1, 5.3_3.
Modifier, precedence of, 2.1_3, modified 3.1_5.
Monosyllables, comparison 10.2_2.

Mood ch XVIII; indicative and subjunctive 18.2_1, form 18.2_3 ff., conditional clauses 18.3 ff., temporal 18.4, wishes 18.5, intention and purpose 18.6_1 ff., content-clauses with *lest* 18.6_3, concessive clauses 18.6_4, indir. speech 18.7_1 f., indir. questions 18.7_3, indef. rel. clauses 18.7_4 f., imaginative *were* 18.7_6.
moon, she 5.8_3, *the* 14.1_4.
Moore Smith on *me*, etc, 7.2_3.
more, without *of* 9.7_4, comparative 10.1_1 f., before comp. 11.1_1, not repeated 11.3_6, 10.4_8, repeated 10.4_7, 'greater number' 11.7_4, 11.7_6.
more than, style tertiary 2.6_3, comparison 11.5_2 f.
-more, comp. ending 10.5_6.
most, comparison 10.1_1, repeated 10.4_7, not repeated 10.4_8, 11.3_6, before superl. 11.1_1, = strengthened *very* 11.7_2 f., 'greatest number' 11.7_4 ff., high degree (with *a*) 13.3_3, *the* 14.7_7, *the*, tertiary 14.7_3, *the most (of)* 14.8_5.
-most, superlative ending 10.5_4 ff., 10.5_9.
mostly, word-order 2.7_3.
mother, zero 15.1_5.
Motor-car, *she* 5.8_1.
Mountains and mountain ranges, names of, 16.2_1.
Mr., Mrs. 16.4_3.
much, introductory 2.4_9, com-

General Index. 675

parison 11.3_1, 11.7_7, 11.8_1, = 'nearly' 11.8_2, before comparatives 11.8_4, before *different* 11.8_5, before superl. 11.8_7.
mummy 5.2_1.
my 4.2_5, *my darling*, etc, 4.3_2.

N.

name, names 8.8_1, 9.2_6, *name of* 9.8.
nanny, zero 15.1_5.
nature, she 5.8_3.
near, comparison 11.2_7, *near* : *nearly* 1.5_5.
necessary, needful, the, 14.8_3.
Negation, word-order 2.2_4.
Negative left out 3.3_7.
neither 17.8_1, position 2.2_3 f., *neither .. nor* 4.5.
nethermost 10.5_7.
never, position 2.8_2 ff.
new, newly 1.5_5.
next 11.2_7, *next door* 8.6_5, *the* 14.7_9.
Nexus 2.1_3, loosely connected 6.4_4.
Nexus-substantive with genitive 9.2_5.
nigh, comparison 11.2_7.
night, nights, tertiary 8.5_2, *stay the night* 15.3_8.
no, none 17.1_7, 17.8_2 f., 17.9_2 f.; *no more*, word-order 2.2_4, left out before *more* 3.3_7, *no earthly* 3.5_5, *no end* 8.3_6, before superl. 11.6_5, 14.7_5, and *any* 17.5_7, compounds 17.8_3.
no- 5.5_1.

Nominative 6.1_3 ff., 6.2_1 ff., 6.2_6, 6.3_2.
Non-reflexive use of *self*-forms 4.9_3.
none see *no*.
nor, word-order 2.2_4, after *neither* 17.8_1.
nor-combinations 12.8_5.
north, etc, see *east*.
not often, word-order 2.7_3.
Notional subject 6.4_1 ff., 7.5_3.
nought 17.2_8.
now, word-order 2.7_3.
Nulli-generic 12.6_6.
Numerals, 17.1_2 ff., with or without *of* 9.7_3, *one* 17.1_3 ff., word-order 17.1_4 ff., long numerals 17.1_9, foreign 17.2_1, uncertainty of number 17.2_2, approximate number 17.2_3, *or two, or so, two-three* 17.2_4, fractions 17.2_6, distributive use 17.2_7, 'nothing' 17.2_8, *once, twice, thrice* 17.3_1 ff.
nurse, Nurse 15.1_5, 16.4_4.

O.

O (=*nought*) 17.2_8.
Object ch II passim; word-order 2.2_7, 2.8_1, omitted 18.5_5.
'Objective' genitive 9.2_5.
Oblique case 6.1_4 ff., as subject 7.5_2 ff.
Oceans, names of, 16.1_6.
odd after numeral 17.2_2.
Østerberg (numerals) 17.2_3.
of ch IX; word-order 2.3_5, *of it* 4.6_{11}, competing with gen.

43*

and poss. 9.2_3 ff., combinations with conjunctions 9.3_3, *of man (men)* 9.3_6, with junction 9.3_7, with composite prep. 9.3_9, *death of, look of* 9.4_2, various uses 9.4_3 ff., *sake of* 9.5_2, *that of, those of* 9.5_9, other employments 9.6, partitive 9.7, specializing 9.8, appositional 9.9, *a* (etc) *stripling of a page* 9.9_5, *of all others* 11.6_2, before zero 12.8_2.

off, word-order 2.4_4.
often not, word-order 2.7_3.
old, comparison 11.1_3 ff.
on, 4.8_5, 2.3_5, 12.8_2.
once 17.3_1 f., word-order 2.7_3, 'if once' 18.4_2.
one, generic person 4.7_4 f., with *a* 12.5_{12}, quantifier 17.1_3 ff.
oneself 4.7_5, *one's self* 4.8_1.
only 2.4_3, 2.7_3, *only less, only more* 11.8_6, after *one* 17.1_7.
or; or two, or so 17.2_4, after *either* 17.7_1, after *neither* 17.8_1, *or ever* 18.4_1.
or-combinations 8.9_6, 12.8_5.
Ordinals, as secondaries 13.3_1 ff., articles with, 14.7, in fractions 17.2_5.
other than 11.4_4.
otherwise 8.7_3.
ought ($=nought$) 17.2_8.
ourself 4.8_1.
out 2.4_4, *out for* *out of* 9.6_3.
outer 10.5_3; *outermore, outermost* 10.5_6 f.
outmost 10.5_6 f.

over 4.8_5, word-order 2.4_4.
own 4.9_5, comparison 10.2_2.
ox 5.4_1.

P.

pair of stairs 8.6_4.
Pairs of words, tertiaries 8.9, zero 12.8_4 ff., sententious phrases 12.8_7.
Palmer on case 6.7_{12}, *anybody* 17.5_6.
pantheress, pantherine 5.4_2.
papa 15.1_5.
Paradise 16.7_2.
Parliament 15.2_4.
parson 15.1_5.
Participial adjectives 2.1_5.
Participles, word-order 2.7_9, in junction 13.2_1, past ptc. and agent-noun 12.8_5.
Particle left out 3.3_2.
Parti-generic sense, masswords 12.6_4, plurals 12.6_8 ff.
passion of 9.9_5.
Passive construction 4.7_1.
pater 14.5_2, 15.1_5.
Pedersen, Holger, on gender 5.1_1.
people, generic 4.7_3.
perhaps 2.7_4.
Periphrastic comparison chs X—XI, 11.3_5 f.
person, a, generic person 4.7_6.
Person ch IV; the three persons 4.1, first 4.2, second 4.3, third 4.4, in verbs 4.5, *they* + numeral, *them* adjunct 4.5_9, *it* 4.6 ff., generic 4.7, 14.3, reflexive 4.8, reflexive possessive 4.9.

Personal name 16.1_2, with *the* 14.2_4, 16.3_8, titles before, 16.4.

Personification 5.8_3, 9.5_4, 16.1_5, esp. 16.5.

Phonetic influence on case-forms ch VII.

pity, genitive 9.5_3, *a* or zero 12.7_8.

Place-names 16.1_3 ff.

places, tertiary 8.6_6.

plain, plainly 1.5_5.

Plants, names of, 14.3_6, gender 5.4_4, pronouns for, 5.7.

play, obj with zero 12.7_1, obj with typical *the* 14.2_1, *play (the) second fiddle* 14.3_9.

plenty (of) 9.7_1.

Plural, after *there is* 3.1_4, represented by *it* 4.6_7, tertiary 8.5_2, zero 12.6_8 ff., after *of* 12.6_{10}, zero after prep. 12.8_2 f., in junctions 13.3_5, place-names 16.1_3 ff.

poetess 5.3_3.

Pope, the, 14.1_4.

Possessive pronoun ch IX; 3rd pers. pl. 9.1_1, from *it* 9.1_2, construction 9.2_3 f., meaning 9.2_5 ff., with composite prep. 9.3_9, and *of* 9.4_2, before appositional *of* 9.9_5.

post; ride post, post-haste 8.7_4.

Precedence of modifier 2.1_3.

Predicate left out 3.5_6.

Predicative ch II passim; adj or adv 1.5_4, front-position 2.3, in sentence with *there* 3.2_3, gender 5.3_7, neuter 5.5_5, case 6.4_3, 6.7, tertiary of measure 8.4_4, articles in, 12.5_5, 12.7_2 ff., 14.2_2 ff.

prefer than 11.5_6.

Preparatory *it* 4.6_3 ff., *there* 3.1_3.

preparatory to 1.5_6.

Preposition, at end of sentence 2.2_9, 2.3_4 ff., 4.8_4 f., case 6.3_1 ff. — Cf Prep. group.

Prepositional group, before ptc. 2.7_9, in tertiary 8.9, regimen with zero 12.8_1 ff., 12.8_6, in junction 13.2_1, *the idea of it*, etc, 14.5_4.

pretty, prettily 1.5_5.

previous(ly) to 1.5_6.

Price, indications of 8.4_6, 8.9_8.

priestess 5.3_4.

Prince, Princess 16.4_1.

prisoner 15.1_6.

Pronoun, after tertiary 2.8_7, gender 5.5, case chs VI—VII, versus article 12.9_2, of totality 17.4_1 ff., 17.9_2 f.

Proper names ch XVI; with *a* 12.5_8, and mass-words $.12.6_3$, as predicatives 12.7_{10}, in junctions 13.1_3, 13.2_3, meaning 16.1_1, personal names 16.1_2, place-names, etc, 16.1_3 ff., typical and honorific *the* before, 16.3_8, titles before, 16.4, personification 16.5, adjs before 16.6, quasi-proper names 16.7.

Prosiopesis 3.3_2 ff., 12.3_4 f., 15.3_9.

Proverbs 3.6_3, 12.6_5, 12.6_8.

Providence 5.5₄, 9.2₇, 13.2₄, 16.7₁.
Purgatory 16.7₂.
Purpose see Intention.

Q.

Quantifiers ch XVII; quantifier tertiaries 2.6₈, before pl 12.6₁₀, before *the* + comparative 14.6₃, numerals 17.1₂ ff., pronouns of totality 17.4₁ ff., adjs 17.9₁, survey 17.9₂.
quarter of, *quarter past* 12.3₄, *quarter to five* 15.3₉.
Quarters of the world, names of, 8.6₉.
Quasi-proper names 16.6₂, 16.7.
Quasi-subject *there* 3.1₄.
queen 5.3₄, 16.4₁.
Question, incomplete 2.1₁, word-order 2.2₂, indirect 18.7₃.
question, prosiopesis 12.3₅.
quick, *quickly* 1.5₅.
quite 2.6₂, 2.7₃, 11.8₄.
Quotation as obj 2.2₈.
quoth he 2.2₈.

R.

-*r*- pronounced in comp. and superl. 10.1₅.
Railway stations, names of, 16.3₅.
rather 10.2₆, 11.4₉, *rather .. than* 2.6₃.
ready, the, 14.8₃.

rector 15.1₅.
Reflexive pronouns 4.8.
Regent's Park 16.2₃.
Regimen of prep. see Preposition and Prep. group.
Relative adverbs in -*ever* 3.5₈.
Relative attraction 6.2₂, 6.2₅ f., 6.7₅, 6.7₇.
Relative clause, form of vb 4.5₅, with *self*-form 4.9₃.
Relative pronouns 6.2₅, in -*ever* 3.5₈.
Relative weight 2.1₅, 2.4₄.
remember, case 6.9₂.
Representative *it* 4.6₃ ff.
Request, inarticulate 3.6₁.
rest, case 6.9₂.
Rhythm 2.1₆.
right, rightly 1.5₅, 10.2₂.
river, he 5.8₃.
River-names 16.1₄ ff.
Roads, names of, 16.2₅ f.
rooster 5.4₁.
round 4.8₅, *round : roundly* 1.5₅.
Royen on gender 5.1₂.
run, case 6.9₂.

S.

'*s*- in terms of imprecation 9.2₆, omitted 9.2₆.
-*s*, -*s'*, genitive 9.2₂.
sake, in terms of imprecation 9.2₆, gen. or *of* 9.5₂.
same, prosiopesis 12.3₅.
Satan 16.7₁.
Sattler on gender 5.6₃.
save, case 6.3₂.
Saviour, the, 14.1₄.

'Sblood 9.2$_6$.
scarce, scarcely 1.5$_5$, scarcely than 11.4$_6$.
Schmidt, Al., on thee 6.9$_3$.
Schröter on river-names 16.1$_4$.
Scottish, a body 4.7$_6$, no partitive of 9.7$_2$, honorific the 16.3$_8$.
Scripture 14.1$_4$.
'Sdeath 9.2$_6$.
sea, gender 5.8$_3$.
Seas, names of, 16.1$_6$.
second fiddle 14.3$_9$, second nature, time, etc, 13.3$_2$.
self, sb 4.9$_4$, in compounds 4.9$_5$.
self-pronouns 4.8$_1$, non-reflexive use 4.9$_3$, case 6.9$_3$ f.
Semi-articulate sentences 3.6.
Sentence-structure chs II-III; abbreviated sentences 3.3$_1$ ff.
servant, compounds 5.3$_9$.
Sex ch V.
sex, the, 14.4$_6$.
'Sfoot 9.2$_6$.
shade, the, 14.4$_6$.
shall's, shall us 6.8$_2$ f.
'Sham subject' (there) 3.1$_4$.
shame, a or zero 12.7$_8$.
she 4.4, 5.3$_9$, 5.5$_1$ ff., 5.6, 6.1$_4$ f.
ship, genitive 9.5$_3$.
Ships, she 5.8$_1$, names of, 16.3$_6$.
short, shortly 1.5$_5$.
shrew 5.3$_6$.
side (of) 8.6$_3$, 9.6$_3$.
silence, (a), 12.6$_2$.
sir 5.3$_1$, 16.4$_1$.
sister 15.1$_5$.
sit, case 6.9$_2$.

Situational basis, ordinary 14.1$_3$, constant 14.1$_4$.
slattern, slut gender 5.3$_6$.
so, position 2.3$_3$, 2.7$_3$, so much us 2.6$_3$, elliptical 3.5$_3$, very or much 11.8$_1$, ever so 11.8$_4$, = 'if (only)', so be 18.3$_6$.
some 17.6$_1$ ff., 17.9$_2$ f., compounds 5.5$_1$, 17.6$_6$, some times, sometimes 8.5$_1$, before one 17.1$_7$, something after numeral 17.2$_2$, and any 17.5$_4$.
Somerset dial., person in, 4.4$_4$.
soon, comparison 11.4$_2$.
sort of, style tertiary 2.6$_4$.
soul, she 5.8$_3$.
sound, soundly 1.5$_5$.
south, etc, see east.
spouse 5.2$_6$.
Squire, zero 15.1$_5$.
Stages of familiarity see Familiarity, stages of.
stand, stay, case 6.9$_2$.
-ster 5.3$_6$.
still, stilly 1.5$_5$, still with comparative 11.6$_1$.
straight, straightly 1.5$_5$.
Straits, names of, 16.1$_6$.
strange, comparison 10.2$_2$.
Straumann on headlinese 3.6$_5$.
Streets, names of, 16.2$_4$ ff.
Stress 2.1$_6$, distinctive 4.4$_4$.
stroke, zero 15.1$_6$.
strong, strongly 1.5$_5$, comparison 10.1$_5$.
Style-tertiaries 2.6$_2$ ff.
Subject, ch II passim; in sentence with there 3.1$_1$ ff.,

3.3_4 f., left out 3.3_3, 18.5_6, case 6.8.
subject to 1.5_6.
'Subjective' genitive 9.2_5.
Subjunctive ch XVIII passim; 2.2_2. — Cf Mood.
subsequent to, subsequently 1.5_6.
Substantives, formation 1.2, sex and gender 5.2, case ch VIII, comparison 10.4_9, superl. in *-most* 10.5_5, meaning with indef. art. 12.5_4, in junction 13.2_1.
such as, case 6.3_4.
sun, he 5.8_3, *the* 14.1_4, 14.4_6.
Superlatives ch X—XI passim; as secondary 13.3_1 ff., articles with, 14.7.
sure, surely 1.5_6.
Svartengren on gender 5.8_1.
Swear-words see Imprecation, terms of.
Sweet on gender 5.1_1, 5.6_1, on case 7.2_1, 7.4_3, on *-ed, -ing* 10.3_3.
swift, swiftly 1.5_5.

T.

take; take place 2.2_7, 3.2_2, *take root* 2.2_7, case 6.9_2, obj with zero 12.7_1.
teacher, gender 5.3_6, zero 15.1_5.
Temporal clauses 18.4_1 f.
Tertiaries, word-order 2.4 ff., 2.6_1 ff., 2.6_2 ff., with vbs 2.8_2 ff., common case 8.3, of measure 8.3_2, of time 8.3_4, 8.4_1 ff., 8.5, of space 8.6, of manner 8.7.

Thames, (the), 16.1_4.
than, word-order 2.4_6, 2.7_1, case 6.3_7, *than whom* 6.5_6, not expressed 11.3_7, contamination 11.4_3 ff., *than what* 11.4_7, *than otherwise* 11.4_9, *more than kind*, etc 11.5_2 f., *prefer than* 11.5_6, after comparative 11.6_2.
that, in *there*-sentence 3.2_3, in predicative 5.5_5, before appositional *of* 9.9_5, after introductory sentence 14.1_1, *that the* 14.7_{10}.
the see Definite article.
þe 7.3_1.
thee 4.3_1, 6.1_4 ff., with imperative 6.9, *th'* 7.3_3, pronunciation 7.3_5 f., Quakers' 7.3_7, nom. 7.3_7.
their(s) 4.4_2, 9.1_1.
them 4.4, 6.1_4 ff., adjunct 4.5_9, as subj 7.5_6.
there, word-order 2.4_3, empty *there* 3.1_1 ff., case with, 6.8_1.
these two 4.5_9.
they 4.4, 5.5_1, 6.1_4 f., *they two* 4.5_9, generic 4.7_3.
th'hast, th'art 7.3_3.
thick, with tertiary 8.4_3.
thine 4.3_5.
thing, ref. to human being 5.5_3, to neuter 5.5_6, to pl 5.5_7, prosiopesis 12.3_5.
things, word-order 2.8_8.
think, case 6.6_5.
this 5.5_5, in tertiary 8.5_1, before appositional *of* 9.9_5, after introductory sentence 14.1_1, *this the* 14.7_{10}.

those in *there*-sentence 3.2_3, *those two* 4.5_9.

thou 4.3_1, 4.5, 5.5_2, 6.1_4 ff., 7.3_5 f.

though, word-order 2.7_3.

thrice 17.3_1 f.

þu, weakened 7.3_1.

thus, word-order 2.5_2.

thy 4.3_5.

tiger, tigress 5.4_2.

till, conj. 18.4_1.

Time, periods of, 5.8_5, tertiaries of, 2.6_7, 8.5, 8.9_2, articles with indications of, 15.3.

time, time enough 8.5_3, articles with, 12.7_9, *all the time* 14.8_6.

times, tertiary 8.4_7, 8.5_1.

Titles before personal names 16.4, — Cf Book-titles.

title of 9.8.

to 4.8_5, word-order 2.3_5, *to it* 4.6_{11}, before subj 6.8_4, with Lat. comparatives 11.7_7, before zero 12.8_2.

tomboy 5.3_9.

tomcat 5.4_3.

too 2.7_3, 11.5_5, 11.8_4.

top (of) 9.6_3.

topmost 10.5_5, 10.5_9.

Totality, pronouns of, 17.4_1 ff.

Toto-generic sense 12.6_5, 12.6_8.

towards 4.8_5.

Towns, *she, it* 5.8_5, names of, gen. or *of* 9.3_1, *the* or zero 16.2_2.

town, zero 15.2_5.

Tradition in word-order 2.1_8.

Train, *she* 5.8_1.

trouble is, truth is 12.3_5.

tsar, tsarevitch, tsarina, the, 16.4_2.

turn, case 6.9_2.

Typical *the* 14.2, before proper names 16.3_8.

U.

'um = them 4.4_1.

Uncountables, with *a* 12.6_1 ff., junctions 13.1_2.

undermost 10.5_7.

Unification of mass-words 12.6.

"Uniques" 14.1_4.

Unit-word 12.4_2, 12.6_3. — Cf Class-nouns.

Unspecified *it* 4.6_9 ff.

universe, the, 14.1_4.

until 18.4_1.

up, word-order 2.4_4, *one up* 8.3_3.

upmost 10.5_6, 10.5_9.

upon 4.8_5, word-order 2.3_5.

upper 10.5_3, *uppermost* 10.5_6, 10.5_9.

us 4.2_1, 6.1_4 f., for *me* 4.2_3, subj 6.8_2, *us two* 7.4_1.

usual, usually 1.5_5.

utmost 10.5_4, 10.5_6 f.

utter 10.5_3, 10.5_7, 11.1_8, *utterly* 10.4_2, *uttermost* 10.5_6 f.

V.

Verbs, formation 1.4, position chs II — III passim, left out 3.3_4, 3.4, person in vbs 4.5, requiring *-self* 4.8_5, obj with zero 12.7_1.

Verbless sentences 3.6$_3$ f.
very 11.8$_1$, before comparative 11.8$_4$, before superl. 11.8$_7$.
vessel, genitive 9.5$_3$.
vicar, zero 15.1$_5$.
virgin 5.3$_6$.
Viscount, zero (or *the*) 16.4$_2$.
vixen 5.4$_3$.
vote, the, 14.4$_6$.

W.

walk, etc, as tertiary 8.7$_4$ f.
way, tertiary 8.6$_2$, 8.7$_1$.
we 4.2$_1$, 4.2$_3$, 6.1$_4$ f., for *you* 4.3$_2$, generic 4.7$_1$, "royal" and "editorial" 7.3$_7$, adjunct 7.4$_1$.
Webster on mood 18.2$_2$.
Weekley on case 6.7$_{12}$.
Weight 2.1$_5$.
well might 2.4$_8$, *well,* comparison 10.5$_1$.
west (go west) 8.6$_9$. — Cf *east.*
Western on sentence-rhythm 2.1$_6$.
wether 5.4$_1$.
what 5.5$_1$, 5.5$_5$.
whatever 3.5$_8$.
Wheeler on *he* or *she* 5.6$_2$.
whensoever 3.5$_8$.
where, clauses with, 2.3$_8$.
wherefore, wherewithal, the, 14.8$_{10}$.
which 5.5$_1$, 5.5$_5$, animals, plants 5.7, *the which* 14.8$_8$.
whichever 3.5$_8$.
while, tertiary 8.5$_4$.
who, 5.5$_1$ 5.5$_5$, 6.1$_4$ f., 6.6$_8$, animals, plants 5.7, as obj 6.5, *than whom* 6.5$_6$, *the who(m), whose* 14.8$_9$.
whoever 3.5$_8$.
whole 5.5$_4$, 17.4$_6$.
whom 6.1$_4$.
why, the, 14.8$_{10}$.
wide, widely 1.5$_5$.
widow, widower 5.3$_2$, *(the) Widow* 16.4$_4$.
wife, the, 14.5$_2$.
wise, tertiary 8.7$_3$.
Wishes 18.5$_1$ ff., word-order 2.2$_2$.
witch 5.3$_1$, 5.3$_6$.
with 4.8$_5$, *with, withal, without* 2.3$_5$, in verbless sentence 3.6$_1$.
withal see *with.*
within 4.8$_5$.
without see *with.*
witness 15.1$_6$.
wits' end 9.5$_3$.
wizard 5.3$_6$.
woe 18.5$_4$.
wolverine 5.4$_2$.
woman, generic 4.7$_6$, 14.3$_4$, OE gender 5.1$_2$, compounds 5.2$_5$.
womankind 5.2$_4$.
word of 9.8.
Word-classes ch I.
Word-group in junction 13.2$_1$.
Word-order chs II—III, with *self*-forms 4.9$_3$, case 6.4$_5$ ff., *one-and-twenty : twenty-one* 17.1$_4$ ff.
world, genitive 9.3$_1$, *the* 14.1$_4$.
worse 11.3$_1$ f., *worser* 11.3$_2$.
worst 11.3$_1$ f.
worth, worthy with common

case 8.2, *worth* after gen. 9.5$_6$.
would, confused with *had* 6.6$_9$, *would to God* 6.8$_5$.
Wright on *he* or *she* 5.8$_2$.
wrong, wrongly 1.5$_5$.

Y.

y changed into *i* 10.1$_7$.
y'are 7.3$_3$ f.
ye 4.3$_1$, 6.1$_4$ f., 7.3$_2$ ff., pronunciation 7.3$_5$, one person 7.3$_7$.
yet, word-order 2.7$_3$.
you 4.3, 6.1$_4$ f., 7.3$_2$ ff., generic 4.7$_1$ f., gender 5.5$_1$, with imperative 6.9$_1$ ff., weakened 7.3$_2$, pronunciation 7.3$_5$, one person 7.3$_7$, emphatic nom. 7.3$_7$, orig. dative 7.5$_8$.
you'll 7.3$_4$.
your(s) 4.3$_5$, *Your Majesty*, etc, 4.3$_2$, 4.5$_8$.
youth 5.2$_1$, 5.2$_6$.

Z.

zero 17.2$_8$.
Zero article chs XII—XVI; 12.1, stages of familiarity 12.4$_2$, 12.4$_4$, mass-word, proper name 12.6$_3$, meaning of mass-words 12.6$_4$ f., plurals 12.6$_8$ ff., object 12.7$_1$, predicative 12.7$_2$ ff., prep. phrases 12.8$_1$ ff., junctions ch XIII, in exclamations 14.5$_7$, with superl. and ordinals 14.7$_5$ ff.; Stage III ch XV; address 15.1$_1$, 15.1$_4$, familiar persons 15.1$_5$ ff., names of meals 15.2$_1$ f., institutions 15.2$_3$ f., indications of time 15.3, personal names 16.1$_2$, place-names 16.1$_4$ ff., other names 16.3$_6$ f., titles 16.4, personification 16.5, adjs before proper names 16.6, quasi-proper names 16.7.
zigzag, tertiary 8.8$_2$.
Zodiac, the, 14.1$_4$.

GEORGE ALLEN & UNWIN LTD

Head Office:
40 Museum Street, London WC1
Telephone: 01-405-8577

Sales, Publicity, Distribution and Accounts Departments:
Park Lane, Hemel Hempstead, Hertfordshire HP2 4TE
Telephone: 0442 3244
Argentina: Defensa 681-5J, Buenos Aires
Australia: Australasian Publishing Company Pty. Ltd.,
Corner Bridge Road and Jersey Street, Hornsby, N.S.W. 2077
Bangladesh: Provincial Book Depot,
Empire Buildings, Victoria Park South, Dacca
Canada: Methuen Ltd.,
2330 Midland Avenue, Agincourt, Ontario
East Africa: University of London Press Ltd.,
P.O. Box 30583, Nairobi, Kenya
Europe: Rock House, Edington, Nr. Bridgwater, Somerset
Greece, Turkey & The Middle East: I.P.R.
3 Mitropoleous Street, Athens 118
India: Blackie & Son Ltd.,
103/5 Walchand Hirachand Marq., P.O. Box 21, Bombay 1 BR
285J Bepin Behari Ganguli Street, Calcutta 12
2/18 Mount Road, Madras 2
4/21-22B Asaf Ali Road, New Delhi 1
Japan: Eastern Book Service
29/13 Hongo 5 Chome, Bunkyo ku, Tokyo 113
Malaysia: Eastern Book Service
Resident Office, 54 Jalan-Pudu, Room 303, Kuala Lumpar
New Zealand: Book Reps (N.Z.) Ltd.,
46 Lake Road, Northcote, Auckland 9
Pakistan: Hamiedkhan Ltd.,
22 Faletti's Hotel, Egerton Road, Lahore
Karachi Chambers, McLeod Road, Karachi
Philippines: Eastern Book Service
U.P., P.O. Box 10, Quezon City D-505
Singapore & Hong Kong: Eastern Book Service
53L Anson Road, 11th Floor Anson Centre, Singapore 2
South Africa: Macmillan (S.A.) Ltd.,
P.O. Box 31487, Braamfontein, Johannesburg
South America: Oxford University Press Ltd.,
Ely House, 37 Dover Street, London W.1
Thailand: Eastern Book Service
P.O. Box 6/1, Bangkok,
West Africa: University of London Press Ltd.,
P.O. Box 62, Ibadan, Nigeria
West Indies: Rockley New Road, St. Lawrence 4. Barbados

by Otto Jespersen

HOW TO TEACH A FOREIGN LANGUAGE

Cr. 8vo

'This very suggestive work has been well translated, and ought to be read by all heads of schools and teachers of foreign languages in Great Britain and other countries where speakers of English live.'

Athenaeum

'Professor Jespersen is well known to English students . . . not only a skilled philologist, but also a profound thinker. The present volume demonstrates that he is besides an experienced teacher.' *Journal of Education*

'We recommend this very lucid, readable and practical book to all language teachers and learners.'

Schoolmaster

LANGUAGE: ITS NATURE, DEVELOPMENT AND ORIGIN

Demy 8vo

'A book which ought to be widely read, and we think that many who had never previously attempted such a book might easily be fascinated.' *Westminster Gazette*

'Wherever it is tapped it yields evidence of the magic of words and of the author's extraordinary power of bringing it out. His enthusiasm and humour work more spells even than his encyclopædic knowledge.'

Birmingham Gazette

'A delightful and fascinating book.' *Daily Herald*

by Otto Jespersen

THE PHILOSOPHY OF GRAMMAR

Demy 8vo

' A fascinating storehouse of the wonderful devices of language, and as its illustrations are largely taken from English, its appeal is not merely to linguists, but may be appreciated by anyone.' *Spectator*

' Indispensable to all students of language and invaluable to every teacher of grammar.' *Education*

' A fascinating book ... In its originality, its erudition, and its breadth, this is quite the best book on grammar we have seen.' *Birmingham Gazette*

' He realizes, as many grammarians do not, that grammar, if it is to become a science, must be based upon a logic and a psychology definitely addressed to the problems of language as well as upon linguistic history, formal analysis and the comparison of usages ... both destructively and constructively the book has notable merits.' *Mind*

ESSENTIALS OF ENGLISH GRAMMAR

Cr. 8vo

' Far more logical and far more elastic than the traditional methods. ... He writes with the ease of perfect mastery.' *Teachers' World*

' Every student of English should get a copy of this grammar.' *Aberdeen Press and Journal*

' All readers will find in the work a masterly exposition of the combination of life and logic in the grammar of a living tongue.' *Schoolmaster*

by Otto Jespersen

NOVIAL LEXIKE
An International Dictionary

La. Cr. 8vo   5s. 6d. net

'I have studied your system with great admiration and sympathy. Your principles are unobjectionable, and Novial surpasses the other international languages in all respects.' C. C. UHLENBACH, *President of the First International Congress of Linguistics*

'Its vocabulary is natural, its grammatical structure is simple and logical, it employs no sounds that are not familiar to everyone, and it shows a considerable euphony.' H. L. MENCKEN in *The American Mercury*

MANKIND, NATION AND INDIVIDUAL

Cr. 8vo   9s. 6d. net

Why did languages break up in the past? What makes for new and wider units, culminating eventually in a supra-national auxiliary medium? What part did London play in the shaping of common English? What is Standard English and who are its best speakers? What is meant by 'correctness'? Are synonyms an unqualified blessing? Where do Ministries of Education concern themselves with linguistic questions? How do class-distinctions assert themselves in speech? What is slang? What have our school-boys in common with the Maoris of New Zealand? Why do identical sound changes occur at widely separated places? What made the little girl think that 'hig' was a nicer word than 'death'? Where do 'cant,' 'na poo,' etc. hail from? These are but a few items from Jespersen's rich and attractively arranged bill of fare.

LANGUAGE

by Leonard Bloomfield

Demy 8vo

'Packed with the fruit of extremely wide reading in many fields but never so abstruse as not to be followed with ease by the intelligent reader. Despite—or is it because of—its wealth of learning, it presents sanely and moderately its author's opinions with which this reviewer at any rate is much in sympathy.' A. LLOYD JAMES in *The Sunday Times*

'Simple and straight-forward, and the bearing of language on human affairs is shown very adequately. Prof. Bloomfield's work is both an encyclopædia of, and an introduction to, this fascinating field of study.'
The Schoolmaster

LANGUAGE IN THOUGHT AND ACTION

by S. I. Hayakawa

Demy 8vo

It is a stimulating guide to accurate thinking, reading, listening and writing, and shows how men use words and how words use men.

Part one is concerned with the functions of language and deals with symbols; the language of reports; social cohesion and social control; and the double task of language.

Part two is concerned with language and thought and deals with words and their meanings; the different meanings attached to the same word when applied to the speaker's actions and to other people's actions; the use of words; and pitfalls in debate.

THE LOOM OF LANGUAGE
by Frederick Bodmer

Illustrated

'Dr. Bodmer has achieved remarkable success in a venture of some complexity. He has presented a truly popular introduction to important problems of linguistic science without sacrificing accuracy, has unified theory by summoning a host of concrete examples drawn from a wide range of languages and . . . has paid special attention to social backgrounds and social applications.' PROFESSOR W. E. COLLINSON

'This history and treatise on all matters linguistic from the hieroglyph onwards is huge, enthralling, encyclopædic.' IVOR BROWN in *The Observer*

THE STORY OF LANGUAGE
by Mario Pei Demy 8vo

'Dr. Pei's book is very readable; his style and his excellent choice of examples will delight his readers. Moreover, his philological views are, in general, correct—and such a happy state of affairs is rare in popular works on linguistics.' *Birmingham Post*

'It would be difficult to imagine a more comprehensive and erudite yet readable analysis of the spoken and the written word viewed in every conceivable aspect.' *John O'London's Weekly*

The Story of Language is a volume which can be read aloud to the family; it can be studied carefully; it can be kept on the shelf next to the dictionary as an indispensable reference book. It certainly belongs in any self-respecting library.

THE WORLD'S CHIEF LANGUAGES
by Mario Pei

Demy 8vo

The author describes the world's main languages and their geographical distribution, the linguistic families and the elementary relationships among their members, the identification of the written and possibly the spoken form of several important tongues, and lastly the description of the sounds and grammatical structure, together with a selective vocabulary, of seven of the world's most widely-spoken languages.

'The book contains an immense amount of well arranged information for anyone interested in language study.' *John O'London's Weekly*

THE NEW ENGLISH GRAMMAR
by R. A. Close

Demy 8vo.

This is the book for students promised in the preface of the author's *English as a Foreign Language*.

Part One lays a basis for good pronunciation (including stress and intonation) and accurate spelling. Part Two deals with nouns, articles, adjectives, adjuncts, pronouns, verbs, tenses, adverbs, prepositions, the construction of the simple sentence, and word-order. Parts Three and Four follow.

The New English Grammar is intended for intelligent beginners requiring proficiency in English for their general education, as well as for more advanced students—including many teachers—who may need a thorough revision of the elements or a handy book of reference.

GEORGE ALLEN AND UNWIN LTD